Ve

The Best of Jules Verne

The Central Sea.

The Best of JULES VERNE

Three complete, illustrated novels

Around the World in Eighty Days
The Clipper of the Clouds
Journey to the Center of the Earth

With original illustrations

▲

Selected and introduced by
ALAN K. RUSSELL

▲

CASTLE BOOKS

Sources

Around the World in Eighty Days was first published in English, translated by George M. Towle, by Sampson Low, Marston & Co. in 1874. Illustrations by Neuville and Benet. The first French edition was published in 1873.

The Clipper of the Clouds was first published in English by Sampson Low, Marston & Co. in 1887. Illustrations by Benet. The first French edition, entitled *Robur le Conquérant*, was published in 1886.

Journey to the Centre of the Earth was first published in English in 1872 by Griffith and Farran who published from the "West Corner of St. Paul's Churchyard". Illustrated by Riou. The first French edition was published in 1864.

Jules Verne at Home by Mrs. Marie A. Belloc was published in *The Strand*, February, 1895.

Jules Verne was born on 8 February 1828 and died 24 March 1905.

The Best of Jules Verne
Selection, editing and introduction © Alan K. Russell 1978.

© Copyright 1978 by Castle Books
A division of Book Sales, Inc.,
Secaucus, New Jersey
ISBN #0-89009-270-2
Manufactured in the United States of America

Jacket design © copyright 1978 by Castle Books

Contents

Never had an eclipse produced such a wonderful
display of optical instruments.

The World of Jules Verne

Here are three complete novels of sheer flamboyant adventure and imagination. The adventurous imagination of Jules Verne, who created these three novels, was prolific and dozens of books poured from his pen. He explored the future, basing his books on the latest scientific ideas. He took the latest thinking and extrapolated it with greater verve and variety than anyone else has ever done. Verne filled his books with characters who have become world famous, and his stories have been staged, paperbacked, filmed (sometimes badly), dramatised for radio, inspired music,

Phileas Fogg, the English adventurer in *Around the World in Eighty Days*, made Verne a fortune. The book was an immense bestseller. It was presented as theatrical entertainment with miraculous moving sets (with real snakes, an elephant, and so forth), and went on to be presented in other media, including the award-winning film by Mike Todd, with David Niven playing the part of Fogg. Todd's film included a balloon fight which you will not find in this volume, for it was injected into the film from another book by Verne! There are several claims for having been the inspiration behind *Around the World in Eighty Days*. One is that Verne was inspired by the 1871 announcement by Thomas Cook of the first round the world tour, which conducted its tourists around the globe in 222 days. The others lie with two Americans. Mr. George F. Train made the journey in 1870, and who knew Verne's friend Dumas, and a real life Fogg, Mr. William Perry Fogg, who made the journey in 1869/1871 and whose own book was called *Round the World* (1872). Certainly, however, after Verne's book was published the idea caught on and there were many who raced around the globe, including, recently, S. J. Perelman. As Mike Todd added to the film, Verne also made subtle alterations to the book. One such was on pages 6 and 7, where the travel schedule is provided. After the publication of the book it was pointed out to the author that the Reform Club, which was a liberal establishment, would not have taken that staunchly conservative newspaper *The Daily Telegraph*. In later editions of *Around The World in Eighty Days* the newspaper's name was changed to *The Daily Chronicle*.

The thrills and adventures in *Around the World* were checked by Verne to gazetteers and the memoirs of travellers, but sometimes prejudice or misconception from a century ago show through, as when Fogg is in an Indian law court, or the election in California.

The Clipper of the Clouds shows Verne's genius in foretelling the future. Here, years before the Wright brothers got off the ground, Verne set out to show that the heavier-than-air flight would be the future of flight, whereas at that time the dirigible balloon was not only in use but believed to be how people would fly in the future. Verne, indeed, was at one time secretary of the French Society for Aerial Navigation which sponsored balloon flight. Robur, the inventor and captain of the 'aeronef' *Albatross*, is one of Verne's memorable characters, a creation to stand alongside Nemo. Robur returned to terrorise the world in *Master of the World* (1904).

For *A Journey to the Centre of the Earth* Verne took endless trouble to check his facts. He took the advice of Charles Sainte-Claire Deville, a French geologist who had explored volcanos; studied the work of an American, John Cleves Symmes, who believed the world to be hollow and open at the Poles; inhabited his fictional Iceland with real life people; and included in the book the latest information on fossil discoveries. One little mystery of this oft lyrical book is that the first English edition named the German professor as von Hardwigg, instead of Lidenbrock as the original French, and Harry was also originally called Alex.

As a bonus to *The Best of Jules Verne* there is a rare glimpse of the author, in the form of an interview which appeared in *The Strand* in 1895. This interview, which we believe has never before been reprinted (although cited in many works about Verne), is from the British magazine from which we have drawn material for the *Original Illustrated Sherlock Holmes, The Science Fiction of HG Wells* and *The Rivals of Sherlock Holmes*. It was a splendid journal full of the best reading matter of its day.

The complete books in this volume present Verne at his best: thrilling, provocative, stimulating and inventive. He took the best and most up-to-date ideas of his times, when new worlds in science were being discovered almost daily, and made them into novels peopled by memorable characters. As the stories take you racing along with Verne's imagination it is difficult to believe that he was born 150 years ago. In telling his stories Verne was inevitably to some extent the product of his times, he sometimes portrayed stereotype characters and images, which today, when readers are so much better informed, seem ill-conceived. But the sheer verve of his creativeness will take you zooming past any motes in the eye of the fastidious modern reader. Read, and enjoy!

Finally, with such a prolific output how do you select 'the best'? Amongst candidates for inclusion must be *Twenty Thousand Leagues Under the Sea, From the Earth to the Moon, Five Weeks in a Balloon, The Mysterious Island, Master of the World* and—well, watch out for *The Best of Jules Verne 2.*

Alan K. Russell.

Around the World in Eighty Days

Phileas Fogg.

Around the World in Eighty Days

CHAPTER I.

IN WHICH PHILEAS FOGG AND PASSEPARTOUT ACCEPT EACH OTHER, THE ONE AS MASTER, THE OTHER AS MAN.

MR. PHILEAS FOGG lived, in 1872, at No. 7, Saville Row, Burlington Gardens, the house in which Sheridan died in 1814. He was one of the most noticeable members of the Reform Club, though he seemed always to avoid attracting attention; an enigmatical personage, about whom little was known, except that he was a polished man of the world. People said that he resembled Byron,—at least that his head was Byronic; but he was a bearded, tranquil Byron, who might live on a thousand years without growing old.

Certainly an Englishman it was more doubtful whether Phileas Fogg was a Londoner. He was never seen on 'Change, nor at the Bank, nor in the counting-rooms of the "City"; no ships ever came into London docks of which he was the owner; he had no public employment; he had never been entered at any of the Inns of Court, either at the Temple, or Lincoln's Inn, or Gray's Inn; nor had his voice ever resounded in the Court of Chancery, or in the Exchequer, or the Queen's Bench, or the Ecclesiastical Courts. He certainly was not a manufacturer; nor was he a merchant or a gentleman farmer. His name was strange to the scientific and learned societies, and he never was known to take part in the sage deliberations of the Royal Institution or the London Institution, the Artisan's Association or the Institution of Arts and Sciences. He belonged, in fact, to none of the numerous societies which swarm in the English capital, from the Harmonic to that of the Entomologists, founded mainly for the purpose of abolishing pernicious insects.

Phileas Fogg was a member of the Reform, and that was all.

The way in which he got admission to this exclusive club was simple enough.

He was recommended by the Barings, with whom he had an open credit. His checks were regularly paid at sight from his account current, which was always flush.

Was Phileas Fogg rich? Undoubtedly. But those who knew him best could not imagine how he had made his fortune, and Mr. Fogg was the last person to whom to apply for the information. He was not lavish, nor, on the contrary, avaricious; for whenever he knew that money was needed for a noble, useful, or benevolent purpose, he supplied it quietly, and sometimes anonymously. He was, in short, the least communicative of men. He talked very little, and seemed all the more mysterious for his taciturn manner. His daily habits were quite open to observation; but whatever he did was so exactly the same thing that he had always done before, that the wits of the curious were fairly puzzled.

Had he travelled? It was likely, for no one seemed to know the world more familiarly; there was no spot so secluded that he did not appear to have an intimate acquaintance with it. He often corrected, with a few clear words, the thousand conjectures advanced by members of the club as to lost and unheard-of travellers, pointing out the true probabilities, and seeming as if gifted with a sort of second sight, so often did events justify his predictions. He must have travelled everywhere, at least in the spirit.

It was at least certain that Phileas Fogg had not absented himself from London for many years. Those who were honoured by a better acquaintance with him than the rest, declared that nobody could pretend to have ever seen him anywhere else. His sole pastimes were reading the papers and playing whist. He often won at this game, which, as a silent one, harmonized with his nature; but his winnings never went into his purse, being reserved as a fund for his charities. Mr. Fogg played, not to win, but for the sake of playing. The game was in his eyes a contest, a struggle with a difficulty, yet a motionless, unwearying struggle, congenial to his tastes.

Phileas Fogg was not known to have either wife or children, which may happen to the most honest people; either relatives or near friends, which is certainly more unusual. He lived alone in his house in Saville Row, whither none penetrated. A single domestic sufficed to serve him. He breakfasted and dined at the club, at hours mathematically fixed, in the same room, at the same table, never taking his meals with other members, much less bringing a guest with him; and went home at exactly

1

Jean Passepartout.

midnight, only to retire at once to bed. He never used the cosy chambers which the Reform provides for its favoured members. He passed ten hours out of the twenty-four in Saville Row, either in sleeping or making his toilet. When he chose to take a walk, it was with a regular step in the entrance hall with its mosaic flooring, or in the circular gallery with its dome supported by twenty red porphyry Ionic columns, and illumined by blue painted windows. When he breakfasted or dined, all the resources of the club—its kitchens and pantries, its buttery and dairy—aided to crowd his table with their most succulent stores; he was served by the gravest waiters, in dress coats, and shoes with swan-skin soles, who proffered the viands in special porcelain, and on the finest linen; club decanters, of a lost mould, contained his sherry, his port, and his cinnamon-spiced claret; while his beverages were refreshingly cooled with ice, brought at great cost from the American lakes.

If to live in this style is to be eccentric, it must be confessed that there is something good in eccentricity!

The mansion in Saville Row, though not sumptuous, was exceedingly comfortable. The habits of its occupant were such as to demand but little from the sole domestic; but Phileas Fogg required him to be almost superhumanly prompt and regular. On this very 2nd of October he had dismissed James Forster, because that luckless youth had brought him shaving-water at eighty-four degrees Fahrenheit instead of eighty-six; and he was awaiting his successor, who was due at the house between eleven and half-past.

Phileas Fogg was seated squarely in his arm-chair, his feet close together like those of a grenadier on parade, his hands resting on his knees, his body straight, his head erect; he was steadily watching a complicated clock which indicated the hours, the minutes, the seconds, the days, the months, and the years. At exactly half-past eleven Mr. Fogg would, according to his daily habit, quit Saville Row, and repair to the Reform.

A rap at this moment sounded on the door of the cosy apartment where Phileas Fogg was seated, and James Forster, the dismissed servant, appeared.

"The new servant," said he.

A young man of thirty advanced and bowed.

"You are a Frenchman, I believe," asked Phileas Fogg, "and your name is John?"

"Jean, if monsieur pleases," replied the new-comer, "Jean Passepartout, a surname which has clung to me because I have a natural aptness for going out of one business into another. I believe I'm honest, monsieur, but, to be outspoken, I've had several trades. I've been an itinerant singer, a circus-rider, when I used to vault like Leotard, and dance on a rope like Blondin. Then I got to be a professor of gymnastics, so as to make better use of my talents; and then I was a sergeant fireman at Paris, and assisted at many a big fire. But I quitted France five years ago, and, wishing to taste the sweets of domestic life, took service as a valet here in England. Finding myself out of place, and hearing that Monsieur Phileas Fogg was the most exact and settled gentleman in the United Kingdom, I have come to monsieur in the hope of living with him a tranquil life, and forgetting even the name of Passepartout."

"Passepartout suits me," responded Mr. Fogg. "You are well recommended to me; I hear a good report of you. You know my conditions?"

"Yes, monsieur."

"Good. What time is it?"

"Twenty-two minutes after eleven," returned Passepartout, drawing an enormous silver watch from the depths of his pocket.

"You are too slow," said Mr. Fogg.

"Pardon me, monsieur, it is impossible—"

"You are four minutes too slow. No matter; it's enough to mention the error. Now from this moment, twenty-nine minutes after eleven, a.m., this Wednesday, October 2nd, you are in my service."

Phileas Fogg got up, took his hat in his left hand, put it on his head with an automatic motion, and went off without a word.

Passepartout heard the street door shut once; it was his new master going out. He heard it shut again; it was his predecessor, James Forster, departing in his turn. Passepartout remained alone in the house in Saville Row.

CHAPTER II.

IN WHICH PASSEPARTOUT IS CONVINCED THAT HE HAS AT LAST FOUND HIS IDEAL.

"FAITH," muttered Passepartout, somewhat flurried, "I've seen people at Madame Tussaud's as lively as my new master!"

Madame Tussaud's "people," let it be said, are of wax, and are much visited in London; speech is all that is wanting to make them human.

During his brief interview with Mr. Fogg, Passepartout had been carefully observing him. He appeared to be a man about forty years of age, with fine, handsome features, and a tall, well-shaped figure; his hair and whiskers were light, his forehead compact and unwrinkled, his face rather pale, his teeth magnificent. His countenance possessed in the highest degree what physiognomists call "repose in action," a quality of those who act rather than talk. Calm and phlegmatic, with a clear eye, Mr. Fogg seemed a perfect type of that English composure which Angelica Kauffmann has so skilfully represented on canvas. Seen in the various phases of his daily life, he gave the idea of being perfectly well-balanced, as exactly regulated as a Leroy chronometer. Phileas Fogg was, indeed, exactitude personified, and this was betrayed even in the expression of his very hands and feet; for in men, as well as in animals, the limbs themselves are expressive of the passions.

He was so exact that he was never in a hurry, was always ready, and was economical alike of his steps and his motions. He never took one step too many, and always went to his destination by the shortest cut; he made no superfluous gestures, and was never seen to be moved or agitated. He was the most deliberate person in the world, yet always reached his destination at the exact moment.

He lived alone, and so to speak, outside of every social relation; and as he knew that in this world account must be taken of friction, and that friction retards, he never rubbed against anybody.

As for Passepartout, he was a true Parisian of Paris. Since he had abandoned his own country for England, taking service as a valet, he had in vain searched for a master after his own heart. Passepartout was by no means one of those pert dunces depicted by Molière, with a bold gaze and a nose held high in the air; he was an honest fellow, with a pleasant face, lips a trifle protruding, soft-mannered and serviceable, with a good round head, such as one likes to see on the shoulders of a friend. His eyes were blue, his complexion rubicund, his figure almost portly and well built, his body muscular, and his physical powers fully developed by the exercises of his younger days. His brown hair was somewhat tumbled; for while the ancient sculptors are said to have known eighteen methods of arranging Minerva's tresses, Passepartout was familiar with but one of dressing his own: three strokes of a large-tooth comb completed his toilet.

It would be rash to predict how Passepartout's lively nature would agree with Mr. Fogg. It was impossible to tell whether the new servant would turn out as absolutely methodical as his master required; experience alone could solve the question. Passepartout had been a sort of vagrant in his early years, and now yearned for repose; but so far he had failed to find it, though he had already served in ten English houses. But he could not take root in any of these; with chagrin he found his masters invariably whimsical and irregular, constantly running about the country, or on the look-out for adventure. His last master, young Lord Longferry, Member of Parliament, after passing his nights in the Haymarket taverns, was too often brought home in the morning on policemen's shoulders. Passepartout, desirous of respecting the gentleman whom he served, ventured a mild remonstrance on such conduct; which being ill received, he took his leave. Hearing that Mr. Phileas Fogg was looking for a servant, and that his life was one of unbroken regularity, that he neither travelled nor stayed from home overnight, he felt sure that this would be the place he was after. He presented himself, and was accepted, as has been seen.

At half-past eleven, then, Passepartout found himself alone in the house in Saville Row. He began its inspection without delay, scouring it from cellar to garret. So clean, well-arranged, solemn a mansion pleased him; it seemed to him like a snail's shell, lighted and warmed by gas, which sufficed for both these purposes. When Passepartout reached the second story, he recognized at once the room which he was to inhabit, and he was well satisfied with it. Electric bells and speaking-tubes afforded communication with the lower stories; while on the mantel stood an electric clock, precisely like that in Mr. Fogg's bed-chamber, both beating the same second at the same instant. "That's good, that'll do," said Passepartout to himself.

He suddenly observed, hung over the clock, a card which, upon inspection, proved to be a programme of the daily routine of the house. It comprised all that was required of the servant, from eight in the morning, exactly at which hour Phileas Fogg rose, till half-past eleven, when he left the house for the Reform Club,— all the details of service, the tea and toast at twenty-three minutes past eight, the shaving-water at thirty-seven minutes past nine, and the toilet at twenty minutes before ten. Everything was regulated and foreseen that was to be done from half-past eleven a.m. till midnight, the hour at which the methodical gentleman retired.

Mr. Fogg's wardrobe was amply supplied and in the best taste. Each pair of trousers, coat, and vest bore a number, indicating the time of year and season at which they were in turn to be laid out for wearing; and the same system was applied to the master's shoes. In short, the house in Saville Row, which must have been a very temple of disorder and unrest under the illustrious but dissipated Sheridan, was cosiness, comfort, and method idealized. There was no study, nor were there books, which would have been quite useless to Mr. Fogg; for at the Reform two libraries, one of general literature and the other of law and politics, were at his service. A moderate-sized safe stood in his bedroom, constructed so as to defy fire as well as burglars; but Passepartout found neither arms nor hunting weapons anywhere; everything betrayed the most tranquil and peaceable habits.

Having scrutinized the house from top to bottom, he rubbed his hands, a broad smile overspread his features, and he said joyfully, "This is just what I wanted! Ah, we shall get on together, Mr. Fogg and I! What a domestic and regular gentleman! A real machine; well, I don't mind serving a machine.

Around the World in Eighty Days

CHAPTER III.

IN WHICH A CONVERSATION TAKES PLACE WHICH SEEMS LIKELY TO COST PHILEAS FOGG DEAR.

PHILEAS FOGG, having shut the door of his house at half-past eleven, and having put his right foot before his left five hundred and seventy-five times, and his left foot before his right five hundred and seventy-six times, reached the Reform Club, an imposing edifice in Pall Mall, which could not have cost less than three millions. He repaired at once to the dining-room, the nine windows of which open upon a tasteful garden, where the trees were already gilded with an autumn colouring; and took his place at the habitual table, the cover of which had already been laid for him. His breakfast consisted of a side-dish, a broiled fish with Reading sauce, a scarlet slice of roast-beef garnished with mushrooms, a rhubarb and gooseberry tart, and a morsel of Cheshire cheese, the whole being washed down with several cups of tea, for which the Reform is famous. He rose at thirteen minutes to one, and directed his steps towards the large hall, a sumptuous apartment adorned with lavishly-framed paintings. A flunkey handed him an uncut *Times*, which he proceeded to cut with a skill which betrayed familiarity with this delicate operation. The perusal of this paper absorbed Phileas Fogg until a quarter before four, whilst the *Standard*, his next task, occupied him till the dinner hour. Dinner passed as breakfast had done, and Mr. Fogg reappeared in the reading-room and sat down to the *Pall Mall* at twenty minutes before six. Half an hour later several members of the Reform came in and drew up to the fireplace, where a coal fire was steadily-burning. They were Mr. Fogg's usual partners at whist: Andrew Stuart, an engineer; John Sullivan and Samuel Fallentin, bankers; Thomas Flanagan, a brewer; and Gauthier Ralph, one of the Directors of the Bank of England;—all rich and highly respectable personages, even in a club which comprises the princes of English trade and finance.

"Well, Ralph," said Thomas Flanagan, "what about that robbery?"

"Oh," replied Stuart, "the bank will lose the money."

"On the contrary," broke in Ralph, "I hope we may put our hands on the robber. Skilful detectives have been sent to all the principal ports of America and the Continent, and he'll be a clever fellow if he slips through their fingers."

"But have you got the robber's description?" asked Stuart.

"In the first place, he is no robber at all," returned Ralph, positively.

"What! a fellow who makes off with fifty-five thousand pounds, no robber?"

"No."

"Perhaps he's a manufacturer, then."

"The *Daily Telegraph* says that he is a gentleman."

It was Phileas Fogg, whose head now emerged from behind his newspapers, who made this remark. He bowed to his friends, and entered into the conversation. The affair which formed its subject, and which was town talk, had occurred three days before at the Bank of England. A package of bank-notes, to the value of fifty-five thousand pounds, had been taken from the principal cashier's table, that functionary being at the moment engaged in registering the receipt of three shillings and sixpence. Of course he could not have his eyes everywhere. Let it be observed that the Bank of England reposes a touching confidence in the honesty of the public. There are neither guards nor gratings to protect its treasures; gold, silver, banknotes are freely exposed, at the mercy of the first comer. A keen observer of English customs relates that, being in one of the rooms of the Bank one day, he had the cuiosity to examine a gold ingot weighing some seven or eight pounds. He took it up, scrutinized it, passed it to his neighbour, he to the next man, and so on until the ingot, going from hand to hand, was transferred to the end of a dark entry; not did it return to its place for half an hour. Meanwhile, the cashier had not so much as raised his head. But in the present instance things had not gone so smoothly. The package of notes not being found when five o'clock sounded from the ponderous clock in the "drawing office," the amount was passed to the account of profit and loss. As soon as the robbery was discovered, picked detectives hastened off to Liverpool, Glasgow, Havre,

Suez, Brindisi, New York, and other ports, inspired by the proffered reward of two thousand pounds, and five per cent. on the sum that might be recovered. Detectives were also charged with narrowly watching those who arrived at or left London by rail, and a judicial examination was at once entered upon.

There were real grounds for supposing, as the *Daily Telegraph* said, that the thief did not belong to a professional band. On the day of the robbery a well-dressed gentleman of polished manners, and with a well-to-do air, had been observed going to and fro in the paying-room, where the crime was committed. A description of him was easily procured, and sent to the detectives; and some hopeful spirits, of whom Ralph was one, did not despair of his apprehension. The papers and clubs were full of the affair, and everywhere people were discussing the probabilities of a successful pursuit; and the Reform Club was especially agitated, several of its members being Bank officials.

Ralph would not concede that the work of the detectives was likely to be in vain, for he thought that the prize offered would greatly stimulate their zeal and activity. But Stuart was far from sharing this confidence; and as they placed themselves at the whist-table, they continued to argue the matter. Stuart and Flanagan played together, while Phileas Fogg had Fallentin for his partner. As the game proceeded the conversation ceased, excepting between the rubbers, when it revived again.

"I maintain," said Stuart, "that the chances are in favour of the thief, who must be a shrewd fellow."

"Well, but where can he fly to?" asked Ralph. "No country is safe for him."

"Pshaw!"

"Where could he go, then?"

"Oh, I don't know that. The world is big enough."

"It was once," said Phileas Fogg, in a low tone. "Cut, sir," he added, handing the cards to Thomas Flanagan.

The discussion fell during the rubber, after which Stuart took up its thread.

"What do you mean by 'once'? Has the world grown smaller?"

"Certainly," returned Ralph. "I agree with Mr. Fogg. The world *has* grown smaller, since a man can now go round it ten times more quickly than a hundred years ago. And that is why the search for this thief will be more likely to succeed."

"And also why the thief can get away more easily."

"Be so good as to play, Mr. Stuart," said Phileas Fogg.

But the incredulous Stuart was not convinced, and when the hand was finished, said eagerly: "You have a strange way, Ralph, of proving that the world has grown smaller. So, because you can go round it in three months—"

"In eighty days," interrupted Phileas Fogg.

"That is true, gentlemen," added John Sullivan. "Only eighty days, now that the section between Rothal and Allahabad, on the Great Indian Peninsula Railway, has been opened. Here is the estimate made by the *Daily Telegraph:*—

From London to Suez *viâ* Mont Cenis and Brindisi, by rail and steamboats	7 days
From Suez to Bombay, by steamer	13 days
From Bombay to Calcutta, by rail	3 days
From Calcutta to Hong Kong, by steamer	13 days
From Hong Kong to Yokohama (Japan), by steamer	6 days
From Yokohama to San Francisco, by steamer	22 days
From San Francisco to New York, by rail	7 days
From New York to London, by steamer and rail	9 days
	—
Total	80 days

"Yes, in eighty days!" exclaimed Stuart, who in his excitement made a false deal. "But that doesn't take into account bad weather, contrary winds, shipwrecks, railway accidents, and so on."

"All included," returned Phileas Fogg, continuing to play despite the discussion.

"But suppose the Hindoos or Indians pull up the rails," replied Stuart; "suppose they stop the trains, pillage the luggage-vans, and scalp the passengers!"

"All included," calmly retorted Fogg; adding, as he threw down the cards, "Two trumps."

Stuart, whose turn it was to deal, gathered them up, and went on: "You are right theoretically, Mr. Fogg, but practically—"

"Practically also, Mr. Stuart."

"I'd like to see you do it in eighty days."

"It depends on you. Shall we go?"

"Heaven preserve me! But I would wager four thousand pounds that such a journey, made under these conditions, is impossible."

"Quite possible, on the contrary," returned Mr. Fogg.

"Well, make it, then!"

"Well, Mr. Fogg," said he, "it shall be so : I will wager £4000 on it."

"The journey round the world in eighty days?"

"Yes."

"I should like nothing better."

"When?"

"At once. Only I warn you that I shall do it at your expense."

"It's absurd!" cried Stuart, who was beginning to be annoyed at the persistency of his friend. "Come, let's go on with the game."

"Deal over again, then," said Phileas Fogg. "There's a false deal."

Stuart took up the pack with a feverish hand; then suddenly put them down again.

"Well, Mr. Fogg," said he, "it shall be so: I will wager the four thousand on it."

"Calm yourself, my dear Stuart," said Fallentin. "It's only a joke."

"When I say I'll wager," returned Stuart, "I mean it."

"All right," said Mr. Fogg; and, turning to the others, he continued, "I have a deposit of twenty thousand at Baring's which I will willingly risk upon it."

"Twenty thousand pounds!" cried Sullivan. "Twenty thousand pounds, which you would lose by a single accidental delay!"

"The unforeseen does not exist," quietly replied Phileas Fogg.

"But, Mr. Fogg, eighty days are only the estimate of the least possible time in which the journey can be made."

"A well-used minimum suffices for everything."

"But, in order not to exceed it, you must jump mathematically from the trains upon the steamers, and from the steamers upon the trains again."

"I will jump—mathematically."

"You are joking."

"A true Englishman doesn't joke when he is talking about so serious a thing as a wager," replied Phileas Fogg, solemnly. "I will bet twenty thousand pounds against any one who wishes, that I will make the tour of the world in eighty days or less; in nineteen hundred and twenty hours, or a hundred and fifteen thousand two hundred minutes. Do you accept?"

"We accept," replied Messrs. Stuart, Fallentin, Sullivan, Flanagan, and Ralph, after consulting each other.

"Good," said Mr. Fogg. "The train leaves for Dover at a quarter before nine. I will take it."

"This very evening?" asked Stuart.

"This very evening," returned Phileas Fogg. He took out and consulted a pocket almanac, and added, "As today is Wednesday, the second of October, I shall be due in London, in this very room of the Reform Club, on Saturday, the twenty-first of December, at a quarter before nine p.m.; or else the twenty thousand pounds, now deposited in my name at Baring's, will belong to you, in fact and in right, gentlemen. Here is a check for the amount."

A memorandum of the wager was at once drawn up and signed by the six parties, during which Phileas Fogg preserved a stoical composure. He certainly did not bet to win, and had only staked the twenty thousand pounds, half of his fortune, because he foresaw that he might have to expend the other half to carry out this difficult, not to say unattainable, project. As for his antagonists, they seemed much agitated; no so much by the value of their stake, as because they had some scruples about betting under conditions so difficult to their friend.

The clock struck seven, and the party offered to suspend the game so that Mr. Fogg might make his preparations for departure.

"I am quite ready now," was his tranquil response "Diamonds are trumps: be so good as to play, gentlemen."

Around the World in Eighty Days

CHAPTER IV.

IN WHICH PHILEAS FOGG ASTOUNDS PASSEPARTOUT, HIS SERVANT.

HAVING won twenty guineas at whist, and taken leave of his friends, Phileas Fogg, at twenty-five minutes past seven, left the Reform Club.

Passepartout, who had conscientiously studied the programme of his duties, was more than surprised to see his master guilty of the inexactness of appearing at this unaccustomed hour; for, according to rule, he was not due in Saville Row until precisely midnight.

Mr. Fogg repaired to his bedroom, and called out, "Passepartout!"

Passepartout did not reply. It could not be he who was called; it was not the right hour.

"Passepartout!" repeated Mr. Fogg, without raising his voice.

Passepartout made his appearance.

"I've called you twice," observed his master.

"But it is not midnight," responded the other, showing his watch.

"I know it; I don't blame you. We start for Dover and Calais in ten minutes."

A puzzled grin overspread Passepartout's round face; clearly he had not comprehended his master.

"Monsieur is going to leave home?"

"Yes," returned Phileas Fogg. "We are going round the world."

Passepartout opened wide his eyes, raised his eyebrows, held up his hands, and seemed about to collapse, so overcome was he with stupefied astonishment.

"Round the world!" he murmured.

"In eighty days," responded Mr. Fogg. "So we haven't a moment to lose."

"But the trunks?" gasped Passepartout, unconsciously swaying his head from right to left.

"We'll have no trunks; only a carpet-bag, with two shirts and three pairs of stockings for me, and the same for you. We'll buy our clothes on the way. Bring down my mackintosh and travelling-cloak, and some stout shoes, though we shall do little walking. Make haste!"

Passepartout tried to reply, but could not. He went out, mounted to his own room, fell into a chair, and muttered: "That's good, that is! And I, who wanted to remain quiet!"

He mechanically set about making the preparations for departure. Around the world in eighty days! Was his master a fool? No. Was this a joke, then? They were going to Dover; good. To Calais; good again. After all, Passepartout, who had been away from France five years, would not be sorry to set foot on his native soil again. Perhaps they would go as far as Paris, and it would do his eyes good to see Paris once more. But surely a gentleman so chary of his steps would stop there; no doubt,—but, then, it was none the less true that he was going away, this so domestic person hitherto!

By eight o'clock Passepartout had packed the modest carpet-bag, containing the wardrobes of his master and himself; then, still troubled in mind, he carefully shut the door of his room, and descended to Mr. Fogg.

Mr. Fogg was quite ready. Under his arm might have been observed a red-bound copy of "Bradshaw's Continental Railway Steam Transit and General Guide," with its time-tables showing the arrival and departure of steamers and railways. He took the carpet-bag, opened it, and slipped into it a goodly roll of Bank of England notes, which would pass wherever he might go.

"You have forgotten nothing?" asked he.

"Nothing, monsieur."

"My mackintosh and cloak?"

"Here they are."

"Good. Take this carpet-bag," handing it to Passepartout. "Take good care of it, for there are twenty thousand pounds in it."

Passepartout nearly dropped the bag, as if the twenty thousand pounds were in gold, and weighed him down.

Master and man then descended, the street-door was double-locked, and at the end of Saville Row they took a cab and drove rapidly to Charing Cross. The cab stopped before the railway station at twenty minutes past eight. Passepartout jumped off the box and followed his master, who, after paying the cabman, was about to enter the station, when a poor beggar-woman, with a child in her arms, her naked feet smeared with mud, her head covered with a wretched bonnet, from which hung a tattered feather, and her shoulders shrouded in a ragged

A poor mendicant.

shawl, approached, and mournfully asked for alms.

Mr. Fogg took out the twenty guineas he had just won at whist, and handed them to the beggar, saying, "Here, my good woman. I'm glad that I met you"; and passed on.

Passepartout had a moist sensation about the eyes; his master's action touched his susceptible heart.

Two first-class tickets for Paris having been speedily purchased, Mr. Fogg was crossing the station to the train, when he perceived his five friends of the Reform.

"Well, gentlemen," said he, "I'm off, you see; and if you will examine my passport when I get back, you will be able to judge whether I have accomplished the journey agreed upon."

"Oh, that would be quite unnecessary, Mr. Fogg," said Ralph, politely. "We will trust your word, as a gentleman of honour."

"You do not forget when you are due in London again?" asked Stuart.

"In eighty days; on Saturday, the 21st of December, 1872, at a quarter before nine p.m. Good-bye, gentlemen."

Phileas Fogg and his servant seated themselves in a first-class carriage at twenty minutes before nine; five minutes later the whistle screamed, and the train slowly glided out of the station.

The night was dark, and a fine, steady rain was falling. Phileas Fogg, snugly ensconced in his corner, did not open his lips. Passepartout, not yet recovered from his stupefaction, clung mechanically to the carpet-bag, with its enormous treasure.

Just as the train was whirling through Sydenham, Passepartout suddenly uttered a cry of despair.

"What's the matter?" asked Mr. Fogg.

"Alas! In my hurry—I—I forgot—"

"What?"

"To turn off the gas in my room!"

"Very well, young man," returned Mr. Fogg, coolly; "it will burn—at your expense."

Around the World in Eighty Days

CHAPTER V.

IN WHICH A NEW SPECIES OF FUNDS, UNKNOWN TO THE MONEYED MEN, APPEARS ON 'CHANGE.

PHILEAS FOGG rightly suspected that his departure from London would create a lively sensation at the West End. The news of the bet spread through the Reform Club, and afforded an exciting topic of conversation to its members. From the Club it soon got into the papers throughout England. The boasted "tour of the world" was talked about, disputed, argued with as much warmth as if the subject were another Alabama claim. Some took sides with Phileas Fogg, but the large majority shook their heads and declared against him; it was absurd, impossible, they declared, that the tour of the world could be made, except theoretically and on paper, in this minimum of time, and with the existing means of travelling. The *Times, Standard, Morning Post*, and *Daily News*, and twenty other highly respectable newspapers scouted Mr. Fogg's project as madness; the *Daily Telegraph* alone hesitatingly supported him. People in general thought him a lunatic, and blamed his Reform Club friends for having accepted a wager which betrayed the mental aberration of its proposer.

Articles no less passionate than logical appeared on the question, for geography is one of the pet subjects of the English; and the columns devoted to Phileas Fogg's venture were eagerly devoured by all classes of readers. At first some rash individuals, principally of the gentler sex, espoused his cause, which became still more popular when the *Illustrated London News* came out with his portrait, copied from a photograph in the Reform Club. A few readers of the *Daily Telegraph* even dared to say, "Why not, after all? Stranger things have come to pass."

At last a long article appeared, on the 7th of October, in the bulletin of the Royal Geographical Society, which treated the question from every point of view, and demonstrated the utter folly of the enterprise.

Everything, it said, was against the travellers, every obstacle imposed alike by man and by nature. A miraculous agreement of the times of departure and arrival, which was impossible, was absolutely necessary to his success. He might, perhaps, reckon on the arrival of trains at the designated hours, in Europe, where the distances were relatively moderate; but when he calculated upon crossing India in three days, and the United States in seven, could he rely beyond misgiving upon accomplishing his task? There were accidents to machinery, the liability of trains to run off the line, collisions, bad weather, the blocking up by snow,—were not all these against Phileas Fogg? Would he not find himself, when travelling by steamer in winter, at the mercy of the winds and fogs? Is it uncommon for the best ocean steamers to be two or three days behind time? But a single delay would suffice to fatally break the chain of communication; should Phileas Fogg once miss, even by an hour, a steamer, he would have to wait for the next, and that would irrevocably render his attempt vain.

This article made a great deal of noise, and being copied into all the papers, seriously depressed the advocates of the rash tourist.

Everybody knows that England is the world of betting men, who are of a higher class than mere gamblers; to bet is in the English temperament. Not only the members of the Reform, but the general public, made heavy wagers for or against Phileas Fogg, who was set down in the betting books as if he were a race-horse. Bonds were issued, and made their appearance on 'Change; "Phileas Fogg bonds" were offered at par or at a premium, and a great business was done in them. But five days after the article in the bulletin of the Geographical Society appeared, the demand began to subside: "Phileas Fogg" declined. They were offered by packages, at first of five, then of ten, until at last nobody would take less than twenty, fifty, a hundred!

Lord Albemarle, an elderly paralytic gentleman, was now the only advocate of Phileas Fogg left. This noble lord, who was fastened to his chair, would have given his fortune to be able to make the tour of the world, if it took ten years; and he bet five thousand pounds on Phileas Fogg. When the folly as well as the uselessness of the adventure was pointed out to him, he contented himself with replying, "If the thing is feasible, the first to do it ought to be an Englishman."

The Fogg party dwindled more and more,

Readers of all classes devoured the news relating to Phileas Fogg.

everybody was going against him, and the bets stood a hundred and fifty and two hundred to one; and a week after his departure, an incident occurred which deprived him of backers at any price.

The commissioner of police was sitting in his office at nine o'clock one evening, when the following telegraphic despatch was put into his hands:—

Suez to London.

ROWAN, COMMISSIONER OF POLICE, SCOTLAND YARD: I've found the bank robber, Phileas Fogg. Send without delay warrant of arrest to Bombay.

FIX, *Detective.*

The effect of this despatch was instantaneous. The polished gentleman disappeared to give place to the bank robber. His photograph, which was hung with those of the rest of the members at the Reform Club, was minutely examined, and it betrayed, feature by feature, the description of the robber which had been provided to the police. The mysterious habits of Phileas Fogg were recalled; his solitary ways, his sudden departure; and it seemed clear that, in undertaking a tour round the world on the pretext of a wager, he had had no other end in view than to elude the detectives, and throw them off his track.

CHAPTER VI.

IN WHICH FIX, THE DETECTIVE, BETRAYS A VERY NATURAL IMPATIENCE.

THE circumstances under which this telegraphic despatch about Phileas Fogg was sent were as follows:—

The steamer "Mongolia," belonging to the Peninsula and Oriental Company, built of iron, of two thousand eight hundred tons burden, and five hundred horse-power, was due at eleven o'clock a.m. on Wednesday, the 9th of October, at Suez. The "Mongolia" plied regularly between Brindisi and Bombay *viâ* the Suez Canal, and was one of the fastest steamers belonging to the company, always making more than ten knots an hour between Brindisi and Suez, and nine and a half between Suez and Bombay.

Two men were promenading up and down the wharves, among the crowd of natives and strangers who were sojourning at this once straggling village—now, thanks to the enterprise of M. Lesseps, a fast-growing town. One was the British consul at Suez, who, despite the prophecies of the English Government, and the unfavourable predictions of Stephenson, was in the habit of seeing, from his office window, English ships daily passing to and fro on the great canal, by which the old roundabout route from England to India by the Cape of Good Hope was abridged by at least a half. The other was a small, slight-built personage, with a nervous, intelligent face, and bright eyes peering out from under eyebrows which he was incessantly twitching. He was just now manifesting unmistakable signs of impatience, nervously pacing up and down, and unable to stand still for a moment. This was Fix, one of the detectives who had been despatched from England in search of the bank robber; it was his task to narrowly watch every passenger who arrived at Suez, and to follow up all who seemed to be suspicious characters, or bore a resemblance to the description of the criminal, which he had received two days before from the police head-quarters at London. The detective was evidently inspired by the hope of obtaining the splendid reward which would be the prize of success, and awaited with a feverish impatience, easy to understand, the arrival of the steamer "Mongolia."

"So you say, consul," asked he for the twentieth time, "that this steamer is never behind time?"

"No, Mr. Fix," replied the consul. "She was bespoken yesterday at Port Said, and the rest of the way is of no account to such a craft. I repeat that the 'Mongolia' has been in advance of the time required by the company's regulations, and gained the prize awarded for excess of speed."

"Does she come directly from Brindisi?"

"Directly from Brindisi; she takes on the Indian mails there, and she left there Saturday at five p.m. Have patience, Mr. Fix; she will not be late. But really I don't see how, from the description you have, you will be able to recognize your man, even if he is on board the 'Mongolia.'"

"A man rather feels the presence of these fellows, consul, than recognizes them. You must have a scent for them, and a scent is like a sixth sense which combines hearing, seeing, and smelling. I've arrested more than one of these gentlemen in my time, and if my thief is on board, I'll answer for it, he'll not slip through my fingers."

"I hope so, Mr. Fix, for it was a heavy robbery."

"A magnificent robbery, consul; fifty-five thousand pounds! We don't often have such windfalls. Burglars are getting to be so contemptible nowadays! A fellow gets hungs for a handful of shillings!"

"Mr. Fix," said the consul, "I like your way of talking, and hope you'll succeed; but I fear you will find it far from easy. Don't you see, the description which you have there has a singular resemblance to an honest man?"

"Consul," remarked the detective, dogmatically, "great robbers *always* resemble honest folks. Fellows who have rascally faces have only one course to take, and that is to remain honest; otherwise they would be arrested off-hand. The artistic thing is, to unmask honest countenances; it's no light task, I admit, but a real art."

Mr. Fix evidently was not wanting in a tinge of self-conceit.

Little by little the scene on the quay became more animated; sailors of various nations, merchants, ship-brokers, porters, fellahs, bustled to and fro as if the steamer were

Detective Fix.

HILDIBRAND

After vigorously repulsing the fellahs who offered their assistance.

immediately expected. The weather was clear, and slightly chilly. The minarets of the town loomed above the houses in the pale rays of the sun. A jetty pier, some two thousand yards long, extended into the roadstead. A number of fishing-smacks and coasting boats, some retaining the fantastic fashion of ancient galleys, were discernible on the Red Sea.

As he passed among the busy crowd, Fix, according to habit, scrutinized the passers-by with a keen, rapid glance.

It was now half-past ten.

"The steamer doesn't come!" he exclaimed, as the port clock struck.

"She can't be far off now," returned his companion.

"How long will she stop at Suez?"

"Four hours; long enough to get in her coal. It is thirteen hundred and ten miles from Suez to Aden, at the other end of the Red Sea, and she has to take in a fresh coal supply."

"And does she go from Suez directly to Bombay?"

"Without putting in anywhere."

"Good," said Fix. "If the robber is on board, he will no doubt get off at Suez, so as to reach the Dutch or French colonies in Asia by some other route. He ought to know that he would not be safe an hour in India, which is English soil."

"Unless," objected the consul, "he is exceptionally shrewd. An English criminal, you know, is always better concealed in London than anywhere else."

This observation furnished the detective food for thought, and meanwhile the consul went away to his office. Fix, left alone, was more impatient than ever, having a presentiment that the robber was on board the "Mongolia." If he had indeed left London intending to reach the New World, he would naturally take the route *via* India, which was less watched and more difficult to watch than

that of the Atlantic. But Fix's reflections were soon interrupted by a succession of sharp whistles, which announced the arrival of the "Mongolia." The porters and fellahs rushed down the quay, and a dozen boats pushed off from the shore to go and meet the steamer. Soon her gigantic hull appeared passing along between the banks, and eleven o'clock struck as she anchored in the road. She brought an unusual number of passengers, some of whom remained on deck to scan the picturesque panorama of the town, while the greater part disembarked in the boats, and landed on the quay.

Fix took up a position, and carefully examined each face and figure which made its appearance. Presently one of the passengers, after vigorously pushing his way through the importunate crowd of porters, came up to him, and politely asked if he could point out the English consulate, at the same time showing a passport which he wished to have *visaed*. Fix instinctively took the passport, and with a rapid glance read the description of its bearer. An involuntary motion of suprise nearly escaped him, for the description in the passport was identical with that of the bank robber which he had received from Scotland Yard.

"Is this your passport?" asked he.

"No, it's my master's."

"And your master is—"

"He stayed on board."

"But he must go to the consul's in person, so as to establish his identity."

"Oh, is that necessary?"

"Quite indispensable."

"And where is the consulate?"

"There, on the corner of the square," said Fix, pointing to a house two hundred steps off.

"I'll go and fetch my master, who won't be much pleased, however, to be disturbed."

The passenger bowed to Fix, and returned to the steamer.

Around the World in Eighty Days

CHAPTER VII.

WHICH ONCE MORE DEMONSTRATES THE USELESSNESS OF PASSPORTS AS AIDS TO DETECTIVES.

THE detective passed down the quay, and rapidly made his way to the consul's office, where he was at once admitted to the presence of that official.

"Consul," said he, without preamble, "I have strong reasons for believing that my man is a passenger on the 'Mongolia.'" And he narrated what had just passed concerning the passport.

"Well, Mr. Fix," replied the consul, "I shall not be sorry to see the rascal's face; but perhaps he won't come here,—that is, if he is the person you suppose him to be. A robber doesn't quite like to leave traces of his flight behind him; and besides, he is not obliged to have his passport countersigned."

"If he is as shrewd as I think he is, consul, he will come."

"To have his passport *visaed?*"

"Yes. Passports are only good for annoying honest folks, and aiding in the flight of rogues. I assure you it will be quite the thing for him to do; but I hope you will not *visa* the passport."

"Why not? If the passport is genuine, I have no right to refuse."

"Still I must keep this man here until I can get a warrant to arrest him from London."

"Ah, that's your look-out. But I cannot—"

The consul did not finish his sentence, for as he spoke a knock was heard at the door, and two strangers entered, one of whom was the servant whom Fix had met on the quay. The other, who was his master, held out his passport with the request that the consul would do him the favour to *visa* it. The consul took the document and carefully read it, whilst Fix observed, or rather devoured, the stranger with his eyes from a corner of the room.

"You are Mr. Phileas Fogg?" said the consul, after reading the passport.

"I am."

"And this man is your servant?"

"He is; a Frenchman, named Passepartout."

"You are from London?"

"Yes."

"And you are going—"

"To Bombay."

"Very good, sir. You know that a *visa* is useless, and that no passport is required?"

"I know it, sir," replied Phileas Fogg; "but I wish to prove, by your *visa*, that I came by Suez."

"Very well, sir."

The consul proceeded to sign and date the passport, after which he added his official seal. Mr. Fogg paid the customary fee, coldly bowed, and went out, followed by his servant.

"Well?" queried the detective.

"Well, he looks and acts like a perfectly honest man," replied the consul.

"Possibly; but that is not the question. Do you think, consul, that this phlegmatic gentleman resembles, feature by feature, the robber whose description I have received?"

"I concede that; but then, you know, all descriptions—"

"I'll make certain of it," interrupted Fix. "The servant seems to me less mysterious than the master; besides, he's a Frenchman, and can't help talking. Excuse me for a little while, consul."

Fix started off in search of Passepartout.

Meanwhile Mr. Fogg, after leaving the consulate, repaired to the quay, gave some orders to Passepartout, went off to the "Mongolia" in a boat, and descended to his cabin. He took up his note-book, which contained the following memoranda:—

"Left London, Wednesday, October 2nd, at 8.45 p.m.

"Reached Paris, Thursday, October 3rd, at 7.20 a.m.

"Left Paris, Thursday, at 8.40 a.m.

"Reached Turin by Mont Cenis, Friday, October 4th, at 6.35 a.m.

"Left Turin, Friday, at 7.20 a.m.

"Arrived at Brindisi, Saturday, October 5th, at 4 p.m.

"Sailed on the 'Mongolia,' Saturday, at 5 p.m.

"Reached Suez, Wednesday, October 9th, at 11 a.m.

"Total of hours spent, 158½; or, in days, six days and a half."

These dates were inscribed in an itinerary divided into columns, indicating the month, the day of the month, and the day for the stipulated and actual arrivals at each principal point,—

Paris, Brindisi, Suez, Bombay, Calcutta, Singapore, Hong Kong, Yokohama, San Francisco, New York, and London,—from the 2nd of October to the 21st of December; and giving a space for setting down the gain made or the loss suffered on arrival at each locality. This methodical record thus contained an account of everything needed, and Mr. Fogg always knew whether he was behindhand or in advance of his time. On this Friday, October 9th, he noted his arrival at Suez, and observed that he had as yet neither gained nor lost. He sat down quietly to breakfast in his cabin, never once thinking of inspecting the town, being one of those Englishmen who are wont to see foreign countries through the eyes of their domestics.

CHAPTER VIII.

IN WHICH PASSEPARTOUT TALKS RATHER MORE, PERHAPS, THAN IS PRUDENT.

FIX soon rejoined Passepartout, who was lounging and looking about on the quay, as if he did not feel that he, at least, was obliged not to see anything.

"Well, my friend," said the detective, coming up with him, "is your passport *visaed?*"

"Ah, it's you, is it, monsieur?" responded Passepartout. "Thanks, yes, the passport is all right."

"And you are looking about you?"

"Yes; but we travel so fast that I seem to be journeying in a dream. So this is Suez?"

"Yes."

"In Egypt?"

"Certainly, in Egypt."

"And in Africa?"

"In Africa."

"In Africa!" repeated Passepartout. "Just think, monsieur, I had no idea that we should go farther than Paris; and all that I saw of Paris was between twenty minutes past seven and twenty minutes before nine in the morning, between the Northern and the Lyons stations, through the windows of a car, and in a driving rain! How I regret not having seen once more Père la Chaise and the circus in the Champs Elysées!"

"You are in a great hurry, then?"

"I am not, but my master is. By the way, I must buy some shoes and shirts. We came away without trunks, only with a carpet-bag."

"I will show you an excellent shop for getting what you want."

"Really, monsieur, you are very kind."

And they walked off together, Passepartout chatting volubly as they went along.

"Above all," said he, "don't let me lose the steamer."

"You have plenty of time; it's only twelve o'clock."

Passepartout pulled out his big watch. "Twelve!" he exclaimed; "why it's only eight minutes before ten."

"Your watch is slow."

"My watch? A family watch, monsieur, which has come down from my great-grandfather! It doesn't vary five minutes in the year, it's a perfect chronometer, look you."

"I see how it is," said Fix. "You have kept London time, which is two hours behind that of Suez. You ought to regulate your watch at noon in each country."

"I regulate my watch? Never!"

"Well, then, it will not agree with the sun."

"So much the worse for the sun, monsieur. The sun will be wrong, then!"

And the worthy fellow returned the watch to its fob with a defiant gesture. After a few minutes' silence, Fix resumed: "You left London hastily, then?"

"I rather think so! Last Friday at eight o'clock in the evening, Monsieur Fogg came home from his club, and three quarters of an hour afterwards we were off."

"But where is your master going?"

"Always straight ahead. He is going round the world."

"Round the world?" cried Fix.

"Yes, and in eighty days! He says it is on a wager; but, between us, I don't believe a word of it. That wouldn't be common sense. There's something else in the wind."

"Ah! Mr. Fogg is a character, is he?"

"I should say he was."

"Is he rich?"

"No doubt, for he is carrying an enormous sum in brand-new bank notes with him. And he doesn't spare the money on the way, either: he has offered a large reward to the engineer of the 'Mongolia' if he gets us to Bombay well in advance of time."

"And you have known your master a long time?"

"Why, no; I entered his service the very day we left London."

The effect of these replies upon the already suspicious and excited detective may be imagined. The hasty departure from London soon after the robbery; the large sum carried by Mr. Fogg; his eagerness to reach distant countries; the pretext of an eccentric and foolhardy bet,—all confirmed Fix in his theory. He continued to pump poor Passepartout, and learned that he really knew little or nothing of his master, who lived a solitary existence in London, was said to be rich, though no one knew whence came his riches, and was

My watch? a family watch!''

mysterious and impenetrable in his affairs and habits. Fix felt sure that Phileas Fogg would not land at Suez, but was really going on to Bombay.

"Is Bombay far from here?" asked Passepartout.

"Pretty far. It is a ten days' voyage by sea."

"And in what country is Bombay?"

"India."

"In Asia?"

"Certainly."

"The deuce! I was going to tell you,—there's one thing that worries me,—my burner!"

"What burner?"

"My gas-burner, which I forgot to turn off, and which is at this moment burning—at my expense. I have calculated, monsieur, that I lose two shillings every four and twenty hours, exactly sixpence more than I earn; and you will understand that the longer our journey—"

Did Fix pay any attention to Passepartout's trouble about the gas? It is not probable. He was not listening, but was cogitating a project. Passepartout and he had now reached the shop, where Fix left his companion to make his purchases, after recommending him not to miss the steamer, and hurried back to the consulate. Now that he was fully convinced, Fix had quite recovered his equanimity.

"Consul," said he, "I have no longer any doubt. I have spotted my man. He passed himself off as an odd stick, who is going round the world in eighty days."

"Then he's a sharp fellow," returned the consul, "and counts on returning to London after putting the police of the two continents off his track."

"We'll see about that," replied Fix.

"But are you not mistaken?"

"I am not mistaken."

"Why was this robber so anxious to prove, by the *visa*, that he had passed through Suez?"

"Why? I have no idea; but listen to me."

He reported in a few words the most important parts of his conversation with Passepartout.

"In short," said the consul, "appearances are wholly against this man. And what are you going to do?"

"Send a despatch to London for a warrant of arrest to be despatched instantly to Bombay, take passage on board the 'Mongolia,' follow my rogue to India, and there, on English ground, arrest him politely, with my warrant in my hand, and my hand on his shoulder."

Having uttered these words with a cool, careless air, the detective took leave of the consul, and repaired to the telegraph office, whence he sent the despatch which we have seen to the London police office. A quarter of an hour later found Fix, with a small bag in his hand, proceeding on board the "Mongolia"; and ere many moments longer, the noble steamer rode out at full steam upon the waters of the Red Sea.

Around the World in Eighty Days

CHAPTER IX.

IN WHICH THE RED SEA AND THE INDIAN OCEAN PROVE PROPITIOUS TO THE DESIGNS OF PHILEAS FOGG.

THE distance between Suez and Aden is precisely thirteen hundred and ten miles, and the regulations of the company allow the steamers one hundred and thirty-eight hours in which to traverse it. The "Mongolia," thanks to the vigorous exertions of the engineer, seemed likely, so rapid was her speed, to reach her destination considerably within that time. The greater part of the passengers from Brindisi were bound for India—some for Bombay, others for Calcutta by way of Bombay, the nearest route thither, now that a railway crosses the Indian peninsula. Among the passengers was a number of officials and military officers of various grades, the latter being either attached to the regular British forces, or commanding the Sepoy troops and receiving high salaries ever since the central government has assumed the powers of the East India Company; for the sub-lieutenants get 280*l.*, brigadiers, 2400*l.*, and generals of division, 4000*l.* What with the military men, a number of rich young Englishmen on their travels, and the hospitable efforts of the purser, the time passed quickly on the "Mongolia." The best of fare was spread upon the cabin tables at breakfast, lunch, dinner and the eight o'clock supper, and the ladies scrupulously changed their toilets twice a day; and the hours were whiled away, when the sea was tranquil, with music, dancing, and games.

But the Red Sea is full of caprice, and often boisterous, like most long and narrow gulfs. When the wind came from the African or Asian coast, the "Mongolia," with her long hull, rolled fearfully. Then the ladies speedily disappeared below; the pianos were silent; singing and dancing suddenly ceased. Yet the good ship ploughed straight on, unretarded by wind or wave, towards the straits of Bab-el-Mandeb. What was Phileas Fogg doing all this time? It might be thought that, in his anxiety, he would be constantly watching the changes of the wind, the disorderly raging of the billows—every chance, in short, which might force the "Mongolia" to slacken her speed, and thus interrupt his journey. But if he thought of these possibilities, he did not betray the fact by any outward sign.

Always the same impassible member of the Reform Club, whom no incident could supervise, as unvarying as the ship's chronometers, and seldom having the curiosity even to go upon the deck, he passed through the memorable scenes of the Red Sea with cold indifference; did not care to recognize the historic towns and villages which, along its borders, raised their picturesque outlines against the sky; and betrayed no fear of the dangers of the Arabic Gulf, which the old historians always spoke of with horror, and upon which the ancient navigators never ventured without propitiating the gods by ample sacrifices. How did this eccentric personage pass his time on the "Mongolia?" He made his four hearty meals every day, regardless of the most persistent rolling and pitching on the part of the steamer; and he played whist indefatigably, for he had found partners as enthusiastic in the game as himself. A tax-collector, on the way to his post at Goa; the Rev. Decimus Smith, returning to his parish at Bombay; and a brigadier-general of the English army, who was about to rejoin his brigade at Benares, made up the party, and, with Mr. Fogg, played whist by the hour together in absorbing silence.

As for Passepartout, he, too, had escaped sea-sickness, and took his meals conscientiously in the forward cabin. He rather enjoyed the voyage, for he was well fed and well lodged, took a great interest in the scenes which they were passing, and consoled himself with the delusion that his master's whim would end at Bombay. He was pleased, on the day after leaving Suez, to find on deck the obliging person with whom he had walked and chatted on the quays.

"If I am not mistaken," said he, approaching this person with his most amiable smile, "you are the gentleman who so kindly volunteered to guide me at Suez?"

"Ah! I quite recognize you. You are the servant of the strange Englishman—"

"Just so, Monsieur—"

"Fix."

"Monsieur Fix," resumed Passepartout,

Mr. Fix on the watch.

"I'm charmed to find you on board. Where are you bound?"

"Like you, to Bombay."

"That's capital! Have you made this trip before?"

"Several times. I am one of the agents of the Peninsula Company."

"Then you know India?"

"Why—yes," replied Fix, who spoke cautiously.

"A curious place, this India?"

"Oh, very curious. Mosques, minarets, temples, fakirs, pagodas, tigers, snakes, elephants! I hope you will have ample time to see the sights."

"I hope so, Monsieur Fix. You see, a man of sound sense ought not to spend his life jumping from a steamer upon a railway train, and from a railway train upon a steamer again, pretending to make the tour of the world in eighty days! No; all these gymnastics, you may be sure, will cease at Bombay."

"And Mr. Fogg is getting on well?" asked Fix, in the most natural tone in the world.

"Quite well, and I too. I eat like a famished ogre; it's the sea air."

"But I never see your master on deck."

"Never; he hasn't the least curiosity."

"Do you know, Mr. Passepartout, that this pretended tour in eighty days may conceal some secret errand—perhaps a diplomatic mission?"

"Faith, Monsieur Fix, I assure you I know nothing about it, nor would I give half-a-crown to find out."

After this meeting, Passepartout and Fix got into the habit of chatting together, the latter making it a point to gain the worthy man's confidence. He frequently offered him a glass of whiskey or pale ale in the steamer bar-room, which Passepartout never failed to accept with graceful alacrity, mentally pronouncing Fix the best of good fellows.

Meanwhile the "Mongolia" was pushing forward rapidly; on the 13th, Mocha, surrounded by its ruined walls whereon date-trees were growing, was sighted, and on the mountains beyond were espied vast coffee-fields. Passepartout was ravished to behold this celebrated place, and thought that, with its circular walls and dismantled fort, it looked like an immense coffee pot and saucer. The following night they passed through the Strait of Bab-el-Mandeb, which means in Arabic "The Bridge of Tears," and the next day they put in at Steamer Point, north-west of Aden harbour, to take in coal. This matter of fuelling steamers is a serious one at such distances from the coal mines; it costs the Peninsula Company some eight hundred thousand pounds a year. In these distant seas, coal is worth three or four pounds sterling a ton.

The "Mongolia" had still sixteen hundred and fifty miles to traverse before reaching Bombay, and was obliged to remain four hours at Steamer Point to coal up. But this delay, as it was foreseen, did not affect Phileas Fogg's programme; besides, the "Mongolia," instead of reaching Aden on the morning of the 15th, when she was due, arrived there on the evening of the 14th, a gain of fifteen hours.

Mr. Fogg and his servant went ashore at Aden to have the passport again *visaed*; Fix, unobserved, followed them. The *visa* procured, Mr. Fogg returned on board to resume his former habits; while Passepartout, according to custom, sauntered about among the mixed population of Somanlis, Banyans, Parsees, Jews, Arabs, and Europeans who comprise the twenty-five thousand inhabitants of Aden. He gazed with wonder upon the fortifications which make this place the Gibraltar of the Indian Ocean, and the vast cisterns where the English engineers were still at work, two thousand years after the engineers of Solomon.

"Very curious, *very* curious," said Passepartout to himself, on returning to the steamer. "I see that it is by no means useless to travel, if a man wants to see something new." At six p.m. the "Mongolia" slowly moved out of the roadstead, and was soon once more on the Indian Ocean. She had a hundred and sixty-eight hours in which to reach Bombay, and the sea was favourable, the wind being in the north-west, and all sails aiding the engine. The steamer rolled but little, the ladies, in fresh toilets, reappeared on deck, and the singing and dancing were resumed. The trip was being accomplished most successfully, and Passepartout was enchanted with the congenial companion which chance had secured him in the person of the delightful Fix. On Sunday, October 20th, towards noon, they came in sight of the Indian coast: two hours later the pilot came on board. A range of hills lays against the sky in the horizon, and soon the rows of palms which adorn Bombay came distinctly into view. The steamer entered the road formed by the islands in the bay, and at half-past four she hauled up at the quays of Bombay.

Phileas Fogg was in the act of finishing the thirty-third rubber of the voyage, and his partner and himself having, by a bold stroke, captured all thirteen of the tricks, concluded this fine campaign with a brilliant victory.

The "Mongolia" was due at Bombay on the

Passepartout, following his usual custom, takes a stroll.

They put in at Steamer Point.

22nd; she arrived on the 20th. This was a gain to Phileas Fogg of two days since his departure from London, and he calmly entered the fact in the itinerary, in the column of gains.

Around the World in Eighty Days

CHAPTER X.

IN WHICH PASSEPARTOUT IS ONLY TOO GLAS TO GET OFF WITH THE LOSS OF HIS SHOES.

EVERYBODY knows that the great reversed triangle of land, with its base in the north and its apex in the south, which is called India, embraces fourteen hundred thousand square miles, upon which is spread unequally a population of one hundred and eighty millions of souls. The British Crown exercises a real and despotic dominion over the larger portion of this vast country, and has a governor-general stationed at Calcutta, governors at Madras, Bombay, and in Bengal, and a lieutenant-governor at Agra.

But British India, properly so called, only embraces seven hundred thousand square miles, and a population of from one hundred to one hundred and ten millions of inhabitants. A considerable portion of India is still free from British authority; and there are certain ferocious rajahs in the interior who are absolutely independent. The celebrated East India Company was all-powerful from 1756, when the English first gained a foothold on the spot where now stands the city of Madras, down to the time of the great Sepoy insurrection. It gradually annexed province after province, purchasing them of the native chiefs, whom it seldom paid, and appointed the governor-general and his subordinates, civil and military. But the East India Company has now passed away, leaving the British possessions in India directly under the control of the Crown. The aspect of the country, as well as the manners and distinctions of race, is daily changing.

Formerly one was obliged to travel in India by the old cumbrous methods of going on foot or on horseback, in palanquins or unwieldy coaches; now, fast steamboats ply on the Indus and the Ganges, and a great railway, with branch lines joining the main line at many points on its route, traverses the peninsula from Bombay to Calcutta in three days. This railway does not run in a direct line across India. The distance between Bombay and Calcutta, as the bird flies, is only from one thousand to eleven hundred miles; but the deflections of the road increase this distance by more than a third.

The general route of the Great Indian Peninsula Railway is as follows:—Leaving Bombay, it passes through Salcette, crossing to the continent opposite Tannah, goes over the chain of the Western Ghauts, runs thence north-east as far as Burhampoor, skirts the nearly independent territory of Bundelcund, ascends to Allahabad, turns thence eastwardly, meeting the Ganges at Benares, then departs from the river a little, and, descending south-eastward by Burdivan and the French town of Chandernagor, has its terminus at Calcutta.

The passengers of the "Mongolia" went ashore at half-past four p.m.; at exactly eight the train would start for Calcutta.

Mr. Fogg, after bidding good-bye to his whist partners, left the steamer, gave his servant several errands to do, urged it upon him to be at the station promptly at eight, and, with his regular step, which beat to the second, like an astronomical clock, directed his steps to the passport office. As for the wonders of Bombay—its famous city hall, its splendid library, its forts and docks, its bazaars, mosques, synagogues, its Armenian churches, and the noble pagoda on Malebar Hill with its two polygonal towers—he cared not a straw to see them. He would not deign to examine even the masterpieces of Elephanta, or the mysterious hypogea, concealed south-east from the docks, or those fine remains of Buddhist architecture, the Kanherian grottoes of the island of Salcette.

Having transacted his business at the passport office, Phileas Fogg repaired quietly to the railway station, where he ordered dinner. Among the dishes served up to him, the landlord especially recommended a certain giblet of "native rabbit," on which he prided himself.

Mr. Fogg accordingly tasted the dish, but, despite its spiced sauce, found it far from palatable. He rang for the landlord, and on his appearance, said, fixing his clear eyes upon him, "Is this rabbit, sir?"

"Yes, my lord," the rogue boldly replied, "rabbit from the jungles."

"And this rabbit did not mew when he was killed?"

"Mew, my lord! what, a rabbit mew! I swear to you—"

"Be so good, landlord, as not to swear, but remember this: cats were formerly considered, in India, as sacred animals. That was a good time."

"For the cats, my lord?"

"Perhaps for the travellers as well!"

After which Mr. Fogg quietly continued his dinner Fix had gone on shore shortly after Mr. Fogg, and his first destination was the headquarters of the Bombay police. He made himself known as a London detective, told his business at Bombay, and the position of affairs relative to the supposed robber, and nervously asked if a warrant had arrived from London. It has not reached the office; indeed, there had not yet been time for it to arrive. Fix was sorely disappointed, and tried to obtain an order of arrest from the director of the Bombay police. This the director refused, as the matter concerned the London office, which alone could legally deliver the warrant. Fix did not insist, and was fain to resign himself to await the arrival of the important document; but he was determined not to lose sight of the mysterious rogue as long as he stayed in Bombay. He did not doubt for a moment, any more than Passepartout, that Phileas Fogg would remain there, at least until it was time for the warrant to arrive.

Passepartout, however, had no sooner heard his master's orders on leaving the "Mongolia," than he saw at once that they were to leave Bombay as they had done Suez and Paris, and that the journey would be extended at least as far as Calcutta, and perhaps beyond that place. He began to ask himself if this bet that Mr. Fogg talked about was not really in good earnest, and whether his fate was not in truth forcing him, despite his love of repose, around the world in eighty days!

Having purchased the usual quota of shirts and shoes, he took a leisurely promenade about the streets, where crowds of people of many nationalities—Europeans, Persians with pointed caps, Banyas with round turbans, Sindes with square bonnets, Parsees with black mitres, and long-robed Armenians—were collected. It happened to be the day of a Parsee festival. These descendants of the sect of Zoroaster—the most thrifty, civilized, intelligent, and austere of the East Indians, among whom are counted the riches native merchants of Bombay—were celebrating a sort of religious carnival, with processions and shows, in the midst of which Indian dancing-girls, clothed in rose-coloured gauze, looped up with gold and silver, danced airily, but with perfect modesty, to the sound of viols and the clanging of tambourines. It is needless to say that Passepartout watched these curious ceremonies with staring eyes and gaping mouth, and that his countenance was that of the greenest booby imaginable.

Unhappily for his master, as well as himself, his curiosity drew him unconsciously farther off than he intended to go. At last, having seen the Parsee carnival wind away in the distance, he was turning his steps towards the station, when he happened to espy the splendid pagoda on Malebar Hill, and was seized with an irresistible desire to see its interior. He was quite ignorant that it is forbidden to Christians to enter certain Indian temples, and that even the faithful must not go in without first leaving their shoes outside the door. It may be said here that the wise policy of the British Government severely punishes a disregard of the practices of the native religions.

Passepartout, however, thinking no harm, went in like a simple tourist, and was soon lost in admiration of the splendid Brahmin ornamentation which everywhere met his eyes, when of a sudden he found himself sprawling on the sacred flagging. He looked up to behold three enraged priests, who forthwith fell upon him, tore off his shoes, and began to beat him with loud, savage exclamations. The agile Frenchman was soon upon his feet again, and lost no time in knocking down two of his long-gowned adversaries with his fists and a vigorous application of his toes; then, rushing out of the pagoda as fast as his legs could carry him, he soon escaped the third priest by mingling with the crowd in the streets.

At five minutes before eight, Passepartout, hatless, shoeless, and having in the squabble lost his package of shirts and shoes, rushed breathlessly into the station.

Fix, who had followed Mr. Fogg to the station, and saw that he was really going to leave Bombay, was there, upon the platform. He had resolved to follow the supposed robber to Calcutta, and farther, if necessary. Passepartout did not observe the detective, who stood in an obscure corner; but Fix heard him relate his adventures in a few words to Mr. Fogg.

"I hope that this will not happen again," said Phileas Fogg, coldly, as he got into the train. Poor Passepartout, quite crestfallen, followed his master without a word. Fix was on the point of entering another carriage, when an idea struck him which induced him to alter his plan.

"No, I'll stay," muttered he. "An offence has been committed on Indian soil. I've got my man."

Just then the locomotive gave a sharp screech, and the train passed out into the darkness of the night.

He knocked down two of his adversaries.

Around the World in Eighty Days

CHAPTER XI.

IN WHICH PHILEAS FOGG SECURES A CURIOUS MEANS OF CONVEYANCE AT A FABULOUS PRICE.

THE train had started punctually. Among the passengers were a number of officers, Government officials, and opium and indigo merchants, whose business called them to the eastern coast. Passepartout rode in the same carriage with his master, and a third passenger occupied a seat opposite to them. This was Sir Francis Cromarty, one of Mr. Fogg's whist partners on the "Mongolia," now on his way to join his corps at Benares. Sir Francis was a tall, fair man of fifty, who had greatly distinguished himself in the last Sepoy revolt. He made India his home, only paying brief visits to England at rare intervals; and was almost as familiar as a native with the customs, history, and character of India and its people. But Phileas Fogg, who was not travelling, but only describing a circumference, took no pains to inquire into these subjects; he was a solid body, traversing an orbit around the terrestrial globe, according to the laws of rational mechanics. He was at this moment calculating in his mind the number of hours spent since his departure from London, and, had it been in his nature to make a useless demonstration, would have rubbed his hands for satisfaction. Sir Francis Cromarty had observed the oddity of his travelling companion —although the only opportunity he had for studying him had been while he was dealing the cards, and between two rubbers—and questioned himself whether a human heart really beat beneath this cold exterior, and whether Phileas Fogg had any sense of the beauties of nature. The brigadier-general was free to mentally confess, that, of all the eccentric persons he had ever met, none was comparable to this product of the exact sciences.

Phileas Fogg had not concealed from Sir Francis his design of going round the world, nor the circumstances under which he set out; and the general only saw in the wager a useless eccentricity, and a lack of sound commonsense. In the way this strange gentleman was going on, he would leave the world without having done any good to himself or anybody else.

An hour after leaving Bombay the train had passed the viaducts and the island of Salcette, and had got into the open country. At Callyan they reached the junction of the branch line which descends towards south-eastern India by Kandallah and Pounah; and, passing Pauwell, they entered the defiles of the mountains, with their basalt bases, and their summits crowned with thick and verdant forests. Phileas Fogg and Sir Francis Cromarty exchanged a few words from time to time, and now Sir Francis, reviving the conversation, observed, "Some years ago, Mr. Fogg, you would have met with a delay at this point, which would probably have lost you your wager."

"How so, Sir Francis?"

"Because the railway stopped at the base of these mountains, which the passengers were obliged to cross in palanquins or on ponies to Kandallah, on the other side."

"Such a delay would not have deranged my plans in the least," said Mr. Fogg. "I have constantly foreseen the likelihood of certain obstacles."

"But, Mr. Fogg," pursued Sir Francis, "you run the risk of having some difficulty about this worthy fellow's adventure at the pagoda." Passepartout, his feet comfortably wrapped in his travelling-blanket, was sound asleep, and did not dream that anybody was talking about him. "The Government is very severe upon that kind of offence. It takes particular care that the religious customs of the Indians should be respected, and if your servant were caught—"

"Very well, Sir Francis," replied Mr. Fogg; "if he had been caught he would have been condemned and punished, and then would have quietly returned to Europe. I don't see how this affair could have delayed his master."

The conversation fell again. During the night the train left the mountains behind, and passed Nassik, and the next day proceeded over the flat, well-cultivated country of the Khandeish, with its straggling villages, above which rose the minarets of the pagodas. This fertile territory is watered by numerous small rivers and limpid streams, mostly tributaries of the Godavery.

Passepartout, on waking and looking out, could not realize that he was actually crossing India in a railway train. The locomotive, guided by an English engineer and fed with English coal, threw out its smoke upon cotton, coffee,

The smoke formed into spiral columns.

nutmeg, clove, and pepper plantations, while the steam curled in spirals around groups of palm-trees, in the midst of which were seen picturesque bungalows, viharis (a sort of abandoned monasteries), and marvellous temples enriched by the exhaustless ornamentation of Indian architecture. Then they came upon vast tracts extending to the horizon, with jungles inhabited by snakes and tigers, which fled at the noise of the train; succeeded by forests penetrated by the railway, and still haunted by elephants which, with pensive eyes, gazed at the train as it passed. The travellers crossed, beyond Malligaum, the fatal country so often stained with blood by the sectaries of the goddess Kali. Not far off rose Ellora, with its graceful pagodas, and the famous Aurunga-bad, capital of the ferocious Aureng-Zeb, now the chief town of one of the detached provinces of the kingdom of the Nizam. It was there-abouts that Feringhea, the Thuggee chief, king of the stranglers, held his sway. These ruffians, united by a secret bond, strangled victims of every age in honour of the goddess Death, without ever shedding blood; there was a period when this part of the country could scarcely be travelled over without corpses being found in every direction. The English Government has succeeded in greatly diminishing these murders, though the Thuggees still exist, and pursue the exercise of their horrible rites.

At half-past twelve the train stopped at Burhampoor, where Passepartout was able to purchase some Indian slippers, ornamented with false pearls, in which, with evident vanity, he proceeded to incase his feet. The travellers made a hasty breakfast, and started off for Assurghur, after skirting for a little the banks of the small river Tapty, which empties into the Gulf of Cambray, near Surat.

Passepartout was now plunged into absorbing reverie. Up to his arrival at Bombay, he had entertained hopes that their journey would end there; but now that they were plainly whirling across India at full speed, a sudden change had come over the spirit of his dreams. His old vagabond nature returned to him; the fantastic ideas of his youth once more took possession of him. He came to regard his master's project as intended in good earnest, believed in the reality of the bet, and therefore in the tour of the world, and the necessity of making it without fail within the designated period. Already he began to worry about possible delays, and accidents which might happen on the way. He recognized himself as being personally interested in the wager, and trembled at the thought that he might have been the means of

losing it by his unpardonable folly of the night before. Being much less cool-headed than Mr. Fogg, he was much more restless, counting and recounting the days passed over, uttering maledictions when the train stopped, and accusing it of sluggishness, and mentally blaming Mr. Fogg for not having bribed the engineer. The worthy fellow was ignorant that, while it was possible by such means to hasten the rate of a steamer, it could not be done on the railway.

The train entered the defiles of the Sutpour Mountains, which separate the Khandeish from Bundelcund, towards evening. The next day Sir Francis Cromarty asked Passepartout what time it was; to which, on consulting his watch, he replied that it was three in the morning. This famous timepiece, always regulated on the Greenwich meridian, which was now some seventy-seven degrees westward, was at least four hours slow. Sir Francis corrected Passepartout's time, whereupon the latter made the same remark that he had done to Fix; and upon the general insisting that the watch should be regulated in each new meridian, since he was constantly going eastward, that is in the face of the sun, and therefore the days were shorter by four minutes for each degree gone over, Passepartout obstinately refused to alter his watch, which he kept at London time. It was an innocent delusion which could harm no one.

The train stopped, at eight o'clock, in the midst of a glade some fifteen miles beyond Rothal, where there were several bungalows and workmen's cabins. The conductor, passing along the carriages, shouted, "Passengers will get out here!"

Phileas Fogg looked at Sir Francis Cromarty for an explanation; but the general could not tell what meant a halt in the midst of this forest of dates and acacias.

Passepartout, not less surprised, rushed out and speedily returned, crying, "Monsieur, no more railway!"

"What do you mean?" asked Sir Francis.

"I mean to say that the train isn't going on."

The general at once stepped out, while Phileas Fogg calmly followed him, and they proceeded together to the conductor.

"Where are we?" asked Sir Francis.

"At the hamlet of Kholby."

"Do we stop here?"

"Certainly. The railway isn't finished."

"What! not finished?"

"No. There's still a matter of fifty miles to be laid from here to Allahabad, where the line begins again."

"But the papers announced the opening of the railway throughout."

"What would you have, officer? The papers were mistaken."

"Yet you sell tickets from Bombay to Calcutta," retorted Sir Francis, who was growing warm.

"No doubt," replied the conductor; "but the passengers know that they must provide means of transportation for themselves from Kholby to Allahabad."

Sir Francis was furious. Passepartout would willingly have knocked the conductor down, and did not dare to look at his master.

"Sir Francis," said Mr. Fogg, quietly, "we will, if you please, look about for some means of conveyance to Allahabad."

"Mr. Fogg, this is a delay greatly to your disadvantage."

"No, Sir Francis; it was foreseen."

"What! You knew that the way—"

"Not at all; but I knew that some obstacle or other would sooner or later arise on my route. Nothing, therefore, is lost. I have two days which I have already gained to sacrifice. A steamer leaves Calcutta for Hong Kong at noon, on the 25th. This is the 22nd, and we shall reach Calcutta in time."

There was nothing to say to so confident a response.

It was but too true that the railway came to a termination at this point. The papers were like some watches, which have a way of getting too fast, and had been premature in their announcement of the completion of the line. The greater part of the travellers were aware of this interruption, and leaving the train, they began to engage such vehicles as the village could provide — four-wheeled palkigharis, waggons drawn by zebus, carriages that looked like perambulating pagodas, palanquins, ponies, and what not.

Mr. Fogg and Sir Francis Cromarty, after searching the village from end to end, came back without having found anything.

"I shall go afoot," said Phileas Fogg.

Passepartout, who had now rejoined his master, made a wry grimace, as he thought of his magnificent, but too frail Indian shoes. Happily he too had been looking about him, and, after a moment's hesitation, said, "Monsieur, I think I have found a means of conveyance."

"What?"

"An elephant! An elephant that belongs to an Indian who lives but a hundred steps from here."

"Let's go and see the elephant," replied Mr. Fogg.

They soon reached a small hut, near which, enclosed within some high palings, was the animal in question. An Indian came out of the hut, and, at their request, conducted them within the enclosure. The elephant, which its owner had reared, not for a beast of burden, but for warlike purposes, was half domesticated. The Indian had begun already, by often irritating him, and feeding him every three months on sugar and butter, to impart to him a ferocity not in his nature, this method being often employed by those who train the Indian elephants for battle. Happily, however, for Mr. Fogg, the animal's instruction in this direction had not gone far, and the elephant still preserved his natural gentleness. Kiouni—this was the name of the beast—could doubtless travel rapidly for a long time, and, in default of any other means of conveyance, Mr. Fogg resolved to hire him. But elephants are far from cheap in India, where they are becoming scarce; the males, which alone are suitable for circus shows, are much sought, especially as but few of them are domesticated. When, therefore, Mr. Fogg proposed to the Indian to hire Kiouni, he refused point-blank. Mr. Fogg persisted, offering the excessive sum of ten pounds an hour for the loan of the beast to Allahabad. Refused. Twenty pounds? Refused also. Forty pounds? Still refused. Passepartout jumped at each advance; but the Indian declined to be tempted. Yet the offer was an alluring one, for, supposing it took the elephant fifteen hours to reach Allahabad, his owner would receive no less than six hundred pounds sterling.

Phileas Fogg, without getting in the least flurried, then proposed to purchase the animal outright, and at first offered a thousand pounds for him. The Indian, perhaps thinking he was going to make a great bargain, still refused.

Sir Francis Cromarty took Mr. Fogg aside, and begged him to reflect before he went any further; to which that gentleman replied that he was not in the habit of acting rashly, that a bet of twenty thousand pounds was at stake, that the elephant was absolutely necessary to him, and that he would secure him if he had to pay twenty times his value. Returning to the Indian, whose small, sharp eyes, glistening with avarice, betrayed that with him it was only a question of how great a price he could obtain, Mr. Fogg offered first twelve hundred, then fifteen hundred, eighteen hundred, two thousand pounds. Passepartout, usually so rubicund, was fairly white with suspense.

There they found themselves in the presence of an animal.

At two thousand pounds the Indian yielded.

"What a price, good heaven!" cried Passepartout, "for an elephant!"

It only remained now to find a guide, which was comparatively easy. A young Parsee, with an intelligent face, offered his services, which Mr. Fogg accepted, promising so generous a reward as to materially stimulate his zeal. The elephant was led out and equipped. The Parsee, who was an accomplished elephant driver, covered his back with a sort of saddle-cloth, and attached to each of his flanks some curiously uncomfortable howdahs.

Phileas Fogg paid the Indian with some bank-notes which he extracted from the famous carpet-bag, a proceeding that seemed to deprive poor Passepartout of his vitals. Then he offered to carry Sir Francis to Allahabad, which the brigadier gratefully accepted, as one traveller the more would not be likely to fatigue the gigantic beast. Provisions were purchased at Kholby, and while Sir Francis and Mr. Fogg took the howdahs on either side, Passepartout got astride the saddle-cloth between them. The Parsee perched himself on the elephant's neck, and at nine o'clock they set out from the village, the animal marching off through the dense forest of palms by the shortest cut.

Around the World in Eighty Days

CHAPTER XII.

IN WHICH PHILEAS FOGG AND HIS COMPANIONS VENTURE ACROSS THE INDIAN FORESTS, AND WHAT ENSUED.

IN order to shorten the journey, the guide passed to the left of the line where the railway was still in process of being built. This line, owing to the capricious turnings of the Vindhia Mountains, did not pursue a straight course. The Parsee, who was quite familiar with the roads and paths in the district, declared that they would gain twenty miles by striking directly through the forest.

Phileas Fogg and Sir Francis Cromarty, plunged to the neck in the peculiar howdahs provided for them, were horribly jostled by the swift trotting of the elephant, spurred on as he was by the skilful Parsee; but they endured the discomfort with true British phlegm, talking little, and scarcely able to catch a glimpse of each other. As for Passepartout, who was mounted on the beast's back, and received the direct force of each concussion as he trod along, he was very careful, in accordance with his master's advice, to keep his tongue from between his teeth, as it would otherwise have been bitten off short. The worthy fellow bounced from the elephant's neck to his rump, and vaulted like a clown on a spring-board; yet he laughed in the midst of his bouncing, and from time to time took a piece of sugar out of his pocket, and inserted it in Kiouni's trunk, who received it without in the least slackening his regular trot.

After two hours the guide stopped the elephant, and gave him an hour for rest, during which Kiouni, after quenching his thirst at a neighbouring spring, set to devouring the branches and shrubs round about him. Neither Sir Francis nor Mr. Fogg regretted the delay, and both descended with a feeling of relief. "Why, he's made of iron!" exclaimed the general, gazing admiringly on Kiouni.

"Of forged iron," replied Passepartout, as he set about preparing a hasty breakfast.

At noon the Parsee gave the signal of departure. The country soon presented a very savage aspect. Copses of dates and dwarf-palms, dotted with scanty shrubs, and sown with great blocks of syenite. All this portion of Bundelcund, which is little frequented by travellers, is inhabited by a fanatical population, hardened in the most horrible practices of the Hindoo faith. The English have not been able to secure complete dominion over this territory, which is subjected to the influence of rajahs, whom it is almost impossible to reach in their inaccessible mountain fastnesses. The travellers several times saw bands of ferocious Indians, who, when they perceived the elephant striding across country, made angry and threatening motions. The Parsee avoided them as much as possible. Few animals were observed on the route; even the monkeys hurried from their path with contortions and grimaces which convulsed Passepartout with laughter.

In the midst of his gaiety, however, one thought troubled the worthy servant. What would Mr. Fogg do with the elephant, when he got to Allahabad? Would he carry him on with him? Impossible! The cost of transporting him would make him ruinously expensive. Would he sell him, or set him free? The estimable beast certainly deserved some consideration. Should Mr. Fogg choose to make him, Passepartout, a present of Kiouni, he would be very much embarrassed; and these thoughts did not cease worrying him for a long time.

The principal chain of the Vindhias was crossed by eight in the evening, and another halt was made on the northern slope, in a ruined bungalow. They had gone nearly twenty-five miles that day, and an equal distance still separated them from the station of Allahabad.

The night was cold. The Parsee lit a fire in the bungalow with a few dry branches, and the warmth was very grateful. The provisions purchased at Kholby sufficed for supper, and the travellers ate ravenously. The conversation, beginning with a few disconnected phrases, soon gave place to loud and steady snores. The guide watched Kiouni, who slept standing, bolstering himself against the trunk of a large tree. Nothing occurred during the night to disturb the slumberers, although occasional growls from panthers and chatterings of monkeys broke the silence; the more formidable beasts made no cries or hostile demonstration against the occupants of the bungalow. Sir Francis slept heavily, like an honest soldier overcome with fatigue. Passepartout was

Passepartout's uneasy ride on the back of the Elephant.

Bands of Hindoos of both sexes

wrapped in uneasy dreams of the bouncing of the day before. As for Mr. Fogg, he slumbered as peacefully as if he had been in his serene mansion in Saville Row.

The journey was resumed at six in the morning; the guide hoped to reach Allahabad by evening. In that case, Mr. Fogg would only lose a part of the forty-eight hours saved since the beginning of the tour. Kiouni, resuming his rapid gait, soon descended the lower spurs of the Vindhias, and towards noon they passed by the village of Kallenger, on the Cani, one of the branches of the Ganges. The guide avoided inhabited places, thinking it safer to keep the open country, which lies along the first depressions of the basin of the great river. Allahabad was now only twelve miles to the north-east. They stopped under a clump of bananas, the fruit of which, as healthy as bread and as succulent as cream, was amply partaken of and appreciated.

At two o'clock the guide entered a thick forest which extended several miles; he preferred to travel under cover of the woods. They had not as yet had any unpleasant encounters, and the journey seemed on the point of being successfully accomplished, when the elephant, becoming restless, suddenly stopped.

It was then four o'clock.

"What's the matter?" asked Sir Francis, putting out his head.

"I don't know, officer," replied the Parsee, listening attentively to a confused murmur which came through the thick branches.

The murmur soon became more distinct; it now seemed like a distant concert of human voices accompanied by brass instruments. Passepartout was all eyes and ears. Mr. Fogg patiently waited without a word. The Parsee jumped to the ground, fastened the elephant to a tree, and plunged into the thicket. He soon returned, saying,—

"A procession of Brahmins is coming this way. We must prevent their seeing us, if possible."

The guide unloosed the elephant and led him into a thicket, at the same time asking the travellers not to stir. He held himself ready to bestride the animal at a moment's notice, should flight become necessary; but he evidently thought that the procession of the faithful would pass without perceiving them amid the thick foliage, in which they were wholly concealed.

The discordant tones of the voices and instruments drew nearer, and now droning songs mingled with the sound of the tambourines and cymbals. The head of the procession soon appeared beneath the trees, a hundred paces away; and the strange figures who performed the religious ceremony were easily distinguished through the branches. First came the priests, with mitres on their heads, and clothed in long lace robes. They were surrounded by men, women, and children, who sang a kind of lugubrious psalm, interrupted at regular intervals by the tambourines and cymbals; while behind them was drawn a car with large wheels, the spokes of which represented serpents entwined with each other. Upon the car, which was drawn by four richly caparisoned zebus, stood a hideous statue with four arms, the body coloured a dull red, with haggard eyes, dishevelled hair, protruding tongue, and lips tinted with betel. It stood upright upon the figure of a prostrate and headless giant.

Sir Francis, recognizing the statue, whispered, "The goddess Kali; the goddess of love and death."

"Of death, perhaps," muttered back Passepartout, "but of love—that ugly old hag? Never!"

The Parsee made a motion to keep silence.

A group of old fakirs were capering and making a wild ado around the statue; these were striped with ochre, and covered with cuts whence their blood issued drop by drop,—stupid fanatics, who, in the great Indian ceremonies, still throw themselves under the wheels of Juggernaut. Some Brahmins, clad in all the sumptuousness of Oriental apparel, and leading a woman who faltered at every step, followed. This woman was young, and as fair as a European. Her head and neck, shoulders, ears, arms, hands, and toes, were loaded down with jewels and gems,—with bracelets, earrings, and rings; while a tunic bordered with gold, and covered with a light muslin robe, betrayed the outline of her form.

The guards who followed the young woman presented a violent contrast to her, armed as they were with naked sabres hung at their waists, and long damasceened pistols, and bearing a corpse on a palanquin. It was the body of an old man, gorgeously arrayed in the habiliments of a rajah, wearing, as in life, a turban embroidered with pearls, a robe of tissue of silk and gold, a scarf of cashmere sewed with diamonds, and the magnificent weapons of a Hindoo prince. Next came the musicians and a rearguard of capering fakirs, whose cries sometimes drowned the noise of the instruments; these closed the procession.

Sir Francis watched the procession with a sad

It was a young woman.

countenance, and, turning to the guide, said, "A suttee."

The Parsee nodded, and put his finger to his lips. The procession slowly wound under the trees, and soon its last ranks disappeared in the depths of the wood. The songs gradually died away; occasionally cries were heard in the distance, until at last all was silence again.

Phileas Fogg had heard what Sir Francis said, and, as soon as the procession had disappeared, asked, "What is a 'suttee'?"

"A suttee," returned the general, "is a human sacrifice, but a voluntary one. The woman you have just seen will be burned tomorrow at the dawn of day."

"Oh, the scoundrels!" cried Passepartout, who could not repress his indignation.

"And the corpse?" asked Mr. Fogg.

"Is that of the prince, her husband," said the guide; "an independent rajah of Bundelcund."

"Is it possible," resumed Phileas Fogg, his voice betraying not the least emotion, "that these barbarous customs still exist in India, and that the English have been unable to put a stop to them?"

"These sacrifices do not occur in the larger portion of India," replied Sir Francis; "but we have no power over these savage territories, and especially here in Bundelcund. The whole district north of the Vindhias is the theatre of incessant murders and pillage."

"The poor wretch!" exclaimed Passepartout, "to be burned alive!"

"Yes," returned Sir Francis, "burned alive. And if she were not, you cannot conceive what treatment she would be obliged to submit to from her relatives. They would shave off her hair, feed her on a scanty allowance of rice, treat her with contempt; she would be looked upon as an unclean creature, and would die in some corner, like a scurvy dog. The prospect of so frightful an existence drives these poor creatures to the sacrifice much more than love or religious fanaticism. Sometimes, however, the sacrifice is really voluntary, and it requires the active interference of the Government to prevent it. Several years ago, when I was living at Bombay, a young widow asked permission of the governor to be burned along with her husband's body; but, as you may imagine, he refused. The woman left the town, took refuge with an independent rajah, and there carried out her self-devoted purpose."

While Sir Francis was speaking, the guide shook his head several times, and now said, "The sacrifice which will take place to-morrow at dawn is not a voluntary one."

"How do you know?"

"Everybody knows about this affair in Bundelcund."

"But the wretched creature did not seem to be making any resistance," observed Sir Francis.

"That was because they had intoxicated her with fumes of hemp and opium."

"But where are they taking her?"

"To the pagoda of Pillaji, two miles from here; she will pass the night there."

"And the sacrifice will take place—"

"To-morrow, at the first light of dawn."

The guide now led the elephant out of the thicket, and leaped upon his neck. Just at the moment that he was about to urge Kiouni forward with a peculiar whistle, Mr. Fogg stopped him, and, turning to Sir Francis Cromarty, said, "Suppose we save this woman."

"Save the woman, Mr. Fogg!"

"I have yet twelve hours to spare; I can devote them to that."

"Why, you are a man of heart!"

"Sometimes," replied Phileas Fogg, quietly; "when I have the time."

Around the World in Eighty Days

CHAPTER XIII.

IN WHICH PASSEPARTOUT RECEIVES A NEW PROOF THAT FORTUNE FAVOURS THE BRAVE.

THE project was a bold one, full of difficulty, perhaps impracticable. Mr. Fogg was going to risk life, or at least liberty, and therefore the success of his tour. But he did not hesitate, and he found in Sir Francis Cromarty an enthusiastic ally.

As for Passepartout, he was ready for anything that might be proposed. His master's idea charmed him; he perceived a heart, a soul, under that icy exterior. He began to love Phileas Fogg.

There remained the guide: what course would he adopt? would he not take part with the Indians? In default of his assistance, it was necessary to be assured of his neutrality.

Sir Francis frankly put the question to him.

"Officers," replied the guide, "I am a Parsee, and this woman is a Parsee. Command me as you will."

"Excellent," said Mr. Fogg.

"However," resumed the guide, "it is certain, not only that we shall risk our lives, but horrible tortures, if we are taken."

"That is foreseen," replied Mr. Fogg. "I think we must wait till night before acting."

"I think so," said the guide.

The worthy Indian then gave some account of the victim, who, he said, was a celebrated beauty of the Parsee race, and the daughter of a wealthy Bombay merchant. She had received a thoroughly English education in that city, and, from her manners and intelligence, would be thought an European. Her name was Aouda. Left an orphan, she was married against her will to the old rajah of Bundelcund; and, knowing the fate that awaited her, she escaped, was retaken, and devoted by the rajah's relatives, who had an interest in her death, to the sacrifice from which it seemed she could not escape.

The Parsee's narrative only confirmed Mr. Fogg and his companions in their generous design. It was decided that the guide should direct the elephant towards the pagoda of Pillaji, which he accordingly approached as quickly as possible. They halted, half an hour afterwards, in a copse, some five hundred feet from the pagoda, where they were well concealed; but they could hear the groans and cries of the fakirs distinctly.

They then discussed the means of getting at the victim. The guide was familiar with the pagoda of Pillaji, in which, as he declared, the young woman was imprisoned. Could they enter any of its doors while the whole party of Indians was plunged in a drunken sleep, or was it safer to attempt to make a hole in the walls? This could only be determined at the moment and the place themselves; but it was certain that the abduction must be made that night, and not when, at break of day, the victim was led to her funeral pyre. Then no human intervention could save her.

As soon as night fell, about six o'clock, they decided to make a reconnoissance around the pagoda. The cries of the fakirs were just ceasing; the Indians were in the act of plunging themselves into the drunkenness caused by liquid opium mingled with hemp, and it might be possible to slip between them to the temple itself.

The Parsee, leading the others, noiselessly crept through the wood, and in ten minutes they found themselves on the banks of a small stream, whence, by the light of the rosin torches, they perceived a pyre of wood, on the top of which lay the embalmed body of the rajah, which was to be burned with his wife. The pagoda, whose minarets loomed above the trees in the deepening dusk, stood a hundred steps away.

"Come!" whispered the guide.

He slipped more cautiously than ever through the brush, followed by his companions; the silence around was only broken by the low murmuring of the wind among the branches.

Soon the Parsee stopped on the borders of the glade, which was lit up by the torches. The ground was covered by groups of the Indians, motionless in their drunken sleep; it seemed a battle-field strewn with the dead. Men, women, and children lay together.

In the background, among the trees, the pagoda of Pillaji loomed indistinctly. Much to the guide's disappointment, the guards of the rajah, lighted by torches, were watching at the doors and marching to and fro with naked sabres; probably the priests, too, were watching within.

The Rajah's Guards.

The Parsee, now convinced that it was impossible to force an entrance to the temple, advanced no farther, but led his companions back again. Phileas Fogg and Sir Francis Cromarty also saw that nothing could be attempted in that direction. They stopped, and engaged in a whispered colloquy.

"It is only eight now," said the brigadier, "and these guards may also go to sleep."

"It is not impossible," returned the Parsee.

They lay down at the foot of a tree, and waited.

The time seemed long; the guide ever and anon left them to take an observation on the edge of the wood, but the guards watched steadily by the glare of the torches, and a dim light crept through the windows of the pagoda.

They waited till midnight; but no change took place among the guards, and it became apparent that their yielding to sleep could not be counted on. The other plan must be carried out; an opening in the walls of the pagoda must be made. It remained to ascertain whether the priests were watching by the side of their victim as assiduously as were the soldiers at the door.

After a last consultation, the guide announced that he was ready for the attempt, and advanced, followed by the others. They took a roundabout way, so as to get at the pagoda on the rear. They reached the walls about half-past twelve, without having met any one; here there was no guard, nor were there either windows or doors.

The night was dark. The moon, on the wane, scarcely left the horizon, and was covered with heavy clouds; the height of the trees deepened the darkness.

It was not enough to reach the walls; an opening in them must be accomplished, and to attain this purpose the party only had their pocket-knives. Happily the temple walls were built of brick and wood, which could be penetrated with little difficulty; after one brick had been taken out, the rest would yield easily.

They set noiselessly to work, and the Parsee on one side and Passepartout on the other began to loosen the bricks' so as to make an aperture two feet wide. They were getting on rapidly, when suddenly a cry was heard in the interior of the temple, followed almost instantly by other cries replying from the outside. Passepartout and the guide stopped. Had they been heard? Was the alarm being given? Common prudence urged them to retire, and they did so, followed by Phileas Fogg and Sir Francis. They again hid themselves in the wood, and waited till the disturbance, whatever it might be, ceased, holding themselves ready to resume their attempt without delay. But, awkwardly enough, the guards now appeared at the rear of the temple, and there installed themselves, in readiness to prevent a surprise.

It would be difficult to describe the disappointment of the party, thus interrupted in their work. They could not now reach the victim; how, then, could they save her? Sir Francis shook his fists, Passepartout was beside himself, and the guide gnashed his teeth with rage. The tranquil Fogg waited, without betraying any emotion.

"We have nothing to do but to go away," whispered Sir Francis.

"Nothing but to go away," echoed the guide.

"Stop," said Fogg. "I am only due at Allahabad to-morrow before noon."

"But what can you hope to do?" asked Sir Francis. "In a few hours it will be daylight, and—"

"The chance which now seems lost may present itself at the last moment."

Sir Francis would have liked to read Phileas Fogg's eyes.

What was this cool Englishman thinking of? Was he planning to make a rush for the young woman at the very moment of the sacrifice, and boldly snatch her from her executioners?

This would be utter folly, and it was hard to admit that Fogg was such a fool. Sir Francis consented, however, to remain to the end of this terrible drama. The guide led them to the rear of the glade, where they were able to observe the sleeping groups.

Meanwhile Passepartout, who had perched himself on the lower branches of a tree, was revolving an idea which had at first struck him like a flash, and which was now firmly lodged in his brain.

He had commenced by saying to himself, "What folly!" and then he repeated, "Why not, after all? It's a chance,—perhaps the only one; and with such sots!" Thinking thus, he slipped, with the suppleness of a serpent, to the lowest branches, the ends of which bent almost to the ground.

The hours passed, and the lighter shades now announced the approach of day, though it was not yet light. This was the moment. The slumbering multitude became animated, the tambourines sounded, songs and cries arose; the hour of the sacrifice had come. The doors of the pagoda swung open, and a bright light escaped from its interior, in the midst of which Mr. Fogg and Sir Francis espied the victim. She seemed, having shaken off the stupor of intoxication, to be striving to escape from her executioner. Sir Francis's heart throbbed; and

There was a cry of terror.

convulsively seizing Mr. Fogg's hand, found in it an open knife. Just at this moment the crowd began to move. The young woman had again fallen into a stupor, caused by the fumes of hemp, and passed among the fakirs, who escorted her with their wild, religious cries.

Phileas Fogg and his companions, mingling in the rear ranks of the crowd, followed; and in two minutes they reached the banks of the stream, and stopped fifty paces from the pyre, upon which still lay the rajah's corpse. In the semi-obscurity they saw the victim, quite senseless, stretched out beside her husband's body. Then a torch was brought, and the wood, soaked with oil, instantly took fire.

At this moment Sir Francis and the guide seized Phileas Fogg, who, in an instant of mad generosity, was about to rush upon the pyre. But he had quickly pushed them aside, when the whole scene suddenly changed. A cry of terror arose. The whole multitude prostrated themselves, terror-stricken, on the ground.

The old rajah was not dead, then, since he rose of a sudden, like a spectre, took up his wife in his arms, and descended from the pyre in the midst of the clouds of smoke, which only heightened his ghostly appearance.

Fakirs and soldiers and priests, seized with instant terror, lay there, with their faces on the ground, not daring to lift their eyes and behold such a prodigy.

The inanimate victim was borne along by the vigorous arms which supported her, and which she did not seem in the least to burden. Mr. Fogg and Sir Francis stood erect, the Parsee bowed his head, and Passepartout was, no doubt, scarcely less stupefied.

The resuscitated rajah approached Sir Francis and Mr. Fogg, and, in an abrupt tone, said, "Let us be off!"

It was Passepartout himself, who had slipped upon the pyre in the midst of the smoke and, profiting by the still overhanging darkness, had delivered the young woman from death! It was Passepartout who, playing his part with a happy audacity, had passed through the crowd amid the general terror.

A moment after all four of the party had disappeared in the woods, and the elephant was bearing them away at a rapid pace. But the cries and noise, and a ball which whizzed through Phileas Fogg's hat, apprised them that the trick had been discovered.

The old rajah's body, indeed, now appeared upon the burning pyre; and the priests, recovered from their terror, perceived that an abduction had taken place. They hastened into the forest, followed by the soldiers, who fired a volley after the fugitives; but the latter rapidly increased the distance between them, and ere long found themselves beyond the reach of the bullets and arrows.

Around the World in Eighty Days

CHAPTER XIV.

IN WHICH PHILEAS FOGG DESCENDS THE WHOLE LENGTH OF THE BEAUTIFUL VALLEY OF THE GANGES WITHOUT EVER THINKING OF SEEING IT.

THE rash exploit had been accomplished; and for an hour Passepartout laughed gaily at his success. Sir Francis pressed the worthy fellow's hand, and his master said, "Well done!" which, from him, was high commendation; to which Passepartout replied that all the credit of the affair belonged to Mr. Fogg. As for him, he had only been struck with a "queer" idea; and he laughed to think that for a few moments he, Passepartout, the ex-gymnast, ex-sergeant fireman, had been the spouse of a charming woman, a venerable, embalmed rajah! As for the young Indian woman, she had been unconscious throughout of what was passing, and now, wrapped up in a travelling-blanket, was reposing in one of the howdahs.

The elephant, thanks to the skilful guidance of the Parsee, was advancing rapidly through the still darksome forest, and, an hour after leaving the pagoda, had crossed a vast plain. They made a halt at seven o'clock, the young woman being still in a state of complete prostration. The guide made her drink a little brandy and water, but the drowsiness which stupefied her could not yet be shaken off. Sir Francis, who was familiar with the effects of the intoxication produced by the fumes of hemp, reassured his companions on her account. But he was more disturbed at the prospect of her future fate. He told Phileas Fogg that, should Aouda remain in India, she would inevitably fall again into the hands of her executioners. These fanatics were scattered throughout the country, and would, despite the English police, recover their victim at Madras, Bombay, or Calcutta. She would only be safe by quitting India for ever.

Phileas Fogg replied that he would reflect upon the matter.

The station at Allahabad was reached about ten o'clock, and the interrupted line of railway being resumed, would enable them to reach Calcutta in less than twenty-four hours. Phileas Fogg would thus be able to arrive in time to take the steamer which left Calcutta the next day, October 25th, at noon, for Hong Kong.

The young woman was placed in one of the waiting-rooms of the station, whilst Passepartout was charged with purchasing for her various articles of toilet, a dress, shawl, and some furs; for which his master gave him unlimited credit. Passepartout started off forthwith, and found himself in the streets of Allahabad, that is, the "City of God," one of the most venerated in India, being built at the junction of the two sacred rivers Ganges and Jumna, the waters of which attract pilgrims from every part of the peninsula. The Ganges, according to the legends of the Ramayana, rises in heaven, whence, owing to Brahma's agency, it descends to the earth.

Passepartout made it a point, as he made his purchases, to take a good look at the city. It was formerly defended by a noble fort, which has since become a state prison; its commerce has dwindled away, and Passepartout in vain looked about him for such a bazaar as he used to frequent in Regent Street. At last he came upon an elderly, crusty Jew, who sold second-hand articles, and from whom he purchased a dress of Scotch stuff, a large mantle, and a fine otter-skin pelisse, for which he did not hesitate to pay seventy-five pounds. He then returned triumphantly to the station.

The influence to which the priests of Pillaji had subjected Aouda began gradually to yield, and she became more herself, so that her fine eyes resumed all their soft Indian expression.

When the poet-king, Ucaf Uddaul, celebrates the charms of the queen of Ahmehnagara, he speaks thus:—

"Her shining tresses, divided in two parts, encircle the harmonious contour of her white and delicate cheeks, brilliant in their glow and freshness. Her ebony brows have the form and charm of the bow of Kama, the god of love, and beneath her long silken lashes the purest reflections and a celestial light swim, as in the sacred lakes of Himalaya, in the black pupils of her great clear eyes. Her teeth, fine, equal, and white, glitter between her smiling lips like dew-drops in a passion-flower's half-enveloped breast. Her delicately formed ears, her vermilion hands, her little feet, curved and tender as the lotus-bud, glitter with the brilliancy of the loveliest pearls of Ceylon, the most dazzling diamonds of Golconda. Her narrow and supple waist, which a hand may clasp around, sets forth the outline of her rounded figure and the beauty of her bosom,

Passepartout not at all frightened.

where youth in its flower displays the wealth of its treasures; and beneath the silken folds of her tunic she seems to have been modelled in pure silver by the godlike hand of Vicvarcarma, the immortal sculptor.''

It is enough to say, without applying this poetical rhapsody to Aouda, that she was a charming woman, in all the European acceptation of the phrase. She spoke English with great purity, and the guide had not exaggerated in saying that the young Parsee had been transformed by her bringing up.

The train was about to start from Allahabad, and Mr. Fogg proceeded to pay the guide the price agreed upon for his service, and not a farthing more; which astonished Passepartout, who remembered all that his master owed to the guide's devotion. He had, indeed, risked his life in the adventure at Pillaji, and if he should be caught afterwards by the Indians, he would with difficulty escape their vengeance. Kiouni, also, must be disposed of. What should be done with the elephant, which had been so dearly purchased? Phileas Fogg had already determined this question.

"Parsee," said he to the guide, "you have been serviceable and devoted. I have paid for your service, but not for your devotion. Would you like to have this elephant? He is yours."

The guide's eyes glistened.

"Your honour is giving me a fortune!" cried he.

"Take him, guide," returned Mr. Fogg, "and I shall still be your debtor."

"Good!" exclaimed Passepartout; "take him, friend. Kiouni is a brave and faithful beast." And, going up to the elephant, he gave him several lumps of sugar, saying, "Here, Kiouni, here, here."

The elephant grunted out his satisfaction, and, clasping Passepartout around the waist with his trunk, lifted him as high as his head. Passepartout, not in the least alarmed, caressed the animal, which replaced him gently on the ground.

Soon after, Phileas Fogg, Sir Francis Cromarty, and Passepartout, installed in a carriage with Aouda, who had the best seat, were whirling at full speed towards Benares. It was a run of eighty miles, and was accomplished in two hours. During the journey, the young woman fully recovered her senses. What was her astonishment to find herself in this carriage, on the railway, dressed in European habiliments, and with travellers who were quite strangers to her! Her companions first set about fully reviving her with a little liquor, and then Sir Francis narrated to her what had

passed, dwelling upon the courage with which Phileas Fogg had not hesitated to risk his life to save her, and recounting the happy sequel of the venture, the result of Passepartout's rash idea. Mr. Fogg said nothing; while Passepartout, abashed, kept repeating that "it wasn't worth telling."

Aouda pathetically thanked her deliverers, rather with tears than words; her fine eyes interpreted her gratitude better than her lips. Then, as her thoughts strayed back to the scene of the sacrifice, and recalled the dangers which still menaced her, she shuddered with terror.

Phileas Fogg understood what was passing in Aouda's mind, and offered, in order to reassure her, to escort her to Hong Kong, where she might remain safely until the affair was hushed up—an offer which she eagerly and gratefully accepted. She had, it seems, a Parsee relation, who was one of the principal merchants of Hong Kong, which is wholly an English city, though on an island on the Chinese coast.

At half-past twelve the train stopped at Benares. The Brahmin legends assert that this city is built on the site of the ancient Casi, which, like Mahomet's tomb, was once suspended between heaven and earth; though the Benares of to-day, which the Orientalists call the Athens of India, stands quite unpoetically on the solid earth. Passepartout caught glimpses of its brick houses and clay huts, giving an aspect of desolation to the place, as the train entered it.

Benares was Sir Francis Cromarty's destination, the troops he was rejoining being encamped some miles northward of the city. He bade adieu to Phileas Fogg, wishing him all success, and expressing the hope that he would come that way again in a less original but more profitable fashion. Mr. Fogg lightly pressed him by the hand. The parting of Aouda, who did not forget what she owed to Sir Francis, betrayed more warmth; and, as for Passepartout, he received a hearty shake of the hand from the gallant general.

The railway, on leaving Benares, passed for a while along the valley of the Ganges. Through the windows of their carriage the travellers had glimpses of the diversified landscape of Behar, with its mountains clothed in verdure, its fields of barley, wheat, and corn, its jungles peopled with green alligators, its neat villages, and its still thickly-leaved forests. Elephants were bathing in the waters of the sacred river, and groups of Indians, despite the advanced season and chilly air, were performing solemnly their pious ablutions. These were fervent Brahmins, the bitterest foes of Buddhism, their deities being Vishnu, the solar god, Shiva, the divine impersonation of natural forces, and Brahma, the supreme ruler of priests and legislators. What would these divinities think of India, anglicized as it is to-day, with steamers whistling and scudding along the Ganges, frightening the gulls which float upon its surface, the turtles swarming along its banks, and the faithful dwelling upon its borders?

The panorama passed before their eyes like a flash, save when the steam concealed it fitfully from the view; the travellers could scarcely discern the fort of Chupenie, twenty miles south-westward from Benares, the ancient stronghold of the rajahs of Behar; or Ghazipur and its famous rose-water factories; or the tomb of Lord Cornwallis, rising on the left bank of the Ganges; the fortified town of Buxar, or Patna, a large manufacturing and trading place, where is held the principal opium market of India; or Monghir, a more than European town, for it is as English as Manchester or Birmingham, with its iron foundries, edge-tool factories, and high

chimneys puffing clouds of black smoke heavenward.

Night came on; the train passed on at full speed, in the midst of the roaring of the tigers, bears, and wolves which fled before the locomotive; and the marvels of Bengal, Golconda, ruined Gour, Murshedabad, the ancient capital, Burdwan, Hugly, and the French town of Chandernagor, where Passepartout would have been proud to see his country's flag flying, were hidden from their view in the darkness.

Calcutta was reached at seven in the morning, and the packet left for Hong Kong at noon; so that Phileas Fogg had five hours before him.

According to his journal, he was due at Calcutta on the 25th of October, and that was the exact date of his actual arrival. He was therefore neither behindhand nor ahead of time. The two days gained between London and Bombay had been lost, as has been seen, in the journey across India. But it is not to be supposed that Phileas Fogg regretted them.

CHAPTER XV.

IN WHICH THE BAG OF BANK-NOTES DISGORGES SOME THOUSANDS OF POUNDS MORE.

THE train entered the station, and Passepartout, jumping out first, was followed by Mr. Fogg, who assisted his fair companion to descend. Phileas Fogg intended to proceed at once to the Hong Kong steamer, in order to get Aouda comfortably settled for the voyage. He was unwilling to leave her while they were still on dangerous ground.

Just as he was leaving the station a policeman came up to him, and said, "Mr. Phileas Fogg?"

"I am he."

"Is this man your servant?" added the policeman, pointing to Passepartout.

"Yes."

"Be so good, both of you, as to follow me."

Mr. Fogg betrayed no surprise whatever. The policeman was a representative of the law, and law is sacred to an Englishman. Passepartout tried to reason about the matter, but the policeman tapped him with his stick, and Mr. Fogg made him a signal to obey.

"May this young lady go with us?" asked he.

"She may," replied the policeman.

Mr. Fogg, Aouda, and Passepartout were conducted to a "palki-gari," a sort of four-wheeled carriage, drawn by two horses, in which they took their places and were driven away. No one spoke during the twenty minutes which elapsed before they reached their destination. They first passed through the "black town," with its narrow streets, its miserable, dirty huts, and squalid population; then through the "European town," which presented a relief in its bright brick mansions, shaded by cocoanut-trees and bristling with masts, where, although it was early morning, elegantly dressed horsemen and handsome equipages were passing back and forth.

The carriage stopped before a modest-looking house, which, however, did not have the appearance of a private mansion. The policeman having requested his prisoners—for so, truly, they might be called—to descend, conducted them into a room with barred windows, and said, "You will appear before Judge Obadiah at half-past eight."

He then retired, and closed the door.

"Why, we are prisoners!" exclaimed Passepartout, falling into a chair.

Aouda, with an emotion she tried to conceal, said to Mr. Fogg, "Sir, you must leave me to my fate! It is on my account that you receive this treatment; it is for having saved me!"

Phileas Fogg contented himself with saying that it was impossible. It was quite unlikely that he should be arrested for preventing a suttee. The complainants would not dare present themselves with such a charge. There was some mistake. Moreover, he would not in any event abandon Aouda, but would escort her to Hong Kong.

"But the steamer leaves at noon!" observed Passepartout, nervously.

"We shall be on board by noon," replied his master, placidly.

It was said so positively, that Passepartout could not help muttering to himself, "Parbleu, that's certain! Before noon we shall be on board." But he was by no means reassured.

At half-past eight the door opened, the policeman appeared, and, requesting them to follow him, led the way to an adjoining hall. It was evidently a court-room, and a crowd of Europeans and natives already occupied the rear of the apartment.

Mr. Fogg and his two companions took their places on a bench opposite the desks of the magistrate and his clerk. Immediately after, Judge Obadiah, a fat, round man, followed by the clerk, entered. He proceeded to take down a wig which was hanging on a nail, and put it hurriedly on his head.

"The first case," said he; then, putting his hand to his head, he exclaimed, "Heh! This is not my wig!"

"No, your worship," returned the clerk, "it is mine."

"My dear Mr. Oysterpuff, how can a judge give a wise sentence in a clerk's wig?"

The wigs were exchanged.

Passepartout was getting nervous, for the hands on the face of the big clock over the judge seemed to go round with terrible rapidity.

"The first case," repeated Judge Obadiah.

"Phileas Fogg?" demanded Oysterpuff.

"I am here," replied Mr. Fogg.

"Passepartout?"

"Present!" responded Passepartout.

"Good," said the judge. "You have been looked for, prisoners, for two days on the trains from Bombay."

"But of what are we accused?" asked Passepartout, impatiently.

"You are about to be informed."

"I am an English subject, sir," said Mr. Fogg, "and I have the right—"

"Have you been ill-treated?"

"Not at all."

"Very well; let the complainants come in."

A door was swung open by order of the judge, and three Indian priests entered.

"That's it," muttered Passepartout; "these are the rogues who were going to burn our young lady."

The priests took their places in front of the judge, and the clerk proceeded to read in a loud voice a complaint of sacrilege against Phileas Fogg and his servant, who were accused of having violated a place held consecrated by the Brahmin religion.

"You hear the charge?" asked the judge.

"Yes, sir," replied Mr. Fogg, consulting his watch, "and I admit it."

"You admit it?"

"I admit it, and I wish to hear these priests admit, in their turn, what they were going to do at the pagoda of Pillaji."

The priests looked at each other; they did not seem to understand what was said.

"Yes," cried Passepartout, warmly; "at the pagoda of Pillaji, where they were on the point of burning their victim."

The judge stared with astonishment, and the priests were stupefied.

"What victim?" said Judge Obadiah. "Burn whom? In Bombay itself?"

"Bombay?" cried Passepartout.

"Certainly. We are not talking of the pagoda of Pillaji, but of the pagoda of Malebar Hill, at Bombay."

"And as a proof," added the clerk, "here are the desecrator's very shoes, which he left behind him."

Whereupon he placed a pair of shoes on his desk.

"My shoes!" cried Passepartout, in his surprise permitting this imprudent exclamation to escape him.

The confusion of master and man, who had quite forgotten the affair at Bombay, for which they were now detained at Calcutta, may be imagined.

Fix, the detective, had foreseen the advantage which Passepartout's escapade gave him, and, delaying his departure for twelve hours, had consulted the priests of Malebar Hill. Knowing that the English authorities dealt very severely with this kind of misdemeanour, he promised them a goodly sum in damages, and sent them forward to Calcutta by the next train. Owing to the delay caused by the rescue of the young widow, Fix and the priests reached the Indian capital before Mr. Fogg and his servant, the magistrates having been already warned by a despatch to arrest them, should they arrive. Fix's disappointment when he learned that Phileas Fogg had not made his appearance in Calcutta, may be imagined. He made up his mind that the robber had stopped somewhere on the route and taken refuge in the southern provinces. For twenty-four hours Fix watched the station with feverish anxiety; at last he was rewarded by seeing Mr. Fogg and Passepartout arrive, accompanied by a young woman, whose presence he was wholly at a loss to explain. He hastened for a policeman; and this was how the party came to be arrested and brought before Judge Obadiah.

Had Passepartout been a little less preoccupied, he would have espied the detective ensconced in a corner of the court-room, watching the proceedings with an interest easily understood; for the warrant had failed to reach him at Calcutta, as it had done at Bombay and Suez.

Judge Obadiah had unfortunately caught Passepartout's rash exclamation, which the poor fellow would have given the world to recall.

"The facts are admitted?" asked the judge.

"Admitted," replied Mr. Fogg, coldly.

"Inasmuch," resumed the judge, "as the English law protects equally and sternly the religions of the Indian people, and as the man Passepartout has admitted that he violated the sacred pagoda of Malebar Hill, at Bombay, on the 20th of October, I condemn the said Passepartout to imprisonment for fifteen days and a fine of three hundred pounds."

"Three hundred pounds!" cried Passepartout, startled at the largeness of the sum.

"Silence!" shouted the constable.

"And inasmuch," continued the judge, "as it is not proved that the act was not done by the connivance of the master with the servant, and as the master in any case must be held responsible for the acts of his paid servant, I condemn Phileas Fogg to a week's imprisonment and a fine of one hundred and fifty pounds."

Fix rubbed his hands softly with satisfaction; if Phileas Fogg could be detained in Calcutta a week, it would be more than time for the

"My shoes!" cried Passepartout.

warrant to arrive. Passepartout was stupefied. This sentence ruined his master. A wager of twenty thousand pounds lost, because he, like a precious fool, had gone into that abominable pagoda!

Phileas Fogg, as self-composed as if the judgment did not in the least concern him, did not even lift his eyebrows while it was being pronounced. Just as the clerk was calling the next case, he rose, and said, "I offer bail."

"You have that right," returned the judge.

Fix's blood ran cold, but he resumed his composure when he heard the judge announce that the bail required for each prisoner would be one thousand pounds.

"I will pay it at once," said Mr. Fogg, taking a roll of bank-bills from the carpet-bag, which Passepartout had by him, and placing them on the clerk's desk.

"This sum will be restored to you upon your release from prison," said the judge. "Meanwhile, you are liberated on bail."

"Come!" said Phileas Fogg to his servant.

"But let them at least give me back my shoes!" cried Passepartout, angrily.

"Ah, these are pretty dear shoes!" he muttered, as they were handed to him. "More than a thousand pounds apiece; besides, they pinch my feet."

Mr. Fogg, offering his arm to Aouda, then departed, followed by the crestfallen Passepartout. Fix still nourished hopes that the robber would not, after all, leave the two thousand pounds behind him, but would decide to serve out his week in jail, and issued forth on Mr. Fogg's traces. That gentleman took a carriage, and the party were soon landed on one of the quays.

The "Rangoon" was moored half a mile off in the harbour, its signal of departure hoisted at the mast-head. Eleven o'clock was striking; Mr. Fogg was an hour in advance of time. Fix saw them leave the carriage and push off in a boat for the steamer, and stamped his feet with disappointment.

"The rascal is off, after all!" he exclaimed. "Two thousand pounds sacrificed! He's as prodigal as a thief! I'll follow him to the end of the world if necessary; but at the rate he is going on, the stolen money will soon be exhausted."

The detective was not far wrong in making this conjecture. Since leaving London, what with travelling-expenses, bribes, the purchase of the elephant, bails, and fines, Mr. Fogg had already spent more than five thousand pounds on the way, and the percentage of the sum recovered from the bank robber, promised to the detectives, was rapidly diminishing.

Around the World in Eighty Days

CHAPTER XVI.

IN WHICH FIX DOES NOT SEEM TO UNDERSTAND IN THE LEAST WHAT IS SAID TO HIM.

THE "Rangoon"—one of the Peninsular and Oriental Company's boats plying in the Chinese and Japanese seas—was a screw steamer, built of iron, weighing about seventeen hundred and seventy tons, and with engines of four hundred horse-power. She was as fast, but not as well fitted up, as the "Mongolia," and Aouda was not as comfortably provided for on board of her as Phileas Fogg could have wished. However, the trip from Calcutta to Hong Kong only comprised some three thousand five hundred miles, occupying from ten to twelve days, and the young woman was not difficult to please.

During the first days of the journey Aouda became better acquainted with her protector, and constantly gave evidence of her deep gratitude for what he had done. The phlegmatic gentleman listened to her, apparently at least, with coldness, neither his voice nor his manner betraying the slightest emotion; but he seemed to be always on the watch that nothing should be wanting to Aouda's comfort. He visited her regularly each day at certain hours, not so much to talk himself as to sit and hear her talk. He treated her with the strictest politeness, but with the precision of an automaton, the movements of which had been arranged for this purpose. Aouda did not quite know what to make of him, though Passepartout had given her some hints of his master's eccentricity, and made her smile by telling her of the wager which was sending him round the world. After all, she owed Phileas Fogg her life, and she always regarded him through the exalting medium of her gratitude.

Aouda confirmed the Parsee guide's narrative of her touching history. She did, indeed, belong to the highest of the native races of India. Many of the Parsee merchants have made great fortunes there by dealing in cotton; and one of them, Sir Jametsee Jeejeebhoy, was made a baronet by the English government. Aouda was a relative of this great man, and it was his cousin, Jeejeeh, whom she hoped to join at Hong Kong. Whether she would find a protector in him she could not tell; but Mr. Fogg essayed to calm her anxieties, and to assure her that everything would be mathematically—he used the very word—arranged. Aouda fastened her great eyes, "clear as the sacred lakes of the Himalaya," upon him; but the intractable Fogg, as reserved as ever, did not seem at all inclined to throw himself into this lake.

The first few days of the voyage passed prosperously, amid favourable weather and propitious winds, and they soon came in sight of the great Andaman, the principal of the islands in the Bay of Bengal, with its picturesque Saddle Peak, two thousand four hundred feet high, looming above the waters. The steamer passed along near the shores, but the savage Papuans, who are in the lowest scale of humanity, but are not, as has been asserted, cannibals, did not make their appearance.

The panorama of the islands, as they steamed by them, was superb. Vast forests of palms, arecs, bamboo, teak-wood, of the gigantic mimosa, and tree-like ferns covered the foreground, while behind, the graceful outlines of the mountains were traced against the sky; and along the coasts swarmed by thousands the precious swallows whose nests furnish a luxurious dish to the tables of the Celestial Empire. The varied landscape afforded by the Andaman Islands was soon passed, however, and the "Rangoon" rapidly approached the Straits of Malacca, which give access to the China seas.

What was detective Fix, so unluckily drawn on from country to country, doing all this while? He had managed to embark on the "Rangoon" at Calcutta without being seen by Passepartout, after leaving orders that, if the warrant should arrive, it should be forwarded to him at Hong Kong; and he hoped to conceal his presence to the end of the voyage. It would have been difficult to explain why he was on board without awaking Passepartout's suspicions, who thought him still at Bombay. But necessity impelled him, nevertheless, to renew his acquaintance with the worthy servant, as will be seen.

All the detective's hopes and wishes were now centred on Hong Kong; for the steamer's stay at Singapore would be too brief to enable him to take any steps there. The arrest must be

She showed him the most lively gratitude.

made at Hong Kong, or the robber would probably escape him for ever. Hong Kong was the last English ground on which he would set foot; beyond, China, Japan, America offered to Fogg an almost certain refuge. If the warrant should at last make its appearance at Hong Kong, Fix could arrest him and give him into the hands of the local police, and there would be no further trouble. But beyond Hong Kong, a simple warrant would be of no avail; an extradition warrant would be necessary, and that would result in delays and obstacles, of which the rascal would take advantage to elude justice.

Fix thought over these probabilities during the long hours which he spent in his cabin, and kept repeating to himself, "Now, either the warrant will be at Hong Kong, in which case I shall arrest my man, or it will not be there; and this time it is absolutely necessary that I should delay his departure. I have failed at Bombay, and I have failed at Calcutta: if I fail at Hong Kong, my reputation is lost. Cost what it may, I *must* succeed! But how shall I prevent his departure, if that should turn out to be my last resource?"

Fix made up his mind that, if worst came to worst, he would make a confidant of Passepartout, and tell him what kind of a fellow his master really was. That Passepartout was not Fogg's accomplice, he was very certain. The servant, enlightened by his disclosure, and afraid of being himself implicated in the crime, would doubtless become an ally of the detective. But this method was a dangerous one, only to be employed when everything else had failed. A word from Passepartout to his master would ruin all. The detective was therefore in a sore strait. But suddenly a new idea struck him. The presence of Aouda on the "Rangoon," in company with Phileas Fogg, gave him new material for reflection.

Who was this woman? What combination of events had made her Fogg's travelling companion? They had evidently met somewhere between Bombay and Calcutta; but where? Had they met accidentally, or had Fogg gone into the interior purposely in quest of this charming damsel? Fix was fairly puzzled. He asked himself whether there had not been a wicked elopement; and this idea so impressed itself upon his mind that he determined to make use of the supposed intrigue. Whether the young woman were married or not, he would be able to create such difficulties for Mr. Fogg at Hong Kong, that he could not escape by paying any amount of money.

But could he even wait till they reached Hong Kong? Fogg had an abominable way of jumping from one boat to another, and, before anything could be effected, might get full under weigh again for Yokohama.

Fix decided that he must warn the English authorities, and signal the "Rangoon" before her arrival. This was easy to do, since the steamer stopped at Singapore, whence there is a telgraphic wire to Hong Kong. He finally resolved, moreover, before acting more positively, to question Passepartout. It would not be difficult to make him talk; and, as there was no time to lose, Fix prepared to make himself known.

It was now the 30th of October, and on the following day the "Rangoon" was due at Singapore.

Fix emerged from his cabin and went on deck. Passepartout was promenading up and down in the forward part of the steamer. The detective rushed forward with every appearance of extreme surprise, and exclaimed, "You here, on the 'Rangoon'?"

"What. Monsieur Fix, are you on board?" returned the really astonished Passepartout, recognizing his crony of the "Mongolia."

"Why, I left you at Bombay, and here you are, on the way to Hong Kong! Are you going round the world too?"

"No, no," replied Fix; "I shall stop at Hong Kong—at least for some days."

"Hum!" said Passepartout, who seemed for an instant perplexed. "But how is it I have not seen you on board since we left Calcutta?"

"Oh, a trifle of seasickness,—I've been staying in my berth. The Gulf of Bengal does not agree with me as well as the Indian Ocean. And how is Mr. Fogg?"

"As well and as punctual as ever, not a day behind time! But, Monsieur Fix, you don't know that we have a young lady with us."

"A young lady?" replied the detective, not seeming to comprehend what was said.

Passepartout thereupon recounted Aouda's history, the affair in the Bombay pagoda, the purchase of the elephant for two thousand pounds, the rescue, the arrest and sentence of the Calcutta court, and the restoration of Mr. Fogg and himself to liberty on bail. Fix, who was familiar with the last events, seemed to be equally ignorant of all that Passepartout related; and the latter was charmed to find so interested a listener.

"But does your master propose to carry this young woman to Europe?"

"Not at all. We are simply going to place her under the protection of one of her relatives, a rich merchant at Hong Kong."

"Nothing to be done there," said Fix to himself, concealing his disappointment. "A glass of gin, Mr. Passepartout?"

"Willingly, Monsieur Fix. We must at least have a friendly glass on board the 'Rangoon.'"

Around the World in Eighty Days

CHAPTER XVII.

SHOWING WHAT HAPPENED ON THE VOYAGE FROM SINGAPORE TO HONG KONG.

THE detective and Passepartout met often on deck after this interview, though Fix was reserved, and did not attempt to induce his companion to divulge any more facts concerning Mr. Fogg. He caught a glimpse of that mysterious gentleman once or twice; but Mr. Fogg usually confined himself to the cabin, where he kept Aouda company, or, according to his inveterate habit, took a hand at whist.

Passepartout began very seriously to conjecture what strange chance kept Fix still on the route that his master was pursuing. It was really worth considering why this certainly very amiable and complacent person, whom he had first met at Suez, had then encountered on board the "Mongolia," who disembarked at Bombay, which he announced as his destination, and now turned up so unexpectedly on the "Rangoon," was following Mr. Fogg's tracks step by step. What was Fix's objcct? Passepartout was ready to wager his Indian shoes— which he religiously preserved—that Fix would also leave Hong Kong at the same time with them, and probably on the same steamer.

Passepartout might have cudgelled his brain for a century without hitting upon the real object which the detective had in view. He never could have imagined that Phileas Fogg was being tracked as a robber around the globe. But as it is in human nature to attempt the solution of every mystery, Passepartout suddenly discovered an explanation of Fix's movements, which was in truth far from unreasonable. Fix, he thought, could only be an agent of Mr. Fogg's friends at the Reform Club, sent to follow him up, and to ascertain that he really went round the world as had been agreed upon.

"It's clear!" repeated the worthy servant to himself, proud of his shrewdness. "He's a spy sent to keep us in view! That isn't quite the thing, either, to be spying Mr. Fogg, who is so honourable a man! Ah, gentlemen of the Reform, this shall cost you dear!"

Passepartout, enchanted with his discovery, resolved to say nothing to his master, lest he should be justly offended at this mistrust on the part of his adversaries. But he determined to chaff Fix, when he had the chance, with mysterious allusions, which, however, need not betray his real suspicions.

During the afternoon of Wednesday, October 30th, the "Rangoon" entered the Strait of Malacca, which separates the peninsula of that name from Sumatra. The mountainous and craggy islets intercepted the beauties of this noble island from the view of the travellers. The "Rangoon" weighed anchor at Singapore the next day at four a.m., to receive coal, having gained half a day on the prescribed time of her arrival. Phileas Fogg noted this gain in his journal, and then, accompanied by Aouda, who betrayed a desire for a walk on shore, disembarked.

Fix, who suspected Mr. Fogg's every movement, followed them cautiously, without being himself perceived; while Passepartout, laughing in his sleeve at Fix's manoeuvres, went about his usual errands.

The island of Singapore is not imposing in aspect, for there are no mountains; yet its appearance is not without attractions. It is a park checkered by pleasant highways and avenues. A handsome carriage, drawn by a sleek pair of New Holland horses, carried Phileas Fogg and Aouda into the midst of rows of palms with brilliant foliage, and of clove-trees whereof the cloves form the heart of a half-open flower. Pepper plants replaced the prickly hedges of European fields; sago-bushes, large ferns with gorgeous branches, varied the aspect of this tropical clime; while nutmeg-trees in full foliage filled the air with a penetrating perfume. Agile and grinning bands of monkeys skipped about in the trees, nor were tigers wanting in the jungles.

After a drive of two hours through the country, Aouda and Mr. Fogg returned to the town, which is a vast collection of heavy-looking, irregular houses, surrounded by charming gardens rich in tropical fruits and plants; and at ten o'clock they re-embarked, closely followed by the detective, who had kept them constantly in sight.

Passepartout, who hard been purchasing several dozen mangoes—a fruit as large as good-sized apples, of a dark-brown colour outside and a bright red within, and whose white pulp, melting in the mouth, affords

In a fine equipage, drawn by splendid horses, Aouda and Phileas Fogg drove through the rich forest scenery.

gourmands a delicious sensation—was waiting for them on deck. He was only too glad to offer some mangoes to Aouda, who thanked him very gracefully for them.

At eleven o'clock the "Rangoon" rode out of Singapore harbour, and in a few hours the high mountains of Malacca, with their forests inhabited by the most beautifully-furred tigers in the world, were lost to view. Singapore is distant some thirteen hundred miles from the island of Hong Kong, which is a little English colony near the Chinese coast. Phileas Fogg hoped to accomplish the journey in six days, so as to be in time for the steamer which would leave on the 6th of November for Yokohama, the principal Japanese port.

The "Rangoon" had a large quota of passengers, among whom disembarked at Singapore, among them a number of Indians, Ceylonese, Chinamen, Malays, and Portuguese, mostly second-class travellers.

The weather, which had hitherto been fine, changed with the last quarter of the moon. The sea rolled heavily, and the wind at intervals rose almost to a storm, but happily blew from the south-west, and thus aided the steamer's progress. The captain as often as possible put up his sails, and under the double action of steam and sail, the vessel made rapid progress along the coasts of Anam and Cochin China. Owing to the defective construction of the "Rangoon," however, unusual precautions became necessary in unfavourable weather; but the loss of time which resulted from this cause, while it nearly drove Passepartout out of his senses, did not seem to affect his master in the least. Passepartout blamed the captain, the engineer, and the crew, and consigned all who were connected with the ship to the land where the pepper grows. Perhaps the thought of the gas, which was remorselessly burning at his expense in Saville Row, had something to do with his hot impatience.

"You are in a great hurry, then," said Fix to him one day, "to reach Hong Kong?"

"A very great hurry!"

"Mr. Fogg, I suppose, is anxious to catch the steamer for Yokohama?"

"Terribly anxious."

"You believe in this journey around the world, then?"

"Absolutely. Don't you, Mr. Fix?"

"I? I don't believe a word of it."

"You're a sly dog!" said Passepartout, winking at him.

This expression rather disturbed Fix, without his knowing why. Had the Frenchman guessed his real purpose? He knew not what to think.

But how could Passepartout have discovered that he was a detective? Yet, in speaking as he did, the man evidently meant more than he expressed.

Passepartout went still further the next day; he could not hold his tongue.

"Mr. Fix," said he, in a bantering tone; "shall we be so unfortunate as to lose you when we get to Hong Kong?"

"Why," responded Fix, a little embarrassed, "I don't know; perhaps—"

"Ah, if you would only go on with us! An agent of the Peninsular Company, you know, can't stop on the way! You were only going to Bombay, and here you are in China. America is not far off, and from America to Europe is only a step."

Fix looked intently at his companion, whose countenance was as serene as possible, and laughed with him. But Passepartout persisted in chaffing him by asking him if he made much by his present occupation.

"Yes, and no," returned Fix; "there is good and bad luck in such things. But you must understand that I don't travel at my own expense."

"Oh, I am quite sure of that!" cried Passepartout, laughing heartily.

Fix, fairly puzzled, descended to his cabin and gave himself up to his reflections. He was evidently suspected; somehow or other the Frenchman had found out that he was a detective. But had he told his master? What part was he playing in all this: was he an accomplice or not? Was the game, then, up? Fix spent several hours turning these things over in his mind, sometimes thinking that all was lost, then persuading himself that Fogg was ignorant of his presence, and then undecided what course it was best to take.

Nevertheless, he preserved his coolness of mind, and at last resolved to deal plainly with Passepartout. If he did not find it practicable to arrest Fogg at Hong Kong, and if Fogg made preparations to leave that last foothold of English territory, he, Fix, would tell Passepartout all. Either the servant was the accomplice of his master, and in this case the master knew of his operations, and he should fail; or else the servant knew nothing about the robbery, and then his interest would be to abandon the robber.

Such was the situation between Fix and Passepartout. Meanwhile Phileas Fogg moved about above them in the most majestic and unconscious indifference. He was passing methodically in his orbit around the world, regardless of the lesser stars which gravitated around him. Yet there was near by what the astronomers would call a disturbing star, which might have produced an agitation in this gentleman's heart. But no! the charms of Aouda failed to act, to Passepartout's great surprise; and the disturbances, if they existed, would have been more difficult to calculate than those of Uranus which led to the discovery of Neptune.

It was every day an increasing wonder to Passepartout, who read in Aouda's eyes the depths of her gratitude to his master. Phileas Fogg, though brave and gallant, must be, he thought, quite heartless. As to the sentiment which this journey might have awakened in him, there was clearly no trace of such a thing; while poor Passepartout existed in perpetual reveries.

One day he was leaning on the railing of the engine-room, and was observing the engine, when a sudden pitch of the steamer threw the screw out of the water. The steam came hissing out of the valves; and this made Passepartout indignant.

"The valves are not sufficiently charged!" he exclaimed. "We are not going. Oh, these English! If this was an American craft, we should blow up, perhaps, but we should at all events go faster!"

Around the World in Eighty Days

CHAPTER XVIII.

IN WHICH PHILEAS FOGG, PASSEPARTOUT, AND FIX GO EACH ABOUT HIS BUSINESS.

THE weather was bad during the latter days of the voyage. The wind, obstinately remaining in the north-west, blew a gale, and retarded the steamer. The "Rangoon" rolled heavily, and the passengers became impatient of the long, monstrous waves which the wind raised before their path. A sort of tempest arose on the 3rd of November, the squall knocking the vessel about with fury, and the waves running high. The "Rangoon" reefed all her sails, and even the rigging proved too much, whistling and shaking amid the squall. The steamer was forced to proceed slowly, and the captain estimated that she would reach Hong Kong twenty hours behind time, and more if the storm lasted.

Phileas Fogg gazed at the tempestuous sea, which seemed to be struggling especially to delay him, with his habitual tranquillity. He never changed countenance for an instant, though a delay of twenty hours, by making him too late for the Yokohama boat, would almost inevitably cause the loss of the wager. But this man of nerve manifested neither impatience nor annoyance; it seemed as if the storm were a part of his programme, and had been foreseen. Aouda was amazed to find him as calm as he had been from the first time she saw him.

Fix did not look at the state of things in the same light. The storm greatly pleased him. His satisfaction would have been complete had the "Rangoon" been forced to retreat before the violence of wind and waves. Each delay filled him with hope, for it became more and more probable that Fogg would be obliged to remain some days at Hong kong; and now the heavens themselves became his allies, with the gusts and squalls. It mattered not that they made him sea-sick—he made no account of this inconvenience; and whilst his body was writhing under their effects, his spirit bounded with hopeful exultation.

Passepartout was enraged beyond expression by the unpropitious weather. Everything had gone so well till now! Earth and sea had seemed to be at his master's service; steamers and railways obeyed him; wind and steam united to speed his journey. Had the hour of adversity come? Passepartout was as much excited as if the twenty thousand pounds were to come from his own pocket. The storm exasperated him, the gale made him furious, and he longed to lash the obstinate sea into obedience. Poor fellow! Fix carefully concealed from him his own satisfaction, for, had he betrayed it, Passepartout could scarcely have restrained himself from personal violence.

Passepartout remained on deck as long as the tempest lasted, being unable to remain quiet below, and taking it into his head to aid the progress of the ship by lending a hand with the crew. He overwhelmed the captain, officers, and sailors, who could not help laughing at his impatience, with all sorts of questions. He wanted to know exactly how long the storm was going to last; whereupon he was referred to the barometer, which seemed to have no intention of rising. Passepartout shook it, but with no perceptible effect; for neither shaking nor maledictions could prevail upon it to change its mind.

On the 4th, however, the sea became more calm, and the storm lessened its violence; the wind veered southward, and was once more favourable. Passepartout cleared up with the weather. Some of the sails were unfurled, and the "Rangoon" resumed its most rapid speed. The time lost could not, however, be regained. Land was not signalled until five o'clock on the morning of the 6th; the steamer was due on the 5th. Phileas Fogg was twenty-four hours behindhand, and the Yokohama steamer would of course be missed.

The pilot went on board at six, and took his place on the bridge, to guide the "Rangoon" through the channels to the port of Hong Kong. Passepartout longed to ask him if the steamer had left for Yokohama; but he dared not, for he wished to preserve the spark of hope which still remained till the last moment. He had confided his anxiety to Fix, who—the sly rascal!—tried to console him by saying that Mr. Fogg would be in time if he took the next boat; but this was only put Passepartout in a passion.

Mr. Fogg, bolder than his servant, did not hesitate to approach the pilot, and tranquilly ask him if he knew when a steamer would leave Hong Kong for Yokohama.

He took a hand at everything and astonished the crew.

"At high tide to-morrow morning," answered the pilot.

"Ah!" said Mr. Fogg, without betraying any astonishment.

Passepartout, who heard what passed, would willingly have embraced the pilot, while Fix would have been glad to twist his neck.

"What is the stamer's name?" asked Mr. Fogg.

"The 'Carnatic.'"

"Ought she not to have gone yesterday?"

"Yes, sir; but they had to repair one of her boilers, and so her departure was postponed till to-morrow."

"Thank you," returned Mr. Fogg, descending mathematically to the saloon.

Passepartout clasped the pilot's hand and shook it heartily in his delight, exclaiming, "Pilot, you are the best of good fellows!"

The pilot probably does not know to this day why his responses won him this enthusiastic greeting. He remounted the bridge, and guided the steamer through the flotilla of junks, tankas, and fishing-boats which crowd the harbour of Hong Kong.

At one o'clock the "Rangoon" was at the quay, and the passengers were going ashore.

Chance had strangely favoured Phileas Fogg, for, had not the "Carnatic" been forced to lie over for repairing her boilers, she would have left on the 6th of November, and the passengers for Japan would have been obliged to await for a week the sailing of the next steamer. Mr. Fogg was, it is true, twenty-four hours behind his time; but this could not seriously imperil the remainder of his tour.

The steamer which crossed the Pacific from Yokohama to San Francisco made a direct connexion with that from Hong Kong, and it could not sail until the latter reached Yokohama; and if Mr. Fogg was twenty-four hours late on reaching Yokohama, this time would no doubt be easily regained in the voyage of twenty-two days across the Pacific. He found himself, then, about twenty-four hours behind-hand, thirty-five days after leaving London.

The "Carnatic" was announced to leave Hong Kong at five the next morning. Mr. Fogg had sixteen hours in which to attend to his business there, which was to deposit Aouda safely with her wealthy relative.

On landing, he conducted her to a palanquin, in which they repaired to the Club Hotel. A room was engaged for the young woman, and Mr. Fogg, after seeing that she wanted for nothing, set out in search of her cousin Jejeeh. He instructed Passepartout to remain at the hotel until his return, that Aouda might not be left entirely alone.

Mr. Fogg repaired to the Exchange, where, he did not doubt, every one would know so wealthy and considerable a personage as the Parsee merchant. Meeting a broker, he made the inquiry, to learn that Jejeeh had left China two years before, and, retiring from business with an immense fortune, had taken up his residence in Europe—in Holland, the broker thought, with the merchants of which country he had principally traded. Phileas Fogg returned to the hotel, begged a moment's conversation with Aouda, and, without more ado, apprised her that Jejeeh was no longer at Hong Kong, but probably in Holland.

Arouda at first said nothing. She passed her hand across her forehead, and reflected a few moments. Then, in her sweet, soft voice, she said, "What ought I to do, Mr. Fogg?"

"It is very simple," responded the gentleman. "Go on to Europe."

"But I cannot intrude—"

"You do not intrude, nor do you in the least embarrass my project. Passepartout!"

"Monsieur."

"Go to the 'Carnatic,' and engaged three cabins."

Passepartout, delighted that the young woman, who was very gracious to him, was going to continue the journey with them, went off at a brisk gait to obey his master's order.

Around the World in Eighty Days

CHAPTER XIX.

IN WHICH PASSEPARTOUT TAKES A TOO GREAT INTEREST IN HIS MASTER, AND WHAT COMES OF IT.

HONG KONG is an island which came into the possession of the English by the treaty of Nankin, after the war of 1842; and the colonizing genius of the English has created upon it an important city and an excellent port. The island is situated at the mouth of the Canton River, and is separated by about sixty miles from the Portuguese town of Macao, on the opposite coast. Hong Kong has beaten Macao in the struggle for the Chinese trade, and now the greater part of the transportation of Chinese goods finds its depôt at the former place. Docks, hospitals, wharves, a Gothic cathedral, a government house, macadamized streets give to Hong Kong the appearance of a town in Kent or Surrey transferred by some strange magic to the antipodes.

Passepartout wandered, with his hands in his pockets, towards the Victoria port, gazing as he went at the curious palanquins and other modes of conveyance, and the groups of Chinese, Japanese, and Europeans who passed to and fro in the streets. Hong Kong seemed to him not unlike Bombay, Calcutta, and Singapore, since, like them, it betrayed everywhere the evidence of English supremacy. At the Victoria port he found a confused mass of ships of all nations, English, French, American, and Dutch, men-of-war and trading vessels, Japanese and Chinese junks, sempas, tankas, and flower-boats, which formed so many floating parterres. Passepartout noticed in the crowd a number of the natives who seemed very old and were dressed in yellow. On going into a barber's to get shaved, he learned that these ancient men were all at least eighty years old, at which age they are permitted to wear yellow, which is the Imperial colour. Passepartout, without exactly knowing why, thought this very funny.

On reaching the quay where they were to embark on the "Carnatic," he was not astonished to find Fix walking up and down. The detective seemed very much disturbed and disappointed.

"This is bad," muttered Passepartout, "for the gentlemen of the Reform Club!" He accosted Fix with a merry smile, as if he had not perceived that gentleman's chagrin. The detective had, indeed, good reasons to inveigh against the bad luck which pursued him. The warrant had not come! It was certainly on the way, but as certainly it could not now reach Hong Kong for several days; and this being the last English territory on Mr. Fogg's route, the robber would escape, unless he could manage to detain him.

"Well, Monsieur Fix," said Passepartout, "have you decided to go on with us as far as America?"

"Yes," returned Fix, through his set teeth.

"Good!" exclaimed Passepartout, laughing heartily. "I knew you could not persuade yourself to separate from us. Come and engage your berth."

They entered the steamer office and secured cabins for four persons. The clerk, as he gave them the tickets, informed them that, the repairs on the "Carnatic" having been completed, the steamer would leave that very evening, and not next morning as had been announced.

"That will suit my master all the better," said Passepartout. "I will go and let him know."

Fix now decided to make a bold move; he resolved to tell Passepartout all. It seemed to be the only possible means of keeping Phileas Fogg several days longer at Hong Kong. He accordingly invited his companion into a tavern which caught his eye on the quay. On entering, they found themselves in a large room handsomely decorated, at the end of which was a large camp-bed furnished with cushions. Several persons lay upon this bed in a deep sleep. At the small tables which were arranged about the room some thirty customers were drinking English beer, porter, gin, and brandy; smoking, the while, long red clay pipes stuffed with little balls of opium mingled with essence of rose. From time to time one of the smokers, overcome with the narcotic, would slip under the table, whereupon the waiters, taking him by the head and feet, carried and laid him upon the bed. The bed already supported twenty of these stupefied sots.

Fix and Passepartout saw that they were in a smoking-house haunted by those wretched, cadaverous, idiotic creatures, to whom the

In his stroll Passepartout came across a number of old natives.

English merchants sell every year the miserable drug called opium, to the amount of one million four hundred thousand pounds—thousands devoted to one of the most despicable vices which afflict humanity! The Chinese government has in vain attempted to deal with the evil by stringent laws. It passed gradually from the rich, to whom it was at first exclusively reserved, to the lower classes, and then its ravages could not be arrested. Opium is smoked everywhere, at all times, by men and women, in the Celestial Empire; and, once accustomed to it, the victims cannot dispense with it, except by suffering horrible bodily contortions and agonies. A great smoker can smoke as many as eight pipes a day; but he dies in five years. It was in one of these dens that Fix and Passepartout in search of a friendly glass, found themselves. Passepartout had no money, but willingly accepted Fix's invitation in the hope of returning the obligation at some future time.

They ordered two bottles of port, to which the Frenchman did ample justice, whilst Fix observed him with close attention. They chatted about the journey, and Passepartout was especially merry at the idea that Fix was going to continue it with them. When the bottles were empty, however, he rose to go and tell his master of the change in the time of the sailing of the "Carnatic."

Fix caught him by the arm, and said, "Wait a moment."

"What for, Mr. Fix?"

"I want to have a serious talk with you."

"A serious talk!" cried Passepartout, drinking up the little wine that was left in the bottom of his glass. "Well, we'll talk about it to-morrow; I haven't time now."

"Stay! What I have to say concerns your master."

Passepartout at this, looked attentively at his companion. Fix's face seemed to have a singular expression. He resumed his seat.

"What is it that you have to say?"

Fix placed his hand upon Passepartout's arm and, lowering his voice, said, "You have guessed who I am?"

"Parbleu!" said Passepartout, smiling.

"Then I'm going to tell you everything—"

"Now that I know everything, my friend! Ah! that's very good. But go on, go on. First, though, let me tell you that those gentlemen have put themselves to a useless expense."

"Useless!" said Fix. "You speak confidently. It's clear that you don't know how large the sum is."

"Of course I do," returned Passepartout.

"Twenty thousand pounds."

"Fify-five thousand!" answered Fix, pressing his companion's hand.

"What!" cried the Frenchman. "Has Monsieur Fogg dared—fifty-five thousand pounds! Well, there's all the more reason for not losing an instant," he continued, getting up hastily.

Fix pushed Passepartout back in his chair, and resumed: "Fify-five thousand pounds; and if I succeed, I get two thousand pounds. If you'll help me, I'll let you have five hundred of them."

"Help you?" cried Passepartout, whose eyes were standing wide open.

"Yes; help me keep Mr. Fogg here for two or three days."

"Why, what are you saying? Those gentlemen are not satisfied with following my master and suspecting his honour, but they must try to put obstacles in his way! I blush for them!"

"What do you mean?"

"I mean that it is a piece of shameful trickery. They might as well waylay Mr. Fogg and put his money in their pockets!"

"That's just what we count on doing."

"It's a conspiracy, then," cried Passepartout, who became more and more excited as the liquor mounted in his head, for he drank without perceiving it. "A real conspiracy! And gentlemen, too. Bah!"

Fix began to be puzzled.

"Members of the Reform Club!" continued Passepartout. "You must know, Monsieur Fix, that my master is an honest man, and that, when he makes a wager, he tries to win it fairly!"

"But who do you think I am?" asked Fix, looking at him intently.

"Parbleu! An agent of the members of the Reform Club, sent out here to interrupt my master's journey. But, though I found you out some time ago, I've taken good care to say nothing about it to Mr. Fogg."

"He knows nothing, then?"

"Nothing," replied Passepartout, again emptying his glass.

The detective passed his hand across his forehead, hesitating before he spoke again. What should he do? Passepartout's mistake seemed sincere, but it made his design more difficult. It was evident that the servant was not the master's accomplice, as Fix had been inclined to suspect.

"Well," said the detective to himself, "as he is not an accomplice, he will help me."

He had no time to lose: Fogg must be

"Listen," said Fix in an undertone.

detained at Hong Kong; so he resolved to make a clean breast of it.

"Listen to me," said Fix abruptly. "I am not, as you think, an agent of the members of the Reform Club—"

"Bah!" retorted Passepartout, with an air of raillery.

"I am a police detective, sent out here by the London office."

"You, a detective?"

"I will prove it. Here is my commission."

Passepartout was speechless with astonishment when Fix displayed this document, the genuineness of which could not be doubted.

"Mr. Fogg's wager," resumed Fix, "is only a pretext, of which you and the gentlemen of the Reform are dupes. He had a motive for securing your innocent complicity."

"But why?"

"Listen. On the 28th of last September a robbery of fifty-five thousand pounds was committed at the Bank of England by a person whose description was fortunately secured. Here is this description; it answers exactly to that of Mr. Phileas Fogg."

"What nonsense!" cried Passepartout, striking the table with his fist. "My master is the most honourable of men!"

"How can you tell? You know scarcely anything about him. You went into his service the day he came away; and he came away on a foolish pretext, without trunks, and carrying a large amount in bank-notes. And yet you are bold enough to assert that he is an honest man!"

"Yes, yes," repeated the poor fellow, mechanically.

"Would you like to be arrested as his accomplice?"

Passepartout, overcome by what he had heard, held his head between his hands, and did not dare to look at the detective. Phileas Fogg, the saviour of Aouda, that brave and generous man, a robber! And yet how many presumptions there were against him! Passepartout essayed to reject the suspicions which forced themselves upon his mind; he did not wish to believe that his master was guilty.

"Well, what do you want of me?" said he, at last, with an effort.

"See here," replied Fix; "I have tracked Mr. Fogg to this place, but as yet I have failed to receive the warrant of arrest for which I sent to London. You must help me to keep him here in Hong Kong—"

"I! But I—"

"I will share with you the two-thousand-pounds reward offered by the Bank of England."

"Never!" replied Passepartout, who tried to rise, but fell back, exhausted in mind and body.

"Mr. Fix," he stammered, "even should what you say be true—if my master is really the robber you are seeking for—which I deny—I have been, am, in his service; I have seen his generosity and goodness; and I will never betray him—not for all the gold in the world, I come from a village where they don't eat that kind of bread!"

"You refuse?"

"I refuse."

"Consider that I've said nothing," said Fix; "and let us drink."

"Yes; let us drink!"

Passepartout felt himself yielding more and more to the effects of the liquor. Fix, seeing that he must, at all hazards, be separated from his master, wished to entirely overcome him. Some pipes full of opium lay upon the table. Fix slipped one into Passepartout's hand. He took it, put it between his lips, lit it, drew several puffs, and his head, becoming heavy under the influence of the narcotic, fell upon the table.

"At last!" said Fix, seeing Passepartout unconscious. "Mr. Fogg will not be informed of the time of the 'Carnatic's' departure; and, if he is, he will have to go without this cursed Frenchman!"

And, after paying his bill, Fix left the tavern.

Around the World in Eighty Days

CHAPTER XX.

IN WHICH FIX COMES FACE TO FACE WITH PHILEAS FOGG.

WHILE these events were passing at the opium-house Mr. Fogg, unconscious of the danger he was in of losing the steamer, was quietly escorting Aouda about the streets of the English quarter, making the necessary purchases for the long voyage before them. It was all very well for an Englishman like Mr. Fogg to make the tour of the world with a carpet-bag; a lady could not be expected to travel comfortably under such conditions. He acquitted his task with characteristic serenity, and invariably replied to the remonstrances of his fair companion, who was confused by his patience and generosity,—

"It is in the interest of my journey—a part of my programme."

The purchases made, they returned to the hotel, where they dined at a sumptuously served *table-d'hôte;* after which Aouda, shaking hands with her protector after the English fashion, retired to her room for rest. Mr. Fogg absorbed himself throughout the evening in the perusal of the *Times* and *Illustrated London News.*

Had he been capable of being astonished at anything, it would have been not to see his servant return at bed-time. But, knowing that the steamer was not to leave for Yokohama until the next morning, he did not disturb himself about the matter. When Passepartout did not appear the next morning, to answer his master's bell, Mr. Fogg, not betraying the least vexation, contented himself with taking his carpet-bag, calling Aouda, and sending for a palanquin.

It was then eight o'clock; at half-past nine, it being then high tide, the "Carnatic" would leave the harbour. Mr. Fogg and Aouda got into the palanquin, their luggage being brought after on a wheelbarrow, and half an hour later stepped upon the quay whence they were to embark. Mr. Fogg then learned that the "Carnatic" had sailed the evening before. He had expected to find not only the steamer, but his domestic, and was forced to give up both; but no sign of disappointment appeared on his face, and he merely remarked to Aouda, "It is an accident, madam; nothing more."

At this moment a man who had been observing him attentively approached. It was Fix, who, bowing, addressed Mr. Fogg: "Were you not, like me, sir, a passenger by the 'Rangoon,' which arrived yesterday?"

"I was, sir," replied Mr. Fogg coldly. "But I have not the honour—"

"Pardon me; I thought I should find your servant here."

"Do you know where he is, sir?" asked Aouda anxiously.

"What!" responded Fix, feigning surprise. "Is he not with you?"

"No," said Aouda. "He has not made his appearance since yesterday. Could he have gone on board the 'Carnatic' without us?"

"Without you, madam?" answered the detective. "Excuse me, did you intend to sail in the 'Carnatic'?"

"Yes, sir."

"So did I, madam, and I am excessively disappointed. The 'Carnatic,' its repairs being completed, left Hong Kong twelve hours before the stated time, without any notice being given; and we must now wait a week for another steamer."

As he said "a week" Fix felt his heart leap for joy. Fogg detained at Hong Kong a week! There would be time for the warrant to arrive, and fortune at last favoured the representative of the law. His horror may be imagined when he heard Mr. Fogg say, in his placid voice, "But there are other vessels besides the 'Carnatic,' it seems to me, in the harbour of Hong Kong."

And, offering his arm to Aouda, he directed his steps toward the docks in search of some craft about to start. Fix, stupefied, followed; it seemed as if he were attached to Mr. Fogg by an invisible thread. Chance, however, appeared really to have abandoned the man it had hitherto served so well. For three hours Phileas Fogg wandered about the docks, with the determination, if necessary, to charter a vessel to carry him to Yokohama; but he could only find vessels which were loading or unloading, and which could not therefore set sail. Fix began to hope again.

But Mr. Fogg, far from being discouraged, was continuing his search, resolved not to stop

"Is your honour looking for a vessel?"

if he had to resort to Macao, when he was accosted by a sailor on one of the wharves.

"Is your honour looking for a boat?"

"Have you a boat ready to sail?"

"Yes, your honour; a pilot-boat—No. 43—the best in the harbour."

"Does she go fast?"

"Between eight and nine knots the hour. Will you look at her?"

"Yes."

"Your honour will be satisfied with her. Is it for a sea excursion?"

"No; for a voyage."

"A voyage?"

"Yes; will you agree to take me to Yokohama?"

The sailor leaned on the railing, opened his eyes wide, and said, "Is your honour joking?"

"No. I have missed the 'Carnatic,' and I must get to Yokohama by the 14th at the latest, to take the boat for San Francisco."

"I am sorry," said the sailor, "but it is impossible."

"I offer you a hundred pounds per day, and an additional reward of two hundred pounds if I reach Yokohama in time."

"Are you in earnest?"

"Very much so."

The pilot walked away a little distance, and gazed out to sea, evidently struggling between the anxiety to gain a large sum and the fear of venturing so far. Fix was in mortal suspense.

Mr. Fogg turned to Aouda and asked her, "You would not be afraid, would you, madam?"

"Not with you, Mr. Fogg," was her answer.

The pilot now returned, shuffling his hat in his hands.

"Well, pilot?" said Mr. Fogg.

"Well, your honour," replied he, "I could not risk myself, my men, or my little boat of scarcely twenty tons on so long a voyage at this time of year. Besides, we could not reach Yokohama in time, for it is sixteen hundred and sixty miles from Hong Kong."

"Only sixteen hundred," said Mr. Fogg.

"It's the same thing."

Fix breathed more freely.

"But," added the pilot, "it might be arranged another way."

Fix ceased to breathe at all.

"How?" asked Mr. Fogg.

"By going to Nagasaki, at the extreme south of Japan, or even to Shanghai, which is only eight hundred miles from here. In going to Shanghai we should not be forced to sail wide of the Chinese coast, which would be a great advantage, as the currents run northward, and would aid us."

"Pilot," said Mr. Fogg, "I must take the American steamer at Yokohama, and not at Shanghai or Nagasaki."

"Why not?" returned the pilot. "The San Francisco steamer does not start from Yokohama. It puts in at Yokohama and Nagasaki, but it starts from Shanghai."

"You are sure of that?"

"Perfectly."

"And when does the boat leave Shanghai?"

"On the 11th, at seven in the evening. We have, therefore, four days before us, that is ninety-six hours; and in that time, if we had good luck and a south-west wind, and the sea was calm, we could make those eight hundred miles to Shanghai."

"And you could go—"

"In an hour; as soon as provisions could be got aboard and the sails put up."

"It is a bargain. Are you the master of the boat?"

"Yes; John Bunsby, master of the 'Tankadere.'"

"Would you like some earnest-money?"

"If it would not put your honour out—"

"Here are two hundred pounds on account. Sir," added Phileas Fogg, turning to Fix, "if you would like to take advantage—"

"Thanks, sir; I was about to ask the favour."

"Very well. In half an hour we shall go on board."

"But poor Passepartout?" urged Aouda, who was much disturbed by the servant's disappearance.

"I shall do all I can to find him," replied Phileas Fogg.

While Fix, in a feverish, nervous state, repaired to the pilot-boat the others directed their course to the police-station at Hong Kong. Phileas Fogg there gave Passepartout's description, and left a sum of money to be spent in the search for him. The same formalities having been gone through at the French consulate, and the palanquin having stopped at the hotel for the luggage, which had been sent back there, they returned to the wharf.

It was now three o'clock; and pilot-boat No. 43, with its crew on board, and its provisions stored away, was ready for departure.

The "Tankadere" was a neat little craft of twenty tons, as gracefully built as if she were a racing yacht. Her shining copper sheathing, her galvanized iron-work, her deck, white as ivory, betrayed the pride taken by John Bunsby in making her presentable. Her two masts leaned a trifle backward; she carried brigantine, foresail, storm-jib, and standing-jib, and was

"I regret having nothing better to offer you," said Mr. Fogg to Fix.

well rigged for running before the wind; and she seemed capable of brisk speed, which, indeed, she had already proved by gaining several prizes in pilot-boat races. The crew of the "Tanka-dere" was composed of John Bunsby, the master, and four hardy mariners, who were familiar with the Chinese seas. John Bunsby himself, a man of forty-five or thereabouts, vigorous, sunburnt, with a sprightly expression of the eye, and energetic and self-reliant countenance, would have inspired confidence in the most timid.

Phileas Fogg and Aouda went on board, where they found Fix already installed. Below deck was a square cabin, of which the walls bulged out in the form of cots, above a circular divan; in the centre was a table provided with a swinging lamp. The accommodation was confined, but neat.

"I am sorry to have nothing better to offer you," said Mr. Fogg to Fix, who bowed without responding.

The detective had a feeling akin to humilia-tion in profiting by the kindness of Mr. Fogg.

"It's certain," thought he, "though rascal as he is, he is a polite one!"

The sails and the English flag were hoisted at ten minutes past three. Mr. Fogg and Aouda, who were seated on deck, cast a last glance at the quay, in the hope of espying Passepartout. Fix was not without his fears lest chance should direct the steps of the unfortunate servant, whom he had so badly treated, in this direction; in which case an explanation the reverse of satisfactory to the detective must have ensued. But the Frenchman did not appear, and, without doubt, was still lying under the supify-ing influence of the opium.

John Bunsby, master, at length gave the order to start, and the "Tankadere," taking the wind under her brigantine, foresail, and standing-jib, bounded briskly forward over the waves.

Around the World in Eighty Days

CHAPTER XXI.

IN WHICH THE MASTER OF THE "TANKADERE" RUNS GREAT RISK OF LOSING A REWARD OF TWO HUNDRED POUNDS.

THIS voyage of eight hundred miles was a perilous venture, on a craft of twenty tons, and at that season of the year. The Chinese seas are usually boisterous, subject to terrible gales of wind, and especially during the equinoxes; and it was now early November.

It would clearly have been to the master's advantage to carry his passengers to Yokohama, since he was paid a certain sum per day; but he would have been rash to attempt such a voyage, and it was imprudent even to attempt to reach Shanghai. But John Bunsby believed in the "Tankadere," which rode on the waves like a sea-gull; and perhaps he was not wrong.

Late in the day they passed through the capricious channels of Hong Kong, and the "Tankadere," impelled by favourable winds, conducted herself admirably.

"I do not need, pilot," said Phileas Fogg, when they got into the open sea, "to advise you to use all possible speed."

"Trust me, your honour. We are carrying all the sail the wind will let us. The poles would add nothing, and are only used when we are going into port."

"It's your trade, not mine, pilot, and I confide in you."

Phileas Fogg, with body erect and legs wide apart, standing like a sailor, gazed without staggering at the swelling waters. The young woman, who was seated aft, was profoundly affected as she looked out upon the ocean, darkening now with the twilight, on which she had ventured in so frail a vessel. Above her head rustled the white sails, which seemed like great white wings. The boat, carried forward by the wind, seemed to be flying in the air.

Night came. The moon was entering her first quarter, and her insufficient light would soon die out in the mist on the horizon. Clouds were rising from the east, and already overcast a part of the heavens.

The pilot had hung out his lights, which was very necesssary in these seas crowded with vessels bound landward; for collisions are not uncommon occurrences, and, at the speed she was going the least shock would shatter the gallant little craft.

Fix, seated in the bow, gave himself up to meditation. He kept apart from his fellow-travellers, knowing Mr. Fogg's taciturn tastes; besides, he did not quite like to talk to the man whose favours he had accepted. He was thinking, too, of the future. It seemed certain that Fogg would not stop at Yokohama, but would at once take the boat for San Francisco; and the vast extent of America would insure him impunity and safety. Fogg's plan appeared to him the simplest in the world. Instead of sailing directly from England to the United States, like a common villain, he had traversed three quarters of the globe, so as to gain the American continent more surely; and there, after throwing the police off his track, he would quietly enjoy himself with the fortune stolen from the bank. But, once in the United States, what should he, Fix, do? Should he abandon this man? No, a hundred times no! Until he had secured his extradition, he would not lose sight of him for an hour. It was his duty, and he would fulfil it to the end. At all events, there was one thing to be thankful for: Passepartout was not with his master; and it was above all important, after the confidences Fix had imparted to him, that the servant should never have speech with his master.

Phileas Fogg was also thinking of Passepartout, who had so strangely disappeared. Looking at the matter from every point of view, it did not seem to him impossible that, by some mistake, the man might have embarked on the "Carnatic" at the last moment; and this was also Aouda's opinion, who regretted very much the loss of the worthy fellow to whom she owed so much. They might then find him at Yokohama; for if the "Carnatic" was carrying him thither, it would be easy to ascertain if he had been on board.

A brisk breeze arose about ten o'clock; but, though it might have been prudent to take in a reef, the pilot, after carefully examining the heavens, let the craft remain rigged as before. The "Tankadere" bore sail admirably, as she drew a great deal of water, and everything was prepared for high speed in case of a gale.

Mr. Fogg and Aouda descended into the cabin at midnight, having been already preceded by Fix, who had lain down on one of the cots. The pilot and crew remained on deck all night.

The young woman, sitting in the stern, was lost in contemplation.

At sunrise the next day, which was November 8th, the boat had made more than one hundred miles. The log indicated a mean speed of between eight and nine miles. The "Tankadere" still carried all sail, and was accomplishing her greatest capacity of speed. If the wind held as it was, the chances would be in her favour. During the day she kept along the coast, where the currents were favourable; the coast, irregular in profile, and visible sometimes across the clearings, was at most five miles distant. The sea was less boisterous, since the wind came off land—a fortunate circumstance for the boat, which would suffer, owing to its small tonnage, by a heavy surge on the sea.

The breeze subsided a little towards noon, and set in from the south-west. The pilot put up his poles, but took them down again within two hours, as the wind freshened up anew.

Mr. Fogg and Aouda, happily unaffected by the roughness of the sea, ate with a good appetite, Fix being invited to share their repast, which he accepted with secret chagrin. To travel at this man's expense and live upon his provisions was not palatable to him. Still, he was obliged to eat, and so he ate.

When the meal was over, he took Mr. Fogg apart, and said, "Sir,"—this "sir" scorched his lips, and he had to control himself to avoid collaring this "gentleman,"—"sir, you have been very kind to give me a passage on this boat. But, though my means will not admit of my expending them as freely as you, I must ask to pay my share—"

"Let us not speak of that, sir," replied Mr. Fogg.

"But, if I insist—

"No, sir," repeated Mr. Fogg, in a tone which did not admit of a reply. "This enters into my general expenses."

Fix, as he bowed, had a stifled feeling, and going forward, where he ensconced himself, did not open his mouth for the rest of the day.

Meanwhile they were progressing famously, and John Bunsby was in high hope. He several times assured Mr. Fogg that they would reach Shanghai in time; to which that gentleman responded that he counted upon it. The crew set to work in good earnest, inspired by the reward to be gained. There was not a sheet which was not tightened, not a sail which was not vigorously hoisted; not a lurch could be charged to the man at the helm. They worked as desperately as if they were contesting in a Royal Yacht regatta.

By evening, the log showed that two hundred and twenty miles had been accomplished from Hong Kong, and Mr. Fogg might hope that he would be able to reach Yokohama without recording any delay in his journal; in which case, the only misadventure which had overtaken him since he left London would not seriously affect his journey.

The "Tankadere" entered the Straits of Fo-Kien, which separate the island of Formosa from the Chinese coast, in the small hours of the night, and crossed the Tropic of Cancer. The sea was very rough in the straits, full of eddies formed by the counter currents, and the chopping waves broke her course, whilst it became very difficult to stand on deck.

At daybreak the wind began to blow hard again, and the heavens seemed to predict a gale. The barometer announced a speedy change, the mercury rising and falling capriciously; the sea also, in the south-east, raised long surges which indicated a tempest. The sun had set the evening before in a red mist, in the midst of the phosphorescent scintillations of the ocean.

John Bunsby long examined the threatening aspect of the heavens, muttering indistinctly between his teeth. At last he said in a low voice to Mr. Fogg, "Shall I speak out to your honour?"

"Of course."

"Well, we are going to have a squall."

"Is the wind north or south?" asked Mr. Fogg quietly.

"South. Look! a typhoon is coming up."

"Glad it's a typhoon from the south, for it will carry us forward."

"Oh, if you take it that way," said John Bunsby, "I've nothing more to say." John Bunsby's suspicions were confirmed. At a less advanced season of the year the typhoon, according to a famous meteorologist, would have passed away like a luminous cascade of electric flame; but in the winter equinox, it was to be feared that it would burst upon them with great violence.

The pilot took his precautions in advance. He reefed all sail, the pole-masts were dispensed with; all hands went forward to the bows. A single triangular sail, of strong canvas, was hoisted as a storm-jib, so as to hold the wind from behind. Then they waited.

John Bunsby had requested his passengers to go below; but this imprisonment in so narrow a space, with little air, and the boat bouncing in the gale, was far from pleasant. Neither Mr. Fogg, Fix, nor Aouda consented to leave the deck.

The storm of rain and wind descended upon them towards eight o'clock. With but its bit of sail, the "Tankadere" was lifted like a feather

The "Tankadère" was tossed about like a feather.

by a wind an idea of whose violence can scarcely be given. To compare her speed to four times that of a locomotive going on full steam would be below the truth.

The boat scudded thus northward during the whole day, borne on by monstrous waves, preserving always, fortunately, a speed equal to theirs. Twenty times she seemed almost to be submerged by these mountains of water which rose behind her; but the adroit management of the pilot saved her. The passengers were often bathed in spray, but they submitted to it philosophically. Fix cursed it, no doubt; but Aouda, with her eyes fastened upon her protector, whose coolness amazed her, showed herself worthy of him, and bravely weathered the storm. As for Phileas Fogg, it seemed just as if the typhoon were a part of his programme.

Up to this time the "Tankadere" had always held her course to the north; but towards evening the wind, veering three quarters, bore down from the north-west. The boat, now lying in the trough of the waves, shook and rolled terribly; the sea struck her with fearful violence. At night the tempest increased in violence. John Bunsby saw the approach of darkness and the rising of the storm with dark misgivings. He thought awhile, and then asked his crew if it was not time to slacken speed. After a consultation he approached Mr. Fogg, and said, "I think, your honour, that we should do well to make for one of the ports on the coast."

"I think so too."

"Ah!" said the pilot. "But which one?"

"I know of but one," returned Mr. Fogg tranquilly.

"And that is—"

"Shanghai."

The pilot, at first, did not seem to comprehend; he could scarcely realize so much determination and tenacity. Then he cried, "Well—yes! Your honour is right. To Shanghai!"

So the "Tankadere" kept steadily on her northward track.

The night was really terrible; it would be a miracle if the craft did not founder. Twice it would have been all over with her, if the crew had not been constantly on the watch. Aouda was exhausted, but did not utter a complaint. More than once Mr. Fogg rushed to protect her from the violence of the waves.

Day reappeared. The tempest still raged with undiminished fury; but the wind now returned to the south-east. It was a favourable change, and the "Tankadere" again bounded forward on this mountainous sea, though the waves crossed each other, and imparted shocks and counter-shocks which would have crushed a craft less solidly built. From time to time the coast was visible through the broken mist, but no vessel was in sight. The "Tankadere" was alone upon the sea.

There were some signs of a calm at noon, and these became more distinct as the sun descended toward the horizon. The tempest had been as brief as terrific. The passengers, thoroughly exhausted, could not eat a little, and take some repose.

The night was comparatively quiet. Some of the sails were again hoisted, and the speed of the boat was very good. The next morning at dawn the espied the coast, and John Bunsby was able to assert that they were not one hundred miles from Shanghai. A hundred miles, and only one day to traverse them! That very evening Mr. Fogg was due at Shanghai, if he did not wish to miss the steamer to Yokohama. Had there been no storm, during which several hours were lost, they would be at this moment within thirty miles of their destination.

The wind grew decidedly calmer, and happily the sea fell with it. All sails were now hoisted, and at noon the "Tankadere" was within forty-five miles of Shanghai. There remained yet six hours in which to accomplish that distance. All on board feared that it could not be done and every one—Phileas Fogg, no doubt, excepted—felt his heart beat with impatience. The boat must keep up an average of nine miles an hour, and the wind was becoming calmer every moment! It was a capricious breeze, coming from the coast, and after it passed the sea became smooth. Still, the "Tankadere" was so light, and her fine sails caught the fickle zephyrs so well, that, with the aid of the current, John Bunsby found himself at six o'clock not more than ten miles from the mouth of Shanghai River. Shanghai itself is situated at least twelve miles up the stream. At seven they were still three miles from Shanghai. The pilot swore an angry oath; the reward of two hundred pounds was evidently on the point of escaping him. He looked at Mr. Fogg. Mr. Fogg was perfectly tranquil; and yet his whole fortune was at this moment at stake.

At this moment, also, a long black funnel, crowned with wreaths of smoke, appeared on the edge of the waters. It was the American steamer, leaving for Yokohama at the appointed time.

"Confound her!" cried John Bunsby, pushing back the rudder with a desperate jerk.

"Signal her!" said Phileas Fogg quietly.

A small brass cannon stood on the forward deck of the "Tankadere," for making signals in the fogs. It was loaded to the muzzle; but just as the pilot was about to apply a red-hot coal to the touchhole, Mr. Fogg said, "Hoist your flag!"

The flag was run up at halfmast, and, this being the signal of distress, it was hoped that the American steamer, perceiving it, would change her course a little, so as to succour the pilot-boat.

"Fire!" said Mr. Fogg. And the booming of the little cannon resounded in the air.

Around the World in Eighty Days

CHAPTER XXII.

IN WHICH PASSEPARTOUT FINDS OUT THAT, EVEN AT THE ANTIPODES, IT IS CONVENIENT TO HAVE SOME MONEY IN ONE'S POCKET.

THE "Carnatic," setting sail from Hong Kong at half-past six on the 7th of November, directed her course at full steam towards Japan. She carried a large cargo and a well-filled cabin of passengers. Two state-rooms in the rear, were, however, unoccupied,—those which had been engaged by Phileas Fogg.

The next day a passenger, with a half-stupefied eye, staggering gait, and disordered hair, was seen to emerge from the second cabin, and to totter to a seat on deck.

It was Passepartout; and what had happened to him was as follows:—Shortly after Fix left the opium den, two waiters had lifted the unconscious Passepartout, and had carried him to the bed reserved for the smokers. Three hours later, pursued even in his dreams by a fixed idea, the poor fellow awoke, and struggled against the stupefying influence of the narcotic. The thought of a duty unfulfilled shook off his torpor, and he hurried from the abode of drunkenness. Staggering and holding himself up by keeping against the walls, falling down and creeping up again, and irresistibly impelled by a kind of instinct, he kept crying out, "The 'Carnatic!' the 'Carnatic!'"

The steamer lay puffing alongside the quay, on the point of starting. Passepartout had but few steps to go; and, rushing upon the plank, he crossed it, and fell unconscious on the deck, just as the "Carnatic" was moving off. Several sailors, who were evidently accustomed to this sort of scene, carried the poor Frenchman down into the second cabin, and Passepartout did not wake until they were one hundred and fifty miles away from China. Thus he found himself the next morning on the deck of the "Carnatic," and eagerly inhaling the exhilarating sea-breeze. The pure air sobered him. He began to collect his senses, which he found a difficult task; but at last he recalled the events of the evening before, Fix's revelation, and the opium-house.

"It is evident," said he to himself, "that I have been abominably drunk! What will Mr. Fogg say? At least I have not missed the steamer, which is the most important thing."

Then, as Fix occurred to him:—"As for that rascal, I hope we are well rid of him, and that he has not dared, as he proposed, to follow us on board the "Carnatic." A detective on the track of Mr. Fogg, accused of robbing the Bank of England! Pshaw! Mr. Fogg is no more a robber than I am a murderer."

Should he divulge Fix's real errand to his master? Would it do to tell the part the detective was playing? Would it not be better to wait until Mr. Fogg reached London again, and then impart to him that an agent of the metropolitan police had been following him round the world, and have a good laugh over it? No doubt; at least, it was worth considering. The first thing to do was to find Mr. Fogg, and apologize for his singular behaviour.

Passepartout got up and proceeded, as well as he could with the rolling of the steamer, to the after-deck. He saw no one who resembled either his master or Aouda. "Good!" muttered he; "Aouda has not got up yet, and Mr. Fogg has probably found some partners at whist."

He descended to the saloon. Mr. Fogg was not there. Passepartout had only, however, to ask the purser the number of his master's stateroom. The purser replied that he did not know any passenger by the name of Fogg.

"I beg your pardon," said Passepartout persistently. "He is a tall gentleman, quiet, and not very talkative, and has with him a young lady—"

"There is no young lady on board," interrupted the purser. "Here is a list of the passengers; you may see for yourself."

Passepartout scanned the list, but his master's name was not upon it. All at once an idea struck him.

"Ah! am I on the 'Carnatic?'"

"Yes."

"On the way to Yokohama?"

"Certainly."

Passepartout had for an instant feared that he was on the wrong boat; but, though he was really on the "Carnatic," his master was not there.

He fell thunderstruck on a seat. He saw it all now. He remembered that the time of sailing had been changed, that he should have informed his master of that fact, and that he had not done so. It was his fault, then, that Mr.

Fogg and Aouda had missed the steamer. Yes, but it was still more the fault of the traitor who, in order to separate him from his master, and detain the latter at Hong Kong, had inveigled him into getting drunk! He now saw the detective's trick; and at this moment Mr. Fogg was certainly ruined, his bet was lost, and he himself perhaps arrested and imprisoned! At this thought Passepartout tore his hair. Ah, if Fix ever came within his reach, what a settling of accounts there would be!

After his first depression, Passepartout became calmer, and began to study his situation. It was certainly not an enviable one. He found himself on the way to Japan, and what should he do when he got there? His pocket was empty; he had not a solitary shilling—not so much as a penny. His passage had fortunately been paid for in advance; and he had five or six days in which to decide upon his future course. He fell to at meals with an appetite, and ate for Mr. Fogg, Aouda, and himself. He helped himself as generously as if Japan were a desert, where nothing to eat was to be looked for.

At dawn on the 13th the "Carnatic" entered the port of Yokohama. This is an important way-station in the Pacific, where all the mail-steamers, and those carrying travellers between North America, China, Japan, and the Oriental islands, put in. It is situated in the bay of Yeddo, and at but a short distance from that second capital of the Japanese Empire, and the residence of the Tycoon, the civil Emperor, before the Mikado, the spiritual Emperor, absorbed his office in his own. The "Carnatic" anchored at the quay near the custom-house, in the midst of a crowd of ships bearing the flags of all nations.

Passepartout went timidly ashore on this so curious territory of the Sons of the Sun. He had nothing better to do than, taking chance for his guide, to wander aimlessly through the streets of Yokohama. He found himself at first in a thoroughly European quarter, the houses having low fronts, and being adorned with verandas, beneath which he caught glimpses of neat peristyles. This quarter occupied, with its streets, squares, docks and warehouses, all the space between the "promontory of the Treaty" and the river. Here, as at Hong Kong and Calcutta, were mixed crowds of all races,—Americans and English, Chinamen and Dutchmen, mostly merchants ready to buy or sell anything. The Frenchman felt himself as much alone among them as if he had dropped down in the midst of Hottentots.

He had, at least, one resource,—to call on the French and English consuls at Yokohama for assistance. But he shrank from telling the story of his adventures, intimately connected as it was with that of his master: and, before doing so, he determined to exhaust all other means of aid. As chance did not favour him in the European quarter, he penetrated that inhabited by the native Japanese, determined, if necessary, to push on to Yeddo.

The Japanese quarter of Yokohama is called Benten, after the goddess of the sea, who is worshipped on the islands round about. There Passepartout beheld beautiful fir and cedar groves, sacred gates of a singular architecture, bridges half hid in the midst of bamboos and reeds, temples shaded by immense cedar-trees, holy retreats where were sheltered Buddhist priests and sectaries of Confucius, and interminable streets, where a perfect harvest of rose-tinted and red-cheeked children, who looked as if they had been cut out of Japanese screens, and who were playing in the midst of short-legged poodles and yellowish cats, might have been gathered.

The streets were crowded with people. Priests were passing in processions, beating their dreary tambourines; police and custom-house officers with pointed hats encrusted with lac, and carrying two sabres hung to their waists; soldiers, clad in blue cotton with white stripes, and bearing guns; the Mikado's guards, enveloped in silken doublets, hauberks, and coats of mail; and numbers of military folk of all ranks—for the military profession is as much respected in Japan as it is despised in China—went hither and thither in groups and pairs. Passepartout saw, too, begging friars, long-robed pilgrims, and simple civilians, with their warped and jet-black hair, big heads, long busts, slender legs, short stature, and complexions varying from copper-colour to a dead white, but never yellow, like the Chinese, from whom the Japanese widely differ. He did not fail to observe the curious equipages,—carriages and palanquins, barrows supplied with sails, and litters made of bamboo; nor the women—whom he thought not especially handsome,—who took little steps with their little feet, whereon they wore canvas shoes, straw sandals, and clogs of worked wood, and who displayed tight-looking eyes, flat chests, teeth fashionably blackened, and gowns crossed with silken scarfs, tied in an enormous knot behind,—an ornament which the modern Parisian ladies seem to have borrowed from the dames of Japan.

Passepartout wandered for several hours in the midst of this motley crowd, looking in at the windows of the rich and curious shops, the

Night came on, and Passepartout returned to the town.

jewellery establishments glittering with quaint Japanese ornaments, the restaurants decked with streamers and banners, the tea-houses, where the odorous beverage was being drunk with "saki," a liquor concocted from the fermentation of rice, and the comfortable smoking-houses, where they were puffing, not opium, which is almost unknown in Japan, but a very fine, stringy tobacco. He went on till he found himself in the fields, in the midst of vast rice plantations. There he saw dazzling camelias expanding themselves, with flowers which were giving forth their last colours and perfumes, not on bushes, but on trees; and within bamboo enclosures, cherry, plum, and apple trees, which the Japanese cultivate rather for their blossoms than their fruit, and which queerly-fashioned grinning scarescrows protected from the sparrows, pigeons, ravens, and other voracious birds. On the branches of the cedars were perched large eagles; amid the foliage of the weeping willows were herons, solemnly standing on one leg; and on every hand were crows, ducks, hawks, wild birds, and a multitude of cranes, which the Japanese consider sacred, and which to their minds symbolize long life and prosperity.

As he was strolling along, Passepartout espied some violets among the shrubs.

"Good!" said he; "I'll have some supper."

But, on smelling them, he found that they were odourless.

"No chance there," thought he.

The worthy fellow had certainly taken good care to eat as hearty a breakfast as possible before leaving the "Carnatic"; but as he had been walking about all day, the demands of hunger were becoming importunate. He observed that the butchers' stalls contained neither mutton, goat, nor pork; and knowing also that it is a sacrilege to kill cattle, which are preserved solely for farming, he made up his mind that meat was far from plentiful in Yokohama,—nor was he mistaken; and in default of butcher's meat, he could have wished for a quarter of wild boar or deer, a partridge, or some quails, some game or fish, which, with rice, the Japanese eat almost exclusively. But he found it necessary to keep up a stout heart, and to postpone the meal he craved till the following morning. Night came, and Passepartout re-entered the native quarter, where he wandered through the streets, lit by vari-coloured lanterns, looking on at the dancers who were executing skilful steps and boundings, and the astrologers who stood in the open air with their telescopes. Then he came to the harbour, which was lit up by the rosin torches of the fishermen, who were fishing from their boats.

The streets at last became quiet, and the patrol, the officers of which, in their splendid costumes, and surrounded by their suites, Passepartout thought seemed like ambassadors, succeeded the bustling crowd. Each time a company passed, Passepartout chuckled, and said to himself, "Good! another Japanese embassy departing for Europe!"

Around the World in Eighty Days

CHAPTER XXIII.

IN WHICH PASSEPARTOUT'S NOSE BECOMES OUTRAGEOUSLY LONG.

THE next morning poor, jaded, famished Passepartout said to himself that he must get something to eat at all hazards, and the sooner he did so the better. He might, indeed, sell his watch; but he would have starved first. Now or never he must use the strong, if not melodious voice which nature had bestowed upon him. He knew several French and English songs, and resolved to try them upon the Japanese, who must be lovers of music, since they were for ever pounding on their cymbals, tam-tams, and tambourines, and could not but appreciate European talent.

It was, perhaps, rather early in the morning to get up a concert, and the audience, prematurely aroused from their slumbers, might not, possibly, pay their entertainer with coin bearing the Mikado's features. Passepartout therefore decided to wait several hours; and, as he was sauntering along, it occurred to him that he would seem rather too well dressed for a wandering artist. The idea struck him to change his garments for clothes more in harmony with his project; by which he might also get a little money to satisfy the immediate cravings of hunger. The resolution taken, it remained to carry it out.

It was only after a long search that Passepartout discovered a native dealer in old clothes, to whom he applied for an exchange. The man liked the European costume, and ere long Passepartout issued from his shop accoutred in an old Japanese coat, and a sort of one-sided turban, faded with long use. A few small pieces of silver, moreover, jingled in his pocket.

"Good!" thought he. "I will imagine I am at the Carnival!"

His first care, after being thus "Japanesed," was to enter a tea-house of modest appearance, and, upon half a bird and a little rice, to breakfast like a man for whom dinner was as yet a problem to be solved.

"Now," thought he, when he had eaten heartily, "I mustn't lose my head. I can't sell this costume again for one still more Japanese. I must consider how to leave this country of the Sun, of which I shall not retain the most delightful of memories, as quickly as possible."

It occurred to him to visit the steamers which were about to leave for America. He would offer himself as a cook or servant, in payment of his passage and meals. Once at San Francisco, he would find some means of going on. The difficulty was, how to traverse the four thousand seven hundred miles of the Pacific which lay between Japan and the New World.

Passepartout was not the man to let an idea go begging, and directed his steps towards the docks. But, as he approached them, his project, which at first had seemed so simple, began to grow more and more formidable to his mind. What need would they have of a cook or servant on an American steamer, and what confidence would they put in him, dressed as he was? What references could he give?

As he was reflecting in this wise, his eyes fell upon an immense placard which a sort of clown was carrying through the streets. This placard, which was in English, read as follows:—

"ACROBATIC JAPANESE TROUPE,

HONOURABLE WILLIAM BATULCAR,
PROPRIETOR,

LAST REPRESENTATIONS,

PRIOR TO THEIR DEPARTURE FOR THE
UNITED STATES

OF THE

LONG NOSES! LONG NOSES!

UNDER THE DIRECT PATRONAGE OF
THE GOD TINGOU!

GREAT ATTRACTION!"

"The United States!" said Passepartout; "that's just what I want!"

He followed the clown, and soon found himself once more in the Japanese quarter. A quarter of an hour later he stopped before a large cabin, adorned with several clusters of streamers, the exterior walls of which were designed to represent, in violent colours and without perspective, a company of jugglers.

This was the Honourable William Batulcar's establishment. That gentleman was a sort of Barnum, the director of a troupe of mountebanks, jugglers, clowns, acrobats, equilibrists,

Passepartout went out muffled up in an old Japanese robe.

and gymnasts, who, according to the placard, was giving his last performances before leaving the Empire of the Sun for the States of the Union.

Passepartout entered and asked for Mr. Batulcar, who straightaway appeared in person.

"What do you want?" said he to Passepartout, whom he at first took for a native.

"Would you like a servant, sir?" asked Passepartout.

"A servant!" cried Mr. Batulcar, caressing the thick gray beard which hung from his chin. "I already have two who are obedient and faithful, have never left me, and serve me for their nourishment,—and here they are," added he, holding out his two robust arms, furrowed with veins as large as the strings of a bass-viol.

"So I can be of no use to you?"

"None."

"The devil! I should so like to cross the Pacific with you!"

"Ah!" said the Honourable Mr. Batulcar. "You are no more a Japanese than I am a monkey! Why are you dressed up in that way?"

"A man dresses as he can."

"That's true. You are a Frenchman, aren't you?"

"Yes; a Parisian of Paris."

"Then you ought to know how to make grimaces?"

"Why," replied Passepartout, a little vexed that his nationality should cause this question, "we Frenchmen know how to make grimaces, it is true,—but not any better than the Americans do."

"True. Well, if I can't take you as a servant, I can as a clown. You see, my friend, in France they exhibit foreign clowns, and in foreign parts French clowns."

"Ah!"

"You are pretty strong, eh?"

"Especially after a good meal."

"And you can sing?"

"Yes," returned Passepartout, who had formerly been wont to sing in the streets.

"But can you sing standing on your head, with a top spinning on your left foot, and a sabre balanced on your right?"

"Humph! I think so," replied Passepartout, recalling the exercises of his younger days.

"Well, that's enough," said the Honourable William Batulcar.

The engagement was concluded there and then.

Passepartout had at last found something to do. He was engaged to act in the celebrated Japanese troupe. It was not a very dignified position, but within a week he would be on his way to San Francisco.

The performance, so noisily announced by the Honourable Mr. Batulcar, was to commence at three o'clock, and soon the deafening instruments of a Japanese orchestra resounded at the door. Passepartout, though he had not been able to study or rehearse a part, was designated to lend the aid of his sturdy shoulders in the great exhibition of the "human pyramid," executed by the Long Noses of the god Tingou. This "great attraction" was to close the performance.

Before three o'clock the large shed was invaded by the spectators, comprising Europeans and natives, Chinese and Japanese, men, women, and children, who precipitated themselves upon the narrow benches and into the boxes opposite the stage. The musicians took up a position inside, and were vigorously performing on their gongs, tam-tams, flutes, bones, tambourines, and immense drums.

The performance was much like all acrobatic displays; but it must be confessed that the Japanese are the first equilibrists in the world.

One, with a fan and some bits of paper, performed the graceful trick of the butterflies and the flowers; another traced in the air, with the odorous smoke of his pipe, a series of blue words, which composed a compliment to the audience; while a third juggled with some lighted candles, which he extinguished successively as they passed his lips, and relit again without interrupting for an instant his juggling. Another reproduced the most singular combinations with a spinning-top; in his hands the revolving tops seemed to be animated with a life of their own in their interminable whirling; they ran over pipe-stems, the edges of sabres, wires, and even hairs stretched across the stage; they turned around on the edges of large glasses, crossed bamboo ladders, dispersed into all the corners, and produced strange musical effects by the combination of their various pitches of tone. The jugglers tossed them in the air, threw them like shuttlecocks with wooden battledores, and yet they kept on spinning; they put them into their pockets, and took them out still whirling as before.

It is useless to describe the astonishing performances of the acrobats and gymnasts. The turning on ladders, poles, balls, barrels, &c., was executed with wonderful precision.

But the principal attraction was the exhibition of the Long Noses, a show to which Europe is as yet a stranger.

The Long Noses form a peculiar company, under the direct patronage of the god Tingou.

The monument collapsed like a castle of cards.

Followed by Passepartout with the wings on his back.

Attired after the fashion of the Middle Ages, they bore upon their shoulders a splendid pair of wings; but what especially distinguished them was the long noses which were fastened to their faces, and the uses which they made of them. These noses were made of bamboo, and were five, six, and even ten feet long, some straight, others curved, some ribboned, and some having imitation warts upon them. It was upon these appendages, fixed tightly on their real noses, that they performed their gymnastic exercises. A dozen of these sectaries of Tingou lay flat upon their backs, while others, dressed to represent lightning-rods, came and frolicked on their noses, jumping from one to another, and performing the most skilful leapings and somersaults.

As a last scene, a "human pyramid" had been announced, in which fifty Long Noses were to represent the Car of Juggernaut. But, instead of forming a pyramid by mounting each other's shoulders, the artists were to group themselves on top of the noses. It happened that the performer who had hitherto formed the base of the Car had quitted the troupe, and as, to fill this part, only strength and adroitness were necessary, Passepartout had been chosen to take his place.

The poor fellow really felt sad when—melancholy reminiscence of his youth!—he donned his costume, adorned with vari-coloured wings, and fastened to his natural feature a false nose six feet long. But he cheered up when he thought that this nose was winning him something to eat.

He went upon the stage, and took his place beside the rest who were to compose the base of the Car of Juggernaut. They all stretched themselves on the floor, their noses pointing to the ceiling. A second group of artists disposed themselves on these long appendages, then a third above these, then a fourth, until a human monument reaching to the very cornices of the theatre soon arose on top of the noses. This elicited loud applause, in the midst of which the orchestra was just striking up a deafening air, when the pyramid tottered, the balance was lost, one of the lower noses vanished from the pyramid, and the human monument was shattered like a castle built of cards!

It was Passepartout's fault. Abandoning his position, clearing the footlights without the aid of his wings, and clambering up to the right-hand gallery, he fell at the feet of one of the spectators, crying, "Ah, my master! my master!"

"You here?"

"Myself."

"Very well; then let us go to the steamer, young man!"

Mr. Fogg, Aouda, and Passepartout passed through the lobby of the theatre to the outside, where they encountered the Honourable Mr. Batulcar, furious with rage. He demanded damages for the "breakage" of the pyramid; and Phileas Fogg appeased him by giving him a handful of bank-notes.

At half-past six, the very hour of departure, Mr. Fogg and Aouda, followed by Passepartout, who in his hurry had retained his wings, and nose six feet long, stepped upon the American steamer.

Around the World in Eighty Days

CHAPTER XXIV.

DURING WHICH MR. FOGG AND PARTY CROSS THE PACIFIC OCEAN.

WHAT happened when the pilot-boat came in sight of Shanghai will be easily guessed. The signals made by the "Tankadere" had been seen by the captain of the Yokohama steamer, who, esplying the flag at half-mast, had directed his course towards the little craft. Phileas Fogg, after paying the stipulated price of his passage to John Bunsby, and rewarding that worthy with the additional sum of five hundred and fifty pounds, ascended the steamer with Aouda and Fix; and they started at once for Nagasaki and Yokohama.

They reached their destination on the morning of the 14th of November. Phileas Fogg lost no time in going on board the "Carnatic," where he learned, to Aouda's great delight—and perhaps to his own, though he betrayed no emotion—that Passepartout, a Frenchman, had really arrived on her the day before.

The San Francisco steamer was announced to leave that very evening, and it became necessary to find Passepartout, if possible, without delay. Mr. Fogg applied in vain to the French and English consuls, and, after wandering through the streets a long time, began to despair of finding his missing servant. Chance, or perhaps a kind of presentiment, at last led him into the Honourable Mr. Batulcar's theatre. He certainly would not have recognized Passepartout in the eccentric mountebank's costume; but the latter, lying on his back, perceived his master in the gallery. He could not help starting, which so changed the position of his nose as to bring the "pyramid" pell-mell upon the stage.

All this Passepartout learned from Aouda, who recounted to him what had taken place on the voyage from Hong Kong to Shanghai on the "Tankadere," in company with one Mr. Fix.

Passepartout did not change countenance on hearing this name. He thought that the time had not yet arrived to divulge to his master what had taken place between the detective and himself; and in the account he gave of his absence, he simply excused himself for having been overtaken by drunkenness, in smoking opium at a tavern in Hong Kong.

Mr. Fogg heard this narrative coldly, without a word; and then furnished his man with funds necessary to obtain clothing more in harmony with his position. Within an hour the Frenchman had cut off his nose and parted with his wings, and retained nothing about him which recalled the sectary of the god Tingou.

The steamer which was about to depart from Yokohama to San Fancisco belonged to the Pacific Mail Steamship Company, and was named the "General Grant." She was a large paddle-wheel steamer of two thousand five hundred tons, well equipped and very fast. The massive walking-beam rose and fell above the deck; at one end a piston-rod worked up and down; and at the other was a connecting-rod which, in changing the rectilinear motion to a circular one, was directly connected with the shaft of the paddles. The "General Grant" was rigged with three masts, giving a large capacity for sails, and thus materially aiding the steam power. By making twelve miles an hour, she would cross the ocean in twenty-one days. Phileas Fogg was therefore justified in hoping that he would reach San Francisco by the 2nd of December, New York by the 11th, and London on the 20th,—thus gaining several hours on the fatal 21st of December.

There was a full complement of passengers on board, among them English, many Americans, a large number of Coolies on their way to California, and several East Indian officers, who were spending their vacation in making the tour of the world. Nothing of moment happened on the voyage; the steamer, sustained on its large paddles, rolled but little, and the "Pacific" almost justified its name. Mr. Fogg was as calm and taciturn as ever. His young companion felt herself more and more attached to him by other ties than gratitude; his silent but generous nature impressed her more than she thought; and it was almost unconsciously that she yielded to emotions which did not seem to have the least effect upon her protector. Aouda took the keenest interest in his plans, and became impatient at any incident which seemed likely to retard his journey.

She often chatted with Passepartout, who did not fail to perceive the state of the lady's heart; and, being the most faithful of domestics, he never exhausted his eulogies of Phileas Fogg's honesty, generosity, and devotion. He took pains to calm Aouda's doubts of a successful termination of the journey, telling her that the most difficult part of it had passed, that now they were beyond the fantastic countries of Japan and China, and were fairly on their way to civilized places again. A railway train from San Francisco to New York, and a transatlantic steamer from New York to Liverpool, would doubtless bring them to the end of this impossible journey round the world within the period agreed upon.

On the ninth day after leaving Yokohama, Phileas Fogg had traversed exactly one half of the terrestrial globe. The "General Grant" passed, on the 23rd of November, the one hundred and eightieth meridian, and was at the very antipodes of London. Mr. Fogg had, it is true, exhausted fifty-two of the eighty days in which he was to complete the tour, and there were only twenty-eight left. But, though he was only half-way by the difference of meridians, he had really gone over two-thirds of the whole journey; for he had been obliged to make long circuits from London to Aden, from Aden to Bombay, from Calcutta to Singapore, and from Singapore to Yokohama. Could he have followed without deviation the fiftieth parallel, which is that of London, the whole distance would only have been about twelve thousand miles; whereas he would be forced, by the irregular methods of locomotion, to traverse twenty-six thousand, of which he had, on the 23rd of November, accomplished seventeen thousand five hundred. And now the course was a straight one, and Fix was no longer there to put obstacles in their way!

It happened also, on the 23rd of November, that Passepartout made a joyful discovery. It will be remembered that the obstinate fellow had insisted on keeping his famous family watch at London time, and on regarding that of the countries he had passed through as quite false and unreliable. Now, on this day, though he had not changed the hands, he found that his watch exactly agreed with the ship's chronometers. His triumph was hilarious. He would have liked to know what Fix would say if he were aboard!

"The rogue told me a lot of stories," repeated Passepartout, "about the meridians, the sun, and the moon! Moon, indeed! moonshine more likely! If one listened to that sort of people, a pretty sort of time one would keep! I was sure that the sun would some day regulate itself by my watch!"

Passepartout was ignorant that, if the face of his watch had been divided into twenty-four hours, like the Italian clocks, he would have no reason for exultation; for the hands of his watch would then, instead of as now indicating nine o'clock in the morning, indicate nine o'clock in the evening, that is the twenty-first hour after midnight,—precisely the difference between London time and that of the one hundred and eightieth meridian. But if Fix had been able to explain this purely physical effect, Passepartout would not have admitted, even if he had comprehended it. Moreover, if the detective had been on board at that moment, Passepartout would have joined issue with him on a quite different subject, and in an entirely different manner.

Where was Fix at that moment?

He was actually on board the "General Grant."

On reaching Yokohama, the detective, leaving Mr. Fogg, whom he expected to meet again during the day, had repaired at once to the English consulate, where he at last found the warrant of arrest. It had followed him from Bombay, and had come by the "Carnatic," on which steamer he himself was supposed to be. Fix's disappointment may be imagined when he reflected that the warrant was now useless. Mr. Fogg had left English ground, and it was now necessary to procure his extradition!

"Well," thought Fix, after a moment of anger, "my warrant is not good here, but it will be in England. The rogue evidently intends to return to his own country, thinking he has thrown the police off his track. Good! I will follow him across the Atlantic. As for the money, Heaven grant there may be some left! But the fellow has already spent in travelling, rewards, trials, bail, elephants, and all sorts of charges, more than five thousand pounds. Yet, after all, the Bank is rich!"

His course decided on, he went on board the "General Grant," and was there when Mr. Fogg and Aouda arrived. To his utter amazement, he recognized Passepartout, despite his theatrical disguise. He quickly concealed himself in his cabin, to avoid an awkward explanation, and hoped—thanks to the number of passengers—to remain unperceived by Mr. Fogg's servant.

On that very day, however, he met Passepartout face to face on the forward deck. The latter, without a word, made a rush for him, grasped him by the throat, and, much to the amusement of a group of Americans, who immediately began to bet on him, administered to the detective a perfect volley of blows, which proved the great superiority of French over English pugilistic skill.

When Passepartout had finished, he found

himself relieved and comforted. Fix got up in a somewhat rumpled condition, and, looking at his adversary, coldly said, "Have you done?"

"For this time—yes."

"Then let me have a word with you."

"But I—"

"In your master's interest."

Passepartout seemed to be vanquished by Fix's coolness, for he quietly followed him, and they sat down aside from the rest of the passengers.

"You have given me a thrashing," said Fix. "Good I expected it. Now, listen to me. Up to this time I have been Mr. Fogg's adversary. I am now in his game."

"Aha!" cried Passepartout; "you are convinced he is an honest man?"

"No," replied Fix Coldly, "I think him a rascal. Sh! don't budge, and let me speak. As long as Mr. Fogg was on English ground, it was for my interest to detain him there until my warrant of arrest arrived. I did everything I could to keep him back. I sent the Bombay priests after him, I got you intoxicated at Hong Kong, I separated you from him, and I made him miss the Yokohama steamer."

Passepartout listened, with closed fists.

"Now," resumed Fix, "Mr. Fogg seems to be going back to England. Well, I will follow him there. But hereafter I will do as much to keep obstacles out of his way as I have done up to this time to put them in his path. I've changed my game, you see, and simply because it was for my interest to change it. Your interest is the same as mine; for it is only in England that you will ascertain whether you are in the service of a criminal or an honest man."

Passepartout listened very attentively to Fix, and was convinced that he spoke with entire good faith.

"Are we friends?" asked the detective.

"Friends?—no," replied Passepartout; "but allies, perhaps. At the least sign of treason, however, I'll twist your neck for you."

"Agreed," said the detective quietly.

Eleven days later, on the 3rd of December, the "General Grant" entered the bay of the Golden Gate, and reached San Francisco.

Mr. Fogg had neither gained nor lost a single day.

Around the World in Eighty Days

CHAPTER XXV.

IN WHICH A SLIGHT GLIMPSE IS HAD OF SAN FRANCISCO.

IT was seven in the morning when Mr. Fogg, Aouda, and Passepartout set foot upon the American continent, if this name can be given to the floating quay upon which they disembarked. These quays, rising and falling with the tide, thus facilitate the loading and unloading of vessels. Alongside them were clippers of all sizes, steamers of all nationalities, and the steamboats, with several decks rising one above the other, which ply on the Sacramento and its tributaries. There were also heaped up the products of a commerce which extends to Mexico, Chili, Peru, Brazil, Europe, Asia, and all the Pacific islands.

Passepartout, in his joy on reaching at last the American continent, thought he would manifest it by executing a perilous vault in fine style; but, tumbling upon some worm-eaten planks, he fell through them. Put out of countenance by the manner in which he thus "set foot" upon the New World, he uttered a loud cry, which so frightened the innumerable cormorants and pelicans that are always perched upon these movable quays, that they flew noisily away.

Mr. Fogg, on reaching shore, proceeded to find out at what hour the first train left for New York, and learned that this was at six o'clock p.m.; he had, therefore, an entire day to spend in the Californian capital. Taking a carriage at a charge of three dollars, he and Aouda entered it, while Passepartout mounted the box beside the driver, and they set out for the International Hotel.

From his exalted position Passepartout observed with much curiosity the wide streets, the low, evenly ranged houses, the Anglo-Saxon Gothic churches, the great docks, the palatial wooden and brick warehouses, the numerous conveyances, omnibuses, horse-cars, and upon the side-walks, not only Americans and Europeans, but Chinese and Indians. Passepartout was surprised at all he saw. San Francisco was no longer the legendary city of 1849,—a city of banditti, assassins, and incendiaries, who had flocked hither in crowds in pursuit of plunder; a paradise of outlaws, where they gambled with gold-dust, a revolver in one hand and a bowie-knife in the other: it was now a great commercial emporium.

The lofty tower of its City Hall overlooked the whole panorama of the streets and avenues, which cut each other at right angles, and in the midst of which appeared pleasant, verdant squares, while beyond appeared the Chinese quarter, seemingly imported from the Celestial Empire in a toy-box. Sombreros and red shirts and plumed Indians were rarely to be seen; but there were silk hats and black coats everywhere worn by a multitude of nervously active, gentlemanly-looking men. Some of the streets —especially Montgomery Street, which is to San Francisco what Regent Street is to London, the Boulevard des Italiens to Paris, and Broadway to New York—were lined with splendid and spacious stores, which exposed in their windows the products of the entire world.

When Passepartout reached the International Hotel, it did not seem to him as if he had left England at all.

The ground floor of the hotel was occupied by a large bar, a sort of restaurant freely open to all passers-by, who might partake of dried beef, oyster soup, biscuits, and cheese, without taking out their purses. Payment was made only for the ale, porter, or sherry which was drunk. This seemed "very American" to Passepartout. The hotel refreshment-rooms were comfortable, and Mr. Fogg and Aouda, installing themselves at a table, were abundantly served on diminutive plates by negroes of darkest hue.

After breakfast, Mr. Fogg, accompanied by Aouda, started for the English consulate to have his passport *visaed*. As he was going out, he met Passepartout, who asked him if it would not be well, before taking the train, to purchase some dozens of Enfield rifles and Colt's revolvers. He had been listening to stories of attacks upon the trains by the Sioux and Pawnees. Mr. Fogg thought it a useless precaution, but told him to do as he thought best, and went on to the consulate.

He had not proceeded two hundred steps, however, when, "by the greatest chance in the world," he met Fix. The detective seemed wholly taken by surprise. What! Had Mr. Fogg and himself crossed the Pacific together, and not met on the steamer! At least Fix felt honoured to behold once more the gentleman

The planks were rotten.

to whom he owed so much, and as his business recalled him to Europe, he should be delighted to continue the journey in such pleasant company.

Mr. Fogg replied that the honour would be his; and the detective—who was determined not to lose sight of him—begged permission to accompany them in their walk about San Francisco—a request which Mr. Fogg readily granted.

They soon found themselves in Montgomery Street, where a great crowd was collected; the side-walks, street, horse-car rails, the shop-doors, the windows of the houses, and even the roofs, were full of people. Men were going about carrying large posters, and flags and streamers were floating in the wind; while loud cries were heard on every hand.

"Hurrah for Camerfield!"

"Hurrah for Mandiboy!"

It was a political meeting; at least so Fix conjectured, who said to Mr. Fogg, "Perhaps we had better not mingle with the crowd. There may be danger in it."

"Yes," returned Mr. Fogg; "and blows, even if they are political, are still blows."

Fix smiled at this remark; and in order to be able to see without being jostled about, the party took up a position on the top of a flight of steps situated at the upper end of Montgomery Street. Opposite them, on the other side of the street, between a coal wharf and a petroleum warehouse, a large platform had been erected in the open air, towards which the current of the crowd seemed to be directed.

For what purpose was this meeting? What was the occasion of this excited assemblage? Phileas Fogg could not imagine. Was it to nominate some high official—a governor or member of Congress? It was not improbable, so agitated was the multitude before them.

Just at this moment there was an unusual stir in the human mass. All the hands were raised in the air. Some, tightly closed, seemed to disappear suddenly in the midst of the cries—an energetic way, no doubt, of casting a vote. The crowd swayed back, the banners and flags wavered, disappeared an instant, then reappeared in tatters. The undulations of the human serge reached the steps, while all the heads floundered on the surface like a sea agitated by a squall. Many of the black hats disappeared, and the greater part of the crowd seemed to have diminished in height.

"It is evidently a meeting," said Fix, "and its object must be an exciting one. I should not wonder if it were about the 'Alabama,' despite the fact that that question is settled."

"Perhaps," replied Mr. Fogg simply.

"At least, there are two champions in presence of each other, the Honourable Mr. Camerfield and the Honourable Mr. Mandiboy."

Aouda, leaning upon Mr. Fogg's arm, observed the tumultuous scene with surprise, while Fix asked a man near him what the cause of it all was. Before the man could reply, a fresh agitation arose; hurrahs and excited shouts were heard; the staffs of the banners began to be used as offensive weapons; and fists flew about in every direction. Thumps were exchanged from the tops of the carriages and omnibuses which had been blocked up in the crowd. Boots and shoes went whirling through the air, and Mr. Fogg thought he even heard the crack of revolvers mingling in the din. The rout approached the stairway, and flowed over the lower step. One of the parties had evidently been repulsed; but the mere lookers-on could not tell whether Mandiboy or Camerfield had gained the upper hand.

"It would be prudent for us to retire," said Fix, who was anxious that Mr. Fogg should not receive any injury, at least until they got back to London. "If there is any question about England in all this, and we were recognized, I fear it would go hard with us."

"An English subject—" began Mr. Fogg.

He did not finish his sentence; for a terrific hubbub now arose on the terrace behind the flight of steps where they stood, and there were frantic shouts of, "Hurrah for Mandiboy! Hip, hip, hurrah!"

It was a band of voters coming to the rescue of their allies, and taking the Camerfield forces in flank. Mr. Fogg, Aouda, and Fix found themselves between two fires; it was too late to escape. The torrent of men, armed with loaded canes and sticks, was irresistible. Phileas Fogg and Fix were roughly hustled in their attempts to protect their fair companion; the former, as cool as ever, tried to defend himself with the weapons which nature has placed at the end of every Englishman's arm, but in vain. A big brawny fellow with a red beard, flushed face, and broad shoulders, who seemed to be the chief of the band, raised his clenched fist to strike Mr. Fogg, whom he would have given a crushing blow, had not Fix rushed in and received it in his stead. An enormous bruise immediately made its appearance under the detective's silk hat, which was completely smashed in.

"Yankee!" exclaimed Mr. Fogg, darting a contemptuous look at the ruffian.

If Fix had not received the blow.

"Englishman!" returned the other. "We will meet again!"

"When you please."

"What is your name?"

"Phileas Fogg. And yours?"

"Colonel Stamp Proctor."

The human tide now swept by, after overturning Fix, who speedily got upon his feet again, though with tattered clothes. Happily, he was not seriously hurt. His travelling overcoat was divided into two unequal parts, and his trousers resembled those of certain Indians, which fit less compactly than they are easy to put on. Aouda had escaped unharmed, and Fix alone bore marks of the fray in his black and blue bruise.

"Thanks," said Mr. Fogg to the detective, as soon as they were out of the crowd.

"No thanks are necessary," replied Fix; "but let us go."

"Where?"

"To a tailors."

Such a visit was, indeed, opportune. The clothing of both Mr. Fogg and Fix was in rags, as if they had themselves been actively engaged in the contest between Camerfield and Mandiboy. An hour after, they were once more suitably attired, and with Aouda returned to the International Hotel.

Passepartout was waiting for his master, armed with half a dozen six-barrelled revolvers. When he perceived Fix, he knit his brows; but Aouda having, in a few words, told him of their adventure, his countenance resumed its placid expression. Fix evidently was no longer an enemy, but an ally; he was faithfully keeping his word.

Dinner over, the coach which was to convey the passengers and their luggage to the station drew up to the door. As he was getting in, Mr. Fogg said to Fix, "You have not seen this Colonel Proctor again?"

"No."

"I will come back to America to find him," said Phileas Fogg calmly. "It would not be right for an Englishman to permit himself to be treated in that way, without retaliating."

The detective smiled, but did not reply. It was clear that Mr. Fogg was one of those Englishmen, who, while they do not tolerate duelling at home, fight abroad when their honour is attacked.

At a quarter before six the travellers reached the station, and found the train ready to depart. As he was about to enter it, Mr. Fogg called a porter, and said to him, "My friend, was there not some trouble to-day in San Francisco?"

"It was a political meeting, sir," replied the porter.

"But I thought there was a great deal of disturbance in the streets."

"It was only a meeting assembled for an election."

"The election of a general-in-chief, no doubt?" asked Mr. Fogg.

"No, sir; of a justice of the peace."

Phileas Fogg got into the train, which started off at full speed.

Around the World in Eighty Days

CHAPTER XXVI.

IN WHICH PHILEAS FOGG AND PARTY TRAVEL BY THE PACIFIC RAILROAD.

"FROM ocean to ocean,"—so say the Americans; and these four words compose the general designation of the "great trunk line" which crosses the entire width of the United States. The Pacific Railroad is, however, really divided into two distinct lines: the Central Pacific, between San Francisco and Ogden, and the Union Pacific, between Ogden and Omaha. Five main lines connect Omaha with New York.

New York and San Francisco are thus united by an uninterrupted metal ribbon, which measures no less than three thousand seven hundred and eighty-six miles. Between Omaha and the Pacific the railway crosses a territory which is still infested by Indians and wild beasts, and a large tract which the Mormons, after they were driven from Illinois in 1845, began to colonize.

The journey from New York to San Francisco consumed, formerly, under the most favourable conditions, at least six months. It is now accomplished in seven days.

It was in 1862 that, in spite of the Southern Members of Congress, who wished a more southerly route, it was decided to lay the road between the forty-first and forty-second parallels. President Lincoln himself fixed the end of the line at Omaha, in Nebraska. The work was at once commenced, and pursued with true American energy; nor did the rapidity with which it went on injuriously affect its good execution. The road grew, on the prairies, a mile and a half a day. A locomotive, running on the rails laid down the evening before, brought the rails to be laid on the morrow, and advanced upon them as fast as they were put in position.

The Pacific Railroad is joined by several branches in Iowa, Kansas, Colorado, and Oregon. On leaving Omaha, it passes along the left bank of the Platte River as far as the junction of its northern branch, follows its southern branch, crosses the Laramie territory and the Wahsatch Mountains, turns the Great Salt Lake, and reaches Salt Lake City, the Mormon capital, plunges into the Tuilla Valley, across the American Desert, Cedar and Humboldt Mountains, the Sierra Nevada, and descends, *viâ* Sacramento, to the Pacific,—its grade, even on the Rocky Mountains, never exceeding one hundred and twelve feet to the mile.

Such was the road to be traversed in seven days, which would enable Phileas Fogg—at least, so he hoped—to take the Atlantic steamer at New York on the 11th for Liverpool.

The car which he occupied was a sort of long omnibus on eight wheels, and with no compartments in the interior. It was supplied with two rows of seats, perpendicular to the direction of the train on either side of an aisle which conducted to the front and rear platforms. These platforms were found throughout the train, and the passengers were able to pass from one end of the train to the other. It was supplied with saloon cars, balcony cars, restaurants, and smoking cars; theatre cars alone were wanting, and they will have these some day.

Book and news dealers, sellers of edibles, drinkables, and cigars, who seemed to have plenty of customers, were continually circulating in the aisles.

The train left Oakland station at six o'clock. It was already night, cold and cheerless, the heavens being overcast with clouds which seemed to threaten snow. The train did not proceed rapidly; counting the stoppages, it did not run more than twenty miles an hour, which was a sufficient speed, however, to enable it to reach Omaha within its designated time.

There was but little conversation in the car, and soon many of the passengers were overcome with sleep. Passepartout found himself beside the detective; but he did not talk to him. After recent events, their relations with each other had grown somewhat cold; there could no longer be mutual sympathy or intimacy between them. Fix's manner had not changed; but Passepartout was very reserved, and ready to strangle his former friend on the slightest provocation.

Snow began to fall an hour after they started, a fine snow, however, which happily could not obstruct the train; nothing could be seen from the windows but a vast, white sheet, against which the smoke of the locomotive had a grayish aspect.

At eight o'clock a steward entered the car and announced that the time for going to bed had

This was a sleeping car.

arrived; and in a few minutes the car was transformed into a dormitory. The backs of the seats were thrown back, bedsteads carefully packed were rolled out by an ingenious system, berths were suddenly improvised, and each traveller had soon at his disposition a comfortable bed, protected from curious eyes by thick curtains. The sheets were clean and the pillows soft. It only remained to go to bed and sleep—which everybody did—while the train sped on across the State of California.

The country between San Francisco and Sacramento is not very hilly. The Central Pacific, taking Sacramento for its starting-point, extends eastward to meet the road from Omaha. The line from San Francisco to Sacramento runs in a north-easterly direction, along the American River, which empties into San Pablo Bay. The one hundred and twenty miles between these cities were accomplished in six hours, and towards midnight, while fast asleep, the travellers passed through Sacramento; so that they saw nothing of that important place, the seat of the State government, with its fine quays, its broad streets, its noble hotels, squares, and churches.

The train, on leaving Sacramento, and passing the junction, Roclin, Auburn, and Colfax, entered the range of the Sierra Nevada. Cisco was reached at seven in the morning; and an hour later the dormitory was transformed into an ordinary car, and the travellers could observe the picturesque beauties of the mountain region through which they were steaming. The railway track wound in and out among the passes, now approaching the mountain sides, now suspended over precipices, avoiding abrupt angles by bold curves, plunging into narrow defiles, which seemed to have no outlet. The locomotive, its great funnel emitting a weird light, with its sharp bell, and its cow-catcher extended like a spur, mingled its shrieks and bellowings with the noise of torrents and cascades, and twined its smoke among the branches of the gigantic pines.

There were few or no bridges or tunnels on the route. The railway turned around the sides of the mountains, and did not attempt to violate nature by taking the shortest cut from one point to another.

The train entered the State of Nevada through the Carson valley about nine o'clock, going always north-easterly; and at midday reached Reno, where there was a delay of twenty minutes for breakfast.

From this point the road, running along Humboldt River, passed northward for several miles by its banks; then it turned eastward, and kept by the river until it reached the Humboldt Range, nearly at the extreme eastern limit of Nevada.

Having breakfasted, Mr. Fogg and his companions resumed their places in the car, and observed the varied landscape which unfolded itself as they passed along; the vast prairies, the mountains lining the horizon, and the creeks with their frothy, foaming streams. Sometimes a great herd of buffaloes, massing together in the distance, seemed like a movable dam. These innumerable multitudes of ruminating beasts often form an insurmountable obstacle to the passage of the trains; thousands of them have been seen passing over the track for hours together, in compact ranks. The locomotive is then forced to stop and wait till the road is once more clear.

This happened, indeed, to the train in which Mr. Fogg was travelling. About twelve o'clock, a troop of ten or twelve thousand head of buffalo encumbered the track. The locomotive, slackening its speed, tried to clear the way with its cow-catcher; but the mass of animals was too great. The buffaloes marched along with a tranquil gait, uttering now and then deafening bellowings. There was no use of interrupting them, for, having taken a particular direction, nothing can moderate and change their course; it is a torrent of living flesh which no dam could contain.

The travellers gazed on this curious spectacle from the platforms; but Phileas Fogg, who had the most reason of all to be in a hurry, remained in his seat, and waited philosophically until it should please the buffaloes to get out of the way.

Passepartout was furious at the delay they occasioned, and longed to discharge his arsenal of revolvers upon them.

"What a country!" cried he. "Mere cattle stop the trains, and go by in a procession, just as if they were not impeding travel! Parbleu! I should like to know if Mr. Fogg foresaw this mishap in his programme! And here's an engineer who doesn't dare to run the locomotive into this herd of beasts?"

The engineer did not try to overcome the obstacle, and he was wise. He would have crushed the first buffaloes, no doubt, with the cow-catcher; but the locomotive, however powerful, would soon have been checked, the train would inevitably have been thrown off the track, and would then have been helpless.

The best course was to wait patiently, and regain the lost time by greater speed when the obstacle was removed. The procession of buffaloes lasted three full hours, and it was

A herd of ten or twelve thousand buffalo barred the track.

night before the track was clear. The last ranks of the herd were now passing over the rails, while the first had already disappeared below the southern horizon.

It was eight o'clock when the train passed through the defiles of the Humboldt Range, and half-past nine when it penetrated Utah, the region of the Great Salt Lake, the singular colony of the Mormons.

CHAPTER XXVII.

IN WHICH PASSEPARTOUT UNDERGOES, AT A SPEED OF TWENTY MILES AN HOUR, A COURSE OF MORMON HISTORY.

DURING the night of the 5th of December, the train ran south-easterly for about fifty miles; then rose an equal distance in a north-easterly direction, towards the Great Salt Lake.

Passepartout, about nine o'clock, went out upon the platform to take the air. The weather was cold, the heavens gray, but it was not snowing. The sun's disc, enlarged by the mist, seemed an enormous ring of gold, and Passepartout was amusing himself by calculating its value in pounds sterling, when he was diverted from this interesting study by a strange-looking personage who made his appearance on the platform.

This personage, who had taken the train at Elko, was tall and dark, with black moustaches, black stockings, a black silk hat, a black waistcoat, black trousers, a white cravat, and dogskin gloves. He might have been taken for a clergyman. He went from one end of the train to the other, and affixed to the door of each car a notice written in manuscript.

Passepartout approached and read one of these notices, which stated that Elder William Hitch, Mormon missionary, taking advantage of his presence on train No. 48, would deliver a lecture on Mormonism, in car No. 117, from eleven to twelve o'clock; and that he invited all who were desirous of being instructed concerning the mysteries of the religion of the "Latter Day Saints" to attend.

"I'll go," said Passepartout to himself. He knew nothing of Mormonism except the custom of polygamy, which is its foundation.

The news quickly spread through the train, which contained about one hundred passengers, thirty of whom, at most, attracted by the notice, esconced themselves in car No. 117. Passepartout took one of the front seats. Neither Mr. Fogg nor Fix cared to attend.

At the appointed hour Elder William Hitch rose, and, in an irritated voice, as if he had already been contradicted, said, "I tell you that Joe Smith is a martyr, that his brother Hiram is a martyr, and that the persecutions of the United States Government against the prophets will also make a martyr of Brigham Young. Who dares to say the contrary?"

No one ventured to gainsay the missionary, whose excited tone contrasted curiously with his naturally calm visage. No doubt his anger arose from the hardships to which the Mormons were actually subjected. The government had just succeeded, with some difficulty, in reducing these independent fanatics to its rule. It had made itself master of Utah, and subjected that territory to the laws of the Union, after imprisoning Brigham Young on a charge of rebellion and polygamy. The disciples of the prophet had since redoubled their efforts, and resisted, by words at least, the authority of Congress. Elder Hitch, as is seen, was trying to make proselytes on the very railway trains.

The, emphasizing his words with his loud voice and frequent gestures, he related the history of the Mormons from Biblical times: how that, in Israel, a Mormon prophet of the tribe of Joseph published the annals of the new religion, and bequeathed them to his son Morom; how, many centuries later, a translation of this precious book, which was written in Egyptian, was made by Joseph Smith, Junior, a Vermont farmer, who revealed himself as a mystical prophet in 1825; and how, in short, a celestial messenger appeared to him in an illuminated forest, and gave him the annals of the Lord.

Several of the audience, not being much interested in the missionary's narrative, here left the car; but Elder Hitch, continuing his lecture, related how Smith, Junior, with his father, two brothers, and a few disciples, founded the church of the "Latter Day Saints," which, adopted not only in America, but in England, Norway and Sweden, and Germany, counts many artisans, as well as men engaged in the liberal professions, among its members; how a colony was established in Ohio, a temple erected there at a cost of two hundred thousand dollars, and a town built at Kirkland; how Smith became an enterprising banker, and received from a simple mummy showman a papyrus scroll written by Abraham and several famous Egyptians.

The Elder's story became somewhat wearisome, and his audience grew gradually less, until it was reduced to twenty passengers. But this did not disconcert the enthusiast, who proceeded with the story of Joseph Smith's bank-

"And you, my faithful friend."

ruptcy in 1837, and how his ruined creditors gave him a coat of tar and feathers; his reappearance some years afterwards, more honourable and honoured than ever, at Independence, Missouri, the chief of a flourishing colony of three thousand disciples, and his pursuit thence by outraged Gentiles, and retirement into the far West.

Ten hearers only were now left, among them honest Passepartout, who was listening with all his ears. Thus he learned that, after long persecutions, Smith reappeared in Illinois, and in 1839 founded a community at Nauvoo, on the Mississippi, numbering twenty-five thousand souls, of which he became mayor, chief justice, and general-in-chief; that he announced himself, in 1843, as a candidate for the Presidency of the United States; and that finally, being drawn into ambuscade at Carthage, he was thrown into prison, and assassinated by a band of men disguised in masks.

Passepartout was now the only person left in the car, and the Elder, looking him full in the face, reminded him that, two years after the assassination of Joseph Smith, the inspired prophet, Brigham Young, his successor, left Nauvoo for the banks of the great Salt Lake, where, in the midst of that fertile region, directly on the route of the emigrants who crossed Utah on their way to California, the new colony, thanks to the polygamy practised by the Mormons, had flourished beyond expectation.

"And this," added Elder William Hitch,—"this is why the jealousy of Congress has been aroused against us! Why have the soldiers of the Union invaded the soil of Utah? Why has Brigham Young, our chief, been imprisoned, in contempt of all justice? Shall we yield to force? Never! Driven from Vermont, driven from Illinois, driven from Ohio, driven from Missouri, driven from Utah, we shall yet find some independent territory on which to plant our tents. And you, my brother," continued the Elder, fixing his angry eye upon his single auditor, "will you not plant yours there, too, under the shadow of our flag?"

"No!" replied Passepartout courageously, in his turn retiring from the car, and leaving the Elder to preach to vacancy.

During the lecture the train had been making good progress, and towards half-past twelve it reached the north-west border of the Great Salt Lake. Thence the passengers could observe the vast extent of this interior sea, which is also called the Dead Sea, and into which flows an American Jordan. It is a picturesque expanse, framed in lofty crags in large strata, encrusted with white salt,—a superb sheet of water, which was formerly of larger extent than now, its shores having encroached with the lapse of time, and thus at once reduced its breadth and increased its depth.

The Salt Lake, seventy miles long and thirty-five miles wide, is situated three miles eight hundred feet above the sea. Quite different from Lake Asphaltite, whose depression is twelve hundred feet below the sea, it contains considerable salt, and one quarter of the weight of its water is solid matter, its specific weight being 1170, and, after being distilled, 1000. Fishes are of course unable to live in it, and those which descend through the Jordan, the Weber, and other streams, soon perish.

The country around the lake was well cultivated, for the Mormons are mostly farmers; while ranches and pens for domesticated animals, fields of wheat, corn, and other cereals, luxuriant prairies, hedges of wild rose, clumps of acacias and milk-wort, would have been seen six months later. Now the ground was covered with a thin powdering of snow.

The train reached Ogden at two o'clock, where it rested for six hours. Mr. Fogg and his party had time to pay a visit to Salt Lake City, connected with Ogden by a branch road; and they spent two hours in this strikingly American town, built on the pattern of other cities of the Union, like a checker-board, "with the sombre sadness of right angles," as Victor Hugo expresses it. The founder of the City of the Saints could not escape from the taste for symmetry which distinguishes the Anglo-Saxons. In this strange country, where the people are certainly not up to the level of their institutions, everything is done "squarely."—cities, houses, and follies.

The travellers, then, were promenading, at three o'clock, about the streets of the town built between the banks of the Jordan and the spurs of the Wahsatch Range. They saw few or no churches, but the prophet's mansion, the court-house, and the arsenal, blue-brick houses with verandahs and porches, surrounded by gardens bordered with acacias, palms, and locusts. A clay and pebble wall, built in 1853, surrounded the town; and in the principal street were the market and several hotels adorned with pavilions. The place did not seem thickly populated. The streets were almost deserted, except in the vicinity of the Temple, which they only reached after having traversed several quarters surrounded by palisades. There were many women, which was easily accounted for by the "peculiar institution" of the Mormons;

The Great Salt Lake.

but it must not be supposed that all the Mormons are polygamists. They are free to marry or not, as they please; but it is worth noting that it is mainly the female citizens of Utah who are anxious to marry, as, according to the Mormon religion, maiden ladies are not admitted to the possession of its highest joys. These poor creatures seemed to be neither well off nor happy. Some—the more well-to-do, no doubt—wore short, open black silk dresses, under a hood or modest shawl; others were habited in Indian fashion.

Passepartout could not behold without a certain fright these women, charged, in groups, with conferring happiness on a single Mormon. His common sense pitied, above all, the husband. It seemed to him a terrible thing to have to guide so many wives at once across the vicissitudes of life, and to conduct them, as it were, in a body to the Mormon paradise, with the prospect of seeing them in the company of the glorious Smith, who doubtless was the chief ornament of that delightful place, to all eternity. He felt decidedly repelled from such a vocation, and he imagined—perhaps he was mistaken—that the fair ones of Salt Lake City cast rather alarming glances on his person. Happily, his stay there was but brief. At four the party found themselves again at the station, took their places in the train, and the whistle sounded for starting. Just at the moment, however, that the locomotive wheels began to move, cries of "Stop! stop!" were heard.

Trains, like time and tide, stop for no one. The gentleman who uttered the cries was evidently a belated Mormon. He was breathless with running. Happily for him, the station had neither gates nor barriers. He rushed along the track, jumped on the rear platform of the train, and fell exhausted into one of the seats.

Passepartout, who had been anxiously watching this amateur gymnast, approached him with lively interest, and learned that he had taken flight after an unpleasant domestic scene.

When the Mormon had recovered his breath, Passepartout ventured to ask him politely how many wives he had; for, from the manner in which he had decamped, it might be thought that he had twenty at least.

"One, sir," replied the Mormon, raising his arms heavenward,—"one, and that was enough!"

Around the World in Eighty Days

CHAPTER XXVIII.

IN WHICH PASSEPARTOUT DOES NOT SUCCEED IN MAKING ANYBODY LISTEN TO REASON.

THE train, on leaving Great Salt Lake at Ogden, passed northward for an hour as far as Weber River, having completed nearly nine hundred miles from San Francisco. From this point it took an easterly direction towards the jagged Wahsatch Mountains. It was in the section included between this range and the Rocky Mountains that the American engineers found the most formidable difficulties in laying the road, and that the government granted a subsidy of forty-eight thousand dollars per mile, instead of sixteen thousand allowed for the work done on the plains. But the engineers, instead of violating nature, avoided its difficulties by winding around, instead of penetrating the rocks. One tunnel only, fourteen thousand feet in length, was pierced in order to arrive at the great basin.

The track up to this time had reached its highest elevation at the Great Salt Lake. From this point it described a long curve, descending towards Bitter Creek Valley, to rise again to the dividing ridge of the waters between the Atlantic and the Pacific. There were many creeks in this mountainous region, and it was necessary to cross Muddy Creek, Green Creek, and others, upon culverts.

Passepartout grew more and more impatient as they went on, while Fix longed to get out of this difficult region, and was more anxious than Phileas Fogg himself to be beyond the danger of delays and accidents, and set foot on English soil.

At ten o'clock at night the train stopped at Fort Bridger station, and twenty minutes later entered Wyoming Territory, following the valley of Bitter Creek throughout. The next day, December 7th, they stopped for a quarter of an hour at Green River station. Snow had fallen abundantly during the night, but, being mixed with rain, it had half melted, and did not interrupt their progress. The bad weather, however, annoyed Passepartout; for the accumulation of snow, by blocking the wheels of the cars, would certainly have been fatal to Mr. Fogg's tour.

"What an idea!" he said to himself. "Why did my master make this journey in winter? Couldn't he have waited for the good season to increase his chances?"

While the worthy Frenchman was absorbed in the state of the sky and the depression of the temperature, Aouda was experiencing fears from a totally different cause.

Several passengers had got off at Green River, and were walking up and down the platforms; and among these Aouda recognized Colonel Stamp Proctor, the same who had so grossly insulted Phileas Fogg at the San Francisco meeting. Not wishing to be recognized, the young woman drew back from the window, feeling much alarm at her discovery. She was attached to the man, who however coldly, gave her daily evidences of the most absolute devotion. She did not comprehend, perhaps, the depth of the sentiment with which her protector inspired her, which she called gratitude, but which, though she was unconscious of it, was really more than that. Her heart sank within her when she recognized the man whom Mr. Fogg desired, sooner or later, to call to account for his conduct. Chance alone, it was clear, had brought Colonel Proctor on this train; but there he was, and it was necessary, at all hazards, that Phileas Fogg should not perceive his adversary.

Aouda seized a moment when Mr. Fogg was asleep, to tell Fix and Passepartout whom she had seen.

"That Proctor on this train!" cried Fix. "Well, reassure yourself, madam; before he settles with Mr. Fogg, he had got to deal with me! It seems to me that I was the more insulted of the two."

"And besides," added Passepartout, "I'll take charge of him, colonel as he is."

"Mr. Fix," resumed Aouda, "Mr. Fogg will allow no one to avenge him. He said that he would come back to America to find this man. Should he perceive Colonel Proctor, we could not prevent a collision which might have terrible results. He must not see him."

"You are right, madam," replied Fix; "a meeting between them might ruin all. Whether he were victorious or beaten, Mr. Fogg would be delayed, and—"

"And," added Passepartout, "that would play the game of the gentlemen of the Reform

Club. In four days we shall be in New York. Well, if my master does not leave this car during those four days, we may hope that chance will not bring him face to face with this confounded American. We must, if possible, prevent his stirring out of it."

The conversation dropped. Mr. Fogg had just woke up, and was looking out of the window. Soon after Passepartout, without being heard by his master or Aouda, whispered to the detective, "Would you really fight for him?"

"I would do anything," replied Fix, in a tone which betrayed determined will, "to get him back, living, to Europe!"

Passepartout felt something like a shudder shoot through his frame, but his confidence in his master remained unbroken.

Was there any means of detaining Mr. Fogg in the car, to avoid a meeting between him and the colonel? It ought not to be a difficult task, since that gentleman was naturally sedentary and little curious. The detective, at least, seemed to have found a way; for, after a few moments, he said to Mr. Fogg, "These are long and slow hours, sir, that we are passing on the railway."

"Yes," replied Mr. Fogg; "but they pass."

"You were in the habit of playing whist," resumed Fix, "on the steamers."

"Yes; but it would be difficult to do so here. I have neither cards nor partners."

"Oh, but we can easily buy some cards, for they are sold on all the American trains. And as for partners, if madam plays—"

"Certainly, sir," Aouda quickly replied; "I understand whist. It is part of an English education."

"I myself have some pretensions to playing a good game. Well, here are three of us, and a dummy—"

"As you please, sir," replied Phileas Fogg, heartily glad to resume his favourite pastime,— even on the railway.

Passepartout was despatched in search of the steward, and soon returned with two packs of cards, some pins, counters, and a shelf covered with cloth.

The game commenced. Aouda understood whist sufficiently well, and even received some compliments on her playing from Mr. Fogg. As for the detective, he was simply an adept, and worthy of being matched against his present opponent.

"Now," thought Passepartout, "we've got him. He won't budge."

At eleven in the morning the train had reached the dividing ridge of the waters at Bridger Pass, seven thousand five hundred and twenty-four feet above the level of the sea, one of the highest points attained by the track in crossing the Rocky Mountains. After going about two hundred miles, the travellers at last found themselves on one of those vast plains which extend to the Atlantic, and which nature has made so propitious for laying the iron road.

On the declivity of the Atlantic basin the first streams, branches of the North Platte River, already appeared. The whole northern and eastern horizon was bounded by the immense semicircular curtain which is formed by the southern portion of the Rocky Mountains, the highest being Laramie Peak. Between this and the railway extended vast plains, plentifully irrigated. On the right rose the lower spurs of the mountainous mass which extends southward to the sources of the Arkansas River, one of the great tributaries of the Missouri.

At half past twelve the travellers caught sight for an instant of Fort Halleck, which commands that section; and in a few more hours the Rocky Mountains were crossed. There was reason to hope, then, that no accident would mark the journey through this difficult country. The snow had ceased falling, and the air became crisp and cold. Large birds, frightened by the locomotive, rose and flew off in the distance. No wild beast appeared on the plain. It was a desert in its vast nakedness.

After a comfortable breakfast, served in the car, Mr. Fogg and his partners had just resumed whist, when a violent whistling was heard, and the train stopped. Passepartout put his head out of the door, but saw nothing to cause the delay; no station was in view.

Aouda and Fix feared that Mr. Fogg might take it into his head to get out; but that gentleman contented himself with saying to his servant, "See what is the matter."

Passepartout rushed out of the car. Thirty or forty passengers had already descended, amongst them Colonel Stamp Proctor.

The train had stopped before a red signal which blocked the way. The engineer and conductor were talking excitedly with a signal-man, whom the station-master ay Medicine Bow, the next stopping place, had sent on before. The passengers drew around and took part in the discussion, in which Colonel Proctor, with his insolent manner, was conspicuous.

Passepartout, joining the group, heard the signal-man say, "No! you can't pass! The bridge at Medicine Bow is shaky, and would not bear the weight of the train."

This was a suspension-bridge thrown over

some rapids, about a mile from the place where they now were. According to the signal-man, it was in a ruinous condition, several of the iron wires being broken; and it was impossible to risk the passage. He did not in any way exaggerate the condition of the bridge. It may be taken for granted that, rash as the Americans usually are, when they are prudent there is good reason for it.

Passepartout, not daring to apprise his master of what he heard, listened with set teeth, immovable as a statue.

"Hum!" cried Colonel Proctor; "but we are not going to stay here, I imagine, and take root in the snow?"

"Colonel," replied the conductor, "we have telegraphed to Omaha for a train, but it is not likely that it will reach Medicine Bow in less than six hours."

"Six hours!" cried Passepartout.

"Certainly," returned the conductor. "Besides, it will take us as long as that to reach Medicine Bow on foot."

"But it is only a mile from here," said one of the passengers.

"Yes, but it's on the other side of the river."

"And can't we cross that in a boat?" asked the colonel.

"That's impossible. The creek is swelled by the rains. It is a rapid, and we shall have to make a circuit of ten miles to the north to find a ford."

The colonel launched a volley of oaths, denouncing the railway company and the conductor; and Passepartout, who was furious, was not disinclined to make common cause with him. Here was an obstacle, indeed, which all his master's bank-notes could not remove.

There was a general disappointment among the passengers, who, without reckoning the delay, saw themselves compelled to trudge fifteen miles over a plain covered with snow. They grumbled and protested, and would certainly have thus attracted Phileas Fogg's attention, if he had not been completely absorbed in his game.

Passepartout found that he could not avoid telling his master what had occurred, and, with hanging head he was turning towards the car, when the engineer—a true Yankee, named Forster—called out, "Gentlemen, perhaps there is a way, after all, to get over."

"On the bridge?" asked a passenger.

"On the bridge."

"With our train?"

"With our train."

Passepartout stopped short, and eagerly listened to the engineer.

"But the bridge is unsafe," urged the conductor.

"No matter," replied Forster; "I think that by putting on the very highest speed we might have a chance of getting over."

"The devil!" muttered Passepartout.

But a number of the passengers were at once attracted by the engineer's proposal, and Colonel Proctor was especially delighted, and found the plan a very feasible one. He told stories about engineers leaping their trains over rivers without bridges, by putting on full steam; and many of those present avowed themselves of the engineer's mind.

"We have fifty chances out of a hundred of getting over," said one.

"Eighty! ninety!"

Passepartout was astounded, and, though ready to attempt anything to get over Medicine Creek, thought the experiment proposed a little too American. "Besides," thought he, "there's a still more simple way, and it does not even occur to any of these people! Sir," said he aloud to one of the passengers, "the engineer's plan seems to me a little dangerous, but—"

"Eighty chances!" replied the passenger, turning his back on him.

"I know it," said Passepartout, turning to another passenger, "but a simple idea—"

"Ideas are no use," returned the American, shrugging his shoulders, "as the engineer assures us that we can pass."

"Doubtless," urged Passepartout, "we can pass, but perhaps it would be more prudent—"

"What! Prudent!" cried Colonel Proctor, whom this word seemed to excite prodigiously. "At full speed, don't you see, at full speed!"

"I know—I see," repeated Passepartout; "but it would be, if not more prudent, since that word displeases you, at least more natural—"

"Who! What! What's the matter with this fellow?" cried several.

The poor fellow did not know to whom to address himself.

"Are you afraid?" asked Colonel Proctor.

"I afraid! Very well; I will show these people that a Frenchman can be as American as they!"

"All aboard!" cried the conductor.

"Yes, all aboard!" repeated Passepartout, and immediately. "But they can't prevent me from thinking that it would be more natural for us to cross the bridge on foot, and let the train come after!"

But no one heard this sage reflection, nor would any one have acknowledged its justice. The passengers resumed their places in the cars. Passepartout took his seat without telling what

The bridge, completely ruined, fell with a crash.

had passed. The whist-players were quite absorbed in their game.

The locomotive whistled vigorously; the engineer, reversing the steam, backed the train for nearly a mile—retiring, like a jumper, in order to take a longer leap. Then, with another whistle, he began to move forward; the train increased its speed, and soon its rapidity became frightful; a prolonged screech issued from the locomotive; the piston worked up and down twenty strokes to the second. They perceived that the whole train, rushing on at the rate of a hundred miles an hour, hardly bore upon the rails at all.

And they passed over! It was like a flash. No one saw the bridge. The train leaped, so to speak, from one bank to the other, and the engineer could not stop it until it had gone five miles beyond the station. But scarcely had the train passed the river, when the bridge, completely ruined, fell with a crash into the rapids of Medicine Bow.

Around the World in Eighty Days

CHAPTER XXIX.

IN WHICH CERTAIN INCIDENTS ARE NARRATED WHICH ARE ONLY TO BE MET WITH ON AMERICAN RAILROADS.

THE train pursued its course, that evening, without interruption, passing Fort Saunders, crossing Cheyene Pass, and reaching Evans Pass. The road here attained the highest elevation of the journey, eight thousand and ninety-one feet above the level of the sea. The travellers had now only to descend to the Atlantic by limitless plains, levelled by nature. A branch of the "grand trunk" led off southward to Denver, the capital of Colorado. The country round about is rich in gold and silver, and more than fifty thousand inhabitants are already settled there.

Thirteen hundred and eighty-two miles had been passed over from San Francisco, in three days and three nights; four days and nights more would probably bring them to New York. Phileas Fogg was not as yet behindhand.

During the night Camp Walbach was passed on the left; Lodge Pole Creek ran parallel with the road, marking the boundary between the territories of Wyoming and Colorado. They entered Nebraska at eleven, passed near Sedgwick, and touched at Julesburg, on the southern branch of the Platte River.

It was here that the Union Pacific Railroad was inaugurated on the 23rd of October, 1867, by the chief engineer, General Dodge. Two powerful locomotives, carrying nine cars of invited guests, amongst whom was Thomas C. Durant, vice-president of the road, stopped at this point; cheers were given, the Sioux and Pawnees performed as imitation Indian battle, fireworks were let off, and the first number of the *Railway Pioneer* was printed by a press brought on the train. Thus was celebrated the inauguration of this great railroad, a mighty instrument of progress and civilization, thrown across the desert, and destined to link together cities and towns which do not yet exist. The whistle of the locomotive, more powerful than Amphion's lyre, was about to bid them rise from American soil.

Fort McPherson was left behind at eight in the morning, and three hundred and fifty-seven miles had yet to be traversed before reaching Omaha. The road followed the capricious windings of the southern branch of the Platte River, on its left bank. At nine the train stopped at the important town of North Platte, built between the two arms of the river, which rejoin each other around it and form a single artery,—a large tributary whose waters empty into the Missouri a little above Omaha.

The one hundred and first meridian was passed.

Mr. Fogg had his partners had resumed their game; no one—not even the dummy—complained of the length of the trip. Fix had begun by winning several guineas, which he seemed likely to lose; but he showed himself a not less eager whist-player than Mr. Fogg. During the morning, chance distinctly favoured that gentleman. Trumps and honours were showered upon his hands.

Once, having resolved on a bold stroke, he was on the point of playing a space, when a voice behind him said, "I should play a diamond."

Mr. Fogg, Aouda, and Fix raised their heads, and beheld Colonel Proctor.

Stamp Proctor and Phileas Fogg recognized each other at once.

"Ah! it's you, is it, Englishman?" cried the colonel; "it's you who are going to play a spade!"

"And who plays it," replied Phileas Fogg coolly, throwing down the ten of spades.

"Well, it pleases me to have it diamonds," replied Colonel Proctor, in an insolent tone.

He made a movement as if to seize the card which had just been played, adding, "You don't understand anything about whist."

"Perhaps I do, as well as another," said Phileas Fogg, rising.

"You have only to try, son of John Bull," replied the colonel.

Aouda turned pale, and her blood ran cold. She seized Mr. Fogg's arm, and gently pulled him back. Passepartout was ready to pounce upon the American, who was staring insolently at his opponent. But Fix got up, and going to Colonel Proctor, said, "You forget that it is I with whom you have to deal, sir; for it was I whom you not only insulted, but struck!"

"Mr. Fix," said Mr. Fogg, "pardon me, but this affair is mine, and mine only. The colonel has again insulted me, by insisting that I should

"I should play a diamond."

play a space, and he shall give me satisfaction for it.''

"When and where you will," replied the American, "and with whatever weapon you choose."

Aouda in vain attempted to retain Mr. Fogg; as vainly did the detective endeavour to make the quarrel his. Passepartout wished to throw the colonel out of the window, but a sign from his master checked him. Phileas Fogg left the car, and the American followed him upon the platform.

"Sir," said Mr. Fogg to his adversary, "I am in a great hurry to get back to Europe, and any delay whatever will be greatly to my disadvantage."

"Well, what's that to me?" replied Colonel Proctor.

"Sir," said Mr. Fogg, very politely, "after our meeting at San Francisco, I determined to return to America and find you as soon as I had completed the business which called me to England."

"Really!"

"Will you appoint a meeting for six months hence?"

"Why not ten years hence?"

"I say six months," returned Phileas Fogg, "and I shall be at the place of meeting promptly."

"All this is an evasion," cried Stamp Proctor. "Now or never!"

"Very good. You are going to New York?"

"No."

"To Chicago?"

"No."

"To Omaha?"

"What difference is it to you? Do you know Plum Creek?"

"No," replied Mr. Fogg.

"It's the next station. The train will be there in an hour, and will stop there ten minutes. In ten minutes several revolver-shots could be exchanged."

"Very well," said Mr. Fogg. "I will stop at Plum Creek."

"And I guess you'll stay there too," added the American insolently.

"Who knows?" replied Mr. Fogg, returning to the car as coolly as usual. He began to reassure Aouda, telling her that blusterers were never to be feared, and begged Fix to be his second at the approaching duel, a request which the detective could not refuse. Mr. Fogg resumed the interrupted game with perfect calmness.

At eleven o'clock the locomotive's whistle announced that they were approaching Plum Creek station. Mr. Fogg rose, and, followed by Fix, went out upon the platform. Passepartout accompanied him, carrying a pair of revolvers. Aouda remained in the car, as pale as death.

The door of the next car opened, and Colonel Proctor appeared on the platform, attended by a Yankee of his own stamp as his second. But just as the combatants were about to step from the train, the conductor hurried up, and shouted, "You can't get off, gentlemen!"

"Why not?" asked the colonel.

"We are twenty minutes late, and we shall not stop."

"But I am going to fight a duel with this gentleman."

"I am sorry," said the conductor, "but we shall be off at once. There's the bell ringing now."

The train started.

"I'm really very sorry, gentlemen," said the conductor. "Under any other circumstances I should have been happy to oblige you. But, after all, as you have not had time to fight here, why not fight as we go along?"

"That wouldn't be convenient, perhaps, for this gentleman," said the colonel, in a jeering tone.

"It would be perfectly so," replied Phileas Fogg.

"Well, we are really in America," thought Passepartout, "and the conductor is a gentleman of the first order!"

So muttering, he followed his master.

The two combatants, their seconds, and the conductor passed through the cars to the rear of the train. The last car was only occupied by a dozen pasengers, whom the conductor politely asked if they would not be so kind as to leave it vacant for a few moments, as two gentlemen had an affair of honour to settle. The passengers granted the request with alacrity, and straightway disappeared on the platform.

The car, which was some fifty feet long, was very convenient for their purpose. The adversaries might march on each other in the aisle, and fire at their ease. Never was duel more easily arranged. Mr. Fogg and Colonel Proctor, each provided with two six-barrelled revolvers, entered the car. The seconds, remaining outside, shut them in. They were to begin firing at the first whistle of the locomotive. After an interval of two minutes, what remained of the two gentlemen would be taken from the car.

Nothing could be more simple. Indeed, it was all so simple that Fix and Passepartout felt their hearts beating as if they would crack. They were listening for the whistle agreed upon, when

They had forced the doors, and were fighting hand to hand with the travellers.

suddenly savage cries resounded in the air, accompanied by reports which certainly did not issue from the car where the duellists were. The reports continued in front and the whole length of the train. Cries of terror proceeded from the interior of the cars.

Colonel Proctor and Mr. Fogg, revolvers in hand, hastily quitted their prison, and rushed forward where the noise was most clamorous. They then perceived that the train was attacked by a band of Sioux.

This was not the first attempt of these daring Indians, for more than once they had waylaid trains on the road. A hundred of them had, according to their habit, jumped upon the steps without stopping the train, with the ease of a clown mounting a horse at full gallop.

The Sioux were armed with guns, from which came the reports, to which the passengers, who were almost all armed, responded by revolver-shots.

The Indians had first mounted the engine, and half stunned the engineer and stoker with blows from their muskets. A Sioux chief, wishing to stop the train, but not knowing how to work the regulator, had opened wide instead of closing the steam-valve, and the locomotive was plunging forward with terrific velocity.

The Sioux had at the same time invaded the cars, skipping like enraged monkeys over the roofs, thrusting open the doors, and fighting hand to hand with the passengers. Penetrating the baggage-car, they pillaged it, throwing the trunks out of the train. The cries and shots were constant.

The travellers defended themselves bravely; some of the cars were barricaded, and sustained a siege, like moving forts, carried along at a speed of a hundred miles an hour.

Aouda behaved courageously from the first. She defended herself, like a true heroine, with a revolver, which she shot through the broken windows whenever a savage made his appearance. Twenty Sioux had fallen mortally wounded to the ground, and the wheels crushed those who fell upon the rails as if they had been worms. Several passengers, shot or stunned, lay on the seats.

It was necessary to put an end to the struggle, which had lasted for ten minutes, and which would result in the triumph of the Sioux if the train was not stopped. Fort Kearney station, where there was a garrison, was only two miles distant; but, that once passed, the Sioux would be masters of the train between Fort Kearney and the station beyond.

The conductor was fighting beside Mr. Fogg, when he was shot and fell. At the same moment he cried, "Unless the train is stopped in five minutes, we are lost!"

"It shall be stopped," said Phileas Fogg, preparing to rush from the car.

"Stay, monsieur," cried Passepartout; "I will go."

Mr. Fogg had not time to stop the brave fellow who, opening a door unperceived by the Indians, succeeded in slipping under the car; and while the struggle continued, and the balls whizzed across each other over his head, he made use of his old acrobatic experience, and with amazing agility worked his way under the cars, holding on to the chains, aiding himself by the brakes and edges of the sashes, creeping from one car to another with marvellous skill, and thus gaining the forward end of the train.

There, suspended by one hand between the baggage-car and the tender, with the other he loosened the safety chains; but, owing to the traction, he would never have succeeded in unscrewing the yoking-bar, had not a violent concussion jolted this bar out. The train, now detached from the engine, remained a little behind, whilst the locomotive rushed forward with increased speed.

Carried on by the force already acquired, the train still moved for several minutes; but the brakes were worked, and at last they stopped, less than a hundred feet from Kearney station.

The soldiers of the fort, attracted by the shots, hurried up; the Sioux had not expected them, and decamped in a body before the train entirely stopped.

But when the passengers counted each other on the station platform several were found missing; among others the courageous French-man, whose devotion had just saved them.

Hanging by one hand between the tender and the luggage van, he . . .

CHAPTER XXX.

IN WHICH PHILEAS FOGG SIMPLY DOES HIS DUTY.

THREE passengers—including Passepartout—had disappeared. Had they been killed in the struggle? Were they taken prisoners by the Sioux? It was impossible to tell.

There were many wounded, but none mortally. Colonel Proctor was one of the most seriously hurt; he had fought bravely, and a ball had entered his groin. He was carried into the station with the other wounded passengers, to receive such attention as could be of avail.

Aouda was safe; and Phileas Fogg, who had been in the thickest of the fight, had not received a scratch. Fix was slightly wounded in the arm. But Passepartout was not to be found, and tears coursed down Aouda's cheeks.

All the passengers had got out of the train, the wheels of which were stained with blood. From the tires and spokes hung ragged pieces of flesh. As far as the eye could reach on the white plain behind, red trails were visible. The last Sioux were disappearing in the south, along the banks of Republican River.

Mr. Fogg, with folded arms, remained motionless. He had a serious decision to make. Aouda, standing near him, looked at him without speaking, and he understood her look. If his servant was a prisoner, ought he not to risk everything to rescue him from the Indians? "I will find him, living or dead," said he quietly to Aouda.

"Ah, Mr.—Mr. Fogg!" cried she, clasping his hands and covering them with tears.

"Living," added Mr. Fogg, "if we do not lose a moment."

Phileas Fogg, by this resolution, inevitably sacrificed himself; he pronounced his own doom. The delay of a single day would make him lose the steamer at New York, and his bet would be certainly lost. But as he thought, "It is my duty," he did not hesitate.

The commanding officer of Fort Kearney was there. A hundred of his soldiers had placed themselves in a position to defend the station, should the Sioux attack it.

"Sir," said Mr. Fogg to the captain, "three passengers have disappeared."

"Dead?" asked the captain.

"Dead or prisoners; that is the uncertainty which must be solved. Do you propose to pursue the Sioux?"

"That's a serious thing to do, sir," returned the captain. "These Indians may retreat beyond the Arkansas, and I cannot leave the fort unprotected."

"The lives of three men are in question, sir," said Phileas Fogg.

"Doubtless; but can I risk the lives of fity men to save three?"

"I don't know whether you can, sir; but you ought to do so."

"Nobody here," returned the other, "has a right to teach me my duty."

"Very well,' said Mr. Fogg, coldly. "I will go alone."

"You, sir!" cried Fix coming up; "you go alone in pursuit of the Indians?"

"Would you have me leave this poor fellow to perish,—him to whom every one present owes his life? I shall go."

"No, sir, you shall not go alone," cried the captain, touched in spite of himself. "No! you are a brave man. Thirty volunteers!" he added, turning to the soldiers.

The whole company started forward at once. The captain had only to pick his men. Thirty were chosen, and an old sergeant placed at their head.

"Thanks, captain," said Mr. Fogg.

"Will you let me go with you?" asked Fix.

"Do as you please, sir. But if you wish to do me a favour, you will remain with Aouda. In case anything should happen to me—"

A sudden pallor overspread the detective's face. Separate himself from the man whom he had so persistently followed step by step! Leave him to wander about in this desert! Fix gazed attentively at Mr. Fogg, and, despite his suspicions and of the struggle which was going on within him, he lowered his eyes before that calm and frank look.

"I will stay," said he.

A few moments after, Mr. Fogg pressed the young woman's hand, and, having confided to her his precious carpet-bag, went off with the sergeant and his little squad. But, before going, he had said to the soldiers, "My friends, I will divide five thousand dollars among you, if we save the prisoners."

It was then a little past noon.

Aouda retired to a waiting-room, and there

An enormous shadow, preceded by a flickering yellow glare.

she waited alone, thinking of the simple and noble generosity, the tranquil courage of Phileas Fogg. He had sacrificed his fortune, and was now risking his life, all without hesitation, from duty, in silence.

Fix did not have the same thoughts, and could scarcely conceal his agitation. He walked feverishly up and down the platform, but soon resumed his outward composure. He now saw the folly of which he had been guilty in letting Fogg go alone. What! This man, whom he had just followed around the world, was permitted now to separate himself from him! He began to accuse and abuse himself, and, as if he were director of police, administered to himself a sound lecture for his greenness.

"I have been an idiot!" he thought, "and this man will see it. He has gone, and won't come back! But how is it that I, Fix, who have in my pocket a warrant for his arrest, have been so fascinated by him? Decidedly, I am nothing but an ass!"

So reasoned the detective, while the hours crept by all too slowly. He did not know what to do. Sometimes he was tempted to tell Aouda all; but he could not doubt how the young woman would receive his confidences. What course should he take? He thought of pursuing Fogg across the vast white plains; it did not seem impossible that he might overtake him. Footsteps were easily printed on the snow! But soon, under a new sheet, every imprint would be effaced.

Fix became discouraged. He felt a sort of insurmountable longing to abandon the game altogether. He could now leave Fort Kearney station, and pursue his journey homeward in peace.

Towards two o'clock in the afternoon, while it was snowing hard, long whistles were heard approaching from the east. A great shadow, preceded by a wild light, slowly advanced, appearing still larger through the mist, which gave it a fantastic aspect. No train was expected from the east, neither had there been time for the succour asked for by telegraph to arrive; the train from Omaha to San Francisco was not due till the next day. The mystery was soon explained.

The locomotive, which was slowly approaching with deafening whistles, was that which, having been detached from the train, had continued its route with such terrific rapidity, carrying off the unconscious engineer and stoker. It had run several miles, when, the fire becoming low for want of fuel, the steam had slackened; and it had finally stopped an hour after, some twenty miles beyond Fort Kearney.

Neither the engineer nor the stoker was dead, and, after remaining for some time in their swoon, had come to themselves. The train had then stopped. The engineer, when he found himself in the desert, and the locomotive without cars, understood what had happened. He could not imagine how the locomotive had becomes separated from the train; but he did not doubt that the train left behind was in distress.

He did not hesitate what to do. It would be prudent to continue on to Omaha, for it would be dangerous to return to the train, which the Indians might still be engaged in pillaging. Nevertheless, he began to rebuild the fire in the furnace; the pressure again mounted, and the locomotive returned, running backwards to Fort Kearney. This it was which was whistling in the mist.

The travellers were glad to see the locomotive resume its place at the head of the train. They could now continue the journey so terribly interrupted.

Aouda, on seeing the locomotive come up, hurried out of the station, and asked the conductor, "Are you going to start?"

"At once, madam."

"But the prisoners—our unfortunate fellow-travellers—"

"I cannot interrupt the trip," replied the conductor. "We are already three hours behind time."

"And when will another train pass here from San Francisco?"

"To-morrow evening, madam."

"To-morrow evening! But then it will be too late! We must wait—"

"It is impossible," responded the conductor. "If you wish to go, please get in."

"I will not go," said Aouda.

Fix had heard this conversation. A little while before, when there was no prospect of procceding on the journey, he had made up his mind to leave Fort Kearney; but now that the train was there, ready to start, and he had only to take his seat in the car, an irresistible influence held him back. The station platform burned his feet, and he could not stir. The conflict in his mind again began; anger and failure stifled him. He wished to struggle on to the end.

Meanwhile the passengers and some of the wounded, among them Colonel Proctor, whose injuries were serious, had taken their places in the train. The buzzing of the overheated boiler was heard, and the steam was escaping from the valves. The engineer whistled, the train started, and soon disappeared, mingling its white

The Frenchman had stunned three with his fists.

smoke with the eddies of the densely falling snow.

The detective had remained behind.

Several hours passed. The weather was dismal, and it was very cold. Fix sat motionless on a bench in the station; he might have been thought asleep. Aouda, despite the storm, kept coming out of the waiting-room, going to the end of the platform, and peering through the tempest of snow, as if to pierce the mist which narrowed the horizon around her, and to hear, if possible, some welcome sound. She heard and saw nothing. Then she would return, chilled through, to issue out again after the lapse of a few moments, but always in vain.

Evening came, and the little band had not returned. Where could they be? Had they found the Indians, and were they having a conflict with them, or were they still wandering amid the mist? The commander of the fort was anxious, though he tried to conceal his apprehensions. As night approached, the snow fell less plentifully, but it became intensely cold. Absolute silence rested on the plains. Neither flight of bird nor passing of beast troubled the perfect calm.

Throughout the night Aouda, full of sad forebodings, her heart stifled with anguish, wandered about on the verge of the plains. Her imagination carried her far off, and showed her innumerable dangers. What she suffered through the long hours it would be impossible to describe.

Fix remained stationary in the same place, but did not sleep. Once a man approached and spoke to him, and the detective merely replied by shaking his head.

Thus the night passed. At dawn, the half-extinguished disk of the sun rose above a misty horizon; but it was now possible to recognize objects two miles off. Phileas Fogg and the squad had gone southward; in the south all was still vacancy. It was then seven o'clock.

The captain, who was really alarmed, did not know what course to take. Should he send another detachment to the rescue of the first? Should he sacrifice more men, with so few chances of saving those already sacrificed? His hesitation did not last long, however. Calling one of his lieutenants, he was on the point of ordering a reconnoissance, when gunshots were heard. Was it a signal? The soldiers rushed out of the fort, and half a mile off they perceived a little band returning in good order.

Mr. Fogg was marching at their head, and just behind him were Passepartout and the other two travellers, rescued from the Sioux.

They had met and fought the Indians ten miles south of Fort Kearney. Shortly before the detachment arrived, Passepartout and his companions had begun to struggle with their captors, three of whom the Frenchman had felled with his fists, when his master and the soldiers hastened up to their relief.

All were welcomed with joyful cries. Phileas Fogg distributed the reward he had promised to the soldiers, while Passepartout, not without reason, muttered to himself, "It must certainly be confessed that I cost my master dear!"

Fix, without saying a word, looked at Mr. Fogg, and it would have been difficult to analyze the thoughts which struggled within him. As for Aouda, she took her protector's hand and pressed it in her own, too much moved to speak.

Meanwhile, Passepartout was looking about for the train; he thought he should find it there, ready to start for Omaha, and he hoped that the time lost might be regained.

"The train! the train!" cried he.

"Gone," replied Fix.

"And when does the next train pass here?" asked Phileas Fogg.

"Not till this evening."

"Ah!" returned the impassible gentleman quietly.

Around the World in Eighty Days

CHAPTER XXXI.

IN WHICH FIX THE DETECTIVE CONSIDERABLY FURTHERS THE INTERESTS OF PHILEAS FOGG.

PHILEAS FOGG found himself twenty hours behind time. Passepartout, the involuntary cause of this delay, was desperate. He had ruined his master!

At this moment the detective approached Mr. Fogg, and, looking him intently in the face, said,—

"Seriously, sir, are you in great haste?"

"Quite seriously."

"I have a purpose in asking," resumed Fix. "Is it absolutely necessary that you should be in New York on the 11th, before nine o'clock in the evening, the time that the steamer leaves for Liverpool?"

"It is absolutely necessary."

"And, if your journey had not been interrupted by these Indians, you would have reached New York on the morning of the 11th?"

"Yes; with eleven hours to spare before the steamer left."

"Good! you are therefore twenty hours behind. Twelve from twenty leaves eight. You must regain eight hours. Do you wish to try to do so?"

"On foot?" asked Mr. Fogg.

"No; on a sledge," replied Fix. "On a sledge with sails. A man has proposed such a method to me."

It was the man who had spoken to Fix during the night, and whose offer he had refused.

Phileas Fogg did not reply at once; but Fix having pointed out the man, who was walking up and down in front of the station, Mr. Fogg went up to him. An instant after, Mr. Fogg and the American, whose name was Mudge, entered a hut built just below the fort.

There Mr. Fogg examined a curious vehicle, a kind of frame on two long beams, a little raised in front like the runners of a sledge, and upon which there was room for five or six persons. A high mast was fixed on the frame, held firmly by metallic lashings, to which was attached a large brigantine sail. This mast held an iron stay upon which to hoist a jib-sail. Behind, a sort of rudder served to guide the vehicle. It was, in short, a sledge rigged like a sloop. During the winter, when the trains are blocked up by the snow, these sledges make extremely rapid journeys across the frozen plains from one station to another. Provided with more sail than a cutter, and with the wind behind them, they slip over the surface of the prairies with a speed equal if not superior to that of the express trains.

Mr. Fogg readily made a bargain with the owner of this land-craft. The wind was favourable, being fresh, and blowing from the west. The snow had hardened, and Mudge was very confident of being able to transport Mr. Fogg in a few hours to Omaha. Thence the trains eastward run frequently to Chicago and New York. It was not impossible that the lost time might yet be recovered; and such an opportunity was not to be rejected.

Not wishing to expose Aouda to the discomforts of travelling in the open air, Mr. Fogg proposed to leave her with Passepartout at Fort Kearney, the servant taking upon himself to escort her to Europe by a better route and under more favourable conditions. But Aouda refused to separate from Mr. Fogg, and Passepartout was delighted with her decision; for nothing could induce him to leave his master while Fix was with him.

It would be difficult to guess the detective's thoughts. Was his conviction shaken by Phileas Fogg's return, or did he still regard him as an exceedingly shrewd rascal, who, his journey round the world completed, would think himself absolutely safe in England? Perhaps Fix's opinion of Phileas Fogg was somewhat modified; but he was nevertheless resolved to do his duty, and to hasten the return of the whole party to England as much as possible.

At eight o'clock the sledge was ready to start. The passengers took their places on it, and wrapped themselves up closely in their travelling-cloaks. The two great sails were hoisted, and under the pressure of the wind the sledge slid over the hardened snow with a velocity of forty miles an hour.

The distance between Fort Kearney and Omaha, as the birds fly, is at most two hundred miles. If the wind held good, the distance might be traversed in five hours; if no accident happened the sledge might reach Omaha by one o'clock.

The cold, increased by the tremendous speed, deprived them of the power of speech.

What a journey! The travellers, huddled close together, could not speak for the cold, intensified by the rapidity at which they were going. The sledge sped on as lightly as a boat over the waves. When the breeze came, skimming the earth, the sledge seemed to be lifted off the ground by its sails. Mudge, who was at the rudder, kept in a straight line, and by a turn of his hand checked the lurches which the vehicle had a tendency to make. All the sails were up, and the jib was so arranged as not to screen the brigantine. A topmast was hoisted, and another jib, held out to the wind, added its force to the other sails. Although the speed could not be exactly estimated, the sledge could not be going at less than forty miles an hour.

"If nothing breaks," said Mudge, "we shall get there!"

Mr. Fogg had made it for Mudge's interest to reach Omaha within the time agreed on, by the offer of a handsome reward.

The prairie, across which the sledge was moving in a straight line, was as flat as a sea. It seemed like a vast frozen lake. The railroad which ran through this section ascended from the south-west to the north-west by Great Island, Columbus, an important Nebraska town, Schuyler, and Fremont, to Omaha. It followed throughout the right bank of the Platte River. The sledge, shortening this route, took the chord of the arc described by the railway. Mudge was not afraid of being stopped by the Platte River, because it was frozen. The road, then, was quite clear of obstacles, and Phileas Fogg had but two things to fear,—an accident to the sledge, and a chance or calm in the wind.

But the breeze, far from lessening its force, blew as if to bend the mast, which, however, the metallic lashings held firmly. These lashings, like the chords of a stringed instrument, resounded as if vibrated by a violin bow. The sledge slid along in the midst of a plaintively intense melody.

"Those chords give the fifth and the octave," said Mr. Fogg.

These were the only words he uttered during the journey. Aouda, cosily packed in furs and cloaks, was sheltered as much as possible from the attacks of the freezing wind. As for Passepartout, his face was as red as the sun's disk when it sets in the mist, and he laboriously inhaled the biting air. With his natural buoyancy of spirits, he began to hope again. They would reach New York on the evening, if not on the morning, of the 11th, and there were still some chances that it would be before the steamer sailed for Liverpool.

Passepartout even felt a strong desire to grasp his ally, Fix, by the hand. He remembered that it was the detective who procured the sledge, the only means of reaching Omaha in time; but, checked by some presentiment, he kept his usual reserve. One thing, however, Passepartout would never forget, and that was the sacrifice which Mr. Fogg had made, without hesitation, to rescue him from the Sioux. Mr. Fogg had risked his fortune and his life. No! His servant would never forget that!

While each of the party was absorbed in reflections so different, the sledge flew fast over the vast carpet of snow. The creeks it passed over were not perceived. Fields and streams disappeared under the uniform whiteness. The plain was absolutely deserted. Between the Union Pacific road and the branch which unites Kearney with Saint Joseph it formed a great uninhabited island. Neither village, station, nor fort appeared. From time to time they sped by some phantom-like tree, whose white skeleton twisted and rattled in the wind. Sometimes flocks of wild birds rose, or bands of gaunt, famished, ferocious prairie-wolves ran howling after the sledge. Passepartout, revolver in hand, held himself ready to fire on those which came too near. Had an accident then happened to the sledge, the travellers, attacked by these beasts, would have been in the most terrible danger; but it held on its even course, soon gained on the wolves, and ere long left the howling band at a safe distance behind.

About noon Mudge perceived by certain landmarks that he was crossing the Platte River. He said nothing, but he felt certain that he was now within twenty miles of Omaha. In less than an hour he left the rudder and furled his sails, whilst the sledge, carried forward by the great impetus the wind had given it, went on half a mile further with its sails unspread.

It stopped at last, and Mudge, pointing to a mass of roofs white with snow, said, "We have got here!"

Arrived! Arrived at the station which is in daily communication, by numerous trains, with the Atlantic seaboard!

Passepartout and Fix jumped off, stretched their stiffened limbs, and aided Mr. Fogg and the young woman to descend from the sledge. Phileas Fogg generously rewarded Mudge, whose hand Passepartout warmly grasped, and the party directed their steps to the Omaha railway station.

The Pacific Railroad proper finds its terminus at this important Nebraska town. Omaha is connected with Chicago by the

And sometimes a pack of prairie wolves.

Chicago and Rock Island Railroad, which runs directly east, and passes fifty stations.

A train was ready to start when Mr. Fogg and his party reached the station, and they only had time to get into the cars. They had seen nothing of Omaha; but Passepartout confessed to himself that this was not to be regretted, as they were not travelling to see the sights.

The train passed rapidly across the State of Iowa, by Council Bluffs, Des Moines, and Iowa City. During the night it crossed the Mississippi at Davenport, and by Rock Island entered Illinois. The next day, which was the 10th, at four in the evening, it reached Chicago, already risen from its ruins, and more proudly seated than ever on the borders of its beautiful Lake Michigan.

Nine hundred miles separated Chicago from New York; but trains are not wanting at Chicago. Mr. Fogg passed at once from one to the other, and the locomotive of the Pittsburg, Fort Wayne, and Chicago Railway left at full speed, as if it fully comprehended that that gentleman had no time to lose. It traversed Indiana, Ohio, Pennsylvania, and New Jersey like a flash, rushing through towns with antique names, some of which had streets and car-tracks, but as yet no houses. At last the Hudson came into view; and at a quarter-past eleven in the evening of the 11th, the train stopped in the station on the right bank of the river, before the very pier of the Cunard line.

The "China," for Liverpool, had started three quarters of an hour before!

Around the World in Eighty Days

CHAPTER XXXII.

IN WHICH PHILEAS FOGG ENGAGES IN A DIRECT STRUGGLE WITH BAD FORTUNE.

THE "China," in leaving, seemed to have carried off Phileas Fogg's last hope. None of the other steamers were able to serve his projects. The "Pereire," of the French Transatlantic Company, whose admirable steamers are equal to any in speed and comfort, did not leave until the 14th; the Hamburg boats did not go directly to Liverpool or London, but to Havre; and the additional trip from Havre to Southampton would render Phileas Fogg's last efforts of no avail. The Inman steamer did not depart till the next day, and could not cross the Atlantic in time to save the wager.

Mr. Fogg learned all this in consulting his "Bradshaw," which gave him the daily movements of the transatlantic steamers.

Passepartout was crushed; it overwhelmed him to lose the boat by three quarters of an hour. It was his fault, for, instead of helping his master, he had not ceased putting obstacles in his path! And when he recalled all the incidents of the tour, when he counted up the sums expended in pure loss and on his own account, when he thought that the immense stake, added to the heavy charges of this useless journey, would completely ruin Mr. Fogg, he overwhelmed himself with bitter self-accusations. Mr. Fogg, however, did not reproach him; and, on leaving the Cunard pier, only said, "We will consult about what is best to-morrow. Come."

The party crossed the Hudson in the Jersey City ferry-boat, and drove in a carriage to the St. Nicholas Hotel, on Broadway. Rooms were engaged, and the night passed, briefly to Phileas Fogg, who slept profoundly, but very long to Aouda and the others, whose agitation did not permit them to rest.

The next day was the 12th of December. From seven in the morning of the 12th, to a quarter before nine in the evening of the 21st, there were nine days, thirteen hours, and forty-five minutes. If Phileas Fogg had left in the "China," one of the fastest steamers on the Atlantic, he would have reached Liverpool, and then London, within the period agreed upon.

Mr. Fogg left the hotel alone, after giving Passepartout instructions to await his return, and inform Aouda to be ready at an instant's notice. He proceeded to the banks of the Hudson, and looked about among the vessels moored or anchored in the river, for any that were about to depart. Several had departure signals, and were preparing to put to sea at morning tide; for in this immense and admirable port, there is not one day in a hundred that vessels do not set out for every quarter of the globe. But they were mostly sailing vessels, of which, of course, Phileas Fogg could make no use.

He seemed about to give up all hope, when he espied, anchored at the Battery, a cable's length off at most, a trading vessel, with a screw, well-shaped, whose funnel, puffing a cloud of smoke, indicated that she was getting ready for departure.

Phileas Fogg hailed a boat, got into it, and soon found himself on board the "Henrietta," iron-hulled, wood-built above. He ascended to the deck, and asked for the captain, who forthwith presented himself. He was a man of fifty, a sort of sea-wolf, with big eyes, a complexion of oxidized copper, red hair and thick neck, and a growling voice.

"The captain?" asked Mr. Fogg.

"I am the captain."

"I am Phileas Fogg, of London."

"And I am Andrew Speedy, of Cardiff."

"You are going to put to sea?"

"In an hour."

"You are bound for—"

"Bordeaux."

"And your cargo?"

"No freight. Going in ballast."

"Have you any passengers?"

"No passengers. Never have passengers. Too much in the way."

"Is your vessel a swift one?"

"Between eleven and twelve knots. The 'Henrietta,' well known."

"Will you carry me and three other persons to Liverpool?"

"To Liverpool? Why not to China?"

"I said Liverpool."

"No!"

"No?"

"No. I am setting out for Bordeaux, and shall go to Bordeaux."

"Money is no object?"

"None."

The captain spoke in a tone which did not admit of a reply.

"But the owners of the 'Henrietta'—" resumed Phileas Fogg.

"The owners are myself," replied the captain. "The vessel belongs to me."

"I will freight it for you."

"No."

"I will buy it off you."

"No."

Phileas Fogg did not betray the least disappointment; but the situation was a grave one. It was not at New York as at Hong Kong, nor with the captain of the "Henrietta" as with the captain of the "Tankadere." Up to this time money had smoothed away every obstacle. Now money failed.

Still, some means must be found to cross the Atlantic on a boat, unless by balloon,—which would have been venturesome, besides not being capable of being put in practice. It seemed that Phileas Fogg had an idea, for he said to the captain, "Well, will you carry me to Bordeaux?"

"No, not if you paid me two hundred dollars."

"I offer you two thousand."

"Apiece?"

"Apiece."

"And there are four of you?"

"Four."

Captain Speedy began to scratch his head. There were eight thousand dollars to gain, without changing his route; for which it was well worth conquering the repugnance he had for all kinds of passengers. Besides, passengers at two thousand dollars are no longer passengers, but valuable merchandise. "I start at nine o'clock," said Captain Speedy, simply. "Are you and your party ready?"

"We will be on board at nine o'clock," replied, no less simply, Mr. Fogg.

It was half-past eight. To disembark from the "Henrietta," jump into a hack, hurry to the St. Nicholas, and return with Aouda, Passepartout, and even the inseparable Fix, was the work of a brief time, and was performed by Mr. Fogg with the coolness which never abandoned him. They were on board when the "Henrietta" made ready to weigh anchor.

When Passepartout heard what this last voyage was going to cost, he uttered a prolonged "Oh!" which extended throughout his vocal gamut.

As for Fix, he said to himself that the Bank of England would certainly not come out of this affair well indemnified. When they reached England, even if Mr. Fogg did not throw some handfuls of bank-bills into the sea, more than seven thousand pounds would have been spent!

CHAPTER XXXIII.

IN WHICH PHILEAS FOGG SHOWS HIMSELF EQUAL TO THE OCCASION.

AN hour after, the "Henrietta" passed the lighthouse which marks the entrance of the Hudson, turned the point of Sandy Hook, and put to sea. During the day she skirted Long Island, passed Fire Island, and directed her course rapidly eastward.

At noon the next day, a man mounted the bridge to ascertain the vessel's position. It might be thought that this was Captain Speedy. Not the least in the world. It was Phileas Fogg, Esquire. As for Captain Speedy, he was shut up in his cabin under lock and key, and was uttering loud cries, which signified an anger at once pardonable and excessive.

What had happened was very simple. Philas Fogg wished to go to Liverpool, but the captain would not carry him there. Then Phileas Fogg had taken passage for Bordeaux, and, during the thirty hours he had been on board, had so shrewdly managed with is bank-notes that the sailors and stokers, who were only an occasional crew, and were not on the best terms with the captain, went over to him in a body. This was why Phileas Fogg was in command instead of Captain Speedy; why the captain was a prisoner in his cabin; and why, in short, the "Henrietta" was directing her course towards Liverpool. It was very clear, to see Mr. Fogg manage the craft, that he had been a sailor.

How the adventure ended will be seen anon. Aouda was anxious, though she said nothing. As for Passepartout, he thought Mr. Fogg's manoeuvre simply glorious. The captain had said "between eleven and twelve knots," and the "Henrietta" confirmed his prediction.

If, then—for there were "ifs" still—the sea did not become too boisterous, if the wind did not veer round to the east, if no accident happened to the boat or its machinery, the "Henrietta" might cross the three thousand miles from New York to Liverpool in the nine days, between the 12th and the 21st of December. It is true that, once arrived, the affair on board the "Henrietta," added to that of the Bank of England, might create more difficulties for Mr. Fogg than he imagined or could desire.

During the first days, they went along smoothly enough. The sea was not very unpropitious, the wind seemed stationary in the north-east, the sails were hoisted, and the "Henrietta" ploughed across the waves like a real transatlantic steamer.

Passepartout was delighted. His master's last exploit, the consequences of which he ignored, enchanted him. Never had the crew seen so jolly and dexterous a fellow. He formed warm friendships with the sailors, and amazed them with his acrobatic feats. He thought they managed the vessel like gentlemen, and that the stokers fired up like heroes. His loquacious good-humour infected every one. He had forgotten the past, its vexations and delays. He only thought of the end, so nearly accomplished; and sometimes he boiled over with impatience, as if heated by the furnaces of the "Henrietta." Often, also, the worthy fellow revolved around Fix, looking at him with a keen, distrustful eye; but he did not speak to him, for their old intimacy no longer existed.

Fix, it must be confessed, understood nothing of what was going on. The conquest of the "Henrietta," the bribery of the crew, Fogg managing the boat like a skilled seaman, amazed and confused him. He did not know what to think. For, after all, a man who began by stealing fifty-five thousand pounds might end by stealing a vessel; and Fix was not unnaturally inclined to conclude that the "Henrietta," under Fogg's command, was not going to Liverpool at all, but to some part of the world where the robber, turned into a pirate, would quietly put himself in safety. The conjecture was at least a plausible one, and the detective began to seriously regret that he had embarked in the affair.

As for Captain Speedy, he continued to howl and growl in his cabin; and Passepartout, whose duty it was to carry him his meals, courageous as he was, took the greatest precautions. Mr. Fogg did not seem even to know that there was a captain on board.

On the 13th they passed the edge of the Banks of Newfoundland, a dangerous locality; during the winter, especially, there are frequent fogs and heavy gales of wind. Ever since the evening before the barometer, suddenly falling, had indicated an approaching change in the atmosphere; and during the night the tempera-

"Pirate!" cried Andrew Speedy.

ture varied, the cold became sharper, and the wind veered to the south-east.

This was a misfortune. Mr. Fogg, in order not to deviate from his course, furled his sails and increased the force of the steam; but the vessel's speed slackened, owing to the state of the sea, the long waves of which broke against the stern. She pitched violently, and this retarded her progress. The breeze little by little swelled into a tempest, and it was to be feared that the "Henrietta" might not be able to maintain herself upright on the waves.

Passepartout's visage darkened with the skies, and for two days the poor fellow experienced constant fright. But Phileas Fogg was a bold mariner, and knew how to maintain headway against the sea; and he kept on his course, without even decreasing his steam. The "Henrietta," when she could not rise upon the waves, crossed them, swamping her deck, but passing safely. Sometimes the screw rose out of the water, beating its protruding end, when a mountain of water raised the stern above the waves; but the craft always kept straight ahead.

The wind, however, did not grow as boisterous as might have been feared; it was not one of those tempests which burst, and rush on with a speed of ninety miles an hour. It continued fresh, but, unhappily, it remained obstinately in the south-east, rendering the sails useless.

The 16th of December was the seventy-fifth day since Phileas Fogg's departure from London, and the "Henrietta" had not yet been seriously delayed. Half of the voyage was almost accomplished, and the worst localities had been passed. In summer, success would have been well-nigh certain. In winter, they were at the mercy of the bad season. Passepartout said nothing; but he cherished hope in secret, and comforted himself with the reflection that, if the wind failed them, they might still count on the steam.

On this day the engineer came on deck, went up to Mr. Fogg, and began to speak earnestly with him. Without knowing why—it was a presentiment, perhaps—Passepartout became vaguely uneasy. He would have given one of his ears to hear with the other what the engineer was saying. He finally managed to catch a few words, and was sure he heard his master say, "You are certain of what you tell me?"

"Certain, sir," replied the engineer. "You must remember that, since we started, we have kept up hot fires in all our furnaces, and though we had coal enough to go on short steam from New York to Bordeaux, we haven't enough to

go with all steam from New York to Liverpool."

"I will consider," replied Mr. Fogg.

Passepartout understood it all; he was seized with mortal anxiety. The coal was giving out! "Ah, if my master can get over that," muttered he, "he'll be a famous man!" He could not help imparting to Fix what he had overheard.

"The you believe that we really are going to Liverpool?"

"Of course."

"Ass!" replied the detective, shrugging his shoulders and turning on his heel.

Passepartout was on the point of vigorously resenting the epithet, the reason of which he could not for the life of him comprehend; but he reflected that the unfortunate Fix was probably very much disappointed and humiliated in his self-esteem, after having so awkwardly followed a false scent around the world, and refrained.

And now what course would Phileas Fogg adopt? It was difficult to imagine. Nevertheless he seemed to have decided upon one, for that evening he sent for the engineer, and said to him, "Feed all the fires until the coal is exhausted."

A few moments after, the funnel of the "Henrietta" vomited forth torrents of smoke. The vessel continued to proceed with all steam on; but on the 18th, the engineer, as he had predicted, announced that the coal would give out in the course of the day.

"Do not let the fires go down," replied Mr. Fogg. "Keep them up to the last. Let the valves be filled."

Towards noon Phileas Fogg, having ascertained their position, called Passepartout, and ordered him to go for Captain Speedy. It was as if the honest fellow had been commanded to unchain a tiger. He went to the poop, saying to himself, "He will be like a madman!"

In a few moments, with cries and oaths, a bomb appeared on the poop-deck. The bomb was Captain Speedy. It was clear that he was on the point of bursting. "Where are we?" were the first words his anger permitted him to utter. Had the poor man been apoplectic, he could never have recovered from his paroxysm of wrath.

"Where are we?" he repeated, with purple face.

"Seven hundred and seventy miles from Liverpool," replied Mr. Fogg, with imperturbable calmness.

"Pirate!" cried Captain Speedy.

"I have sent for you, sir—"

"Pickaroon!"

The crew evinced an incredible zeal.

"—Sir," continued Mr. Fogg, "to ask you to sell me your vessel."

"No! By all the devils, no!"

"But I shall be obliged to burn her."

"Burn the 'Henrietta'!"

"Yes; at least the upper part of her. The coal has given out."

"Burn my vessel!" cried Captain Speedy, who could scarcely pronounce the words. "A vessel worth fifty thousand dollars!"

"Here are sixty thousand," replied Phileas Fogg, handing the captain a roll of bank bills. This had a prodigious effect on Andrew Speedy. An American can scarcely remain unmoved at the sight of sixty thousand dollars. The captain forgot in an instant his anger, his imprisonment, and all his grudges against his passenger. The "Henrietta" was twenty years old; it was a great bargain. The bomb would not go off after all. Mr. Fogg had taken away the match.

"And I shall still have the iron hull," said the captain in a softer tone.

"The iron hull and the engine. Is it agreed?"

"Agreed."

And Andrew Speedy, seizing the bank-notes, counted them, and consigned them to his pocket.

During this colloquy, Passepartout was as white as a sheet, and Fix seemed on the point of having an apoplectic fit. Nearly twenty thousand pounds had been expended, and Fogg left the hull and engine to the captain, that is, near the whole value of the craft! It was true, however, that fifty-five thousand pounds had been stolen from the bank.

When Andrew Speedy had pocketed the money, Mr. Fogg said to him, "Don't let this astonish you, sir. You must know that I shall lose twenty thousand pounds, unless I arrive in London by a quarter before nine on the evening of the 21st of December. I missed the steamer at New York, and as you refused to take me to Liverpool—"

"And I did well!" cried Andrew Speedy; "for I have gained at least forty thousand dollars by it!" He added, more sedately, "Do you know one thing, Captain—"

"Fogg."

"Captain Fogg, you've got something of the Yankee about you."

And, having paid his passenger what he considered a high compliment, he was going away, when Mr. Fogg said, "The vessel now belongs to me?"

"Certainly, from the keel to the truck of the masts,—all the wood, that is."

"Very well. Have the interior seats, bunks, and frames pulled down, and burn them."

It was necessary to have dry wood to keep the steam up to the adequate pressure, and on that day the poop, cabins, bunks, and the spare deck were sacrificed. On the next day, the 19th of December, the mast, rafts, and spars were burned; the crew worked lustily, keeping up the fires. Passepartout hewed, cut, and sawed away with all his might. There was a perfect rage for demolition.

The railings, fittings, the greater part of the deck, and top sides disappeared on the 20th, and the "Henrietta" was not only a flat hulk. But on this day they sighted the Irish coast and Fastnet Light. By ten in the evening they were passing Queenstown. Phileas Fogg had only twenty-four hours more in which to get to London; that length of time was necessary to reach Liverpool, with all steam on. And the steam was about to give out altogether!

"Sir," said Captain Speedy, who was now deeply interested in Mr. Fogg's project, "I really commiserate you. Everything is against you. We are only opposite Queenstown."

"Ah," said Mr. Fogg, "is that place where we see the lights Queenstown?"

"Yes."

"Can we enter the harbour?"

"Not under three hours. Only at high tide."

"Stay," replied Mr. Fogg calmly, without betraying in his features that by a supreme inspiration he was about to attempt once more to conquer ill-fortune.

Queenstown is the Irish port at which the transatlantic steamers stop to put off the mails. These mails are carried to Dublin by express trains always held in readiness to start; from Dublin they are sent on to Liverpool by the most rapid boats, and thus gain twelve hours on the Atlantic steamers.

Phileas Fogg counted on gaining twelve hours in the same way. Instead of arriving at Liverpool the next evening by the "Henrietta," he would be there by noon, and would therefore have time to reach London before a quarter before nine in the evening.

The "Henrietta" entered Queenstown harbour at one o'clock in the morning, it then being high tide; and Phileas Fogg, after being grasped heartily by the hand by Captain Speedy, left that gentleman on the levelled hulk of his craft, which was still worth half what he had sold it for.

The party went on shore at once. Fix was greatly tempted to arrest Mr. Fogg on the spot; but he did not. Why? What struggle was going on within him? Had he changed his mind about "his man?" Did he understand that he had made a grave mistake? He did not, however,

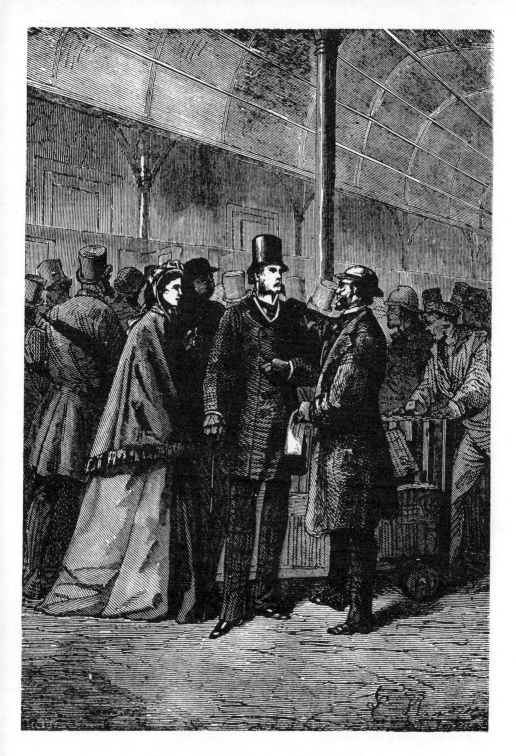

"I arrest you in the name of the Queen."

abandon Mr. Fogg. They all got upon the train, which was just ready to start, at half-past one; at dawn of day they were in Dublin; and they lost no time in embarking on a steamer which, disdaining to rise upon the waves, invariably cut through them.

Phileas Fogg at last disembarked on the Liverpool quay, at twenty minutes before twelve, December 21st. He was only six hours distant from London.

But at this moment Fix came up, put his hand upon Mr. Fogg's shoulder, and, showing his warrant, said, "You are really Phileas Fogg?"

"I am."

"I arrest you in the Queen's name!"

Around the World in Eighty Days

CHAPTER XXXIV.

IN WHICH PHILEAS FOGG AT LAST REACHES LONDON.

PHILEAS FOGG was in prison. He had been shut up in the Custom House, and he was to be transferred to London the next day.

Passepartout, when he saw his master arrested, would have fallen upon Fix, had he not been held back by some policemen. Aouda was thunderstruck at the suddenness of an event which she could not understand. Passepartout explained to her how it was that the honest and courageous Fogg was arrested as a robber. The young woman's heart revolted against so heinous a charge, and when she saw that she could attempt or do nothing to save her protector, wept bitterly.

As for Fix, he had arrested Mr. Fogg because it was his duty, whether Mr. Fogg were guilty or not.

The thought then struck Passepartout, that he was the cause of this new misfortune! Had he not concealed Fix's errand from his master? When Fix revealed his true character and purpose, why had he not told Mr. Fogg? If the latter had been warned, he would no doubt have given Fix proof of his innocence, and satisfied him of his mistake; at least, Fix would not have continued his journey at the expense and on the heels of his master, only to arrest him the moment he set foot on English soil. Passepartout wept till he was blind, and felt like blowing his brains out.

Aouda and he had remained, despite the cold, under the portico of the Custom House. Neither wished to leave the place; both were anxious to see Mr. Fogg again.

That gentleman was really ruined, and that at the moment when he was about to attain his end. This arrest was fatal. Having arrived at Liverpool at twenty minutes before twelve on the 21st of December, he had till a quarter before nine that evening to reach the Reform Club, that is, nine hours and a quarter; the journey from Liverpool to London was six hours.

If any one, at this moment, had entered the Custom House, he would have found Mr. Fogg seated, motionless, calm, and without apparent anger, upon a wooden bench. He was not, it is true, resigned; but this last blow failed to force him into an outward betrayal of any emotion. Was he being devoured by one of those secret rages, all the more terrible because contained, and which only burst forth, with an irresistible force, at the last moment? No one could tell. There he sat, calmly waiting—for what? Did he still cherish hope? Did he still believe, now that the door of this prison was closed upon him, that he would succeed?

However that may have been, Mr. Fogg carefully put his watch upon the table, and observed its advancing hands. Not a word escaped his lips, but his look was singularly set and stern. The situation, in any event, was a terrible one, and might be thus stated: If Phileas Fogg was honest, he was ruined. If he was a knave, he was caught.

Did escape occur to him? Did he examine to see if there were any practicable outlet from his prison? Did he think of escaping from it? Possibly; for once he walked slowly around the room. But the door was locked, and the window heavily barred with iron rods. He sat down again, and drew his journal from his pocket. On the line where these words were written, "December 21st, Saturday, Liverpool," he added, "80th day, 11.40 A.M.," and waited.

The Custom House clock struck one. Mr. Fogg observed that his watch was two hours too fast.

Two hours! Admitting that he was at this moment taking an express train, he could reach London and the Reform Club by a quarter before nine, P.M. His forehead slightly wrinkled.

At thirty-three minutes past two he heard a singular noise outside, then a hasty opening of doors. Passepartout's voice was audible, and immediately after that of Fix. Phileas Fogg's eyes brightened for an instant.

The door swung open, and he saw Passepartout, Aouda, and Fix, who hurried towards him.

Fix was out of breath, and his hair was in disorder. He could not speak. "Sir," he stammered, "sir—forgive me—a most—unfortunate resemblance—robber arrested three days ago—you—are free!"

Phileas Fogg was free! He walked to the detective, looked him steadily in the face, and with the only rapid motion he had ever made in his life, or which he ever would make, drew back his arms, and with the precision of a machine, knocked Fix down.

"Well hit!" cried Passepartout. "Parbleu! that's what you might call a good application of English fists!"

Fix, who found himself on the floor, did not utter a word. He had only received his deserts. Mr. Fogg, Aouda, and Passepartout left the Custom House without delay, got into a cab, and in a few moments descended at the station.

Phileas Fogg asked if there was an express train about to leave for London. It was forty minutes past two. The express train had left thirty-five minutes before.

Phileas Fogg then ordered a special train.

There were several rapid locomotives on hand; but the railway arrangements did not permit the special train to leave until three o'clock.

At that hour Phileas Fogg, having stimulated the engineer by the offer of a generous reward, at last set out towards London with Aouda and his faithful servant.

It was necessary to make the journey in five hours and a half; and this would have been easy on a clear road throughout. But there were forced delays, and when Mr. Fogg stepped from the train at the terminus, all the the clocks in London were striking ten minutes before nine.*

Having made the tour of the world, he was behindhand five minutes. He had lost the wager!

*A somewhat remarkable eccentricity on the part of the London clocks!—Translator.

Around the World in Eighty Days

CHAPTER XXXV.

IN WHICH PHILEAS FOGG DOES NOT HAVE TO REPEAT HIS ORDERS TO PASSEPARTOUT TWICE

THE dwellers in Saville Row would have been surprised, the next day, if they had been told that Phileas Fogg had returned home. His doors and windows were still closed; no appearance of change was visible.

After leaving the station, Mr. Fogg gave Passepartout instructions to purchase some provisions, and quietly went to his domicile.

He bore his misfortune with his habitual tranquillity. Ruined! And by the blundering of the detective! After having steadily traversed that long journey, overcome a hundred obstacles, braved many dangers, and still found time to do some good on his way, to fail near the goal by a sudden event which he could not have foreseen, and against which he was unarmed; it was terrible! But a few pounds were left of the large sum he had carried with him. There only remained of his fortune the twenty thousand pounds deposited at Barings, and this amount he owed to his friends of the Reform Club. So great had been the expense of his tour, that, even had he won, it would not have enriched him; and it is probable that he had not sought to enrich himself, being a man who rather laid wagers for honour's sake than for the stake proposed. But this wager totally ruined him.

Mr. Fogg's course, however, was fully decided upon; he knew what remained for him to do.

A room in the house in Saville Row was set apart for Aouda, who was overwhelmed with grief at her protector's misfortune. From the words which Mr. Fogg dropped, she saw that he was meditating some serious project.

Knowing that Englishmen governed by a fixed idea sometimes resort to the desperate expedient of suicide, Passepartout kept a narrow watch upon his master, though he carefully concealed the appearance of so doing.

First of all, the worthy fellow had gone up to his room, and had extinguished the gas-burner, which had been burning for eighty days. He had found in the letter-box a bill from the gas company, and he thought it more than time to put a stop to this expense, which he had been doomed to bear.

The night passed. Mr. Fogg went to bed, but did he sleep? Aouda did not once close her eyes. Passepartout watched all night, like a faithful dog, at his master's door.

Mr. Fogg called him in the morning, and told him to get Aouda's breakfast, and a cup of tea and a chop for himself. He desired Aouda to excuse him from breakfast and dinner, as his time would be absorbed all day in putting his affairs to rights. In the evening he would ask permission to have a few moments' conversation with the young lady.

Passepartout, having received his orders, had nothing to do but obey them. He looked at his imperturbable master, and could scarcely bring his mind to leave him. His heart was full, and his conscience tortured by remorse; for he accused himself more bitterly than ever of being the cause of the irretrievable disaster. Yes! if he had warned Mr. Fogg, and had betrayed Fix's projects to him, his master would certainly not have given the detective passage to Liverpool, and then—

Passepartout could hold in no longer.

"My master! Mr. Fogg!" he cried, "why do you not curse me? It was my fault that—"

"I blame no one," returned Phileas Fogg, with perfect calmness. "Go!"

Passepartout left the room, and went to find Aouda, to whom he delivered his master's message.

"Madam," he added, "I can do nothing myself—nothing! I have no influence over my master; but you, perhaps—"

"What influence could I have?" replied Aouda. "Mr. Fogg is influenced by no one. Has he ever understood that my gratitude to him is overflowing? Has he ever read my heart? My friend, he must not be left alone an instant! You say he is going to speak with me this evening?"

"Yes, madam; probably to arrange for your protection and comfort in England."

"We shall see," replied Aouda, becoming suddenly pensive.

Throughout this day (Sunday) the house in Saville Row was as if uninhabited, and Phileas Fogg, for the first time since he had lived in that house, did not set out for his club when Westminster clock struck half-past eleven.

He had found a bill from the Gas Company.

Why should he present himself at the Reform? His friends no longer expected him there. As Phileas Fogg had not appeared in the saloon on the evening before (Saturday, the 21st of December, at a quarter before nine), he had lost his wager. It was not even necessary that he should go to his bankers for the twenty thousand pounds; for his antagonists already had his check in their hands, and they had only to fill it out and send it to the Barings to have the amount transferred to their credit.

Mr. Fogg, therefore, had no reason for going out, and so he remained at home. He shut himself up in his room, and busied himself putting his affairs in order. Passepartout

a corner, and looked ruefully at the young woman. Aouda was still pensive.

About half-past seven in the evening Mr. Fogg sent to know if Aouda would receive him, and in a few moments he found himself alone with her.

Phileas Fogg took a chair, and sat down near the fireplace, opposite Aouda. No emotion was visible on his face. Fogg returned was exactly the Fogg who had gone away; there was the same calm, the same impassibility.

He sat several minutes without speaking; then, bending his eyes on Aouda, "Madam," said he, "will you pardon me for bringing you to England?"

Passepartout putting out the gas-light.

continually ascended and descended the stairs. The hours were long for him. He listened at his master's door, and looked through the keyhole, as if he had a perfect right so to do, and as if he feared that something terrible might happen at any moment. Sometimes he thought of Fix, but no longer in anger. Fix, like all the world, had been mistaken in Phileas Fogg, and had only done his duty in tracking and arresting him; while he, Passepartout— This thought haunted him, and he never ceased cursing his miserable folly.

Finding himself too wretched to remain alone, he knocked at Aouda's door, went into her room, seated himself, without speaking, in

"I, Mr. Fogg!" replied Aouda, checking the pulsations of her heart.

"Please let me finish," returned Mr. Fogg. "When I decided to bring you far away from the country which was so unsafe for you, I was rich, and counted on putting a portion of my fortune at your disposal; then your existence would have been free and happy. But now I am ruined."

"I know it, Mr. Fogg," replied Aouda; "and I ask you in my turn, will you forgive me for having followed you, and—who knows?—for having, perhaps, delayed you, and thus contributed to your ruin?"

"Madam, you could not remain in India, and

your safety could only be assured by bringing you to such a distance that your persecutors could not take you."

"So, Mr. Fogg," resumed Aouda, "not content with rescuing me from a terrible death, you thought yourself bound to secure my comfort in a foreign land?"

"Yes, madam; but circumstances have been against me. Still, I beg to place the little I have left at your service."

"But what will become of you, Mr. Fogg?"

"As for me, madam," replied the gentleman, coldly, "I have need of nothing."

"But how do you look upon the fate, sir, which awaits you?"

"As I am in the habit of doing."

"At least," said Aouda, "want should not overtake a man like you. Your friends—"

"I have no friends, madam."

"Your relatives—"

I have no longer any relatives."

"I pity you, then, Mr. Fogg, for solitude is a sad thing, with no heart to which to confide your griefs. They say, though, that misery itself, shared by two sympathetic souls may be borne with patience."

"They say so, madam."

"Mr. Fogg," said Aouda, rising, and seizing his hand, "do you wish at once a kinswoman and friend? Will you have me for your wife?"

Mr. Fogg, at this, rose in his turn. There was an unwonted light in his eyes, and a slight trembling of his lips. Aouda looked into his face. The sincerity, rectitude, firmness, and sweetness of this soft glance of a noble woman, who could dare all to save him to whom she owed all, at first astonished, then penetrated him. He shut his eyes for an instant, as if to avoid her look. When he opened them again, "I love you!" he said, simply. "Yes, by all that is holiest, I love you, and I am entirely yours!"

"Ah!" cried Aouda, pressing his hand to her heart.

Passepartout was summoned and appeared immediately. Mr. Fogg still held Aouda's hand in his own; Passepartout understood, and his big, round face became as radiant as the tropical sun at its zenith.

Mr. Fogg asked him if it was not too late to notify the Reverend Samuel Wilson, of Marylebone Parish, that evening.

Passepartout smiled his most genial smile, and said, "Never too late."

It was five minutes past eight.

"Will it be for to-morrow, Monday?"

"For to-morrow, Monday," said Mr. Fogg, turning to Aouda.

"Yes; for to-morrow, Monday," she replied.

Passepartout hurried off as fast as his legs could carry him.

Around the World in Eighty Days

CHAPTER XXXVI.

IN WHICH PHILEAS FOGG'S NAME IS ONCE MORE AT A PREMIUM ON 'CHANGE.

IT is time to relate what a change took place in English public opinion, when it transpired that the real bank-robber, a certain James Strand, had been arrested, on the 17th of December, at Edinburgh. Three days before, Phileas Fogg had been a criminal, who was being desperately followed up by the police; now he was an honourable gentleman, mathematically pursuing his eccentric journey round the world.

The papers resumed their discussion about the wager; all those who had laid bets, for or against him, revived their interest, as if by magic; the "Phileas Fogg bonds" again became negotiable, and many new wagers were made. Phileas Fogg's name was once more at a premium on 'Change.

His five friends of the Reform Coub passed these three days in a state of feverish suspense. Would Phileas Fogg whom they had forgotten, reappear before their eyes! Where was he at this moment? The 17th of December, the day of James Strand's arrest, was the seventy-sixth since Phileas Fogg's departure, and no news of him had been received. Was he dead? Had he abandoned the effort, or was he continuing his journey along the route agreed upon? And would he appear on Saturday, the 21st of December, at a quarter before nine in the evening, on the threshold of the Reform Club saloon?

The anxiety in which, for three days, London society existed, cannot be described. Telegrams were sent to America and Asia for news of Phileas Fogg. Messengers were despatched to the house in Saville Row morning and evening. No news. The police were ignorant what had become of the detective, Fix, who had so unfortunately followed up a false scent. Bets increased, nevertheless, in number and value. Phileas Fogg, like a racehorse, was drawing near his last turning-point. The bonds were quoted, no longer at a hundred below par, but at twenty, at ten, and at five; and paralytic old Lord Albemarle bet even in his favour.

A great crowd was collected in Pall Mall and the neighbouring streets on Saturday evening; it seemed like a multitude of brokers permanently established around the Reform Club. Circulation was impeded, and everywhere disputes, discussions, and financial transactions were going on. The police had great difficulty in keeping back the crowd, and as the hour when Phileas Fogg was due approached, the excitement rose to its highest pitch.

The five antagonists of Phileas Fogg had met in the great saloon of the club. John Sullivan and Samuel Fallentin, the bankers, Andrew Stuart, the engineer, Gauthier Ralph, the director of the Bank of England, and Thomas Flanagan, the brewer, one and all waited anxiously.

When the clock indicated twenty minutes past eight, Andrew Stuart got up, saying, "Gentlemen, in twenty minutes the time agreed upon between Mr. Fogg and ourselves will have expired."

"What time did the last train arrive from Liverpool?" asked Thomas Flanagan.

"At twenty-three minutes past seven," replied Gauthier Ralph; "and the next does not arrive till ten minutes after twelve."

"Well, gentlemen," resumed Andrew Stuart, "if Phileas Fogg had come in the 7.23 train, he would have got here by this time. We can therefore regard the bet as won."

"Wait; don't let us be too hasty," replied Samuel Fallentin. "You know that Mr. Fogg is very eccentric. His punctuality is well known; he never arrives too soon, or too late; and I should not be surprised if he appeared before us at the last minute."

"Why," said Andrew Stuart nervously, "if I should see him, I should not believe it was he."

"The fact is," resumed Thomas Flanagan, "Mr. Fogg's project was absurdly foolish. Whatever his punctuality, he could not prevent the delays which were certain to occur; and a delay of only two or three days would be fatal to his tour."

"Observe, too," added John Sullivan, "that we have received no intelligence from him, though there are telegraphic lines all along his route."

"He has lost, gentlemen," said Andrew Stuart,—"he has a hundred times lost! You know, besides, that the 'China'—the only steamer he could have taken from New York to get here in time—arrived yesterday. I have seen a list of the passengers, and the name of Phileas Fogg is not among them. Even if we admit that

"Here I am, gentlemen," said he.

fortune has favoured him, he can scarcely have reached America. I think he will be at least twenty days behindhand, and that Lord Albermarle will lose a cool five thousand.''

"It is clear,'' replied Gauthier Ralph; "and we have nothing to do but to present Mr. Fogg's check at Barings to-morrow.''

At this moment, the hands of the club clock pointed to twenty minutes to nine.

"Five minutes more,'' said Andrew Stuart.

The five gentlemen looked at each other. Their anxiety was becoming intense; but, not wishing to betray it, they readily assented to Mr. Fallentin's proposal of a rubber.

"I wouldn't give up my four thousand of the bet,'' said Andrew Stuart, as he took his seat, "for three thousand nine hundred and ninety-nine.''

The clock indicated eighteen minutes to nine.

The players took up their cards, but could not keep their eyes off the clock. Certainly, however secure they felt, minutes had never seemed so long to them!

"Seventeen minutes to nine,'' said Thomas Flanagan, as he cut the cards which Ralph handed to him.

Then there was a moment of silence. The great saloon was perfectly quiet; but the murmurs of the crowd outside were heard, with now and then a shrill cry. The pendulum beat the seconds, which each player eagerly counted, as he listened, with mathematical regularity.

"Sixteen minutes to nine!'' said John Sullivan, in a voice which betrayed his emotion.

One minute more, and the wager would be won. Andrew Stuart and his partners suspended their game. They left their cards, and counted the seconds.

At the fortieth second, nothing. At the fiftieth, still nothing.

At the fifty-fifth, a loud cry was heard in the street, followed by applause, hurrahs, and some fierce growls.

The players rose from their seats.

At the fifty-seventh second the door of the saloon opened; and the pendulum had not beat the sixtieth second when Phileas Fogg appeared, followed by an excited crowd who had forced their way through the club doors, and in his calm voice, said, "Here I am, gentlemen!''

Around the World in Eighty Days

CHAPTER XXXVII.

IN WHICH IT IS SHOWN THAT PHILEAS FOGG GAINED NOTHING BY HIS TOUR AROUND THE WORLD, UNLESS IT WERE HAPPINESS.

YES; Phileas Fogg in person.

The reader will remember that at five minutes past eight in the evening—about five and twenty hours after the arrival of the travellers in London—Passepartout had been sent by his master to engage the services of the Reverend Samuel Wilson in a certain marriage ceremony, which was to take place the next day.

Passepartout went on his errand enchanted. He soon reached the clergyman's house, but found him not at home. Passepartout waited a good twenty minutes, and when he left the reverend gentleman, it was thirty-five minutes past eight. But in what a state he was! With his hair in disorder, and without his hat, he ran along the street as never man was seen to run before, overturning passers-by, rushing over the sidewalk like a waterspout.

In three minutes he was in Saville Row again, and staggered breathlessly into Mr. Fogg's room.

He could not speak.

"What is the matter?" asked Mr. Fogg.

"My master!" gasped Passepartout,—"marriage—impossible—"

"Impossible?"

"Impossible—for to-morrow."

"Why so?"

"Because to-morrow—is Sunday!"

"Monday," replied Mr. Fogg.

"No—to-day—is Saturday."

"Saturday? Impossible!"

"Yes, yes, yes, yes!" cried Passepartout. "You have made a mistake of one day! We arrived twenty-four hours ahead of time; but there are only ten minutes left!"

Passepartout had seized his master by the collar, and was dragging him along with irresistible force.

Phileas Fogg, thus kidnapped, without having time to think, left his house, jumped into a cab, promised a hundred pounds to the cabman, and, having run over two dogs and overturned five carriages, reached the Reform Club.

The clock indicated a quarter before nine when he appeared in the great saloon.

Phileas Fogg had accomplished the journey round the world in eighty days!

Phileas Fogg had won his wager of twenty thousand pounds!

How was it that a man so exact and fastidious could have made this error of a day? How came he to think that he had arrived in London on Saturday, the twenty-first day of December, when it was really Friday, the twentieth, the seventy-ninth day only from his departure?

The cause of the error is very simple.

Phileas Fogg had, without suspecting it, gained one day on his journey, and this merely because he had travelled constantly *eastward*; he would, on the contrary, have lost a day, had he gone in the opposite direction, that is, *westward*.

In journeying eastward he had gone towards the sun, and the days therefore diminished for him as many times four minutes as he crossed degrees in this direction. There are three hundred and sixty degrees on the circumference of the earth; and these three hundred and sixty degrees, multiplied by four minutes, gives precisely twenty-four hours—that is, the day unconsciously gained. In other words, while Phileas Fogg, going eastward, saw the sun pass the meridian *eighty* times, his friends in London only saw it pass the meridian *seventy-nine* times. This is why they awaited him at the Reform Club on Saturday, and not Sunday, as Mr. Fogg thought.

And Passepartout's famous family watch, which had always kept London time, would have betrayed this fact, if it had marked the days as well as the hours and minutes!

Phileas Fogg, then, had won the twenty thousand pounds; but as he had spent nearly nineteen thousand on the way, the pecuniary gain was small. His object was, however, to be victorious, and not to win money. He divided the one thousand pounds that remained between Passepartout and the unfortunate Fix, against whom he cherished no grudge. He deducted, however, from Passepartout's share the cost of the gas which had burned in his room for nineteen hundred and twenty hours, for the sake of regularity.

That evening, Mr. Fogg, as tranquil and phlegmatic as ever, said to Aouda, "Is our marriage still agreeable to you?"

His hair all in disorder, without a hat, knocking down foot-passengers, on he ran.

"Mr. Fogg," replied she, "it is for me to ask that question. You were ruined, but now you are rich again."

"Pardon me, madam; my fortune belongs to you. If you had not suggested our marriage, my servant would not have gone to the Reverend Samuel Wilson's, I should not have been apprised of my error, and—"

"Dear Mr. Fogg!" said the young woman.

"Dear Aouda!" replied Phileas Fogg.

It need not be said that the marriage took place forty-eight hours after, and that Passepartout, glowing and dazzling, gave the bride away. Had he not saved her, and was he not entitled to this honour?

The next day, as soon as it was light, Passepartout rapped vigorously at his master's door. Mr. Fogg opened it, and asked, "What's the matter, Passepartout?"

"What is it, sir? Why, I've just this instant found out—"

"What?"

"That we might have made the tour of the world in only seventy-eight days."

"No doubt," returned Mr. Fogg, "by not crossing India. But if I had not crossed India, I should not have saved Aouda; she would not have been my wife, and—"

Mr. Fogg quietly shut the door.

Phileas Fogg had won his wager, and had made his journey around the world in eighty days. To do this, he had employed every means of conveyance—steamers, railways, carriages, yachts, trading-vessels, sledges, elephants. The eccentric gentleman had throughout displayed all his marvellous qualities of coolness and exactitude. But what then? What had he really gained by all this trouble? What had he brought back from this long and weary journey?

Nothing, say you? Perhaps so; nothing but a charming woman, who, strange as it may appear, made him the happiest of men!

Truly, would you not for less than that make the tour around the world?

The Clipper of the Clouds

The Clipper of the Clouds

CHAPTER I.

MYSTERIOUS SOUNDS

"BANG! Bang!"

The pistol-shots were almost simultaneous. A cow peacefully grazing fifty yards away received one of the bullets in her back. She had nothing to do with the quarrel all the same.

Neither of the adversaries was hit.

Who were these two gentlemen? We do not know, although this would be an excellent opportunity to hand down their names to posterity. All we can say is that the elder was an Englishman and the younger an American, and both of them were old enough to know better.

So far as recording in what locality the inoffensive ruminant had just tasted her last tuft of herbage, nothing can be easier. It was on the left bank of the Niagara, not far from the suspension bridge which joins the American to the Canadian bank three miles from the falls.

The Englishman stepped up to the American.

"I contend, nevertheless, that it was 'Rule Britannia!'"

"And I say it was 'Yankee Doodle!'" replied the other.

The dispute was about to begin again when one of the seconds—doubtless in the interests of the milk trade—interposed.

"Suppose we say it was 'Rule Doodle' and 'Yankee Britannia,' and adjourn to breakfast?"

This compromise between the national airs of Great Britain and the United States was adopted to the general satisfaction. The Americans and Englishmen walked up the left bank of the Niagara on their way to Goat Island, the neutral ground between the falls. Let us leave them in the presence of the boiled eggs and traditional ham, and floods enough of tea to make the cataract jealous, and trouble ourselves no more about them. It is extremely unlikely that we shall again meet with them in this story.

Which was right; the Englishman or the American? It is not easy to say. Anyhow the duel shows how great was the excitement, not only in the new but also in the old world, with regard to an inexplicable phenomenon which for a month or more had driven everybody to distraction.

Never had the sky been so much looked at since the appearance of man on the terrestrial globe. The night before an aerial trumpet had blared its brazen notes through space immediately over that part of Canada between Lake Ontario and Lake Erie. Some people had heard those notes as "Yankee Doodle," others had heard them as "Rule Britannia," and hence the quarrel between the Anglo-Saxons, which ended with the breakfast on Goat Island. Perhaps it was neither one nor the other of these patriotic tunes, but what was undoubted by all was that these extraordinary sounds had seemed to descend from the sky to the earth.

What could it be? Was it some exuberant aeronaut rejoicing on that sonorous instrument of which the Renommée makes such obstreperous use?

No! There was no balloon and there were no aeronauts. Some strange phenomenon had occurred in the higher zones of the atmosphere, a phenomenon of which neither the nature nor the cause could be explained. To-day it appeared over America; forty-eight hours afterwards it was over Europe; a week later it was in Asia over the Celestial Empire.

Hence in every country of the world— empire, kingdom, or republic—there was anxiety which it was important to allay. If you hear in your house strange and inexplicable noises, do you not at once endeavour to discover the cause? And if your search is in vain, do you not leave your house and take up your quarters in another? Yes, of course you do! But in this case the house was the terrestrial globe! There are no means of leaving that house for the moon, or Mars, or Venus, or Jupiter, or any other planet of the solar system. And so of necessity we have to find out what it is that takes place, not in the infinite void, but within the atmospherical zones. In fact, if there is no air there is no noise, and as there was a noise— that famous trumpet to wit—the phenomenon must occur in the air, the density of which invariably diminishes, and which does not extend for more than six miles round our spheroid.

Naturally the newspapers took up the question in their thousands, and treated it in every form, throwing on it both light and

Both of them were old enough to know better.

darkness, recording many things about it true or false, alarming and tranquillizing their readers—as the sale required—and almost driving ordinary people mad. At one blow party politics dropped unheeded—and the affairs of the world went on none the worse for it.

But what could this thing be?

There was not an observatory that was not applied to. If an observatory could not give a satisfactory answer, what was the use of observatories? If astronomers, who doubled and tripled the stars a hundred thousand million miles away, could not explain a phenomenon occurring only a few miles off, what was the use of astronomers?

How many eye-glasses, spectacles, field-glasses, sea-glasses, binoculars, monoculars, reflectors, and refractors, were pointed at the sky during the clear summer nights it would be impossible to say. There were hundreds of thousands of them at the least. Ten times, twenty times as many as the stars that can be seen by the naked eye on the celestial sphere. Never had an eclipse, observed simultaneously over half the globe, produced such a wonderful display of optical instruments.

The observatories gave their answers, but the answers were very unsatisfactory. Each offered an opinion, but each opinion differed from the others, and therefore during the last weeks of April and the early weeks of May there arose an intestine war in the scientific world.

The observatory at Paris was very guarded in what it said. In the mathematical section they had not thought the statement worth noticing; in the meridional section they knew nothing about it; in the physical observatory they had not come across it; in the geodetic section they had had no observation; in the meteorological section there had been no record; in the calculating-room they had had nothing to deal with. At any rate this confession was a frank one, and the same frankness characterized the replies from the observatory of Montsouris and the magnetic station in the park of St. Maur. The same respect for the truth distinguished the Bureau des Longitudes.

The provinces were slightly more affirmative. Perhaps in the night of the fifth and morning of the sixth of May there had appeared a flash of light of electrical origin which lasted about twenty seconds. At the Pic du Midi this light appeared between nine and ten in the evening. At the Meteorological Observatory on the Puy de Dome the light had been observed between one and two o'clock in the morning; at Mont Ventoux in Provence it had been seen between two and three o'clock; at Nice it had been noticed between three and four o'clock; while at the Semnoz Alps between Annecy, Le Bourget, and Le Léman, it had been detected just as the zenith was paling with the dawn.

Now it evidently would not do to disregard these observations altogether. There could be no doubt that a light had been observed at different places, in succession, at intervals, during some hours. Hence, whether it had been produced from many centres in the terrestrial atmosphere, or from one centre, it was plain that the light must have travelled at a speed of over one hundred and twenty miles an hour.

But had there been anything abnormal in the air during the day?

Nothing of the sort.

Had the trumpet been heard in the aerial domain?

No note of a trumpet had been detected between sunrise and sundown.

In the United Kingdom there was much perplexity. The observatories were not in agreement. Greenwich would not consent to the proposition of Oxford. They were agreed on one point, however, and that was—

"It was nothing at all!"

But, said one,

"It was an optical illusion!"

While the other contended that

"It was an acoustical illusion!"

And so they disputed. Something, however, was, it will be seen, common to both.

"It was an illusion."

Between the observatory of Berlin and the observatory of Vienna the discussion threatened to end in international complications; but Russia, in the person of the director of the observatory at Pulkowa, showed that both were right. It all depended on the point of view from which they attacked the phenomenon, which, though impossible in theory, was possible in practice.

In Switzerland, at the observatory of Sautis in the canton of Appenzell, at the Righi, at the Gäbriss, in the passes of the St. Gothard, at the St. Bernard, at the Julier, at the Simplon, at Zurich, at Somblick in the Tyrolean Alps, there was a very strong disinclination to say anything about what nobody could prove—and that was nothing but reasonable.

But in Italy, at the meteorological stations on Vesuvius, on Etna in the old Casa Inglesi, at Monte Cavo, the observers made no hesitation in admitting the materiality of the phenomenon, particularly as they had seen it by day in the form of a small cloud of vapour, and by night in that of a shooting star. But of what it was they knew nothing.

Scientists began at last to tire of the mystery, while they continued to disagree about it, and even to frighten the lowly and the ignorant, who, thanks to one of the wisest laws of nature, have formed, form, and will form the immense majority of the world's inhabitants. Astronomers and meteorologists would soon have dropped the subject altogether had not, on the night of the 26th and 27th, the observatory of Kautokeino at Finmark, in Norway, and during the night of the 28th and 29th that of Isfjord at Spitzbergen—Norwegian one and Swedish the other—found themselves agreed in recording that in the centre of an aurora borealis there had appeared a sort of huge bird, an aerial monster, whose structure they were unable to determine, but who, there was no doubt, was showering off from his body certain corpuscles which exploded like bombs.

In Europe not a doubt was thrown on this observation of the stations in Finmark and Spitzbergen. But what appeared the most phenomenal about it was that the Swedes and Norwegians could find themselves in agreement on any subject whatever.

There was a laugh at the asserted discovery in all the observatories of South America, in Brazil, Peru, and La Plata, and in those of Australia at Sydney, Adelaide, and Melbourne; and Australian laughter is very catching.

To sum up, only one chief of a meteorological station ventured on a decided answer to this question, notwithstanding the sarcasms that his solution provoked. This was a Chinaman, the director of the observatory at Zi-Ka-Wey which rises in the centre of a vast plateau less than thirty miles from the sea, having an immense horizon and wonderfully pure atmosphere.

"It is possible," said he, "that the object was an aviform apparatus—a flying machine!"

What nonsense!

But if the controversy was keen in the old world, we can imagine what it was like in that portion of the new of which the United States occupy so vast an area.

A Yankee, we know, does not waste time on the road. He takes the street that leads him straight to his end. And the observatories of the American Federation did not hesitate to do their best. If they did not hurl their objectives at each other's heads, it was because they would have had to put them back just when they most wanted to use them. In this much-disputed question the observatories of Washington in the district of Columbia, and Cambridge in

Massachusetts, found themselves opposed by those of Dartmouth College in Connecticut, and Ann Arbor in Michigan. The subject of their dispute was not the nature of the body observed, but the precise moment of its observation. All of them claimed to have seen it the same night, the same hour, the same minute, the same second, although the trajectory of the mysterious voyager took it but a moderate height above the horizon. Now from Massachusetts to Michigan, from Connecticut to Columbia, the distance is too great for this double observation, made at the same moment, to be considered possible.

Dudley at Albany, in the State of New York, and West Point, the Military Academy, showed that their colleagues were wrong by an elaborate calculation of the right ascension and declination of the aforesaid body.

But later on it was discovered that the observers had been deceived in the body, and that what they had seen was an aerolite. This aerolite could not be the object in question, for how could an aerolite blow a trumpet?

It was in vain that they tried to get rid of this trumpet as an acoustical illusion. The ears were no more deceived than the eyes. Something had assuredly been seen, and something had assuredly been heard. In the night of the 12th and 13th of May—a very dark night—the observers at Yale College, in the Sheffield Science School, had been able to take down a few bars of a musical phrase in D major, common time, which gave note for note, rhythm for rhythm, the chorus of the Chant du Départ.

"Good," said the Yankee wags. "There is a French band well up in the air."

"But to joke is not to answer." Thus said the observatory at Boston, founded by the Atlantic Iron Works Society, whose opinions in matters of astronomy and meteorology began to have much weight in the world of science.

Then there intervened the observatory at Cincinnati, founded in 1870 on Mount Lookout, thanks to the generosity of Mr. Kilgour, and known for its micrometrical measurements of double stars. Its director declared with the utmost good faith that there had certainly been something, that a travelling body had shown itself at very short periods at different points in the atmosphere, but what were the nature of this body, its dimensions, its speed, and its trajectory, it was impossible to say.

It was then that a journal whose publicity is immense—the *New York Herald*—received the anonymous contribution hereunder.

"There will be in the recollection of most

people the rivalry which existed a few years ago between the two heirs of the Begum of Ragginahra, the French doctor Sarrasin, in the city of Franceville, and the German engineer Schultze, in the city of Stahlstadt, both in the south of Oregon in the United States.

"It will not have been forgotten that, with the object of destroying Franceville, Herr Schultze launched a formidable engine, intended to beat down the town and annihilate it at a single blow.

"Still less will it be forgotten that this engine, whose initial velocity as it left the mouth of the monster cannon had been erroneously calculated, had flown off at a speed exceeding by sixteen times that of ordinary projectiles—or about four hundred and fifty miles an hour—that it did not fall to the ground, and that it passed into an aerolitic stage, so as to circle for ever round our globe.

"Why should not this be the body in question?"

Very ingenious, Mr. Correspondent of the *New York Herald!* but how about the trumpet? There was no trumpet in Herr Schultze's projectile!

So all the explanations explained nothing, and all the observers had observed in vain. There remained only the suggestion offered by the director of Zi-Ka-Wey. But the opinion of a Chinaman! . . . .

The discussion continued, and there was no sign of agreement. Then came a short period of rest. Some days elapsed without any object, aerolite or otherwise, being descried, and without any trumpet notes being heard in the atmosphere. The body then had fallen on some part of the globe where it had been difficult to trace it; in the sea, perhaps. Had it sunk in the depths of the Atlantic, the Pacific, or the Indian Ocean? What was to be said in this matter?

But then, between the 2nd and 9th of June, there came a new series of facts which could not possibly be explained by the unaided existence of a cosmic phenomenon.

In a week the Hamburgers at the top of St. Michael's Tower, the Turks on the highest minaret of St. Sophia, the Rouennais at the end of the metal spire of their cathedral, the Strasburgers at the summit of their minster, the Americans on the head of the Liberty statue at the entrance of the Hudson and on the Washington monument at Boston, the Chinese at the spike of the temple of the Four Hundred Genii at Canton, the Hindoos on the sixteenth terrace of the pyramid of the temple at Tanjore, the San Pietrini at the cross of St. Peter's at Rome, the English at the cross of St. Paul's in London, the Egyptians at the apex of the Great Pyramid of Ghizeh, the Parisians at the lightning conductor of the iron tower of the Exposition of 1889, a thousand feet high, all of them beheld a flag floating from some one of these inaccessible points.

And the flag was black, dotted with stars, and it bore a golden sun in its centre.

The Clipper of the Clouds

CHAPTER II.

AGREEMENT IMPOSSIBLE

"AND the first who says the contrary—"

"Indeed! But we will say the contrary so long as there is a place to say it in!"

"And in spite of your threats—"

"Mind what you are saying, Bat Fynn!"

"Mind what you are saying, Uncle Prudent!"

"I maintain that the screw ought to be behind!"

"And so do we! And so do we!" replied half a hundred voices confounded in one.

"No! It ought to be in front!" shouted Phil Evans.

"In front!" roared fifty other voices, with a vigour in no whit less remarkable.

"We shall never agree!"

"Never! Never!"

"Then what is the use of a dispute?"

"It is not a dispute! It is a discussion!"

One would not have thought so to listen to the taunts, objurgations, and vociferations which filled the lecture-room for a good quarter of an hour.

The room was one of the largest in the Weldon Institute, the well-known club in Walnut Street, Philadelphia, Pennsylvania, U.S.A.

The evening before there had been an election of a lamplighter, occasioning many public manifestations, noisy meetings, and even interchanges of blows, resulting in an effervescence which had not yet subsided, and which would account for some of the excitement just exhibited by the members of the Weldon Institute. For this was merely a meeting of balloonists, discussing the burning question of the direction of balloons.

It took place in a town of the United States whose development has been more rapid than that of New York, Chicago, Cincinnati, or San Francisco, a city which is neither a port nor a mining centre for coal or petroleum, nor an agglomeration of manufactories, nor a terminus of radiating railways; a town larger than Manchester, Edinburgh, Liverpool, Vienna, Petersburg, or Dublin; a town possessing a park in which the seven parks of the English capital could all be packed together; a town containing over a million people; the fourth of fifth town of the world after London, Paris, and New York.

Philadelphia is almost a city of marble, with its palatial houses and its unrivalled public establishments. The most important of the colleges of the New World is the Girard College, and it is at Philadelphia. The largest iron bridge on the globe is that across the Schuylkill, and that is at Philadelphia. The finest temple of the Freemasons is the Masonic Temple at Philadelphia. And the largest club of experts in aerial navigation is at Philadelphia, and if we had visited it on this evening of the 12th of June we might have found something to interest us.

In this great saloon there were struggling, pushing, gesticulating, shouting, arguing, disputing, a hundred balloonists, all with their hats on, under the authority of a president, assisted by a secretary and treasurer. They were not engineers by profession, but simply amateurs of all that appertained to aerostatics, and they were amateurs in a fury, and especially foes of those who would oppose to aerostats "apparatuses heavier than the air," flying machines, aerial ships, or what not. That these people might one day discover the method of guiding balloons is possible. There could be no doubt that their president had considerable difficulty in guiding them.

This president, well known in Philadelphia, was the famous Uncle Prudent, Prudent being his family name. There is nothing surprising in America in the qualificative uncle, for you can there be uncle without having either nephew or niece. There they speak of uncle as in other places they speak of father, though the father may have had no children.

Uncle Prudent was a personage of consideration, and in spite of his name was well known for his audacity. He was very rich, and that is no drawback even in the United States; and how could it be otherwise when he owned the greater part of the shares in Niagara Falls? A society of engineers had just been founded at Buffalo for working the cataract. It seemed to be an excellent speculation. The seven thousand five hundred cubic metres that Niagara passes over in a second would produce seven millions of horse-power. This enormous power, distributed amongst all the workshops within a radius of three hundred miles, would return an annual income of three hundred million dollars, of which the greater part would find its way into the pocket of Uncle Prudent. He was a bachelor, he lived quietly, and for his only servant had his valet Frycollin, who was hardly worthy of being the servant of so audacious a master.

Uncle Prudent was rich, and therefore he had friends, as was natural; but he also had enemies, although he was president of the club —among others all those who envied his position. Amongst his bitterest foes we may mention the secretary of the Weldon Institute.

This was Phil Evans, who was also very rich, being the manager of the Wheelem Watch Company, an important manufactory, which makes every day five hundred movements equal in every respect to the best Swiss workmanship. Phil Evans would have passed for one of the happiest men in the world, and even in the United States, if it had not been for Uncle Prudent. Like him he was in his forty-sixth year; like him of invariable health; like him of undoubted boldness. They were two men made to thoroughly understand each other, but they did not, for both were of extreme violence of character. Uncle Prudent was furiously hot; Phil Evans was abnormally cool.

And why had not Phil Evans been elected president of the club? The votes were exactly divided between Uncle Prudent and him. Twenty times there had been a scrutiny, and twenty times the majority had not declared for either one of the other. The position was embarrassing, and it might have lasted for the lifetime of the candidates.

One of the members of the club then proposed a way out of the difficulty. This was Jem Chip, the treasurer of the Weldon Institute. Chip was a confirmed vegetarian, a proscriber of all animal nourishment, of all fermented liquors, half a Mussulman, half a Brahman. On this occasion Jem Chip was supported by another member of the club, William T. Forbes, the manager of a large factory where they made glucose by treating rags with sulphuric acid. A man of good standing was this William T. Forbes, the father of two charming girls—Miss Dorothy, called Doll, and Miss Martha, called Mat, who gave the tone to the best society in Philadelphia.

It followed, then, on the proposition of Jem Chip, supported by William T. Forbes and others, that it was decided to elect the president

"on the centre point."

This mode of election can be applied in all cases when it is desired to elect the most worthy; and a number of Americans of high intelligence are already thinking of employing it in the nomination of the President of the Republic of the United States.

On two boards of perfect whiteness a black line is traced. The length of each of these lines is mathematically the same, for they have been determined with as much accuracy as the base of the first triangle in a trigonometrical survey. That done, the two boards were erected on the same day in the centre of the conference room, and the two candidates, each armed with a fine needle, marched towards the board that had fallen to his lot. The man who planted his needle nearest the centre of the line would be proclaimed President of the Weldon Institute.

The operation must be done at once—no guide-marks or trial-shots allowed; nothing but sureness of eye. The man must have a compass in his eye, as the saying goes; that was all.

Uncle Prudent had approached the centre moment as Phil Evans did his. Then there began the measurement to discover which of the two competitors had most nearly approached the centre.

Wonderful! Such had been the precision of the shots that the measures gave no appreciable difference. If they were not exactly in the mathematical centre of the line, the distance between the needles was so small as to be invisible to the naked eye.

The meeting was much embarrassed.

Fortunately one of the members, Truck Milnor, insisted that the measurements should be remade by means of a rule graduated by the micrometrical machine of M. Perreaux, which can divide a millimetre into fifteen hundred parts. This rule, dividing the fifteen-hundredths of a millimetre with a diamond splinter, was brought to bear on the lines, and on reading the divisions through a microscope the following were the results:—

Unce Prudent had approached the centre within less than six fifteen-hundredths of a millimetre. Phil Evans was within nine fifteen-hundredths.

And that is why Phil Evans was only secretary of the Weldon Institute, whereas Uncle Prudent was president. A difference of three fifteen-hundredths of a millimetre! And on account of it Phil Evans vowed against Uncle Prudent one of those hatreds which are none the less fierce for being latent.

The meeting was much embarrassed.

The Clipper of the Clouds

CHAPTER III.

A VISITOR IS ANNOUNCED

THE many experiments made during this last quarter of the nineteenth century have given considerable impetus to the question of guidable balloons. The cars furnished with propellers attached in 1852 to the aerostats of the elongated form introduced by Henry Giffard, the machines of Dupuy de Lome in 1872, of the Tissandier brothers in 1883, and of Captains Krebs and Renard in 1884, yielded many important results. But if these machines, moving in a medium heavier than themselves, manoeuvring under the propulsion of a screw, working at an angle to the direction of the wind, and even against the wind, to return to their point of departure, had been really "guidable," they had only succeeded under very favourable conditions. In large covered halls their success was perfect. In a calm atmosphere they did very well. In a light wind of five or six yards a second they still moved. But nothing practical had been obtained. Against a miller's wind—nine yards a second—the machines had remained almost stationary. Against a fresh breeze—eleven yards a second—they would have advanced backwards. In a storm—twenty-seven to thirty-three yards a second—they would have been blown about like a feather. In a hurricane —sixty yards a second—they would have run the risk of being dashed to pieces. And in one of those cyclones which exceed a hundred yards a second not a fragment of them would have been left. It remained, then, even after the striking experiments of Captains Krebs and Renard, that though guidable aerostats had gained a little speed, they could not be kept going in a moderate breeze. Hence the impossibility of making practical use of this mode of aerial locomotion.

With regard to the means employed to give the aerostat its motion a great deal of progress had been made. For the steam-engines of Henry Giffard, and the muscular force of Dupuy de Lome, electric motors had gradually been substituted. The batteries of bichromate of potassium of the Tissandier brothers had given a speed of four yards a second. The dynamo-electric machines of Captains Krebs and Renard had developed a force of twelve-horse power and yielded a speed of six and a half yards per second.

With regard to this motor, engineers and electricians had been approaching more and more to that desideratum which is known as a steam-horse in a watch-case. Gradually the results of the pile of which Captains Krebs and Renard had kept the secret had been surpassed, and aeronauts had become able to avail themselves of motors whose lightness increased at the same time as their power.

In this there was much to encourage those who believed in the utilization of guidable balloons. But yet how many good people there are who refuse to admit the possibility of such a thing! If the aerostat finds support in the air it belongs to the medium in which it moves; under such conditions, how can its mass, which offers so much resistance to the currents of the atmosphere, make its way against the wind?

In this struggle of the inventors after a light and powerful motor, the Americans had most nearly attained what they sought. A dynamo-electric apparatus, in which a new pile was employed the composition of which was still a mystery, had been bought from its inventor, a Boston chemist up to then unknown. Calculations made with the greatest care, diagrams drawn with the utmost exactitude, showed that by means of this apparatus driving a screw of given dimensions a displacement could be obtained of from twenty to twenty-two yards a second.

Now this was magnificent!

"And it is not dear," said Uncle Prudent, as he handed to the inventor in return for his formal receipt the last instalment of the hundred thousand paper dollars he had paid for his invention.

Immediately the Weldon Institute set to work. When there comes along a project of practical utility the money leaps nimbly enough from American pockets. The funds flowed in even without its being necessary to form a syndicate. Three hundred thousand dollars came into the club's account at the first appeal. The work began under the superintendence of the most celebrated aeronaut of the United States, Harry W. Tinder, immortalized by three of his ascents out of a thousand, one in which he rose to a height of twelve thousand yards, higher than Gay Lussac, Coxwell, Sivet,

The third, which ended in a frightful fall.

Crocé-Spinelli, Tissandier, Glaisher; another in which he had crossed America from New York to San Francisco, exceeding by many hundred leagues the journeys of Nadar, Godard, and others, to say nothing of that of John Wise, who accomplished eleven hundred and fifty miles from St. Louis to Jefferson county; the third, which ended in a frightful fall from fifteen hundred feet at the cost of a slight sprain in the right thumb, while the less fortunate Pilâtre de Rozier fell only seven hundred feet, and yet killed himself on the spot!

At the time this story begins the Weldon Institute had got their work well in hand. In the Turner yard at Philadelphia there reposed an enormous aerostat, whose strength had been tried by highly compressed air. It well merited the name of the monster balloon.

How large was Nadar's Géant? Six thousand cubic metres. How large was John Wise's balloon? Twenty thousand cubic metres. How large was the Giffard balloon at the 1878 Exhibition? Twenty-five thousand cubic metres. Compare these three aerostats with the aerial machine of the Weldon Institute, whose volume amounted to forty thousand cubic metres, and you will understand why Uncle Prudent and his colleagues were so justifiably proud of it.

This balloon not being destined for the exploration of the higher strata of the atmosphere, was not called the Excelsior, a name which is rather too much held in honour among the citizens of America. No! It was called, simply, the Go-ahead, and all it had to do was to justify its name by going ahead obediently to the wishes of its commander.

The dynamo-electric machine, according to the patent purchased by the Weldon Institute, was nearly ready. In less than six weeks the Go-ahead would start for its first cruise through space.

But, as we have seen, all the mechanical difficulties had not been overcome. Many evenings had been devoted to discussing, not the form of its screw not its dimensions, but whether it ought to be put behind, as the Tissandier brothers had done, or before as Captains Krebs and Renard had done. It is unnecessary to add that the partisans of the two systems had almost come to blows. The group of "Beforists" were equalled in number by the group of "Behindists." Uncle Prudent, who ought to have given the casting vote—Uncle Prudent, brought up doubtless in the school of Professor Buridan—could not bring himself to decide.

Hence the impossibility of getting the screw into place. The dispute might last for some time, unless the Government interfered. But in the United States the Government meddles with private affairs as little as it possibly can. And it is right.

Things were in this state at this meeting on the 13th of June, which threatened to end in a riot—insults exchanged, fisticuffs succeeding the insults, cane thrashings succeeding the fisticuffs, revolver shots succeeding the cane thrashings—when at thirty-seven minutes past eight there occurred a diversion.

The porter of the Weldon Institute coolly and calmly, like a policeman amid the storm of the meeting, approached the presidential desk. On it he placed a card. He awaited the orders that Uncle Prudent found it convenient to give.

Uncle Prudent turned on the steam whistle, which did duty for the presidential bell, for even the Kremlin clock would have struck in vain! But the tumult slackened not.

Then the president removed his hat. Thanks to this extreme measure a semi-silence was obtained.

"A communication!" said Uncle Prudent, after taking a huge pinch from the snuff-box which never left him.

"Speak up!" answered eighty-nine voices, accidentally in agreement on this one point.

"A stranger, my dear colleagues, asks to be admitted to the meeting."

"Never!" replied every voice.

"He desires to prove to us, it would appear," continued Uncle Prudent, "that to believe in guiding balloons is to believe in the absurdest of Utopias!"

"Let him in! Let him in!"

"What is the name of this singular personage?" asked secretary Phil Evans.

"Robur," replied Uncle Prudent.

"Robur! Robur! Robur!" yelled the assembly. And the welcome accorded so quickly to the curious name was chiefly due to the Weldon Institute hoping to vent its exasperation on the head of him who bore it!

The Clipper of the Clouds

CHAPTER IV.

IN WHICH A NEW CHARACTER APPEARS

"CITIZENS of the United States! My name is Robur. I am worthy of the name! I am forty years old, although I look but thirty, and I have a constitution of iron, a healthy vigour that nothing can shake, a muscular strength that few can equal, and a digestion that would be thought first-class even in an ostrich!"

They were listening! Yes! The riot was quelled at once by the totally unexpected fashion of the speech. Was this fellow a madman or a hoaxer? Whoever he was, he kept his audience in hand. There was not a whisper in the meeting in which but a few minutes ago the storm was in full fury.

And Robur looked the man he said he was. Of middle height and geometric breadth, his figure was a regular trapezium with the greatest of its parallel sides formed by the line of his shoulders. On this line attached by a robust neck there rose an enormous spheroidal head. The head of what animal did it resemble from the point of view of passional analogy? The head of a bull; but a bull with an intelligent face. Eyes which at the least opposition would glow like coals of fire; and above them a permanent contraction of the superciliary muscle, an invariable sign of extreme energy. Short hair, slightly woolly, with metallic reflections; large chest rising and falling like a smith's bellows; arms, hands, legs, feet, all worthy of the trunk. No moustaches, no whiskers, but a large American goatee, revealing the attachments of the jaw whose masseter muscles were evidently of formidable strength. It has been calculated—what has not been calculated?—that the pressure of the jaw of an ordinary crocodile can reach four hundred atmospheres, while that of a hound can only amount to one hundred. From this the following curious formula has been deduced:—If a kilogram of dog produces eight kilograms of masseteric force, a kilogram of crocodile could produce twelve. Now, a kilogram of the aforesaid Robur would not produce less than ten, so that he came between the dog and the crocodile.

From what country did this remarkable specimen come? It was difficult to say. One thing was noticeable, and that was that he expressed himself fluently in English without a trace of the drawling twang that distinguishes the Yankees of New England.

He continued:—

"And now, honourable citizens, for my mental faculties. You see before you an engineer whose nerves are in no way inferior to his muscles. I have no fear of anything or anybody. I have a strength of will that has never had to yield. When I have decided on a thing, all America, all the world, may strive in vain to keep me from it. When I have an idea I allow no one to share it, and I do not permit any contradiction. I insist on these details, honourable citizens, because it is necessary you should quite understand me. Perhaps you think I am talking too much about myself? It does not matter if you do! And now consider a little before you interrupt me, as I have come to tell you something that you may not be particularly pleased to hear."

A sound as of the surf on the beach began to rise along the first rows of seats—a sign that the sea would not be long in getting stormy again.

"Speak, stranger!" said Uncle Prudent, who had some difficulty in restraining himself.

And Robur spoke as follows, without troubling himself any more about his audience.

"Yes! I know it well! After a century of experiments that have led to nothing, and trials giving no result, there still exist ill-balanced minds who believe in guiding balloons. They imagine that a motor of some sort, electric or otherwise, might be applied to their pretentious skin bags which are at the mercy of every current in the atmosphere. They persuade themselves that they can be masters of an aerostat as they can be masters of a ship on the surface of the sea. Because a few inventors in calm or nearly calm weather have succeeded in working on an angle with the wind, or even beating to windward in a gentle breeze, they think that the steering of aerial apparatus lighter than the air is a practicable matter. Well, now, look here; You hundred, who believe in the realization of your dreams, are throwing your thousands of dollars not into water but into space! You are fighting the impossible!"

Strange it was that at this affirmation the members of the Weldon Institute did not move. Had they become as deaf as they were patient?

169

"My name is Robur!"

Or were they reserving themselves to see how far this audacious contradicter would dare to go?

Robur continued:—

"What? A balloon! When to obtain the raising of a couple of pounds you require a cubic yard of gas. A balloon pretending to resist the wind by aid of its mechanism, when the pressure of a light breeze on a vessel's sails is not less than that of four hundred horse-power; when in the accident at the Tay Bridge you saw the storm produce a pressure of eight and a half hundredweight on a square yard. A balloon, when on such a system nature has never constructed anything flying, whether furnished with wings like birds, or membranes like certain fish, or certain mammalia—"

"Mammalia?" exclaimed one of the members of the club.

"Yes! Mammalia! The bat, which flies, if I am not mistaken! Is the gentleman unaware that this flyer is a mammal? Did he ever see an omelette made of bat's eggs?"

And the interrupter reserved himself for future interruption, and Robur resumed:—

"But does that mean that man is to give up the conquest of the air, and the transformation of the domestic and political manners of the old world, by the use of this admirable means of locomotion? By no means. As he has become master of the seas with the ship, by the oar, the sail, the wheel, and the screw, so shall he become master of atmospherical space by apparatus heavier than the air—for it must be heavier to be stronger than the air!"

And then the assembly exploded. What a broadside of yells escaped from all these mouths, aimed at Robur like the muzzles of so many guns! Was not this hurling a declaration of war into the very camp of the balloonists? Was not this a stirring up of strife between "the lighter" and "the heavier" than air?

Robur did not even frown. With folded arms he waited bravely till silence was obtained.

By a gesture Uncle Prudent ordered the firing to cease.

"Yes," continued Robur, "the future is for the flying-machine. The air affords a solid fulcrum. If you will give a column of air an ascensional movement of forty-five metres a second, a man can support himself on the top of it if the soles of his boots have a superficies of only the eighth of a square metre. And if the speed be increased to ninety metres, he can walk on it with naked feet. Or if, by means of a screw, you drive a mass of air at this speed, you get the same result."

What Robur said had been said before by all the partisans of aviation, whose work slowly but surely is leading on to the solution of the problem. To Ponton d'Amécourt, La Landelle, Nadar, De Luzy, De Louvrié, Liais, Beleguir, Moreau, the brothers Richard, Babinet, Jobert, Du Temple, Salives, Penaud, De Villeneuve, Gauchot and Tatin, Michel Loup, Edison, Planavergne, and so many others, belongs the honour of having brought forward ideas of such simplicity. Abandoned and resumed times without number, they are sure some day to triumph. To the enemies of aviation, who urge that the bird only sustains himself by warming the air he strikes, their answer is ready. Have they not proved that an eagle weighing five kilograms would have to fill fifty cubic metres with his warm fluid merely to sustain himself in space?

This is what Robur demonstrated with undeniable logic amid the uproar that arose on all sides. And in conclusion these are the words he hurled in the faces of the balloonists:—

"With your aerostats you can do nothing—you will arrive at nothing—you dare do nothing! The boldest of your aeonauts, John Wise, although he has made an aerial voyage of twelve hundred miles above the American continent, has had to give up his project of crossing the Atlantic! And you have not advanced a step—not one step—towards your end."

"Sir," said the president, who in vain endeavoured to keep himself cool, "you forget what was said by our immortal Franklin at the first appearance of the fire balloon, 'It is but a child, but it will grow!' It was but a child, and it has grown."

"No, Mr. President, it has not grown! It has got fatter—and that is not the same thing!"

This was a direct attack on the Weldon Institute, which had decreed, helped, and paid for the making of a monster balloon. And so propositions of the following kind began to fly about the room:—

"Turn him out!"

"Throw him off the platform:"

"Prove that he is heavier than the air!"

And many others.

But these were only words, not means to an end.

Robur remained impassible, and continued, "There is no progress for your aerostats, my citizen balloonists; progress, is for flying machines. The bird flies, and he is not a balloon, he is a piece of mechanism!"

"Yes, he flies!" exclaimed the fiery Bat. T. Fynn; "but he flies against all the laws of mechanics."

"Indeed!" said Robur, shrugging his shoulders.

And, resuming, "Since we have begun the study of the flight of large and small birds one simple idea has prevailed—to imitate nature, which never makes mistakes. Between the albatross, which gives hardly ten beats of the wing per minute, between the pelican, which gives seventy—"

"Seventy-one," said the voice of a scoffer.

"And the bee, which gives one hundred and ninety-two per second—"

"One hundred and ninety-three!" said the facetious individual.

"And the common house-fly, which gives three hundred and thirty—"

"And a half!"

"And the mosquito, which gives millions—"

"No, milliards!"

But Robur, the interrupted, interrupted not his demonstration.

"Between these different rates—" he continued.

"There is a difference," said a voice.

"There is a possibility of finding a practical solution. When De Lucy showed that the stag-beetle, an insect weighing only two grammes, could lift a weight of four hundred grammes, or two hundred times its own weight, the problem of aviation was solved. Besides, it has been shown that the wing surface decreases in proportion to the increase of the size and weight of the animal. Hence we can look forward to such contrivances—"

"Which would never fly!" said secretary Phil Evans.

"Which have flown, and which will fly," said Robur, without being in the least disconcerted, "and which we can call streophores, helicopters, orthopters—or, in imitation of the word 'nef,' which comes from 'navis,' call them from 'avis,' 'efs,'—by means of which man will become the master of space. The helix—"

"Ah, the helix!" replied Phil Evans. "But the bird has no helix; that we know!"

"So," said Robur; "but Penaud has shown that in reality the bird makes a helix, and its flight is helicopteral. And the motor of the future is the screw—"

"From such a maladee
Saint Helix keep us free!"

sung out one of the members, who had accidentally hit upon the air from Herold's "Zampa."

And they all took up the chorus:—

"From such a maladee
Saint Helix keep us free!"

with such intonations and variations as would have made the French composer groan in his grave.

As the last notes died away in a frightful discord Uncle Prudent took advantage of the momentary calm to say,—

"Stranger, up to now, we let you speak without interruption."

It seemed that for the president of the Weldon Institute shouts, yells, and catcalls were not interruptions, but only an exchange of arguments.

"But I may remind you, all the same, that the theory of aviation is condemned beforehand, and rejected by the majority of American and foreign engineers. It is a system which was the cause of the death of the Flying Saracen at Constantinople, of the monk Volador at Lisbon, of De Letur in 1852, of De Groof in 1864, besides the victims I forget since the mythological Icarus—"

"A system," replied Robur, "no more to be condemned than that whose martyrology contains the names of Pilâtre de Rozier at Calais, of Blanchard at Paris, of Donaldson and Grimwood in Lake Michigan, of Sivel and of Crocé-Spinelli of Eloy, and so many others whom it takes good care to forget."

This was a counter-thrust with a vengeance.

"Besides," continued Robur, "with your balloons as good as you can make them you will never obtain any speed worth mentioning. It would take you ten years to go round the world —and a flying-machine could do it in a week!"

Here arose a new tempest of protests and denials, which lasted for three long minutes. And then Phil Evans took up the word.

"Mr. Aviator," he said, "you who talk so much of the benefits of aviation, have you ever aviated?"

"I have."

"And made the conquest of the air?"

"Not unlikely."

"Hooray for Robur the Conqueror!" shouted an ironical voice.

"Well, yes! Robur the Conqueror! I accept the name and I will bear it, for I have a right to it."

"We beg to doubt it!" said Jem Chip.

"Gentlemen," said Robur, and his brows knit, "when I have just seriously stated a serious thing I do not permit any one to reply to me by a flat denial, and I shall be glad to know the name of the interrupter."

"My name is Chip, and I am a vegetarian."

"You are not Americans."

"Citizen Chip," said Robur, "I knew that vegetarians had longer alimentary canals than other men—a good foot longer at the least. That is quite long enough; and so do not compel me to make yours any longer by beginning at your ears and—"

"Throw him out."

"Into the street with him!"

"Limb him!"

"Lynch him!"

"Helix him!"

The rage of the balloonists burst forth at last.

They rushed at the platform. Robur disappeared amid a sheaf of hands that were thrown about as if caught in a storm. In vain the steam-whistle screamed its fanfares on to the assembly. Philadelphia might well think that a fire was devouring one of its quarters and that all the waters of the Schuylkill could not put it out.

Suddenly there was a recoil in the tumult.

Robur had put his hands into his pockets and now held them out at the front ranks of the infuriated mob.

In each hand was one of those American institutions known as revolvers which the mere pressure of the fingers is enough to fire—pocket mitrailleuses in fact.

And taking advantage not only of the recoil of his assailants but also of the silence which accompanied it,—

"Decidedly," said he, "it was not Amerigo that discovered the New World, it was Cabot! You are not Americans, citizen balloonists! You are only Cabo—"

Four or five pistol-shots cracked out, fired into space. They hurt nobody. Amid the smoke the engineer vanished; and when it had thinned away there was no trace of him. Robur the conqueror had flown, as if some apparatus of aviation had borne him into the air.

The Clipper of the Clouds

CHAPTER V.

ANOTHER DISAPPEARANCE

THIS was not the first occasion on which, at the end of their stormy discussions, the members of the Weldon Institute had filled Walnut Street and its neighbourhood with their tumult. Several times had the inhabitants complained of the noisy way in which the proceedings ended, and more than once had the policemen had to interfere to clear the thoroughfare for the passers-by, who for the most part were supremely indifferent on this question of aerial navigation. But never before had the tumult attained such proportions, never had the complaints been better founded, never had the intervention of the police been more necessary.

But there was some excuse for the members of the Weldon Institute. They had been attacked in their own house. To these enthusiasts for "lighter than air" a no less enthusiast for "heavier than air" had said things absolutely abhorrent. And at the moment they were about to treat him as he deserved he had disappeared.

And so they cried aloud for vengeance. To leave such insults unpunished was impossible to all with American blood in their veins. Had not the sons of Amerigo been called the sons of Cabot? Was not that an insult as unpardonable as it happened to be just—historically?

The members of the club in several groups rushed down Walnut Street, then into the adjoining streets, and then all over the neighbourhood. They woke up the house-holders; they compelled them to search their houses, prepared to indemnify them later on for the outrage on their privacy. Vain were all their trouble and searching. Robur was nowhere to be found; there was no trace of him. He might have gone off in the Go-ahead, the balloon of the Institute, for all they could tell. After an hour's hunt the members had to give in and separate, not before they had agreed to extend their search over the whole territory of the twin Americas that form the new continent.

By eleven o'clock quiet had been restored in the neighbourhood of Walnut Street. Philadelphia was able to sink again into that sound sleep which is the privilege of non-manufacturing towns. The different members of the club parted to seek their respective houses. To mention the most distinguished amongst them, William T. Forbes sought his large sugar establishment, where Miss Doll and Miss Mat had prepared for him his evening tea, sweetened with his own glucose. Truck Milnor took the road to his factory in the distant suburb, where the engines worked day and night. Treasurer Jim Chip, publicly accused of possessing an alimentary canal twelve inches longer than that of other men, returned to the vegetable soup that was waiting for him.

Two of the most important balloonists—two only—did not seem to think of returning so soon to their domicile. They availed themselves of the opportunity to discuss the question with more than usual acrimony. These were the irreconcilables, Uncle Prudent and Phil Evans, the president and secretary of the Weldon Institute.

At the door of the club the valet Frycollin waited for Uncle Prudent, his master, and at last he went after him, though he cared but little for the subject which had set the two colleagues at loggerheads.

It is only by an euphemism that the verb "discuss" can be used to express the way in which the duet between the president and secretary was being performed. As a matter of fact they were in full wrangle with an energy born of their old rivalry.

"No, sir, no," said Phil Evans. "If I had had the honour of being president of the Weldon Institute, there never, no, never, would have been such a scandal."

"And what would you have done, if you had had the honour?" demanded Uncle Prudent.

"I would have stopped the insulter before he had opened his mouth."

"It seems to me it would have been impossible to stop him until he had opened his mouth."

"Not in America, sir; not in America."

And exchanging such observations, increasing in bitterness as they went, they walked on through the streets farther and farther from their homes, until they reached a part of the city whence they had to go a long way round to get back.

Frycollin followed, by no means at ease to see his master plunging into such deserted spots. He did not like deserted spots, particularly after midnight. In fact the darkness was profound

They had reached the centre of a wide clump of trees.

and the moon was only a thin crescent just beginning its monthly life.

Frycollin kept a look-out to the left and right of him to see if he was followed. And he fancied he could see five or six hulking fellows dogging his footsteps.

Instinctively he drew nearer to his master, but not for the world would he have dared to break in on the conversation of which the fragments reached him.

In short it so chanced that the president and secretary of the Weldon Institute found themselves on the road to Fairmont Park. In the full heat of their dispute they crossed the Schuylkill river by the famous iron bridge. They met only a few belated wayfarers, and pressed on across a wide open tract where the immense prairie was broken every now and then by the patches of thick woodland which make the park different to any other in the world.

There Frycollin's terror became acute, particularly as he saw the five or six shadows gliding after him across the Schuylkill bridge. The pupils of his eyes broadened out to the circumference of his iris, and his limbs seemed to diminish as if endowed with the contractility peculiar to the mollusca and certain of the articulata; for Frycollin, the valet, was an egregious coward.

He was a pure South Carolina negro, with the head of a fool and the carcase of an imbecile. Being only one-and-twenty, he had never been a slave, not even by birth, but that made no difference to him. Grinning and greedy and idle, and a magnificent poltroon, he had been the servant of Uncle Prudent for about three years. Over and over again had his master threatened to kick him out, but had kept him on for fear of doing worse. With a master ever ready to venture on the most audacious enterprises, Frycollin's cowardice had brought him many arduous trials. But he had some compensation. Very little had been said about his gluttony, and still less about his laziness.

Ah, Valet Frycollin, if you could only have read the future! Why, oh why, Frycollin, did you not remain at Boston with the Sneffels, and not have given them up when they talked of going to Switzerland? Was not that a much more suitable place for you than this of Uncle Prudent's, where danger was daily welcomed.

But here he was, and his master had become used to his faults. He had one advantage, and that was a consideration. Although he was a negro by birth he did not speak like a negro, and nothing is so irritating as that hateful jargon in which all the pronouns are possessive and all the verbs infinitive.

Let it be understood, then, that Frycollin was a thorough coward.

And now it was midnight, and the pale crescent of the moon began to sink in the west behind the trees in the park. The rays streaming fitfully through the branches made the shadows darker than ever.

Frycollin looked around him anxiously.

"Brrr!" he said. "There are those fellows there all the time. Positively they are getting nearer! . . . Master Uncle!" he shouted.

It was thus he called the president of the Weldon Institute, and thus did the president desire to be called.

At the moment the dispute of the rivals had reached its maximum, and as they hurled their epithets at each other they walked faster and faster, and drew farther and farther away from the Schuylkill bridge.

They had reached the centre of a wide clump of trees, whose summits were just tipped by the parting rays of the moon. Beyond the trees was a large clearing—an oval field, a complete amphitheatre. Not a hillock was there to hinder the gallop of the horses, not a bush to stop the view of the spectators.

And if Uncle Prudent and Phil Evans had not been so deep in their dispute, and had used their eyes as they were accustomed to, they would have found the clearing was not in its usual state. Was it a flour-mill that had anchored on it during the night? It looked like it, with its wings and sails—motionless and mysterious in the gathering gloom.

But neither the president nor the secretary of the Weldon Institute noticed the strange modification in the landscape of Fairmont Park; and neither did Frycollin. It seemed to him that the thieves were approaching, and preparing for their attack; and he was seized with convulsive fear, paralyzed in his limbs, with every hair he could boast on the bristle. His terror was extreme.

His knees bent under him, but he had just strength enough to exclaim for the last time,—

"Master Uncle! Master Uncle!"

"What is the matter with you?" asked Uncle Prudent. Perhaps the disputants would not have been sorry to have relieved their fury at the expense of the unfortunate valet. But they had no time; and neither even had he time to answer.

A whistle was heard. A flash of electric light shot across the clearing.

A signal, doubtless? The moment had come for the deed of violence!

In less time than it takes to tell, six men came leaping across from under the trees, two on to

They were carried bodily off across the clearing.

Uncle Prudent, two on to Phil Evans, two on to Frycollin—there was no need for the two last, for the negro was incapable of defending himself.

The president and secretary of the Weldon Institute, although taken by surprise, would have resisted.

They had neither time nor strength to do so. In a second they were rendered speechless by a gag, blind by a bandage, thrown down, pinioned and carried bodily off across the clearing. What could they think except that they had fallen into the hands of people who intended to rob them? The people did nothing of the sort, however. They did not even touch Uncle Prudent's pockets, although, according to his custom, they were full of paper dollars.

Within a minute of the attack, without a word being passed, Uncle Prudent, Phil Evans, and Frycollin felt themselves laid gently down, not on the grass, but on a sort of plank that creaked beneath them. They were laid down side by side.

A door was shut; and the grating of a bolt in a staple told them that they were prisoners.

Then there came a continuous buzzing, a quivering, a frrrr, with the rrr unending.

And that was the only sound that broke the quiet of the night.

*   *   *   *   *   *   *

Great was the excitement next morning in Philadelphia! Very early was it known what had passed at the meeting of the Institute. Every one knew of the appearance of the mysterious engineer named Robur—Robur the Conqueror—and the tumult among the balloonists, and his inexplicable disappearance.

But it was quite another thing when all the town heard that the president and secretary of the club had also disappeared during the night.

Long and keen was the search in the city and neighbourhood! Useless! The newspapers of Philadelphia, the newspapers of Pennsylvania, the newspapers of the United States reported the facts and explained them in a hundred ways, not one of which was the right one. Heavy rewards were offered, and placards were pasted up, but all to no purpose. The earth seemed to have opened and bodily swallowed the president and secretary of the Weldon Institute.

The Clipper of the Clouds

CHAPTER VI.

THE PRESIDENT AND SECRETARY SUSPEND HOSTILITIES

A BANDAGE over the eyes, a gag in the mouth, a cord round the wrists, a cord round the ankles, unable to see, to speak, or to move. Uncle Prudent, Phil Evans, and Frycollin were anything but pleased with their position. Knowing not who had seized them, nor in what they had been thrown like parcels in a goods waggon, nor where they were, not what was reserved for them—it was enough to exasperate even the most patient of the ovine race, and we know that the members of the Weldon Institute were not precisely sheep as far as patience went. With his violence of character we can easily imagine how Uncle Prudent felt.

One thing was evident, that Phil Evans and he would find it difficult to attend the club next evening.

As to Frycollin, with his eyes shut and his mouth closed; it was impossible for him to think of anything. He was more dead than alive.

For an hour the position of the prisoners remained unchanged. No one came to visit them, or to give them that liberty of movement and speech of which they lay in such need. They were reduced to stifled sighs, to grunts emitted over and under their gags, to everything that betrayed anger kept dumb and fury imprisoned, or rather bound down. Then after many fruitless efforts they remained for some time as though lifeless. Then as the sense of sight was denied them they tried by their sense of hearing to obtain some indication of the nature of this disquieting state of things. But in vain did they seek for any other sound than an interminable and inexplicable f-r-r-r which seemed to envelop them in a quivering atmosphere.

At last something happened. Phil Evans, regaining his coolness, managed to slacken the cord which bound his wrists. Little by little the knot slipped, his fingers slipped over each other, and his hands regained their usual freedom.

A vigorous rubbing restored the circulation. A moment after he had slipped off the bandage which bound his eyes, taken the gag out of his mouth, and cut the cords round his ankles with his knife. An American who has not a bowie-knife in his pocket is no longer an American.

But if Phil Evans had regained the power of moving and speaking, that was all. His eyes were useless to him—at present at any rate. The prison was quite dark, though about six feet above him a feeble gleam of light came in through a kind of loophole.

As may be imagined, Phil Evans did not hesitate to at once set free his rival. A few cuts with the bowie settled the knots which bound him foot and hand.

Immediately Uncle Prudent rose to his knees and snatched away his bandage and his gag.

"Thanks," said he, in stifled voice.

"No!" said the other, "no thanks."

"Phil Evans?"

"Uncle Prudent?"

"Here we are no longer the president and secretary of the Weldon Institute. We are adversaries no more."

"You are right," answered Evans. "We are now only two men agreed to avenge ourselves on a third whose attempt deserves severe reprisals. And this third is—"

"Robur!"

"It is Robur!"

On this point both were absolutely in accord. On this subject there was no fear of dispute.

"And your servant?" said Evans, pointing to Frycollin, who was puffing like a grampus. "We must set him free."

"Not yet," said Uncle Prudent. "He would overwhelm us with his jeremiads, and we have something else to do than abuse each other."

"What is that Uncle Prudent?"

"To save ourselves if possible."

"And even if it is impossible."

"You are right; even if it is impossible."

There could be no doubt that this kidnapping was due to Robur, for an ordinary thief would have relieved them of their watches, jewellery, and purses, and thrown their bodies into the Schuylkill with a good gash in their throats instead of throwing them to the bottom of— Of what? That was a serious question, which would have to be answered before attempting an escape with any chance of success.

"Phil Evans," began Uncle Prudent, "if, when we came away from out meeting, instead of indulging in amenities to which we need not recur, we had kept our eyes more open, this would not have happened. Had we remained in the streets of Philadelphia there would have been none of this. Evidently Robur foresaw what would happen at the club, and had placed some of his bandits on guard at the door. When we left Walnut Street these fellows must have watched us and followed us, and when we imprudently ventured into Fairmont Park they went in for their little game.''

"Agreed," said Evans. "We were wrong not to go straight home."

"It is always wrong not to be right," said Prudent.

Here a long-drawn sigh escaped from the darkest corner of the prison.

"What is that?" asked Evans.

"Nothing! Frycollin is dreaming."

"Between the moment we were seized a few steps out into the clearing and the moment we were thrown in here only two minutes elapsed. It is thus evident that these people did not take us out of Fairmount Park.

"And if they had done so we should have felt we were being moved."

"Undoubtedly: and consequently we must be in some vehicle, perhaps some of those long prairie waggons, or some show-caravan—"

"Evidently! For if we were in a boat moored on the Schuylkill we should have noticed the movement due to the current—"

"That is so; and as we are still in the clearing, I think that now is the time to get away, and we can return later to settle with this Robur—"

"And make him pay for this attempt on the liberty of two citizens of the United States."

"And he shall pay pretty dearly!"

"But who is this man? Where does he come from? Is he English, or German, or French—"

"He is a scoundrel, that is enough!" said Uncle Prudent. "Now to work."

And then the two men, with their hands stretched out and their fingers wide apart, began to feel round the walls to find a joint or crack.

Nothing. Nothing; not even at the door. It was closely shut and it was impossible to shoot back the lock. All that could be done was to make a hole, and escape through the hole. It remained to be seen if the knives could cut into the walls.

"But whence comes this never-ending rustling?" asked Evans, who was much impressed at the continuous f-r-r-r.

"The wind, doubtless," said Uncle Prudent.

"The wind! But I thought the night was quite calm."

"So it was. But if it isn't the wind, what can it be?"

Phil Evans got out the best blade of his knife and set to work on the wall near the door. Perhaps he might make a hole which would enable him to open it from the outside should it be only bolted or should the key have been left in the lock.

He worked away for some minutes. The only result was to nip up his knife, to snip off its point, and transform what was left of the blade into a saw.

"Doesn't it cut?" asked Uncle Prudent.

"No."

"Is the wall made of sheet iron?"

"No; it gives no metallic sound when you hit it."

"Is it of ironwood?"

"No; it isn't iron and it isn't wood."

"What is it then?"

"Impossible to say. But, anyhow, steel doesn't touch it."

Uncle Prudent, in a sudden outburst of fury, began to rave and stamp on the sonorous planks, while his hands sought to strangle an imaginary Robur.

"Be calm, Prudent, be calm! You have a try."

Uncle Prudent had a try, but the bowie-knife could do nothing against a wall which its best blades could not even scratch. The wall seemed to be made of crystal.

So it became evident that all flight was impracticable except through the door, and for a time they must resign themselves to their fate —not a very pleasant thing for the Yankee temperament, and very much to the disgust of these eminently practical men. But this conclusion was not arrived at without many objurgations and loud-sounding phrases hurled at this Robur—who, from what had been seen of him at the Weldon Institute, was not the sort of man to trouble himself much about them.

Suddenly Frycollin began to give unequivocal signs of being unwell. He began to writhe in a most lamentable fashion, either with cramp in his stomach or in his limbs; and Uncle Prudent, thinking it his duty to put an end to these gymnastics, cut the cords that bound him.

He had cause to be sorry for it. Immediately there was poured forth an interminable litany, in which the terrors of fear were mingled with the tortures of hunger. Frycollin was no worse in his brain than in his stomach, and it would have been difficult to decide to which organ the chief cause of the trouble should be assigned.

"Frycollin!" said Uncle Prudent.

"Master Uncle! Master Uncle!" answered the negro between two of his lugubrious howls.

"It is possible that we are doomed to die of

"It is unbreakable glass."

hunger in this prison, but we have made up our minds not to succumb until we have availed ourselves of every means of alimentation to prolong our lives.''

"To eat me?'' exclaimed Frycollin.

"As is always done with a negro under such circumstances! So you had better not make yourself too obvious—''

"Or you'll have your bones picked!'' said Evans.

And as Frycollin saw he might be used to prolong two existences more precious than his own, he contented himself thenceforth with groaning on the quiet.

The time went on, and all attempts to force the door or get through the wall proved fruitless. What the wall was made of was impossible to say. It was not metal; it was not wood; it was not stone. And all the cell seemed to be made of the same stuff. When they stamped on the floor it gave a peculiar sound that Uncle Prudent found it difficult to describe; and the floor seemed to sound hollow, as if it was not resting directly on the ground of the clearing. And the inexplicable f-r-r-r-r seemed to sweep along below it. All of which was rather alarming.

"Uncle Prudent!'' said Phil Evans.

"Well?''

"Do you think our prison has been moved at all?''

"Not that I know of.''

"Because when we were first caught I distinctly remember the fresh fragrance of the grass and the resinous odour of the park trees. While now, when I take in a good sniff of the air, it seems as though all that had gone.''

"So it has.''

"Why?''

"We cannot say why unless we admit that the prison has moved; and I say again that if the prison had moved, either as a vehicle on the road or a boat on the stream, we should have felt it.''

Here Frycollin gave vent to a long groan, which might have been taken for his last had he not followed it up with several more.

"I expect Robur will soon have us brought before him,'' said Phil Evans.

"I hope so,'' said Uncle Prudent. "And I shall tell him—''

"What?''

"That he began by being rude and ended in being unbearable.''

Here Phil Evans noticed that day was beginning to break. A gleam, still faint, filtered through the narrow window opposite the door. It ought thus to be about four o'clock in the morning, for it is at that hour in the month of June in this latitude that the horizon of Philadelphia is tinged by the first rays of the dawn.

But when Uncle Prudent sounded his repeater—which was a masterpiece from his colleague's factory—the tiny gong only gave a quarter to three, and the watch had not stopped.

"That is strange!'' said Phil Evans. "At a quarter to three it ought still to be night.''

"Perhaps my watch has got slow,'' answered Uncle Prudent.

"A watch of the Wheelton Watch Company!'' exclaimed Phil Evans.

Whatever might be the reason, there was no doubt that the day was breaking. Gradually the window became white in the deep darkness of the cell. However, if the dawn appeared sooner than the fortieth parallel permitted, it did not advance with the rapidity peculiar to lower latitudes.

This was another observation of Uncle Prudent's—a new inexplicable phenomenon.

"Couldn't we get up to the window and see where we are?''

"We might,'' said Uncle Prudent. "Frycollin, get up!''

The negro arose.

"Put your back against the wall,'' continued Prudent, "and you, Evans, get on his shoulders while I buttress him up.''

"Right!'' said Evans.

An instant afterwards his knees were on Frycollin's shoulders, and his eyes were level with the window. The window was not of lenticular glass like those on shipboard, but was a simple flat pane. It was small, and Phil Evans found his range of view was much limited.

"Break the glass,'' said Prudent, "and perhaps you will be able to see better.''

Phil Evans gave it a sharp knock with the handle of his bowie-knife. It gave back a silvery sound, but it did not break.

Another and more violent blow. The same result.

"It is unbreakable glass!'' said Evans.

It appeared as though the pane was made of glass toughened on the Siemens system, as after several blows it remained intact.

The light had now increased, and Phil Evans could see for some distance within the radius allowed by the frame.

"What do you see?'' asked Uncle Prudent.

"Nothing.''

"What? Not any trees?''

"No.''

"Not even the top branches?''

"No.''

And what did they see?

"Then we are not in the clearing?"

"Neither in the clearing nor in the park."

"Don't you see any roofs of houses or monuments?" said Prudent, whose disappointment and anger were increasing rapidly.

"No."

"What! Not a flagstaff, nor a church tower, nor a chimney?"

"Nothing but space."

As he uttered the words the door opened. A man appeared on the threshold.

It was Robur.

"Honourable balloonists!" he said, in a serious voice, "you are now free to go and come as you like."

"Free!" exclaimed Uncle Prudent.

"Yes—within the limits of the Albatross!"

Uncle Prudent and Phil Evans rushed out of their prison.

And what did they see?

Four thousand feet below them the face of a country they sought in vain to recognize.

The Clipper of the Clouds

CHAPTER VII.

ON BOARD THE ALBATROSS

"WHEN will man cease to crawl in the depths to live in the azure and quiet of the sky?"

To this question of Camille Flammarion's the answer is easy. It will be when the progress of mechanics has enabled us to solve the problem of aviation. And in a few years—as we can foresee—a more practical utilization of electricity will do much towards that solution.

In 1783, before the Montgolfier brothers had built their fire-balloon, and Charles, the physician, had devised his first aerostat, a few adventurous spirits had dreamt of the conquest of space by mechanical means. The first inventors did not think of apparatus lighter than air; for that the science of their time did not allow them to imagine. It was to contrivances heavier than air, to flying machines in imitation of the birds, that they trusted to realize aerial locomotion.

This was exactly what had been done by that madman Icarus, the son of Daedalus, whose wings, fixed together with wax, had melted as they approached the sun.

But without going back to mythologic times, without dwelling on Archytas of Tarentum, we find in the works of Dante of Perugia, of Leonardo da Vinci and Guidotti, the idea of machines made to move through the air. Two centuries and a half afterwards inventors began to multiply. In 1742 the Marquis de Bacqueville designed a system of wings, tried it over the Seine, and fell and broke his arm. In 1768 Paucton conceived the idea of an apparatus with two screws, suspensive and propulsive. In 1781 Meerwein, the architect of the Prince of Baden, built an orthopteric machine, and protested against the tendency of the aerostats which had just been invented. In 1784 Launoy and Bienvenu had manoeuvred a helicopter worked by springs. In 1808 there were the attempts at flight by the Austrian Jacques Degen. In 1810 came the pamphlet by Deniau of Nantes, in which the principles of "heavier than air" are laid down. From 1811 to 1840 came the inventions and researches of Berblinger, Vigual, Sarti, Dubochet, and Cagniard de Latour. In 1842 we have the Englishman Henson, with his system of inclined planes and screws worked by steam. In 1845 came Crossus and his ascensional screws. In 1847 came Camille Vert and his helicopter made of birds' wings. In 1852 came Letur with his system of guidable parachutes, whose trial cost him his life; and in the same year came Michael Loup with his plan of gliding through the air on four revolving wings. In 1853 came Béléguic and his aeroplane with the traction screws, Vaussin-Chardannes with his guidable kite, and George Cauley with his flying-machines driven by gas. From 1854 to 1863 appeared Joseph Pline with several patents for aerial systems. Bréant, Carlingford, Le Bris, Du Temple, Bright, whose ascensional screws were left-handed; Smythies, Panafieu, Crosnier, &c. At length, in 1863, thanks to the efforts of Nadar, a society of "heavier than air" was founded in Paris. There the inventors could experiment with the machines, of which many were patented. Ponton d'Amécourt and his steam helicopter, La Landelle and his system of combining screws with inclined planes and parachutes, Louvrié and his aeroscaph, Esterno and his mechanical bird, Groof and his apparatus with wings worked by levers. The impetus was given, inventors invented, calculators calculated all that could render aerial locomotion practicable. Bourcart, Le Bris, Kaufmann, Smyth, Stringfellow, Prigent, Danjard, Pomés and De la Pauze, Moy, Pénaud, Jobert, Haureau de Villeneuve, Achenbach, Garapon, Duchesne, Danduran, Parisel, Dieuaide, Melkisff, Forlanini, Brearey, Tatin, Dandrieux, Edison, some with wings or screws, others with inclined planes, imagined, created, constructed, perfected, their flying machines, ready to do their work, once there came to be applied to them by some inventor a motor of adequate power and excessive lightness.

This list may be a little long, but that will be forgiven, for it is necessary to give the various steps in the ladder of aerial locomotion, on the top of which appeared Robur the Conqueror. Without these attempts, these experiments of his predecessors, how could the inquirer have conceived so perfect an apparatus? And though he had but contempt for those who obstinately worked away in the direction of balloons, he held in high esteem all those partisans of "heavier than air," English, American, Italian,

The Clipper of the Clouds.

Austrian, French—and particularly French,—whose work had been perfected by him, and led him to design and then to build this flying engine known as the Albatross, which he was guiding through the currents of the atmosphere.

"The pigeon flies!" had exclaimed one of the most persistent adepts at aviation.

"They will crowd the air as they crowd the earth!" said one of his most excited partisans.

"From the locomotive to the aeromotive!" shouted the noisiest of all, who had turned on the trumpet of publicity to awaken the Old and New Worlds.

Nothing, in fact, is better established, by experiment and calculation, than that the air is highly resistant. A circumference of only a yard in diameter in the shape of a parachute can not only impede descent in air, but can render it isochronous. That is a fact.

It is equally well known that when the speed is great the work of the weight varies in almost inverse ratio to the square of the speed, and becomes almost insignificant.

It is also known that as the weight of a flying animal increases, the less is the proportional increase in the surface beaten by the wings in order to sustain it, although the motion of the wings becomes slower.

A flying machine must therefore be constructed to take advantage of these natural laws, to imitate the bird, "that admirable type of aerial locomotion," according to Dr. Marcy, of the Institute of France.

In short, the contrivances likely to solve the problem are of three kinds:—

1. Helicopters or spiralifers, which are simply screws with vertical axes.

2. Orthopters, machines which endeavour to reproduce the natural flight of birds.

3. Aeroplanes, which are merely inclined planes like kites, but towed or driven by horizontal screws.

Each of these systems has had and still has its partisans obstinately resolved to give way in not the slightest particular.

However, Robur, for many reasons, had rejected the two first.

The orthopter, or mechanical bird, offers certain advantages, no doubt. That the work and experiments of M. Renard in 1884 have sufficiently proved. But, as has been said, it is not necessary to copy Nature servilely. Locomotives are not copied from the hare, nor are ships copied from the fish. To the first we have put wheels which are not legs; to the second we have put screws which are not fins. And they do not do so badly. Besides, what is this mechanical movement in the flight of birds, whose action is so complex? Has not Doctor Marcy suspected that the feathers open during the return of the wing so as to let the air through them? And is not that rather a difficult operation for an artificial machine?

On the other hand, aeroplanes have given many good results. Screws opposing a slanting plane to the bed of air will produce an ascensional movement, and the models experimented on have shown that the disposable weight, that is to say, the weight it is possible to deal with as distinct from that of the apparatus, increases with the square of the speed. Herein the aeroplane has the advantage over the aerostat even when the aerostat is furnished with the means of locomotion.

Nevertheless Robur had thought that the simpler his contrivance the better. And the screws—the Saint Helices that had been thrown in his teeth at the Weldon Institute—had sufficed for all the needs of his flying machine. One series could hold it suspended in the air, the other could drive it along under conditions that were marvellously adapted for speed and safety.

If the orthopter—striking like the wings of a bird—raised itself by beating the air, the helicopter raised itself by striking the air obliquely with the fins of the screw as it mounted on an inclined plane. These fins, or arms, are in reality wings, but wings disposed as a helix instead of as a paddle-wheel. The helix advances in the direction of its axis. Is the axis vertical? Then it moves vertically. Is the axis horizontal? Then it moves horizontally.

The whole of Robur's flying apparatus depended on these two movements, as will be seen from the following detailed description, which can be divided under three heads—the platform, the engines of suspension and propulsion, and the machinery.

Platform.—This was a framework a hundred feet long and twelve wide, a ship's deck in fact, with a projecting prow. Beneath was a hull solidly built, enclosing the engines, stores, and provisions of all sorts, including the water-tanks. Round the deck a few light uprights supported a wire trellis that did duty for bulwarks. On the deck were three houses, whose compartments were used as cabins for the crew, or as machine-rooms. In the centre house was the machine which drove the suspensory helices, in that forward was the machine that drove the bow screw, in that aft was the machine that drove the stern screw. In the bow there were the cook's galley and the crew's quarters; in the stern were several cabins, including that of the engineer, the saloon, and above them all a glass house in which stood the helmsman, who steered the vessel by means of a powerful rudder. All these cabins were lighted by portholes filled with toughened glass, which has ten times the resistance of ordinary glass. Beneath the hull was a system of flexible springs to ease off the concussion when it became advisable to land.

Engines of suspension and propulsion.— Above the deck rose thirty-seven vertical axes, fifteen along each side, and seven, more elevated, in the centre. The albatross might be called a clipper with thirty-seven masts. But these masts instead of sails bore each two horizontal screws, not very large in spread or diameter, but driven at prodigious speed. Each of these axes had its movement independent of the rest, and each alternate one spun round in a different direction from the others, so as to avoid any tendency to gyration. Hence the screws as they rose on the vertical column of air retained their equilibrium by their horizontal resistance. Consequently the apparatus was furnished with seventy-four suspensory screws, whose three branches were connected by a metallic circle which economized their motive force. In front and behind, mounted on horizontal axes, were two propelling screws, each with four arms. These screws were of much larger diameter than the suspensory ones, but could be worked at quite their speed. In fact, the vessel combined the systems of Cossus, La Landelle, and Ponton d'Amécourt, as perfected by Robur. But it was in the choice and application of his motive force that he could claim to be an inventor.

Machinery.—Robur had not availed himself of the vapour of water or other liquids, nor compressed air and other elastic gases, nor explosive mixtures capable of producing mechanical motion. He employed electricity, that agent which one day will be the soul of the industrial world. But he required no electro-motor to produce it. All he trusted to was piles and accumulators. What were the elements of these piles, and what were the acids he used, Robur only knew. And the construction of the accumulators was kept equally secret. Of what were their positive and negative plates? None can say. The engineer took good care—and not unreasonably—to keep his secret unpatented. One thing was unmistakable, and that was that the piles were of extraordinary strength; and the accumulators left those of Faure-Sellon-Volckmar very far behind in yielding currents whose ampères ran into figures up to then unknown. Thus there was obtained a power to drive the screws and communicate a suspending and propelling force in excess of all his requirements under any circumstances.

But—it is as well to repeat it—this belonged entirely to Robur. He kept it a close secret. And, if the president and secretary of the Weldon Institute did not happen to discover it, it would probably be lost to humanity.

It need not be shown that the apparatus possessed sufficient stability. Its centre of gravity proved that at once. There was no danger of its making alarming angles with the horizontal, still less of its capsizing.

And now for the metal used by Robur in the construction of his aeronef—a name which can be exactly applied to the Albatross. What was this material, so hard that the bowie-knife of Phil Evans could not scratch it, and Uncle Prudent could not explain its nature? Simply paper!

For some years this fabrication had been making considerable progress. Unsized paper, with the sheets impregnated with dextrin and starch and squeezed in hydraulic presses, will form a material as hard as steel. there are made of it pulleys, rails, and waggon-wheels, much more solid than metal wheels, and far lighter. And it was this lightness and solidity which Robur availed himself of in building his aerial locomotive. Everything—framework, hull, houses, cabins—was made of straw-paper turned hard as metal by compression, and— what was not to be despised in an apparatus flying at great heights—incombustible. The different parts of the engines and the screws were made of gelatinized fibre, which combined in sufficient degree flexibility with resistance. This material could be used in every form. It was insoluble in most gases and liquids, acids or essences, to say nothing of its insulating properties, and it proved most valuable in the electric machinery of the Albatross.

Robur, his mate Tom Turner, an engineer and two assistants, two steersmen and a cook— eight men all told—formed the crew of the aeronef, and proved ample for all the manoeuvres required in aerial navigation. There were arms of the chase and of war; fishing appliances; electric lights; instruments of observation, compasses, and sextants for checking the course, thermometers for studying the temperature, different barometers, some for estimating the heights attained, others for indicating the variations of atmospheric pressure; a storm-glass for forecasting tempests; a small library; a portable printing-press; a field-piece mounted on a pivot, breech-

Above the deck rose thirty-seven vertical axes.

loading, and throwing a three-inch shell; a supply of powder, bullets, dynamite cartridges; a cooking-stove, warmed by currents from the accumulators; a stock of preserves, meats, and vegetables sufficient to last for months. Such were the outfit and stores of the aeronef—in addition to the famous trumpet.

There was besides a light india-rubber boat, insubmersible, which could carry eight men on the surface of a river, a lake, or a calm sea.

But were there any parachutes in case of accident? No. Robur did not believe in accidents of that kind. The axes of the screws were independent. The stoppage of a few would not affect the motion of the others; and if only half were working, the Albatross could keep afloat in her natural element.

"And with her," said Robur to his guests—guests in spite of themselves—"I am master of the seventh part of the world, larger than Africa, Oceania, Asia, America, and Europe, this aerial Icarian sea, which millions of Icarians will one day people."

The Clipper of the Clouds

CHAPTER VIII.

THE BALLOONISTS REFUSE TO BE CONVINCED

THE president of the Weldon Institute was stupefied; his companion was astonished. But neither of them would allow any of their very natural amazement to be visible.

The valet Frycollin did not conceal his terror at finding himself borne through space on such a machine, and he took no pains whatever to hide it.

The suspensory screws were rapidly spinning overhead. Fast as they were going, they would have to triple their speed if the Albatross was to ascend to higher zones. The two propellers were running very easily and driving the ship at about eleven knots an hour.

As they leaned over the rail the passengers of the Albatross could perceive a long sinuous liquid ribbon which meandered like a mere brook through a varied country amid the gleaming of many lagoons obliquely struck by the rays of the sun. The brook was a river, one of the most important in that district. Along its left bank was a chain of mountins extending out of sight.

"And will you tell us where we are?" asked Uncle Prudent, in a voice tremulous with anger.

"I have nothing to teach you," answered Robur.

"And will you tell us where we are going?" said Phil Evans.

"Through space."

"And how long will that last?"

"Until it ends."

"Are we going round the world?" asked Phil Evans, ironically.

"Further than that," said Robur.

"And if this voyage does not suit us?" asked Uncle Prudent.

"It will have to suit you."

That is a foretaste of the nature of the relations that were to obtain between the master of the Albatross and his guests, not to say his prisoners. Manifestly he wished to give them time to cool down, to admire the marvellous apparatus which was bearing them through the air, and doubtless to compliment the inventor. And so he went off to the other end of the deck, leaving them to examine the arrangement of the machinery and the management of the ship or to give their whole attention to the landscape which was unrolling beneath them.

"Uncle Prudent," said Evans, "unless I am mistaken we are flying over Central Canada. That river in the north-west is the St. Lawrence. That town we are leaving behind is Quebec."

It was indeed the old city of Champlain, whose zinc roofs were shining like reflectors in the sun. The Albatross must thus have reached the forty-sixth degree of north latitude, and thus was explained the premature advance of the day with the abnormal prolongation of the dawn.

"Yes," said Phil Evans, "there is the town in its amphitheatre, the hill with its citadel, the Gibraltar of North America. There are the cathedrals. There is the Custom House with its dome surmounted by the British flag!"

Phil Evans had not finished before the Canadian city began to slip into the distance.

The clipper entered a zone of light clouds, which gradually shut off the view of the ground.

Robur, seeing that the president and secretary of the Weldon Institute had directed their attention to the external arrangements of the Albatross, walked up to them and said,—

"Well, gentlemen, do you believe in the possibility of aerial locomotion by machines heavier than air?"

It would have been difficult not to succumb to the evidence. But Uncle Prudent and Phil Evans did not reply.

"You are silent," continued the engineer. "Doubtless hunger makes you dumb! But if I undertook to carry you through the air, I did not think of feeding you on such a poorly nutritive fluid. Your first breakfast is waiting for you."

As Uncle Prudent and Phil Evans were feeling the pangs of hunger somewhat keenly they did not care to stand upon ceremony. A meal would commit them to nothing; and when Robur put them back on the ground they could resume full liberty of action.

And so they followed into a small dining-room in the aftermost house. There they found a well-laid table at which they could take their meals during the voyage. There were different preserves; and, among other things, was a sort of bread made of equal parts of flour and meat reduced to powder and worked together with a

A meal would commit them to nothing.

little lard, which boiled in water made excellent soup; and there were rashers of fried ham; and for drink there was tea.

Neither had Frycollin been forgotten. He was taken forward, and there found some strong soup made of this bread. In truth, he had to be very hungry to eat at all, for his jaws shook with fear, and almost refused to work.

"If it was to break!—if it was to break!" said the unfortunate negro.

Hence continual faintings. Only think! A fall of over four thousand feet, which would smash him to a jelly!

An hour afterwards Uncle Prudent and Phil Evans appeared on the deck. Robur was no longer there. At the stern the man at the wheel in his glass cage, his eyes fixed on the compass, followed imperturbably without hesitation the route given by the engineer.

As for the rest of the crew, breakfast probably kept them from their posts. An assistant engineer, examining the machinery, went from one house to the other.

If the speed of the ship was great the two colleagues could only estimate it imperfectly, for the Albatross had passed through the cloud zone which the sun showed some four thousand feet below.

"I can hardly believe it," said Phil Evans.

"Don't believe it!" said Uncle Prudent. And going to the bow they looked out towards the western horizon.

"Another town!" said Phil Evans.

"Do you recognize it?"

"Yes! It seems to me to be Montreal."

"Montreal? But we only left Quebec two hours ago!"

"That proves that we must be going at a speed of seventy five miles an hour."

Such was the speed of the aeronef; and if the passengers were not inconvenienced by it, it was because they were going with the wind. In a calm such speed would have been difficult and the rate would have sunk to that of an express. In a head-wind the speed would have been unbearable.

Phil Evans was not mistaken. Below the Albatross appeared Montreal, easily recognizable by the Victoria Bridge, a tubular bridge thrown over the St. Lawrence like the railway viaduct over the Venice lagoon. Soon they could distinguish the town's wide streets, its huge shops, its palatial banks, its cathedral, recently built on the model of St. Peter's at Rome, and then Mount Royal, which commands the city and forms a magnificent park.

Luckily Phil Evans had visited the chief towns of Canada, and could recognize them without asking Robur. After Montreal they passed Ottawa, whose falls seen from above, looked like a vast cauldron in ebullition, throwing off masses of steam with grand effect.

"There is the Parliament House."

And he pointed out a sort of Nuremburg toy planted on a hill top. This toy with its polychrome architecture resembled the Houses of Parliament in London much as the Montreal cathedral resembles St. Peter's at Rome. But that was of no consequence; there could be no doubt it was Ottawa.

Soon the city faded off towards the horizon, and formed but a luminous spot on the ground.

It was almost two hours before Robur appeared. His mate, Tom Turner, accompanied him. He said only three words. These were transmitted to the two assistant-engineers in the fore and aft engine-houses. At a sign the helmsman changed the direction of the Albatross a couple of points to the south-west; at the same time Uncle Prudent and Phil Evans felt that a greater speed had been given to the propellers.

In fact, the speed had been doubled, and now surpassed anything that had ever been attained by terrestrial engines. Torpedo-boats do their twenty-two knots an hour; railway trains do their sixty miles an hour; the ice-boats on the frozen Hudson do their sixty-five miles an hour; a machine built by the Patterson company, with a cogged wheel, has done its eighty miles; and another locomotive between Trenton and Jersey has done its eighty-four.

But the Albatross, at full speed, could do her hundred and twenty miles an hour, or 176 feet per second. This speed is that of the storm which tears up trees by the roots. It is the mean speed of the carrier pigeon, and is only surpassed by the flight of the swallow (220 feet per second) and that of the swift (274 feet per second).

In a word, as Robur had said, the Albatross, by using the whole force of her screws, could make the tour of the globe in two hundred hours, or less than eight days.

Is it necessary to say so? The phenomenon whose appearance had so much puzzled the people of both worlds was the aeronef of the engineer. The trumpet which blared its startling fanfares through the air was that of the mate, Tom Turner. The flag planted on the chief monuments of Europe, Asia, America, was the flag of Robur the Conqueror and his Albatross.

And if up to then the engineer had taken many precautions against being recognized, if by preference he travelled at night, clearing the way with his electric lights, and during the day

Tom Turner.

vanishing into the zones above the clouds, he seemed now to have no wish to keep his secret hidden. And if he had come to Philadelphia and presented himself at the meeting of the Weldon Institute, was it not that they might share in his prodigious discovery, and convince *ipso facto* the most incredulous? We know how he had been received, and we see what reprisals he had taken on the president and secretary of the club.

Again did Robur approach his prisoners, who affected to be in no way surprised at what they saw, of what had succeeded in spite of them. Evidently beneath the cranium of these two Anglo-Saxon heads there was a thick crust of obstinacy, which would not be easy to remove.

On his part, Robur did not seem to notice anything particular, and coolly continued the conversation which he had begun two hours before.

"Gentlemen," said he, "you ask yourselves doubtless if this apparatus, so marvellously adapted for aerial locomotion, is susceptible of receiving greater speed. It is not worth while to conquer space if we cannot devour it. I wanted the air to be a solid support to me, and it is. I saw that to struggle against the wind I must be stronger than the wind, and I am. I had no need of sails to drive me, nor oars nor wheels to push me, nor rails to give me a faster road. Air is what I wanted, that was all. Air surrounds me as it surrounds the submarine boat, and in it my propellers act like the screws of a steamer. That is how I solved the problem of aviation. That is what a balloon will never do, nor will any machine that is lighter than air."

Silence, absolute, on the part of the colleagues, which did not for a moment disconcert the engineer. He contented himself with a half-smile, and continued in his interrogative style,—

"Perhaps you ask if to this power of the Albatross to move horizontally there is added an equal power of vertical movement—in a word, if, when, we visit the higher zones of the atmosphere, we can compete with an aerostat? Well, I should not advise you to enter the Go-ahead against her!"

The two colleagues shrugged their shoulders. That was probably what the engineer was waiting for.

Robur made a sign. The propelling screws immediately stopped, and after running for a mile the Albatross pulled up, motionless.

At a second gesture from Robur the suspensory helices revolved at a speed that can only be compared to that of a siren in acoustical experiments. Their f-r-r-r-r rose nearly an octave in the scale of sound, diminishing gradually in intensity as the air became more rarified, and the machine rose vertically, like a lark singing his song in space.

"Master! Master!" shouted Frycollin. "See that it doesn't break!"

A smile of disdain was Robur's only reply. In a few minutes the Albatross had attained the height of 8700 feet, and extended the range of vision by seventy miles, the barometer having fallen 480 millimetres.

Then the Albatross descended. The diminution of the pressure in high altitudes leads to the diminution of oxygen in the air, and consequently in the blood. This has been the cause of several serious accidents which have happened to aeronauts, and Robur saw no reason to run any risk.

The Albatross thus returned to the height she seemed to prefer, and her propellers beginning again, drove her off to the south-west.

"Now, sirs, if that is what you wanted you can reply."

Then, leaning over the rail, he remained absorbed in contemplation.

When he raised his head the president and secretary of the Weldon Institute stood by his side.

"Engineer Robur," said Uncle Prudent, in vain endeavouring to control himself, "we have nothing to ask about what you seem to believe, but we wish to ask you a question which we think you would do well to answer."

"Speak."

"By what right did you attack us in Philadelphia in Fairmont Park? By what right did you shut us up in that prison? By what right have you brought us against out will on board this flying machine?"

"And by what right, Messieurs Balloonists, did you insult and threaten me in your club in such a way that I am astonished I came out of it alive?"

"To ask is not to answer," said Phil Evans, "and I repeat, by what right?"

"Do you wish to know?"

"If you please."

"Well, by the right of the strongest!"

"That is cynical."

"But it is true."

"And for how long, citizen engineer," asked Uncle Prudent, who was nearly exploding, "for how long do you intend to exercise that right?"

"How can you?" said Robur, ironically, "how can you ask me such a question when you have only to cast down your eyes to enjoy a spectacle unparalleled in the world?"

The Albatross was then sweeping across the

The Falls of Niagara.

immense expanse of Lake Ontario. She had just crossed the country so poetically described by Cooper. Then she followed the southern shore and headed for the celebrated river which pours into it the waters of Lake Erie, breaking them to powder in its cataracts.

In an instant a majestic sound, a roar as of the tempest, mounted towards them; and, as if a humid fog had been projected into the air, the atmosphere sensibly freshened.

Below were the liquid masses. They seemed like an enormous flowing sheet of crystal amid a thousand rainbows due to refraction as it decomposed the solar rays. The sight was sublime.

Before the falls a foot-bridge, stretching like a thread, united one bank to the other. Three miles below was a suspension-bridge, across which a train was crawling from the Canadian to the American bank.

"The falls of Niagara!" exclaimed Phil Evans. And as the exclamation escaped him, Uncle Prudent was doing all he could to admire nothing of these wonders.

A minute afterwards the Albatross had crossed the river which separates the United States from Canada, and was flying over the vast territories of the West.

The Clipper of the Clouds

CHAPTER IX.

ACROSS THE PRAIRIE

IN one of the cabins of the after-house Uncle Prudent and Phil Evans had found two excellent berths, with clean linen, change of clothes, and travelling-cloaks and rugs. No Atlantic liner could have offered them more comfort. If they did not sleep soundly it was that they did not wish to do so, or rather that their very real anxiety prevented them. In what adventure had they embarked? To what series of experiments had they been invited? How would the business end? and above all, what was Robur going to do with them?

Frycollin, the valet, was quartered forward in a cabin adjoining that of the cook. The neighbourhood did not displease him; he liked to rub shoulders with the great in this world. But if he finally went to sleep it was to dream of fall after fall, of projections through space, which made his sleep a horrible nightmare.

However, nothing could be quieter than this journey through the atmosphere, whose currents had grown weaker with the evening. Beyond the rustling of the blades of the screws there was not a sound, except now and then the whistle from some terrestrial locomotive, or the calling of some animal. Strange instinct! These terrestrial beings felt the aeronef glide over them, and uttered cries of terror as it passed. On the morrow, 14th June, at five o'clock, Uncle Prudent and Phil Evans were walking on the deck of the Albatross. Nothing had changed since the evening; there was a look-out forward, and the helmsman was in his glass cage.

Why was there a look-out? Was there any chance of collision with another such machine? Certainly not. Robur had not yet found imitators. The chance of encountering an aerostat gliding through the air was too remote to be regarded. In any case it would be all the worse for the aerostat—the earthen pot and the iron pot. The Albatross had nothing to fear from the collision.

But what could happen? The aeronef might find herself like a ship on a lee shore if a mountain than could not be outflanked or passed barred the way. These are the reefs of the air, and they have to be avoided as a ship avoids the reefs of the sea. The engineer, it is true, had given the course, and in doing so had taken into account the altitude necessary to clear the summits of the high lands in the district. But as the aeronef was rapidly nearing a mountainous country, it was only prudent to keep a good lookout, in case some slight deviation from the course became necessary.

Looking at the country beneath them, Uncle Prudent and Phil Evans noticed a large lake, whose lower southern end the Albatross had just reached. They concluded, therefore, that during the night the whole length of Erie had been traversed, and that, as they were going due west, they would soon be over Lake Michigan. "There can be no doubt of it," said Phil Evans, "and that group of roofs on the horizon is Chicago."

He was right. It was indeed the city from which the seventeen railways diverge, the Queen of the West, the vast reservoir into which flow the products of Indiana, Ohio, Wisconsin, Missouri, and all the States which form the western half of the Union.

Uncle Prudent, through an excellent telescope he had found in his cabin, easily recognized the principal buildings. His colleague pointed out to him the churches and public edifices, the numerous "elevators" or mechanical granaries, and the huge Sherman Hotel, whose windows seemed like a hundred glittering points on each of its faces.

"If that is Chicago," said Uncle Prudent, "it is obvious that we are going farther west than is convenient for us if we are to return to our starting-place."

And, in fact, the Albatross was travelling in a straight line from the Pennsylvanian capital.

But if Uncle Prudent wished to ask Robur to take him eastwards he could not then do so. That morning the engineer did not leave his cabin. Either he was occupied in some work, or else he was asleep, and the two colleagues sat down to breakfast without seeing him.

The speed was the same as that during last evening. The wind being easterly the rate was not interfered with at all, and as the thermometer only falls a degree centigrade for every seventy metres of elevation the temperature was not insupportable. And so, in chatting and thinking and waiting for the engineer, Uncle Prudent and Phil Evans walked about beneath the forest of screws, whose gyratory movement gave their arms the appearance of semi-diaphanous disks.

The State of Illinois was left by its northern frontier in less than two hours and a half; and they crossed the Father of Waters, the Mississippi, whose double-decked steamboats seemed no bigger than canoes. Then the Albatross flew over Iowa after having sighted Iowa city about eleven o'clock in the morning.

A few chains of hills, "bluffs" as they are called, curved across the face of the country trending from the south to the north-west, whose moderate height necessitated no rise in the course of the aeronef. Soon the bluffs gave place to the large plains of western Iowa and Nebraska—immense prairies extending all the way to the foot of the Rocky Mountains. Here and there were many rios, affluents or minor affluents of the Missouri. On their banks were towns and villages, growing more scattered as the Albatross sped farther west.

Nothing particular happened during this day. Uncle Prudent and Phil Evans were left entirely to themselves. They hardly noticed Frycollin sprawling at full length in the bow, keeping his eyes shut so that he could see nothing. And they were not attacked by vertigo, as might have been expected. There was no guiding mark, and there was nothing to cause the vertigo, as there would have been on the top of a lofty building. The abyss has no attractive power when it is gazed at from the car of a balloon or deck of an aeronef. It is not an abyss that opens beneath the aeronaut, but an horizon that rises round him on all sides like a cup.

In a couple of hours the Albatross was over Omaha, on the Nebraska frontier—Omaha city, the real head of the Pacific Railway, that long line of rails, four thousand five hundred miles in length, stretching from New York to San Francisco. For a moment they could see the yellow waters of the Missouri, then the town, with its houses of wood and brick in the centre of a rich basin, like a buckle in the iron belt which clasps North America round the waist. Doubtless, also, as the passengers in the aeronef could observe all these details, the inhabitants of Omaha noticed the strange machine. But their astonishment at seeing it gliding overhead could be no greater than that of the president and secretary of the Weldon Insitute at finding themselves on board.

Anyhow, the journals of the Union would be certain to notice the fact. It would be the explanation of the astonishing phenomenon which the whole world had been wondering over for some time.

In an hour the Albatross had left Omaha and crossed the Plate River, whose valley is followed by the Pacific Railway in its route across the prairie. Things looked serious for Uncle Prudent and Phil Evans.

"It is serious, then, this absurd project of taking us to the Antipodes."

"And whether we like it or not!" exclaimed the other. "Robur had better take care! I am not the man to stand that sort of thing."

"Nor am I!" replied Phil Evans. "But be calm, Uncle Prudent, be calm."

"Be calm!"

"And keep your temper until it is wanted."

By five o'clock they had crossed the Black Mountains covered with pines and cedars, and the Albatross was over the appropriately named Bad Lands of Nebraska—a chaos of ochre-coloured hills, of mountainous fragments fallen on the soil and broken in their fall. At a distance these blocks take the most fantastic shapes. Here and there amid this enormous game of knucklebones there could be traced the imaginary ruins of mediaeval cities with forts and dungeons, pepper-box turrets, and machicolated towers. And in truth these Bad Lands are an immense ossuary where lie bleaching in the sun myriads of fragments of pachyderms, chelonians, and even, some would have us believe, fossil men, over-whelmed by unknown cataclysms ages and ages ago.

When evening came the whole basin of the Plate River had been crossed, and the plain extended to the extreme limits of the horizon, which rose high owing to the altitude of the Albatross.

During the night there were no more shrill whistles of locomotives or deeper notes of the river steamers to trouble the quiet of the starry firmament. Long bellowings occasionally reached the aeronef from the herds of buffalo that roamed over the prairie in search of water and pasturage. And when they ceased, the trampling of the grass under their feet produced a dull roaring similar to the rushing of a flood, and very different from the continuous f-r-r-r-r of the screws.

Then from time to time came the howl of a wolf, a fox, a wild cat, or a coyote, the *Canis latrans*, whose name is justified by his sonorous bark.

Occasionally came penetrating odours of mint, and sage, and absinthe, mingled with the more powerful fragrance of the conifers which rose floating through the night air.

At last came a menacing yell, which was not due to the coyote. It was the shout of a Redskin, which no Tenderfoot would confound with the cry of a wild beast.

The Clipper of the Clouds

CHAPTER X.

WESTWARD—BUT WHITHER?

THE next day, the 15th of June, about five o'clock in the morning, Phil Evans left his cabin. Perhaps he would today have a chance of speaking to Robur? Desirous of knowing why he had not appeared the day before, Evans addressed himself to the mate, Tom Turner.

Tom Turner was an Englishman of about forty-five, broad in the shoulders and short in the legs, a man of iron, with one of those enormous characteristic heads that Hogarth rejoiced in.

"Shall we see Mr. Robur to-day?" asked Phil Evans.

"I don't know," said Turner.

"I need not ask if he has gone out."

"Perhaps he has."

"And when will he come back?"

"When he has finished his cruise."

And Tom went into his cabin.

With this reply they had to be contented. Matters did not look promising, particularly as on reference to the compass it appeared that the Albatross was still steering south-west.

Great was the contrast between the barren tract of the Bad Lands passed over during the night and the landscape then unrolling beneath them.

The aeronef was now more than six hundred miles from Omaha, and over a country which Phil Evans could not recognize because he had never been there before. A few forts to keep the Indians in order crowned the bluffs with their geometric lines, formed oftener of palisades than walls. There were few villages and few inhabitants, the country differing widely from the auriferous lands of Colorado many leagues to the south.

In the distance a long line of mountain crests, in great confusion as yet, began to appear. They were the Rocky Mountains.

For the first time that morning Uncle Prudent and Phil Evans were sensible of a certain lowness of temperature which was not due to a change in the weather, for the sun shone in superb splendour.

"It is because of the Albatross being higher in the air," said Phil Evans.

In fact the barometer outside the central deck-house had fallen 540 millimeters, thus indicating an elevation of about 10,000 feet above the sea. The aeronef was at this altitude owing to the elevation of the ground. An hour before she had been at a height of 13,000 feet, and behind her were mountains covered with perpetual snow.

There was nothing Uncle Prudent and his companion could remember which would lead them to discover where they were. During the night the Albatross had made several stretches north and south at tremendous speed, and that was what had put them out of their reckoning.

After talking over several hypotheses more or less plausible they came to the conclusion that this country encircled with mountains must be the district declared by an Act of Congress in March, 1872, to be the National Park of the United States. A strange region it was. It well merited the name of a park—a park with mountains for hills, with lakes for ponds, with rivers for streamlets, and with geysers of marvellous power instead of fountains.

In a few minutes the Albatross glided across the Yellowstone River, leaving Mount Stevenson on the right, and coasting the large lake which bears the name of the stream. Great was the variety on the banks of this basin, ribbed as they were with obsidian and tiny crystals, reflecting the sunlight on their myriad facets. Wonderful was the arrangement of the islands on its surface; magnificent were the blue reflections of the gigantic mirror. And around the lake, one of the highest in the globe, were multitudes of pelicans, swans, gulls and geese, bernicles and divers. In places the steep banks were clothed with green trees, pines and larches, and at the foot of the escarpments there shot upwards innumerable white fuma-roles, the vapour escaping from the soil as from an enormous reservoir in which the water is kept in permanent ebullition by subterranean fire.

The cook might have seized the opportunity of securing an ample supply of trout, the only fish the Yellowstone Lake contains in myriads. But the Albatross kept on at such a height that there was no chance of indulging in a catch which assuredly would have been miraculous.

In three quarters of an hour the lake was overpassed, and a little farther on the last was seen of the geyser region, which rivals the finest in Iceland. Leaning over the rail, Uncle Prudent

It was really extraordinary.

and Phil Evans watched the liquid columns which leaped up as though to furnish the aeronef with a new element. There were the Fan, with the jets shot forth in rays, the Fortress, which seemed to be defended by waterspouts, the Faithful Friend, with her plume crowned with the rainbows, the Giant, spurting forth a vertical torrent twenty feet round and more than two hundred feet high.

Robur must evidently have been familiar with this incomparable spectacle, unique in the world, for he did not appear on deck. Was it, then, for the sole pleasure of his guests that he had brought the aeronef above the national domain? If so, he came not to receive their thanks. He did not even trouble himself during the daring passage of the Rocky Mountains, which the Albatross approached at about seven o'clock.

As we know, this orographical system stretches like an enormous backbone throughout the length of North America, and is prolonged into the Mexican Andes. It extends for over two thousand miles, its highest point being James Peak, which attains a height of twelve thousand feet.

By increasing the speed of her wings, as a bird rising in its flight, the Albatross would clear the highest ridges of the chain, and sink again over Oregon or Utah. But the manoeuvre was unnecessary. The passes allowed the barrier to be crossed without ascending for the higher ridges. There are many of these canyons, or steep valleys, more or less narrow, through which they could glide, such as Bridger Gap, through which runs the Pacific Railway into the Mormon territory, and others to the north and south of it.

It was through one of these that the Albatross headed, after slackening speed so as not to dash against the walls of the canyon. The steersman, with a sureness of hand rendered more effective by the sensitiveness of the rudder, manoeuvred his craft as if she were a crack racer in a Royal Victoria match. It was really extraordinary. In spite of all the jealousy of the two enemies of "lighter than air," they could not help being surprised at the perfection of this engine of aerial locomotion.

In less than two hours and a half they were through the Rockies, and the Albatross had resumed her former speed of sixty-two miles an hour. She was steering south-west so as to cut across Utah diagonally as she neared the ground. She had even dropped several hundred yards when the sound of a whistle attracted the attention of Uncle Prudent and Phil Evans.

It was a train on the Pacific Railway on the road to Salt Lake City.

And then, in obedience to an order secretly given, the Albatross dropped still lower so as to chase the train, which was going at full speed. She was immediately sighted. A few heads showed themselves at the doors of the cars. Then numerous passengers crowded the gangways. Some did not hesitate to climb on the roof to get a better view of the flying machine. Cheers came floating up through the air, but no Robur appeared in answer to them.

The Albatross continued her descent, slowing her suspensory screws and moderating her speed so as not to leave the train behind. She flew about it like an enormous beetle or a gigantic bird of prey. She headed off to the right and left, and swept on in front, and hung behind, and proudly displayed her flag with the golden sun, to which the conductor of the train replied by waving the Stars and Stripes.

In vain the prisoners, in their desire to take advantage of the opportunity, endeavoured to make themselves known to those below. In vain the president of the Weldon Institute roared forth at the top of his voice,—

"I am Uncle Prudent of Philadelphia!"

And the secretary followed suit with,—

"I am Phil Evans, his colleague!"

Their shouts were lost in the thousands of cheers with which the passengers greeted the aeronef.

Three or four of the crew of the Albatross had appeared on the deck, and one of them, like sailors when passing a ship less speedy than their own, held out a rope, an ironical way of offering to tow them.

And then the Albatross resumed her original speed, and in half an hour the express was out of sight.

About one o'clock there appeared a vast disk, which reflected the solar rays as if it were an immense mirror.

"That ought to be the Mormon capital, Salt Lake City," said Uncle Prudent.

And so it was, and the disk was the roof of the Tabernacle, where ten thousand saints can worship at their ease. This vast dome, like a convex mirror, threw off the rays of the sun in all directions.

There was a great city, at the foot of the Wasatch Mountains, clothed half way with cedars and pines, on the banks of the River Jordan, through which the Utah waters enter the lake. Beneath the aeronef lay the draughtboard in which so many American cities are planned. Around was a well-cultivated country in which the flocks of sheep were countable in thousands.

It was a train on the Pacific Railway.

But the draught-board vanished like a shadow, and the Albatross sped on her way to the south-west with a speed that was not felt, because it surpassed that of the chasing wind. Soon she was in Nevada, over the silver regions, which the Sierra separates from the golden lands of California.

"We shall certainly reach San Francisco before night," said Phil Evans.

"And then?" asked Uncle Prudent.

It was six o'clock precisely when the Sierra Nevada was crossed by the same pass as that taken by the railway. Only a hundred and eighty miles then separated them from San Francisco, the Californian capital.

At the speed the Albatross was going she would be over the dome by eight o'clock.

At this moment Robur appeared on deck.

The colleagues walked up to him.

"Engineer Robur," said Uncle Prudent, "we are now on the confines of America! We think the time has come for this joke to end."

"I never joke," said Robur.

He raised his hand. The Albatross swiftly dropped towards the ground, and at the same time such speed was given her as to drive the prisoners into their cabin.

As soon as the door was shut, Uncle Prudent exclaimed,—

"I could strangle him!"

"We must try to escape!" said Phil Evans.

"Yes; cost what it may!"

A long murmut greeted their eats.

It was the beating of the surf on the seashore. It was the Pacific Ocean!

The Clipper of the Clouds

CHAPTER XI.

THE WIDE PACIFIC

UNCLE PRUDENT and Phil Evans had quite made up their minds to escape. If they had not had to deal with the eight particularly vigorous men who composed the crew of the aeronef they might have tried to succeed by main force. But as they were only two—for Frycollin could only be considered as a quantity of no importance—force was not to be thought of. Hence recourse must be had to strategy as soon as the Albatross again took the ground. Such was what Phil Evans endeavoured to impress on his irascible colleague, though he was in constant fear of Prudent aggravating matters by some premature outbreak.

In any case the present was not the time to attempt anything of the sort. The aeronef was sweeping along over the North Pacific. On the following morning, that of June 16th, the coast was out of sight. And as the coast curves off from Vancouver Island up to the Aleutians—belonging to that portion of America ceded by Russia to the United States in 1867—it was highly probable that the Albatross would cross it at the end of the curve, if her course remained unchanged.

How long the night appeared to be to the two friends! How eager they were to get out of their cabins! When they came on deck in the morning the dawn had for some hours been silvering the eastern horizon. They were nearing the June solstice, the longest day of the year in the northern hemisphere, when there is hardly any night along the sixtieth parallel.

Either from custom or intention Robur was in no hurry to leave his deck-house. When he came out this morning he contented himself with bowing to his two guests as he passed them in the stern of the aeronef.

And now Frycollin ventured out of his cabin. His eyes red with sleeplessness, and dazed in their look, he tottered along like a man whose foot feels it is not on solid ground. His first glance was at the suspensory screws, which were working with gratifying regularity without any signs of haste.

That done, the negro stumbled along to the rail, and grasped it with both hands, so as to make sure of his balance. Evidently he wished to view the country over which the Albatross was flying at the height of seven hundred feet or more.

At first he kept himself well back behind the rail. Then he shook it to make sure it was firm; then he drew himself up; then he bent forward; then he stretched out his head. It need not be said that while he was executing these different manoeuvres he kept his eyes shut. At last he opened them.

What a shout! And how quickly he fled! And how deeply his head sank back into his shoulders!

At the bottom of the abyss he had seen the immense ocean. His hair would have risen on end—if it had not been wool.

"The sea! the sea!" he cried.

And Frycollin would have fallen on the deck had not the cook opened his arms to receive him.

This cook was a Frenchman, and probably a Gascon, his name being Francois Tapage. If he was not a Gascon he must in his infancy have inhaled the breezes of the Garonne. How did this Francois Tapage find himself in the service of the engineer? By what chain of accidents had he become one of the crew of the Albatross? We can hardly say; but in any case he spoke English like a Yankee.

"Eh, stand up!" said he, lifting the negro by a vigorous clutch at the waist.

"Master Tapage!" said the poor fellow, giving a despairing look at the screws.

"At your service, Frycollin."

"Did this thing ever smash?"

"No, but it will end by smashing."

"Why? Why?"

"Because everything must end."

"And the sea is beneath us!"

"If we are to fall, it is better to fall in the sea."

"We shall be drowned."

"We shall be drowned, but we shall not be smashed to a jelly."

The next moment Frycollin was on all fours, creeping to the back of his cabin.

During this day the aeronef was only driven at moderate speed. She seemed to skim the placid surface of the sea, which lay glistening in the sunshine about a hundred feet beneath. Uncle Prudent and his companion remained in their cabin, so that they did not meet with

Robur, who walked about smoking alone or talking to the mate. Only half the screws were working, yet that was enough to keep the apparatus afloat in the lower zones of the atmosphere.

The crew, as a change from the ordinary routine, would have endeavoured to catch a few fish, had there been any sign of them; but all that could be seen on the surface of the sea were a few of those yellow-bellied whales which measure about eighty feet in length. These are the most formidable cetaceans in the northern seas, and whalers are very careful in attacking them, for their strength is prodigious. However, in harpooning one of these whales, either with the ordinary harpoon, the Fletcher fuse, or the javelin-bomb, of which there was an assortment on board, there would have been no danger to the men of the Albatross.

But what was the good of such useless massacre? Doubtless to show off the powers of the aeronef to the members of the Weldon Institute. And so Robur gave orders for the capture of one of these monstrous cetaceans.

At the shout of "A whale! a whale!" Uncle Prudent and Phil Evans came out of their cabin. Perhaps there was a whaler in sight! In that case all they had to do to escape from their flying prison was to jump into the sea, and chance being picked up by the vessel.

The crew were all on deck.

"Shall we try, sir?" asked Tom Turner.

'Yes," said Robur.

In the engine-room the engineer and his assistant were at their posts ready to obey the orders signalled to them. The Albatross dropped towards the sea, and remained about fifty feet above it.

There was no ship in sight—of that the two colleagues soon assured themselves—nor was there any land to be seen to which they could swim, providing Robur made no attempt to recapture them.

Several jets of water from the spout holes soon announced the presence of the whales as they came to the surface to breathe.

Tom Turner and one of the men were in the bow. Within his reach was one of those javelin-bombs, of Californian make, which are shot from an arquebus, and which are shaped as a metallic cylinder terminated by a cylindrical shell armed with a shaft having a barbed point. Robur was a little farther aft, and with his right hand signalled to the engineers, while with his left he directed the steersman. He thus controlled the aeronef in every way, horizontally and vertically, and it is almost impossible to conceive with what speed and precision the

Albatross answered to his orders. She seemed a living being, of which he was the soul.

"A whale! a whale!" shouted Tom Turner, as the back of a cetacean emerged from the surface about four cable-lengths in front of the Albatross.

The Albatross swept towards it, and when she was within sixty feet of it she stopped dead.

Tom Turner seized the arquebus, which was resting against a cleat on the rail. He fired, and the projectile, attached to a long line, entered the whale's body. The shell, filled with an explosive compound, burst, and shot out a small harpoon with two branches, which fastened into the animal's flesh.

"Look out!" shouted Turner.

Uncle Prudent and Phil Evans, much against their will, became greatly interested in the spectacle.

The whale, seriously wounded, gave the sea such a slap with his tail, that the water dashed up over the bow of the aeronef. Then he plunged to a great depth, while the line, which had been previously wetted in a tub of water to prevent its taking fire, ran out like lightning. When the whale rose to the surface he started off at full speed in a northerly direction.

It may be imagined with what speed the Albatross was towed in pursuit. Besides, the propellers had been stopped. The whale was let go as he would, and the ship followed him. Turner stood ready to cut the line in case a fresh plunge should render this towing dangerous.

For half an hour, and perhaps for a distance of six miles, the Albatross was thus dragged along, but it was obvious that the whale was tiring. Then, at a gesture from Robur, the assistant engineers started the propellers astern, so as to oppose a certain resistance to the whale, who was gradually getting closer.

Soon the aeronef was gliding about twenty-five feet above him. His tail was beating the waters with incredible violence, and as he turned over on his back an enormous wave was produced.

Suddenly the whale turned up again, so as to take a header, as it were, and then dived with such rapidity that Turner had barely time to cut the line.

The aeronef was dragged to the very surface of the water. A whirlpool was formed where the animal had disappeared. A wave dashed up on to the deck as if the aeronef were a ship driving against wind and tide.

Luckily, with a blow of the hatchet the mate severed the line, and the Albatross, freed from her tug, sprang aloft six hundred feet under the impulse of her ascensional screws.

With a blow of the hatchet the mate severed the line.

Robur had manoeuvred his ship without losing his coolness for a moment.

A few minutes afterwards the whale returned to the surface—dead. From every side the birds flew down on to the carcass, and their cries were enough to deafen a congress. The Albatross, without stopping to share in the spoil, resumed her course to the west.

In the morning of the 17th of June, at about six o'clock, land was sighted on the horizon. This was the peninsula of Alaska, and the long range of breakers of the Aleutian Islands.

The Albatross glided over the barrier where the fur seals swarm for the benefit of the Russo-American Company. An excellent business is the capture of these amphibians, which are from six to seven feet long, russet in colour, and weigh from three hundred to four hundred pounds. There they were in interminable files, ranged in line of battle, and countable by thousands.

Although they did not move at the passage of the Albatross, it was otherwise with the ducks, divers, and loons, whose husky cries filled the air as they disappeared beneath the waves and fled terrified from the aerial monster.

The twelve hundred miles of the Behring Sea between the first of the Aleutians and the extreme end of Kamtschatka were traversed during the twenty-four hours of this day and the following night. Uncle Prudent and Phil Evans found that there was no present chance of putting their project of escape into execution. Flight was not to be thought of among the deserts of Eastern Asia, nor on the coast of the sea of Okhotsk. Evidently the Albatross was bound for Japan or China, and there, although it was not perhaps quite safe to trust themselves to the mercies of the Chinese or Japanese, the two friends had made up their minds to run if the aeronef stopped.

But would she stop? She was not like a bird which grows fatigued by too long a flight, or like a balloon which has to descend for want of gas. She still had food for many weeks, and her organs were of marvellous strength, defying all weakness and weariness.

During the 18th of June she swept over the peninsula of Kamtschatka, and during the day there was a glimpse of Petropaulovski and the volcano of Kloutschew. Then she rose again to cross the Sea of Okhotsk, running down by the Kurile Isles, which seemed to be a breakwater pierced by hundreds of channels. On the 19th, in the morning, the Albatross was over the strait of La Perouse between Saghalien and Northern Japan, and had reached the mouth of the great Siberian river, the Amoor.

Then there came on a fog so dense that the aeronef had to rise above it. At the altitude she was there was no obstacle to be feared, no elevated monuments to hinder her passage, no mountains against which there was risk of being shattered in her flight. The country was only slightly varied. But the fog was very disagreeable, and made everything on board very damp.

All that was necessary was to get above this bed of mist, which was nearly thirteen hundred feet thick, and the ascensional screws being increased in speed, the Albatross was soon clear of the fog and in the sunny regions of the sky. Under these circumstances, Uncle Prudent and Phil Evans would have found some difficulty in carrying out their plan of escape, even admitting that they could leave the aeronef.

During the day, as Robur passed them, he stopped for a moment, and without seeming to attach any importance to what he said, addressed them carelessly as follows:—

"Gentlemen, a sailing-ship or a steamship caught in a fog from which it cannot escape is always much delayed. It must not move unless it keeps its whistle or its horn going. It must reduce its speed, and any instant a collision may be expected. The Albatross has none of these things to fear. What does fog matter to her? She can leave it when she chooses. The whole of space is hers."

And Robur continued his stroll without waiting for an answer, and the puffs of his pipe were lost in the sky.

"Uncle Prudent," said Phil Evans, "it seems that this astonishing Albatross never has anything to fear."

"That we shall see!" answered the president of the Weldon Institute.

The fog lasted three days, the 19th, 20th, and 21st of June, with regrettable persistence. An ascent had to be made to clear the Japanese mountain of Fusiyama. When the curtain of mist was drawn aside there lay below them an immense city, with palaces, villas, gardens, and parks. Even without seeing it Robur had recognized it by the barking of the innumerable dogs, the cries of the birds of prey, and above all, by the cadaverous odour which the bodies of its executed criminals gave off into space.

The two colleagues were out on the deck while the engineer was taking his observations in case he thought it best to continue his course through the fog.

"Gentlemen," said he, "I have no reason for concealing from you that this town is Tokio, the capital of Japan."

Uncle Prudent did not reply. In the presence

This town is Tokio, the capital of Japan.''

of the engineer he was almost choked, as if his lungs were short of air.

"This view of Tokio," continued Robur, "is very curious."

"Curious as it may be—" replied Phil Evans.

"It is not as good as Pekin?" interrupted the engineer. "That is what I think, and very shortly you shall have an opportunity of judging."

Impossible to be more agreeable!

The Albatross then gliding south-east, had her course changed four points, so as to head to the eastward.

The Clipper of the Clouds

CHAPTER XII.

THROUGH THE HIMALAYAS

DURING the night the fog cleared off. There were symptoms of an approaching typhoon—a rapid fall of the barometer, a disappearance of vapour, large clouds of ellipsoid form clinging to a copper sky, and, on the opposite horizon, long streaks of carmine on a slate-coloured field, with a large sector quite clear in the north. Then the sea was smooth and calm and at sunset assumed a deep scarlet hue.

Fortunately the typhoon broke more to the south, and had no other result than to sweep away the mist which had been accumulating during the last three days.

In an hour they had traversed the hundred and twenty-five miles of the Corean strait, and while the typhoon was raging on the coast of China, the Albatross was over the Yellow Sea. During the 22nd and 23rd she was over the Gulf of Pechelee, and on the 24th she was ascending the valley of the Peiho on her way to the capital of the Celestial Empire.

Leaning over the rail, the two colleagues, as the engineer had told them, could see distinctly the immense city, the wall which divides it into two parts—the Manchoo town and the Chinese town—the twelve suburbs which surround it, the large boulevards which radiate from its centre, the temples with their green and yellow roofs bathed in the rising sun, the grounds surrounding the houses of the mandarins; then in the middle of the Manchoo town the eighteen hundred acres of the Yellow town, with its pagodas, its imperial gardens, its artificial lakes, its mountain of coal which towers above the capital; and in the centre of the Yellow town, like a square of a Chinese puzzle enclosed in another, the Red town, that is the imperial palace, with all the peaks of its outrageous architecture.

Below the Albatross the air was filled with a singular harmony. It seemed to be a concert of Aeolian harps. In the air were a hundred kites of different forms, made of sheets of palm-leaf, and having at their upper end a sort of bow of light wood with a thin slip of bamboo beneath. In the breath of the wind these slips, with all their notes varied like those of a harmonicon, gave forth a most melancholy murmuring. It seemed as thought they were breathing musical oxygen.

It suited Robur's whim to run close up to this aerial orchestra, and the Albatross slowed as she glided through the sonorous waves which the kites gave off through the atmosphere.

But immediately an extraordinary effect was produced amongst the innumerable population. Beatings of the tomtoms and sounds of other formidable instruments of the Chinese orchestra, gun reports by the thousand, mortars fired in hundreds, all were brought into play to scare away the aeronef. Although the Chinese astronomers may have recognized the aerial machine as the moving body that had given rise to such disputes, it was to the Celestial million, from the humblest tankader to the best-buttoned mandarin, an apocalyptical monster appearing in the sky of Buddha.

The crew of the Albatross troubled themselves very little about these demonstrations. But the strings which held the kites, and were tied to fixed pegs in the imperial gardens, were cut or quickly hauled in; and the kites were either drawn in rapidly, sounding louder as they sank, or else fell like a bird shot through both wings, whose song ends with its last sigh.

A noisy fanfare escaped from Tom Turner's trumpet, and drowned the final notes of the aerial concert. It did not interrupt the terrestrial fusillade. At last a shell exploded a few feet below the Albatross, and then she mounted into the inaccessible regions of the sky.

Nothing happened during the few following days of which the prisoners could take advantage. The aeronef kept on her course to the south-west, thereby showing that it was intended to take her to India. Twelve hours after leaving Pekin Uncle Prudent and Phil Evans caught a glimpse of the Great Wall in the neighbourhood of Chen-Si. Then, avoiding the Lung Mountains, they passed over the valley of the Hoangho and crossed the Chinese border on the Thibet side.

Thibet consists of high table-lands without vegetation, with here and there snowy peaks and barren ravines, torrents fed by glaciers, depressions with glittering beds of salt, lakes surrounded by luxurious forests, with icy winds sweeping over all.

The barometer falling seventeen-tenths of an inch indicated an altitude of thirteen thousand

Avoiding the Lung Mountains.

feet above the level of the sea. At that height the temperature, although it was in the warmest months of the northern hemisphere, was only a little above freezing. This cold, combined with the speed of the Albatross, made the voyage somewhat trying, and although the friends had warm travelling wraps, they preferred to keep to their cabin.

It need hardly be said that to keep the aeronef in this rarefied atmosphere the suspensory screws had to be driven at extreme speed. But they worked with perfect regularity, and the sound of their wings almost acted as a lullaby.

During this day, appearing from below about the size of a carrier pigeon, she passed over Garlock, a town of western Thibet, the capital of the province of Gari Khorsum.

On the 27th of June, Uncle Prudent and Phil Evans sighted an enormous barrier, broken here and there by several peaks, lost in the snows that bounded the horizon.

Leaning against the fore-cabin, so as to keep their places notwithstanding the speed of the ship, they watched these colossal masses, which seemed to be running away from the aeronef.

"The Himalayas, evidently," said Phil Evans; "and probably Robur is going round their base, so as to pass into India."

"So much the worse," answered Uncle Prudent. "On that immense territory we shall perhaps be able to—"

"Unless he goes round by Burmah to the east, or Nepaul to the west."

"Anyhow, I defy him to go through them."

"Indeed!" said a voice.

The next day, the 28th of June, the Albatross was in front of the huge mass above the province of Zzang. On the other side of the chain was the province of Nepaul.

These ranges block the road into India from the north. The two northern ones, between which the aeronef was gliding like a ship between enormous reefs, are the first steps of the Central Asian barrier. The first was the Kuen Lung, the other the Karakorum, bordering the longitudinal valley parallel to the Himalayas, from which the Indus flows to the west and the Brahmapootra to the east.

What a superb orographical system! More than two hundred summits have been measured, seventeen of which exceed twenty-five thousand feet. In front of the Albatross, at a height of twenty-nine thousand feet, towered Mount Everest. To the right was Dhawalagiri, reaching twenty-six thousand eight hundred feet, and relegated to second place since the measurement of Mount Everest.

Evidently Robur did not intend to go over the top of these peaks; but probably he knew the passes of the Himalayas, among others that of Ibi Ganim, which the brothers Schlagintweit traversed in 1856 at a height of twenty-two thousand feet. And towards it he went.

Several hours palpitation, becoming quite painful, followed; and although the rarefaction of the air was not such as to necessitate recourse being had to the special apparatus for renewing the oxygen in the cabins, the cold was excessive.

Robur stood in the bow, his sturdy figure wrapped in a great-coat. He gave the orders, while Tom Turner was at the helm. The engineer kept an attentive watch on his batteries, the acid in which fortunately ran no risk of congelation. The screws, running at the full strength of the current, gave forth a note of intense shrillness in spite of the trifling density of the air. The barometer showed twenty-three thousand feet in altitude.

Magnificent was the grouping of the chaos of mountains! Everywhere were brilliant white summits. There were no lakes, but glaciers descending ten thousand feet towards the base. There was no herbage, only a few phanerogams on the limit of vegetable life. Down on the lower flanks of the range were splendid forests of pines and cedars. Here were none of the gigantic ferns and interminable parasites stretching from tree to tree as in the thickets of the jungle. There were no animals—no wild horses, or yaks, or Thibetan bulls. Occasionally a sacred gazelle showed itself far down the slopes. There were no birds, save a couple of those crows which can rise to the utmost limits of the respirable air.

The pass at last was traversed. The Albatross began to descend. Coming from the hills out of the forest region there was now beneath them an immense plain stretching far and wide.

Then Robur stepped up to his guests, and in a pleasant voice remarked,—

"India, gentlemen!"

Gliding like a ship between enormous reefs.

The Clipper of the Clouds

CHAPTER XIII.

OVER THE CASPIAN

THE engineer had no intention of taking his ship over the wondrous lands of Hindostan. To cross the Himalayas was to show how admirable was the machine he commanded; to convince those who would not be convinced was all he wished to do.

But if in their hearts Uncle Prudent and his colleague could not help admiring so perfect an engine of aerial locomotion, they allowed none of their admiration to be visible. All they thought of was how to escape. They did not even admire the superb spectacle that lay beneath them as the Albatross flew along the river banks of the Punjab.

At the base of the Himalayas there runs a marshy belt of country, the home of malarious vapours, the Terai, in which fever is endemic. But this offered no obstacle to the Albatross, or in any way affected the health of her crew. She kept on without undue haste towards the angle where India joins on to China and Turkestan, and on the 29th of June, in the early hours of the morning, there opened to view the incomparable valley of Cashmere.

Yes! incomparable is this gorge between the major and minor Himalayas—furrowed by the buttresses in which the mighty range dies out in the basin of the Hydaspes, and watered by the capricious windings of the river which saw the struggle between the armies of Porus and Alexander, when India and Greece contended for Central Asia. The Hydaspes is still there, although the two towns founded by the Macedonian in remembrance of his victory have long since disappeared.

During the morning the aeronef was over Serinuggur, which is better known under the name of Cashmere. Uncle Prudent and his companion beheld the superb city clustered along both banks of the river; its wooden bridges stretching across like threads, its villas and their balconies standing out in bold outline, its hills shaded by tall poplars, its roofs grassed over and looking like molehills; its numerous canals, with boats like nut-shells, and boatmen like ants; its palaces, temples, kiosks, mosques, and bungalows on the outskirts; and its old citadel of Hari-Pawata on the slope of the hill like the most important of the forts of Paris on the slope of Mont Valerien.

"That would be Venice," said Phil Evans, "if we were in Europe."

"And if we were in Europe," answered Uncle Prudent, "we should know how to find the way to America."

The Albatross did not linger over the lake through which the river flows, but continued her flight down the valley of the Hydaspes.

For half an hour only did she descend to within thirty feet of the river, and remained stationary. Then, by means of an india-rubber pipe, Tom Turner and his men replenished their water-supply, which was drawn up by a pump worked by the accumulators. Uncle Prudent and Phil Evans stood watching the operation. The same idea occurred to each of them. They were only a few feet from the surface of the stream. They were both good swimmers. A plunge would give them their liberty; and once they had reached the river, how could Robur get them back again? For his propellers to work, he must keep at least six feet above the ground.

In a moment all the chances pro and con. were run over in their minds. In a moment they were considered, and the prisoners rushed to throw themselves overboard, when several pairs of hands seized them by the shoulders.

They had been watched; and flight was impossible. This time they did not yield without resisting. They tried to throw off those who held them. But these men of the Albatross were no children.

"Gentlemen," said the engineer, "when people have the pleasure of travelling with Robur the Conqueror, as you have so well named him, on board his admirable Albatross, they do not leave him in that way. I may add you never leave him."

Phil Evans drew away his colleague, who was about to commit some act of violence. They retired to their cabin, resolved to escape, even if it cost them their lives.

Immediately the Albatross resumed her course to the west. During the day at moderate speed she passed over the territory of Cabulistan, catching a momentary glimpse of its capital, and crossed the frontier of the kingdom of Herat, nearly seven hundred miles from Cashmere.

They tried to throw off those who held them.

In these much-disputed countries, the open road for the Russians to the English possessions in India, there were seen many columns and convoys, and, in a word, everything that constitutes in men and material an army on the march. There were heard also the roar of the cannon and the crackling of musketry. But the engineer never meddled with the affairs of others where his honour or humanity was not concerned. He passed above them. If Herat, as we are told, is the key of Central Asia, it mattered little to him if it was kept in an English or Muscovite pocket. Terrestrial interests were nothing to him who had made the air his domain.

Besides, the country soon disappeared in one of those sandstorms which are so frequent in these regions. The wind called the "tebbad" bears along the seeds of fever in the impalpable dust it raises in its passage. And many are the caravans that perish in its eddies.

To escape this dust, which might have interfered with the working of the screws, the Albatross shot up some six thousand feet into a purer atmosphere.

And thus vanished the Persian frontier and the extensive plains. The speed was not excessive, although there were no rocks ahead, for the mountains marked on the map are of very moderate altitude. But as the ship approached the capital, she had to steer clear of Demavend, whose snowy peak rises some twenty-two thousand feet, and the chain of Elbruz, at whose foot is built Teheran.

As soon as the day broke on the 2nd of July the peak of Demavend appeared above the sandstorm, and the Albatross was steered so as to pass over the town, which the wind had wrapped in a mantle of dust.

However, about six o'clock her crew could see the large ditches that surround it, and the Shah's palace, with its walls covered with porcelain tiles, and its ornamental lakes, which seemed like huge turquoises of beautiful blue.

It was but a hasty glimpse. The Albatross now headed for the north, and a few hours afterwards she was over a little hill at the northern angle of the Persian frontier, on the shores of a vast extent of water which stretched away out of sight to the north and east.

The town was Ashurada, the most southerly of the Russian stations. The vast extent of water was a sea. It was the Caspian.

The eddies of sand had been passed. There was a view of a group of European houses rising along a promontory, with a church tower in the midst of them.

The Albatross swooped down towards the surface of the sea. Towards evening she was running along the coast—which formerly belonged to Turkestan, but now belongs to Russia—and in the morning of the 3rd of July she was about three hundred feet above the Caspian.

There was no land in sight, either on the Asiatic or European side. On the surface of the sea a few white sails were bellying in the breeze. These were native vessels recognizable by their peculiar rig—kesebeys, with two masts; kayuks, the old pirate-boats, with one mast; teimils, and smaller craft for trading and fishing. Here and there a few puffs of smoke rose up to the Albatross from the funnels of the Ashurada steamers, which the Russians keep as the police of these Turcoman waters.

That morning Tom Turner was talking to the cook, Tapage, and to a question of his replied,—

"Yes; we shall be about forty-eight hours over the Caspian."

"Good!" said the cook; "then we can have some fishing."

"Just so."

They were to remain for forty-eight hours over the Caspian, which is some six hundred and twenty-five miles long and two hundred wide, because the speed of the Albatross had been much reduced, and while the fishing was going on she would be stopped altogether.

The reply was heard by Phil Evans, who was then in the bow, where Frycollin was overwhelming him with piteous pleadings to be put "on the ground."

Without replying to this preposterous request, Evans returned aft to Uncle Prudent; and there, taking care not to be overheard, he reported the conversation that had taken place.

"Phil Evans," said Uncle Prudent, "I think there can be no mistake as to this scoundrel's intention with regard to us."

"None," said Phil Evans. "He will only give us our liberty when it suits him, and perhaps not at all."

"In that case we must do all we can to get away from the Albatross."

"A splendid craft she is, I must admit."

"Perhaps so," said Uncle Prudent; "but she belongs to a scoundrel who detains us on board in defiance of all right. For us and ours she is a constant danger. If we do not destroy her—"

"Let us begin by saving ourselves!" answered Phil Evans; "we can see about the destruction afterwards."

"Just so," said Uncle Prudent. "And we must avail ourselves of every chance that comes along. Evidently the Albatross is going to cross the Caspian into Europe, either by the north into Russia or by the west into the southern countries. Well, no matter where we stop, before we get to the Atlantic we shall be safe. And we ought to be ready at any moment."

"But," asked Evans, "how are we to get out?"

"Listen to me," said Uncle Prudent. "It may happen during the night that the Albatross may drop to within a few hundred feet of the ground. Now there are on board several ropes of that length, and, with a little pluck we might slip down them—"

"Yes," said Evans. "If the case is desperate I don't mind—"

"Nor I. During the night there's no one about except the man at the wheel. And if we can drop one of the ropes forward without being seen or heard—"

"Good! I am glad to see you are so cool; that means business. But just now we are over the Caspian. There are several ships in sight. The Albatross is going down to fish. Cannot we do something now?"

"Sh! They are watching us much more than you think," said Uncle Prudent. "You saw that when we tried to jump into the Hydaspes."

"And who knows that they don't watch us at night?" asked Evans.

"Well, we must end this; we must finish with this Albatross and her master."

It will be seen how in the excitement of their anger the colleagues—Uncle Prudent in particular—were prepared to attempt the most hazardous things. The sense of their powerlessness, the ironical disdain with which Robur treated them, the brutal remarks he indulged in—all contributed towards intensifying the aggravation which daily grew more manifest.

This very day something occurred which gave rise to another most regrettable altercation between Robur and his guests. This was provoked by Frycollin, who, finding himself above the boundless sea, was seized with another fit of terror. Like a child, he gave himself over to groaning and protesting and crying, and writhing in a thousand contortions and grimaces.

"I want to get out! I want to get out! I am not a bird! Boohoo! I don't want to fly, I want to get out!"

Uncle Prudent, as may be imagined, did not attempt to quiet him. In fact, he encouraged him, and particularly as the incessant howling seemed to have a strangely irritating effect on Robur.

When Tom Turner and his companions were getting ready for fishing, the engineer ordered them to shut up Frycollin in his cabin. But the negro never ceased his jumping about, and began to kick at the wall and yell with redoubled power.

It was noon. The Albatross was only about fifteen or twenty feet above the water. A few ships, terrified at the apparition, sought safety in flight.

As may be guessed, a sharp look-out was kept on the prisoners, whose temptation to escape could not but be intensified. Even supposing they jumped overboard they would have been picked up by the india-rubber boat. As there was nothing to do during the fishing, in which Phil Evans intended to take part, Uncle Prudent, raging furiously as usual, retired to his cabin.

The Caspian Sea is a volcanic depression. Into it flow the waters of the Volga, the Ural, the Kour, the Kouma, the Jemba, and others. Without the evaporation which relieves it of its overflow, this basin, with an area of 17,000 square miles, and a depth of from sixty to four hundred feet, would flood the low marshy ground to its north and east. Although it is not in communication with the Black Sea or the Sea of Aral, being at a much lower level than they are, it contains an immense number of fish—such fish, be it understood, as can live in its bitter waters, the bitterness being due to the naphtha which pours in from the springs on the south.

The crew of the Albatross made no secret of their delight at the change in their food the fishing would bring them.

"Look out!" shouted Turner, as he harpooned a good-sized fish, not unlike a shark.

It was a splendid sturgeon seven feet long, called by the Russians belouga, the eggs of which mixed up with salt, vinegar, and white wine form caviare. Sturgeons from the river are, it may be, rather better than those from the sea; but these were welcomed warmly enough on board the Albatross.

But the best catches were made with the drag-nets, which brought up at each haul carp, bream, salmon, salt-water pike, and a number of medium-sized sterlets, which wealthy gourmets have sent them alive to Astrakhan, Moscow, and Petersburg, and which now passed direct from their natural element into the cook's kettle without any charge for transport.

An hour's work sufficed to fill up the larders of the aeronef, and she resumed her course to the north.

During the fishing Frycollin had continued

An hour's work sufficed to fill up the larders.

shouting and kicking at his cabin wall and making a tremendous noise.

"That wretched nigger will not be quiet, then?" said Robur, almost out of patience.

"It seems to me, sir, he had a right to complain," said Phil Evans.

"Yes, and I have a right to look after my ears," replied Robur.

"Engineer Robur!" said Uncle Prudent, who had just appeared on deck.

"President of the Weldon Institute!"

They had stepped up to one another, and were looking into the whites of each other's eyes.

Then Robur shrugged his shoulders.

"Put him at the end of a line," he said.

Turner saw his meaning at once.

Frycollin was dragged out of his cabin.

Loud were his cries when the mate and one of the men seized him and tied him into a tub, which they hitched on to a rope—one of those very ropes, in fact, that Uncle Prudent had intended to use as we know.

The negro at first thought he was going to be hanged. No! he was only going to be towed!

The rope was paid out for a hundred feet and Frycollin found himself hanging in space.

He could then shout at his ease. But fright contracted his larynx, and he was mute.

Uncle Prudent and Phil Evans endeavoured to prevent this performance. They were thrust aside.

"It is scandalous! It is cowardly!" said Uncle Prudent, quite beside himself with rage.

"Indeed!" said Robur.

"It is an abuse of power against which I protest."

"Protest away!"

"I will be avenged, Mr. Robur."

"Avenge when you like, Mr. Prudent."

"I will have my revenge on you and yours."

The crew began to close up with anything but peaceful intentions. Robur motioned them away.

"Yes, on you and yours!" said Uncle Prudent, whom his colleague in vain tried to keep quiet.

"Whenever you please!" said the engineer.

"And in every possible way!"

"That is enough now," said Robur, in a threatening tone. "There are other ropes on board. And if you don't be quiet, I'll treat you as I have done your valet!"

Uncle Prudent was silent, not because he was afraid, but because his wrath had nearly choked him; and Phil Evans led him off to his cabin.

During the last hour the air had been strangely troubled. The symptoms could not be mistaken. A storm was threatening. The electric saturation of the atmosphere had become so great that about half-past two o'clock Robur witnessed a phenomenon that was new to him.

In the north, whence the storm was travelling, were spirals of half-luminous vapour due to the difference in the electric charges of the various beds of cloud. The reflections of these bands came running along the waves in myriads of lights, growing in intensity as the sky darkened.

The Albatross and the storm were sure to meet, for they were exactly in front of each other.

And Frycollin? Well! Frycollin was being towed—and towed is exactly the word, for the rope made such an angle with the aeronef, now going at over sixty knots an hour, that the tub was a long way behind her.

The crew were busy in preparing for the storm, for the Albatross would either have to rise above it or drive through its lowest layers. She was about three thousand feet above the sea when a clap of thunder was heard. Suddenly the squall struck her. In a few seconds the fiery clouds swept on around her.

Phil Evans went to intercede for Frycollin, and asked for him to be taken on board again.

But Robur had already given orders to that effect, and the rope was being hauled in, when suddenly there took place an inexplicable slackening in the speed of the screws.

The engineer rushed to the central deck-house.

"Power! More power!" he shouted. "We must rise quickly and get over the storm!"

"Impossible, sir!"

"What is the matter?"

"The currents are troubled! They are intermittent!" And, in fact, the Albatross was falling fast.

As with telegraph wires on land during a storm, so was it with the accumulators of the aeronef. But what is only an inconvenience in the case of messages was here a terrible danger.

"Let her down, then," said Robur, "and get out of the electric zone! Keep cool, my lads!"

He stepped on to his quarter-deck and his crew went to their stations.

Although the Albatross had sunk several hundred feet she was still in the thick of the cloud, and the flashes played across her as if they were fireworks. It seemed as though she was struck. The screws ran more and more slowly, and what began as a gentle descent threatened to become a collapse.

In less than a minute it was evident they

Frycollin, of course, had a bath.

would get down to the surface of the sea. Once they were immersed no power could drag them from the abyss.

Suddenly the electric cloud appeared above them. The Albatross was only sixty feet from the crest of the waves. In two or three seconds the deck would be under water.

But Robur, seizing the propitious moment, rushed to the central house and seized the levers. He turned on the currents from the piles no longer neutralized by the electric tension of the surrounding atmosphere. In a moment the screws had regained their normal speed and checked the descent; and the Albatross remained at her slight elevation while her propellers drove her swiftly out of reach of the storm.

Frycollin, of course, had a bath—though only for a few seconds. When he was dragged on deck he was as wet as if he had been to the bottom of the sea. As may be imagined, he cried no more.

In the morning of the 4th of July the Albatross had passed over the northern shore of the Caspian.

The Clipper of the Clouds

CHAPTER XIV.

THE AERONEF AT FULL SPEED

IF ever Uncle Prudent and Phil Evans despaired of escaping from the Albatross it was during the two days that followed. It may be that Robur considered it more difficult to keep a watch on his prisoners while he was crossing Europe, and he certainly knew that they had made up their minds to get away.

But any attempt to have done so would have been simply committing suicide. To jump from an express going sixty miles an hour is to risk your life, but to jump from a machine going one hundred and twenty miles an hour would be to seek your death.

And it was at this speed, the greatest that could be given to her, that the Albatross tore along. Her speed exceeded that of the swallow, which is one hundred and twelve miles an hour.

At first the wind was in the north-east, and the Albatross had it fair, her general course being a westerly one. But the wind began to drop, and it soon became impossible for the colleagues to remain on the deck without having their breath taken away by the rapidity of the flight. And on one occasion they would have been blown overboard if they had not been dashed up against the deck-house by the pressure of the wind.

Luckily the steersman saw them through the windows of his cage, and by the electric bell gave the alarm to the men in the fore-cabin. Four of them came aft, creeping along the deck.

Those who have been at sea, beating to windward in half a gale of wind, will understand what the pressure was like. Only here it was the Albatross that by her incomparable speed made her own wind.

To allow Uncle Prudent and Phil Evans to get back to their cabin the speed had to be reduced. Inside the deck-houses the Albatross bore with her a perfectly breathable atmosphere.

To stand such driving the strength of the apparatus must have been prodigious. The propellers spun round so swiftly that they seemed immovable, and it was with irresistible penetrative power that they screwed themselves through the air.

The last town that had been noted was Astrakhan, situated at the north end of the Caspian Sea. The Star of the Desert—it must have been a poet who so called it—has now sunk from the first rank to the fifth or sixth. A momentary glance was afforded at its old walls, with their useless battlements, the ancient towers in the centre of the city, the mosques and modern churches, the cathedral with its five domes, gilded and dotted with stars as if it were a piece of the sky, as they rose from the bank of the Volga, which here, as it joins the sea, is over a mile in width.

Thenceforward the flight of the Albatross became quite a race through the heights of the sky, as if she had been harnessed to one of those fabulous hippogriffs which cleared a league at every sweep of the wing.

At ten o'clock in the morning of the 4th of July the aeronef, heading north-west, followed for a little the valley of the Volga. The steppes of the Don and the Ural stretched away on each side of the river. Even if it had been possible to get a glimpse of these vast territories there would have been no time to count the towns and villages. In the evening the aeronef passed over Moscow without saluting the flag on the Kremlin. In ten hours she had covered the twelve hundred miles which separate Astrakhan fron the ancient capital of all the Russias.

From Moscow to St. Petersburg the railway line measures about seven hundred and fifty miles. This was but a half-day's journey, and the Albatross, as punctual as the mail, reached St. Petersburg and the banks of the Neva at two o'clock in the morning.

Then came the Gulf of Finland, the Archipelago of Abo, the Baltic, Sweden in the latitude of Stockholm, and Norway in the latitude of Christiania. Ten hours only for these twelve hundred miles! Verily it might be thought that no human power would henceforth be able to check the speed of the albatross, and as if the resultant of her force of projection and the attraction of the earth would maintain her in an unvarying trajectory round the globe.

But she did stop nevertheless, and that was over the famous fall of the Rjukanfos in Norway. Gousta, whose summit dominates this

225

Away from the others.

The lamps of the Albatross were turned on.

wonderful region of Tellemarken, stood in the west like a gigantic barrier apparently impassable. And when the Albatross resumed her journey at full speed her head had been turned to the south.

And during this extraordinary flight what was Frycollin doing? Frycollin remained silent in a corner of his cabin, sleeping as well as he could, except at meal-times.

Tapage then favoured him with his company —and amused himself at his expense.

"Eh! eh! my boy!" said he. "So you are not crying any more? Perhaps it hurt you too much? That two hours' hanging cured you of it! At our present rate, what a splendid air-bath you have for your rheumatics!"

"It seems to me we shall soon go to pieces!"

"Perhaps so; but we shall go so fast we shan't have time to fall! That is some comfort!"

"Do you think so?"

"I do."

To tell the truth, and not to exaggerate like Tapage, it was only reasonable that owing to the excessive speed the work of the suspensory screws should be somewhat lessened. The Albatross glided on its bed of air like a Congreve rocket.

"And shall we last long like that?" asked Frycollin.

"Long? Oh, no; only as long as we live!"

"Oh!" said the negro, beginning his lamentations.

"Take care, Fry, take care! for, as they say in my country, the master may send you to the seesaw!"

And Frycollin gulped down his sobs as he gulped down the meat which, in double doses, he was hastily swallowing.

Meanwhile Uncle Prudent and Phil Evans, who were not men to waste time in wrangling when nothing could come of it, agreed upon doing something. It was evident that escape was not to be thought of. But if it was impossible for them to again set foot on the terrestrial globe, could they not make known to its inhabitants what had become of them since their disappearance, and tell them by whom they had been carried off, and provoke—how was not very clear—some audacious attempt on the part of their friends to rescue them from Robur?

Communicate? But how?

Should they follow the example of sailors in distress and enclose in a bottle a document giving the place of shipwreck and throw it into the sea?

But here the sea was the atmosphere. The bottle would not swim. And if it did not fall on somebody and crack his skull it might never be found.

The colleagues were about to sacrifice one of the bottles on board when an idea occurred to Uncle Prudent. He took snuff, as we know, and we may pardon this fault in an American, who might do worse. And as a snuff-taker he possessed a snuff-box, which was now empty. This box was made of aluminium. If it was thrown overboard any honest citizen that found it would pick it up, and, being an honest citizen, he would take it to the police-office, and there they would open it and discover from the document what had become of the two victims of Robur the Conqueror!

And this is what was done. The note was short, but it told all, and it gave the address of the Weldon Institute, with a request that it might be forwarded. Then Uncle Prudent folded up the note, shut it in the box, and bound the box round with a piece of worsted so as to keep it from opening as it fell. And then all that had to be done was to wait for a favourable opportunity.

During this marvellous flight over Europe it was not an easy thing to leave the cabin and creep along the deck at the risk of being suddenly and secretly blown away, and it would not do for the snuff-box to fall into the sea or a gulf or a lake or a watercourse, for it would then perhaps be lost. At the same time it was not impossible that the colleagues might in this way get into communication with the habitable globe.

It was then growing daylight, and it seemed as though it would be better to wait for the night and take advantage of a slackening of speed or a halt to go out on deck and drop the precious snuff-box into some town.

When all these points had been thought over and settled, the prisoners found they could not put their plan into execution—on that day, at all events—for the Albatross, after leaving Gousta, had kept her southerly course, which took her over the North Sea, much to the consternation of the thousands of coasting craft engaged in the English, Dutch, French, and Belgian trade. Unless the snuff-box fell on the deck of one of these vessels there was every chance of its going to the bottom of the sea, and Uncle Prudent and Phil Evans were obliged to wait for a better opportunity. And, as we shall immediately see, an excellent chance was soon to be offered them.

At ten o'clock that evening the Albatross reached the French coast near Dunkerque. The night was rather dark. For a moment they could see the lighthouse at Grisnez cross its electric beam with the lights from Dover on the other side of the strait. Then the Albatross flew over the French territory at a mean height of three thousand feet.

There was no diminution in her speed. She shot like a rocket over the towns and villages so numerous in northern France. She was flying straight on to Paris, and after Dunkerque came Doullens, Amiens, Creil, Saint Denis. She never left the line; and about midnight she was over the "city of light," which merits its name even when its inhabitants are asleep—or ought to be.

By what strange whim was it that she was stopped over the city of Paris? We do not know; but down she came till she was within a few hundred feet of the ground. Robur then came out of his cabin, and the crew came on to the deck to breathe the ambient air.

Uncle Prudent and Phil Evans took care not to miss such an excellent opportunity. They left their deck-house and walked off away from the others so as to be ready at the propitious moment. It was important their action should not be seen.

The Albatross, like a huge coleopter, glided gently over the mighty city. She took the line of the boulevards, then brilliantly lighted by the Edison lamps. Up to her there floated the rumble of the vehicles as they drove along the streets, and the roll of the trains on the numerous railways that converge into Paris. Then she glided over the highest monuments as if she was going to knock the ball off the Pantheon or the cross off the Invalides. She hovered over the two minarets of the Trocadero and the metal tower of the Champ de Mars, where the enormous reflector was inundating the whole capital with its electric rays.

This aerial promenade, this nocturnal loitering, lasted for about an hour. It was a halt for breath before the voyage was resumed.

And probably Robur wished to give the Parisians the sight of a meteor quite unforeseen by their astronomers. The lamps of the albatross were turned on. Two brilliant sheaves of light shot down and moved along over the squares, the gardens, the palaces, the sixty thousand houses, and swept the space from one horizon to the other.

Assuredly the Albatross was seen this time—and not only well seen but heard, for Tom Turner brought out his trumpet and blew a rousing tarantaratara.

At this moment Uncle Prudent leant over the rail, opened his hand, and let his snuff-box fall.

Immediately the Albatross shot upwards, and past her, higher still, there mounted the noisy cheering of the crowd then thick on the boulevards—a hurrah of stupefaction to greet the imaginary meteor.

Then the lamps of the aeronef were turned off, and the darkness and the silence closed in around as the voyage was resumed at the rate of one hundred and twenty miles an hour.

This was all that was to be seen of the French capital. At four o'clock in the morning the Albatross had crossed the whole country obliquely; and so as to lose no time in traversing the Alps or the Pyrenees, she flew over the face of Provence to the cape of Antibes. At nine o'clock next morning the San Pietrini assembled on the terrace of St. Peter at Rome were astounded to see her pass over the eternal city. Two hours afterwards she crossed the Bay of Naples and hovered for an instant over the fulginous wreaths of Vesuvius. Then, after cutting obliquely across the Mediterranean, in the early hours of the afternoon she was signalled by the look-outs at La Goulette on the Tunisian coast.

After America, Asia! After Asia, Europe! More than eighteen thousand miles had this wonderful machine accomplished in less than twenty-three days!

And now she was off over the known and unknown regions of Africa!

*   *   *   *   *   *

It may be interesting to know what had happened to the famous snuff-box after its fall?

It had fallen in the Rue de Rivoli, opposite No. 200, when the street was deserted. In the morning it was picked up by an honest sweeper, who took it to the prefecture of police.

There it was at first supposed to be an infernal machine. And it was untied, examined, and opened with extreme care.

Suddenly a sort of explosion took place. It was a terrific sneeze on the part of the inspector.

The document was then extracted from the snuff-box, and, to the general surprise, read as follows:—

"Messrs. Prudent and Phil Evans, president and secretary of the Weldon Institute, Philadelphia, have been carried off in the aeronef Albatross belonging to Robur the engineer.

"Please inform our friends and acquaintances."

"P. and P.E."

Thus was the strange phenomenon at last

explained to the people of the two worlds. Thus was peace given to the scientists of the numerous observatories on the surface of the terrestrial globe.

CHAPTER XV.

A SKIRMISH IN DAHOMEY

AT this point in the circumaviatory voyage of the Albatross it is only natural that some such questions as the following should be asked.

Who was this Robur, of whom up to the present we know nothing but the name? Did he pass his life in the air? Did his aeronef never rest? Had he not some retreat in some inaccessible spot in which, if he had need of repose or revictualling, he could betake himself? It would be very strange if it were not so. The most powerful flyers have always an eyrie or nest somewhere.

And what was the engineer going to do with his prisoners? Was he going to keep them in his power and condemn them to perpetual aviation? Or was he going to take them on a trip over Africa, South America, Australasia, the Indian Ocean, the Atlantic, and the Pacific, to convince them against their will, and then dismiss them with, "And now, gentlemen, I hope you will believe a little more in heavier than air?"

To these questions it is now impossible to reply. They are the secrets of the future. Perhaps the answers will be revealed.

Anyhow the bird-like Robur was not seeking his nest on the northern frontier of Africa. By the end of the day he had traversed Tunis from Cape Bon to Cape Carthage, sometimes hovering, and sometimes darting along at top speed. Soon he reached the interior, and flew down the beautiful valley of Medjeida above its yellow stream hidden under its luxuriant bushes of cactus and oleander; and scared away the hundreds of parrots that perch on the telegraph wires and seem to wait for the messages to pass to bear them away beneath their wings.

When night came the Albatross was over the frontiers of Kroumiria, and if a Kroumir then existed, he, of course, fell on his face and uttered an invocation to Allah at the apparition of the gigantic eagle.

In the morning she was over Bona and the hills in the neighbourhood; then she reached Philippeville, now a small Algiers, with its new wharves and arcades and its admirable vineyards, whose verdant shoots clothe the country-side, which seems to be a slice brought hither from Burgundy or the Bordelais.

This promenade of three hundred miles into great and little Kabylia was brought to an end about noon over the Kasbah at Algiers. What a view it was for the passengers on the aeronef—the open roadstead between Cape Matifou and Point Pescade, the shore dotted with palaces, marabouts, villas, irregular valleys clothed in their vineyard mantles, the Mediterranean so blue ploughed by the huge liners now dwarfed to canoes! And so it was at Oran the picturesque, whose inhabitants, loitering in the gardens of the citadel, saw the Albatross appear among the earliest stars of the night.

Two hours after sunset the helm was put up and the Albatross bore off to the south-east; and on the morrow, after clearing the Tell Mountains, she saw the rising of the morning star over the sands of the Sahara.

On the 30th of July there was seen from the aeronef the little village of Geryville, founded like Laghouat on the frontier of the desert to facilitate the future conquest of Kabylia. Next, not without difficulty, the peaks of Stillero were passed against a somewhat boisterous wind. Then the desert was crossed, sometimes leisurely, over the Ksars or green oases, sometimes at terrific speed that far outstripped the flight of the vultures. Often the crew had to fire into the flocks of these birds which, a dozen or so at a time, fearlessly hurled themselves on to the aeronef to the extreme terror of Frycollin.

But if the vultures could only reply with cries and blows of beaks and talons, the natives, in no way less savage, were not sparing of their musket-shots, particularly when crossing the Mountain of Sel, whose green and violet slope bore its cape of white. Then the Albatross was at last over the grand Sahara; and at once she rose into the higher zones so as to escape from a simoom which was sweeping a wave of ruddy sand along the surface of the ground like a bore on the surface of the sea.

Then the desolate table-lands of Chetka scattered their ballast in blackish waves up to the fresh and verdant valley of Ain-Massin. It is difficult to conceive the variety of the territories which could be seen at one view. To the green hills covered with trees and shrubs there succeeded long grey undulations draped like the folds of an Arab burnous and broken in

231

picturesque masses. In the distance could be seen the wadys with their torrential waters, their forests of palm-trees, and blocks of small houses grouped on a hill around a mosque, among them Metlili, where there vegetates a religious chief, the grand marabout Sidi Chick.

Before night several hundred miles had been accomplished above a flattish country ridged occasionally with large sand-hills. If the Albatross had halted, she would have come to the earth in the depths of the Wargla oasis hidden beneath an immense forest of palm-trees. The town was clearly enough displayed with its three distinct quarters, the ancient palace of the Sultan, a kind of fortified Kasbah, houses of brick which had been left to the sun to bake, and artesian wells dug in the valley where the aeronef could have renewed her water supply. But, thanks to her extraordinary speed, the waters of the Hydaspes taken in the vale of Cashmere still filled her tanks in the centre of the African deserts.

Was the Albatross seen by the Arabs, the Mozabites, and the negroes who share amongst them the town of Wargla? Certainly, for she was saluted with many hundred gunshots, and the bullets fell back before they reached her.

Then came the night, that silent night in the desert of which Felicien David has so poetically told us the secrets.

During the following hours the course lay south-westerly, cutting across the routes of El Golea, one of which was explored in 1859 by the intrepid Duveyrier.

The darkness was profound. Nothing could be seen ot the Trans-Saharan Railway constructing on the plans of Duponchel—a long ribbon of iron destined to bind together Algiers and Timbuctoo by way of Laghouat and Gardaia, and destined eventually to run down into the Gulf of Guinea.

Then the Albatross entered the equatorial region below the tropic of Cancer. Six hundred miles from the northern frontier of the Sahara she crossed the route on which Major Laing met his death in 1846, and crossed the road of the caravans from Morocco to the Soudan, and that part of the desert swept by the Tuaregs, where could be heard what is called "the song of the sand," a soft and plaintive murmur that seems to escape from the ground.

Only one thing happened. A cloud of locusts came flying along, and there fell such a cargo of them on board as to threaten to sink the ship. But all hands set to work to clear the deck, and the locusts were thrown over except a few hundred kept by Tapage for his larder. And he

served them up in so succulent a fashion that Frycollin forgot for the moment his perpetual trances and said,—

"These are as good as prawns."

The aeronef was then eleven hundred miles from the Wargla oasis and almost on the northern frontier of the Soudan. About two o'clock in the afternoon a city appeared in the bend of a large river. The river was the Niger. The city was Timbuctoo.

If, up to then, this African Mecca had only been visited by the travellers of the ancient world, Batouta, Khazan, Imbert, Mungo Park, Adams, Laing, Caillé, Barth, Lenz, on that day by a most singular chance the two Americans could boast of having seen, heard, and smelt it, on their return to America—if they ever got back there.

Of having seen it, because their view included the whole triangle of three or four miles in circumference; of having heard it, because the day was one of some rejoicing and the noise was terrible; of having smelt it, because the olfactory nerve could not but be very disagreeably affected by the odours of the Youbou-Kamo square, where the meat-market stands close to the palace of the ancient Somai kings.

The engineer had no notion of allowing the president and secretary of the Weldon Institute to be ignorant that they had the extreme honour of contemplating the Queen of the Soudan, now in the power of the Tuaregs of Taganet.

"Gentlemen, Timbuctoo!" he said, in the same tone as twelve days before he had said,—

"Gentlemen, India!"

Then he continued,—

"Timbuctoo is an important city of from twelve to thirteen thousand inhabitants, formerly illustrious in science and art. Perhaps you would like to stay there for a day or two?"

Such a proposal could only have been made ironically. "But," continued he, "it would be dangerous among the Negroes, Berbers, and Foullanes who occupy it—particularly as our arrival in an aeronef might prejudice them against you."

"Sir," said Phil Evans, in the same tone, "for the pleasure of leaving you we would willingly risk an unpleasant reception from the natives. Prison for prison, we would rather be in Timbuctoo than on the Albatross."

"That is a matter of taste," answered the engineer. "Anyhow, I shall not try the adventure, for I am responsible for the safety of the guests who do me the honour to travel with me."

"And so," said Uncle Prudent, explosively,

Flocks of elephants and buffaloes.

"you are not content with being our gaoler, but you insult us."

"Oh! a little irony, that is all!"

"Are there any weapons on board?"

"Oh! quite an arsenal."

"Two revolvers will do, if I hold one and you the other."

"A duel!" exclaimed Robur, "a duel, which would perhaps cause the death of one of us."

"Which certainly would cause it."

"Well! No, Mr. President of the Weldon Institute, I very much prefer keeping you alive."

"To be sure of living yourself. That is wise."

"Wise or not, it suits me. You are at liberty to think as you like, and to complain to those who have the power to help you—if you can."

"And that we have done, Mr. Robur."

"Indeed!"

"Was it so difficult when we were crossing the inhabited parts of Europe to drop a letter overboard?"

"Did you do that?" said Robur, in a paroxysm of rage.

"And if we have done it?"

"If you have done it—you deserve—"

"What, sir?"

"To follow your letter overboard."

"Throw us over, then. We did do it."

Robur stepped towards them. At a gesture from him Tom Turner and some of the crew ran up. The engineer was seriously tempted to put his threat into execution, and, fearful perhaps of yielding to it, he precipitately rushed into his cabin.

"Good!" exclaimed Phil Evans.

"And what he dare not do," said Uncle Prudent, "I will do! Yes, I will do!"

At the moment the population of Timbuctoo were crowding into the squares and roads and the terraces built like amphitheatres. In the rich quarters of Sankere and Sarahama, as in the miserable huts at Raguidi, the priests from the minarets were thundering their loudest maledictions against the aerial monster. These were more harmless than the rifle-bullets; though assuredly if the aeronef had come to earth she would have been torn to pieces.

For some miles noisy flocks of storks, francolins, and ibises escorted the Albatross and tried to race her, but in her rapid flight she soon distanced them.

The evening came. The air was troubled by the roarings of the numerous flocks of elephants and buffaloes which wander over this land, whose fertility is simply marvellous. For forty-eight hours the whole of the region between the prime meridian and the second degree, in the bend of the Niger, was viewed from the Albatross.

If a geographer had only such an apparatus at his command, with what facility could he map the country, note the elevations, fix the courses of the rivers and their affluents, and determine the positions of the towns and villages! There would then be no huge blanks on the map of Africa, no dotted lines, no vague designations which are the despair of cartographers.

In the morning of the 11th the Albatross crossed the mountains of northern Guinea, between the Soudan and the gulf which bears their name. On the horizon was the confused outline of the Kong mountains in the kingdom of Dahomey.

Since the departure from Timbuctoo Uncle Prudent and Phil Evans noticed that the course had been due south. If that direction was persisted in they would cross the equator in six more degrees. The Albatross would then abandon the continents and fly not over the Behring Sea, or the Caspian Sea, or the North Sea, or the Mediterranean, but over the Atlantic Ocean.

This look-out was not particularly pleasing to the two friends, whose chances of escape had sunk to zero.

But the Albatross had slackened speed as though hesitating to leave Africa behind. Was Robur thinking of going back? No; but his attention had been particularly attracted to the country which he was then crossing.

We know—and he knew—that the kingdom of Dahomey is one of the most powerful on the West Coast of Africa. Strong enough to hold its own with its neighbour Ashantee, its area is somewhat small, being contained within three hundred and sixty leagues from north to south, and one hundred and eighty from east to west. But its population numbers some seven or eight hundred thousand, including the neighbouring independent territories of Whydah and Ardrah.

If Dahomey is not a large country, it is often talked about. It is celebrated for the frightful cruelties which signalize its annual festivals, and by its human sacrifices—fearful hecatombs intended to honour the sovereign it has lost and the sovereign who has succeeded him. It is even a matter of politeness when the King of Dahomey receives a visit from some high personage or some foreign ambassador to give him a surprise present of a dozen heads, cut off in his honour by the minister of justice, the "minghan," who is wonderfully skilful in that branch of his duties.

When the Albatross came flying over Dahomey the old King Bahadou had just died, and the whole population was proceeding to the enthronization of his successor. Hence there was great agitation all over the country, and it did not escape Robur that everybody was on the move.

Long lines of Dahomians were hurrying along the roads from the country into the capital, Abomey. Well-kept roads radiating among vast plains clothed with giant trees, immense fields of manioc, magnificent forests or palms, cocoa-trees, mimosas, orange-trees, mango-trees—such was the country whose perfumes mounted to the Albatross, while thousands of parrots and cardinals swarmed among the trees.

The engineer, leaning over the rail, seemed deep in thought, and exchanged but a few words with Tom Turner.

It did not look as though the Albatross had attracted the attention of those moving masses, which were often invisible under the impenetrable roof of trees. This was doubtless due to her keeping at a good altitude amid a bank of light cloud.

About eleven o'clock in the morning the capital was sighted, surrounded by its walls, defended by a fosse measuring twelve miles round, with wide, regular streets on the flat plain, and a large square on the northern side occupied by the king's palace. This huge collection of buildings is commanded by a terrace not far from the place of sacrifice. During the festival days it is from this high terrace that they throw the prisoners tied up in wicker baskets, and it can be imagined with what fury these unhappy wretches are cut in pieces.

In one of the courtyards which divide the king's palace there were drawn up four thousand warriors, one of the contingents of the royal army—and not the least courageous one.

If it is doubtful if there are any Amazons on the river of that name, there is no doubt of there being Amazons at Dahomey. Some have a blue shirt with a blue or red scarf, with white-and-blue striped trousers and a white cap; others, the elephant-huntresses, have a heavy carbine, a short-bladed dagger, and two antelope horns fixed to their heads by a band of iron. The artillery-women have a blue-and-red tunic, and, as weapons, blunderbusses and old cast cannons; and another brigade, consisting of vestal virgins pure as Diana, have blue tunics and white trousers. If we add to these Amazons five or six thousand men in cotton drawers and

shirts, with a knotted tuft to increase their stature, we shall have passed in review the Dahomian army.

Abomey on this day was deserted. The sovereign, the royal family, the masculine and feminine army, and the population had all gone out of the capital to a vast plain a few miles away surrounded by magnificent forests.

On this plain the recognition of the new king was to take place. Here it was that thousands of prisoners taken during recent razzias were to be immolated in his honour.

It was about two o'clock when the Albatross arrived over the plain and began to descend among the clouds which still hid her from the Dahomians.

There were sixteen thousand people at least come from all parts of the kingdom, from Whydah, and Kerapay, and Ardrah, and Tombory, and the most distant villages.

The new king—a sturdy fellow named Bou-Nadi—some five-and-twenty years old, was seated on a hillock shaded by a group of wide-branched trees. Before him stood his male army, his Amazons, and his people.

At the foot of the mound fifty musicians were playing on their barbarous instruments, elephants' tusks giving forth a husky note, deerskin drums, calabashes, guitars, bells struck with an iron clapper, and bamboo flutes, whose shrill whistle was heard over all. Every other second came discharges of guns and blunderbusses, discharges of cannons with the carriages jumping so as to imperil the lives of the artillery-women, and a general uproar so intense that even the thunder would be unheard amidst it.

In one corner of the plain, under a guard of soldiers, were grouped the prisoners destined to accompany the defunct king into the other world. At the obsequies of Ghozo, the father of Bahadou, his son had despatched three thousand, and Bou-Nadi could not do less than his predecessor. For an hour there was a series of discourses, harangues, palavers and dances, executed not only by professionals, but by the Amazons, who displayed much martial grace.

But the time for the hecatomb was approaching. Robur, who knew the customs of Dahomey, did not lose sight of the men, women, and children reserved for butchery.

The mingham was standing at the foot of the hillock. He was brandishing his executioner's sword, with its curved blade surmounted by a metal bird, whose weight rendered the cut more certain.

This time he was not alone. He could not have performed the task. Near him were

The little gun shot forth its shrapnel.

Exploded like so many small shells.

grouped a hundred executioners, all accustomed to cut off heads at one blow.

The Albatross came slowly down in an oblique direction. Soon she emerged from the bed of clouds which hid her till she was within three hundred feet of the ground, and for the first time she was visible from below.

Contrary to what had hitherto happened, the savages saw in her a celestial being come to render homage to King Bahadou. The enthusiasm was indescribable, the shouts were interminable, the prayers were terrific—prayers addressed to this supernatural hippo-—griff, which had doubtless come to take the king's body to the higher regions of the Dahomian heaven.

And now the first head fell under the minghan's sword, and the prisoners were led up in hundreds before the horrible executioners.

Suddenly a gun was fired from the Albatross. The minister of justice fell dead on his face.

"Well aimed, Tom!" said Robur.

His comrades, armed as he was, stood ready to fire when the order was given.

But a change came over the crowd below. They had understood. The winged monster was not a friendly spirit, it was a hostile spirit. And after the fall of the minghan loud shouts for revenge arose on all sides. Almost immediately a fusillade resounded over the plain.

These menaces did not prevent the Albatross from descending boldly to within a hundred and fifty feet of the ground. Uncle Prudent and Phil Evans, whatever were their feelings towards Robur, could not help joining him in such a work of humanity.

"Let us free the prisoners!" they shouted.

"That is what I am going to do!" said the engineer.

And the magazine rifles of the Albatross in the hands of the colleagues, as in the hands of the crew, began to rain down the bullets, of which not one was lost in the masses below. And the little gun shot forth its shrapnel, which really did marvels.

The prisoners, although they did not understand how the help had come to them, broke their bonds, while the soldiers were firing at the aeronef. The stern screw was shot through by a bullet, and a few holes were made in the hull. Frycollin, crouching in his cabin, received a graze from a bullet that came through the deck-house.

"Ah! They will have them!" said Tom Turner. And, rushing to the magazine, he returned with a dozen dynamite cartridges, which he distributed to the men. At a sign from Robur these cartridges were fired at the hillock, and as they reached the ground exploded like so many small shells.

The king and his court and army and people were stricken with fear at the turn things had taken. They fled under the trees, while the prisoners ran off without anybody thinking of pursuing them.

In this way was the festival interfered with. And in this way did Uncle Prudent and Phil Evans recognize the power of the aeronef and the services it could render to humanity.

Soon the Albatross rose again to a moderate height, and passing over Whydah lost to view this savage coast which the south-west wind hems round with an inaccessible surf. And she flew out over the Atlantic.

The Clipper of the Clouds

CHAPTER XVI.

OVER THE ATLANTIC

YES, the Atlantic! The fears of the two colleagues were realized; but it did not seem as though Robur had the least anxiety about venturing over this vast ocean. Both he and his men seemed quite unconcerned about it, and had gone back to their stations.

Whither was the Albatross bound? Was she going more than round the world as Robur had said? Even if she were, the voyage must end somewhere. That Robur spent his life in the air on board the aeronef and never came to the ground was impossible. How could he make up his stock of provisions and the materials required for working his machines? He must have some retreat, some harbour of refuge in some unknown and inaccessible spot where the Albatross could revictual. That he had broken off all connection with the inhabitants of the land might be true, but with every point on the surface of the earth, certainly not.

That being the case, where was this point? How had the engineer come to choose it? Was he expected by a little colony of which he was the chief? Could he there find a new crew?

What means had he that he should be able to build so costly a vessel as the Albatross and keep her building secret? It is true his living was not expensive. But, finally, who was this Robur? Where did he come from? What had been his history? Here were riddles impossible to solve; and Robur was not the man to willingly assist in their solution.

It is not to be wondered at that these insoluble problems drove the colleagues almost to frenzy. To find themselves whipped off into the unknown without knowing what the end might be, doubting even if the adventure would end, sentenced to perpetual aviation, was this not enough to drive the president and secretary of the Weldon Institute to extremities.

Meanwhile the Albatross drove along above the Atlantic, and in the morning when the sun rose there was nothing to be seen but the circular line where earth met sky. Not a spot of land was in sight in this huge field of vision. Africa had vanished beneath the northern horizon.

When Frycollin ventured out of his cabin and saw all this water beneath him, fear took possession of him.

Beneath him is hardly the correct phrase; we should have said around him, for to an observer above the earth the abyss seems to curve up like a bowl to the horizon on a level with his eye, and the edge of the horizon seems to travel away as he moves towards it.

It is probable that Frycollin could not explain this effect physically, but he felt it all the same, and it produced on him that horror of the abyss from which certain people, brave though they may be, cannot free themselves. The negro was wise enough to say nothing. With eyes shut he felt his way back to his cabin, resolving to stay there for some considerable time.

Of the hundred and forty-five million square miles of which the area of the world's waters consists, the Atlantic claims about a quarter; and it seemed as though the engineer was in no hurry to cross it. There was now no going at full speed, none of the hundred and twenty miles an hour at which the Albatross had flown over Europe. Here, where the south-west winds prevail, the wind was ahead of them, and though it was not very strong, it would not do to defy it. And the Albatross was sent along at a moderate speed, which, however, easily out-stripped that of the fastest mail-boat.

On the 13th of July she crossed the line, and the fact was duly announced to the crew. It was then that Uncle Prudent and Phil Evans ascertained that they were bound for the southern hemisphere. The crossing of the line took place without any of the Neptunian ceremonies that still linger on certain ships. Tapage was the only one to mark the event, and he did so by pouring a pint of water down Frycollin's neck.

On the morning of the 15th the Albatross passed between the islands of Ascension and St. Helena approaching the last, whose higher ground showed above the horizon for some hours. In the evenings of the 16th and 17th of July there was a curious phenomenon at sunset. In a higher latitude it might have been taken for the aurora borealis. The sun as it disappeared shot forth a number of multi-coloured rays, some of which were of a vivid green.

Was this due to cosmic dust which the earth was then passing through, and which reflected the last beams of the day? Some observers have

A volcanic eruption had projected this cloud into the air.

assigned such an origin to these crepuscular lights, but their explanation would not have been maintained for long had they been on board the aeronef, where it was found that there were floating in the air tiny crystals of pyroxene, and glassy globes and slender needles of magnetic iron, analogous to the matter ejected by certain volcanoes. There could be no doubt that a volcanic eruption had projected this cloud into the air, where it was held in suspension while it drifted over the Atlantic.

And other phenomena were observed. On several occasions the sky took a strange greyish tint, and when the curtain of vapour was passed its surface seemed ridged with white feathery clouds and dotted with solid spangles, giving an appearance which could only be explained as due to a form of hail.

In the night between the 17th and 18th there appeared a greenish lunar bow, owing to the aeronef being between the full moon and a curtain of fine rain which went off into vapour before it reached the sea.

Did these phenomena portend a change in the weather? Perhaps. Anyhow, the wind, which had blown from the south-west since their leaving the coast of Africa, had now dropped to a calm. And in this tropical zone it was extremely cold, for Robur had risen to get the benefit of the higher air-currents, and taken steps to screen himself from the direct rays of the sun, which would have been almost insupportable.

In the southern hemisphere the month of July answers to the month of January in the northern, that is to say, it is the depth of winter, and if the Albatross was kept on her southerly course she would soon feel the effect of this.

On the 18th of July, when beyond the tropic of Capricorn, another phenomenon was noticed, which would have been somewhat alarming to a ship on the sea.

A strange succession of luminous waves widened out over the surface of the ocean with a speed estimated at quite sixty miles an hour. The waves ran along at about eighty feet from one another, tracing two furrows of light. As night fell a bright reflection rose even to the Albatross, so that she might have been taken for a flaming aerolite. Never before had Robur sailed on a sea of fire—a fire without heat—which there was no need to flee from as it mounted upwards into the sky.

The cause of this light must have been electricity; it could not be attributed to a bank of fish spawn, nor to a crowd of those animalculae that give phosphorescence to the sea, and this showed that the electrical tension of the atmosphere was considerable.

In the morning an ordinary ship would probably have been lost. But the Albatross played with the winds and waves like the powerful bird whose name she bore. If she did not walk on their surface like the petrels, she could like the eagles find calm and sunshine in the higher zones.

They had now passed the forty-seventh parallel. The day was but little over seven hours long, and would become even less as they approached the Pole.

About one o'clock in the afternoon the Albatross was floating along in a lower current than usual, about a hundred feet from the level of the sea. The air was calm, but in certain parts of the sky were thick black clouds, massed in mountains on their upper surface, and ruled off below by a sharp horizontal line. From these clouds a few lengthy protuberances escaped, and their points as they fell seemed to draw up hills of foaming water to meet them.

Suddenly the water shot up in the form of a gigantic hour-glass, and the Albatross was enveloped in the eddy of an enormous water-spout, while twenty others, black as ink, raged around her. Fortunately the gyratory move-ment of the water was opposite to that of the suspensory screws, otherwise the aeronef would have been hurled into the sea. But she began to spin round on herself with frightful rapidity.

The danger was immense, and perhaps impossible to escape, for the engineer could not get through the spout which sucked him back in defiance of his propellers. The men, thrown to the ends of the deck by centrifugal force, were grasping the rail to save themselves from being shot off.

"Keep cool!" shouted Robur.

They wanted all their coolness, and their patience too.

Uncle Prudent and Phil Evans, who had just come out of their cabin, were hurled back at the risk of flying overboard.

As she spun the Albatross was carried along by the spout, which pirouetted along the waves with a speed enough to make the helices jealous. And if she escaped from the spout she might be caught by another, and jerked to pieces with the shock.

"Get the gun ready!" said Robur.

The order was given to Tom Turner, who was crouching behind the swivel amidships where the effect of the centrifugal force was least felt. He understood. In a moment he had opened the breech and slipped in a cartridge from the ammunition-box at hand. The gun went off,

Enveloped in the eddy of an enormous waterspout.

and the waterspouts collapsed, and with them vanished the platform of cloud they seemed to bear above them.

"Nothing broken on board?" asked Robur.

"No," answered Tom Turner. "But we don't want to have another game of humming-top like that!"

For ten minutes or so the Albatross had been in extreme peril. Had it not been for her extraordinary strength of build she would have been lost.

During this passage of the Atlantic many were the hours whose monotony was unbroken by any phenomenon whatever. The days grew shorter and shorter, and the cold became keen. Uncle Prudent and Phil Evans saw little of Robur. Seated in his cabin, the engineer was busy laying out his course and marking it on his maps, taking his observations whenever he could, recording the readings of his barometers, thermometers, and chronometers, and making full entries in his log-book.

The colleagues wrapped themselves well up and eagerly watched for the sight of land to the southward. At Uncle Prudent's request Frycollin tried to pump the cook as to whither the engineer was bound. But what reliance could be placed on the information given by this Gascon? Sometimes Robur was an ex-minister of the Argentine Republic, sometimes a lord of the Admiralty, sometimes an ex-President of the United States, sometimes a Spanish general temporarily retired, sometimes a Viceroy of the Indies who had sought a more elevated position in the air. Sometimes he possessed millions, thanks to successful razzias in the aeronef, and he had been proclaimed for piracy. Sometimes he had been ruined by making the aeronef, and had been forced to fly aloft to escape from his creditors. As to knowing if he were going to stop anywhere, no! But if he thought of going to the moon, and found there a convenient anchorage, he would anchor there!

"Eh! Fry! my boy! That would just suit you to see what was going on up there."

"I shall not go! I refuse!" said the negro, who took all these things seriously.

"And why, Fry, why? You might get married to some pretty bouncing Lunarian!"

Frycollin reported this conversation to his master, who saw it was evident that nothing was to be learnt about Robur. And so he thought still more of how he could have his revenge on him.

"Phil," said he one day, "is it quite certain that escape is impossible?"

"Impossible."

"Be it so! But a man is always his own property; and if necessary, by sacrificing his life—"

"If we are to make that sacrifice," said Phil Evans, "the sooner the better. It is almost time to end this. Where is the Albatross going? Here we are flying obliquely over the Atlantic, and if we keep on we shall get to the coast of Patagonia or Tierra del Fuego. And what are we to do then? Get into the Pacific, or go to the continent at the South Pole? Everything is possible with this Robur. We shall be lost in the end. It is thus a cage of legitimate self-defence, and if we must perish—"

"Which we shall not do," answered Uncle Prudent, "without being avenged, without annihilating this machine and all she carries."

The colleagues had reached a stage of impotent fury and were prepared to sacrifice themselves if they could only destroy the inventor and his secret. A few months only would then be the life of this prodigious aeronef, of whose superiority in aerial locomotion they had such convincing proofs! The idea took such hold of them that they thought of nothing else but how to put it into execution. And how? By seizing on some of the explosives on board and simply blowing her up. But could they get at the magazine!

Fortunately for them, Frycollin had no suspicion of their scheme. At the thought of the Albatross exploding in mid air, he would not have shrunk from betraying his master.

It was on the 23rd of July that the land reappeared in the south-west near Cape Virgins at the entrance of the Straits of Magellan. Under the fifty-second parallel at this time of year the night was eighteen hours long and the temperature was six below freezing.

At first the Albatross, instead of keeping on to the south, followed the windings of the coast as if to enter the Pacific. After passing Lomas Bay, leaving Mount Gregory to the north and the Brecknocks to the west, they sighted Puerto Arena, a small Chilian village, at the moment the church-bells were in full swing; and a few hours later they were over the old settlement at Port Famine.

If the Patagonians, whose fires could be seen occasionally, were really above the average in stature, the passengers in the aeronef were unable to say, for to them they seemed to be dwarfs. But what a magnificent landscape opened around during these short hours of the southern day! Rugged mountains, peaks eternally capped with snow, with thick forest rising on their flanks, inland seas, bays deep set amid the peninsulas and islands of the Archipelago. Clarence Island, Dawson Island,

Here was work for the cook.

and the Land of Desolation, straits and channels, capes and promontories, all in inextricable confusion, and bound by the ice in one solid mass from Cape Forward, the most southerly point of the American continent, to Cape Horn the most southerly point of the New World.

When she reached Port Famine the Albatross resumed her course to the south. Passing between Mount Tarn on the Brunswick Peninsula and Mount Graves, she steered for Mount Sarmiento, an enormous peak wrapped in snow, which commands the Straits of Magellan, rising six thousand four hundred feet from the sea. And now they were over the land of the Fuegians, Tierra del Fuego, the land of fire. Six months later, in the height of summer, with days from fifteen to sixteen hours long, how beautiful and fertile would most of this country be, particularly in its northern portion! Then, all around would be seen valleys and pasturages that could form the feeding-grounds of thousands of animals; then would appear virgin forests, gigantic trees—birches, beeches, ash-trees, cypresses, tree-ferns—and broad plains overrun by herds of guanacos, vicunas, and ostriches. Now there were armies of penguins and myriads of birds; and when the Albatross turned on her electric lamps the guillemots, ducks, and geese came crowding on board enough to fill Tapage's larder a hundred times and more.

Here was work for the cook, who knew how to bring out the flavour of the game and keep down its peculiar oiliness. And here was work for Frycollin in plucking dozen after dozen of such interesting feathered friends.

That day, as the sun was setting about three o'clock in the afternoon, there appeared in sight a large lake framed in a border of superb forest. The lake was completely frozen over, and a few natives with long snowshoes on their feet were swiftly gliding over it.

At the sight of the Albatross, the Fuegians, overwhelmed with terror, scattered in all directions, and when they could not get away they hid themselves, taking, like the animals, to the holes in the ground.

The Albatross still held her southerly course, crossing the Beagle Channel, and Navarin Island and Wollaston Island, on the shores of the Pacific. Then, having accomplished 4700 miles since she left Dahomey, she passed the last islands of the Magellanic archipelago, whose most southerly outpost, lashed by the everlasting surf, is the terrible Cape Horn.

The Clipper of the Clouds

CHAPTER XVII.

THE SHIPWRECKED CREW

NEXT day was the 24th of July; and the 24th of July in the southern hemisphere corresponds to the 24th of January in the northern. The fifty-sixth degree of latitude had been left behind. The similar parallel in northern Europe runs through Edinburgh.

The thermometer kept steadily below freezing, so that the machinery was called upon to furnish a little artificial heat in the cabins. Although the days begin to lengthen after the 21st of June in the southern hemisphere, yet the advance of the Albatross towards the Pole more than neutralized this increase, and consequently the daylight became very short. There was thus very little to be seen. At night time the cold became very keen; but as there was no scarcity of clothing on board, the colleagues, well wrapped up, remained a good deal on deck thinking over their plans of escape, and watching for an opportunity. Little was seen of Robur; since the high words that had been exchanged in the Timbuctoo country, the engineer had left off speaking to his prisoners.

Frycollin seldom came out of the cookhouse, where Tapage treated him most hospitably, on condition that he acted as his assistant. This position was not without its advantages, and the negro, with his master's permission, very willingly accepted it. Shut up in the galley, he saw nothing of what was passing outside, and might even consider himself beyond the reach of danger. He was, in fact, very like the ostrich, not only in his stomach, but in his folly.

But whither went the Albatross? Was she in mid-winter bound for the southern seas or continents round the Pole? In this icy atmosphere, even granting the the elements of the batteries were unaffected by such frost, would not all the crew succumb to a horrible death from the cold? That Robur should attempt to cross the Pole in the warm season was bad enough, but to attempt such a thing in the depth of the winter night would be the act of a madman.

Thus reasoned the President and Secretary of the Weldon Institute, now they had been brought to the end of the continent of the New World, which is still America, although it does not belong to the United States.

What was this intractable Robur going to do? Had not the time arrived for them to end the voyage by blowing up the ship?

It was noticed that during the 24th of July the engineer had frequent consultations with his mate. He and Tom Turner kept constant watch on the barometer—not so much to keep themselves informed of the height at which they were travelling as to be on the look-out for a change in the weather. Evidently some indications had been observed of which it was necessary to make careful note.

Uncle Prudent also remarked that Robur had been taking stock of the provisions and stores, and everything seemed to show that he was contemplating turning back.

"Turning back!" said Phil Evans. "But where to?"

"Where he can re-provision the ship," said Uncle Prudent.

"That ought to be in some lonely island in the Pacific with a colony of scoundrels worthy of their chief."

"That is what I think. I fancy he is going west, and with the speed he can get up it would not take him long to get home."

"But we should not be able to put our plan into execution. If we get there—"

"We shall not get there!"

The colleagues had partly guessed the engineer's intentions. During the day it became no longer doubtful that when the Albatross reached the confines of the Antarctic Sea her course was to be changed. When the ice has formed about Cape Horn the lower regions of the Pacific are covered with ice-fields and icebergs. The floes then form an impenetrable barrier to the strongest ships and the boldest navigators.

Of course, by increasing the speed of her wings the Albatross could clear the mountain of ice accumulated on the ocean as she could the mountains of earth on the polar continent—if it is a continent that forms the cap of the southern pole. But would she attempt it in the middle of the polar night, in an atmosphere of sixty below freezing?

After she had advanced about a hundred miles to the south the Albatross headed westerly, as if for some unknown island of the Pacific. Beneath her stretched the liquid plain between Asia and America. The waters now had assumed that singular colour which has earned for them the name of the Milky Sea. In the half shadow, which the enfeebled rays of the sun were unable to dissipate, the surface of the Pacific was a milky white. It seemed like a vast snowfield, whose undulations were imperceptible at such a height. If the sea had been solidified by the cold, and converted into an immense icefield, its aspect could not have been much different. They knew that the phenomenon was produced by myriads of luminous particles or phosphorescent corpuscles; but it was surprising to come across such an opalescent mass beyond the limits of the Indian Ocean.

Suddenly the barometer fell after keeping somewhat high during the earlier hours of the day. Evidently the indications were such as a shipmaster might feel anxious at, though the master of an aeronef might despise them. There was every sign that a terrible storm had recently raged in the Pacific.

It was one o'clock in the afternoon when Tom Turner came up to the engineer and said, "Do you see that black spot on the horizon, sir—there away to due north of us? That is not a rock?"

"No, Tom; there is no land out there."

"Then it must be a ship or a boat."

Uncle Prudent and Phil Evans, who were in the bow, looked in the direction pointed out by the mate.

Robur asked for the glass and attentively observed the object.

"It is a boat," said he, "and there are some men in it."

"Shipwrecked?" asked Tom.

"Yes! They have had to abandon their ship, and knowing nothing of the nearest land, are perhaps dying of hunger and thirst! Well, it shall not be said that the Albatross did not come to their help!"

The orders were given, and the aeronef began to sink towards the sea. At three hundred yards from it the descent was stopped, and the propellers drove ahead full speed towards the north.

It was a boat. Her sail flapped against the mast as she rose and fell on the waves. There was no wind, and she was making no progress. Doubtless there was no one on board with strength enough left to work the oars. In the boat were five men asleep or helpless, if they were not dead.

The Albatross had arrived above them, and slowly descended.

On the boat's stern was the name of the ship to which she belonged—the Jeannette of Nantes.

"Hallo, there!" shouted Turner, loud enough for the men to hear, for the boat was only eighty feet below him.

There was no answer.

"Fire a gun!" said Robur.

The gun was fired and the report rang our over the sea.

One of the men looked up feebly. His eyes were haggard and his face was that of a skeleton. As he caught sight of the Albatross he made a gesture as of fear.

"Don't be afraid," said Robur in French, "we have come to help you. Who are you?"

"We belong to the barque Jeanette, and I am the mate. We left her a fortnight ago as she was sinking. We have no water and no food."

The four other men had now sat up. Wan and exhausted, in a terrible state of emaciation, they lifted their hands towards the Albatross.

"Look out!" shouted Robur.

A line was let down, and a pail of fresh water was lowered into the boat. The men snatched at it and drank it with an eagerness awful to see.

"Bread, Bread!" they exclaimed.

Immediately a basket with some food and five pints of coffee descended towards them. The mate with difficulty restrained them in their ravenousness.

"Where are we?" asked the mate at last.

"Fifty miles from the Chili coast and the Chonos Archipelago," answered Robur.

"Thanks. But we are becalmed, and—"

"We are going to tow you."

"Who are you?"

"People who are glad to be of assistance to you," said Robur.

The mate understood that the incognito was to be respected. But had the flying machine sufficient power to tow them through the water?

Yes; and the boat, attached to a hundred feet of rope, began to move off towards the east. At ten o'clock at night the land was sighted—or rather they could see the lights which indicated its position. This rescue from the sky had come just in time for the survivors of the Jeannette, and they had good reason to believe it miraculous.

When they had been taken to the mouth of the channel leading among the Chonos Islands, Robur shouted to them to cast off the tow-line. This, with many a blessing to those who had saved them, they did, and the Albatross headed out to the offing.

"Who are you?"

Certainly there was some good in this aeronef, which could thus help those who were lost at sea! What balloon, perfect as it might be, would be able to perform such a service? And between themselves Uncle Prudent and Phil Evans could not but admit it, although they were quite disposed to deny the evidence of their senses.

The Clipper of the Clouds

CHAPTER XVIII.

OVER THE VOLCANO

THE sea was as rough as ever, and the symptoms became alarming. The barometer fell several millimetres. The wind came in violent gusts, and then for a moment or so failed altogether. Under such circumstances a sailing vessel would have had two reefs in her topsails and a reef in her foresail. Everything showed that the wind was rising in the north-west. The storm-glass became much troubled and its movements were most disquieting.

At one o'clock in the morning the wind came on again with extreme violence. Although the aeronef was going right in its teeth she was still making progress at a rate of from twelve to fifteen miles an hour. But that was the utmost she could do.

Evidently preparations must be made for a cyclone, a very rare occurrence in these latitudes. Whether it be called a hurricane, as in the Atlantic, a typhoon, as in Chinese waters, a simoom, as in the Sahara, or a tornado, as on the western coast, such a storm is always a gyratory one, and most dangerous for any ship caught in the current which increases from the circumference to the centre, and has only one spot of calm, the middle of the vortex.

Robur knew this. He also knew it was best to escape from the cyclone and get beyond its zone of attraction by ascending to the higher strata. Up to then he had always succeeded in doing this, but now he had not an hour, perhaps not a minute, to lose.

In fact the violence of the wind sensibly increased. The crests of the waves were swept off as they rose and blown into white dust on the surface of the sea. It was manifest that the cyclone was advancing with fearful velocity straight towards the regions of the pole.

"Higher!" said Robur.

"Higher it is," said Tom Turner.

An extreme ascensional power was communicated to the aeronef, and she shot up slantingly as if she was travelling on a plane sloping downwards from the south-west. Suddenly the barometer fell more than a dozen millimetres and the Albatross paused in her ascent.

What was the cause of the stoppage? Evidently she was pulled back by the air; some formidable current had diminished the resist-ance to the screws. When a steamer travels up stream more work is got out of her screw than when the water is running between the blades. The recoil is then considerable, and may perhaps be as great as the current. It was thus with the Albatross at this moment.

But Robur was not the man to give in. His seventy-four screws, working perfectly together, were driven at their maximum speed. But the aeronef could not escape; the attraction of the cyclone was irresistible. During the few moments of calm she began to ascend, but the heavy pull soon drew her back, and she sunk like a ship as she founders.

Evidently if the violence of the cyclone went on increasing the Albatross would be but as a straw caught in one of those whirlwinds that root up the trees, carry off roofs, and blow down walls.

Robur and Tom could only speak by signs. Uncle Prudent and Phil Evans clung to the rail and wondered if the cyclone was not playing their game in destroying the aeronef and with her the inventor, and with the inventor the secret of his invention.

But if the Albatross could not get out of the cyclone vertically could she not do something else? Could she not gain the centre, where it was comparatively calm, and where they would have more control over her? Quite so; but to do this she would have to break through the circular currents which were sweeping her round with them. Had she sufficient mechanical power to escape through them?

Suddenly the upper part of the cloud fell in. The vapour condensed in torrents of rain. It was two o'clock in the morning. The barometer, oscillating over a range of twelve millimetres, had now fallen to 27.91, and from this something should be taken on account of the height of the aeronef above the level of the sea.

Strange to say, the cyclone was out of the zone to which such storms are generally restricted, such zone being bounded by the thirtieth parallel of north latitude and the twenty-sixth parallel of south latitude. This may perhaps explain why the eddying storm suddenly turned into a straight one. But what a hurricane! The tempest in Connecticut on the

22nd of March, 1882, could only have been compared to it, and the speed of that was more than three hundred miles an hour.

The Albatross had thus to fly before the wind, or rather she had to be left to be driven by the current, from which she could neither mount nor escape. But in following this unchanging trajectory she was bearing due south, towards those polar regions which Robur had endeavoured to avoid. And now he was no longer master of her course; she would go where the hurricane took her.

Tom Turner was at the helm, and it required all his skill to keep her straight. In the first hours of the morning—if we can so call the vague tint which began to rise over the horizon —the Albatross was fifteen degrees below Cape Horn; twelve hundred miles more and she would cross the antarctic circle. Where she was, in this month of July, the night lasted nineteen hours and a half. The sun's disk—without warmth, without light—only appeared above the horizon to disappear almost immediately. At the pole the night lengthened into one of a hundred and seventy-nine hours. Everything showed that the Albatross was about to plunge into an abyss.

During the day an observation, had it been possible, would have given 66° 40' south latitude. The aeronef was within fourteen hundred miles of the pole.

Irresistibly was she drawn towards this inaccessible corner of the globe, her speed eating up, so to speak, her weight, although she weighed less than before, owing to the flattening of the earth at the pole. It seemed as though she could have dispensed altogether with her suspensory screws. And soon the fury of the storm reached such a height that Robur thought it best to reduce the speed of her helices as much as possible, so as to avoid disaster. And only enough speed was given to keep the aeronef under control of the rudder.

Amid these dangers the engineer retained his imperturbable coolness, and the crew obeyed him as if their leader's mind had entered into them. Uncle Prudent and Phil Evans had not for a moment left the deck; they could remain without being disturbed. The air made but slight resistance. The aeronef was like an aerostat, which drifts with the fluid mass in which it is plunged.

Is the domain of the southern pole a continent or an archipelago? Or is it a paleo-crystic sea, whose ice melts not even during the long summer? We know not. But what we do know is that the southern pole is colder than the northern one—a phenomenon due to the position of the earth in its orbit during winter in the antarctic regions.

During this day there was nothing to show that the storm was abating. It was by the seventy-fifth meridian to the west that the Albatross crossed into the circumpolar region. By what meridian would she come out—if she ever came out?

As she descended more to the south the length of the day diminished. Before long she would be plunged in that continuous night which is illuminated only by the rays of the moon or the pale streamers of the aurora. But the moon was then new, and the companions of Robur might see nothing of the regions whose secret has hitherto defied human curiosity.

There was not much inconvenience on board from the cold, for the temperature was not nearly so low as was expected. It seemed as though the hurricane was a sort of Gulf Stream, carrying a certain amount of heat along with it.

Great was the regret that the whole region was in such profound obscurity. Even if the moon had been in full glory but few observations could have been made. At this season of the year an immense curtain of snow, an icy carapace, covers up the polar surface. There was none of that ice "blink" to be seen, that whitish tint of which the reflection is absent from dark horizons. Under such circumstances how could they distinguish the shape of the ground, the extent of the seas, the position of the islands? How could they recognize the hydrographic network of the country or the orographic configuration, and distinguish the hills and mountains from the icebergs and floes?

A little after midnight an aurora illuminated the darkness. With its silver fringes and spangles radiating over space, it seemed like a huge fan open over half the sky. Its farthest electric effluences were lost in the Southern Cross, whose four bright stars were gleaming overhead. The phenomenon was one of incomparable magnificence, and the light showed the face of the country as a confused mass of white.

It need not be said that they had approached so near to the pole that the compass was constantly affected, and gave no precise indication of the course pursued. Its inclination was such that at one time Robur felt certain they were passing over the magnetic pole discovered by Sir James Ross. And an hour later, in calculating the angle the needle made with the vertical, he exclaimed,—

"The South Pole is beneath us!"

A white cap appeared, but nothing could be seen of what it hid under its ice.

A few minutes afterwards the aurora died away, and the point where all the world's meridians cross is still to be discovered.

If Uncle Prudent and Phil Evans wished to bury in the most mysterious solitudes the aeronef and all she bore, the moment was propitious. If they did not do so it was doubtless because the explosive they required was still denied to them.

The hurricane still raged, and swept along with such rapidity that had a mountain been met with the aeronef would have been dashed to pieces like a ship on a lee shore. Not only had the power gone to steer her horizontally, but the control of her elevation had also vanished.

And it was not unlikely that mountains did exist in these antarctic lands. Any instant a shock might happen which would destroy the Albatross. Such a catastrophe became more probable as the wind shifted more to the east after they passed the prime meridian. Two luminous points then showed themselves ahead of the Albatross. These were the two volcanos of the Ross Mountains—Erebus and Terror. Was the Albatross to be shrivelled up in their flames like a gigantic butterfly?

And hour of intense excitement followed. One of the volcanoes, Erebus, seemed to be rushing at the aeronef, which could not move from the bed of the hurricane. The cloud of flame grew as they neared it. A network of fire barred their road. A brilliant light shone round over all. The figures on board stood out in the bright light as if come from another world. Motionless, without a sound or a gesture, they waited for the terrible moment when the furnace would wrap them in its fires.

But the storm that bore the Albatross saved them from such a fearful fate. The flames of Erebus were blown down by the hurricane as it passed, and the Albatross flew over unhurt. She swept through a hail of ejected material, which was fortunately kept at bay by the centrifugal action of the suspensory screws. And she harmlessly passed over the crater while it was in full eruption.

An hour afterwards the horizon hid from their view the two colossal torches which light the confines of the world during the long polar night.

At two o'clock in the morning Balleny Island was sighted on the coast of Discovery Land, though it could not be recognized owing to its being bound to the mainland by a cement of ice.

And the Albatross emerged from the polar circle on the hundred and seventy-fifth meridian. The hurricane had carried her over the icebergs and icefloes, against which she was

in danger of being dashed a hundred times or more. She was not in the hands of the helmsman, but in the hand of God—and God is a good pilot.

The aeronef sped along to the north, and at the sixtieth parallel the storm showed signs of dying away. Its violence sensibly diminished. The Albatross began to come under control again. And, what was a great comfort, had again entered the lighted regions of the globe; and the day reappeared about eight o'clock in the morning.

Robur had been carried by the storm into the Pacific over the polar region, accomplishing four thousand three hundred and fifty miles in nineteen hours, or about three miles a minute, a speed almost double that which the Albatross was equal to with her propellers under ordinary circumstances. But he did not know where he then was owing to the disturbance of the needle in the neighbourhood of the magnetic pole, and he would have to wait till the sun shone out under convenient conditions for observation. Unfortunately, heavy clouds covered the sky all that day and the sun did not appear.

This was a disappointment more keenly felt as both propelling screws had sustained damage during the tempest. Robur, much disconcerted at this accident, could only advance at a moderate speed during this day, and when he passed over the antipodes of Paris was only going about eighteen miles an hour. It was necessary not to aggravate the damage to the screws, for if the propellers were rendered useless the situation of the aeronef above the vast seas of the Pacific would be a very awkward one. And the engineer began to consider if he could not effect his repairs on the spot, so as to make sure of continuing his voyage.

In the morning of the 27th of July, about seven o'clock, land was sighted to the north. It was soon seen to be an island. But which island was it of the thousands that dot the Pacific? However, Robur decided to stop at it without landing. He thought that he could repair damages during the day and start in the evening.

The wind had died away completely, and this was a favourable circumstance for the manoeuvre he desired to execute. At least, if she did not remain stationary the Albatross would not be carried he knew not where.

A cable one hundred and fifty feet long with an anchor at the end was dropped overboard. When the aeronef reached the shore of the island the anchor dragged up the first few rocks and then got firmly fixed between two large blocks. The cable then stretched to full length under the influence of the suspensory screws, and the Albatross remained motionless, riding like a ship in a roadstead.

It was the first time she had been fastened to the earth since she left Philadelphia.

The Clipper of the Clouds

CHAPTER XIX.

ANCHORED AT LAST

WHEN the Albatross was high in the air the island could be seen to be of moderate size. But on what parallel was it situated? What meridian ran through it? Was it an island in the Pacific, in Australasia, or in the Indian Ocean? When the sun appeared, and Robur had taken his observations, they would know; but although they could not trust to the indications of the compass there was reason to think they were in the Pacific.

At this height—one hundred and fifty feet—the island which measured about fifteen miles round, was like a three-pointed star in the sea.

Off the south-west point was an islet and a range of rocks. On the shore there were no tide-marks, and this tended to confirm Robur in his opinion as to his position for the ebb and flow are almost imperceptible in the Pacific.

At the north-west point there was a conical mountain about two hundred feet high.

No natives were to be seen, but they might be on the opposite coast. In any case, if they had perceived the aeronef, terror had made them hide themselves or run away.

The Albatross had anchored on the south-west point of the island. Not far off, down a little creek, a small river flowed in among the rocks. Beyond were several winding valleys; trees of different kinds; and birds—partridges and bustards—in great numbers. If the island was not inhabited it was habitable. Robur might surely had landed on it; if he had not done so it was probably because the ground was uneven and did not offer a convenient spot to beach the aeronef.

While he was waiting for the sun the engineer began the repairs he reckoned on completing before the day was over. The suspensory screws were undamaged and had worked admirably amid all the violence of the storm, which, as we have said, had considerably lightened their work. At this moment half of them were in action, enough to keep the Albatross fixed to the shore by the taut cable. But the two propellers had suffered, and more than Robur had thought. Their blades would have to be adjusted and the gearing seen to by which they receive their rotatory movement.

It was the screw at the bow which was first attacked under Robur's superintendence. It was the best to commence with, in case the Albatross had to leave before the work was finished. With only this propeller he could easily keep a proper course.

Meanwhile Uncle Prudent and his colleague, after walking about the deck, had sat down aft. Frycollin was strangely reassured. What a difference! To be suspended only one hundred and fifty feet from the ground!

The work was only interrupted for a moment while the elevation of the sun above the horizon allowed Robur to take an horary angle, so that at the time of its culmination he could calculate his position.

The result of the observation, taken with the greatest exactitude, was as follows:—

Longitude, 176 deg. 10 min. west.

Latitude, 44 deg. 25 min. south.

This point on the map answered to the position of the Chatham Islands, and particularly of Pitt Island, one of the group.

"That is nearer than I supposed," said Robur to Tom Turner.

"How far off are we?"

"Forty-six degrees south of X Island, or two thousand eight hundred miles."

"All the more reason to get out propellers into order," said the mate. "We may have the wind against us this passage, and with the little stores we have left we ought to get to X as soon as possible."

"Yes, Tom, and I hope to get under way to-night, even if I go with one screw, and put the other to-rights on the voyage."

"Mr. Robur," said Tom, "What is to be done with those two gentlemen and their servant?"

"Do you think they would complain if they became colonists of X Island?"

But where was this X? It was an island lost in the immensity of the Pacific Ocean between the Equator and the Tropic of Cancer—an island most appropriately named by Robur in this algebraic fashion. It was in the north of the South Pacific, a long way out of the route of inter-oceanic communication. There it was that Robur had founded his little colony, and there the Albatross rested when tired with her flight. There she was provisioned for all her voyages.

254

While they were busy in the bow.

In X Island, Robur, a man of immense wealth, had established a ship-yard, in which he built his aeronef. There he could repair it, and even rebuild it. In his warehouses were materials and provisions of all sorts stored for the fifty inhabitants who lived on the island.

When Robur had doubled Cape Horn a few days before his intention had been to regain X Island by crossing the Pacific obliquely. But the cyclone had seized the Albatross, and the hurricane had carried her away to the south. In fact, he had been brought back to much the same latitude as before, and if his propellers had not been damaged the delay would have been of no importance.

His object was therefore to get back to X Island; but as the mate had said, the voyage would be a long one, and the winds would probably be against them. The mechanical power of the Albatross was, however, quite equal to taking her to her destination, and under ordinary circumstances she would be there in three or four days.

Hence Robur's resolve to anchor on the Chatham Islands. There was there every opportunity for repairing at least the fore-screw. He had no fear that if the wind were to rise he would be driven to the south instead of to the north. When night came the repairs would be finished, and he would have to manoeuvre so as to weight his anchor. If it were too firmly fixed in the rocks he could cut the cable and resume his flight towards the equator.

The crew of the Albatross, knowing there was no time to lose, set to work vigorously.

While they were busy in the bow of the aeronef, Uncle Prudent and Phil Evans held a little conversation together which excep-tionally important consequences.

"Phil Evans," said Uncle Prudent, "you have resolved, as I have, to sacrifice your life?"

"Yes, like you."

"It is evident that we can expect nothing from Robur."

"Nothing."

"Well, Phil Evans, I have made up my mind. If the Albatross leaves this place to-night, the night will not pass without our having accom-plished our task. We will smash the wings of this bird of Robur's! This night I will blow it into the air!"

"The sooner the better," said Phil Evans.

It will be seen that the two colleagues were agreed on all points, even in accepting with indifference the frightful death in store for them.

"Have you all you want?" asked Phil Evans.

"Yes. Last night, while Robur and his people

had enough to do to look after the safety of the ship, I slipped into the magazine and got hold of a dynamite cartridge."

"Let us set to work, Uncle Prudent."

"No. Wait till to-night. When the night comes we will go into our cabin, and you shall see something that will surprise you."

At six o'clock the colleagues dined together as usual. Two hours afterwards they retired to their cabin like men who wished to make up for a sleepless night.

Neither Robur nor any of his companions had a suspicion of the catastrophe that threatened the Albatross.

This was Uncle Prudent's plan.

As he had said, he had stolen into the magazine, and there had possessed himself of some powder and a cartridge like those used by Robur in Dahomey. Returning to his cabin, he had carefully concealed the cartridge with which he had resolved to blow up the Albatross in mid-air.

Phil Evans, screened by his companion, was now examining the infernal machine, which was a metallic canister containing about two pounds of dynamite, enough to shatter the aeronef to atoms. If the explosion did not destroy her at once, it would do so in her fall. Nothing was easier than to place this cartridge in a corner of the cabin, so that it would blow in the deck and tear away the framework of the hull.

But to obtain the explosion it was necessary to adjust the fulminating cap with which the cartridge was fitted. This was the most delicate part of the operation, for the explosion would have to be carefully timed, so as not to occur too soon or too late.

Uncle Prudent had carefully thought over the matter. His conclusions were as follows. As soon as the fore propeller was repaired the aeronef would resume her course to the north, and that done Robur and his crew would probably come aft to put the other screw into order. The presence of these people about the cabin might interfere with his plans, and so he had resolved to make a slow match do duty as a time-fuse.

"When I got the cartridge," said he to Phil Evans, "I took some gunpowder as well. With the powder I will make a fuse that will take some time to burn, and which will lead into the fulminate. My idea is to light it about midnight, so that the explosion will take place about three or four o'clock in the morning."

"Well planned!" said Phil Evans.

The colleagues, as we see, had arrived at such a stage as to look with the greatest nonchalance

Uncle Prudent lighted the end.

on the awful destruction in which they were about to perish. Their hatred against Robur and his people had so increased that they would sacrifice their own lives to destroy the Albatross and all she bore. The act was that of madmen, it was horrible; but at such a pitch had they arrived after five weeks of anger that could not vent itself, of rage that could not be gratified.

"And Frycollin?" asked Phil Evans, "have we the right to dispose of his life?"

"We shall sacrifice ours as well!" said Uncle Prudent.

It is doubtful if Frycollin would have thought the reason sufficient.

Immediately Uncle Prudent set to work, while Evans kept watch in the neighbourhood of the cabin.

The crew were all at work forward. There was no fear of being surprised.

Uncle Prudent began by rubbing a small quantity of the powder very fine; and then, having slightly moistened it, he wrapped it up in a piece of rag in the shape of a match. When it was lighted he calculated it would burn about an inch in five minutes, or a yard in three hours. The match was tried and found to answer, and was then would round with string and attached to the cap of the cartridge. Uncle Prudent had all finished about ten o'clock in the evening without having excited the least suspicion.

During the day the work on the fore screw had been actively carried on, but it had had to be taken on board to adjust the twisted blades. Of the piles and accumulators and the machinery that drove the ship nothing was damaged.

When night fell Robur and his men knocked off work. The fore propeller had not been got into place, and to finish it would take another three hours. After some conversation with Tom Turner it was decided to give the crew a rest, and postpone what required to be done to the next morning.

The final adjustment was a matter of extreme nicety, and the electric lamps did not give so suitable a light for such work as the daylight.

Uncle Prudent and Phil Evans were not aware of this. They had understood that the screw would be in place during the night, and that the Albatross would be on her way to the north.

The night was dark and moonless. Heavy clouds made the darkness deeper. A light breeze began to rise. A few puffs came from the south-west, but they had no effect on the Albatross. She remained motionless at her anchor, and the cable stretched vertically downwards to the ground.

Uncle Prudent and his colleague, imagining they were under way again, sat shut up in their cabin, exchanging but a few words, and listening to the f-r-r-r of the suspensory screws, which drowned every other sound on board. They were waiting till the time of action arrived.

A little before midnight Uncle Prudent said, "It is time!"

Under the berths in the cabin was a sliding box, forming a small locker, and in this locker Uncle Prudent put the dynamite and the slow-match. In this way the match would burn without betraying itself by its smoke or spluttering. Uncle Prudent lighted the end and pushed back the box under the berth with,—

"Now let us go aft, and wait."

They then went out, and were astonished not to find the steersman at his post.

Phil Evans leant out over the rail.

"The Albatross is where she was," said he in a low voice. "The work is not finished. They have not started!"

Uncle Prudent made a gesture of disappointment. "We shall have to put out the match," said he.

"No," said Phil Evans, "we must escape."

"Escape?"

"Yes! down the cable! fifty yards is nothing!"

"Nothing, of course, Phil Evans, and we should be fools not to take the chance now it has come."

But first they went back to the cabin and took away all they could carry, with a view to a more or less prolonged stay on the Chatham Islands. Then they shut the door and noiselessly crept forward, intending to wake Frycollin and take him with them.

The darkness was intense. The clouds were racing up from the south-west, and the aeronef was tugging at her anchor, and thus throwing the cable more and more out of the vertical. There would be no difficulty in slipping down it.

The colleagues made their way along the deck, stopping in the shadow of the deckhouses to listen if there was any sound. The silence was unbroken. No light shone from the portholes. The aeronef was not only silent; she was asleep.

Uncle Prudent was close to Frycollin's cabin when Phil Evans stopped him.

"The look-out!" he said.

A man was crouching near the deck-house. He was only half asleep. All flight would be impossible if he were to give the alarm.

Close by were a few ropes, and pieces of rag and waste used in the work at the screw.

"Down you go."

An instant afterwards the man was gagged and blindfolded and lashed to the rail unable to utter a sound or move an inch.

This was done almost without a whisper.

Uncle Prudent and Phil Evans listened. All was silent within the cabins. Every one on board was asleep.

They reached Frycollin's cabin. Tapage was snoring away in a style worthy of his name, and that promised well.

To his great surprise, Uncle Prudent had not even to push Frycollin's door. It was open. He stepped into the doorway and looked round.

"Nobody here!" he said.

"Nobody! Where can he be?" asked Phil Evans.

They went into the bow, thinking Frycollin might perhaps be asleep in the corner.

Still they found nobody.

"Has the fellow got the start of us?" asked Uncle Prudent.

"Whether he has or not," said Phil Evans, "we can't wait any longer. Down you go."

Without hesitation the fugitives one after the other clambered over the side and, seizing the cable with hands and feet, slipped down it safe and sound to the ground.

Think of their joy at again treading the earth they had lost for so long—at walking on solid ground and being no longer the playthings of the atmosphere!

They were starting up the creek for the interior of the island when suddenly a form rose in front of them.

It was Frycollin.

The valet had had the same idea as his master and the audacity to start without telling him.

But there was no time for recriminations, and Uncle Prudent was in search of a refuge in some distant part of the island when Phil Evans stopped him.

"Uncle Prudent," said he. "Here we are safe from Robur. He is doomed like his companions to a terrible death. He deserves it, we know. But if he would swear on his honour not to take us prisoners again—"

"The honour of such a man—"

Uncle Prudent did not finish his sentence.

There was a noise on the Albatross. Evidently the alarm had been given. The escape was discovered.

"Help! Help!" shouted somebody.

It was the look-out man, who had got rid of his gag. Hurried footsteps were heard on deck. Almost immediately the electric lamps shot beams over a large circle.

"There they are! There they are!" shouted Tom Turner.

The fugitives were seen.

At the same instant an order was given by Robur, and, the suspensory screws being slowed, the cable was hauled in on board, and the Albatross sank towards the ground.

At this moment the voice of Phil Evans was heard shouting,—

"Engineer Robur, will you give us your word of honour to leave us free on this island?"

"Never!" said Robur.

And the reply was followed by the report of a gun, and the bullet grazed Phil's shoulder.

"Ah! The brutes!" said Uncle Prudent.

Knife in hand, he rushed towards the rocks where the anchor had fixed itself. The aeronef was not more than fifty feet from the ground.

In a few seconds the cable was cut, and the breeze, which had increased considerably, striking the Albatross on the quarter, carried her out over the sea.

In a few seconds the cable was cut.

The Clipper of the Clouds

CHAPTER XX.

THE WRECK OF THE ALBATROSS

IT was then twenty minutes after midnight. Five or six shots had been fired from the aeronef. Uncle Prudent and Frycollin, supporting Phil Evans, had taken shelter among the rocks. They had not been hit. For the moment there was nothing to fear.

As the Albatross drifted off from Pitt Island she rose obliquely to nearly three thousand feet. It was necessary to increase the ascensional power to prevent her falling into the sea.

When the look-out man had got clear of his gag and shouted, Robur and Tom Turner had rushed up to him and torn off his bandage. The mate had then run back to the stern cabin. It was empty!

Tapage had searched Frycollin's cabin, and that also was empty.

When he saw that the prisoners had escaped, Robur was seized with a paroxysm of anger. The escape meant the revelation of his secret to the world. He had not been much concerned at the document thrown overboard while they were crossing Europe, for there were so many chances that it would be lost in its fall; but now—!''

As he grew calm,—

"They have escaped," said he. "Be it so! but they cannot get away from Pitt Island, and in a day or so I will go back! I will recapture them! And then—"

In fact, the safety of the three fugitives was by no means assured. The Albatross would be repaired, and return well in hand. Before the day was out they might again be in the power of the engineer.

Before the day was out! But in two hours the Albatross would be annihilated! The dynamite cartridge was like a torpedo fastened to her hull, and would accomplish her destruction in mid-air.

The breeze freshened, and the aeronef was carried to the north-east. Although her speed was but moderate, she would be out of sight of the Chatham Islands before sunrise.

To return against the wind she must have her propellers going, particularly the one in the bow.

"Tom," said the engineer, "turn the lights full on."

"Yes, sir."

"And all hands to work."

"Yes, sir."

There was no longer any idea of putting off the work till to-morrow. There was now no thought of fatigue. Not one of the men of the Albatross failed to share in the feelings of his chief. Not one but was ready to do anything to recapture the fugitives!

As soon as the screw was in place they would return to the island, and drop another anchor, and give chase to the fugitives. Then only would they begin repairing the stern-screw; and then the aeronef could resume her voyage across the Pacific to X Island.

It was important, above all things, that the Albatross should not be carried too far to the north-east, but unfortunately the breeze grew stronger, and she could not head against it, or even remain stationary. Deprived of her propellers she was an unguidable balloon. The fugitives on the shore knew that she would have disappeared before the explosion blew her to pieces.

Robur felt much disappointment at seeing his plans so interfered with. Would it not take him much longer than he thought to get back to his old anchorage?

While the work at the screw was actively pushed on, he resolved to descend to the surface of the sea, in the hope that the wind would there be lighter. Perhaps the Albatross would be able to remain in the neighbourhood until she was again fit to work to windward.

The manoeuvre was instantly executed. If a passing ship had sighted the aerial machine as she sunk through the air, with her electric lights in full blaze, with what terror would she have been seized!

When the Albatross was a few hundred feet from the waves she stopped.

Unfortunately Robur found that the breeze was stronger here than above, and the aeronef drifted off more rapidly. He risked being blown a long way off to the north-east, and that would delay his return to Pitt Island.

In short, after several experiments, he found it better to keep his ship well up in the air, and the Albatross went aloft to about ten thousand feet. There, if she did not remain stationary, the drifting was very slight. The engineer could thus hope that by sunrise at such an altitude he would still be in sight of the island.

Robur did not trouble himself about the reception the fugitives might have received from the natives—if there were any natives. That they might help them mattered little to him. With the powers of offence possessed by the Albatross they would be promptly terrified and dispersed. The capture of the prisoners was certain, and once he had them again,—

"They will not escape from X Island!"

About one o'clock in the morning the fore-screw was finished, and all that had to be done was to get it back to its place. This would take about an hour. That done, the Albatross would be headed south-west and the stern-screw could be taken in hand.

And how about the match that was burning in the deserted cabin?—the match of which more than a third was now consumed? And the spark that was creeping along to the dynamite?

Assuredly if the men of the aeronef had not been so busy one of them would have heard the feeble sputtering that was going on in the deck-house. Perhaps he would have smelt the burning powder! He would doubtless have become uneasy! And told Tom Turner! And then they would have looked about, and found the box and the infernal machine; and then there would have been time to save this wonderful Albatross and all she bore!

But the men were at work in the bow, twenty yards away from the cabin. Nothing brought them to that part of the deck; nothing called off their attention from their work.

Robur was there working with his hands, excellent mechanic as he was. He hurried on the work, but nothing was neglected, everything was carefully done. Was it not necessary that he should again become absolute master of his invention? If he did not recapture the fugitives they would get away home. They would begin inquiring into matters. They might even discover X Island, and there would be an end to this life, which the men of the Albatross had created for themselves, a life that seemed superhuman and sublime.

And here Tom Turner came up to the engineer. It was a quarter past one.

"It seems to me, sir, that the breeze is falling, and going round to the west."

"What does the barometer say?" asked Robur, after looking up at the sky.

"It is almost stationary, and the clouds seem gathering below us."

"So they are, and it may be raining down at the sea; but if we keep above the rain it makes no difference to us. It will not interfere with the work."

"If it is raining it is not a heavy rain," said Tom. "The clouds do not look like it, and probably the wind has dropped altogether."

"Perhaps so, but I think we had better not go down yet. Let us get into going order as soon as we can, and then we can do as we like."

At a few minutes after two the first part of the work was finished. The fore-screw was in its place, and the power was turned on. The speed was gradually increased and the Albatross, heading to the south-west, returned at moderate speed towards the Chatham Islands.

"Tom," said Robur, "it is about two hours and a half since we got adrift. The wind has not changed all the time. I think we ought to be over the island in an hour."

"Yes, sir. We are going about forty feet a second. We ought to be there about half-past three."

"All the better. It would suit us best to get back while it is dark, and even beach the Albatross if we can. Those fellows will fancy we are a long way off to the northward, and never think of keeping a look-out. If we have to stop a day or two on the island—"

"We'll stop, and if we have to fight an army of natives—"

"We'll fight," said Robur. "We'll fight then for out Albatross."

The engineer went forward to the men, who were waiting for orders.

"My lads," he said to them, "we cannot knock off yet. We must work till day comes."

They were all ready to do so.

The stern-screw had now to be treated as the other had been. The damage was the same, a twisting from the violence of the hurricane during the passage across the southern pole.

But to get the screw on board it seemed best to stop the progress of the aeronef for a few minutes, and even to drive her backwards. The engines were reversed. The aeronef began to fall astern, when Tom Turner was surprised by a peculiar odour.

This was from the gas given off by the match, which had accumulated in the box, and was now escaping from the cabin.

"Hallo!" said the mate, with a sniff.

"What is the matter?" asked Robur.

"Don't you smell something? Isn't it burning powder?"

"So it is, Tom."

"And it comes from that cabin."

"Yes, the very cabin—"

"Have those scoundrels set it on fire?"

"Suppose it is something else!" exclaimed

The Albatross dropped into the abyss.

Robur. "Force the door, Tom; drive in the door!"

But the mate had not made one step towards it when a fearful explosion shook the Albatross. The cabins flew into splinters. The lamps went out. The electric current suddenly failed. The darkness was complete. Most of the suspensory screws were twisted or broken, but a few in the bow still revolved.

At the same instant the hull of the aeronef opened just behind the first deck-house, where the engines for the fore-screw were placed; and the after-part of the deck collapsed in space.

Immediately the last suspensory screw stopped spinning, and the Albatross dropped into the abyss.

It was a fall of ten thousand feet for the eight men who were clinging to the wreck; and the fall was even faster that it might have been, for the fore propeller was vertical in the air and still working!

It was then that Robur, with extraordinary coolness, climbed up to the broken deck-house, and seizing the lever reversed the rotation, so that the propeller became a suspender.

The fall continued, but it was checked, and the wreck did not fall with the accelerating swiftness of bodies influenced solely by gravitation; and if it was death to the survivors of the Albatross from their being hurled into the sea, it was not death by asphyxia amid air which the rapidity of descent rendered unbreathable.

Eighty seconds after the explosion, all that remained of the Albatross plunged into the waves!

The Clipper of the Clouds

CHAPTER XXI.

THE INSTITUTE AGAIN

SOME weeks before, on the 13th of June, on the morning after the sitting during which the Weldon Institute had been given over to such stormy discussions, the excitement of all classes of the Philadelphian population, black or white, had been much easier to imagine than to describe.

From a very early hour conversation was entirely occupied with the unexpected and scandalous incident of the night before. A stranger calling himself an engineer, and answering to the name of Robur, a person of unknown origin, of anonymous nationality, had unexpectedly presented himself in the club-room, insulted the balloonists, made fun of the aeronauts, boasted of the marvels of machines heavier than air, and raised a frightful tumult by the remarks with which he greeted the menaces of his adversaries. After leaving the desk, amid a volley of revolver shots, he had disappeared, and, in spite of every endeavour, no trace could be found of him.

Assuredly here was enough to exercise every tongue and excite every imagination. But by how much was this excitement increased when in the evening of the 13th of June it was found that neither the president nor secretary of the Weldon Institute had returned to their homes! Was it by chance only that they were absent? No, or at least there was nothing to lead people to think so. It had even been agreed that in the morning they would be back at the club, one as president, the other as secretary, to take their places during a discussion on the events of the preceding evening.

And not only was there the complete disappearance of these two considerable personages in the state of Pennsylvania, but there was no news of the valet Frycollin. He was as undiscoverable as his master. Never had a negro since Toussaint L'Ouverture, Soulouque, or Dessaline had so much talked about him.

The next day there was no news. Neither the colleagues nor Frycollin had been found. The anxiety became serious. Agitation commenced. A numerous crowd besieged the post and telegraph offices in case any news should be received.

There was no news.

And they had been seen coming out of the Weldon Institute loudly talking together, and with Frycollin in attendance, go down Walnut Street towards Fairmont Park!

Jem Chip, the vegetarian, had even shaken hands with the president and left him with "To-morrow!"

And William T. Forbes, the manufacturer of sugar from rags, had received a cordial shake from Phil Evans who had said to him twice,—

"Au revoir! au revoir!"

Miss Doll and Miss Mat Forbes, so attached to Uncle Prudent by the bonds of purest friendship, could not get over the disappearance, and in order to obtain news of the absent, talked even more than they were accustomed to.

Three, four, five, six days passed. Then a week, then two weeks, and there was nothing to give a clue to the missing three.

The most minute search had been made in every quarter. Nothing! In the streets going down to the harbour. Nothing! In the park, even under the trees and brushwood. Nothing! Always nothing! although here it was noticed that the grass looked to be pressed down in a way that seemed suspicious and certainly was inexplicable; and at the edge of the clearing there were traces of a recent struggle. Perhaps a band of scoundrels had attacked the colleagues here in the deserted park in the middle of the night!

It was possible. The police proceeded with their inquiries in all due form and with all lawful slowness. They dragged the Schuylkill river, and cut into the thick bushes that fringe its banks; and if this was useless it was not quite a waste, for the Schuylkill is in great want of a good weeding, and it got it on this occasion! Practical people are the authorities of Philadelphia!

Then the newspapers were tried. Advertisements and notices and articles were sent to all the journals in the Union without distinction of colour. The "Daily Negro," the special organ of the black race, published a portrait of Frycollin after his latest photograph. Rewards were offered to whoever would give news of the three absentees, and even to those who would find some clue to put the police on the track.

The grass looked to be pressed down.

"Five thousand dollars! five thousand dollars to any citizen who would—"

Nothing was done. The five thousand dollars remained with the treasurer of the Weldon Institute.

Undiscoverable! undiscoverable! undiscoverable! Uncle Prudent and Phil Evans, of Philadelphia!

It need hardly be said that the club was put to serious inconvenience by this disappearance of its president and secretary. And at first the assembly voted urgency to a measure which suspended the work on the Goahead. How, in the absence of the principal promoters of the affair, of those who had devoted to the enterprise a certain part of their fortune in time and money—how could they finish the work when these were not present? It were better, then, to wait.

And just then came the first news of the strange phenomenon which had exercised people's minds some weeks before.

The mysterious object had been again seen at different times in the higher regions of the atmosphere. But nobody dreamt of establishing a connection between this singular reappearance and the no less singular disappearance of the members of the Weldon Institute. In fact, it would have required a very strong dose of imagination to connect one of these facts with the other.

Whatever, it might be, asteroid or aerolite or aerial monster, it had reappeared in such a way that its dimensions and shape could be much better appreciated, first in Canada, over the country between Ottawa and Quebec, on the very morning after the disappearance of the colleagues, and later over the plains of the Far West, where it had tried its speed against an express train on the Union Pacific.

At the end of this day the doubts of the learned world were at an end. The body was not a product of nature, it was a flying machine, the practical application of the theory of "heavier than air." And if the inventor of the aeronef had wished to keep himself unknown he could evidently have done better than to try it over the Far West. As to the mechanical force he required, or the engines by which it was communicated, nothing was known, but there could be no doubt the aeronef was gifted with an extraordinary faculty of locomotion. In fact, a few days afterwards it was reported from the Celestial Empire, then from the southern part of India, then from the Russian steppes.

Who was then this bold mechanician that possessed such powers of locomotion, for whom States had no frontiers and oceans no

limits, who disposed of the terrestrial atmosphere as if it were his domain? Could it be this Robur whose theories had been so brutally thrown in the face of the Weldon Institute the day he led the attack against the utopia of guidable balloons?

Perhaps such a notion occurred to some of the wide-awake people, but none dreamt that the said Robur had anything to do with the disappearance of the president and secretary of the Institute.

Things remained in this state of mystery when a telegram arrived from France through the New York cable at 11.37 a.m. on July 13.

And what was this telegram? It was the text of the document found at Paris in a snuff-box revealing what had happened to the two personages for whom the Union was in mourning.

So, then, the perpetrator of this kidnapping was Robur the engineer, come expressly to Philadelphia to destroy in its egg the theory of the balloonists. He it was who commanded the Albatross! He it was who carried off by way of reprisal Uncle Prudent, Phil Evans, and Frycollin; and they might be considered lost for ever. At least until some means were found of constructing an engine capable of contending with this powerful machine their terrestrial friends would never bring them back to earth.

What excitement! What stupor! The telegram from Paris had been addressed to the members of the Weldon Institute. The members of the club were immediately informed of it. Ten minutes later all Philadelphia received the news through its telephones, and in less than an hour all America heard of it through the innumerable electric wires of the new continent.

No one would believe it! "It is an unseasonable joke," said some. "It is all smoke," said others. How could such a thing be done in Philadelphia, and so secretly, too? How could the Albatross have been beached in Fairmont Park without its appearance having been signalled all over Pennsylvania?

Very good. These were the arguments. The incredulous had the right of doubting. But the right did not last long. Seven days after the receipt of the telegram the French mail-boat Normandie came into the Hudson, bringing the famous snuff-box. The railway took it in all haste from New York to Philadelphia.

It was indeed the snuff-box of the President of the Weldon Institute. Jem Chip would have done better on that day to take some more substantial nourishment, for he fell into a swoon when he recognized it. How many a time had he taken from it the pinch of friendship! And Miss Doll and Miss Mat also recognized it, and so did William T. Forbes, Truck Milnor, Batt T. Fyn, and many other members.

And not only was it the president's snuff-box, it was the president's writing.

Then did the people lament and stretch out their hands in despair to the skies. Uncle Prudent and his colleague carried away in a flying machine, and no one able to deliver them!

The Niagara Falls Company, in which Uncle Prudent was the largest shareholder, thought of suspending its business and turning off its cataracts. The Wheelton Watch Company thought of winding up its machinery now it had lost its manager.

Nothing more was heard of the aeronef. July passed, and there was no news. August ran its course, and the uncertainty on the subject of Robur's prisoners was as great as ever. Had he, like Icarus, fallen a victim to his own temerity?

The first twenty-seven days of September went by without result, but on the 28th a rumour spread through Philadephia that Uncle Prudent and Phil Evans had during the afternoon quietly walked into the president's house. And, what was more extraordinary, the rumour was true, although very few believed it.

They had, however, to give in to the evidence. There could be no doubt these were the two men, and not their shadows. And Frycollin also had come back!

The members of the club, then their friends, then the crowd, swarmed into the president's house, and shook hands with the president and secretary, and cheered them again and again.

Jem Chip was there, having left his luncheon —a joint of boiled lettuces—and William T. Forbes and his daughters, and all the members of the club. It is a mystery how Uncle Prudent and Phil Evans emerged alive from the thousands who welcomed them.

On that evening was the weekly meeting of the Institute. It was expected that the colleagues would take their places at the desk. As they had said nothing of their adventures, it was thought they would then speak, and relate the impressions of their voyage.

But for some reason or other both were silent. And so also was Frycollin, whom his congeners in their delirium had failed to dismember.

But though the colleagues did not tell what had happened to them, that is no reason why we should not.

We know what occurred on the night of the 27th and 28th of July: the daring escape to the earth, the scramble among the rocks, the bullet fired at Phil Evans, the cut cable, and the Albatross deprived of her propellers, drifting off to the north-east at a great altitude.

Her electric lamps rendered her visible for some time. And then she disappeared.

The fugitives had little to fear. How could Robur get back to the island for three or four hours if his screws were out of gear? By that time the Albatross would have been destroyed by the explosion, and be no more than a wreck floating on the sea; those whom she bore would be mangled corpses, which the ocean would not even give up again.

The act of vengeance would be accomplished in all its horror.

Uncle Prudent and Phil Evans looked upon it as an act of legitimate self-defence, and felt no remorse whatever.

Evans was but slightly wounded by the rifle bullet, and the three made their way up from the shore in the hope of meeting some of the natives.

The hope was realized. About fifty natives were living by fishing off the western coast. They had seen the aeronef descend on the island and they welcomed the fugitives as if they were supernatural beings. They worshipped them, we ought rather to say. They accommodated them in the most comfortable of their huts.

As they had expected, Uncle Prudent and Phil Evans saw nothing more of the aeronef. They concluded that the catastrophe had taken place in some high region of the atmosphere, and that they would hear no more of Robur and his prodigious machine.

Meanwhile they had to wait for an opportunity of returning to America. The Chatham Islands are not much visited by navigators, and all August passed without sign of a ship. The fugitives began to ask themselves if they had not exchanged one prison for another.

At last, on September 3rd, a ship came to water at the Chatham Islands. It will not have been forgotten that when Uncle Prudent was seized he had on him several thousand paper dollars, much more than would take him back to America. After thanking their adorers, who were not sparing of their most respectful demonstrations, Uncle Prudent, Phil Evans, and Frycollin embarked for Auckland. They said nothing of their adventures, and in two days landed in New Zealand.

At Auckland, a mail-boat on the 20th of September took them on board as passengers, and after a splendid passage the survivors of the Albatross, stepped ashore at San Francisco.

They worshipped them, we ought rather to say.

They said nothing as to who they were or whence they had come, but as they had paid full price for their berths no American captain would trouble them further.

At San Francisco they took the first train out on the Pacific Railway, and on the 27th they arrived at Philadelphia.

That is the compendious history of what had occurred since the escape of the fugitive. And that is why this very evening the president and secretary of the Weldon Institute took their seats amid a most extraordinary attendance.

But never before had either of them been so calm. To look at them it did not seem as though anything abnormal had happened since the memorable sitting of the 12th of June. Three months and a half had gone, and seemed to be counted as nothing.

After the first round of cheers, which both received without showing the slightest emotion, Uncle Prudent took off his hat and spoke.

"Worthy citizens," said he, "the meeting is now open."

Tremendous applause. And properly so, for if it was not extraordinary that the meeting was open, it was extraordinary that it should be opened by Uncle Prudent and Phil Evans.

The president allowed the enthusiasm to subside in shouts and clappings; then he continued:—

"At our last meeting, gentlemen, the discussion was somewhat animated—(hear, hear)—between the partisans of the screw before and those of the screw behind for our balloon Goahead. (Marks of surprise.) We have found a way to bring the beforists and the behindists in agreement. That way is as follows: we are going to use two screws, one at each end of the car!" (Silence and complete stupefaction.)

That was all.

Yes, all! Of the kidnapping of the president and secretary of the Weldon Institute not a word! Not a word of the Albatross nor of Robur! Not a word of the voyage! Not a word of the way in which the prisoners had escaped! Not a word of what had become of the aeronef, if it still flew through space, or if they were to be prepared for new reprisals on the members of the club!

Of course the balloonists were longing to ask Uncle Prudent and the secretary about all these things, but they looked so close and so serious that they thought it best to respect their attitude. When they thought fit to speak they would do so, and it would be an honour to hear.

After all, there might be in all this some secret which could not yet be divulged.

And then Uncle Prudent, resuming his speech amid a silence up to then unknown in the meetings of the Weldon Institute, said, "Gentlemen, it now only remains for us to finish the aerostat Goahead. It is left to her to effect the conquest of the air! The meeting is at an end!"

The Clipper of the Clouds

CHAPTER XXII.

THE GOAHEAD IS LAUNCHED

ON the following 19th of April, seven months after the unexpected return of Uncle Prudent and Phil Evans, Philadelphia was in a state of unwonted excitement. There were neither elections nor meetings this time. The aerostat Goahead, built by the Weldon Institute, was to take possession of her natural element.

The celebrated Harry W. Tinder, whose name we mentioned at the beginning of this story, had been engaged as aeronaut. He had no assistant, and the only passengers were to be the president and secretary of the Weldon Institute. Did they not merit such an honour? Did it not come to them appropriately to rise in person to protest against any apparatus that was heavier than air?

During the seven months, however, they had said nothing of their adventures; and even Frycollin had not uttered a whisper of Robur and his wonderful clipper. Probably Uncle Prudent and his friend desired that no question should arise as to the merits of the aeronef, or any other flying machine. Although the Goahead might not claim the first place among aerial locomotives, they would have nothing to say about the inventions of other aviators. They believed, and would always believe, that the true atmospheric vehicle was the aerostat, and that to it alone belonged the future.

Besides, he on whom they had been so terribly—and in their idea so justly—avenged, existed no longer. None of those who accompanied him had survived. The secret of the Albatross was buried in the depths of the Pacific!

That Robur had a retreat, an island in the middle of that vast ocean, where he could put into port, was only a hypothesis; and the colleagues reserved to themselves the right of making inquiries on the subject—later on.

The grand experiment which the Weldon Institute had been preparing for so long was at last to take place. The Goahead was the most perfect type of what had up to then been invented in aerostatic art—she was what an Inflexible or a Formidable is in ships of war.

She possessed all the qualities of a good aerostat. Her dimensions allowed of her rising to the greatest height a balloon could attain; her impermeability enabled her to remain for an indefinite time in the atmosphere; her solidity would defy any dilatation of gas or violence of wind or rain; her capacity gave her sufficient ascensional force to lift with all their accessories an electric engine that would communicate to her propellers a power superior to anything yet obtained. The Goahead was of elongated form, so as to facilitate her horizontal displacement. Her car was a platform somewhat like that of the balloon used by Krebs and Renard; and it carried all the necessary outfit, instruments, cables, grapnels, guide-ropes, &c., and the piles and accumulators for the mechanical power. The car had a screw in front, and a screw and rudder behind. But probably the work done by the machines would be very much less than that done by the machines of the Albatross.

The Goahead had been taken to the clearing in Fairmont Park, to the very spot where the aeronef had landed for a few hours.

Her ascensional power was due to the very lightest of gaseous bodies. Ordinary lighting gas possesses an elevating force of about 700 grammes for every cubic metre. But hydrogen possesses an ascensional force estimated at 1100 grammes per cubic metre. Pure hydrogen prepared according to the method of the celebrated Henry Gifford filled the enormous balloon. And as the capacity of the Goahead was 40,000 cubic metres, the ascensional power of the gas she contained was 40,000 multiplied by 1100, or 44,000 kilogrammes.

On this 29th of April everything was ready. Since eleven o'clock the enormous aerostat had been floating a few feet from the ground ready to rise in mid-air. It was splendid weather and seemed to have been made specially for the experiment, although if the breeze had been stronger the results might have been more conclusive. There had never been any doubt that a balloon could be guided in a calm atmosphere; but to guide it when the atmosphere is in motion is quite another thing; and it is under such circumstances that the experiment should be tried.

But there was no wind to-day, nor any sign of any. Strange to say, North America on that day omitted to send on to Europe one of those first-class storms which it seems to have in such

272

"Let go!" shouted Uncle Prudent.

inexhaustible numbers. A better day could not have been chosen for an aeronautic experiment.

The crowd was immense in Fairmont Park; trains had poured into the Pennsylvanian capital sightseers from the neighbouring states; industrial and commercial life came to a standstill that the people might troop to the show—masters, workmen, women, old men, children, members of Congress, soldiers, magistrates, reporters, white natives and black natives, all were there. We need not stop to describe the excitement, the unaccountable movements, the sudden pushings, which made the mass heave and swell. Nor need we recount the number of cheers which rose from all sides like fireworks when Uncle Prudent and Phil Evans appeared on the platform and hoisted the American colours. Need we say that the majority of the crowd had come from afar not so much to see the Goahead as to gaze on these extraordinary men?

Why two and not three? Why not Frycollin? Because Frycollin thought his campaign in the Albatross sufficient for his fame. He had declined the honour of accompanying his master, and he took no part in the frenzied acclamations that greeted the president and secretary of the Weldon Institute.

Of the members of the illustrious assembly not one was absent from the reserved places within the ropes. There were Truck Milnor, Batt T. Fyn, and William T. Forbes with his two daughters on his arm. All had come to affirm by their presence that nothing could separate them from the partisans of "lighter than air."

About twenty minutes past eleven a gun announced the end of the final preparations.

The Goahead only waited the signal to start. At twenty-five minutes past eleven the second gun was fired.

The Goahead was about one hundred and fifty feet above the clearing, and was held by a rope. In this way the platform commanded the excited crowd. Uncle Prudent and Phil Evans stood upright and placed their left hands on their hearts, to signify how deeply they were touched by their reception. Then they extended their right hands towards the zenith, to signify that the greatest of known balloons was about to take possession of the supra-terrestrial domain.

A hundred thousand hands were placed in answer on a hundred thousand hearts, and a hundred thousand other hands were lifted to the sky.

The third gun was fired at half-past eleven. "Let go!" shouted Uncle Prudent; and the Goahead rose "majestically"—an adverb consecrated by custom to all aerostatic ascents.

And it really was a superb spectacle. It seemed as if a vessel were just launched from the stocks. And was she not a vessel launched into the aerial sea?

The Goahead went up in a perfectly vertical line—a proof of the calmness of the atmosphere—and stopped at an altitude of eight hundred feet.

Then she began her horizontal manoeuvring. With her screws going she moved to the east at a speed of twelve yards a second. That is the speed of the whale—not an inappropriate comparison, for the balloon was somewhat of the shape of the giant of the northern seas.

A salvo of cheers mounted towards the skilful aeronauts.

Then, under the influence of her rudder, the Goahead went through all the evolutions that her steersman could give her. She turned in a small circle; she moved forwards and backwards in a way to convince the most refractory disbeliever in the guiding of balloons. And if there had been any disbeliever there he would have been simply annihilated.

But why was there no wind to assist at this magnificent experiment? It was regrettable. Doubtless the spectators would have seen the Goahead unhesitatingly execute all the movements of a sailing vessel in beating to windward, or of a steamer driving in the wind's eye.

At this moment the aerostat rose a few hundred yards.

The manoeuvre was understood below. Uncle Prudent and his companions were going in search of a breeze in the higher zones, so as to complete the experiment. The system of cellular balloons—analogous to the swimming bladder in fishes—into which could be introduced a certain amount of air by pumping, had provided for this vertical motion. Without throwing out ballast or losing gas the aeronaut was able to rise or sink at his will. Of course there was a valve in the upper hemisphere which would permit of a rapid descent if found necessary. All these contrivances are well known, but they were here fitted in perfection.

The Goahead then rose vertically. Her enormous dimensions gradually grew smaller to the eye, and the necks of the crowd were almost ricked as they gazed into the air. Gradually the whale became a porpoise, and the porpoise became a gudgeon.

The ascensional movement did not cease until the Goahead had reached a height of fourteen thousand feet. But the air was so free from mist that she remained clearly visible.

However, she remained over the clearing as if she were a fixture. An immense bell had imprisoned the atmosphere and deprived it of movement; not a breath of wind was there, high or low.

The aerostat manoeuvred without encountering any resistance, seeming very small owing to the distance, much as if she were being looked at through the wrong end of a telescope.

Suddenly there was a shout among the crowd, a shout followed by a hundred thousand more.

All hands were stretched towards a point on the horizon.

That point was the north-west.

There in the deep azure appeared a moving body, which was approaching and growing larger.

Was it a bird beating with its wings the higher zones of space? Was it an aerolite shooting obliquely through the atmosphere? In any case, its speed was terrific, and it would soon be above the crowd.

A suspicion communicated itself electrically to the brains of all on the clearing.

But it seemed as though the Goahead had sighted this strange object. Assuredly it seemed as though she feared some danger, for her speed was increased, and she was going east as fast as she could.

Yes, the crowd saw what it meant! A name uttered by one of the members of the Weldon Institute was repeated by a hundred thousand mouths—

"The Albatross! the Albatross!"

The Clipper of the Clouds

CHAPTER XXIII.

THE GRAND COLLAPSE

IT was indeed the Albatross! It was indeed Robur who had reappeared in the heights of the sky! It was he who like a huge bird of prey was going to strike the Goahead.

And yet, nine months before, the aeronef, shattered by the explosion, her screws broken, her deck smashed in two, had been apparently annihilated.

Without the prodigious coolness of the engineer, who reversed the gyratory motion of the forepropeller and converted it into a suspensory screw, the men of the Albatross would all have been asphyxiated by the fall. But if they had escaped asphyxia, how had they escaped being drowned in the Pacific?

The remains of the deck, the blades of the propellers, the compartments of the cabins, all formed a sort of raft. When a wounded bird falls on the waves its wings keep it afloat. For several hours Robur and his men remained unhelped, at first on the wreck, and afterwards in the india-rubber boat that had fallen uninjured. A few hours after sunrise they were sighted by a passing ship, and a boat was lowered to their rescue.

Robur and his companions were saved, and so was much of what remained of the aeronef. The engineer said that his ship her perished in a collision, and no further questions were asked him.

The ship was an English three-master, the *Two Friends*, bound to Melbourne, where she arrived a few days afterwards.

Robur was in Australia, but a long way from X Island, to which he desired to return as soon as possible.

In the ruins of the aftermost cabin he had found a considerable sum of money, quite enough to provide for himself and companions without applying to any one for help. A short time after he arrived in Melbourne he became the owner of a small brigantine of about a hundred tons, and in her he sailed for X Island.

There he had but one idea—to be avenged. But to secure his vengeance he would have to make another Albatross. This after all was an easy task for him who made the first. He used up what he could of the old material; the propellers and engines he had brought back in the brigantine. The mechanism was fitted with new piles and new accumulators, and, in short, in less than eight months the work was finished and a new Albatross, identical with the one destroyed by the explosion, was ready to take flight. And he had the same crew.

The Albatross left X Island in the first week of April. During this aerial passage Robur did not want to be seen from the earth, and he came along almost always above the clouds. When he arrived over North America he descended in a desolate spot in the Far West. There the engineer, keeping a profound incognito, learnt with considerable pleasure that the Weldon Institute was about to begin its experiments, and that the Goahead, with Uncle Prudent and Phil Evans, was going to start from Philadelphia on the 29th of April.

Here was a chance for Robur and his crew to gratify their longing for revenge! Here was a chance of inflicting on their foes a terrible vengeance, which in the Goahead they could not escape! A public vengeance, which would at the same time prove the superiority of the aeronef to all aerostats and contrivances of that nature!

And that is why, on this very day, like a vulture from the clouds, the aeronef appeared over Fairmont Park.

Yes! it was the Albatross, easily recognized by all those who had never before seen her.

The Goahead was in full flight; but it soon appeared that she could not escape horizontally, and so she sought her safety in a vertical direction, not dropping to the ground, for the aeronef would have cut her off, but rising to a zone where she could not perhaps be reached. This was very daring, and at the same time very logical.

But the Albatross began to rise after her. Although she was smaller than the Goahead, it was a case of the swordfish and the whale.

This could easily be seen from below, and with what anxiety! In a few moments the aerostat had attained a height of sixteen thousand feet.

The Albatross followed her as she rose. She flew round her flanks, and manoeuvred round her in a circle with a constantly diminishing radius. She could have annihilated her at a stroke, and Uncle Prudent and his companions

He was going to save her crew.

would have been dashed to atoms in a frightful fall.

The people, mute with horror, gazed breathlessly; they were seized with that sort of fear which presses on the chest and grips the legs when we see any one fall from a height. An aerial combat was beginning in which there were none of the chances of safety as in a sea-fight. It was the first of its kind, but it would not be the last, for progress is one of the laws of this world. And if the Goahead was flying the American colours, did not the Albatross display the stars and golden sun of Robur the Conqueror.

The Goahead tried to distance her enemy by rising still higher. She threw away the ballast she had in reserve; she made a new leap of three thousand feet; she was now but a dot in space. The Albatross, which followed her round and round at top speed, was now invisible.

Suddenly a shout of terror rose from the crowd. The Goahead increased rapidly in size, and the aeronef appeared dropping with her. This time it was a fall. The gas had dilated in the higher zones of the atmosphere and had burst the balloon, which, half inflated still, was falling rapidly.

But the aeronef, slowing her suspensory screws, came down just as fast. She ran alongside the Goahead when she was not more than four thousand feet from the ground.

Would Robur destroy her?

No; he was going to save her crew!

And so cleverly did he handle his vessel that the aeronaut jumped on board.

Would Uncle Prudent and Phil Evans refuse to be saved by him? They were quite capable of doing so. But the crew threw themselves on them and dragged them by force from the Goahead to the Albatross.

Then the aeronef glided off and remained stationary, while the balloon, quite empty of gas, fell on the trees of the clearing and hung there like a gigantic rag.

An appalling silence reigned on the ground. It seemed as though life were suspended in each of the crowd; and many eyes had been closed so as not to behold the final catastrophe.

Uncle Prudent and Phil Evans had again become the prisoners of the redoubtable Robur. Now he had recaptured them, would he carry them off into space, where it was impossible to follow him?

It seemed so.

However, instead of mounting into the sky the Albatross continued falling. Was she coming down to the ground? It looked like it, and the crowd divided so as to leave a space for her in the centre of the clearing.

The excitement was at its maximum. The Albatross stopped six feet from the ground. Then, amid profound silence, the engineer's voice was heard.

"Citizens of the United States," he said, "the president and secretary of the Weldon Institute are again in my power. In keeping them I am only within my right. But from the passion kindled in them by the success of the Albatross I see that their minds are not prepared for that important revolution which the conquest of the air will one day bring. Uncle Prudent and Phil Evans, you are free!"

The president, the secretary, and the aeronaut had only to jump down.

The Albatross then mounted to about forty feet from the ground.

Then Robur continued:—

"Citizens of the United States, my experiment is finished; but my advice to those present is to be premature in nothing, not even in progress. It is evolution and not revolution that we should seek. In a word, we must not be before our time. I have come too soon to-day to withstand such contradictory and divided interests as yours. Nations are not yet fit for union.

"I go, then; and I take my secret with me. But it will not be lost to humanity. It will belong to you the day you are educated enough to profit by it and wise enough not to abuse it. Citizens of the United States! Good-bye!"

And the Albatross, beating the air with her seventy-four screws, and driven by her propellers, shot off towards the east amid a tempest of cheers.

The two colleagues, profoundly humiliated, as through them was the whole Weldon Institute, did the only thing they could. They went home.

And the crowd by a sudden change of front greeted them with particularly keen sarcasms, and, at their expense, are sarcastic still.

*   *   *   *   *   *

And now, who is this Robur? Shall we ever know?

We know to-day. Robur is the science of the future. Perhaps the science of to-morrow! Certainly the science that will come!

Does the Albatross still cruise in the atmosphere in the realm that none can take from her? There is no reason to doubt it. Will Robur, the Conqueror, appear one day as he said? Yes! He will come to declare the secret of his invention, which will greatly change the social and political conditions of the world.

As for the future of aerial locomotion, it belongs to the aeronef and not the aerostat. It is to the Albatross that the conquest of the air will assuredly fall.

A Journey to the Centre of the Earth

A Journey to the Centre of the Earth

CHAPTER I.

MY UNCLE MAKES A GREAT DISCOVERY

LOOKING back to all that has occurred to me since that eventful day, I am scarcely able to believe in the reality of my adventures. They were truly so wonderful that even now I am bewildered when I think of them.

My uncle was a German, having married my mother's sister, an Englishwoman. Being very much attached to his fatherless nephew, he invited me to study under him in his home in the fatherland. This home was in a large town, and my uncle a Professor of philosophy, chemistry, geology, mineralogy, and many other ologies.

One day, after passing some hours in the laboratory—my uncle being absent at the time—I suddenly felt the necessity of renovating the tissues—*i.e.,* I was hungry, and was about to rouse up our old French cook, when my uncle, Professor Von Hardwigg, suddenly opened the street door, and came rushing up stairs.

Now Professor Hardwigg, my worthy uncle, is by no means a bad sort of man; he is, however, choleric and original. To bear with him means to obey; and scarcely had his heavy feet resounded within our joint domicile than he shouted for me to attend upon him.

"Harry—Harry—Harry—"

I hastened to obey, but before I could reach his room, jumping three steps at a time, he was stamping his right foot upon the landing.

"Harry!" he cried, in a frantic tone, "are you coming up?"

Now to tell the truth, at that moment I was far more interested in the question as to what was to constitute our dinner than in any problem of science; to me soup was more interesting than soda, an omelette more tempting than arithmetic, and an artichoke of ten times more value than any amount of asbestos.

But my uncle was not a man to be kept waiting; so adjourning therefore all minor questions, I presented myself before him.

He was a very learned man. Now most persons in this category supply themselves with information, as pedlars do with goods, for the benefit of others, and lay up stores in order to diffuse them abroad for the benefit of society in general. Not so my excellent uncle, Professor Hardwigg; he studied, he consumed the mid-night oil, he pored over heavy tomes, and digested huge quartos and folios in order to keep the knowledge acquired to himself.

There was a reason, and it may be regarded as a good one, why my uncle objected to display his learning more than was absolutely necessary; he stammered; and when intent upon explaining the phenomena of the heavens, was apt to find himself at fault, and allude in such a vague way to sun, moon, and stars, that few were able to comprehend his meaning. To tell the honest truth, when the right word would not come, it was generally replaced by a very powerful adjective.

In connection with the sciences there are many almost unpronounceable names—names very much resembling those of Welsh villages; and my uncle being very fond of using them, his habit of stammering was not thereby improved. In fact, there were periods in his discourse when he would finally give up, and swallow his discomfiture—in a glass of water.

As I said, my uncle, Professor Hardwigg, was a very learned man; and I now add a most kind relative. I was bound to him by the double ties of affection and interest. I took deep interest in all his doings, and hoped some day to be almost as learned myself. It was a rare thing for me to be absent from his lectures. Like him, I preferred mineralogy to all the other sciences. My anxiety was to gain *real knowledge of the earth*. Geology and mineralogy were to us the sole objects of life, and in connection with these studies many a fair specimen of stone, chalk, or metal did we break with our hammers.

Steel rods, loadstone, glass pipes, and bottles of various acids were oftener before us than our meals. My uncle Hardwigg was once known to classify six hundred different geological specimens by their weight, hardness, fusibility, sound, taste, and smell.

He corresponded with all the great, learned, and scientific men of the age. I was therefore in constant communication with, at all events the letters of, Sir Humphry Davy, Captain Franklin, and other great men.

But before I state the subject on which my uncle wished to confer with me, I must say a word about his personal appearance. Alas! my readers will see a very different portrait of him at a future time, after he has gone through the fearful adventures yet to be related.

My uncle was fifty years old; tall, thin, and wiry. Large spectacles hid, to a certain extent, his vast, round and goggle eyes, while his nose was irreverently compared to a thin file. So much indeed did it resemble that useful article, that a compass was said in his presence to have made considerable N* deviation.

The truth being told, however, the only article really attracted to my uncle's nose was tobacco.

Another peculiarity of his was, that he always stepped a yard at a time, clenched his fists as if he were going to hit you, and was, when in one of his peculiar humours, very far from a pleasant companion.

It is further necessary to observe that he lived in a very nice house, in that very nice street, the Königstrasse at Hamburg. Though lying in the centre of a town, it was perfectly rural in its aspect—half wood, half bricks, with old-fashioned gables—one of the few old houses spared by the great fire of 1842.

When I say a nice house, I mean a handsome house—old, tottering, and not exactly comfort-able to English notions: a house a little off the perpendicular and inclined to fall into the neighbouring canal; exactly the house for a wandering artist to depict; all the more that you could scarcely see it for ivy and a magnificent old tree which grew over the door.

My uncle was rich; his house was his own property, while he had a considerable private income. To my notion the best part of his possessions was his god-daughter Gretchen. And the old cook, the young lady, the Professor and I were the sole inhabitants.

I loved mineralogy, I loved geology. To me there was nothing like pebbles—and if my uncle had been in a little less of a fury, we should have been the happiest of families. To prove the excellent Hardwigg's impatience, I solemnly declare that when the flowers in the drawing-room pots began to grow, he rose every morning at four o'clock to make them grow quicker by pulling the leaves!

Having described my uncle, I will now give an account of our interview.

He received me in his study; a perfect museum, containing every natural curiosity that can well be imagined—minerals, however, predominating. Every one was familiar to me, having been catalogued by my own hand. My uncle, apparently oblivious of the fact that he had summoned me to his presence, was absorbed in a book. He was particularly fond of early editions, tall copies, and unique works.

"Wonderful!" he cried, tapping his forehead. "Wonderful—wonderful!"

It was one of those yellow-leaved volumes now rarely found on stalls, and to me it appeared to possess but little value. My uncle, however, was in raptures.

He admired its binding, the clearness of its characters, the ease with which it opened in his hand, and repeated aloud, half-a-dozen times, that it was very, very old.

To my fancy he was making a great fuss about nothing, but it was not my province to say so. On the contrary, I professed consider-able interest in the subject, and asked him what it was about.

"It is the Heims-Kringla of Snorre Tarleson," he said, "the celebrated Icelandic author of the twelfth century—it is a true and correct account of the Norwegian princes who reigned in Iceland."

My next question related to the language in which it was written. I hoped at all events it was translated into German. My uncle was indignant at the very thought, and declared he wouldn't give a penny for a translation. His delight was to have found the original work in the Icelandic tongue, which he declared to be one of the most magnificent and yet simple idioms in the world—while at the same time its grammatical combinations were the most varied known to students.

"About as easy as German?" was my insidious remark.

My uncle shrugged his shoulders.

"The letters at all events," I said, "are rather difficult of comprehension."

"It is a Runic manuscript, the language of the original population of Iceland, invented by Odin himself," cried my uncle, angry at my ignorance.

I was about to venture upon some misplaced joke on the subject, when a small scrap of parchment fell out of the leaves. Like a hungry man snatching at a morsel of bread, the Professor seized it. It was about five inches by three, and was scrawled over in the most extra-ordinary fashion.

The lines on page 286 are an exact fac-simile of what was written on the venerable piece of parchment—and have wonderful importance, as they induced my uncle to undertake the most wonderful series of adventures which ever fell to the lot of human beings.

My uncle looked keenly at the document for some moments and then declared that it was Runic. The letters were similar to those in the

*(?) Nasal.

Professor Hardwigg's Home in the Königstrasse.

book, but then what did they mean? This was exactly what I wanted to know.

Now as I had a strong conviction that the Runic alphabet and dialect were simply an invention to mystify poor human nature, I was delighted to find that my uncle knew as much about the matter as I did—which was nothing. At all events, the tremulous motion of his fingers made me think so.

"And yet," he muttered to himself, "it is old Icelandic, I am sure of it."

And my uncle ought to have known, for he was a perfect polyglot dictionary in himself. He did not pretend, like a certain learned pundit, to speak the two thousand languages and four thousand idioms made use of in different parts of the globe, but he did know all the more important ones.

It is a matter of great doubt to me now, to what violent measures my uncle's impetuosity might have led him, had not the clock struck two, and our old French cook called out to let us know that dinner was on the table.

"Bother the dinner!" cried my uncle.

But as I was hungry, I sallied forth to the dining room, where I took up my usual quarters. Out of politeness I waited three minutes, but no sign of my uncle, the Professor. I was surprised. He was not usually so blind to the pleasures of a good dinner. It was the acme of German luxury—parsley soup, a ham omelette with sorrel trimmings, an oyster of veal stewed with prunes, delicious fruit, and sparkling Moselle. For the sake of poring over this musty old piece of parchment, my uncle forbore to share our meal. To satisfy my conscience, I ate for both.

The old cook and housekeeper was nearly out of her mind. After taking so much trouble, to find her master not appear at dinner was to her a sad disappointment—which, as she occasionally watched the havoc I was making on the viands, became also alarm. If my uncle were to come to table after all?

Suddenly, just as I had consumed the last apple and drank the last glass of wine, a terrible voice was heard at no great distance. It was my uncle roaring for me to come to him. I made very nearly one leap of it—so loud, so fierce was his tone.

A Journey to the Centre of the Earth

CHAPTER II.

THE MYSTERIOUS PARCHMENT

ᛉ.ᛗᛚᚲᚱᛅ ᛏᛅᛏᚲᚾᛏᚲ �2ᛏᛏᚱI ᛒᚱ
�2ᛝᛏᛐᛅᛑF ᚾᛐᛏᚱIᛏF ᚲ Iᛏᛒᛅᚲᛏ
ᚱᛐᛐ1ᛏᚲ 1ᛏᚮ1ᛏᛏ2 ᛣᚾ Fᛒᚮᚮᚮ
ᛏᛐᛏᚮ1ᛏI ᚾᚮ1ᛏᚱᛐ ᚮᚮ I ᚮ2
1ᛏᚾ11ᚮ .ᚮᛝᚱᚮᚱ I ᛏ11Bᛝ
ᚱᚱᛒᚮᛐᛐI ᛏᛏᚾᛏᚾᛏ Fᚮ1ᚮᛏᚾ
ᛒᛏ₍11ᚱ ᚲᛝᛏIBᚲ ᛉᛏᛒIᛁI

"I DECLARE," cried my uncle, striking the table fiercely with his fist, "I declare to you it is Runic—and contains some wonderful secret, which I must get at, at any price."

I was about to reply when he stopped me.

"Sit down," he said, quite fiercely, "and write to my dictation."

I obeyed.

"I will substitute," he said, "a letter of our alphabet for that of the Runic: we will then see what that will produce. Now, begin and make no mistakes."

The dictation commenced with the following incomprehensible result:—

m.rnlls	esruel	seecJde
sgtssmf	unteief	niedrke
kt,samn	atrateS	Saodrrn
emtnael	nuaect	rrilSa
Atvaar	.nscrc	ieaabs
ccdrmi	eeutul	frantu
dt,iac	oseibo	KediiI

Scarcely giving me time to finish, my uncle snatched the document from my hands and examined it with the most rapt and deep attention.

"I should like to know what it means," he said, after a long period.

I certainly could not tell him, nor did he expect me to—his conversation being uniformly answered by himself.

"I declare it puts me in mind of a cryptograph," he cried, "unless, indeed, the letters have been written without any real meaning; and yet why take so much trouble? Who knows but I may be on the verge of some great discovery?"

My candid opinion was that it was all rubbish! But this opinion I kept carefully to myself, as my uncle's choler was not pleasant to bear. All this time he was comparing the book and the parchment.

"The manuscript volume and the smaller document are written in different hands," he said, "the cryptograph is of much later date than the book; there is an undoubted proof of the correctness of my surmise. [An irrefragable proof I took it to be.] The first letter is a double M, which was only added to the Icelandic language in the twelfth century—this makes the parchment two hundred years posterior to the volume."

The circumstance appeared very probable and very logical, but it was all surmise to me.

"To me it appears probable that this sentence was written by some owner of the book. Now who was the owner, is the next important question. Perhaps by great good luck it may be written somewhere in the volume."

With these words Professor Hardwigg took off his spectacles, and, taking a powerful magnifying glass, examined the book carefully.

On the fly leaf was what appeared to be a blot of ink, but on examination proved to be a line of writing almost effaced by time. This was what he sought; and, after some considerable time, he made out these letters:

1ᚮᚲᛏ ᛝ1ᚱᚾᛝᛝᛏᛉ

"Arne Saknussemm!" he cried in a joyous and triumphant tone, "that is not only an Icelandic name, but of a learned professor of the sixteenth century, a celebrated alchemist."

I bowed as a sign of respect.

"These alchemists," he continued, "Avicena, Bacon, Lully, Paracelsus, were the true, the only learned men of the day. They made surprising discoveries. May not this Saknussemm, nephew mine, have hidden on this bit of parchment some astounding invention? I believe the cryptograph to have a profound meaning—which I must make out."

My uncle walked about the room in a state of excitement almost impossible to describe.

"It may be so, sir," I timidly observed, "but why conceal it from posterity, if it be a useful, a worthy discovery?"

"Why—how should I know? Did not Galileo make a secret of his discoveries in connection

Professor Von Hardwigg.

with Saturn? But we shall see. Until I discover the meaning of this sentence I will neither eat nor sleep.''

"My dear uncle—'' I began.

"Nor you neither,'' he added.

It was lucky I had taken double allowance that day.

"In the first place,'' he continued, "there must be a clue to the meaning. If we could find that, the rest would be easy enough.''

I began seriously to reflect. The prospect of going without food and sleep was not a promising one, so I determined to do my best to solve the mystery. My uncle, meanwhile, went on with his soliloquy.

"The way to discover it is easy enough. In this document there are one hundred and thirty-two letters, giving seventy-nine consonants to fifty-three vowels. This is about the proportion found in most southern languages, the idioms of the north being much more rich in consonants. We may confidently predict, therefore, that we have to deal with a southern dialect.''

Nothing could be more logical.

"Now,'' said Professor Hardwigg, "to trace the particular language.''

"As Shakespeare says, 'that is the question,''' was my rather satirical reply.

"This man Saknussemm,'' he continued, "was a very learned man: now as he did not write in the language of his birth-place, he probably, like most learned men of the sixteenth century, wrote in Latin. If, however, I prove wrong in this guess, we must try Spanish, French, Italian, Greek, and even Hebrew. My own opinion, though, is decidedly in favour of Latin.''

This proposition startled me. Latin was my favourite study, and it seemed sacrilege to believe this gibberish to belong to the country of Virgil.

"Barbarous Latin, in all probability,'' continued my uncle, "but still Latin.''

"Very probably,'' I replied, not to contradict him.

"Let us see into the matter,'' continued my uncle; "here you see we have a series of one hundred and thirty-two letters, apparently thrown pell-mell upon paper, without method or organisation. There are words which are composed wholly of consonants, such as *m.rnlls*, others which are nearly all vowels, the fifth, for instance, which is *unteief*, and one of the last *oseibo*. This appears an extraordinary combination. Probably we shall find that the phrase is arranged according to some mathematical plan. No doubt a certain sentence has been written out and then jumbled up—some plan to which some figure is the clue. Now, Harry, to show your English wit—what is that figure?''

I could give him no hint. My thoughts were indeed far away. While he was speaking I had caught sight of the portrait of my cousin Gretchen, and was wondering when she would return.

We were affianced, and loved one another very sincerely. But my uncle, who never thought even of such sublunary matters, knew nothing of this. Without noticing my abstraction, the Professor began reading the puzzling cryptograph all sorts of ways, according to some theory of his own. Presently, rousing my wandering attention, he dictated one precious attempt to me.

I mildly handed it over to him. It read as follows:—

mmessunkaSenrA.icefdoK.segnittamurtn ecertserrette,rotaivsadua,ednscsedsadne lacartniiiluJsiratracSarbmutabiledmek meretarcsilucoIsleffenSnI.

"I could scarcely keep from laughing, while my uncle, on the contrary, got in a towering passion, struck the table with his fist, darted out of the room, out of the house, and then taking to his heels was presently lost to sight.

A Journey to the Centre of the Earth

CHAPTER III.

AN ASTOUNDING DISCOVERY

"WHAT is the matter?" cried the cook, entering the room; "when will master have his dinner?"

"Never."

"And his supper?"

"I don't know. He says he will eat no more, neither shall I. My uncle has determined to fast and make me fast until he makes out this abominable inscription," I replied.

"You will be starved to death," she said.

I was very much of the same opinion, but not liking to say so, sent her away, and began some of my usual work of classification. But boy as I made myself, nothing could keep me from thinking alternately of the stupid manuscript and of the pretty Gretchen.

Several times I thought of going out, but my uncle would have been angry at my absence. At the end of an hour, my allotted task was done. How to pass the time? I began by lighting my pipe. Like all students, I delighted in tobacco; and, seating myself in the great armchair, I began to think.

Where was my uncle? I could easily imagine him tearing along some solitary road, gesticulating, talking to himself, cutting the air with his cane, and still thinking of the absurd bit of hieroglyphics. Would he hit upon some clue? Would he come home in better humour? While these thoughts were passing through my brain, I mechanically took up the execrable puzzle and tried every imaginable way of grouping the letters. I put them together by twos, by threes, fours, and fives—in vain. Nothing intelligible came out, except that the fourteenth, fifteenth and sixteenth made *ice* in English; the eighty-fourth, eighty-fifth and eighty-sixth, the word *sir;* then at last I seemed to find the Latin words *rota, mutabile, ira, nec, atra.*

"Ha! there seems to be some truth in my uncle's notion," thought I.

Then again I seemed to find the word *luco,* which means sacred wood. Then in the third line I appeared to make out *labiled,* a perfectly Hebrew word, and at the last the syllables *mère, are, mer,* which were French.

It was enough to drive one mad. Four different idioms im this absurd phrase. What connection could there be between ice, sir, anger, cruel, sacred wood, changing, mother, are and sea? The first and the last might, in a sentence connected with Iceland, mean sea of ice. But what of the rest of this monstrous cryptograph?

I was, in fact, fighting against an insurmountable difficulty; my brain was almost on fire; my eyes were strained with staring at the parchment; the whole absurd collection of letters appeared to dance before my vision in a number of black little groups. My mind was possessed with temporary hallucination—I was stifling. I wanted air. Mechanically I fanned myself with the document, of which now I saw the back and then the front.

Imagine my surprise when glancing at the back of the wearisome puzzle, the ink having gone through, I clearly made out Latin words, and among others *craterem* and *terrestre.*

I had discovered the secret!

It came upon me like a flash of lightning. I had got the clue. All you had to do to understand the document was to read it backwards. All the ingenious ideas of the Professor were realised; he had dictated it rightly to me; by a mere accident I had discovered what he so much desired.

My delight, my emotion may be imagined, my eyes were dazzled and I trembled so that at first I could make nothing of it. One look, however, would tell me all I wished to know.

"Let me read," I said to myself, after drawing a long breath.

I spread it before me on the table, I passed my finger over each letter, I spelt it through; in my excitement I read it out.

What horror and stupefaction took possession of my soul. I was like a man who had received a knock-down blow. Was it possible that I really read the terrible secret, and it had really been accomplished! A man had dared to do—what?

No living being should ever know.

"Never!" cried I, jumping up; "Never shall my uncle be made aware of the dread secret. He would be quite capable of undertaking the terrible journey. Nothing would check him, nothing stop him. Worse, he would compel me to accompany him, and we should be lost for ever. But no; such folly and madness cannot be allowed.

I was almost beside myself with rage and fury.

"My worthy uncle is already nearly mad," I cried aloud. "This would finish him. By some accident he may make the discovery; in which case, we are both lost. Perish the fearful secret —let the flames for ever bury it in oblivion."

I snatched up book and parchment, and was about to cast them into the fire, when the door opened and my uncle entered.

I had scarcely time to put down the wretched documents before my uncle was by my side. He was profoundly absorbed. His thoughts were evidently bent on the terrible parchment. Some new combination had probably struck him while taking his walk.

He seated himself in his armchair, and with a pen began to make an algebraical calculation. I watched him with anxious eyes. My flesh crawled as it became probable that he would discover *the* secret.

His combinations I knew now were useless, I having discovered the one only clue. For three mortal hours he continued without speaking a word, without raising his head, scratching, re-writing, calculating over and over again. I knew that in time he must hit upon the right phrase. The letters of every alphabet have only a certain number of combinations. But then years might elapse before he would perhaps arrive at the correct solution.

Still time went on; night came, the sounds in the streets ceased—and still my uncle went on, not even answering our worthy cook when she called us to supper.

I did not dare to leave him, so waved her away, and at last fell asleep on the sofa.

When I awoke my uncle was still at work. His red eyes, his pallid countenance, his matted hair, his feverish hands, his hecticly flushed cheeks, showed how terrible had been his struggle with the impossible, and what fearful fatigue he had undergone during that long sleepless night. It made me quite ill to look at him. Though he was rather severe with me, I loved him, and my heart ached at his sufferings. He was so overcome by one idea that he could not even get in a passion! All his energies were focussed on one point. And I knew that by speaking one little word all this suffering would cease. I could not speak it.

My heart was, nevertheless, inclining towards him. Why, then, did I remain silent? In the interest of my uncle himself.

"Nothing shall make me speak," I muttered. "He will want to follow in the footsteps of the other! I know him well. His imagination is a perfect volcano, and to make discoveries in the interests of geology, he would sacrifice his life. I will therefore be silent and strictly keep the secret I have discovered. To reveal it would be suicidal. He would not only rush, himself, to destruction but drag me with him."

I crossed my arms, looked another way and smoked—resolved never to speak.

When our cook wanted to go out to market, or on any other errand, she found the front door locked and the key taken away. Was this done purposely or not? Surely Professor Hardwigg did not intend the old woman and myself to become martyrs to his obstinate will. Were we to be starved to death? A frightful recollection came to my mind. Once we had fed on bits and scraps for a week while he sorted some curiosities. It gave me the cramp even to think of it!

I wanted my breakfast, and saw no way of getting it. Still my resolution held good. I would starve rather than yield. But the cook began to take me seriously to task. What was to be done? She could not go out; and I dared not.

My uncle continued counting and writing; his imagination seemed to have translated him to the skies. He neither thought of eating nor drinking. In this way twelve o'clock came round. I was hungry, and there was nothing in the house. The cook had eaten the last bit of bread. This could not go on. It did, however, until two, when my sensations were terrible. After all, I began to think the document very absurd. Perhaps it might only be a gigantic hoax. Besides, some means would surely be found to keep my uncle back from attempting any such absurd expedition. On the other hand, if he did attempt anything so Quixotic, I should not be compelled to accompany him. Another line of reasoning partially decided me. Very likely he would make the discovery himself when I should have suffered starvation for nothing. Under the influence of hunger this reasoning appeared admirable. I determined to tell all.

The question now arose as to how it was to be done. I was still dwelling on the thought, when he rose and put on his hat.

What! go out and lock us in? Never!

"Uncle," I began.

He did not appear even to hear me.

"Professor Hardwigg," I cried.

"What," he retorted, "did you speak?"

"How about the key?"

"What key—the key of the door?"

"No—of these horrible hieroglyphics?"

He looked at me from under his spectacles,

Tracing our route.

and started at the odd expression of my face. Rushing forward, he clutched me by the arm and keenly examined my countenance. His very look was an interrogation.

I simply nodded.

With an incredulous shrug of the shoulders, he turned upon his heel. Undoubtedly he thought I had gone mad.

"I have made a very important discovery."

His eyes flashed with excitement. His hand was lifted in a menacing attitude. For a moment neither of us spoke. It is hard to say which was most excited.

"You don't mean to say that you have any idea of the meaning of the scrawl?"

"I do," was my desperate reply. "Look at the sentence as dictated by you."

"Well, but it means nothing," was the angry answer.

"Nothing if you read from left to right, but mark, if from right to left—"

"Backwards!" cried my uncle, in wild amazement. "Oh most cunning Saknussemm; and I to be such a blockhead!"

He snatched up the document, gazed at it with haggard eye, and read it out as I had done. It read as follows:—

In Sneffels yoculis craterem kem delebat Umbra Scartaris Julii intra calendas descende.

Audas viator, et terrestre centrum attinges, Kod feci. Arne Saknussemm.

Which dog-Latin being translated, reads as follows:—

"Descend into the crater of Yocul of Sneffels, which the shade of Scartaris caresses, before the kalends of July, audacious traveller, and you will reach the centre of the earth. I did it. ARNE SAKNUSSEMM."

My uncle leaped three feet from the ground with joy. He looked radiant and handsome. He rushed about the room wild with delight and satisfaction. He knocked over tables and chairs. He threw his books about until at last, utterly exhausted, he fell into his arm-chair.

"What's o'clock?" he asked.

"About three."

"My dinner does not seem to have done me much good," he observed, "Let me have something to eat. We can then start at once. Get my portmanteau ready."

"What for?"

"And your own," he continued. "We start at once."

My horror may be conceived. I resolved however to show no fear. Scientific reasons were the only ones likely to influence my uncle. Now, there were many against this terrible journey. The very idea of going down to the centre of the earth was simply absurd. I determined therefore to argue the point after dinner.

My uncle's rage was now directed against the cook for having no dinner ready. My explanation however satisfied him, and giving her the key she soon contrived to get sufficient to satisfy our voracious appetites.

During the repast my uncle was rather gay than otherwise. He made some of those peculiar jokes which belong exclusively to the learned. As soon however as dessert was over, he called me to his study. We each took a chair on opposite sides of the table.

"Henry," he said, in a soft and winning voice; "I have always believed you ingenious, and you have rendered me a service never to be forgotten. Without you, this great, this wondrous discovery would never have been made. It is my duty, therefore, to insist on your sharing the glory."

"He is in a good humour," thought I; "I'll soon let him know my opinion of glory."

"In the first place," he continued, "you must keep the whole affair a profound secret. There is no more envious race of men than scientific discoverers. Many would start on the same journey. At all events, we will be the first in the field."

"I doubt your having many competitors," was my reply.

"A man of real scientific acquirements would be delighted at the chance. We should find a perfect stream of pilgrims on the traces of Arne Saknussemm, if this document were once made public."

"But, my dear sir, is not this paper very likely to be a hoax?" I urged.

"The book in which we find it is sufficient proof of its authenticity," he replied.

"I thoroughly allow that the celebrated Professor wrote the lines, but only, I believe, as a kind of mystification," was my answer.

Scarcely were the words out of my mouth, when I was sorry I had uttered them. My uncle looked at me with a dark and gloomy scowl, and I began to be alarmed for the results of our conversation. His mood soon changed, however, and a smile took the place of a frown.

"We shall see,' he remarked, with decisive emphasis.

"But see, what is all this about Yocul, and Sneffels, and this Scartaris? I have never heard anything about them."

"The very point to which I am coming. I lately received from my friend, Augustus Peterman, of Leipzig, a map. Take down the

Harry in a Brown Study.

third atlas from the second shelf, series Z, plate 4.

I rose, went to the shelf, and presently returned with the volume indicated.

"This," said my uncle, "is one of the best maps of Iceland. I believe it will settle all your doubts, difficulties and objections."

With a grim hope to the contrary, I stooped over the map.

My uncle's excitement.

A Journey to the Centre of the Earth

CHAPTER IV.

WE START ON THE JOURNEY

"YOU see, the whole island is composed of volcanoes," said the Professor, "and remark carefully that they all bear the name of Yokul. The word is Icelandic, and means a glacier. In most of the lofty mountains of that region the volcanic eruptions come forth from icebound caverns. Hence the name applied to every volcano on this extraordinary island."

"But what does this word Sneffels mean?"

To this question I expected no rational answer. I was mistaken.

"Follow my finger to the western coast of Iceland, there you see Reykjawik, its capital. Follow the direction of one of its innumerable fjords or arms of the sea, and what do you see below the sixty-fifth degree of latitude?"

"A peninsula—very like a thigh-bone in shape."

"And in the centre of it—?"

"A mountain."

"Well, that's Sneffels."

I had nothing to say.

"That is Sneffels—a mountain about five thousand feet in height, one of the most remarkable in the whole island, and certainly doomed to be the most celebrated in the world, for through its crater we shall reach the Centre of the Earth."

"Impossible!" cried I, startled and shocked at the thought.

"Why impossible?" said Professor Hardwigg in his severest tones.

"Because its crater is choked with lava, by burning rocks—by infinite dangers."

"But if it be extinct?"

"That would make a difference."

"Of course it would. There are about three hundred volcanoes on the whole surface of the globe—but the greater number are extinct. Of these Sneffels is one. No eruption had occurred since 1219—in fact, it has ceased to be a volcano at all."

After this what more could I say? Yes—I thought of another objection.

"But what is all this about Scartaris and the kalends of July—?"

My uncle reflected deeply. Presently he gave forth the result of his reflections in a sententious tone.

"What appears obscure to you, to me is light. This very phrase shows how particular Saknussemm is in his directions. The Sneffels' mountain has many craters. He is careful therefore to point the exact one which is the highway into the Interior of the Earth. He lets us know, for this purpose, that about the end of the month of June, the shadow of Mount Scartaris falls upon the one crater. There can be no doubt about the matter."

My uncle had an answer for everything.

"I accept all your explanations," I said, "and Saknussemm is right. He found out the entrance to the bowels of the earth, he has indicated correctly, but that he or any one else ever followed up the discovery, is madness to suppose."

"Why so, young man?"

"All scientific teaching, theoretical and practical, shows it to be impossible."

"I care nothing for theories," retorted my uncle.

"But is it not well-known that heat increases one degree for every seventy feet you descend into the earth? which gives a fine idea of the central heat. All the matters which compose the globe are in a state of incandescence; even gold, platinum, and the hardest rocks are in a state of fusion. What would become of us?"

"Don't be alarmed at the heat, my boy."

"How so?"

"Neither you nor anybody else know anything about the real state of the earth's interior. All modern experiments tend to explode the older theories. Were any such heat to exist, the upper crust of the earth would be shattered to atoms, and the world would be at an end."

A long, learned and not uninteresting discussion followed, which ended in this wise:—

"I do not believe in the dangers and difficulties which you, Henry, seem to multiply; and the only way to learn, is like Arne Saknussemm, to go and see."

"Well," cried I, overcome at last, "let us go and see. Though how we can do that in the dark is another mystery."

"Fear nothing. We shall overcome these, and many other difficulties. Besides, as we

296

Farewell to Home.

approach the Centre, I expect to find it luminous—''

"Nothing is impossible.''

"And now that we have come to a thorough understanding, not a word to any living soul. Our success depends on secrecy and despatch.''

Thus ended our memorable conference, which roused a perfect fever in me. Leaving my uncle, I went forth like one possessed. Reaching the banks of the Elbe, I began to think. Was all I had heard really and truly possible? Was my uncle in his sober senses, and could the interior of the earth be reached? Was I the victim of a madman, or was he a discoverer of rare courage and grandeur of conception?

To a certain extent I was anxious to be off. I was afraid my enthusiasm would cool. I determined to pack up at once. At the end of an hour, however, on my way home, I found that my feelings had very much changed.

"I'm all abroad," I cried; "'tis a nightmare —I must have dreamed it.''

At this moment I came face to face with Gretchen, whom I warmly embraced.

"So you have come to meet me," she said; "how good of you. But what is the matter?''

Well, it was no use mincing the matter, I told her all. She listened with awe, and for some minutes she could not speak.

"Well?" I at last said, rather anxiously.

"What a magnificent journey. If I were only a man! A journey worthy of the nephew of Professor Hardwigg. I should look upon it as an honour to accompany him.''

"My dear Gretchen, I thought you would be the first to cry out against this mad enterprise.''

"No; on the contrary, I glory in it. It is magnificent, splendid—an idea worthy of my father. Henry Lawson, I envy you.''

This was, as it were, conclusive. The final blow of all.

When we entered the house we found my uncle surrounded by workmen and porters, who were packing up. He was pulling and hauling at a bell.

"Where have you been wasting your time. Your portmanteau is not packed—my papers are not in order—the precious tailor has not brought my clothes, nor my gaiters—the key of my carpet bag is gone!''

I looked at him stupefied. And still he tugged away at the bell.

"We are really off, then?" I said.

"Yes—of course, and yet you go out for a stroll, unfortunate boy!''

"And when do we go?''

"The day after to-morrow, at daybreak.''

I heard no more; but darted off to my little bed-chamber and locked myself in. There was no doubt about it now. My uncle had been hard at work all the afternoon. The garden was full of ropes, rope-ladders, torches, gourds, iron clamps, crow-bars, alpenstocks, and pickaxes —enough to load ten men.

I passed a terrible night. I was called early the next day to learn that the resolution of my uncle was unchanged and irrevocable. I also found my cousin and affianced wife as warm on the subject as was her father.

Next day, at five o'clock in the morning, the post chaise was at the door. Gretchen and the old cook received the keys of the house; and, scarcely pausing to wish anyone good-bye, we started on our adventurous journey into the Centre of the Earth.

A Journey to the Centre of the Earth

CHAPTER V.

FIRST LESSONS IN CLIMBING

AT Altona, a suburb of Hamburg, is the Chief Station of the Kiel railway, which was to take us to the shores of the Belt. In twenty minutes from the moment of our departure we were in Holstein, and our carriage entered the station. Our heavy luggage was taken out, weighed, labelled, and placed in a huge van. We then took our tickets, and exactly at seven o'clock were seated opposite each other in a first-class railway carriage.

My uncle said nothing. He was too busy examining his papers, among which of course was the famous parchment, and some letters of introduction from the Danish consul, which were to pave the way to an introduction to the Governor of Iceland. My only amusement was looking out of the window. But as we passed through a flat though fertile country, this occupation was slightly monotonous. In three hours we reached Kiel, and our baggage was at once transferred to the steamer.

We had now a day before us, a delay of about ten hours. Which fact put my uncle in a towering passion. We had nothing to do but to walk about the pretty town and bay. At length, however, we went on board, and at half past ten were steaming down the Great Belt. It was a dark night, with a strong breeze and a rough sea, nothing being visible but the occasional fires on shore, with here and there a lighthouse. At seven in the morning we left Korsör, a little town on the western side of Seeland.

Here we took another railway, which in three hours brought us to the capital, Copenhagen, where, scarcely taking time for refreshment, my uncle hurried out to present one of his letters of introduction. It was to the director of the Museum of Antiquities, who having been informed that we were tourists bound for Iceland, did all he could to assist us. One wretched hope sustained me now. Perhaps no vessel was bound for such distant parts.

Alas! a little Danish schooner, the *Valkyrie*, was to sail on the second of June for Reykjawik. The captain, M. Bjarne, was on board, and was rather surprised at the energy and cordiality with which his future passenger shook him by the hand. To him a voyage to Iceland was merely a matter of course. My uncle, on the other hand, considered the event of sublime importance. The honest sailor took advantage of the Professor's enthusiasm to double the fare.

"On Tuesday morning at seven o'clock be on board," said M. Bjarne, handing us our receipts.

"Excellent! Capital! Glorious!" remarked my uncle as we sat down to a late breakfast; "refresh yourself, my boy, and we will take a run through the town."

Our meal concluded, we went to the Kongens-Nye-Torw; to the king's magnificent palace; to the beautiful bridge over the canal near the Museum; to the immense cenotaph of Thorwaldsen with its hideous naval groups; to the Castle of Rosenberg; and to all the other lions of the place,—none of which my uncle even saw, so absorbed was he in his anticipated triumphs.

But one thing struck his fancy, and that was a certain singular steeple situated on the Island of Amak, which is the south-east quarter of the city of Copenhagen. My uncle at once ordered me to turn my steps that way, and accordingly we went on board the steam ferry boat which does duty on the canal, and very soon reached the noted dockyard quay.

In the first instance we crossed some narrow streets, where we met numerous groups of galley slaves, with parti-coloured trousers, grey and yellow, working under the orders and the sticks of severe task-masters, and finally reached the Vor-Frelser's-Kirk.

This church exhibited nothing remarkable in itself; in fact, the worthy Professor had only been attracted to it by one circumstance, which was, that its rather elevated steeple started from a circular platform, after which there was an exterior staircase, which wound round to the very summit.

"Let us ascend," said my uncle.

"But I never could climb church towers," I cried, "I am subject to dizziness in my head."

"The very reason why you should go up. I want to cure you of a bad habit."

"But my good sir—"

"I tell you to come. What is the use of wasting so much valuable time?"

It was impossible to dispute the dictatorial commands of my uncle. I yielded with a groan.

On payment of a fee, a verger gave us the key. He, for one, was not partial to the ascent. My uncle at once showed me the way, running up the steps like a schoolboy. I followed as well as I could, though no sooner was I outside the tower, than my head began to swim. There was nothing of the eagle about me. The earth was enough for me, and no ambitious desire to soar ever entered my mind. Still things did not go badly until I had ascended 150 steps, and was near the platform, when I began to feel the rush of cold air. I could scarcely stand, when clutching the railings, I looked upwards. The railing was frail enough, but nothing to those which skirted the terrible winding staircase, that appeared, from where I stood, to ascend to the skies.

"Now then, Henry."

"I can't do it!" I cried, in accents of despair.

"Are you, after all, a coward sir?" said my uncle in a pitiless tone. "Go up, I say!"

To this there was no reply possible. And yet the keen air acted violently on my nervous system; sky, earth, all seemed to swim round; while the steeple rocked like a ship. My legs gave way like those of a drunken man. I crawled upon my hands and knees; I hauled myself up slowly, crawling like a snake. Presently I closed my eyes, and allowed myself to be dragged upwards.

"Look around you," said my uncle, in a stern voice, "Heaven knows what profound abysses you may have to look down. This is excellent practice."

Slowly, and shivering all the while with cold, I opened my eyes. What then did I see? My first glance was upwards at the cold fleecy clouds, which as by some optical delusion appeared to stand still, while the steeple, the weathercock, and our two selves were carried swifly along. Far away on one side could be seen the grassy plain, while on the other lay the sea bathed in translucent light. The Sund, or Sound as we call it, could be discovered beyond the point of Elsinore, crowded with white sails, which, at that distance, looked like the wings of seagulls; while to the east could be made out the far-off coast of Sweden. The whole appeared a magic panorama.

But faint and bewildered as I was, there was no remedy for it. Rise and stand up I must. Despite my protestations my first lesson lasted quite an hour. When, nearly two hours later, I reached the bosom of mother earth, I was like a rheumatic old man bent double with pain.

"Enough for one day," said my uncle, rubbing his hands, "we will begin again to-morrow."

There was no remedy. My lessons lasted five days, and at the end of that period, I ascended blithely enough, and found myself able to look down into the depths below, without even winking, and with some degree of pleasure.

A Journey to the Centre of the Earth

CHAPTER VI.

OUR VOYAGE TO ICELAND

THE hour of departure came at last. The night before, the worthy Mr. Thomson brought us the most cordial letters of introduction for Count Trampe, Governor of Iceland, for M. Pictursson, coadjutor to the bishop, and for M. Finsen, mayor of the town of Reykjawik. In return, my uncle nearly crushed his hands, so warmly did he shake them.

On the second of the month, at two in the morning, our precious cargo of luggage was taken on board the good ship *Valkyrie*. We followed, and were very politely introduced by the captain to a small cabin with two standing bed places, neither very well ventilated nor very comfortable. But in the cause of science men are expected to suffer.

"Well, and have we a fair wind?" cried my uncle, in his most mellifluous accents.

"An excellent wind!" replied Captain Bjarne; "we shall leave the Sound, going free with all sails set."

A few minutes afterwards, the schooner started before the wind, under all the canvas she could carry, and entered the channel. An hour later, the capital of Denmark seemed to sink into the waves, and we were at no great distance from the coast of Elsinore. My uncle was delighted; for myself, moody and dissatisfied, I appeared almost to expect a glimpse of the ghost of Hamlet.

"Sublime madman," thought I, "you, doubtless, would approve our proceedings. You might perhaps even follow us to the centre of the earth, there to resolve your eternal doubts."

But no ghost, or anything else appeared upon the ancient walls. The fact is, the castle is much later than the time of the heroic prince of Denmark. It is now the residence of the keeper of the Strait of the Sound, and through that Sound more than fifteen thousand vessels of all nations pass every year.

The castle of Kronborg soon disappeared in the murky atmosphere, as well as the tower of Helsinborg, which raises its head on the Swedish Bank. And here the schooner began to feel in earnest the breezes of the Cattegat. The *Valkyrie* was swift enough, but with all sailing boats there is the same uncertainty. Her cargo was coal, furniture, pottery, woollen clothing, and a load of corn. As usual, the crew was small, five Danes doing the whole of the work.

"How long will the voyage last?" asked my uncle.

"Well, I should think about ten days," replied the skipper, "unless, indeed, we meet with some north-east gales among the Faroe Islands.

"At all events, there will be no very considerable delay," cried the impatient Professor.

"No, Mr. Hardwigg," said the captain, "no fear of that. At all events, we shall get there some day."

Towards evening the schooner doubled Cape Skagen, the northernmost part of Denmark, crossed the Skager-Rak during the night—skirted the extreme point of Norway through the gut of Cape Lindness, and then reached the Northern Seas. Two days later we were not far from the coast of Scotland, somewhere near what Danish sailors call Peterhead, and then the *Valkyrie* stretched out direct for the Faroe Islands, between Orkney and Shetland. Our vessel now felt the full force of the ocean waves, and the wind shifting, we with great difficulty made the Faroe Islands. On the eighth day, the captain made out Myganness, the westernmost of the Isles, and from that moment headed direct for Portland, a cape on the southern shores of the singular island for which we were bound.

The voyage offered no incidents worthy of record. I bore it very well, but my uncle to his great annoyance, and even shame, was remarkably sea-sick! This *mal de mer* troubled him the more, that it prevented him from questioning Captain Bjarne as to the subject of Sneffels, as to the means of communication, and the facilities of transport. All these explanations he had to adjourn to the period of his arrival. His time meanwhile, was spent lying in bed groaning, and dwelling anxiously on the hoped-for termination of the voyage. I didn't pity him.

On the eleventh day we sighted Cape Portland, over which towered Mount Myrdals Yokul, which, the weather being clear, we made out very readily. The cape itself is nothing but a huge mount of granite standing naked and alone to meet the Atlantic waves. The *Valkyrie*

Vor-Frelser's-Kirk Steeple.

kept off the coast, steering to the westward. On all sides were to be seen whole "schools" of whales and sharks. After some hours we came in sight of a solitary rock in the ocean, forming a mighty vault, through which the foaming waves poured with intense fury. The islets of Westman appeared to leap from the ocean, being so low in the water as scarcely to be seen until you were right upon them. From that moment the schooner was steered to the westward in order to round Cape Reykjaness, the western point of Iceland.

My uncle, to his great disgust, was unable even to crawl on deck, so heavy a sea was on, and thus lost the first view of the Land of Promise. Forty-eight hours later, after a storm which drove us far to sea under bare poles, we came once more in sight of land, and were boarded by a pilot, who, after three hours of dangerous navigation, brought the schooner safely to an anchor in the bay of Faxa before Reykjawik.

My uncle came out of his cabin pale, haggard, thin, but full of enthusiasm, his eyes dilated with pleasure and satisfaction. Nearly the whole population of the town was on foot to see us land. The fact was, that scarcely any one of them but expected some goods by the periodical vessel.

Professor Hardwigg was in haste to leave his prison, or rather as he called it, his hospital; but before he attempted to do so, he caught hold of my hand, led me to the quarterdeck of the schooner, took my arm with his left hand, and pointed inland with his right, over the northern part of the bay, to where rose a high two-peaked mountain—a double cone covered with eternal snow.

"Behold," he whispered in an awe-stricken voice, "behold—Mount Sneffels!"

Then without further remark, he put his finger to his lips, frowned darkly, and descended into the small boat which awaited us. I followed, and in a few minutes we stood upon the soil of mysterious Iceland!

Scarcely were we fairly on shore when there appeared before us a man of excellent appearance, wearing the costume of a military officer. He was, however, but a civil servant, a magistrate, the governor of the island—Baron Trampe. The Professor knew whom he had to deal with. He therefore handed him the letters from Copenhagen, and a brief conversation in Danish followed, to which I of course was a stranger, and for a very good reason, for I did not know the language in which they conversed. I afterwards heard, however, that Baron Trampe placed himself entirely at the beck and call of Professor Hardwigg.

My uncle was most graciously received by M. Finsen, the mayor, who as far as costume went, was quite as military as the governor, but also from character and occupation quite as pacific. As for his coadjutor M. Pictursson, he was absent on an episcopal visit to the northern portion of the diocese. We were therefore compelled to defer the pleasure of being presented to him. His absence was, however, more than compensated by the presence of M. Fridriksson, Professor of natural sciences in the college of Reykjawik, a man of invaluable ability. This modest scholar spoke no languages save Icelandic and Latin. When, therefore, he addressed himself to me in the language of Horace, we at once came to understand one another. He was, in fact, the only person that I did thoroughly understand during the whole period of my residence in this benighted island.

Out of three rooms of which his house was composed, two were placed at our service, and in a few hours we were installed with all our baggage, the amount of which rather astonished the simple inhabitants of Reykjawik.

"Now, Harry," said my uncle, rubbing his hands, "all goes well, the worst difficulty is now over."

"How the worst difficulty over?" I cried in fresh amazement.

"Doubtless. Here we are in Iceland. Nothing more remains but to descend into the bowels of the earth."

"Well, sir, to a certain extent you are right. We have only to go down—but, as far as I am concerned, that is not the question. I want to know how we are to get up again."

"That is the least part of the business, and does not in any way trouble me. In the meantime, there is not an hour to lose. I am about to visit the public library. Very likely I may find there some manuscripts from the hand of Saknussemm. I shall be glad to consult them."

"In the meanwhile, I replied, I will take a walk through the town. Will you not likewise do so?"

"I feel no interest in the subject," said my uncle. "What for me is curious in this island, is not what is above the surface, but what is below."

I bowed by way of reply, put on my hat and furred cloak, and went out.

It was not an easy matter to lose oneself in the two streets of Reykjawik; I had therefore no need to ask my way. The town lies on a flat and marshy plain, between two hills. A vast field of lava skirts it on one side, falling away in

View of Reykjawik.

terraces towards the sea. On the other hand is the large bay of Faxa, bordered on the north by the enormous glacier of Sneffels, and in which bay the *Valkyrie* was then the only vessel at anchor. Generally there were one or two English or French gunboats, to watch and protect the fisheries in the offing. They were now, however, absent on duty.

The longest of the streets of Reykjawik runs parallel to the shore. In this street the merchants and traders live in wooden huts made with beams of wood, painted red,—mere log huts, such as you find in the wilds of America. The other street, situated more to the west, runs towards a little lake between the residences of the bishop and the other personages not engaged in commerce.

I had soon seen all I wanted of these weary and dismal thoroughfares. Here and there was a strip of discoloured turf, like an old worn-out bit of woollen carpet; and now and then a bit of kitchen garden, in which grew potatoes, cabbages, and lettuces, almost diminutive enough to suggest the idea of Lilliput.

In the centre of the new commercial street, I found the public cemetery, enclosed by an earthen wall. Though not very large, it appeared not likely to be filled for centuries. From hence I went to the house of the Governor —a mere hut in comparison with the Mansion House of Hamburg—but a palace alongside the other Icelandic houses. Between the little lake and the town was the church, built in simple Protestant style, and composed of calcined stones, thrown up by volcanic action. I have not the slightest doubt that in high winds, its red tiles were blown about, to the great annoyance of the pastor and congregation. Upon an eminence close at hand was the national school, in which were taught Hebrew, English, French and Danish.

In three hours my tour was complete. The general impression upon my mind was sadness. No trees, no vegetation, so to speak—on all sides volcanic peaks—the huts of turf and earth —more like roofs than houses. Thanks to the heat of these residences, grass grows on the roof, which grass is carefully cut for hay. I saw but few inhabitants during my excursion, but I met a crowd on the beach, drying, salting and loading cod-fish, the principal article of exportation. The men appeared robust but heavy; fairhaired like Germans, but of pensive mien—exiles of a higher scale in the ladder of humanity than the Esquimaux, but, I thought, much more unhappy, since with superior perceptions they are compelled to live within the limits of the Polar Circle.

Sometimes they gave vent to a convulsive laugh, but by no chance did they smile. Their costume consists of a coarse capote of black wool, known in Scandinavian countries as the "vadmel," a broad brimmed hat, trousers of red serge, and a piece of leather tied with strings for a shoe—a coarse kind of moccasin. The women, though sad-looking and mournful, had rather agreeable features, without much expression. They wear a boddice and petticoat of sombre vadmel. When unmarried they wear a little brown knitted cap over a crown of plaited hair; but when married, they cover their heads with a coloured handkerchief, over which they tie a white scarf.

High Street of Reykjawik.

A Journey to the Centre of the Earth

CHAPTER VII.

CONVERSATION AND DISCOVERY

WHEN I returned, dinner was ready. This meal was devoured by my worthy relative with avidity and voracity. His shipboard diet had turned his interior into a perfect gulf. The repast, which was more Danish than Icelandic, was in itself nothing, but the excessive hospitality of our host made us enjoy it doubly.

The conversation turned upon scientific matters, and M. Fridriksson asked my uncle what he thought of the public library.

"Library, sir?" cried my uncle; "it appears to me a collection of useless odd volumes, and a beggarly amount of empty shelves."

"What!" cried M. Fridriksson; "why, we have eight thousand volumes of most rare and valuable works—some in the Scandinavian language, besides all the new publications from Copenhagen."

"Eight thousand volumes, my dear sir—why, where are they?" cried my uncle.

"Scattered over the country, Professor Hardwigg. We are very studious, my dear sir, though we do live in Iceland. Every farmer, every labourer, every fisherman can both read and write—and we think that books instead of being locked up in cupboards, far from the sight of students, should be distributed as widely as possible. The books of our library are therefore, passed from hand to hand without returning to the library shelves perhaps for years."

"Then when foreigners visit you, there is nothing for them to see?"

"Well, sir, foreigners have their own libraries, and our first consideration is, that out humbler classes should be highly educated. Fortunately, the love of study is innate in the Icelandic people. In 1816 we founded a Literary Society and Mechanics' Institute; many foreign scholars of eminence are honorary members; we published books destined to educate our people, and these books have rendered valuable services to our country. Allow me to have the honour, Professor Hardwigg, to enrol you as an honorary member?"

My uncle, who already belonged to nearly every literary and scientific institution in Europe, immediately yielded to the amiable wishes of good M. Fridriksson.

"And now," he said, after many expressions of gratitude and good-will, "if you will tell me what books you expected to find, perhaps I may be of some assistance to you."

I watched my uncle keenly. For a minute or two he hesitated, as if unwilling to speak; to speak openly was, perhaps, to unveil his projects. Nevertheless, after some reflection, he made up his mind.

"Well, M. Fridriksson," he said, in an easy unconcerned kind of way. "I was desirous of ascertaining, if among other valuable works, you had any of the learned Arne Saknussemm."

"Arne Saknussemm!" cried the Professor of Reykjawik; "you speak of one of the most distinguished scholars of the sixteenth century, of the great naturalist, the great alchemist, the great traveller."

"Exactly so."

"One of the most distinguished men connected with Icelandic science and literature."

"As you say, sir—"

"A man illustrious above all."

"Yes, sir, all this is true, but his works?"

"We have none of them."

"Not in Iceland?"

"There are none in Iceland or elsewhere," answered the other, sadly.

"Why so?"

"Because Arne Saknussemm was persecuted for heresy, and in 1573 his works were publicly burnt at Copenhagen, by the hands of the common hangman."

"Very good! capital!" murmured my uncle, to the great astonishment of the worthy Icelander.

"You said, sir—"

"Yes, yes, all is clear, I see the link in the chain; everything is explained, and I now understand why Arne Saknussemm, put out of court, forced to hide his magnificent discoveries, was compelled to conceal beneath the veil of an incomprehensible cryptograph, the secret—"

"What secret?"

"A secret—which," stammered my uncle.

"Have you discovered some wonderful manuscript?" cried M. Fridriksson.

"No, no, I was carried away by my enthusiasm. A mere supposition."

"Very good, sir. But, really, to turn to another subject, I hope you will not leave our island without examining into its mineralogical riches."

"Well, the fact is, I am rather late. So many learned men have been here before me."

"Yes, yes, but there is still much to be done," cried M. Fridriksson.

"You think so," said my uncle, his eyes twinkling with hidden satisfaction.

"Yes, you have no idea how many unknown mountains, glaciers, volcanoes there are which remain to be studied. Without moving from where we sit, I can show you one. Yonder on the edge of the horizon, you see Sneffels."

"Oh yes, Sneffels," said my uncle.

"One of the most curious volcanoes in existence, the crater of which has been rarely visited."

"Extinct?"

"Extinct, any time these five hundred years," was the ready reply.

"Well," said my uncle, who dug his nails into his flesh, and pressed his knees tightly together to prevent himself from leaping up with joy. "I have a great mind to begin my studies with an examination of the geological mysteries of this Mount Seffel—Feisel—what do you call it?"

"Sneffels, my dear sir."

This portion of the conversation took place in Latin, and I had therefore understood all that had been said. I could scarcely keep my countenance when I found my uncle so cunningly concealing his delight and satisfaction. I must confess that his artful grimaces, put on to conceal his happiness, made him look a new Mephistopheles.

"Yes, yes," he continued, "your proposition delights me. I will endeavour to climb to the summit of Sneffels, and, if possible, will descend into its crater."

"I very much regret," continued M. Fridriksson, "that my occupation will entirely preclude the possibility of my accompanying you. It would have been both pleasurable and profitable if I could have spared the time."

"No, no, a thousand times no, cried my uncle. "I do not wish to disturb the serenity of any man. I thank you, however, with all my heart. The presence of one so learned as yourself, would no doubt have been most useful, but the duties of your office and profession before everything."

In the innocence of his simple heart, our host did not perceive the irony of these remarks.

"I entirely approve your project," continued the Icelander, after some further remarks. "It is a good idea to begin by examining this volcano. You will make a harvest of curious observations. In the first place, how do you propose to get to Sneffels?"

"By sea. I shall cross the bay. Of course that is the most rapid route."

"Of course. But still it cannot be done."

"Why?"

"We have not an available boat in all Reykjawik," replied the other.

"What is to be done?"

"You must go by land along the coast. It is longer, but much more interesting."

"Then I must have a guide."

"Of course; and I have your very man."

"Somebody on whom I can depend?"

"Yes, an inhabitant of the peninsula on which Sneffels is situated. He is a very shrewd and worthy man, with whom you will be pleased. He speaks Danish like a Dane."

"When can I see him—to-day?"

"No, to-morrow; he will not be here before."

"To-morrow be it," replied my uncle, with a deep sigh.

The conversation ended by compliments on both sides. During the dinner my uncle had learned much as to the history of Arne Saknussemm, the reasons for his mysterious and hieroglyphical document. He also became aware that his host would not accompany him on his adventurous expedition, and that next day we should have a guide.

A Journey to the Centre of the Earth

CHAPTER VIII.

THE EIDER-DOWN HUNTER—OFF AT LAST

THAT evening I took a brief walk on the shore near Reykjawik, after which I returned to an early sleep on my bed of coarse planks, where I slept the sleep of the just. When I awoke I heard my uncle speaking loudly in the next room. I rose hastily and joined him. He was talking in Danish with a man of tall stature, and of perfectly Herculean build. This man appeared to be possessed of very great strength. His eyes, which started rather prominently from a very large head, the face belonging to which was simple and naive, appeared very quick and intelligent. Very long hair, which even in England would have been accounted exceedingly red, fell over his athletic shoulders. This native of Iceland was active and supple in appearance, though he scarcely moved his arms, being in fact one of those men who despise the habit of gesticulation common to southern people.

Everything in this man's manner revealed a calm and phlegmatic temperament. There was nothing indolent about him, but his appearance spoke of tranquillity. He was one of those who never seemed to expect anything from anybody, who liked to work when he thought proper, and whose philosophy nothing could astonish or trouble.

I began to comprehend his character, simply from the way in which he listened to the wild and impassioned verbiage of my worthy uncle. While the excellent Professor spoke sentence after sentence, he stood with folded arms, utterly still, motionless to all my uncle's gesticulations. When he wanted to say No he moved his head from left to right; when he acquiesced he nodded, so slightly that you could scarcely see the undulation of his head. This economy of motion was carried to the length of avarice.

Judging from his appearance I should have been a long time before I had suspected him to be what he was, a mighty hunter. Certainly his manner was not likely to frighten the game. How, then, did he contrive to get at his prey?

My surprise was slightly modified when I knew that this tranquil and solemn personage, was only a hunter of the eider-duck, the down of which is, after all, the greatest source of the Icelanders' wealth.

In the early days of summer, the female of the eider, a pretty sort of duck, builds its nest amid the rocks of the fjords—the name given to all narrow gulfs in Scandinavian countries—with which every part of the island is indented. No sooner has the eider duck made her nest than she lines the inside of it with the softest down from her breast. Then comes the hunter or trader, taking away the nest; the poor bereaved female begins her task over gain, and this continues as long as any eider-down is to be found.

When she can find no more the male bird sets to work to see what he can do. As, however, his down is not so soft, and has therefore no commercial value, the hunter does not take the trouble to rob him of his nest-lining. The nest is accordingly finished, the eggs are laid, the little ones are born, and next year the harvest of eider-down is again collected.

Now, as the eider-duck never selects steep rocks or aspects to build its nest, but rather sloping and low cliffs near to the sea, the Icelandic hunter can carry on his trade operations without much difficulty. He is like a farmer who has neither to plough, to sow, nor to harrow, only to collect his harvest.*

This grave, sententious, silent person, as phlegmatic as an Englishman on the French stage, was named Hans Bjelke. He had called upon us in consequence of the recommendation of M. Fridriksson. He was, in fact, our future guide. It struck me that had I sought the world over, I could not have found a greater contradiction to my impulsive uncle.

They, however, readily understood one another. Neither of them had any thought about money; one was ready to take all that was offered him, the other ready to offer anything that was asked. It may readily be conceived, then, that an understanding was soon come to between them.

Now, the understanding was, that he was to take us to the village of Stapi, situated on the

---

*The birds, however, are not always so accommodating. They are found in the southern part of England as a winter visitant, but in the more northern part of our isle, and in the north of Scotland remain all the year. One of our ablest naturalists says: "Taking these nests is a regular business not unattended with risk, on account of the precipitous localities in which the eider-duck often breeds." Again, "The eider is a shy, retiring bird, placing its nest on islands and rocks projecting well into the sea."

Hans Bjelke, the guide.

southern slope of the peninsula of Sneffels, at the very foot of the volcano. Hans, the guide, told us the distance was about twenty-two miles, a journey which my uncle supposed would take about two days.

But when my uncle came to understand that they were Danish miles, of eight thousand yards each, he was obliged to be more moderate in his ideas, and, considering the horrible roads we had to follow, to allow eight or ten days for the journey.

Four horses were prepared for us, two to carry the baggage, and two to bear the important weight of myself and uncle. Hans declared that nothing ever would make him climb on the back of any animal. He knew every inch of that part of the coast, and promised to take us the very shortest way.

His engagement with my uncle was by no means to cease with out arrival at Stapi; he was further to remain in his service during the whole time required for the completion of his scientific investigations, at the fixed salary of three rix-dollars a week, being exactly fourteen shillings and twopence, minus one farthing, English currency. One stipulation, however, was made by the guide—the money was to be paid to him every Saturday night, failing which, his engagement was at an end.

The day of our departure was fixed. My uncle wished to hand the eider-down hunter an advance, but he refused in one emphatic word—

"*Efter.*"

Which being translated from Icelandic into plain English means—After.

The treaty concluded, our worthy guide retired without another word.

"A splendid fellow," said my uncle; "only he little suspects the marvellous part he is about to play in the history of the world."

"You mean, then," I cried in amazement, "that he should accompany us?"

"To the Interior of the Earth, yes;" replied my uncle. "Why not?"

There were yet forty-eight hours to elapse before we made our final start. To my great regret, our whole time was taken up in making preparations for our journey. All our industry and ability were devoted to packing every object in the most advantageous manner—the instruments on one side, the arms on the other, the tools here and the provisions there. There were, in fact, four distinct groups.

The instruments were of course of the best manufacture:—

1. A centigrade thermometer of Eizel, counting up to 150 degrees, which to me did not appear half enough—or too much. Too hot by half, if the degree of heat was to ascend so high—in which case we should certainly be cooked—not enough, if we wanted to ascertain the exact temperature of springs or metal in a state of fusion.

2. A *manometer* worked by compressed air, an instrument used to ascertain the upper atmospheric pressure on the level of the ocean. Perhaps a common barometer would not have done as well, the atmospheric pressure being likely to increase in proportion as we descended below the surface of the earth.

3. A first-class chronometer made by Boissonnas, of Geneva, set at the meridian of Hamburg, from which Germans calculate, as the English do from Greenwich, and the French from Paris.

4. Two compasses, one for horizontal guidance, the other to ascertain the dip.

5. A night glass.

6. Two Ruhmkorf's coils, which, by means of a current of electricity, would ensure us a very excellent, easy carried, and certain means of obtaining light.

7. A voltaic battery on the newest principle.*

Our arms consisted of two rifles, with two revolving six-shooters. Why these arms were provided it was impossible for me to say. I had every reason to believe that we had neither wild beasts nor savage natives to fear. My uncle, on the other hand, was quite as devoted to his arsenal as to his collection of instruments, and above all was very careful with his provision of fulminating or gun cotton, warranted to keep in any climate, and of which the expansive force was known to be greater than that of ordinary gunpowder.

Our tools consisted of two pickaxes, two crowbars, a silken ladder, three iron-shod Alpine poles, a hatchet, a hammer, a dozen wedges, some pointed pieces of iron, and a quantity of strong rope. You may conceive that the whole made a tolerable parcel, especially

---

*Thermometer (*thermos*, hot, and *metron*, measure); an instrument for measuring the temperature of the air.—Manometer (*manos*, rare, and *metron*, measure); an instrument to show the density of rarity of gases.—Chronometer (*chronos*, time, and *metron*, measure) a time measurer, or superior watch.—Ruhmkorf's coil, an instrument for producing currents of induced electricity of great intensity. It consists of a coil of copper wire, insulated by being covered with silk, surrounded by another coil of fine wire, also insulated, in which a momentary current is induced when a current is passed through the inner coil from a voltaic battery. When the apparatus is in action, the gas becomes luminous, and produces a white and continued light. The battery and wire are carried in a leather bag, which the traveller fastens by a strap to his shoulders. The lantern is in front, and enables the benighted wanderer to see in the most profound obscurity. He may venture without fear of explosion into the midst of the most inflammable gases, and the lantern will burn beneath the deepest waters. M. Ruhmkorff, an able and learned chemist, discovered the induction coil. In 1864 he obtained the great French prize of £2,000 for this ingenious application of electricity.—A voltaic battery, so called from Volta, its designer, is an apparatus consisting of a series of metal plates arranged in pairs and subjected to the action of saline solutions for producing currents of electricity.

when I mention that the ladder itself was three hundred feet long!

Then there came the important question of provisions. The hamper was not very large but tolerably satisfactory, for I knew that in concentrated essence of meat and biscuit there was enough to last six months. The only liquid provided by uncle was scheidam. Of water, not a drop. We had, however, an ample supply of gourds, and my uncle counted on finding water, and enough to fill them, as soon as we commenced our downward journey.

My remarks as to the temperature, the quality, and even as to the possibility of none being found, remained wholly without effect.

To make up the exact list of our travelling gear—for the guidance of future travellers—I will add, that we carried a medicine and surgical chest with all apparatus necessary for wounds, fractures and blows; lint, scissors, lancets—in fact, a perfect collection of horrible-looking instruments; a number of phials containing ammonia, alcohol, ether, goulard water, aromatic vinegar, in fact, every possible and impossible drug—finally, all the materials for working the Ruhmkorff coil!

My uncle had also been careful to lay in a goodly supply of tobacco, several flasks of very fine gunpowder, boxes of tinder, besides a large black belt crammed full of notes and gold. Good boots rendered water-tight were to be found to the number of six in the tool-box.

"My boy, with such clothing, with such boots, and such general equipments," said my uncle, in a state of rapturous delight; "we may hope to travel far."

It took a whole day to put all these matters in order. In the evening we dined with Baron Trampe, in company with the Mayor of Reykjawik, and Doctor Hyaltalin, the great medical man of Iceland. M. Fridriksson was not present, and I was afterwards sorry to hear that he and the governor did not agree on some matters connected with the administration of the island. Unfortunately, the consequence was, that I did not understand a word that was said at dinner—a kind of semi-official reception. One thing I can say, my uncle never left off speaking.

The next day our labour came to an end. Our worthy host delighted my uncle, Professor Hardwigg, by giving him a good map of Iceland, a most important and precious document for a mineralogist.

Our last evening was spent in a long conversation with M. Fridriksson, whom I liked very much—the more that I never expected to see him or any one else again. After this agreeable way of spending an hour or so, I tried to sleep. In vain; with the exception of a few dozes, my night was miserable.

At five o'clock in the morning I was awakened from the only real half hour's sleep of the night, by the loud neighing of horses under my window. I hastily dressed myself and went down into the street. Hans was engaged in putting the finishing stroke to our baggage, which he did in a silent, quiet way that won my admiration, and yet he did it admirably well. My uncle wasted a great deal of breath in giving him directions, but worthy Hans took not the slightest notice of his words.

At six o'clock all our preparations were completed, and M. Fridriksson shook hands heartily with us. My uncle thanked him warmly, in the Icelandic language, for his kind hospitality, speaking truly from the heart.

As for myself, I put together a few of my best Latin phrases and paid him the highest compliments I could. This fraternal and friendly duty performed, we sallied forth and mounted our horses.

As soon as we were quite ready, M. Fridriksson advanced, and by way of farewell, called after me in the words of Virgil—words which appeared to have been made for us, travellers starting for an uncertain destination:—

"*Et quacunque viam dederit fortuna sequamur.*"

("And whichsoever way thou goest, may fortune follow!")

A Journey to the Centre of the Earth

CHAPTER IX.

OUR START—WE MEET WITH ADVENTURES BY THE WAY

THE weather was overcast but settled, when we commenced our adventurous and perilous journey. We had neither to fear fatiguing heat nor drenching rain. It was, in fact, real tourist weather.

As there was nothing I liked better than horse exercise, the pleasure of riding through an unknown country, caused the early part of our enterprise to be particularly agreeable to me.

I began to enjoy the exhilarating delight of travelling, a life of desire, gratification and liberty. The truth is, that my spirits rose so rapidly, that I began to be indifferent to what had once appeared to be a terrible journey.

"After all," I said to myself, "what do I risk? Simply to take a journey through a curious country, to climb a remarkable mountain, and if the worst comes to the worst, to descend into the crater of an extinct volcano."

There could be no doubt that this was all this terrible Saknussemm had done. As to the existence of a gallery, or of subterraneous passages leading into the interior of the earth, the idea was simply absurd, the hallucination of a distempered imagination. All, then, that may be required of me I will do cheerfully, and will create no difficulty.

It was just before we left Reykjawik that I came to this decision.

Hans, our extraordinary guide, went first, walking with a steady, rapid, and unvarying step. Our two horses with the luggage followed of their own accord, without requiring whip or spur. My uncle and I came behind, cutting a very tolerable figure upon our small but vigorous animals.

Iceland is one of the largest islands in Europe. It contains thirty thousand square miles of surface, and has about seventy thousand inhabitants. Geographers have divided it into four parts, and we had to cross the South-west quarter which in the vernacular is called Sudvestr Fjordùngr.

Hans, on taking his departure from Reykjawik, had followed the line of the sea. We took our way through poor and sparse meadows, which make a desperate effort every year to show a little green. They very rarely succeed in a good show of yellow.

The rugged summits of the rocky hills were dimly visible on the edge of the horizon, through the misty fogs; every now and then some heavy flakes of snow showed conspicuous in the morning light, while certain lofty and pointed rocks were first lost in the grey low clouds, their summits clearly visible above, like jagged reefs rising from a troublous sea.

Every now and then a spur of rock came down through the arid ground, leaving us scarcely room to pass. Our horses, however, appeared not only well acquainted with the country, but by a kind of instinct, knew which was the best road. My uncle had not even the satisfaction of urging forward his steed by whip spur, or voice. It was utterly useless to show any signs of impatience. I could not help smiling to see him look so big on his little horse; his long legs now and then touching the ground made him look like a six-footed centaur.

"Good beast, good beast," he would cry. "I assure you, Henry, that I begin to think no animal is more intelligent than an Icelandic horse. Snow, tempest, impracticable roads, rocks, icebergs—nothing stops him. He is brave; he is sober; he is safe; he never makes a false step; never glides or slips from his path. I dare to say that if any river, any fjord has to be crossed—and I have no doubt there will be many—you will see him enter the water without hesitation like an amphibious animal, and reach the opposite side in safety. We must not, however, attempt to hurry him; we must allow him to have his own way, and I will undertake to say that between us we shall do our ten leagues a day."

"We may do so," was my reply, "but what about out worthy guide?"

"I have not the slightest anxiety about him: those sort of people go ahead without knowing even what they are about. Look at Hans. He moves so little that it is impossible for him to become fatigued. Besides, if he were to complain of weariness, he could have the loan of my horse. I should have a violent attack of the cramp if I were not to have some sort of exercise. My arms are right—but my legs are getting a little stiff."

All this while we were advancing at a rapid pace. The country we had reached was already

En Route!

nearly a desert. Here and there could be seen an isolated farm, some solitary boër, or Icelandic house, built of wood, earth, fragments of lava—looking like beggars on the highway of life. These wretched and miserable huts excited in us such pity that we felt half disposed to leave alms at every door. In this country there are no roads, paths are nearly unknown, and vegetation, poor as it was, slowly as it reached perfection, soon obliterated all traces of the few travellers who passed from place to place.

Nevertheless, this division of the province, situated only a few miles from the capital, is considered one of the best cultivated and most thickly peopled in all Iceland. What, then, must be the state of the less known and more distant parts of the island? After travelling fully half a Danish mile, we had met neither a farmer at the door of his hut, nor even a wandering shepherd with his wild and savage flock.

A few stray cows and sheep were only seen occasionally. What, then, must we expect when we come to the upheaved regions—to the districts broken and roughened from volcanic eruptions and subterraneous commotions?

We were to learn this all in good time. I saw, however, on consulting the map, that we avoided a good deal of this rough country, by following the winding and desolate shores of the sea. In reality, the great volcanic movement of the island, and all its attendant phenomena, is concentrated in the interior of the island; there, horizontal layers or strata of rocks, piled one upon the other, eruptions of basaltic origin, and streams of lava, have given this country a kind of supernatural reputation.

Little did I expect, however, the spectacle which awaited us when we reached the peninsula of Sneffels, where agglomerations of nature's ruins form a kind of terrible chaos.

Some two hours or more after we had left the city of Reykjawik, we reached the little town called Aoalkirkja, or the principal church. It consists simply of a few houses—not what in England or Germany we should call a hamlet.

Hans stopped here one half hour. He shared our frugal breakfast, answered yes and no to my uncle's questions as to the nature of the road, and at last when asked where we were to pass the night was as laconic as usual.

"Gardar!" was his one-worded reply.

I took occasion to consult the map, to see where Gardar was to be found. After looking keenly I found a small town of that name on the borders of the Hvalfjord, about four miles from Reykjawik. I pointed this out to my uncle, who made a very energetic grimace.

"Only four miles out of twenty-two? Why it is only a little walk."

He was about to make some energetic observation to the guide, but Hans, without taking the slightest notice of him, went in front of the horses, and walked ahead with the same imperturbable phlegm he had always exhibited.

Three hours later, still travelling over those apparently interminable and sandy prairies, we were compelled to go round the Kollafjord, an easier and shorter cut than crossing the gulfs. Shortly after we entered a place of communal jurisdiction called Ejulberg, and the clock of which would then have struck twelve, if any Icelandic church had been rich enough to possess so valuable and useful an article. These sacred edifices are, however, very much like these people, who do without watches—and never miss them.

Here the horses were allowed to take some rest and refreshment, then following a narrow strip of shore between high rocks and the sea, they took us without farther halt to the "aoalkirkja" of Brantar, and after another mile to "Saurboer Annexia," a chapel of ease, situated on the southern bank of the Hvalfjord.

It was four o'clock in the evening and we had travelled four Danish miles, about equal to twenty English.

The fjord was in this place about half-a-mile in width. The sweeping and broken waves came rolling in upon the pointed rocks; the gulf was surrounded by rocky walls—a mighty cliff, three thousand feet in height, remarkable for its brown strata, separated here and there by beds of tufa of a reddish hue. Now, whatever may have been the intelligence of our horses, I had not the slightest reliance upon them, as a means of crossing a stormy arm of the sea. To ride over salt water upon the back of a little horse seemed to me absurd.

"If they are really intelligent," I said to myself, "they will certainly not make the attempt. In any case, I shall trust rather to my own intelligence than theirs."

But my uncle was in no humour to wait. He dug his heels into the sides of his steed, and made for the shore. His horse went to the very edge of the water, sniffed at the approaching wave and retreated.

My uncle, who was, sooth to say, quite as obstinate as the beast he bestrode, insisted on his making the desired advance. This attempt was followed by a new refusal on the part of the horse which quietly shook its head. This demonstration of rebellion was followed by a volley of words and a stout application of whipcord; also followed by kicks on the part of the horse, which threw its head and heels upwards and tried to throw his rider. At length the sturdy little pony, spreading out his legs, in a stiff and ludicrous attitude, got from under the professor's legs, and left him standing, with both feet on a separate stone, like the Colossus of Rhodes.

"Wretched animal!" cried my uncle, suddenly transformed into a foot passenger— and as angry and ashamed as a dismounted cavalry officer on the field of battle.

"Farja," said the guide, tapping him familiarly on the shoulder.

"What, a ferry boat!"

"*Der*," answered Hans, pointing to where lay the boat in question—"there."

"Well," I cried, quite delighted with the information; "so it is."

"Why did you not say so before," cried my uncle; "why not start at once?"

"Tidvatten," said the guide.

"What does he say?" I asked, considerably puzzled by the delay and the dialogue.

"He says tide," replied my uncle, translating the Danish word for my information.

"Of course I understand—we must wait till the tide serves."

"*For bida*?" asked my uncle.

"*Ja*," replied Hans.

My uncle frowned, stamped his feet and then followed the horses to where the boat lay.

I thoroughly understood and appreciated the necessity for waiting, before crossing the fjord, for that moment when the sea at its highest point is in a state of slack water. As neither the ebb nor flow can then be felt, the ferry boat was in no danger of being carried out to sea, or dashed upon the rocky coast.

The favourable moment did not come until six o'clock in the evening. Then my uncle, myself, and guide, two boatmen and the four horses got into a very awkward flat-bottomed boat. Accustomed as I had been to the steam ferry-boats of the Elbe, I found the long oars of the boatmen but sorry means of locomotion. We were more than an hour in crossing the fjord; but at length the passage was concluded without accident.

Half-an-hour later we reached Gardar.

A Journey to the Centre of the Earth

CHAPTER X.

TRAVELLING IN ICELAND—THE LEPERS

IT ought, one would have thought, to have been night, even in the sixty-fifth parallel of latitude; but still the nocturnal illumination did not surprise me. For in Iceland, during the months of June and July, the sun never sets.

The temperature, however, was very much lower than I expected. I was cold, but even that did not affect me so much as ravenous hunger. Welcome indeed, therefore, was the hut which hospitably opened its doors to us.

It was merely the house of a peasant, but in the matter of hospitality, it was worthy of being the palace of a king. As we alighted at the door the master of the house came forward, held out his hand, and without any further ceremony, signalled to us to follow him.

We followed him, for to accompany him was impossible. A long, narrow, gloomy passage led into the interior of this habitation, made from beams roughly squared by the axe. This passage gave ingress to every room. The chambers were four in number—the kitchen, the workshop, where the weaving was carried on, the general sleeping chamber of the family, and the best room, to which strangers were specially invited. My uncle, whose lofty stature had not been taken into consideration when the house was built, contrived to knock his head against the beams of the roof.

We were introduced into our chamber, a kind of large room with a hard earthern floor, and lighted by a window, the panes of which were made of a sort of parchment from the intestines of sheep—very far from transparent.

The bedding was composed of dry hay thrown into two long red wooden boxes, ornamented with sentences painted in Icelandic. I really had no idea that we should be made so comfortable. There was one objection to the house, and that was, the very powerful odour of dried fish, of macerated meat, and of sour milk, which three fragrances combined, did not at all suit my olfactory nerves.

As soon as we had freed ourselves from our heavy travelling costume, the voice of our host was heard calling to us to come into the kitchen, the only room in which the Icelanders ever make any fire, no matter how cold it may be.

My uncle, nothing loth, hastened to obey this hospitable and friendly invitation. I followed.

The kitchen chimney was made on an antique model. A large stone standing in the middle of the room was the fireplace, above, in the roof, was a hole for the smoke to pass through. This apartment was kitchen, parlour and dining-room all in one.

On our entrance, our worthy host, as if he had not seen us before, advanced cere-moniously, uttered a word which means "be happy," and then kissed each of us on the cheek.

His wife followed, pronounced the same word, with the same ceremonial, then the husband and wife, placing their right hands upon their hearts, bowed profoundly.

This excellent Icelandic woman was the mother of nineteen children, who, little and big, rolled, crawled, and walked about in the midst of volumes of smoke arising from the angular fireplace in the middle of the room. Every now and then I could see a fresh white head, and a slightly melancholy expression of countenance, peering at me through the vapour.

Both my uncle and myself, however, were very friendly with the whole party, and before we were aware of it, there were three or four of these little ones on our shoulders, as many on our boxes, and the rest hanging about our legs. Those who could speak kept crying out *saellvertu* in every possible and impossible key. Those who did not speak only made all the more noise.

This concert was interrupted by the announcement of supper. At this moment our worthy guide, the eider-duck hunter, came in after seeing to the feeding and stabling of the horses—which consisted in letting them loose to browse on the stunted green of the Icelandic prairies. There was little for them to eat, but moss and some very dry and innutritious grass; next day they were ready before the door, some time before we were.

"Welcome," said Hans.

Then tranquilly, with the air of an automaton, without any more expression in one kiss than another, he embraced the host, the hostess and their nineteen children.

This ceremony concluded to the satisfaction of all parties, we all sat down to table, that is

Crossing the Fjord

twenty-four of us, somewhat crowded. Those who were best off had only two juveniles on their knees.

As soon, however, as the inevitable soup was placed on the table, the natural taciturnity, common even to Icelandic babies, prevailed over all else. Our host filled our plates with a portion of *Lichen* soup of Iceland moss, of by no means disagreeable flavour, an enormous lump of fish floating in sour butter. After that there came some "skyr," a kind of curds and whey, served with biscuits and juniper-berry juice. To drink, we had blanda, skimmed milk with water. I was hungry, so hungry, that by way of dessert I finished up with a basin of thick oaten porridge.

As soon as the meal was over, the children disappeared, whilst the grown people sat round the fireplace, on which was placed turf, heather, cow dung and dried fish-bones. As soon as everybody was sufficiently warm, a general dispersion took place, all retiring to their respective couches. Our hostess offered to pull off our stockings and trousers, according to the custom of the country, but as we graciously declined to be so honoured, she left us to our bed of dry fodder.

Next day, at five in the morning, we took our leave of these hospitable peasants. My uncle had great difficulty in making them accept a sufficient and proper remuneration.

Hans then gave the signal to start.

We had scarcely got a hundred yards from Gardar, when the character of the country changed. The soil began to be marshy and boggy, and less favourable to progress. To the right, the range of mountains was prolonged indefinitely like a great system of natural fortifications, of which we skirted the glacis. We met with numerous streams and rivulets which it was necessary to ford, and that without wetting our baggage. As we advanced, the deserted appearance increased, and yet now and then we could see human shadows flitting in the distance. When a sudden turn of the track brought us within easy reach of one of these spectres, I felt a sudden impulse of disgust at the sight of a swollen head, with shining skin, utterly without hair, and whose repulsive and revolting wounds could be seen through his rags. The unhappy wretches never came forward to beg; on the contrary, they ran away; not so quick, however, but that Hans was able to salute them with the universal Saellvertu.

"Spetelsk," said he.

"A leper," explained my uncle.

The very sound of such a word caused a feeling of repulsion. The horrible affection

known as leprosy, which has almost vanished before the effects of modern science, is common in Iceland. It is not contagious but hereditary, so that marriage is strictly prohibited to these unfortunate creatures.

These poor lepers did not tend to enliven our journey, the scene of which was inexpressibly sad and lonely. The very last tufts of grassy vegetation appeared to die at our feet. Not a tree was to be seen, except a few stunted willows about as big as blackberry bushes. Now and then we watched a falcon soaring in the grey and misty air, taking his flight towards warmer and sunnier regions. I could not help feeling a sense of melancholy come over me. I sighed for my own Native Land, and wished to be back with Gretchen.

We were compelled to cross several little fjords, and at last came to a real gulf. The tide was at its height, and we were able to go over at once, and reach the hamlet of Alftanes, about a mile farther.

That evening, after fording the Alfa and the Heta, two rivers rich in trout and pike, we were compelled to pass the night in a deserted house, worthy of being haunted by all the fays of Scandinavian mythology. The King of Cold had taken up his residence there, and made us feel his presence all night.

The following day was remarkable by its lack of any particular incidents. Always the same damp and swampy soil; the same dreary uniformity; the same sad and monotonous aspect of scenery. In the evening, having accomplished the half of our projected journey, we slept at the Annexia of Krosolbt.

For a whole mile we had under out feet nothing but lava. This disposition of the soil is called *hraun*: the crumbled lava on the surface was in some instances like ship cables stretched out horizontally, in others coiled up in heaps; an immense field of lava came from the neighbouring mountains, all extinct volcanoes, but whose remains showed what once they had been. Here and there could be made out the steam from hot water springs.

There was no time, however, for us to take more than a cursory view of these phenomena. We had to go forward with what speed we might. Soon the soft and swampy soil again appeared under the feet of our horses, while at every hundred yards we came upon one or more small lakes. Our journey was now in a westernly direction; we had, in fact, swept round the great bay of Faxa, and the twin white summits of Sneffels rose to the clouds at a distance of less than five miles.

The horses now advanced rapidly. The

The Leper

accidents and difficulties of the soil no longer checked them. I confess that fatigue began to tell severely upon me; but my uncle was as firm and as hard as he had been on the first day. I could not help admiring both the excellent Professor and the worthy guide; for they appeared to regard this rugged expedition as a mere walk!

On Saturday, the 20th June, at six o'clock in the evening, we reached Budir, a small town picturesquely situated on the shore of the ocean; and here the guide asked for his money. My uncle settled with him immediately. It was now the family of Hans himself, that is to say, his uncles, his cousins-german, who offered us hospitality. We were exceedingly well received, and without taking too much advantage of the goodness of these worthy people, I should have liked very much to have rested with them after the fatigues of the journey. But my uncle, who did not require rest, had no idea of anything of the kind; and despite the fact that next day was Sunday, I was compelled once more to mount my steed.

The soil was again affected by the neighbour-hood of the mountains, whose granite peered out of the ground like tops of an old oak. We were skirting the enormous base of the mighty volcano. My uncle never took his eyes from off it; he could not keep from gesticulating, and looking at it with a kind of sullen defiance, as much as to say, "that is the giant I have made up my mind to conquer."

After four hours of steady travelling, the horses stopped of themselves before the door of the presbytery of Stapi.

A Journey to the Centre of the Earth

CHAPTER XI.

WE REACH MOUNT SNEFFELS—THE "REYKIR"

STAPI is a town consisting of thirty huts, built on a large plain of lava, exposed to the rays of the sun, reflected from the volcano. It stretches its humble tenements along the end of a little fjord, surrounded by a basaltic wall of the most singular character.

Basalt is a brown rock of igneous origin. It assumes regular forms, which astonish by their singular appearance. Here we found Nature proceeding geometrically, and working quite after a human fashion, as if she had employed the plummet line, the compass, and the rule. If elsewhere she produces grand artistic effects by piling up huge masses without order or connection—if elsewhere we see truncated cones, imperfect pyramids, with an odd succession of lines; here, as if wishing to give a lesson in regularity, and preceding the architects of the early ages, she has erected a severe order of architecture, which neither the splendours of Babylon nor the marvels of Greece ever surpassed.

I had often heard of the Giants' Causeway in Ireland, the Grotto of Fingal in one of the Hebrides, but the grand spectacle of a real basaltic formation had never yet come before my eyes.

This at Stapi gave us an idea of one in all its wonderful beauty and grace.

The wall of the fjord, like nearly the whole of the peninsula, consisted of a series of vertical columns, in height about thirty feet. These upright pillars of stone, of the finest proportions, supported an archivault of horizontal columns which formed a kind of half-vaulted roof above the sea. At certain intervals, and below this natural basin, the eye was pleased and suprised by the sight of oval openings through which the outward waves came thundering in volleys of foam. Some banks of basalt, torn from their fastenings by the fury of the waves, lay scattered on the ground like the ruins of an ancient temple—ruins eternally young, over which the storms of ages swept without producing any perceptible effect!

This was the last stage of our journey. Hans had brought us along with fidelity and intelligence, and I began to feel somewhat more comfortable when I reflected that he was to accompany us still farther on our way.

When we halted before the house of the Rector, a small and incommodious cabin, neither handsome nor more comfortable than those of his neighbours, I saw a man in the act of shoeing a horse, a hammer in his hand, and a leathern apron tied round his waist.

"Be happy," said the eider-down hunter, using his national salutation in his own language.

"*Good-dag*—good day!" replied the former, in excellent Danish.

"Kyrkoherde," cried Hans, turning round and introducing him to my uncle.

"The Rector," repeated the worthy Professor; "it appears, my dear Harry, that this worthy man is the Rector, and is not above doing his own work."

During the speaking of these few words the guide intimated to the Kyrkoherde what was the true state of the case. The good man, ceasing from his occupation, gave a kind of halloo, upon which a tall woman, almost a giantess, came out of the hut. She was at least six feet high, which in that region is something considerable.

My first impression was one of horror. I thought she had come to give us the Icelandic kiss. I had however, nothing to fear, for she did not even show much inclination to receive us into her house.

The room devoted to strangers appeared to me to be by far the worst in the presbytery; it was narrow, dirty, and offensive. There was, however, no choice about the matter. The Rector had no notion of practising the usual cordial and antique hospitality. Far from it. Before the day was over, I found we had to deal with a blacksmith, a fisherman, a hunter, a carpenter—anything but a clergyman. It must be said in his favour that we had caught him on a week day: probably he appeared to greater advantage on the Sunday.

These poor priests receive from the Danish Government a most ridiculously inadequate salary, and collect one quarter of the tithe of their parish—not more than sixty marks current, or abour £3 10s. sterling. Hence the necessity of working to live. In truth, we soon found that our host did not count civility among the cardinal virtues.

The Fjord of Stapi

My uncle soon became aware of the kind of man he had to deal with. Instead of a worthy and learned scholar, he found a dull ill-mannered peasant. He therefore resolved to start on his great expedition as soon as possible. He did not care about fatigue, and resolved to spend a few days in the mountains.

The preparations for our departure were made the very next day after our arrival at Stapi; Hans now hired three Icelanders to take the place of the horses—which could no longer carry our luggage. When, however, these worthy islanders had reached the bottom of the crater, they were to go back and leave us to ourselves. This point was settled before they would agree to start.

On this occasion, my uncle partially confided in Hans, the eider-duck hunter, and gave him to understand that it was his intention to continue his exploration of the volcano to the last possible limits.

Hans listened calmly, and then nodded his head. To go there, or elsewhere, to bury himself in the bowels of the earth, or to travel over its summits, was all the same to him! As for me, amused and occupied by the incidents of travel, I had begun to forget the inevitable future; but now I was once more destined to realise the actual state of affairs. What was to be done? Run away? But if I really had intended to leave Professor Hardwigg to his fate, it should have been at Hamburg and not at the foot of Sneffels.

One idea, above all others, began to trouble me: a very terrible idea, and one calculated to shake the nerves of a man even less sensitive than myself.

"Let us consider the matter," I said to myself; "we are going to ascend the Sneffels mountain. Well and good. We are about to pay a visit to the very bottom of the crater. Good, still. Others have done it and did not perish from that course.

"That, however, is not the whole matter to be considered. If a road does really present itself by which to descend into the dark and subterraneous bowels of Mother Earth, if this thrice unhappy Saknussemm has really told the truth, we shall be most certainly lost in the midst of the labyrinth of subterraneous galleries of the volcano. Now, we have no evidence to prove that Sneffels is really extinct. What proof have we that an eruption is not shortly about to take place? Because the monster has slept soundly since 1229, does it follow that he is never to wake?

"If he does wake what is to become of us?" These were questions worth thinking about,

and upon them I reflected long and deeply. I could not lie down in search of sleep without dreaming of eruptions. The more I thought, the more I objected to be reduced to the state of dross and ashes.

I could stand it no longer: so I determined at last to submit the whole case to my uncle, in the most adroit manner possible, and under the form of some totally irreconcilable hypothesis.

I sought him. I laid before him my fears, and then drew back in order to let him get his passion over at his ease.

"I have been thinking about the matter," he said, in the quietest tone in the world.

What did he mean? Was he at last about to listen to the voice of reason? Did he think of suspending his projects? It was almost too much happiness to be true.

I however made no remark. In fact, I was only too anxious not to interrupt him, and allowed him to reflect at his leisure. After some moments he spoke out.

"I have been thinking about the matter," he resumed. "Ever since we have been at Stapi, my mind has been almost solely occupied with the grave question which has been submitted to me by yourself—for nothing would be unwiser and more inconsistent than to act with imprudence."

"I heartily agree with you, my dear uncle," was my somewhat hopeful rejoinder.

"It is now six hundred years since Sneffels has spoken—but though now reduced to a state of utter silence, he may speak again. New volcanic eruptions are always preceded by perfectly well-known phenomena. I have closely examined the inhabitants of this region; I have carefully studied the soil, and I beg to tell you emphatically, my dear Harry, there will be no eruption at present."

As I listened to his positive affirmations, I was stupefied and could say nothing.

"I see you doubt my word," said my uncle; "follow me."

I obeyed mechanically.

Leaving the presbytery, the Professor took a road through an opening in the basaltic rock, which led far away from the sea. We were soon in open country, if we could give such a name to a place all covered with volcanic deposits. The whole land seemed crushed under the weight of enormous stones—of trap, of basalt, of granite, of lava, and of all other volcanic substances.

I could see many spouts of steam rising in the air. These white vapours, called in the Icelandic language "reykir," come from hot water fountains, and indicate by their violence the

The "Reykir."

volcanic activity of the soil. Now the sight of these appeared to justify my apprehension. I was, therefore, all the more surprised and mortified when my uncle thus addressed me.

"You see all this smoke, Harry, my boy?"

"Yes, sir."

"Well, as long as you see them thus, you have nothing to fear from the volcano."

"How can that be?"

"Be careful to remember this," continued the Professor. "At the approach of an eruption these spouts of vapour redouble their activity— to disappear altogether during the period of volcanic eruption; for the elastic fluids, no longer having the necessary tension, seek refuge in the interior of the crater, instead of escaping through the fissures of the earth. If, then, the steam remains in its normal or habitual state, if their energy does not increase, and if you add to this, the remark, that the wind is not replaced by heavy atmospheric pressure and dead calm, you may be quite sure that there is no fear of any immediate eruption."

"But—"

"Enough, my boy. When science has sent forth her fiat—it is only to hear and obey."

I came back to the house quite downcast and disappointed. My uncle had completely defeated me with his scientific arguments. Nevertheless, I had still one hope, and that was, when once we were at the bottom of the crater, that it would be impossible in default of a gallery or tunnel, to descend any deeper; and this, despite all the learned Saknussemms in the world.

I passed the whole of the following night with a nightmare on my chest! and, after unheard of miseries and tortures, found myself in the very depths of the earth, from which I was suddenly launched into plantetary space, under the form of an eruptive rock!

Next day, the 23rd June, Hans calmly awaited us outside the presbytery with his two companions loaded with provisions, tools, and instruments. Two iron-shod poles, two guns, and two large game bags, were reserved for my uncle and myself. Hans, who was a man who never forgot even the minutest precautions, had added to our baggage a large skin full of water, as an addition to our gourds. This assured us water for eight days.

It was nine o'clock in the morning when we were quite ready. The rector and his huge wife or servant, I never knew which, stood at the door to see us off. They appeared to be about to inflict on us the usual final kiss of the Icelanders. To our supreme astonishment their adieu took the shape of a formidable bill, in which they even counted the use of the pastoral house, really and truly the most abominable and dirty place I ever was in. The worthy couple cheated and robbed us like a Swiss innkeeper, and made us feel, by the sum we had to pay, the splendours of their hospitality.

My uncle, however, paid without bargaining. A man who had made up his mind to undertake a voyage into the Interior of the Earth, is not the man to haggle over a few miserable rix-dollars.

This important matter settled, Hans gave the signal for departure, and some few moments later we had left Stapi.

A Journey to the Centre of the Earth

CHAPTER XII.

THE ASCENT OF MOUNT SNEFFELS

THE huge volcano which was the first stage of our daring experiment, is above five thousand feet high. Sneffels is the termination of a long range of rocky volcanic mountains, of a different character to the system of the island itself. One of its peculiarities is its two huge pointed summits. From whence we started it was impossible to make out the real outlines of the peak against the grey field of sky. All we could distinguish was a vast dome of white, which fell downwards from the head of the giant.

The commencement of the great undertaking filled me with awe. Now that we had actually started, I began to believe in the reality of the undertaking!

Our party formed quite a procession. We walked in single file, preceded by Hans, the imperturbable eider-duck hunter. He calmly led us by narrow paths where two persons could by no possibility walk abreast. Conversation was wholly impossible. We had all the more opportunity to reflect and admire the awful grandeur of the scene around.

Beyond the extraordinary basaltic wall of the fjord of Stapi we found ourselves making our way through fibrous turf, over which grew a scanty vegetation of grass, the residuum of the ancient vegetation of the swampy peninsula. The vast mass of this combustible, the field of which as yet is utterly unexplored, would suffice to warm Iceland for a whole century. This mighty turf pit, measured from the bottom of certain ravines, is often not less than seventy feet deep, and presents to the eye, the view of successive layers of black burned-up rocky detritus, separated by thin streaks of porous sandstone.

The grandeur of the spectacle was undoubted, as well as its arid and deserted air.

As a true nephew of the great Professor Hardwigg, and despite my pre-occupation and doleful fears of what was to come, I observed with great interest the vast collection of mineralogical curiosities spread out before me in this vast museum of natural history. Looking back to my recent studies, I went over in thought the whole geological history of Iceland.

This extraordinary and curious island must have made its appearance from out the great world of waters at a comparatively recent date. Like the coral islands of the Pacific, it may, for aught we know, be still rising by slow and imperceptible degrees.

If this really be the case, its origin can be attributed to only one cause—that of the continued action of subterranean fires.

This was a happy thought.

If so, if this were true, away with the theories of Sir Humphrey Davy; away with the authority of the parchment of Arne Saknussemm; the wonderful pretensions to discovery on the part of my uncle—and to our journey!

All must end in smoke.

Charmed with the idea, I began more carefully to look about me. A serious study of the soil was necessary to negative or confirm my hypothesis. I took in every item of what I saw, and I began to comprehend the succession of phenomena which had preceded its formation.

Iceland, being absolutely without sedimentary soil, is composed exclusively of volcanic tufa; that is to say, of an agglomeration of stones and of rocks of a porous texture. Long before the existence of volcanoes, it was composed of a solid body of massive trap-rock lifted bodily and slowly out of the sea, by the action of the centrifugal force at work in the interior of the earth.

The internal fires, however, had not as yet burst their bounds and flooded the exterior cake of Mother Earth with hot and raging lava.

My readers must excuse this brief and somewhat pedantic geological lecture. But it is necessary to the complete understanding of what follows.

At a later period in the world's history, a huge and mighty fissure must, reasoning by analogy, have been dug diagonally from the south-west to the north-east of the island, through which by degrees flowed the volcanic crust. The great and wondrous phenomenon then went on without violence—the outpouring was enormous, and the seething fused matter, ejected from the bowels of the earth, spread slowly and peacefully in the form of vast level plains, or what are called mamelons or mounds.

It was at this epoch that the rocks called

The Ascent of Sneffels.

feldspars, syenites, and porphyries appeared.

But as a natural consequence of this overflow, the depth of the island increased. It can readily be believed what an enormous quantity of elastic fluids were piled up within its centre, when at last if afforded no other openings, after the process of cooling the crust had taken place.

At length a time came when despite the enormous thickness and weight of the upper crust, the mechanical forces of the combustible gases below became so great, that they actually upheaved the weighty back and made for themselves huge and gigantic shafts. Hence the volcanoes which suddenly arose through the upper crust, and next the craters, which burst forth at the summit of these new creations.

It will be seen that the first phenomena in connexion with the formation of the island were simply eruptive; to these, however, shortly succeeded the volcanic phenomena.

Through the newly-formed openings, escaped the marvellous mass of basaltic stones with which the plain we were now crossing was covered. We were trampling our way over heavy rocks of dark grey colour, which, while cooling, had been moulded into six-sided prisms. In the "back distance" we could see a number of flattened cones, which formerly were so many fire-vomiting mouths.

After the basaltic eruption was appeased and set at rest, the volcano, the force of which increased with that of the extinct craters, gave free passage to the fiery overflow of lava, and to the mass of cinders and pumice-stone, now scattered over the sides of the mountain, like dishevelled hair on the shoulders of a Bacchante.

Here, in a nutshell, I had the whole history of the phenomena from which Iceland arose. All take their rise in the fierce action of interior fires, and to believe that the central mass did not remain in a state of liquid fire, white hot, was simply and purely madness.

This being satisfactorily proved, (*q. e. d.*) what insensate folly to pretend to penetrate into the interior of the mighty earth!

This mental lecture delivered to myself while proceeding on my journey, did me good. I was quite re-assured as to the fate of our enterprise; and therefore went, like a brave soldier mounting a bristling battery, to the assault of old Sneffels.

As we advanced, the road became every moment more difficult. The soil was broken and dangerous. The rocks broke and gave way under our feet, and we had to be scrupulously careful in order to avoid dangerous and constant falls.

Hans advanced as calmly as if he had been walking over Salisbury Plain; sometimes he would disappear behind huge blocks of stone, and we momentarily lost sight of him. There was a little period of anxiety and then there was a shrill whistle, just to tell us where to look for him.

Occasionally he would take it into his head to stop to pick up lumps of rock, and silently pile them up into small heaps, *in order that we might not lose our way on our return.*

He had no idea of the journey we were about to undertake.

At all events, the precaution was a good one; though how utterly useless and unnecessary— but I must not anticipate.

Three hours of terrible fatigue, walking incessantly, had only brought us to the foot of the great mountain. This will give some notion of what we had still to undergo.

Suddenly, however, Hans cried a halt—that is, he made signs to that effect—and a summary kind of breakfast was laid out on the lava before us. My uncle, who now was simply Professor Hardwigg, was so eager to advance, that he bolted his food like a greedy clown. This halt for refreshment was also a halt for repose. The Professor was therefore compelled to wait the good pleasure of his imperturbable guide, who did not give the signal for departure for a good hour.

The three Icelanders, who were as taciturn as their comrade, did not say a word; but went on eating and drinking very quietly and soberly.

From this, our first real stage, we began to ascend the slopes of the Sneffels volcano. Its magnificent snowy night-cap, as we began to call it, by an optical delusion very common in mountains, appeared to me to be close at hand; and yet how many long weary hours must elapse before we reached its summit. What unheard of fatigue must we endure!

The stones on the mountain side, held together by no cement of soil, bound together by no roots or creeping herbs, gave way continually under our feet, and went rushing below into the plains, like a series of small avalanches.

In certain places the sides of this stupendous mountain were at an angle so steep that it was impossible to climb upwards, and we were compelled to get round these obstacles as best we might.

Those who understand Alpine climbing will comprehend our difficulties. Often we were obliged to help each other along by means of our climbing poles.

I must say this for my uncle, that he stuck as

The Sandstorm.

close to me as possible. He never lost sight of me, and on many occasions his arm supplied me with firm and solid support. He was strong, wiry, and apparently insensible to fatigue. Another great advantage with him was that he had the innate sentiment of equilibrium—for he never slipped or failed in his steps. The Icelanders, though heavily loaded, climbed with the agility of mountaineers.

Looking up, every now and then, at the height of the great volcano of Sneffels, it appeared to me wholly impossible to reach to the summit on that side; at all events, if the angle of inclination did not speedily change.

Fortunately, after an hour of unheard of fatigues, and of gymnastic exercises that would have been trying to an acrobat, we came to a vast field of ice, which wholly surrounded the bottom of the cone of the volcano. The natives called it the table cloth, probably from some such reason as the dwellers in the Cape of Good Hope call their mountain Table Mountain, and their roads Table Bay.

Here, to our mutual surprise, we found an actual flight of stone steps, which wonderfully assisted our ascent. This singular flight of stairs was, like everything else, volcanic. It had been formed by one of those torrents of stones cast up by the eruptions, and of which the Icelandic name is stinâ. If this singular torrent had not been checked in its descent by the peculiar shape of the flanks of the mountain, it would have swept into the sea, and would have formed new islands.

Such as it was, it served us admirably. The abrupt character of the slopes momentarily increased, but these remarkable stone steps, a little less difficult than those of the Egyptian pyramids, were the one simple natural means by which we were enabled to proceed.

About seven in the evening of that day, after having clambered up two thousand of these rough steps, we found ourselves over-looking a kind of spur or projection of the mountain—a sort of buttress upon which the cone-like crater, properly so called, leaned for support.

The ocean lay beneath us at a depth of more than three thousand two hundred feet—a grand and mighty spectacle. We had reached the region of eternal snows.

The cold was keen, searching and intense. The wind blew with extraordinary violence. I was utterly exhausted.

My worthy uncle, the Professor, saw clearly that my legs refused further service, and that, in fact, I was utterly exhausted. Despite his hot and feverish impatience, he decided, with a sigh, upon a halt. He called the eider-duck hunter to his side. That worthy, however, shook his head.

"Ofvanfor," said his sole spoken reply.

"It appears," says my uncle with a woebegone look, "that we must go higher."

He then turned to Hans, and asked him to give some reason for this decisive response.

"Mistour," replied the guide.

"*Ja mistour*—yes, the mistour," cried one of the Icelandic guides in a terrified tone.

It was the first time he had spoken.

"What does this mysterious word signify?" I anxiously enquired.

"Look," said my uncle.

I looked down upon the plain below, and I saw a vast, a prodigious volume of pulverised pumice-stone, of sand, of dust, rising to the heavens in the form of a mighty waterspout. It resembled the fearful phenomenon of a similar character known to travellers in the desert of the great Sahara.

The wind was driving it directly towards that side of Sneffels on which we were perched. This opaque veil standing up between us and the sun projected a deep shadow on the flanks of the mountain. If this sand-spout broke over us, we must all be infallibly destroyed, crushed in its fearful embraces. This extraordinary phenomenon, very common when the wind shakes the glaciers, and sweeps over the arid plains, is in the Icelandic tongue called *mistour*.

"Hastigt, Hastigt!" cried our guide.

Now I certainly knew nothing of Danish, but I thoroughly understood that his gestures were meant to quicken us.

The guide turned rapidly in a direction which would take us to the back of the crater, all the while ascending slightly.

We followed rapidly, despite our excessive fatigue.

A quarter of an hour later Hans paused to enable us to look back. The mighty whirlwind of sand was spreading up the slope of the mountain to the very spot where we had proposed to halt. Huge stones were caught up, cast into the air, and thrown about as during an eruption. We were happily a little out of the direction of the wind, and therefore out of reach of danger. But for the precaution and knowledge of our guide, our dislocated bodies, our crushed and broken limbs, would have been cast to the wind, like dust from some unknown meteor.

Hans, however, did not think it prudent to pass the night on the bare side of the cone. We therefore continued our journey in a zigzag direction. The fifteen hundred feet which remained to be accomplished took us at least five hours. The turnings and windings, the no-thoroughfares, the marches and marches, turned that insignificant distance into at least three leagues. I never felt such misery, fatigue and exhaustion in my life. I was ready to faint from hunger and cold. The rarified air at the same time painfully acted upon my lungs.

At last, when I thought myself at my last gasp, about eleven at night, it being in that region quite dark, we reached the summit of Mount Sneffels! It was in an awful mood of mind, that despite my fatigue, before I descended into the crater which was to shelter us for the night, I paused to behold the sun rise at midnight on the very day of its lowest declension, and enjoyed the spectacle of its ghastly pale rays cast upon the isle which lay sleeping at our feet!

I no longer wondered at people travelling all the way from England to Norway, to behold this magical and wondrous spectacle.

A Journey to the Centre of the Earth

CHAPTER XIII.

THE SHADOW OF SCARTARIS

OUR supper was eaten with ease and rapidity, after which everybody did the best he could for himself within the hollow of the crater. The bed was hard, the shelter unsatisfactory, the situation painful—lying in the open air, five thousand feet above the level of the sea!

Nevertheless, it has seldom happened to me to sleep so well as I did on that particular night. I did not even dream. So much for the effects of what my uncle called "wholesome fatigue."

Next day, when we awoke under the rays of a bright and glorious sun, we were nearly frozen by the keen air. I left my granite couch and made one of the party to enjoy a view of the magnificent spectacle which developed itself, panoramalike, at our feet.

I stood upon the lofty summit of Mount Sneffels' southern peak. Thence I was able to obtain a view of the greater part of the island. The optical delusion, common to all lofty heights, raised the shores of the island, while the central portions appeared depressed. It was by no means too great a flight of fancy to believe that a giant picture was stretched out before me. I could see the deep valleys that crossed each other in every direction. I could see precipices looking like sides of wells, lakes that seemed to be changed into ponds, ponds that looked like puddles, and rivers that were transformed into petty brooks. To my right were glaciers upon glaciers, and multiplied peaks, topped with light clouds of smoke.

The undulation of these infinite numbers of mountains, whose snowy summits made them look as if covered by foam, recalled to my remembrance the surface of a storm-beaten ocean. If I looked towards the west, the ocean lay before me in all its majestic grandeur, a continuation as it were, of these fleecy hill tops.

Where the earth ended and the sea began it was impossible for the eye to distinguish.

I soon felt that strange and mysterious sensation which is awakened in the mind when looking down from lofty hill tops, and now I was able to do so without any feeling of nervousness, having fortunately hardened myself to that kind of sublime contemplation.

I wholly forgot who I was, and where I was. I became intoxicated with a sense of lofty sublimity, without thought of the abysses into which my daring was soon about to plunge me. I was presently, however, brought back to the realities of life, by the arrival of the Professor and Hans, who joined me upon the lofty summit of the peak.

My uncle, turning in a westerly direction, pointed out to me a light cloud of vapour, a kind of haze, with a faint outline of land rising out of the waters.

"Greenland!" said he.

"Greenland?" cried I, in reply.

"Yes," continued my uncle, who always when explaining anything spoke as if he were in a Professor's chair; "we are not more than thirty-five leagues distant from that wonderful land. When the great annual break up of the ice takes place, white bears come over to Iceland, carried by the floating masses of ice from the north. This, however, is a matter of little consequence. We are now on the summit of the great, the transcendent Sneffels, and here are its two peaks, north and south. Hans will tell you the name by which the people of Iceland call that on which we stand."

My uncle turned to the imperturbable guide, who nodded, and spoke as usual—one word.

"*Scartaris.*"

My uncle looked at me with a proud and triumphant glance.

"A crater," he said, "you hear?"

I did hear, but I was totally unable to make reply.

The crater of Mount Sneffels represented an inverted cone, the gaping orifice apparently half a mile across; the depth indefinite feet. Conceive what this *hole* must have been like when full of flame and thunder and lightning. The bottom of the funnel-shaped hollow was about five hundred feet in circumference, by which it will be seen that the slope from the summit to the bottom was very gradual, and we were therefore clearly able to get there without much fatigue or difficulty. Involuntarily, I compared this crater to an enormous loaded cannon; and the comparison completely terrified me.

"To descend into the interior of a cannon," I thought to myself, "when perhaps it is loaded, and will go off at the least shock, is the act of a madman."

Arne Saknussemm.

But there was no longer any opportunity for me to hesitate. Hans, with a perfectly calm and indifferent air, took his usual post at the head of the adventurous little band. I followed without uttering a syllable.

I felt like the lamb led to the slaughter.

In order to render the descent less difficult, Hans took his way down the interior of the cone in rather a zigzag fashion, making, as the sailors say, long tacks to the eastward, followed by equally long ones to the west. It was necessary to walk through the midst of eruptive rocks, some of which, shaken in their balance, went rolling down with thundering clamour to the bottom of the abyss. These continual falls awoke echoes of singular power and effect.

Many portions of the cone consisted of interior glaciers. Hans, whenever he met with one of these obstacles advanced with a great show of precaution, sounding the soil with his long iron pole in order to discover fissures and layers of deep soft snow. In many doubtful or dangerous places, it became necessary for us to be tied together by a long rope in order that should any one of us be unfortunate enough to slip, he would be supported by his companions. This connecting link was doubtless a prudent precaution, but not by any means unattended with danger.

Nevertheless, and despite all the manifold difficulties of the descent, along slopes with which our guide was wholly unacquainted, we made considerable progress without accident. One of our great parcels of rope slipped from one of the Iceland porters, and rushed by a short cut to the bottom of the abyss.

By mid-day we were at the end of our journey. I looked upwards, and saw only the upper orifice of the cone, which served as a circular frame to a very small portion of the sky—a portion which seemed to me singularly beautiful. Should I ever again gaze on that lovely sunlit sky!

The only exception to this extraordinary landscape, was the Peak of Scartaris, which seemed lost in the great void of the heavens.

The bottom of the crater was composed of three separate shafts, through which, during periods of eruption, when Sneffels was in action, the great central furnace sent forth its burning lava and poisonous vapours. Each of these chimneys or shafts gaped open-mouthed in our path. I kept as far away from them as possible, not even venturing to take the faintest peep downwards.

As for the Professor, after a rapid examination of their disposition and characteristics, he became breathless and panting. He ran from one to the other like a delighted schoolboy, gesticulating wildly, and uttering incomprehensible and disjointed phrases in all sorts of languages.

Hans, the guide, and his humbler companions seated themselves on some piles of lava and looked silently on. They clearly took my uncle for a lunatic; and—waited the result.

Suddenly the Professor uttered a wild, unearthly cry. At first I imagined he had lost his footing, and was falling headlong into one of the yawning gulfs. Nothing of the kind. I saw him, his arms spread out to their widest extent, his legs stretched apart, standing upright before an enormous pedestal, high enough and black enough to bear a gigantic statue of Pluto. His attitude and mien were that of a man utterly stupefied. But his stupefaction was speedily changed to the wildest joy.

"Harry! Harry! come here!" he cried; "make haste—wonderful—wonderful!"

Unable to understand what he meant, I turned to obey his commands. Neither Hans, nor the other Icelanders moved a step.

"Look!" said the Professor, in something of the manner of the French general, pointing out the pyramids to his army.

And fully partaking his stupefaction, if not his joy, I read on the eastern side of the huge block of stone, the same characters, half eaten away by the corrosive action of time, the name, to me a thousand times accursed—

"Arne Saknussemm!" cried my uncle, "now, unbeliever, do you begin to have faith?"

It was totally impossible for me to answer a single word. I went back to my pile of lava, in a state of silent awe. The evidence was unanswerable, overwhelming!

In a few moments, however, my thoughts were far away, back in my German home, with Gretchen and the old cook. What would I have given for one of my cousin's smiles, for one of the ancient domestic's omelettes, and for my own feather bed!

How long I remained in this state I know not. All I can say is that when at last I raised my head from between my hands, there remained at the bottom of the crater only myself, my uncle and Hans. The Icelandic porters had been dismissed and were now descending the exterior slopes of Mount Sneffels, on their way to Stapi. Now heartily did I wish myself with them!

Hans slept tranquilly at the foot of a rock in a kind of rill of lava, where he had made himself a rough and ready bed. My uncle was walking about the bottom of the crater like a wild beast in a cage. I had no desire, neither had I the strength, to move from my recumbent position. Taking example by the guide, I gave way to a kind of painful somnolency, during which I seemed both to hear and feel continued heavings and shudderings in the mountain.

In this way we passed our first night in the interior of a crater.

Next morning, a grey, cloudy, heavy sky hung like a funeral-pall over the summit of the volcanic cone. I did not notice it so much from the obscurity that reigned around us, as from the rage with which my uncle was devoured.

I fully understood the reason, and again a glimpse of hope made my heart leap with joy. I will briefly explain the cause.

Of the three openings which yawned beneath our steps, only one could have been followed by the adventurous Saknussemm. According to the words of the learned Icelander, it was only to be known by that one particular mentioned in the cryptograph, that the shadow of Scartaris fell upon it, just touching its mouth in the last days of the month of June.

We were, in fact, to consider the pointed peak as the *stylus* of an immense sun-dial, the shadow of which pointed on one given day, like the inexorable finger of fate, to the yawning chasm which led into the interior of the earth.

Now, as often happens in these regions, should the sun fail to burst through the clouds, no shadow. Consequently, no chance of discovering the right aperture. We had already reached the 25th June. If the kindly heavens would only remain densely clouded for six more days, we should have to put off our voyage of discovery for another year, when certainly there would be one person fewer in the party. I already had sufficient of the mad and monstrous enterprise.

It would be utterly impossible to depict the impotent rage of Professor Hardwigg. The day passed away, and not the faintest outline of a shadow could be seen at the bottom of the crater. Hans the guide never moved from his place. He must have been curious to know what we were about, if indeed he could believe we were about anything. As for my uncle, he never addressed a word to me. He was nursing his wrath to keep it warm! His eyes fixed on the black and foggy atmosphere, his complexion hideous with suppressed passion. Never had his eyes appeared so fierce, his nose so aquiline, his mouth so hard and firm.

On the 26th no change for the better. A mixture of rain and snow fell during the whole day. Hans very quietly built himself a hut of lava into which he retired like Diogenes into his tub. I took a malicious delight in watching the thousand little cascades that flowed down the side of the cone, carrying with them at times a stream of stones into the "vasty deep" below.

My uncle was almost frantic: to be sure it was enough to make even a patient man angry. He had reached to a certain extent the goal of his desires, and yet he was likely to be wrecked in port.

But if the heavens and the elements are capable of causing us much pain and sorrow, there are two sides to a medal. And there was reserved for Professor Hardwigg a brilliant and sudden surprise which was to compensate him for all his sufferings.

Next day the sky was still overcast, but on Sunday, the 26th the last day but one of the months, with a sudden change of wind and a new moon there came a change of weather. The sun poured its beaming rays to the very bottom of the crater.

Each hillock, every rock, every stone, every asperity of the soil had its share of the luminous effulgence, and its shadow fell heavily on the soil. Among others, to his insane delight, the shadow of Scartaris was marked and clear, and moved slowly with the radiant star of day.

My uncle moved with it in a state of mental ecstacy.

At twelve o'clock exactly, when the sun had attained its highest altitude for the day, the shadow fell upon the edge of the central pit!

"Here it is," gasped the Professor in an agony of joy, "here it is—we have found it. Forward, my friends, into the Interior of the Earth."

I looked curiously at Hans to see what reply he would make to this terrific announcement.

"Forüt," said the guide tranquilly.

"Forward it is," answered my uncle, who was now in the seventh heaven of delight.

When we were quite ready, our watches indicated thirteen minutes past one!

A Journey to the Centre of the Earth

CHAPTER XIV.

THE REAL JOURNEY COMMENCES

OUR real journey had now commenced.

Hitherto our courage and determination had overcome all difficulties. We were fatigued at times; and that was all. Now, unknown and fearful dangers we were about to encounter.

I had not as yet ventured to take a glimpse down the horrible abyss into which in a few minutes more I was about to plunge. The fatal moment had, however, at last arrived. I had still the option of refusing or accepting a share in this foolish and audacious enterprise. But I was ashamed to show more fear than the eider-duck hunter. Hans seemed to accept the difficulties of the journey so tranquilly, with such calm indifference, with such perfect reck-lessness of all danger, that I actually blushed to appear less of a man than he!

Had I been alone with my uncle, I should certainly have sat down and argued the point fully; but in the presence of the guide I held my tongue. I gave one moment to the thought of my charming cousin, and then I advanced to the mouth of the central shaft.

It measured about a hundred feet in diameter, which made about three hundred in circumference. I leaned over a rock which stood on its edge, and looked down. My hair stood on end, my teeth chattered, my limbs trembled, I seemed utterly to lose my centre of gravity, while my head was in a sort of whirl, like that of a drunken man. There is nothing more power-ful than this attraction towards an abyss. I was about to fall headlong into the gaping well, when I was drawn back by a firm and powerful hand. It was that of Hans. I had not taken lessons enough at the Frelser's-kirk of Copenhagen in the art of looking down from lofty eminances without blinking!

However, few as the minutes were during which I gazed down this tremendous and even wondrous shaft, I had a sufficient glimpse of it to give me some idea of its physical con-formation. Its sides, which were almost as perpendicular as those of a well, presented numerous projections which doubtless would assist our descent.

It was a sort of wild and savage staircase, without bannister or fence. A rope fastened above, near the surface, would certainly support our weight and enable us to reach the bottom, but how, when we had arrived at its utmost depths, were we to loosen it above? This was, I thought, a question of some importance.

My uncle, however, was one of those men who are nearly always prepared with expedients. He hit upon a very simple method of obviating this difficulty. He unrolled a cord about as thick as my thumb, and at least four hundred feet in length. He allowed about half of it to go down the pit and catch in a hitch over a great block of lava which stood on the edge of the precipice. This done, he threw the second half after the first.

Each of us could now descend by catching the two cords in one hand. When about two hundred feet below, all the explorer had to do was to let go one end and pull away at the other, when the cord would come falling at his feet. In order to go down farther, all that was necessary was to continue the same operation.

This was a very excellent proposition, and no doubt a correct one. Going down appeared to me easy enough, it was the coming up again that now occupied my thoughts.

"Now," said my uncle, as soon as he had completed this important preparation, "let us see about the baggage. It must be divided into three separate parcels, and each of us must carry one on his back. I allude to the more important and fragile articles."

My worthy and ingenious uncle did not appear to consider that we came under that denomination.

"Hans," he continued, "you will take charge of the tools and some of the provisions; you, Harry, must take possession of another third of the provisions and of the arms. I will load myself with the rest of the eatables, and with the more delicate instruments."

"But," I exclaimed, "our clothes, this mass of cord and ladders—who will undertake to carry them down?"

"They will go down of themselves."

"And how so?" I asked.

"You shall see."

My uncle was not fond of half measures, nor did he like anything in the way of hesitation. Giving his orders to Hans he had the whole of the non-fragile articles made up into one bundle; and the packet, firmly and solidly

The Descent of the Crater.

fastened, was simply pitched over the edge of the gulph.

I heard the moaning of the suddenly displaced air, and the noise of falling stones. My uncle leaning over the abyss followed the descent of his luggage with a perfectly self-satisfied air, and did not rise until it had completely disappeared from sight.

"Now then," he cried, "it is our turn."

I put it in good faith to any man of common sense—was it possible to hear this energetic cry without a shudder?

The Professor fastened his case of instruments on his back Hans took charge of the tools, I of the arms. The descent then commenced in the following order. Hans went first, my uncle followed, and I went last. Our progress was made in profound silence—a silence only troubled by the fall of pieces of rock, which breaking from the jagged sides, fell with a roar into the depths below.

I allowed myself to slide, so to speak, holding frantically on to the double cord with one hand and with the other keeping myself off the rocks by the assistance of my iron-shod pole. One idea was all the time impressed upon my brain. I feared that the upper support would fail me. The cord appeared to me far too fragile to bear the weight of three such persons as we were, with out luggage. I made as little use of it as possible, trusting to my own agility and doing miracles in the way of feats of dexterity and strength upon the projecting shelves and spurs of lava which my feet seemed to clutch as strongly as my hands.

The guide went first I have said, and when one of the slippery and frail supports broke from under his feet he had recourse to his usual monosyllabic way of speaking.

"Gifakit—"

"Attention—look out," repeated my uncle.

In about half an hour we reached a kind of small terrace formed by a fragment of rock projecting some distance from the sides of the shaft.

Hans now began to haul upon the cord on one side only, the other going as quietly upward as the other came down. It fell at last, bringing with it a shower of small stones, lava and dust, a disagreeable kind of rain or hail.

While we were seated on this extraordinary bench I ventured once more to look downwards. With a sigh I discovered that the bottom was still wholly invisible. Were we, then, going direct to the interior of the earth?

The performance with the cord recommenced, and a quarter of an hour later, we had reached to the depth of another two hundred feet.

I have very strong doubts if the most determined geologist would, during that descent have studied the nature of the different layers of earth around him. I did not trouble my head much about the matter; whether we were among the combustible carbon, silurians, or primitive soil, I neither knew nor cared to know.

Not so the inveterate Professor. He must have taken notes all the way down, for, at one of our halts, he began a brief lecture.

"The farther we advance," said he, "the greater is my confidence in the result. The disposition of these volcana strata absolutely confirms the theories of Sir Humphrey Davy. We are still within the region of the primordial soil, the soil in which took place the chemical operation of metals becoming inflamed by coming in contact with air and water. I at once regret the old and now for ever exploded theory of a central fire. At all events, we shall soon know the truth."

Such was the everlasting conclusion to which he came. I, however, was very far from being in a humour to discuss the matter. I had something else to think of. My silence was taken for consent; and still we continued to go down.

At the expiration of three hours, we were, to all appearance, as far off as ever from the bottom of the well. When I looked upwards, however, I could see that the upper orifice was every minute decreasing in size. The sides of the shaft were getting closer and closer together, we were approaching the regions of eternal night!

And still we continued to descend!

At length, I noticed that when pieces of stone were detached from the sides of this stupendous precipice, they were swallowed up with less noise than before. The final sound was sooner heard. We were approaching the bottom of the abyss!

As I had been very careful to keep account of all the changes of cord which took place, I was able to tell exactly what was the depth we had reached, as well as the time it had taken.

We had shifted the rope twenty-eight times, each operation taking a quarter of an hour, which in all made seven hours. To this had to be added twenty-eight pauses; in all ten hours and a-half. We started at one, it was now, therefore, about eleven o'clock at night.

It does not require great knowledge of arithmetic to know that twenty-eight times two hundred feet makes five thousand six hundred feet in all (more than an English mile.)

While I was making this mental calculation a

voice broke the dreary silence. It was the voice of Hans.

"Halt!" he cried.

I checked myself very suddenly, just at the moment when I was about to kick my uncle on the head.

"We have reached the end of our journey," said the worthy Professor in a satisfied tone.

"What, the interior of the earth?" said I, slipping down to his side.

"No, you stupid fellow! but we have reached the bottom of the well."

"And I suppose there is no farther progress to be made?" I hopefully exclaimed.

"Oh, yes, I can dimly see a sort of tunnel, which turns off obliquely to the right. At all events, we must see about that to-morrow. Let us sup now, and seek slumber as best we may."

I thought it time, but made no observations on that point. I was fairly launched on a desperate course, and all I had to do was to go forward hopefully and trustingly.

It was not even now quite dark, the light filtering down in a most extraordinary manner.

We opened the provision bag, ate a frugal supper, and each did his best to find a bed amid the pile of stones, dirt, and lava which had accumulated for ages at the bottom of the shaft.

I happened to grope out the pile of ropes, ladders, and clothes which we had thrown down; and upon them I stretched myself. After such a day's labour, my rough bed seemed as soft as down!

For awhile I lay in a sort of pleasant trance.

Presently, after lying quietly for some minutes, I opened my eyes and looked upwards. As I did so I made out a brilliant little dot, at the extremity of this long, gigantic telescope.

It was a star without scintillating rays. According to my calculation, must be   in the constellation of the Little Bear.

After this little bit of astronomical recreation, I dropped into a sound sleep.

A Journey to the Centre of the Earth

CHAPTER XV.

WE CONTINUE OUR DESCENT

AT eight o'clock the next morning, a faint kind of dawn of day awoke us. The thousand and one prisms of the lava, collected the light as it passed and brought it to us like a shower of sparks.

We were able with ease to see objects around us.

"Well, Harry, my boy," cried the delighted Professor, rubbing his hands together, "what say you now? Did you ever pass a more tranquil night in our house in the König Strasse? No deafening sounds of cart-wheels, no cries of hawkers, no bad language from boatmen or watermen!"

"Well, uncle, we are very quiet at the bottom of this well—but to me there is something terrible in this calm."

"Why," said the Professor, hotly, "one would say you were already beginning to be afraid. How will you get on presently? Do you know, that as yet, we have not penetrated one inch into the bowels of the earth."

"What can you mean, sir?" was my bewildered and astonished reply.

"I mean to say that we have only just reached the soil of the island itself. This long vertical tube, which ends at the bottom of the crater of Sneffels, ceases here just about on a level with the sea."

"Are you sure, sir?"

"Quite sure. Consult the barometer."

It was quite true that the mercury, after rising gradually in the instrument, as long as our descent was taking place, had stopped precisely at twenty-nine degrees.

"You perceive," said the Professor, "we have as yet only to endure the pressure of air. I am curious to replace the barometer by the manometer.

The barometer, in fact, was about to become useless—as soon as the weight of the air was greater than what was calculated as above the level of the ocean.

"But," said I, "is it not very much to be feared that this ever-increasing pressure may not in the end turn out very painful and inconvenient?"

"No," said he. "We shall descend very slowly, and our lungs will be gradually accustomed to breathe compressed air. It is well

known that aëronauts have gone so high as to be nearly without air at all—why, then, should we not accustom ourselves to breathe when we have, say, a little too much of it? For myself, I am certain I shall prefer it. Let us not lose a moment. Where is the packet which preceded us in our descent?"

I smilingly pointed it out to my uncle. Hans had not seen it, and believed it caught somewhere above us: "huppe" as he phrased it.

"Now," said my uncle, "let us breakfast, and break fast like people who have a long day's work before them."

Biscuit and dried meat, washed down by some mouthfuls of water flavoured with schiedam, was the material of our luxurious meal.

As soon as it was finished, my uncle took from his pocket a note-book destined to be filled by memoranda of our travels. He had already placed his instruments in order, and this is what he wrote:—

Monday, July 1st.

Chronometer, 8h. 17m. morning.

Barometer, 29 degrees.

Thermometer, 43° Fahr.

Direction, E.S.E.

This last observation referred to the obscure gallery, and was indicated to us by the compass.

"Now Harry," cried the Professor, in an enthusiastic tone of voice, "we are truly about to take our first step into the Interior of the Earth; never before visited by man since the first creation of the world. You may consider, therefore, that at this precise moment our travels really commence."

As my uncle made this remark, he took in one hand the Ruhmkorff coil apparatus, which hung round his neck, and with the other he put the electric current into communication with the worm of the lantern. And a bright light at once illumined that dark and gloomy tunnel!

The effect was magical!

Hans, who carried the second apparatus, had it also put into operation. This ingenious application of electricity to practical purposes enabled us to move along by the light of an artificial day, amid even the flow of the most inflammable and combustible gases.

"Forward!" cried my uncle. Each took up

The Lava Gallery.

his burden. Hans went first, my uncle followed, and I going third, we entered the sombre gallery!

Just as we were about to engulph ourselves in this dismal passage, I lifted up my head, and through the tube-like shaft saw that Iceland sky I was never to see again!

Was it the last I should ever see of any sky?

The stream of lava flowing from the bowels of the earth in 1229, had forced itself a passage through the tunnel. It lined the whole of the inside with its thick and brilliant coating. The electric light added very greatly to the brilliancy of the effect.

The great difficulty of our journey now began. How were we to prevent ourselves from slipping down the steeply-inclined plane? Happily some cracks, abrasures of the soil, and other irregularities, served the place of steps; and we descended slowly; allowing our heavy luggage to slip on before, at the end of a long cord.

But that which served as steps under our feet, became in other places stalactites. The lava, very porous in certain places, took the form of little round blisters. Crystals of opaque quartz, adorned with limpid drops of natural glass suspended to the roof like lustres, seemed to take fire as we passed beneath them. One would have fancied that the genii of romance were illuminating their underground palaces to receive the sons of men.

"Magnificent, glorious!" I cried in a moment of involuntary enthusiasm, "what a spectacle, uncle! Do you not admire these variegated shades of lava, which run through a whole series of colours, from reddish brown to pale yellow—by the most insensible degrees. And these crystals, they appear like luminous globes."

"You are beginning to see the charms of travel, Master Harry," cried my uncle. "Wait a bit, until we advance farther. What we have as yet discovered is nothing—onwards, my boy, onwards!"

It would have been a far more correct and appropriate expression, had he said, "let us slide," for we were going down an inclined plane with perfect ease. The compass indicated that we were moving in a south-easterly direction. The flow of lava had never turned to the right or the left. It had the inflexibility of a straight line.

Nevertheless, to my great surprise, we found no perceptible increase in heat. This proved the theories of Humphrey Davy to be founded on truth, and more than once I found myself examining the thermometer in silent astonish-ment.

Two hours after my departure it only marked 54 degrees Fahrenheit. I had every reason to believe from this that our descent was far more horizontal than vertical. As for discovering the exact depth to which we had attained, nothing could be easier. The Professor, as he advanced measured the angles of deviation and inclination; but he kept the result of his observations to himself.

About eight o'clock in the evening, my uncle gave the signal for halting. Hans seated himself on the ground. The lamps were hung to fissures in the lava rock. We were now in a large cavern where air was not wanting. On the contrary, it abounded. What could be the cause of this—to what atmospheric agitation could be ascribed this draught? But this was a question which I did not care to discuss just then. Fatigue and hunger made me incapable of reasoning. An unceasing march of seven hours had not been kept up without great exhaustion. I was really and truly worn our; and delighted enough I was to hear the word Halt.

Hans laid out some provisions on a lump of lava, and we each supped with keen relish. One thing, however, caused us great uneasiness— our water reserve was already half exhausted. My uncle had full confidence in finding subterranean sources, but hitherto we had completely failed in so doing. I could not help calling my uncle's attention to the circumstance.

"And you are surprised at this total absence of springs?" he said.

"Doubtless—I am very uneasy on the point We have certainly not enough water to last us five days."

"Be quite easy on that matter," continued my uncle. "I answer for it we shall find plenty of water—in fact, far more than we shall want."

"But when?"

"When we once get through this crust of lava. How can you expect springs to force their way through these solid stone walls?"

"But what is there to prove that this concrete mass of lava does not extend to the centre of the earth? I don't think we have as yet done much in a vertical way."

"What puts that into your head, my boy?" asked my uncle, mildly.

"Well, it appears to me that if we had descended very far below the level of the sea— we should find it rather hotter than we have."

"According to your system," said my uncle; "but what does the thermometer say?"

"Scarcely 15 degrees by Reaumur, which is only an increase of 9 since our departure."

"Well, and what conclusion does that bring you to?" enquired the Professor.

"The deduction I draw from this is very simple. According to the most exact observations, the augmentation of the temperature of the interior of the earth is 1 degree for every hundred feet. But certain local causes may considerably modify this figure. Thus at Yakoust in Siberia, it has been remarked that the heat increases a degree every thirty-six feet. The difference evidently depends on the conductibility of certain rocks. In the neighbourhood of an extinct volcano, it has been remarked that the elevation of temperature was only 1 degree on every five-and-twenty feet. Let us, then, go upon this calculation—which is the most favourable—and calculate."

"Calculate away, my boy."

"Nothing easier," said I, pulling out my note-book and pencil. "Nine times one hundred and twenty-five feet, make a depth of eleven hundred and twenty-five feet."

"Archimedes could not have spoken more geometrically."

"Well?"

"Well, according to my observations, we are at least ten thousand feet below the level of the sea."

"Can it be possible?"

"Either my calculation is correct, or there is no truth in figures."

The calculations of the Professor were perfectly correct. We were already six thousand feet deeper down in the bowels of the earth than any one had even been before. The lowest known depth to which man had hitherto penetrated was in the mines of Kitz-Bahl, on the Tyrol, and those of Wuttemburg in Bohemia.

The temperature, which should have been eighty-one, was in this place only fifteen. This was a matter for serious consideration.

A Journey to the Centre of the Earth

CHAPTER XVI.

THE EASTERN TUNNEL

THE next day was Tuesday, the 2nd of July—and at six o'clock in the morning we resumed our journey.

We still continued to follow the gallery of lava, a perfect natural pathway, as easy of descent as some of those inclined planes which, in very old German houses, serve the purpose of staircases. This went on until seventeen minutes past twelve, the precise instant at which we rejoined Hans, who having been somewhat in advance, had suddenly stopped.

"At last," cried my uncle, "we have reached the end of the shaft."

I looked wonderingly about me. We were in the centre of four cross paths—sombre and narrow tunnels. The question now arose as to which it was wise to take; and this of itself was no small difficulty.

My uncle, who did not wish to appear to have any hesitation about the matter before myself or the guide, at once made up his mind. He pointed quietly to the eastern tunnel; and, without delay, we entered within its gloomy recesses.

Besides, had he entertained any feeling of hesitation it might have been prolonged indefinitely, for there was no indication by which to determine on a choice. It was absolutely necessary to trust to chance and good fortune!

The descent of this obscure and narrow gallery was very gradual and winding. Sometimes we gazed through a succession of arches, its course very like the aisles of a Gothic cathedral. The great artistic sculptors and builders of the middle ages might have here completed their studies with advantage. Many most beautiful and suggestive ideas of architectural beauty would have been discovered by them. After passing through this phase of the cavernous way, we suddenly came, about a mile farther on, upon a square system of arch, adopted by the early Romans, projecting from the solid rock, and keeping up the weight of the roof.

Suddenly we would come upon a series of low subterranean tunnels which looked like beaver holes, or the work of foxes. Through whose narrow and winding ways we had literally to crawl!

The heat still remained at quite a supportable degree. With an involuntary shudder, I reflected on what the heat must have been when the volcano of Sneffels was pouring its smoke, flames, and streams of boiling lava—all of which must have come up by the road we were now following. I could imagine the torrents of hot seething stone darting on, bubbling up with accompaniments of smoke, steam, and sulphurous stench!

"Only to think of the consequences," I mused, "if the old volcano were once more to set to work."

I did not communicate these rather unpleasant reflections to my uncle. He not only would not have understood them, but would have been intensely disgusted. His only idea was to go ahead. He walked, he slid, he clambered over piles of fragments, he rolled down heaps of broken lava, with an earnestness and conviction it was impossible not to admire.

At six o'clock in the evening, after a very wearisome journey, but one not so fatiguing as before, we had made six miles towards the southward, but had not gone more than a mile downwards.

My uncle, as usual gave the signal to halt. We ate our meal in thoughtful silence, and then retired to sleep.

Our arrangements for the night were very primitive and simple. A travelling rug, in which each rolled himself, was all our bedding. We had no necessity to fear cold or any unpleasant visit. Travellers who bury themselves in the wilds and depths of the African desert, who seek profit and pleasure in the forests of the New World, are compelled to take it in turn to watch during the hours of sleep; but in this region of the earth absolute solitude and complete security, reigned supreme.

We had nothing to fear either from savages or from wild beasts.

After a night's sweet repose, we awoke fresh and ready for action. There being nothing to detain us, we started on our journey. We continued to burrow through the lava tunnel as before. It was impossible to make out through what soil we were making way. The tunnel, moreover, instead of going down into the

The Cross Roads.

bowels of the earth, became absolutely horizontal.

I even thought, after some examination, that we were actually tending upwards. About ten o'clock in the day this state of things became so clear, that finding the change very fatiguing I was obliged to slacken my pace and finally to come to a halt.

"Well," said the Professor, impatiently, "what is the matter?"

"The fact is, I am dreadfully tired," was my earnest reply.

"What," cried my uncle, "tired after a three hours' walk, and by so easy a road?"

"Easy enough, I daresay, but very fatiguing."

"But how can that be, when all we have to do is to go downwards."

"I beg your pardon, sir. For some time I have noticed that we are going upwards."

"Upwards," cried my uncle, shrugging his shoulders, "how can that be?"

"There can be no doubt about it. For the last half hour the slopes have been upward—and if we go on in this way much longer we shall find ourselves back in Iceland."

My uncle shook his head with the air of a man who does not want to be convinced. I tried to continue the conversation. He would not answer me, but once more gave the signal for departure. His silence I thought was only caused by concentrated ill-temper.

However this might be, I once more took up my load, and boldly and resolutely followed Hans, who was now in advance of my uncle. I did not like to be beaten or even distanced. I was naturally anxious not to lose sight of my companions. The very idea of being left behind, lost in that terrible labyrinth, made me shiver as with the ague.

Besides, if the ascending path was more arduous and painful to clamber, I had one source of secret consolation and delight. It was to all appearances taking us back to the surface of the earth. That of itself was hopeful. Every step I took confirmed me in my belief, and I began already to build castles in the air in relation to my marriage with my pretty little cousin.

About twelve o'clock there was a great and sudden change in the aspect of the rocky sides of the gallery. I first noticed it from the diminution of the rays of light which cast back the reflection of the lamp. From being coated with shining and resplendent lava, it became living rock. The sides were sloping walls, which sometimes became quite vertical.

We were now in what the geological professors call a state of transition, in the period of Silurian stones, so called because this specimen of early formation is very common in England in the counties formerly inhabited by the Celtic nation known as Silures.

"I can see, clearly now," I cried; "the sediment from the waters which once covered the whole earth, formed during the second period of its existence, these schists and these calcareous rocks. We are turning our backs on the granitic rocks, and are like people from Hamburg who would go to Lübeck by way of Hanover.

I might just as well have kept by observations to myself. My geological enthusiasm got the better, however, of my cooler judgment, and Professor Hardwigg heard my observations.

"What is the matter now?" he said, in a tone of great gravity.

"Well," cried I, "do you not see these different layers of calcareous rocks and the first indication of slate strata?"

"Well; what then?"

"We have arrived at that period of the world's existence when the first plants and the first animals made their appearance."

"You think so?"

"Yes, look; examine and judge for youself."

I induced the Professor with some difficulty to cast the light of his lamp on the sides of the long winding gallery. I expected some exclamation to burst from his lips. I was very much mistaken. The worthy Professor never spoke a word.

It was impossible to say whether he understood me or not. Perhaps it was possible that in his pride—my uncle and a learned professor—he did not like to own that he was wrong in having chosen the eastern tunnel, or was he determined at any price to go to the end of it. It was quite evident we had left the region of lava, and that the road by which we were going could not take us back to the great crater of Mount Sneffels.

As we went along I could not help ruminating on the whole question, and asked myself if I did not lay too great a stress on these sudden and peculiar modification of the earth's crust.

After all, I was very likely to be mistaken—and it was within the range of probability and possibility, that we were not making our way through the strata of rocks which I believed I recognised piled on the lower layer of granitic formation.

"At all events, if I am right," I thought to myself, "I must certainly find some remains of primitive plants, and it will be absolutely necessary to give way to such indubitable evidence. Let us have a good search."

I accordingly lost no opportunity of searching, and had not gone more than about a hundred yards, when the evidence I sought for cropped up in the most incontestable manner before my eyes. It was quite natural that I should expect to find these signs, for during the Silurian period the seas contained no fewer than fifteen hundred different animal and vegetable species. My feet, so long accustomed to the hard and arid lava soil, suddenly found themselves treading on a kind of soft dust, the remains of plants and shells.

Upon the walls themselves I could clearly make out the outline, as plain as a sun picture, of the fucus and the lycopodes. The worthy and excellent professor Hardwigg could not of course make any mistake about the matter; but I believe he deliberately closed his eyes, and continued on his way with a firm and unalterable step.

I began to think that he was carrying his obstinacy a great deal too far. I could no longer act with prudence or composure. I stooped on a sudden and picked up an almost perfect shell, which had undoubtedly belonged to some animal very much resembling some of the present day. Having secured the prize, I followed in the wake of my uncle.

"Do you see this?" I said.

"Well," said the Professor, with the most imperturbable tranquillity, "it is the shell of a crustaceous animal of the extinct order of the trilobites; nothing more I assure you."

"But," cried I, much troubled at his coolness, "do you draw no conclusion from it?"

"Well, if I may ask, what conclusion do you draw from it yourself?"

"Well, I thought—"

"I know, my boy, what you would say, and you are right, perfectly and incontestably right. We have finally abandoned the crust of lava and the road by which the lava ascended. It is quite possible that I may have been mistaken, but I shall be unable to discover my error until I get quite to the end of this gallery."

"You are quite right as far as that is concerned," I replied, "and I should highly approve of your decision, if we had not to fear the greatest of all dangers."

"And what is that?"

"Want of water."

"Well, my dear Henry, it can't be helped. We must put ourselves on rations."

And on he went.

A Journey to the Centre of the Earth

CHAPTER XVII.

DEEPER AND DEEPER—THE COAL MINE

IN truth, we were compelled to put ourselves upon rations. Our supply would certainly last not more than three days. I found this out about supper-time. The worst part of the matter was, that in what is called the transition rocks, it was hardly to be expected we should meet with water!

I had read of the horrors of thirst, and I knew that where we were, a brief trial of its sufferings would put an end to our adventures—and our lives! But it was utterly useless to discuss the matter with my uncle. He would have answered by some axiom from Plato.

During the whole of next day we proceeded on our journey through this interminable gallery, arch after arch, tunnel after tunnel. We journeyed without exchanging a word. We had become as mute and reticent as Hans our guide.

The road had no longer an upward tendency; at all events, if it had, it was not to be made out very clearly. Sometimes there could be no doubt that we were going downwards. But this inclination was scarcely to be distinguished, and was by no means reassuring to the Professor, because the character of the strata was in no wise modified, and the transition character of the rocks became more and more marked.

It was a glorious sight to see how the electric light brought out the sparkles in the walls of the calcareous rocks, and the old red sandstone. One might have fancied oneself in one of those deep cuttings in Devonshire, which have given their name to this kind of soil. Some magnificent specimens of marble projected from the sides of the gallery; some of an agate grey with white veins of variegated character, others of a yellow spotted colour, with red veins; farther off might be seen samples of colour in which cherry-tinted seams were to be found in all their brightest shades.

The greater number of these marbles were stamped with the marks of primitive animals. Since the previous evening, nature and creation had made considerable progress. Instead of the rudimentary trilobites, I perceived the remains of a more perfect order. Among others, the fish in which the eye of a geologist has been able to discover the first form of the reptile. The Devonian seas were inhabited by a vast number of animals of this species, which were deposited in tens of thousands in the rocks of new formation.

It was quite evident to me that we were ascending the scale of animal life of which man forms the summit. My excellent uncle, the Professor, appeared not to take notice of these warnings. He was determined at any risk to proceed.

He must have been in expectation of one of two things; either that a vertical well was about to open under his feet, and thus allow him to continue his descent, or that some insurmountable obstacle would compel us to stop and go back by the road we had so long travelled. But evening came again, and, to my horror, neither hope was doomed to be realised!

On Friday, after a night when I began to feel the gnawing agony of thirst, and when in consequence appetite decreased, our little band rose and once more followed the turnings and windings, the ascents and descents, of this interminable gallery. All were silent and gloomy. I could see that even my uncle had ventured too far.

After about ten hours of further progress,— a progress dull and monotonous to the last degree—I remarked that the reverberation, and reflection of our lamps upon the sides of the tunnel had singularly diminished. The marble, the schist, the calcareous rocks, the red sandstone, had disappeared, leaving in their places a dark and gloomy wall, sombre and without brightness. When we reached a remarkably narrow part of the tunnel, I leaned my left hand against the rock.

When I took my hand away, and happened to glance at it, it was quite black. We had reached the coal strata of the Central Earth.

"A coal mine!" I cried.

"A coal mine without miners," responded my uncle, a little severely.

"How can we tell?"

"I can tell," replied my uncle, in a sharp and doctorial tone. "I am perfectly certain that this gallery through successive layers of coal, was not cut by the hand of man. But whether it is the work of nature or not is of little concern to us. The hour for our evening meal has come—let us sup."

Hans, the guide, occupied himself in preparing food. I had come to that point when I could no longer eat. All I cared about were the few drops of water which fell to my share. What I suffered it is useless to record. The guide's gourd, not quite half full, was all that was left for us three!

Having finished their repast, my two companions laid themselves down upon their rugs, and found in sleep a remedy for their fatigue and sufferings. As for me, I could not sleep, I lay counting the hours until morning.

The next morning, Saturday, at six o'clock, we started again. Twenty minutes later we suddenly came upon a vast excavation. From its mighty extent I saw at once that the hand of man could have had nothing to do with this coal mine; the vault above would have fallen in; as it was, it was only held together by some miracle of nature.

This mighty natural cavern was about a hundred feet wide, by about a hundred and fifty high. The earth had evidently been cast apart by some violent subterranean commotion. The mass, giving way to some prodigious upheaving of nature, had split in two, leaving the vast gap into which we inhabitants of the earth had penetrated for the first time.

The whole singular history of the coal period was written on those dark and gloomy walls. A geologist would have been able easily to follow the different phases of its formation. The seams of coal were separated by strata of sandstone, a compact clay, which appeared to be crushed down by the weight from above.

At that period of the world which preceded the secondary epoch, the earth was covered by a coating of enormous and rich vegetation, due to the double action of tropical heat and perpetual humidity. A vast atmospheric cloud of vapour surrounded the earth on all sides, preventing the rays of the sun from ever reaching it.

Hence the conclusion that these intense heats did not arise from this new source of caloric.

Perhaps even the star of day was not quite ready for its brilliant work—to illumine a universe. Climates did not as yet exist, and a level heat pervaded the whole surface of the globe—the same heat existing at the north pole as at the equator.

Whence did it come? From the interior of the earth?

In spite of all the learned theories of Professor Hardwigg, a fierce and vehement fire certainly burned within the entrails of the great spheroid. Its action was felt even to the very topmost crust of the earth; the plants then in existence being deprived of the vivifying rays of the sun, had neither buds, nor flowers, nor odour, but their roots drew a strong and vigorous life from the burning earth of early days.

There were but few of what may be called trees—only herbaceous plants, immense turfs, briers, mosses, rare families, which however in those days were counted by tens and tens of thousands.

It is entirely to this exuberant vegetation that coal owes its origin. The crust of the vast globe still yielded under the influence of the seething, boiling mass, which was for ever at work beneath. Hence arose numerous fissures, and continual falling in of the upper earth. The dense mass of plants being beneath the waters, soon formed themselves into vast agglomerations.

Then came about the action of natural chemistry; in the depths of the ocean the vegetable mass at first became turf, then, thanks to the influence of gases and subterranean fermentation, they underwent the complete process of mineralisation.

In this manner, in early days, were formed those vast and prodigious layers of coal, which an ever increasing consumption must utterly use up in about three centuries more, if people do not find some more economic light than gas, and some cheaper motive power than steam.

All these reflections, the memories of my school studies, came to my mind while I gazed upon these mighty accumulations of coal, whose riches however are scarcely likely to be ever utilised. The working of these mines could only be carried out at an expense that would never yield a profit.

The matter, however, is scarcely worthy consideration, when coal is scattered over the whole surface of the globe, within a few yards of the upper crust. As I looked at these untouched strata, therefore, I knew they would remain as long as the world lasts.

While we still continued our journey, I alone forgot the length of the road, by giving myself up wholly to these geological considerations. The temperature continued to be very much the same as while we were travelling amid the lava and the schists. On the other hand my sense of smell was much affected by a very powerful odour. I immediately knew that the gallery was filled to overflowing with that dangerous gas the miners call fire-damp, the explosion of which has caused such fearful and terrible accidents, making a hundred widows, and hundreds of orphans in a single hour.

Happily, we were able to illumine our

The Coal Mine

progress by means of the Ruhmkorff apparatus. If we had been so rash and imprudent as to explore this gallery, torch in hand, a terrible explosion would have put an end to our travels, simply because no travellers would be left.

Our excursion through this wondrous coal mine in the very bowels of the earth lasted until evening. My uncle was scarcely able to conceal his impatience and dissatisfaction at the road continuing still to advance in a horizontal direction.

The darkness, dense and opaque, a few yards in advance and in the rear, rendered it impossible to make out what was the length of the gallery. For myself, I began to believe that it was simply interminable, and would go on in the same manner for months.

Suddenly, at six o'clock, we stood in front of a wall. To the right, to the left, above, below, nowhere was there any passage. We had reached a spot where the rocks said in unmistakeable accents—No Thoroughfare.

I stood stupefied. The guide simply folded his arms. My uncle was silent.

"Well, well, so much the better," cried my uncle, at last, "I now know what we are about. We are decidedly not upon the road followed by Saknussemm. All we have to do is to go back. Let us take one night's good rest, and before three days are over, I promise you we shall have regained the point where the galleries divided.

"Yes, we may, if our strength lasts as long," I cried, in a lamentable voice.

"And why not?"

"To-morrow, among us three, there will not be a drop of water. It is just gone."

"And your courage with it," said my uncle, speaking in a severe tone.

What could I say? I turned round on my side, and from sheer exhaustion fell into a heavy but troubled sleep. Dreams of water! And I awoke unrefreshed.

I would have bartered a diamond mine for a glass of pure spring water!

A Journey to the Centre of the Earth

CHAPTER XVIII.

THE WRONG ROAD!

NEXT day, our departure took place at a very early hour. There was no time for the least delay. According to my account, we had five days' hard work to get back to the place where the galleries divided.

I can never tell all the sufferings we endured upon our return. My uncle bore them like a man who has been in the wrong—that is, with concentrated and suppressed anger; Hans, with all the resignation of his pacific character; and I—I confess that I did nothing but complain, and despair. I had no heart for this bad fortune.

But there was one consolation. Defeat at the outset would probably upset the whole journey!

As I had expected from the first, our supply of water gave completely out on our first day's march. Our provision of liquids was reduced to our supply of schiedam; but this horrible—nay, I will say it—this infernal liquor burnt the throat, and I could not even bear the sight of it. I found the temperature to be stifling. I was paralysed with fatigue. More than once I was about to fall insensible to the ground. The whole party then halted, and the worthy Icelander and my excellent uncle did their best to console and comfort me. I could, however, plainly see that my uncle was contending painfully against the extreme fatigues of our journey, and the awful torture generated by the absence of water.

At length a time came when I ceased to recollect anything—when all was one awful, hideous, fantastic dream!

At last, on Tuesday, the eighth of the month of July, after crawling on our hands and knees for many hours, more dead than alive, we reached the point of junction between the galleries. I lay like a log, an inert mass of human flesh on the arid lava soil. It was then ten in the morning.

Hans and my uncle, leaning against the wall, tried to nibble away at some pieces of biscuit, while deep groans and sighs escaped from my scorched and swollen lips. Then I fell off into a kind of deep lethargy.

Presently I felt my uncle approach, and lift me up tenderly in his arms.

"Poor boy," I heard him say in a tone of deep commiseration.

I was profoundly touched by these words, being by no means accustomed to signs of womanly weakness in the Professor. I caught his trembling hands in mine and gave them a gentle pressure. He allowed me to do so without resistance, looking at me kindly all the time. His eyes were wet with tears.

I then saw him take the gourd which he wore at his side. To my surprise, or rather to my stupefaction, he placed it to my lips.

"Drink, my boy," he said.

Was it possible my ears had not deceived me? Was my uncle mad? I looked at him, with, I am sure, quite an idiotic expression. I would not understand him. I too much feared the counteraction of disappointment.

"Drink," he said again.

Had I heard aright? Before, however, I could ask myself the question a second time, a mouthful of water cooled my parched lips and throat —one mouthful, but I do believe it brought me back to life.

I thanked my uncle by clasping my hands. My heart was too full to speak.

"Yes," said he, "one mouthful of water, the very last—do you hear, my boy—the very last! I have taken care of it at the bottom of my bottle as the apple of my eye. Twenty times, a hundred times, I have resisted the fearful desire to drink it. But—no—no, Harry, I saved it for you."

"My dear uncle," I exclaimed, and the big tears rolled down my hot and feverish cheeks.

"Yes, my poor boy, I knew that when you reached this place, this cross road in the earth, you would fall down half dead, and I saved my last drop of water in order to restore you."

"Thanks," I cried; "thanks from my heart."

As little as my thirst was really quenched, I had nevertheless partially recovered my strength. The contracted muscles of my throat relaxed—and the inflammation of my lips in some measure subsided. At all events, I was able to speak.

"Well," I said, "there can be no doubt now as to what we have to do. Water has utterly failed us; our journey is therefore at an end. Let us return."

While I spoke thus, my uncle evidently avoided my face: he held down his head; his eyes were turned in every possible direction but the right one.

"Yes," I continued, getting excited by my own words, "we must go back to Sneffels. May heaven give us strength to enable us once more to revisit the light of day. Would that we now stood on the summit of the crater."

"Go back," said my uncle speaking to himself—"and must it be so?"

"Go back—yes, and without losing a single moment," I vehemently cried.

For some moments there was silence under that dark and gloomy vault.

"So, my dear Harry," said the Professor in a very singular tone of voice, "those few drops of water have not sufficed to restore your energy and courage."

"Courage!" I cried.

"I see that you are quite as downcast as before—and still give way to discouragement and despair."

What, then, was the man made of, and what other projects were entering his fertile and audacious brain!

"You are not discouraged, sir?"

"What! give up just as we are on the verge of success," he cried, "never, never shall it be said that Professor Hardwigg retreated."

"Then we must make up our minds to perish," I cried with a helpless sigh.

"No, Harry, my boy, certainly not. Go, leave me, I am very far from desiring your death. Take Hans with you. *I will go on alone.*"

"You ask us to leave you?"

"Leave me, I say. I have undertaken this dangerous and perilous adventure. I will carry it to the end—or I will never return to the surface of Mother Earth. Go,—Harry—once more I say to you—go!"

My uncle as he spoke was terribly excited. His voice, which before had been tender, almost womanly, became harsh and menacing. He appeared to be struggling with desperate energy against the impossible. I did not wish to abandon him at the bottom of that abyss, while, on the other hand, the instinct of preservation told me to fly.

Meanwhile, our guide was looking on with profound calmness and indifference. He appeared to be an unconcerned party, and yet he perfectly well knew what was going on between us. Our gestures sufficiently indicated the different roads each wished to follow—and which each tried to influence the other to undertake. But Hans appeared not to take the slightest interest in what was really a question of life and death for us all, but waited quite ready to obey the signal which should say go

aloft, or to resume his desperate journey into the interior of the earth.

How then I wished with all my heart and soul that I could make him understand my words. My representations, my sighs and groans, the earnest accents in which I should have spoken would have convinced that cold hard nature. Those fearful dangers and perils of which the stolid guide had no idea, I would have pointed them out to him—I would have, as it were, made him see and feel. Between us, we might have convinced the obstinate Professor. If the worst had come to the worst, we could have compelled him to return to the summit of Sneffels.

I quietly approached Hans. I caught his hand in mine. He never moved a muscle. I indicated to him the road to the top of the crater. He remained motionless. My panting form, my haggard countenance, must have indicated the extent of my sufferings. The Icelander gently shook his head and pointed to my uncle.

"*Master,*" he said.

The word is Icelandic as well as English.

"The master!" I cried, beside myself with fury—"madman! no—I tell you he is not the master of our lives; we must fly! we must drag him with us! do you hear me? Do you understand me, I say?"

I have already explained that I held Hans by the arm. I tried to make him rise from his seat. I struggled with him and tried to force him away. My uncle now interposed.

"My good Henry, be calm," he said. "You will obtain nothing from my devoted follower; therefore, listen to what I have to say."

I folded my arms, as well as I could, and looked my uncle full in the face.

"This wretched want of water," he said, "is the sole obstacle to the success of my project. In the entire gallery, composed of lava, schist, and coal, it is true we found not one liquid molecule. It is quite possible that we may be more fortunate in the western tunnel."

My sole reply was to shake my head with an air of incredulity.

"Listen to me to the end," said the Professor in his well-known lecturing voice. "While you lay yonder without life or motion, I undertook a reconnoitering journey into the conformation of this other gallery. I have discovered that it goes directly downwards into the bowels of the earth, and in a few hours will take us to the old granitic formation. In this we shall undoubtedly find innumerable springs. The nature of the rock makes this a mathematical certainty, and instinct agrees with logic to say that it is so. Now, this is the serious proposition

The last drop of water.

which I have to make to you. When Christopher Columbus asked of his men three days to discover the land of promise, his men ill, terrified, and hopeless, yet gave him three days—and the New World was discovered. Now I, the Christopher Columbus of this subterranean region, only ask of you one more day. If, when that time is expired, I have not found the water of which we are in search, I swear to you, I will give up my mighty enterprise and return to the earth's surface."

Despite my irritation and despair, I knew how much it cost my uncle to make this proposition, and to hold such conciliatory language. Under the circumstances, what could I do, but yield?

"Well," I cried, "let it be as you wish, and may heaven reward your super-human energy. But as, unless we discover water, our hours are numbered, let us lose no time, but go ahead."

A Journey to the Centre of the Earth

CHAPTER XIX.

THE WESTERN GALLERY—A NEW ROUTE

OUR descent was now resumed by means of the second gallery. Hans took up his post in front as usual. We had not gone more than a hundred yards when the Professor carefully examined the walls.

"This is the primitive formation—we are on the right road—onwards is our hope!"

When the whole earth got cool in the first hours of the world's morning, the diminution of the volume of the earth produced a state of dislocation in its upper crust, followed by ruptures, crevasses and fissures. The passage was a fissure of this kind, through which, ages ago, had flowed the eruptive granite. The thousand windings and turnings formed an inextricable labyrinth through the ancient soil.

As we descended, successions of layers composing the primitive soil appeared with the utmost fidelity of detail. Geological science considers this primitive soil as the base of the mineral crust, and it has recognised that it is composed of three different strata or layers, all resting on the immoveable rock known as granite.

No mineralogists had ever found themselves placed in such a marvellous position to study nature in all her real and naked beauty. The sounding rod, a mere machine, could not bring to the surface of the earth the objects of value for the study of its internal structure, which we were about to see with our own eyes, to touch with out own hands.

Remember that I am writing this *after* the journey.

Across the streak of the rocks, coloured by beautiful green tints, wound metallic threads of copper, of manganese, with traces of platinum and gold. I could not help gazing at these riches buried in the entrails of mother earth, and of which no man would have the enjoyment to the end of time! These treasures—mighty and inexhaustible, were buried in the morning of the earth's history, at such awful depths, that no crowbar or pickaxe will ever drag them from their tomb!

The light of our Ruhmkorff's coil, increased tenfold by the myriad of prismatic masses of rock, sent their jets of fire in every direction, and I could fancy myself travelling through a huge hollow diamond, the rays of which produced myriads of extraordinary effects.

Towards six o'clock, this festival of light began sensibly and visibly to decrease, and soon almost ceased. The sides of the gallery assumed a crystallized tint, with a sombre hue; white mica began to commingle more freely with feldspar and quartz, to form what may be called the true rock—the stone which is hard above all, that supports, without being crushed, the four stories of the earth's soil.

We were walled by an immense and wondrous prison of granite!

It was now eight o'clock, and still there was no sign of water. The sufferings I endured were horrible. My uncle now kept at the head of our little column. Nothing could induce him to stop. I, meanwhile, had but one real thought. My ear was keenly on the watch to catch the sound of a spring. But no pleasant sound of falling water fell upon my listening ear.

But at last the time came when my limbs refused to longer carry me. I contended heroically against the terrible tortures I endured, because I did not wish to compel my uncle to halt. To him I knew this would be the last fatal stroke.

Suddenly I felt a deadly faintness come over me. My eyes could no longer see; my knees shook. I gave one despairing cry—and fell!

"Help, help, I am dying!"

My uncle turned and slowly retraced his steps. He looked at me with folded arms, and then allowed one sentence to escape, in hollow accents, from his lips—

"All is over."

The last thing I saw was a face fearfully distorted with pain and sorrow; and then my eyes closed.

When I again opened them, I saw my companions lying near me, motionless, wrapped in their huge travelling rugs. Were they asleep or dead? For myself, sleep was wholly out of the question. My fainting fit over, I was wakeful as the lark. I suffered too much for sleep to visit my eyelids—the more, that I thought myself sick unto death—dying. The last words spoken by my uncle seemed to be buzzing in my ears— *all is over!* And it was probable that he was right. In the state of prostration to which I was

A Diamond Mine.

reduced, it was madness to think of ever again seeing the light of day.

Above were miles upon miles of the earth's crust. As I thought of it, I could fancy the whole weight resting on my shoulders. I was crushed, annihilated! and exhausted myself in vain attempts to turn in my granite bed.

Hours upon hours passed away. A profound and terrible silence reigned around us—a silence of the tomb. Nothing could make itself heard through these gigantic walls of granite. The very thought was stupendous.

Presently, despite my apathy, despite the kind of deadly calm into which I was cast, something aroused me. It was a slight but peculiar noise. While I was watching intently, I observed that the tunnel was becoming dark. Then gazing through the dim light that remained, I thought I saw the Icelander taking his departure, lamp in hand.

Why had he acted thus? Did Hans the guide mean to abandon us? My uncle lay fast asleep—or dead. I tried to cry out, and arouse him. My voice, feebly issuing from my parched and fevered lips, found no echo in that fearful place. My throat was dry, my tongue stuck to the roof of my mouth. The obscurity had by this time become intense, and at last even the faint sound of the guide's footsteps was lost in the blank distance. My soul seemed filled with anguish, and death appeared welcome, only let it come quickly.

"Hans is leaving us," I cried. "Hans—Hans, if you are a man, come back."

These words were spoken to myself. They could not be heard aloud. Nevertheless, after the first few moments of terror were over, I was ashamed of my suspicions against a man, who hitherto had behaved so admirably. Nothing in his conduct or character justified suspicion. Moreover, a moment's reflection re-assured me. His departure could not be a flight. Instead of ascending the gallery, he was going deeper down into the gulf. Had he had any bad design, his way would have been upwards.

This reasoning calmed me a little and I began to hope!

The good, and peaceful, and imperturbable Hans would certainly not have arisen from his sleep without some serious and grave motive. Was he bent on a voyage of discovery? During the deep, still silence of the night had he at last heard that sweet murmur about which we were all so anxious?

A Journey to the Centre of the Earth

CHAPTER XX.

WATER, WHERE IS IT? A BITTER DISAPPOINTMENT

DURING a long, long, weary hour, there crossed my wildly delirious brain all sorts of reasons as to what could have aroused our quiet and faithful guide. The most absurd and ridiculous ideas passed through my head, each more impossible than the other. I believe I was either half or wholly mad.

Suddenly, however, there arose, as it were from the depths of the earth, a voice of comfort. It was the sound of footsteps! Hans was returning.

Presently the uncertain light began to shine upon the walls of the passage, and then it came in view far down the sloping tunnel. At length Hans himself appeared.

He approached my uncle, placed his hand upon his shoulder, and gently awakened him. My uncle, as soon as he saw who it was, instantly rose.

"Well!" exclaimed the Professor.

"*Vatten*," said the hunter.

I did not know a single word of the Danish language, and yet by a sort of mysterious instinct I understood what the guide had said.

"Water, water!" I cried, in a wild and frantic tone, clapping my hands, and gesticulating like a madman.

"Water!" murmured my uncle, in a voice of deep emotion and gratitude, "Hvar?" (where.)

"Nedat" (below.)

"Where? below!" I understood every word. I had caught the hunter by the hands, and I shook them heartily, while he looked on with perfect calmness.

The preparations for our departure did not take long, and we were soon making a rapid descent into the tunnel.

An hour later we had advanced a thousand yards, and descended two thousand feet.

At this moment I heard an accustomed and well-known sound running along the floors of the granite rock—a kind of dull and sullen roar, like that of a distant waterfall.

During the first half-hour of our advance, not finding the discovered spring, my feelings of intense suffering appeared to return. Once more I began to lose all hope. My uncle, however, observing how downhearted I was again becoming, took up the conversation.

"Hans was right," he exclaimed, enthusiasti-

cally; "that is the dull roaring of a torrent."

"A torrent," I cried, delighted at even hearing the welcome words.

"There's not the slightest doubt about it," he replied, "a subterranean river is flowing beside us."

I made no reply, but hastened on, once more animated by hope. I began not even to feel the deep fatigue which hitherto had overpowered me. The very sound of this glorious murmuring water already refreshed me. We could hear it increasing in volume every moment. The torrent, which for a long time could be heard flowing over our heads, now ran distinctly along the left wall, roaring, rushing, spluttering, and still falling.

Several times I passed my hand across the rock hoping to find some trace of humidity—of the slightest percolation. Alas! in vain.

Again a half hour elapsed in the same weary toil. Again we advanced.

It now became evident that the hunter, during his absence, had not been able to carry his researches any farther. Guided by an instinct peculiar to the dwellers in mountain regions and water finders, he "smelt" the living spring through the rock. Still he had not seen the precious liquid. He had neither quenched his own thirst, nor brought us one drop in his gourd.

Moreover, we soon made the disastrous discovery, that if our progress continued, we should soon be moving away from the torrent, the sound of which gradually diminished. We turned back. Hans halted at the precise spot where the sound of the torrent appeared nearest.

I could bear the suspense and suffering no longer, and seated myself against the wall, behind which I could hear the water seething and effervescing not two feet away. But a solid wall of granite still separated us from it!

Hans looked keenly at me, and, strange enough, for once I thought I saw a smile on his imperturbable face.

He rose from a stone on which he had been seated, and took up the lamp. I could not help rising and following. He moved slowly along the firm and solid granite wall. I watched him with mingled curiosity and eagerness. Presently

The Boiling Jet.

he halted and placed his ear against the dry stone, moving slowly along and listening with the most extreme care and attention. I understood at once that he was searching for the exact spot where the torrent's roar was most plainly heard. This point he soon found in the lateral wall on the left side, about three feet above the level of the tunnel floor.

I was in a state of intense excitement. I scarcely dared believe what the eider-duck hunter was about to do. It was, however, impossible in a moment more not to both understand and applaud, and even to smother him in my embraces, when I saw him raise the heavy crowbar and commence an attack upon the rock itself.

"Saved," I cried.

"Yes," cried my uncle, even more excited and delighted than myself; "Hans is quite right. Oh, the worthy, excellent man! We should never have thought of such an idea."

And nobody else, I think, would have done so. Such a process, simple as it seemed, would most certainly not have entered our heads. Nothing could be more dangerous than to begin to work with pickaxes in that particular part of the globe. Supposing while he was at work a break-up were to take place, and supposing the torrent once having gained an inch were to take an ell, and come pouring bodily through the broken rock!

Not one of these dangers were chimerical. They were only too real. But at that moment no fear of falling in of roof, or even of inundation was capable of stopping us. Our thirst was so intense, that to quench it we would have dug below the bed of old Ocean itself.

Hans went quietly to work—a work which neither my uncle nor I would have undertaken at any price. Our impatience was so great, that if we had once begun with pickaxe and crowbar, the rock would soon have split into a hundred fragments. The guide, on the contrary, calm, ready, moderate, wore away the hard rock by little steady blows of his instrument, making no attempt at a larger hole than about six inches. As I stood, I heard, or I thought I heard, the roar of the torrent momentarily increasing in loudness, and at times I almost felt the pleasant sensation of water upon my parched lips.

At the end of what appeared an age, Hans had made a hole, which enabled his crowbar to enter two feet into the solid rock. He had been at work exactly an hour. It appeared a dozen. I was getting wild with impatience. My uncle began to think of using more violent measures. I had the greatest difficulty in checking him. He

had indeed just got hold of his crowbar when a loud and welcome hiss was heard. Then a stream, or rather jet of water burst through the wall and came out with such force as to hit the opposite side!

Hans, the guide, who was half upset by the shock, was scarcely able to keep down a cry of pain and grief. I understood his meaning when plunging my hands into the sparkling jet I myself gave a wild and frantic cry. The water was scalding hot!

"Boiling," I cried, in bitter disappointment.

"Well, never mind," said my uncle, "it will soon get cool."

The tunnel began to be filled by clouds of vapour, while a small stream ran away into the interior of the earth. In a short time we had some sufficiently cool to drink. We swallowed it in huge mouthfuls.

Oh what exalted delight—what rich and incomparable luxury! What was this water, whence did it come? To us what was that? The simple fact was—it was water; and, though still with a tinge of warmth about it, it brought back to the heart, that life which, but for it, must surely have faded away. I drank greedily, almost without tasting it.

When, however, I had almost quenched my ravenous thirst, I made a discovery.

"Why, it is ferruginous water."

"Most excellent stomachic," replied my uncle, "and highly mineralised. Here is a journey worth twenty to Spa."

"It's very good," I replied.

"I should think so. Water found six miles underground. There is a peculiarly inky flavour about it, which is by no means disagreeable. Hans may congratulate himself on having made a rare discovery. What do you say, nephew, according to the usual custom of travellers, to name the stream after him?"

"Good," said I.

And the name of "Hans-bach" was at once agreed upon.

Hans was not a bit more proud after hearing our determination than he was before. After having taken a very small modicum of the welcome refreshment, he had seated himself in a corner with his usual imperturbable gravity.

"Now," said I, "it is not worth while letting this water run to waste."

"What is the use," replied my uncle, "the source from which this river rises is inexhaustible."

"Never mind," I continued, "let us fill our goat skin and gourds, and then try to stop the opening up."

My advice, after some hesitation, was

The Guiding Stream.

followed or attempted to be followed. Hans picked up all the broken pieces of granite he had knocked out, and using some two he happened to have about him, tried to shut up the fissure he had made in the wall. All he did was to scald his hands. The pressure was too great, and all our attempts were utter failures.

"It is evident," I remarked, "that the upper surface of these springs is situated at a very great height above—as we may fairly infer from the great pressure of the jet."

"That is by no means doubtful," replied my uncle, "if this column of water is about thirty-two thousand feet high, the atmospheric pressure must be something enormous. But a new idea has just struck me."

"And what is that?"

"Why be at so much trouble to close this aperture?"

"Because—"

I hesitated and stammered, having no real reason.

"When our water bottles are empty, we are not at all sure that we shall be able to fill them," observed my uncle.

"I think that is very probable."

"Well, then, let this water run. It will, of course, naturally follow in our track, and will serve to guide and refresh us."

"I think the idea a good one," I cried, in reply, "and with this rivulet as a companion, there is no further reason why we should not succeed in our marvellous project."

"Ah, my boy," said the professor, laughing, "after all, you are coming round."

"More than that, I am now confident of ultimate success. Forward."

"One moment, nephew mine. Let us begin by taking some hours of repose."

I had utterly forgotten that it was night. The chronometer, however, informed me of the fact. Soon we were sufficiently restored and refreshed, and had all fallen into a profound sleep.

A Journey to the Centre of the Earth

CHAPTER XXI.

UNDER THE OCEAN

BY the next day we had nearly forgotten our past sufferings. The first sensation I experienced was surprise at not being thirsty, and I actually asked myself the reason. The running stream, which flowed in rippling wavelets at my feet, was the satisfactory reply.

We breakfasted with a good appetite, and then drank our fill of the excellent water. I felt myself quite a new man, ready to go anywhere my uncle chose to lead. I began to think. Why should not a man as seriously convinced as my uncle, succeed, with so excellent a guide as worthy Hans, and so devoted a nephew as myself? These were the brilliant ideas which now invaded my brain. Had the proposition now been made to go back to the summit of Mount Sneffels, I should have declined the offer in a most indignant manner.

But fortunately there was no question of going up. We were about to descend farther into the interior of the earth.

"Let us be moving," I cried, awakening the echoes of the old world.

We resumed our march on Thursday at eight o'clock in the morning. The great granite tunnel going round by sinuous and winding ways, presented every now and then sharp turns, and in fact had all the appearance of a labyrinth. Its direction, however, was in general towards the south-west. My uncle made several pauses in order to consult his compass.

The gallery now began to trend downwards in a horizontal direction, with about two inches of fall in every furlong. The murmuring stream flowed quietly at our feet. I could not but compare it to some familiar spirit, guiding us through the earth, and I dabbled my fingers in its tepid water, which sang like a naiad as we progressed. My good humour began to assume a mythological character.

As for my uncle he began to complain of the horizontal character of the road. His route he found began to be indefinitely prolonged, instead of "sliding down the celestial ray," according to his expression.

But we had no choice; and as long as our road lead towards the centre—however little progress we made, there was no reason to complain.

Moreover, from time to time the slopes were much greater; the naiad sang more loudly, and we began to dip downwards in earnest.

As yet, however, I felt no painful sensation. I had not got over the excitement of the discovery of water.

That day and the next we did a considerable amount of horizontal, and relatively very little vertical, travelling.

On Friday evening, the tenth of July, according to our estimation, we ought to have been thirty leagues to the south-east of Reykjawick, and about two leagues and a-half deep. We now received a rather startling surprise.

Under our feet there opened a horrible well. My uncle was so delighted that he actually clapped his hands—as he saw how steep and sharp was the descent.

"Ah, ah!" he cried, in rapturous delight; "this will take us a long way. Look at the projections of the rock. Hah!" he exclaimed, "it's a fearful staircase!"

Hans, however, who in all our troubles had never given up the ropes, took care so to dispose of them as to prevent any accidents. Our descent then began. I dare not call it a perilous descent, for I was already too familiar with that sort of work to look upon it as anything but a very ordinary affair.

This well was a kind of narrow opening in the massive granite of the kind known as a fissure. The contraction of the terrestrial scaffolding, when it suddenly cooled, had been evidently the cause. If it had ever served in former times as a kind of funnel through which passed the eruptive masses vomited by Sneffels, I was at a loss to explain how it had left no mark. We were, in fact, descending a spiral, something like those winding staircases in use in modern houses.

We were compelled every quarter of an hour or thereabouts to sit down in order to rest our legs. Our calves ached. We then seated ourselves on some projecting rock with our legs hanging over, and gossipped while we ate a mouthful—drinking still from the pleasantly-warm running stream which had not deserted us.

It is scarcely necessary to say, that in this curiously-shaped fissure the Hansbach had

A vertical descent.

become a cascade to the detriment of its size. It was still however sufficient, and more, for our wants. Besides we knew that, as soon as the declivity ceased to be so abrupt, the stream must resume its peaceful course. At this moment it reminded me of my uncle, his impatience and rage, while when it flowed more peacefully, I pictured to myself the placidity of the Icelandic guide.

During the whole of two days, the sixth and seventh of July, we followed the extraordinary spiral staircase of the fissure, penetrating two leagues farther into the crust of the earth, which placed us five leagues below the level of the sea. On the eighth, however, at twelve o'clock in the day, the fissure suddenly assumed a much more gentle slope still trending in a south-east direction.

The road now became comparatively easy, and at the same time dreadfully monotonous. It would have been difficult for matters to have turned out otherwise. Our peculiar journey had no chance of being diversified by landscape and scenery. At all events, such was my idea.

At length, on Wednesday the fifteenth, we were actually seven leagues (twenty-one miles,) below the surface of the earth, and fifty leagues distant from the mountain of Sneffels. Though, if the truth be told, we were very tired, our health had resisted all suffering, and was in a most satisfactory state. Our traveller's box of medicaments had not even been opened.

My uncle was careful to note every hour the indications of the compass, of the chronometer, of the manometer, and of the thermometer, all which he afterwards published in his elaborate philosophical and scientific account of our remarkable voyage. He was therefore able to give an exact relation of the situation. When, therefore, he informed me that we were fifty leagues in a horizontal direction distant from our starting point, I could not suppress a loud exclamation.

"What is the matter now?" cried my uncle.

"Nothing very important, only an idea has entered my head," was my reply.

"Well, out with it, my boy."

"It is my opinion that if your calculations are correct we are no longer under Iceland."

"Do you think so?"

"We can very easily find out," I replied, pulling out the map and compasses.

"You see," I said, after careful measurement, "that I am not mistaken. We are far beyond Cape Portland; and those fifty leagues to the south-east will take us into the open sea."

"Under the open sea," cried my uncle, rubbing his hands with a delighted air.

"Yes," I cried, "no doubt old ocean flows over our heads."

"Well, my dear boy, what can be more natural. Do you not know that in the neighbourhood of Newcastle there are coal mines which have been worked far out under the sea?"

Now my worthy uncle the Professor, no doubt regarded this discovery as a very simple fact, but to me the idea was by no means a pleasant one. And yet when one came to think the matter over seriously, what mattered it whether the plains and mountains of Iceland were suspended over our devoted heads, or the mighty billows of the Atlantic Ocean? The whole question rested on the solidity of the granite roof above us. However, I soon got used to the idea, for the passage now level, now running down, and still always to the southeast, kept going deeper and deeper into the profound abysses of Mother Earth.

Three days later, on the eighteenth day of July, on a Saturday, we reached a kind of vast grotto. My uncle here paid Hans his usual rixdollars, and it was decided that the next day should be a day of rest.

A Journey to the Centre of the Earth

CHAPTER XXII.

SUNDAY BELOW GROUND

I AWOKE on Sunday morning without any sense of hurry and bustle attendant on an immediate departure. Though the day to be devoted to repose and reflection was spent under such strange circumstances, and in so wonderful a place, the idea was a pleasant one. Besides, we all began to get used to this kind of existence. I had almost ceased to think of the sun, of the moon, of the stars, of the trees, houses, and towns; in fact, about any terrestrial necessities. In our peculiar position we were far above such reflections.

The grotto was a vast and magnificent hall. Along its granitic soil the stream flowed placidly and pleasantly. So great a distance was it now from its fiery source, that its water was scarcely lukewarm, and could be drank without delay or difficulty.

After a frugal breakfast, the Professor made up his mind to devote some hours to putting his notes and calculations in order.

"In the first place," he said, "I have a good many to verify and prove, in order that we may know our exact position. I wish to be able on our return to the upper regions, to make a map of our journey, a kind of a vertical section of the globe, which will be as it were the profile of the expedition."

"That would indeed be a curious work, uncle; but can you make your observations with anything like certainty and precision?"

"I can. I have never on one occasion failed to note with great care the angles and slopes. I am certain as to having made no mistake. Take the compass and examine how she points."

I looked at the instrument with care.

"East one quarter south-east."

"Very good," resumed the Professor, noting the observation, and going through some rapid calculations. "I make out that we have journeyed two hundred and fifty miles from the point of our departure."

"Then the mighty waves of the Atlantic are rolling over our heads?"

"Certainly."

"And at this very moment it is possible that fierce tempests are raging above, and that men and ships are battling against the angry blasts just over our heads?"

"It is quite within the range of possibility,"

rejoined my uncle smiling.

"And that whales are playing in shoals, thrashing the bottom of the sea, the roof of our adamantine prison?"

"Be quite at rest on that point; there is no danger of their breaking through. But to return to our calculations. We are to the south-east, two hundred and fifty miles from the base of Sneffels, and, according to my preceding notes, I think we have gone sixteen leagues in a downward direction."

"Sixteen leagues—fifty miles!" I cried.

"I am sure of it."

"But that is the extreme limit allowed by science for the thickness of the earth's crust," I replied, referring to my geological studies.

"I do not contravene that assertion," was his quiet answer.

"And at this stage of our journey, according to all known laws on the increase of heat, there should be here a temperature of *fifteen hundred* degrees of Reaumur."

"There should be—you say, my boy."

"In which case this granite would not exist, but be in a state of fusion."

"But you perceive, my boy, that it is not so, and that facts, as usual, are very stubborn things, overruling all theories."

"I am forced to yield to the evidence of my senses, but I am nevertheless very much surprised."

"What heat does the thermometer really indicate?" continued the philosopher.

"Twenty-seven six-tenths."

"So that science is wrong by fourteen hundred and seventy-four degrees and four-tenths. According to which, it is demonstrated that the proportional increase in the temperature is an exploded error. Humphrey Davy here shines forth in all his glory. He is right, and I have acted wisely to believe him. Have you any answer to make to this statement?"

Had I chosen to have spoken, I might have said a great deal. I in no way admitted the theory of Humphrey Davy—I still held out for the theory of proportional increase of heat, though I did not feel it.

I was far more willing to allow that this chimney of an extinct volcano was covered by lava of a kind refractory to heat—in fact a bad conductor—which did not allow the great increase of temperature to percolate through its sides. The hot water jet supported my view of the matter.

But without entering on a long and useless discussion, or seeking for new arguments to controvert my uncle, I contented myself with taking up facts as they were.

"Well, sir, I take for granted that all your calculations are correct, but allow me to draw from them a rigorous and definite conclusion."

"Go on, my boy—have your say," cried my uncle, good-humouredly.

"At the place where we now are, under the latitude of Iceland, the terrestrial depth is about fifteen hundred and eighty-three leagues."

"Fifteen hundred, eighty-three and a quarter."

"Well, suppose we say sixteen hundred in round numbers. Now, out of a voyage of sixteen hundred leagues we have completed sixteen."

"As you say, what then?"

"At the expense of a diagonal journey of no less than eighty-five leagues."

"Exactly."

"We have been twenty days about it."

"Exactly twenty days."

"Now sixteen is the hundredth part of our contemplated expedition. If we go on in this way we shall be two thousand days, that is about five years and a half going down."

The Professor folded his arms, listened, but did not speak.

"Without counting that if a vertical descent of sixteen leagues costs us a horizontal of eighty-five, we shall have to go about eight thousand leagues to the south-east, and we must therefore come out somewhere in the circumference long before we can hope to reach the centre."

"Bother your calculations," cried my uncle in one of his old rages. "On what bases do they rest? How do you know that this passage does not take us direct to the end we require? Moreover, I have in my favour, fortunately, a precedent. What I have undertaken to do, another has done, and he having succeeded, why should I not be equally successful?"

"I hope, indeed, you will, but still, I suppose I may be allowed to—"

"You are allowed to hold your tongue," cried Professor Hardwigg, "when you talk so unreasonably as this."

I saw at once that the old doctorial Professor was still alive in my uncle—and fearful to rouse his angry passions, I dropped the unpleasant subject.

"Now, then," he explained, "consult the manometer. What does that indicate?"

"A considerable amount of pressure."

"Very good. You see, then, that by descending slowly, and by gradually accustoming ourselves to the density of this lower atmosphere, we shall not suffer."

"Well, I suppose not, except it may be a certain amount of pain in the ears," was my rather grim reply.

"That, my dear boy, is nothing, and you will easily get rid of that source of discomfort by bringing the exterior air in communication with the air contained in your lungs."

"Perfectly," said I, for I had quite made up my mind in no wise to contradict my uncle. "I should fancy almost that I should experience a certain amount of satisfaction in making a plunge into this dense atmosphere. Have you taken note of how wonderfully sound is propagated?"

"Of course I have. There can be no doubt that a journey into the interior of the earth would be an excellent cure for deafness."

"But then, uncle," I ventured mildly to observe, "this density will continue to increase."

"Yes—according to a law which, however, is scarcely defined. It is true that the intensity of weight will diminish just in proportion to the depth to which we go. You know very well that it is on the surface of the earth that its action is most powerfully felt, while on the contrary, in the very centre of the earth bodies cease to have any weight at all."

"I know that is the case, but as we progress will not the atmosphere finally assume the density of water?"

"I know it; when placed under the pressure of seven hundred and ten atmospheres," cried my uncle with imperturbable gravity.

"And when we are still lower down?" I asked with natural anxiety.

"Well, lower down, the density will become even greater still."

"Then how shall we be able to make our way through this atmospheric fog?"

"Well, my worthy nephew, we must ballast ourselves by filling our pockets with stones," said Professor Hardwigg.

"Faith, uncle, you have an answer for everything," was my only reply.

I began to feel that it was unwise in me to go any farther into the wide field of hypotheses for I should certainly have revived some difficulty, or rather impossibility that would have enraged the Professsor.

It was evident, nevertheless, that the air

under a pressure which might be multiplied by thousands of atmospheres, would end by becoming perfectly solid, and that then admitting our bodies resisted the pressure, we should have to stop, in spite of the all the reasonings in the world. Facts overcome all arguments.

But I thought it best not to urge this argument. My uncle would simply have quoted the example of Saknussemm. Supposing the learned Icelander's journey ever really to have taken place—there was one simple answer to be made:—

In the sixteenth century neither the barometer nor the manometer had been invented— how, then, could Saknussemm have been able to discover when he did reach the centre of the earth?

This unanswerable and learned objection I, however, kept to myself, and bracing up my courage awaited the course of events—little aware of how adventurous yet were to be the incidents of our remarkable journey.

The rest of this day of leisure and repose was spent in calculation and conversation. I made it a point to agree with the Professor in everything; but I envied the perfect indifference of Hans, who without taking any such trouble about cause and effect, went blindly onwards wherever destiny chose to lead him.

A Journey to the Centre of the Earth

CHAPTER XXIII.

ALONE

IT must in all truth be confessed, things as yet had gone on well, and I should have acted in bad taste to have complained. If the true medium of our difficulties did not increase, it was within the range of possibility that we might ultimately reach the end of our journey. Then what glory would be ours! I began in the newly-aroused ardour of my soul to speak enthusiastically to the Professor. Well, was I serious? The whole state in which we existed was a mystery—and it was impossible to know whether or not I was in earnest.

For several days after our memorable halt, the slopes became more rapid—some were even of a most frightful character—almost vertical, so that we were for ever going down into the solid interior mass. During some days, we actually descended a league and a-half, even two leagues towards the centre of the earth. The descents were sufficiently perilous, and while we were engaged in them we learned fully to appreciate the marvellous coolness of our guide Hans. Without him we should have been wholly lost. The grave and impassible Icelander devoted himself to us with the most incomprehensible *sang froid* and ease; and, thanks to him, many a dangerous pass was got over, where, but for him, we should inevitably have stuck fast.

His silence increased every day. I think that we began to be influenced by this peculiar trait in his character. It is certain that the inanimate objects by which you are surrounded have a direct action on the brain. It must be that a man who shuts himself up between four walls must lose the faculty of associating ideas and words. How many persons condemned to the horrors of solitary confinement have gone mad—simply because the thinking faculties have lain dormant!

During the two weeks that followed our last interesting conversation, there occurred nothing worthy of being especially recorded.

I have, while writing these memoirs, taxed my memory in vain for one incident of travel during this particular period.

But the next event to be related is indeed terrible. Its very memory, even now, makes my soul shudder, and my blood run cold.

It was on the seventh of August. Our constant and successive descents had taken us quite thirty leagues into the interior of the earth, that is to say that there were above us thirty leagues, nearly a hundred miles, of rocks, and oceans and continents and towns, to say nothing of living inhabitants. We were in a south-easterly direction, about two hundred leagues from Iceland.

On that memorable day the tunnel had begun to assume an almost horizontal course.

I was on this occasion walking on in front. My uncle had charge of one of the Ruhmkorff coils, I had possession of the other. By means of its light I was busily examining the different layers of granite. I was completely absorbed in my work.

Suddenly halting and turning round, I found that I was alone!

"Well," thought I to myself, "I have certainly been walking too fast—or else Hans and my uncle have stopped to rest. The best thing I can do is to go back and find them. Luckily, there is very little ascent to tire me."

I accordingly retraced my steps, and while doing so, walked for at least a quarter of an hour. Rather uneasy, I paused and looked eagerly around. Not a living soul. I called aloud. No reply. My voice was lost amid the myriad cavernous echoes it aroused!

I began for the first time to feel seriously uneasy. A cold shiver shook my whole body, and perspiration, chill and terrible, burst upon my skin.

"I must be calm," I said, speaking aloud, as boys whistle to drive away fear. "There can be no doubt that I shall find my companions. There cannot be two roads. It is certain that I was considerably ahead; all I have to do is to go back."

Having come to this determination I ascended the tunnel for at least half an hour, unable to decide if I had ever seen certain landmarks before. Every now and then I paused to discover if any loud appeal was made to me, well knowing that in that dense and intensified atmosphere I should hear it a long way off. But no. The most extraordinary silence reigned in this immense gallery. Only the echoes of my own footsteps could be heard.

At last I stopped. I could scarcely realise the

fact of my isolation. I was quite willing to think that I had made a mistake, but not that I was lost. If I had made a mistake, I might find my way: if lost—I shuddered to think of it.

"Come, come," said I to myself, "since there is only one road, and they must come by it, we shall at last meet. All I have to do is still to go upwards. Perhaps, however, not seeing me, and forgetting I was ahead, they may have gone back in search of me. Still even in this case, if I make haste, I shall get up to them. There can be no doubt about the matter."

But as I spoke these last words aloud, it would have been quite clear to any listener—had there been one—that I was by no means convinced of the fact. Moreover, in order to associate together these simple ideas and to reunite them under the form of reasoning, required some time. I could not all at once bring my brain to think.

Then another dread doubt fell upon my soul. After all, was I ahead. Of course I was. Hans was no doubt following behind preceded by my uncle. I perfectly recollected his having stopped for a moment to strap his baggage on his shoulder. I now remembered this trifling detail. It was, I believed, just at that very moment that I had determined to continue my route.

"Again," thought I, reasoning as calmly as was possible, "there is another sure means of not losing my way, a thread to guide me through the labyrinthine subterraneous retreat, —one which I had forgotten—my faithful river."

This course of reasoning roused my drooping spirits, and I resolved to resume my journey without further delay. No time was to be lost.

It was at this moment that I had reason to bless the thoughtfulness of my uncle, when he refused to allow the eider hunter to close the orifice of the hot spring—that small fissure in the great mass of granite. The beneficent spring after having saved us from thirst during so many days would now enable me to regain the right road.

Having come to this mental decision, I made up my mind, before I started upwards, that ablution would certainly do me a great deal of good.

I stopped to plunge my hands and forehead in the pleasant water of the Hansbach stream, blessing its presence as a certain consolation.

Conceive my horror and stupefaction!—I was treading a hard, dusty, shingly road of granite. The stream on which I reckoned had wholly disappeared!

A Journey to the Centre of the Earth

CHAPTER XXIV.

LOST!

NO words in any human language can depict my utter despair. I was literally buried alive; with no other expectation before me but to die in all the slow horrible torture of hunger and thirst.

Mechanically I crawled about, feeling the dry and arid rock. Never to my fancy had I ever felt anything so dry.

But, I frantically asked myself, how had I lost the course of the flowing stream? There could be no doubt it had ceased to flow in the gallery in which I now was. Now I began to understand the cause of the strange silence which prevailed when last I tried if any appeal from my companions might perchance reach my ear.

It so happened that when I first took an imprudent step in the wrong direction, I did not perceive the absence of the all-important stream.

It was now quite evident that when we halted, another tunnel must have received the waters of the little torrent, and that I had unconsciously entered a different gallery. To what unknown depths had my companions gone? Where was I?

How to get back! Clue or landmark there was absolutely none! My feet left no signs on the granite and shingle. My brain throbbed with agony as I tried to discover the solution of this terrible problem. My situation, after all sophistry and reflection, had finally to be summed up in three awful words—

Lost! LOST!! LOST!!!

Lost at a depth which, to my finite understanding, appeared to be immeasurable.

These thirty leagues of the crust of the earth weighed upon my shoulders like the globe on the shoulders of Atlas. I felt myself crushed by the awful weight. It was indeed a position to drive the sanest man to madness!

I tried to bring my thoughts back to the things of the world so long forgotten. It was with the greatest difficulty that I succeeded in doing so. Hamburg, the house on the Königstrasse, my dear cousin Gretchen—all that world which had before vanished like a shadow floated before my now vivid imagination.

There they were before me, but how unreal.

Under the influence of a terrible hallucination I saw the whole incidents of our journey pass before me like the scenes of a panorama. The ship and its inmates, Iceland, M. Fridriksson, and the great summit of Mount Sneffels! I said to myself that if in my position, I retained the most faint and shadowy outline of a hope it would be a sure sign of approaching delirium. It were better to give way wholly to despair!

In fact, did I but reason with calmness and philosophy, what human power was there in existence able to take me back to the surface of the earth, and ready too, to split asunder, to rend in twain, those huge and mighty vaults which stand above my head? Who could enable me to find my road—and regain my companions?

Insensate folly and madness to entertain even a shadow of hope!

"Oh, uncle!" was my despairing cry.

This was the only word of reproach which came to my lips; for I thoroughly understood how deeply and sorrowfully the worthy Professor would regret my loss, and how in his turn he would patiently seek for me.

When I at last began to resign myself to the fact that no further aid was to be expected from man, and knowing that I was utterly powerless to do anything for my own salvation, I kneeled with earnest fervour and asked assistance from Heaven. The remembrance of my innocent childhood, the memory of my mother, known only in my infancy, came welling forth from my heart. I had recourse to prayer. And little as I had a right to be remembered by Him whom I had forgotten in the hour of prosperity, and whom I so tardily invoked, I prayed earnestly and sincerely.

This renewal of my youthful faith brought about a much greater amount of calm, and I was enabled to concentrate all my strength and intelligence on the terrible realities of my unprecedented situation.

I had about me that which I had at first wholly forgotten—three days' provisions. Moreover, my water bottle was quite full. Nevertheless, the one thing which it was impossible to do was to remain alone. Try to find my companions I must, at any price. But which course should I take? Should I go

"Lost! Lost!"

upwards, or again descend? Doubtless it was right to retrace my steps in an upward direction.

By doing this with care and coolness, I must reach the point where I had turned away from the rippling stream. I must find the fatal bifurcation or fork. Once at this spot, once the river at my feet, I could, at all events, regain the awful crater of Mount Sneffels. Why had I not thought of this before? This, at last, was a reasonable hope of safety. The most important thing, then, to be done was to discover the bed of the Hansbach.

After a slight meal and a draught of water, I rose like a giant refreshed. Leaning heavily on my pole, I began the ascent of the gallery. The slope was very rapid and rather difficult. But I advanced hopefully and carefully, like a man who at last is making his way out of a forest, and knows there is only one road to follow.

During one whole hour nothing happened to check my progress. As I advanced I tried to recollect the shape of the tunnel—to recall to my memory certain projections of rocks—to persuade myself that I had followed certain winding routes before. But no one particular sign could I bring to mind, and I was soon forced to allow that this gallery would never take me back to the point at which I had separated myself from my companions. It was absolutely without issue—a mere blind alley in the earth.

The moment at length came when, facing the solid rock, I knew my fate, and fell inanimate on the arid floor!

To describe the horrible state of despair and fear into which I then fell would now be vain and impossible. My last hope, the courage which had sustained me, drooped before the sight of this pitiless granite rock!

Lost in a vast labyrinth, the sinuosities of which spread in every direction, without guide, clue or compass, it was a vain and useless task to attempt flight. All that remained to me was to lie down and die. To lie down and die the most cruel and horrible of deaths!

In my state of mind, the idea came into my head that one day perhaps, when my fossil bones were found, their discovery so far below the level of the earth might give rise to solemn and interesting scientific discussions.

I tried to cry aloud, but hoarse, hollow and inarticulate sounds alone could make themselves heard through my parched lips. I literally panted for breath.

In the midst of all these horrible sources of anguish and despair, a new horror took possession of my soul. My lamp, by falling down, had got out of order. I had no means of repairing it. Its light was already becoming paler and paler, and soon would expire.

With a strange sense of resignation and despair, I watched the luminous current in the coil getting less and less. A procession of shadows moved flashing along the granite wall. I scarcely dared to lower my eyelids, fearing to lose the last spark of this fugitive light. Every instant it seemed to me that it was about to vanish and to leave me for ever—in utter darkness!

At last, one final trembling flame remained in the lamp; I followed it with all my power of vision; I gasped for breath; I concentrated upon it all the power of my soul, as upon the last scintillation of light I was ever destined to see: and then I was to be lost for ever in Cimmerian and tenebrous shades.

A wild and plaintive cry escaped my lips. On earth during the most profound and comparatively complete darkness, light never allows a complete destruction and extinction of its power. Light is so diffuse, so subtle, that it permeates everywhere, and whatever little may remain, the retina of the eye will succeed in finding it. In this place nothing—not the faintest ray of light. It mazed me!

My head was now wholly lost. I raised my arms, trying the effect of the feeling in getting against the cold stone wall. It was painful in the extreme. Madness must have taken possession of me. I knew not what I did. I began to run, to fly, rushing at haphazard in this inextricable labyrinth, always going downwards, running wildly underneath the terrestrial crust, like an inhabitant of the subterranean furnaces, screaming, roaring, howling, until bruised by the pointed rocks, falling and picking myself up all covered with blood, seeking madly to drink the blood which dripped from my torn features, mad because this blood only trickled over my face, and watching always for this horrid wall which ever presented to me the fearful obstacle against which I could not dash my head.

Where was I going? It was impossible to say. I was perfectly ignorant of the matter.

Several hours passed in this way. After a long time, having utterly exhausted my strength, I fell a heavy inert mass along the side of the tunnel, and lost all consciousness of existence!

A Journey to the Centre of the Earth

CHAPTER XXV.

THE WHISPERING GALLERY

WHEN at last I came back to a sense of life and being, my face was wet; but wet as I soon knew with tears. How long this state of insensibility lasted, it is quite impossible for me now to say. I had no means left to me of taking any account of time. Never since the creation of the world, had such a solitude as mine existed. I was completely abandoned.

After my fall, I lost much blood. I felt myself flooded with the life-giving liquid. My first sensation was perhaps a natural one. Why was I not dead? Because I was alive, there was something left to do. I tried to make up my mind to think no longer. As far as I was able, I drove away all ideas, and utterly overcome by pain and grief, I crouched against the granite wall.

I just commenced to feel the fainting coming on again, and the sensation that this was the last struggle before complete annihilation,—when, on a sudden, a violent uproar reached my ears. It had some resemblance to the prolonged rumbling voice of thunder, and I clearly distinguished sonorous voices, lost one after the other, in the distant depths of the gulf.

Whence came this noise? Naturally, it was to be supposed from new phenomena which were taking place in the bosom of the solid mass of Mother Earth! The explosion of some gaseous vapours, or the fall of some solid, of the granitic or other rock.

Again I listened with deep attention. I was extremely anxious to hear if this strange and inexplicable sound was likely to be renewed! A whole quarter of an hour elapsed in painful expectation. Deep and solemn silence reigned in the tunnel. So still that I could hear the beatings of my own heart. I waited, waited, waited with a strange kind of hopefulness.

Suddenly my ear, which leant accidentally against the wall, appeared to catch as it were the faintest echo of a sound. I thought that I heard vague, incoherent and distant voices. I quivered all over with excitement and hope!

"It must be hallucination," I cried. "It cannot be! it is not true!"

"But no! By listening more attentively, I really did convince myself that what I heard was truly the sound of human voices. To make any meaning out of the sound, however, was beyond my power. I was too weak even to hear distinctly. Still it was a positive fact that some one was speaking. Of that I was quite certain.

There was a moment of fear. A dread fell upon my soul that it might be my own words brought back to me by a distant echo. Perhaps without knowing it, I might have been crying aloud. I resolutely closed my lips, and once more placed my ear to the huge granite wall.

Yes, for certain. It was in truth the sound of human voices.

I now by the exercise of great determination dragged myself along the sides of the cavern, until I reached a point where I could hear more distinctly. But though I could detect the sound, I could only make out uncertain, strange, and incomprehensible words. They reached my ear as if they had been spoken in a low tone— murmured, as it were, afar off.

At last, I made out the word *förlorad* repeated several times in a tone betokening great mental anguish and sorrow.

What could this word mean, and who was speaking it? It must be either my uncle or the guide Hans! If, therefore, I could hear them, they must surely be able to hear me.

"Help," I cried at the top of my voice; "help, I am dying!"

I then listened with scarcely a breath; I panted for the slightest sound in the darkness— a cry, a sight, a question! But silence reigned supreme. No answer came! In this way some minutes passed. A whole flood of ideas flashed through my mind. I began to fear that my voice weakened by sickness and suffering could not reach my companions who were in search of me.

"It must be them," I cried; "what other men can by possibility be buried a hundred miles below the level of the earth?" The mere supposition was preposterous.

I began, therefore, to listen again with the most breathless attention. As I moved my ears along the side of the place I was in, I found a mathematical point as it were, where the voices appeared to attain their maximum of intensity. The word *förlorad* again distinctly reached my ear. Then came again that rolling noise like thunder which had awakened me out of torpor.

"I begin to understand," I said to myself after some little time devoted to reflection; "it

The Whisper Heard.

is not through the solid mass that the sound reaches my ears. The walls of my cavernous retreat are of solid granite, and the most fearful explosion would not make uproar enough to penetrate them. The sound must come along the gallery itself. The place I was in must possess some peculiar acoustic properties of its own.

Again I listened; and this time—yes, this time—I heard my name distinctly pronounced: cast as it were into space.

It was my uncle the Professor who was speaking. He was in conversation with the guide, and the word which had so often reached my ears, *förlorad*, was a Danish expression.

Then I understood it all. In order to make myself heard, I too must speak as it were along the side of the gallery, which would carry the sound of my voice just as the wire carries the electric fluid from point to point.

But there was no time to lose. If my companions were only to remove a few feet from where they stood, the acoustic effect would be over, my Whispering Gallery would be destroyed. I again therefore crawled towards the wall, and said as clearly and distinctly as I could—

"Uncle Hardwigg."

I then awaited a reply.

Sound does not possess the property of travelling with such extreme rapidity. Besides, the density of the air at that depth from light and motion, was very far from adding to the rapidity of circulation. Several seconds elapsed, which to my excited imagination, appeared ages; and these words reached my eager ears, and moved my wildly beating heart—

"Harry, my boy, is that you?"

A short delay between question and answer.

"Yes—yes."

"Where are you?"

"Lost!"

"And your lamp?"

"Out."

"But the guiding stream?"

"Is lost!"

"Keep your courage, Harry. We will do our best."

"One moment, my uncle," I cried; "I have no longer strength to answer your questions. But—for heaven's sake—do you—continue—to speak—to me!"

Absolute silence I felt, would be annihilation.

"Keep up your courage," said my uncle. "As you are so weak do not speak. We have been searching for you in all directions, both by going upwards and downwards in the gallery. My dear boy, I had begun to give over all hope—and you can never know what bitter tears of sorrow and regret I have shed. At last, supposing you to be still on the road beside the Hansbach we again descended, firing off guns as signals. Now, however, that we have found you, and that our voices reach each other, it may be a long time before we actually meet. We are conversing by means of some extraordinary acoustic arrangement of the labyrinth. But do not despair, my dear boy. It is something gained even to hear each other."

While he was speaking my brain was at work reflecting. A certain undefined hope, vague and shapeless as yet, made my heart beat wildly. In the first place, it was absolutely necessary for me to know one thing. I once more therefore leaned my head against the wall, which I almost touched with my lips, and again spoke.

"Uncle."

"My boy," was his ready answer.

"It is of the utmost consequence that we should know how far we are asunder."

"That is not difficult."

"You have your chronometer at hand?" I asked.

"Certainly."

"Well, take it into your hand. Pronounce my name, noting exactly the second at which you speak. I will reply as soon as I hear your words—and you will then note exactly the moment at which my reply reaches you."

"Very good; and the mean time between my question and your answer will be the time occupied by my voice in reaching you."

"That is exactly what I mean, uncle," was my eager reply.

"Are you ready?"

"Yes."

"Well, make ready, I am about to pronounce your name," said the Professor.

I applied my ear close to the sides of the cavernous gallery, and as soon as the word Harry reached my ear, I turned round, and placing my lips to the wall, repeated the sound. "Forty seconds," said my uncle. "There has elapsed forty seconds between the two words. The sound, therefore, takes twenty seconds to ascend. Now, allowing a thousand and twenty feet for every second—we have twenty thousand four hundred feet—a league and a half and one-eighth."

These words fell on my soul like a kind of death-knell.

"A league and a-half," I muttered in a low and despairing voice.

"It shall be got over, my boy," cried my uncle in a cheery tone; "depend on us."

"But do you know whether to ascend or descend?" I asked faintly enough.

"We have to descend, and I will tell you why. You have reached a vast open space, a kind of bare cross road, from which galleries diverge in every direction. That in which you are now lying, must necessarily bring you to this point, for it appears that all these mighty fissures, these fractures of the globe's interior radiate from the vast cavern which we at this moment occupy. Rouse youself, then, have courage and continue your route. Walk if you can, if not drag youself along—slide, if nothing else is possible. The slope must be rather rapid—and you will find strong arms to receive you at the end of your journey. Make a start, like a good fellow."

These words served to rouse some kind of courage in my sinking frame.

"Farewell for the present, good uncle, I am about to take my departure. As soon as I start, our voices will cease to commingle. Farewell, then, until we meet again."

"Adieu, Harry—until we say Welcome." Such were the last words which reached my anxious ears, before I commenced my weary and almost hopeless journey.

This wonderful and surprising conversation which took place through the vast mass of the earth's labyrinth, these words exchanged, the speakers being about five miles apart—ended with hopeful and pleasant expressions. I breathed one more prayer to Heaven, I sent up words of thanksgiving—believing in my inmost heart that He had led me to the only place where the voices of my friends could reach my ears.

This apparently astounding acoustic mystery is easily explainable by simple natural laws; it arose from the peculiar formation of the gallery and from the conductibility of the rock. There are many instances of this singular propagation of sound which are not perceptible in its less mediate positions. In the interior gallery of St. Paul's, and amid the curious caverns in Sicily, these phenomena are observable. The most marvellous of them all is known as the Ear of Dionysius.

These memories of the past, of my early reading and studies, came fresh to my thoughts. Moreover, I began to reason that if my uncle and I could communicate at so great a distance, no serious obstacle could exist between us. All I had to do was to follow the direction whence the sound had reached me; and, logically putting it, I must reach him if my strength did not fail.

I accordingly rose to my feet. I soon found, however, that I could not walk; that I must drag myself along. The slope as I expected, was very rapid; but I allowed myself to slip down.

Soon the rapidity of the descent began to assume frightful proportions; and menaced a fearful fall. I clutched at the sides; I grasped at projections of rocks; I threw myself backwards. All in vain. My weakness was so great I could do nothing to save myself.

Suddenly earth failed me.

I was first launched into a dark, and gloomy void. I then struck against the projecting asperities of a vertical gallery, a perfect well. My head bounded against a pointed rock, and I lost all knowledge of existence. As far as I was concerned, death had claimed me for his own.

A Journey to the Centre of the Earth

CHAPTER XXVI.

A RAPID RECOVERY

WHEN I returned to the consciousness of existence, I found myself surrounded by a kind of semi-obscurity, lying on some thick and soft coverlids. My uncle was watching—his eye fixed intently on my countenance, a grave expression on his face; a tear in his eye. At the first sigh which struggled from my bosom he took hold of my hand. When he saw my eyes open and fix themselves upon his, he uttered a loud cry of joy.

"He lives! he lives!"

"Yes, my good uncle," I whispered.

"My dear boy," continued the grim Professor, clasping me to his heart, "you are saved!"

I was deeply and unaffectedly touched by the tone in which these words were uttered, and even more by the kindly care which accompanied them. The Professor, however, was one of those men who must be severely tried in order to induce any display of affection or gentle emotion. At this moment our friend, Hans, the guide joined us. He saw my hand in that of my uncle, and I venture to say that, taciturn as he was, his eyes beamed with lively satisfaction.

"*God dag*," he said.

"Good day, Hans, good day," I replied, in as hearty a tone as I could assume, "and now, uncle, that we are together, tell me where we are. I have lost all idea of our position, as of everything else."

"To-morrow, Harry, to-morrow," he replied. "To-day you are far too weak. Your head is surrounded with bandages and poultices that must not be touched. Sleep, my boy, sleep, and to-morrow you will know all that you require."

"But," I cried, "let me know what o'clock it is—what day it is?"

"It is now eleven o'clock at night, and this is once more Sunday. It is now the ninth of the month of August. And I distinctly prohibit you from asking any more questions until the tenth of the same."

I was, if the truth be told, very weak indeed, and my eyes soon closed, involuntarily. I did require a good night's rest, and I went off reflecting at the last moment that my perilous adventure in the interior of the earth, in total darkness, had lasted four days!

On the morning of the next day, at my awakening, I began to look around me. My sleeping place, made of all our travelling bedding, was in a charming grotto, adorned with magnificent stalagmites, glittering in all the colours of the rainbow, the floor of soft and silvery sand.

A dim obscurity prevailed. No torch, no lamp was lighted, and yet certain unexplained beams of light penetrated from without, and made their way through the opening of the beautiful grotto.

I, moreover, heard a vague and indefinite murmur, like the ebb and flow of waves upon a strand, and sometimes I verily believed I could hear the sighing of the wind.

I began to believe that, instead of being awake, I must be dreaming. Surely my brain had not been affected by my fall, and all that occurred during the last twenty-four hours was not the frenzied visions of madness? And yet after some reflection, a trial of my faculties, I came to the conclusion that I could not be mistaken. Eyes and ears could not surely both deceive me.

"It is a ray of the blessed daylight," I said to myself, "which has penetrated through some mighty fissure in the rocks. But what is the meaning of this murmur of waves, this unmistakable moaning of the salt sea billows? I can hear, too, plainly enough, the whistling of the wind. But can I be altogether mistaken? If my uncle, during my illness, has but carried me back to the surface of the earth! Has he, on my account, given up his wondrous expedition, or in some strange manner has it come to an end?"

I was puzzling my brain over these and other questions, when the Professor joined me.

"Good-day, Harry," he cried, in a joyous tone. "I fancy you are quite well."

"I am very much better," I replied, actually sitting up in my bed.

"I knew that would be the end of it, as you slept both soundly and tranquilly. Hans and I have each taken turn to watch, and every hour we have seen visible signs of amelioration."

"You must be right, uncle," was my reply, "for I feel as if I could do justice to any meal you could put before me. I am really hungry."

Saved! I fall into the Grotto.

"You shall eat, my boy, you shall eat. The fever has left you. Our excellent friend Hans has rubbed your wounds and bruises, with I know not what ointment, of which the Icelanders alone possess the secret. And they have healed your bruises in the most marvellous manner. Ah, he's a wise fellow, is Master Hans."

While he was speaking, my uncle was placing before me several articles of food, which despite his earnest injunctions, I readily devoured. As soon as the first rage of hunger was appeased, I overwhelmed him with questions, to which he now no longer hesitated to give answers.

I then learned, for the first time, that my providential fall had brought me to the bottom of an almost perpendicular gallery. As I came down, amidst a perfect shower of stones, the least of which falling on me would have crushed me to death, they came to the conclusion that I had carried with me an entire dislocated rock. Riding as it were on this terrible chariot, I was cast headlong into my uncle's arms. And into them I fell, insensible and covered with blood.

"It is indeed a miracle," was the Professor's final remark, "that you were not killed a thousand times over. But let us take care never to separate; for surely we should risk never meeting again."

"Let us take care never again to separate."

These words fell with a sort of chill upon my heart. The journey, then, was not over. I looked at my uncle with surprise and astonishment. My uncle, after an instant's examination of my countenance, said—

"What is the matter, Harry?"

"I want to ask you a very serious question. You say that I am all right in health?"

"Certainly you are."

"And all my limbs are sound and capable of new exertion?" I asked.

"Most undoubtedly."

"But what about my head?" was my next anxious question.

"Well, your head, except that you have one or two contusions, is exactly where it ought to be—on your shoulders," said my uncle, laughing.

"Well, my own opinion is that my head is not exactly right. In fact, I believe myself slightly delirious."

"What makes you think so?"

"I will explain why I fancy I have lost my senses," I cried; "have we not returned to the surface of mother earth?"

"Certainly not."

"Then truly I must be mad, for do I not see the light of day? do I not hear the whistling of the wind? and can I not distinguish the wash of a great sea?"

"And that is all that makes you uneasy?" said my uncle, with a smile.

"Can you explain?"

"I will not make any attempt to explain; for the whole matter is utterly inexplicable. But you shall see and judge for yourself. You will then find that geological science is as yet in its infancy—and that we are doomed to enlighten the world."

"Let us advance, then," I cried eagerly, no longer able to restrain my curiosity.

"Wait a moment, my dear Harry," he responded; "you must take precautions after your illness before going into the open air."

"The open air?"

"Yes, my boy. I have to warn you that the wind is rather violent—and I have no wish for you to expose yourself without necessary precautions."

"But I beg to assure you that I am perfectly recovered from my illness."

"Have just a little patience, my boy. A relapse would be inconvenient to all parties. We have no time to lose—as our approaching sea voyage may be of long duration."

"Sea voyage?" I cried, more bewildered than ever.

"Yes. You must take another day's rest, and we shall be ready to go on board by to-morrow," replied my uncle, with a peculiar smile.

Go on board! The words utterly astonished me.

Go on board—what and how? Had we come upon a river, a lake, had we discovered some inland sea? Was a vessel lying at anchor in some part of the interior of the earth?

My curiosity was worked up to the very highest pitch. My uncle made vain attempts to restrain me. When at last, however, he discovered that my feverish impatience would do more harm than good—and that the satisfaction of my wishes could alone restore me to a calm state of mind, he gave way.

I dressed myself rapidly—and then taking the precaution to please my uncle, of wrapping myself in one of the coverlets, I rushed out of the grotto.

A Journey to the Centre of the Earth

CHAPTER XXVII.

THE CENTRAL SEA

AT first I saw absolutely nothing. My eyes, wholly unused to the effulgence of light, could not bear the sudden brightness; and I was compelled to close them. When I was able to re-open them, I stood still, far more stupefied than astonished. Not all the wildest effects of imagination could have conjured up such a scene!

"The sea—the sea," I cried.

"Yes," replied my uncle, in a tone of pardonable pride; "The Central Sea. No future navigator will deny the fact of my having discovered it; and hence of acquiring a right of giving it a name."

It was quite true. A vast, limitless expanse of water, the end of a lake if not of an ocean, spread before us, until it was lost in the distance. The shore which was very much indented, consisted of a beautiful soft golden sand, mixed with small shells, the long deserted home of some of the creatures of a past age. The waves broke incessantly, and with a peculiarly sonorous murmur—to be found in underground localities.—A slight frothy flake arose as the wind blew along the pellucid waters; and many a dash of spray was blown into my face. The mighty superstructure of rock which rose above to an inconceivable height, left only a narrow opening—but where we stood, there was a large margin of strand. On all sides were capes and promontories and enormous cliffs, partially worn by the eternal breaking of the waves, through countless ages! And as I gazed from side to side, the mighty rocks faded away like a fleecy film of cloud.

It was in reality an ocean, with all the usual characteristics of an inland sea, only horribly wild—so rigid, cold and savage.

One thing startled and puzzled me greatly. How was it that I was able to look upon that vast sheet of water instead of being plunged in utter darkness? The vast landscape before me was lit up like day. But there was wanting the dazzling brilliancy, the splendid irradiation of the sun; the pale cold illumination of the moon; the brightness of the stars. The illuminating power in this subterraneous region, from its trembling and flickering character, its clear dry whiteness, the very slight elevation of its temperature, its great superiority to that of the moon, was evidently electric; something in the nature of the aurora borealis, only that its phenomena were constant, and able to light up the whole of the ocean cavern.

The tremendous vault above our heads, the sky, so to speak, appeared to be composed of a conglomeration of nebulous vapours, in constant motion. I should originally have supposed, that under such an atmospheric pressure as must exist in that place, the evaporation of water could not really take place, and yet from the action of some physical law, which escaped my memory, there were heavy and dense clouds rolling along that mighty vault, partially concealing the roof, Electric currents produced astonishing play of light and shade in the distance, especially around the heavier clouds. Deep shadows were cast beneath, and then suddenly, between two clouds, there would come a ray of unusual beauty, and remarkable intensity. And yet it was not like the sun, for it gave no heat.

The effect was sad and excruciatingly melancholy. Instead of a noble firmament of blue, studded with stars, there was above me a heavy roof of granite, which seemed to crush me.

Gazing around, I began to think of the theory of the English captain, who compared the earth to a vast hollow sphere in the interior of which the air is retained in a luminous state by means of atmospheric pressure, while two stars, Pluto and Proserpine, circled there in their mysterious orbits. After all, suppose the old fellow was right!

In truth, we were imprisoned—bound as it were, in a vast excavation. Its width it was impossible to make out; the shore, on either hand, widening rapidly until lost to sight; while its length was equally uncertain. A haze on the distant horizon bounded our view. As to its height we could see that it must be many miles to the roof. Looking upward, it was impossible to discover where the stupendous roof began. The lowest of the clouds must have been floating at an elevation of two thousand yards, a height greater than that of terrestrial vapours, which circumstance was doubtless owing to the extreme density of the air.

I use the word cavern in order to give an idea

of the place. I cannot describe its awful grandeur; human language fails to convey an idea of its savage sublimity. Whether this singular vacuum had or had not been caused by the sudden cooling of the earth when in a state of fusion, I could not say. I had read of most wonderful and gigantic caverns— but none in any way like this.

The great grotto of Guachara, in Columbia, visited by the learned Humboldt; the vast and partially explored Mammoth Cave in Kentucky; what were these holes in the earth to that in which I stood in speechless admiration! with its vapoury clouds, its electric light, and the mighty ocean slumbering in its bosom! Imagination, not description, can alone give an idea of the splendour and vastness of the cave.

I gazed at these marvels in profound silence. Words were utterly wanting to indicate the sensations of wonder I experienced. I seemed, as I stood upon that mysterious shore, as if I were some wandering inhabitant of a distant planet, present for the first time at the spectacle of some terrestrial phenomena belonging to another existence. To give body and existence to such new sensations, would have required the coinage of new words—and here my feeble brain found itself wholly at fault. I looked on, I thought, I reflected, I admired, in a state of stupefaction not altogether unmingled with fear!

The unexpected spectacle restored some colour to my pallid cheeks. I seemed to be actually getting better under the influence of this novelty. Moreover, the vivacity of the dense atmosphere, reanimated my body, by inflating my lungs with unaccustomed oxygen.

It will be readily conceived that after an imprisonment of forty-seven days, in a dark and miserable tunnel, it was with infinite delight that I breathed this saline air. It was like the genial, reviving influence of the salt sea waves.

My uncle had already got over the first surprise.

With the Latin poet Horace his idea was that—

"Not to admire is all the art I know,

To make man happy and to keep him so."

"Well," he said, after giving me time thoroughly to appreciate the marvels of this underground sea, "do you feel strong enough to walk up and down?"

"Certainly," was my ready answer, "nothing would give me greater pleasure."

"Well then, my boy," he said, "lean on my arm, and we will stroll along the beach."

I accepted his offer eagerly, and we began to walk along the shores of this extraordinary lake. To our left were abrupt rocks, piled one upon the other,—a stupendous titanic pile; down their sides leapt innumerable cascades, which at last, becoming limpid and murmuring streams, were lost in the waters of the lake. Light vapours, which rose here and there, and floated in fleecy clouds from rock to rock, indicated hot springs, which also poured their superfluity into the vast reservoir at our feet.

Among them I recognised our old faithful stream, the Hansbach, which, lost in that wild basin, seemed as if it had been flowing since the creation of the world.

"We shall miss our excellent friend," I remarked, with a deep sigh.

"Bah"! said my uncle, testily, "What matters it. That or another, it is all the same."

I thought the remark ungrateful, and felt almost inclined to say so; but I forbore.

At this moment my attention was attracted by an unexpected spectacle. After we had gone about five hundred yards, we suddenly turned a steep promontory, and found ourselves close to a lofty forest! It consisted of straight trunks with tufted tops, in shape like parasols. The air seemed to have no effect upon these trees— which in spite of a tolerable breeze remained as still and motionless as if they had been petrified.

I hastened forward. I could find no name for these singular formations. Did they not belong to the two thousand and more known trees—or were we to make the discovery of a new growth? By no means. When we at last reached the forest, and stood beneath the trees, my surprise gave way to admiration.

In truth, I was simply in the presence of a very ordinary product of the earth, of singular and gigantic proportions. My uncle unhesitatingly called them by their real names.

"It is only," he said, in his coolest manner, "a forest of mushrooms."

On close examination I found that he was not mistaken. Judge of the development attained by this product of damp hot soils. I had heard that the *lycoperdon giganteum* reaches nine feet in circumference, but here were white mushrooms, nearly forty feet high, and with tops of equal dimensions. They grew in countless thousands—the light could not make its way through their massive substance, and beneath them reigned a gloomy and mystic darkness.

Still I wished to go forward. The cold in the shades of this singular forest was intense. For nearly an hour we wandered about in this darkness visible. At length I left the spot, and

The Mushroom Forest.

once more returned to the shores of the lake, to light and comparative warmth.

But the amazing vegetation of subterraneous land was not confined to gigantic mushrooms. New wonders awaited us at every step. We had not gone many hundred yards, when we came upon a mighty group of other trees with dis-coloured leaves—the common humble trees of mother earth, of an exorbitant and phenomenal size: lycopodes a hundred feet high; flowering ferns as tall as pines; gigantic grasses!

"Astonishing, magnificent, splendid!" cried my uncle; "here we have before us the whole Flora of the second period of the world, that of transition. Behold the humble plants of our gardens, which in the first ages of the world were mighty trees. Look around you, my dear Harry. No botanist ever before gazed on such a sight!"

My uncle's enthusiasm, always a little more than was required, was now excusable.

"You are right, uncle," I remarked. "Provi-dence appears to have designed the preserva-tion in this vast and mysterious hot-houses of antediluvian plants, to prove the sagacity of learned men in figuring them so marvellously on paper."

"Well said, my boy—very well said; it is indeed a mighty hot-house;—but you would also be within the bounds of reason and common sense, if you also added—a vast menagerie."

I looked rather anxiously around. If the animals were as exaggerated as the plants, the matter would certainly be serious.

"A menagerie?"

"Doubtless. Look at the dust we are treading under foot—behold the bones with which the whole soil of the sea shore is covered—"

"Bones," I replied, "yes, certainly, the bones of antediluvian animals."

I stopped down as I spoke, and picked up one or two singular remains, relics of a by-gone age. It was easy to give a name to these gigantic bones, in some instances as big as trunks of trees.

"Here is, clearly, the lower jaw-bone of a mastodon," I cried, almost as warmly and enthusiastically as my uncle, "here are the molars of the dinotherium; here is a leg-bone which belonged to the megatherium. You are right, uncle, it is indeed a menagerie; for the mighty animals to which these bones once belonged, have lived and died on the shores of this subterranean sea, under the shadow of these plants. Look, yonder are whole skeletons —and yet—"

"And yet, nephew?" said my uncle, noticing that I suddenly came to a full stop.

"I do not understand the presence of such beasts in granite caverns, however vast and prodigious," was my reply.

"Why not?" said my uncle, with very much of his old professional impatience.

"Because it is well known that animal life only existed on earth during the secondary period, when the sedimentary soil was formed by the alluviums, and thus replaced the hot and burning rocks of the primitive age."

"I have listened to you earnestly and with patience, Harry, and I have a simple and clear answer to your objections: and that is, that this itself is a sedimentary soil."

"How can that be at such enormous depths from the surface of the earth?"

"The fact can be explained both simply and geologically. At a certain period, the earth consisted only of an elastic crust, liable to alternative upward and downward movements in virtue of the law of attraction. It is very probable that many a landslip took place in those days, and that large portions of sedimen-tary soil were cast into huge and mighty chasms."

"Quite possible," I drily remarked. "But uncle, if these antediluvian animals formerly lived in these subterranean regions, what more likely that one of these huge monsters may at this moment be concealed behind one of yonder mighty rocks."

As I spoke, I looked keenly around, examining with care every point of the horizon; but nothing alive appeared to exist on these deserted shores.

I now felt rather fatigued, and told my uncle so. The walk and the excitement were too much for me in my weak state. I therefore seated myself at the end of a promontory, at the foot of which the waves broke in incessant rolls. I looked round a bay formed by projections of vast granitic rocks. At the extreme end was a little port protected by huge pyramids of stones. A brig and three or four schooners might have lain there with perfect ease. So natural did it seem, that every minute my imagination induced me to expect a vessel coming out under all sail and making for the open sea under the influence of a warm southerly breeze.

But the fantastic illusion never lasted more than a minute. We were the only living creatures in this subterranean world!

During certain periods there was an utter cessation of wind, when a silence deeper, more terrible than the silence of the desert fell upon these solitary and arid rocks—and seemed to

The first bather in these waters. A plunge into the Central Sea.

hang like a leaden weight upon the waters of this singular ocean. I sought, amid the awful stillness, to penetrate through the distant fog, to tear down the veil which concealed the mysterious distance. What unspoken words were murmured by my trembling lips—what questions did I wish to ask and did not! Where did this sea end—to what did it lead? Should we ever be able to examine its distant shores?

But my uncle had no doubts about the matter. He was convinced that our enterprise would in the end be successful. For my part, I was in a state of painful indecision—I desired to embark on the journey and to succeed, and still I feared the result.

After we had passed an hour or more in silent contemplation of the wondrous spectacle, we rose and went down towards the bank on our way to the grotto, which I was not sorry to gain. After a slight repast, I sought refuge in slumber, and at length, after many and tedious struggles, sleep came over my weary eyes.

A Journey to the Centre of the Earth

CHAPTER XXVIII.

LAUNCHING THE RAFT

ON the morning of the next day, to my great surprise, I awoke completely restored. I thought a bath would be delightful after my long illness and sufferings. So, soon after rising, I went and plunged into the waters of this new Mediterranean. The bath was cool, fresh and invigorating.

I came back to breakfast with an excellent appetite. Hans, our worthy guide, thoroughly understood how to cook such eatables as we were able to provide; he had both fire and water at discretion, so that he was enabled slightly to vary the weary monotony of our ordinary repast.

Our morning meal was like a capital English breakfast, with coffee by way of a wind up. And never had this delicious beverage been so welcome and refreshing.

My uncle had sufficient regard for my state of health not to interrupt me in the enjoyment of the meal, but he was evidently delighted when I had finished.

"Now then," said he, "come with me. It is the height of the tide, and I am anxious to study its curious phenomena."

"What," I cried, rising in astonishment, "did you say the tide, uncle?"

"Certainly I did."

"You do not mean to say," I replied, in a tone of respectful doubt, "that the influence of the sun and moon is felt here below."

"And pray why not? Are not all bodies influenced by the law of universal attraction? Why should this vast underground sea be exempt from the general law, the rule of the universe? Besides, there is nothing like that which is proved and demonstrated. Despite the great atmospheric pressure down here, you will notice that this inland sea rises and falls with as much regularity as the Atlantic itself."

As my uncle spoke, we reached the sandy shore, and saw and heard the waves breaking monotonously on the beach. They were evidently rising.

"This is truly the flood," I cried looking at the water at my feet.

"Yes, my excellent nephew," replied my uncle, rubbing his hands with the gusto of a philosopher, "and you see by these several streaks of foam, that the tide rises at least ten or twelve feet."

"It is indeed marvellous."

"By no means," he responded; "on the contrary, it is quite natural."

"It may appear so in your eyes, my dear uncle," was my reply, "but the whole phenomena of the place appear to me to partake of the marvellous. It is almost impossible to believe that which I see. Who in his wildest dreams could have imagined that, beneath the crust of our earth, there could exist a real ocean, with ebbing and flowing tides, with its changes of winds, and even its storms. I for one should have laughed the suggestion to scorn."

"But, Harry, my boy, why not?" enquired my uncle, with a pitying smile, "is there any physical reason in opposition to it?"

"Well, if we give up the great theory of the central heat of the earth, I certainly can offer no reasons why anything should be looked upon as impossible."

"Then you will own," he added, "that the system of Sir Humphrey Davy is wholly justified by what we have seen?"

"I allow that it is—and that point once granted, I certainly can see no reason for doubting the existence of seas and other wonders, even countries, in the interior of the globe."

"That is so—but of course these varied countries are uninhabited?"

"Well, I grant that it is more likely than not: still, I do not see why this sea should not have given shelter to some species of unknown fish."

"Hitherto we have not discovered any, and the probabilities are rather against our ever doing so," observed the Professor.

I was losing my scepticism in the presence of these wonders.

"Well, I am determined to solve the question. It is my intention to try my luck with my fishing line and hook."

"Certainly; make the experiment," said my uncle, pleased with my enthusiasm. "While we are about it, it will certainly be only proper to discover all the secrets of this extraordinary region."

"But, after all, where are we now?" I asked; "all this time I have quite forgotten to ask you a question, which, doubtless, your philosophical instruments have long since answered.''

"Well," replied the Professor, "examining the situation from only one point of view, we are now distant three hundred and fifty leagues from Iceland.''

"So much?" was my exclamation.

"I have gone over the matter several times, and am sure not to have made a mistake of five hundred yards," replied my uncle positively.

"And as to the direction—are we still going to the south-east?''

"Yes, with a western declination* of nineteen degrees, forty-two minutes, just as it is above. As for the inclination** I have discovered a very curious fact.''

"And what may that be, uncle? Your information interests me.''

"Why that the needle, instead of dipping towards the pole as it does on earth, in the northern hemisphere, has an upward tendency.''

"This proves," I cried, "that the great point of magnetic attraction lies somewhere between the surface of the earth and the spot we have succeeded in reaching.''

"Exactly, my observant nephew, exclaimed my uncle, elated and delighted, "and it is quite probable that if we succeed in getting towards the polar regions—somewhere near the seventy-third degree of latitude, where Sir James Ross discovered the magnetic pole, we shall behold the needle point directly upward. We have therefore discovered by analogy, that this great centre of attraction is not situated at a very great depth.''

"Well," said I, rather surprised, "this discovery will astonish experimental philosophers. It was never suspected.''

"Science, great, mighty and in the end unerring," replied my uncle dogmatically, "science has fallen into many errors—errors which have been fortunate and useful rather than otherwise, for they have been the stepping stones to truth.''

After some further discussion, I turned to another matter.

"Have you any idea of the depth we have reached?''

"We are now," continued the Professor, "exactly thirty-five leagues—above a hundred miles—down into the interior of the earth.''

"So," said I, after measuring the distance on the map, "we are now beneath the Scottish Highlands, and have over our heads the lofty Grampian hills.''

"You are quite right," said the Professor laughing, "it sounds very alarming, the weight being heavy—but the vault which supports this vast mass of earth and rock is solid and safe— the mighty Architect of the Universe has constructed it of solid materials. Man, even in his highest flights of vivid and poetic imagination, never thought of such things! What are the finest arches of our bridges, what the vaulted roofs of our cathedrals, to that mighty dome above us, and beneath which floats an ocean with its storms and calms and tides!''

"I admire it all as much as you can, uncle, and have no fear that our granite sky will fall upon our heads. But now that we have discussed matters of science and discovery, what are your future intentions? Are you not thinking of getting back to the surface of our beautiful earth?''

This was said more as a feeler than with any hope of success.

"Go back, nephew," cried my uncle in a tone of alarm, "you are not surely thinking of anything so absurd or cowardly. No; my intention is to advance and continue our journey. We have as yet been singularly fortunate, and henceforth I hope we shall be more so.''

"But," said I, "how are we to cross yonder liquid plain?''

"It is not my intention to leap into it head foremost, or even to swim across it, like Leander over the Hellespont. But as oceans are, after all, only great lakes, inasmuch as they are surrounded by land, so does it stand to reason, that this central sea is circumscribed by granite surroundings.''

"Doubtless," was my natural reply.

"Well, then, do you not think that when once we reach the other end, we shall find some means of continuing our journey?''

"Probably, but what extent do you allow to this internal ocean?''

"Well, I should fancy it to extend about forty or fifty leagues—more or less.''

"But even supposing this approximation to be a correct one—what then?" I asked.

"My dear boy, we have no time for further discussion. We shall embark to-morrow.''

I look around with surprise and incredulity. I could see nothing in the shape of boat or vessel.

"What!" I cried, "we are about to launch out upon an unknown sea; and where, if I may ask, is the vessel to carry us?''

"Well, my boy, it will not be exactly what you would call a vessel. For the present we must be content with a good and solid raft.''

*The declination is the variation of the needle from the true meridian of a place.
**Inclination is the dip of the magnetic needle with a tendency to incline towards the earth.

"A raft," I cried, incredulously, "but down here a raft is as impossible of construction as a vessel—and I am at a loss to imagine—"

"My good Harry—if you were to listen instead of talking so much, you would hear," said my uncle, waxing a little impatient.

"I should hear?"

"Yes—certain knocks with the hammer, which Hans is now employing to make the raft. He has been at work for many hours."

"Making a raft?"

"Yes."

"But where has he found trees suitable for such a construction."

"He found the trees all ready to his hand. Come, and you shall see our excellent guide at work."

More and more amazed at what I heard and saw, I followed my uncle like one in a dream.

After a walk of about a quarter of an hour, I saw Hans at work on the other side of the promontory which formed our natural port. A few minutes more and I was beside him. To my great surprise, on the sand shore lay a half-finished raft. It was made from beams of a very peculiar wood, and a great number of limbs, joints, boughs and pieces lay about, sufficient to have constructed a fleet of ships and boats.

I turned to my uncle, silent with astonishment and awe.

"Where did all this wood come from?" I cried; "what wood is it?"

"Well, there is pine-wood, fir, and the palms of the northern regions, mineralised by the action of the sea," he replied, sententiously.

"Can it be possible?"

"Yes," said the learned Professor, "what you see is called fossil wood."

"But then," cried I, after reflecting for a moment, "like the lignites, it must be as hard and heavy as iron, and therefore will certainly not float."

"Sometimes that is the case. Many of these woods have become true anthracites, but others again, like those you see before you, have only undergone one phase of fossil transformation. But there is no proof like demonstration," added my uncle, picking one or two of these precious waifs and casting them into the sea.

The piece of wood, after having disappeared for a moment, came to the surface, and floated about with the oscillation produced by wind and tide.

"Are you convinced?" said my uncle, with a self-satisfied smile.

"I am convinced," I cried, "that what I see is incredible."

The fact was that my journey into the interior of the earth was rapidly changing all preconceived notions, and day by day preparing me for the marvellous.

I should not have been surprised to have seen a fleet of native canoes afloat upon that silent sea.

The very next evening, thanks to the industry and ability of Hans, the raft was finished. It was about ten feet long and five feet wide. The beams bound together with stout ropes, were solid and firm, and once launched by our united efforts, the improvised vessel floated tranquilly upon the waters of what the Professor had well named the Central Sea.

A Journey to the Centre of the Earth

CHAPTER XXIX.

ON THE WATERS—A RAFT VOYAGE

ON the 13th of August we were up betimes. There was no time to be lost. We now had to inaugurate a new kind of locomotion, which would have the advantage of being rapid and not fatiguing.

A mast, made of two pieces of wood fastened together, to give additional strength, a yard made from another one, the sail a linen sheet from our bed. We were fortunately in no want of cordage, and the whole on trial appeared solid and seaworthy.

At six o'clock in the morning, when the eager and enthusiastic Professor gave the signal to embark, the victuals, the luggage, all our instruments, our weapons, and a goodly supply of sweet water, which we had collected from springs in the rocks, were placed on the raft.

Hans had, with considerable ingenuity, contrived a rudder, which enabled him to guide the floating apparatus with ease. He took the tiller, as a matter of course. The worthy man was as good a sailor as he was a guide and duck-hunter. I then let go the painter which held us to the shore, the sail was brought to the wind, and we made a rapid offing.

Our sea voyage had at length commenced; and once more we were making for distant and unknown regions.

Just as we were about to leave the little port where the raft had been constructed, my uncle, who was very strong as to geographic nomenclature, wanted to give it a name, and among others, suggested mine.

"Well," said I, "before you decide I have another to propose."

"Well; out with it."

"I should like to call it Gretchen. Port Gretchen will sound very well on our future map."

"Well then, Port Gretchen let it be," said the Professor.

And thus it was that the memory of my dear girl was attached to our adventurous and memorable expedition.

When we left the shore the wind was blowing from the northward and eastward. We went directly before the wind at a much greater speed than might have been expected from a raft. The dense layers of atmosphere at that depth had great propelling power and acted upon the sail with considerable force.

At the end of an hour, my uncle, who had been taking careful observations, was enabled to judge of the rapidity with which we moved. It was far beyond anything seen in the upper world.

"If," he said, "we continue to advance at our present rate, we shall have travelled at least thirty leagues in twenty-four hours. With a mere raft this is an almost incredible velocity."

I certainly was surprised, and without making any reply went forward upon the raft. Already the northern shore was fading away upon the edge of the horizon. The two shores appeared to separate more and more, leaving a wide and open space for our departure. Before me I could see nothing but the vast and apparently limitless sea—upon which we floated—the only living objects in sight.

Huge and dark clouds cast their grey shadows below—shadows which seemed to crush that colourless and sullen water by their weight. Anything more suggestive of gloom and of regions of nether darkness I never beheld. Silvery rays of electric light, reflected here and there upon some small spots of water, brought up luminous sparkles in the long wake of our cumbrous bark. Presently we were wholly out of sight of land, not a vestige could be seen, nor any indication of where we were going. So still and motionless did we seem without any distant point to fix our eyes on, that but for the phosphoric light at the wake of the raft I should have fancied that we were still and motionless.

But I knew that we were advancing at a very rapid rate.

About twelve o'clock in the day, vast collections of seaweed were discovered surrounding us on all sides. I was aware of the extraordinary vegetative power of these plants, which have been known to creep along the bottom of the great ocean, and stop the advance of large ships. But never were seaweeds ever seen, so gigantic and wonderful as those of the Central Sea. I could well imagine how, seen at a distance, tossing and heaving on the summit of the billows, the long lines of Algae have been taken for living things, and thus have been the fertile sources of the belief in sea serpents.

Our raft swept past great specimens of fucae or sea-wrack, from three to four thousand feet in length, immense, incredibly long, looking like snakes that stretched our far beyond our horizon. It afforded me great amusement to gaze on their variegated ribbon-like endless lengths. Hour after hour passed without our coming to the termination of these floating weeds. If my astonishment increased, my patience was well-nigh exhausted.

What natural force could possibly have produced such abnormal and extraordinary plants? What must have been the aspect of the globe, during the first centuries of its formation, when under the combined action of heat and humidity, the vegetable kingdom occupied its vast surface to the exclusion of everything else?

These were considerations of never-ending interest for the geologist and the philosopher.

All this while we were advancing on our journey; and at length night came; but as I had remarked the evening before, the luminous state of the atmosphere was in nothing diminished. Whatever was the cause, it was a phenomenon upon the duration of which we could calculate with certainty.

As soon as our supper had been disposed of, and some little speculative conversation indulged in, I stretched myself at the foot of the mass, and presently went to sleep.

Hans remained motionless at the tiller, allowing the raft to rise and fall on the waves. The wind being aft, and the sail square, all he had to do was to keep his oar in the centre.

Ever since we had taken our departure from the newly-named Port Gretchen, my worthy uncle had directed me to keep a regular log of our day's navigation, with instructions to put down even the most minute particulars, every interesting and curious phenomenon, the direction of the wind, our rate of sailing, the distance we went; in a word, every incident of our extraordinary voyage.

From our log, therefore, I tell the story of our voyage on the Central Sea.

Friday, August 14th. A steady breeze from the north-west. Raft progressing with extreme rapidity, and going perfectly straight. Coast still dimly visible about thirty leagues to leeward. Nothing to be seen beyond the horizon in front. The extraordinary intensity of the light neither increases nor diminishes. It is singularly stationary. The weather remarkably fine; that is to say, the clouds have ascended very high, and are light and fleecy,

and surrounded by an atmosphere resembling silver in fusion.

Thermometer + 32 degrees centigrade.

About twelve o'clock in the day our guide Hans having prepared and baited a hook, cast his line into the subterranean waters. The bait he used was a small piece of meat, by means of which he concealed his hook. Anxious as I was, I was for a long time doomed to disappointment. Were these waters supplied with fish or not? That was the important question. No—was my decided answer. Then there came a sudden and rather hard tug. Hans coolly drew it in, and with it a fish, which struggled violently to escape.

"A fish," cried my uncle, putting on his spectacles to examine it.

"It is a sturgeon!" I cried, "certainly a small sturgeon."

The Professor examined the fish carefully, noting every characteristic; and he did not coincide in my opinion. The fish had a flat head, round body, and the lower extremities covered with bony scales; its mouth was wholly without teeth, the pectoral fins, which were highly developed, sprouted direct from the body, which properly speaking had no tail. The animal certainly belonged to the order in which naturalists class the sturgeon, but it differed from that fish in many essential particulars.

My uncle, after all, was not mistaken. After a long and patient examination he said—

"This fish, my dear boy, belongs to a family which has been extinct for ages, and of which no trace has ever been found on earth, except fossil remains in the Devonian strata."

"You do not mean to say," I cried, "that we have captured a live specimen of a fish belonging to the primitive stock that existed before the deluge?"

"We have," said the Professor, who all this time was continuing his observations, "and you may see by careful examination that these fossil fish have no identity with existing species. To hold in one's hand, therefore, a living specimen of the order, is enough to make a naturalist happy for life."

"But," cried I, "to what family does it belong?"

"To the order of Ganoides—an order of fish having angular scales, covered with bright enamel—forming one of the family of the Cephalaspides , of the genus—"

"Well, sir," I remarked, as I noticed my uncle hesitated to conclude.

"To the Genus Pterychtis—yes, I am certain of it. Still, though I am confident of the correctness of my surmise, this fish offers to our notice

The Algae of the Central Sea.

a remarkable peculiarity, never known to exist in any other fish but those which are the natives of subterranean waters, wells, lakes in caverns, and such like hidden pools."

"And what may that be?"

"It is blind."

"Blind!" I cried, much surprised.

"Not only blind," continued the Professor, "but absolutely without organs of sight."

I now examined our discovery for myself. It was singular, to be sure, but it was really a fact. This, however, might be a solitary instance, I suggested. The hook was baited again and once more thrown into the water. This subterranean ocean must have been tolerably well supplied with fish, for in two hours we took a large number of Pterychtis, as well as other fish belonging to another supposed extinct family—the Dipterides (a genus of fish, furnished with two fins only, whence the name,) though my uncle could not class it exactly. All, without exception, however, were blind. This unexpected capture enabled us to renew our stock of provisions in a very satisfactory way.

We were now convinced that this Subterranean Sea contained only fish known to us as fossil specimens—and fish and reptiles alike, were all the more perfect the farther back they dated their origin.

We began to hope that we should find some of those Saurians which science has succeeded in reconstructing from bits of bone or cartilage.

I took up the telescope and carefully examined the horizon—looked over the whole sea; it was utterly and entirely deserted. Doubtless we were still too near the coast.

After an examination of the ocean, I looked upward, towards the strange and mysterious sky. Why should not one of the birds, reconstructed by the immortal Cuvier, flap his stupendous wings aloft in the dull strata of subterranean air? It would, of course, find quite sufficient food from the fish in the sea. I gazed for some time upon the void above. It was as silent and as deserted as the shores we had but lately left.

Nevertheless, though I could neither see nor discover anything, my imagination carried me away into wild hypotheses. I was in a kind of waking dream. I thought I saw on the surface of the water those enormous antediluvian turtles as big as floating islands. Upon those dull and sombre shores passed a spectral row of the mammifers of early days, the great Leptotherium found in the cavernous hollow of the Brazilian hills, the Mesicotherium, a native of the glacial regions of Siberia.

Farther on, the pachydermatous Lophrodon,

that gigantic tapir, which concealed itself behind rocks, ready to do battle for its prey with the Anoplotherium, a singular animal partaking of the nature of the rhinoceros, the horse, the hippopotamus and the camel.

There was the giant Mastodon, twisting and turning his horrid trunk, with which he crushed the rocks of the shore to powder, while the Megatherium—his back raised like a cat in a passion, his enormous claws stretched out, dug into the earth for food, at the same time that he awoke the sonorous echoes of the whole place with his terrible roar.

Higher up still, the first monkey ever seen on the face of the globe clambered, gambling and playing up the granite hills. Still farther away, ran the Pterodactyl, with the winged hand, gliding or rather sailing through the dense and compressed air like a huge bat.

Above all, near the leaden granitic sky, were immense birds, more powerful than the casoar, giants to the ostrich, which spread their mighty wings and fluttered against the huge stone vault of the inland sea.

I thought, such was the effect of my imagination, that I saw this whole tribe of antediluvian creatures. I carried myself back to far ages, long before man existed—when, in fact, the earth was in too imperfect a state for him to live upon it.

My dream was of countless ages before the existence of man. The mammifers first disappeared, then the mighty birds, then the reptiles of the secondary period, presently the fish, the crustacea, the molluscs, and finally the vertebrata. The zoophytes of the period of transition in their turn sank into annihilation.

The whole panorama of the world's life before the historic period, seemed to be born over again, and mine was the only human heart that beat in this unpeopled world! There were no more seasons; there were no more climates; the natural heat of the world increased unceasingly, and neutralised that of the great radiant Sun.

Vegetation was exaggerated in an extraordinary manner. I passed like a shadow in the midst of brushwood as lofty as the giant trees of California, and trod underfoot the moist and humid soil, reeking with a rank and varied vegetation.

I leaned against the huge column-like trunks of giant trees, to which those of Canada were as ferns. Whole ages passed, hundreds upon hundreds of years were concentrated into a single day.

Next, unrolled before me like a panorama, came the great and wondrous series of

The Antediluvian World.

terrestrial transformations. Plants disappeared; the granitic rocks lost all trace of solidity; the liquid state was suddenly substituted for that which had before existed. This was caused by intense heat acting on the organic matter of the earth. The waters flowed over the whole surface of the globe; they boiled; they were volatilised, or turned into vapour; a kind of steam-cloud wrapped the whole earth, the globe itself becoming at last nothing but one huge sphere of gas, indescribable in colour, between white heat and red, as big and as brilliant as the sun.

In the very centre of this prodigious mass, fourteen hundred thousand times as large as our globe, I was whirled round in space, and brought into close conjunction with the planets. My body was subtilised, or rather became volatile, and commingled in a state of atomic vapour, with the prodigious clouds, which rushed forward like a mighty comet into infinite space!

What an extraordinary dream! Where would it finally take me? My feverish hand began to write down the marvellous details—details more like the imaginings of a lunatic than anything sober and real. I had during this period of hallucination forgotten everything—the Professor, the guide, and the raft on which we were floating. My mind was in a state of semi-oblivion.

"What is the matter, Harry?" said my uncle, suddenly.

My eyes, which were wide open like those of a somnambulist, were fixed upon him, but I did not see him, nor could I clearly make out anything around me.

"Take care, my boy," again cried my uncle, "you will fall into the sea."

As he uttered these words, I felt myself seized on the other side by the firm hand of our devoted guide. Had it not been for the presence of mind of Hans, I must infallibly have fallen into the waves and been drowned.

"Have you gone mad?" cried my uncle shaking me on the other side.

"What—what is the matter?" I said at last, coming to myself.

"Are you ill, Henry?" continued the Professor in an anxious tone.

"No-no; but I have had an extraordinary dream. It, however, has passed away. All now seems well," I added, looking around me with strangely puzzled eyes.

"All right," said my uncle; "a beautiful breeze, a splendid sea. We are going along at a rapid rate, and if I am not out in my calculations we shall soon see land. I shall not be sorry to exchange the narrow limits of our raft for the mysterious strand of the Subterranean Ocean."

As my uncle uttered these words, I rose and carefully scanned the horizon. But the line of water was still confounded with the lowering clouds that hung aloft, and in the distance appeared to touch the edge of the water.

A Journey to the Centre of the Earth

CHAPTER XXX.

TERRIFIC SAURIAN COMBAT

SATURDAY, August 15. The sea still retains its uniform monotony. The same leaden hue, the same eternal glare from above. No indication of land being in sight. The horizon appears to retreat before us, more and more as we advance.

My head still dull and heavy from the effects of my extraordinary dream, which I cannot as yet banish from my mind.

The Professor, who has not dreamed, is, however, in one of his morose and unaccountable humours. Spends his time in scanning the horizon, at every point of the compass. His telescope is raised every moment to his eyes, and when he finds nothing to give any clue to our whereabouts, he assumes a Napoleonic attitude and walks anxiously.

I remarked that my uncle, the Professor, had a strong tendency to resume his old impatient character, and I could not but make a note of this disagreeable circumstance in my Journal. I saw clearly that it had required all the influence of my danger and suffering, to extract from him one scintillation of humane feeling. Now that I was quite recovered, his original nature had conquered and obtained the upper hand.

And, after all, what had he to be angry and annoyed about, now more than at any other time? Was not the journey being accomplished under the most favourable circumstance? Was not the raft progressing with the most marvellous rapidity?

What, then, could be the matter? After one or two preliminary hems, I determined to inquire.

"You seem uneasy, uncle," said I, when for about the hundredth time he put down his telescope and walked up and down, muttering to himself.

"No, I am not uneasy," he replied in a dry harsh tone, "by no means."

"Perhaps I should have said impatient," I replied, softening the force of my remark.

"Enough to make me so, I think."

"And yet we are advancing at a rate seldom attained by a raft," I remarked.

"What matters that?" cried my uncle. "I am not vexed at the rate we go at, but I am annoyed to find the sea so much faster than I expected."

I then recollected that the Professor, before

our departure, had estimated the length of this Subterranean Ocean, as at most about thirty leagues. Now we had travelled at least over thrice that distance without discovering any trace of the distant shore. I began to understand my uncle's anger.

"We are not going down," suddenly exclaimed the Professor. "We are not progressing with out great discoveries. All this is utter loss of time. After all, I did not come from home to undertake a party of pleasure. This voyage on a raft over a pond annoys and wearies me."

He called this adventurous journey a party of pleasure, and this great Inland Sea a pond!

"But," argued I, "if we have followed the route indicated by the great Saknussemm, we cannot be going far wrong."

"'That is the question,' as the great, the immortal Shakspere, has it. Are we following the route indicated by that wondrous sage? Did Saknussemm ever fall in with this great sheet of water? If he did, did he cross it? If he did, did he cross it? I begin to fear that the rivulet we adopted for a guide has led us wrong."

"In any case, we can never regret having come thus far. It is worth the whole journey to have enjoyed this magnificent spectacle—it is something to have seen."

"I care nothing about seeing, nor about magnificent spectacles. I came down into the interior of the earth with an object, and that object I mean to attain. Don't talk to me about admiring scenery, or any other sentimental trash."

After this I thought it well to hold my tongue, and allow the Professor to bite his lips until the blood came, without further remark.

At six o'clock in the evening, our matter-of-fact guide, Hans, asked for his week's salary, and receiving his three rix-dollars, put them carefully in his pocket. He was perfectly contented and satisfied.

Sunday, 16th August. Nothing new to record. The same weather as before. The wind has a slight tendency to freshen up, with signs of an approaching gale. When I awoke, my first observation was in regard to the intensity of the light. I keep on fearing, day after day, that the extraordinary electric phenomenon should

The Monster lifts the raft right out of the water.

become first obscured, and then go wholly out, leaving us in total darkness. Nothing, however, of the kind occurs. The shadow of the raft, its mast and sails, is clearly distinguished on the surface of the water.

This wondrous sea is, after all, infinite in its extent. It must be quite as wide as the Mediterranean—or perhaps even as the great Atlantic Ocean. Why, after all, should it not be so?

My uncle has on more than one occasion, tried deep sea soundings. He tied the cross of one of our heaviest crowbars to the extremity of a cord, which he allowed to run out to the extent of two hundred fathoms. We had the greatest difficulty in hoisting in our novel kind of lead.

When the crowbar was finally dragged on board, Hans called my attention to some singular marks upon its surface. The piece of iron looked as if it had been crushed between two very hard substances.

I looked at out worthy guide with an inquiring glance.

"Tänder," said he.

Of course I was at a loss to understand. I turned round towards my uncle, absorbed in gloomy reflections. I had little wish to disturb him from his reverie. I accordingly turned once more towards our worthy Icelander.

Hans very quietly and significantly opened his mouth once or twice, as if in the act of biting, and in this way made me understand his meaning.

"Teeth!" cried I, with stupefaction, as I examined the bar of iron with more attention.

Yes. There can be no doubt about the matter. The indentations on the bar of iron are the marks of teeth! What jaws must the owner of such molars be possessed of! Have we, then, come upon a monster of unknown species, which still exists within the vast waste of waters—a monster more voracious than a shark, more terrible and bulky than the whale. I am unable to withdraw my eyes, from the bar of iron, actually half crushed!

Is, then, my dream about to come true—a dread and terrible reality?

All day my thoughts were bent upon these speculations, and my imagination scarcely regained a degree of calmness and power of reflection until after a sleep of many hours.

This day, as on other Sundays, we observed as a day of rest and pious meditation.

Monday, August 17th. I have been trying to realise from memory the particular instincts of those antediluvian animals of the secondary period, which succeeding to the mollusca, to the crustacea, and to the fish, preceded the appearance of the race of mammifers. The generation of reptiles then reigned supreme upon the earth. These hideous monsters ruled everything in the seas of the secondary period, which formed the strata of which the Jura mountains are composed. Nature had endowed them with perfect organisation. What a gigantic structure was theirs; what vast and prodigious strength they possessed!

The existing Saurians, which include all such reptiles as lizards, crocodiles, and alligators, even the largest and most formidable of their class, are but feeble imitations of their mighty sires, the animals of ages long ago. If there were giants in the days of old, there were also gigantic animals.

I shuddered as I evolved from my mind the idea and recollection of these awful monsters. No eye of man had seen them in the flesh. They took their walks abroad upon the face of the earth thousands of ages before man came into existence, and their fossil bones, discovered in the limestone, have allowed us to reconstruct them anatomically, and thus to get some faint idea of their colossal formation.

I recollect once seeing in the great Museum of Hamburg the skeleton of one of these wonderful Saurians. It measured no less than thirty feet from the nose to the tail. Am I, then, an inhabitant of the earth of the present day, destined to find myself face to face with a representative of this antediluvian family? I can scarcely believe it possible; can hardly believe it true. And yet these marks of powerful teeth upon the bar of iron! can there be a doubt from their shape that the bite is the bite of a crocodile?

My eyes stare wildly and with terror upon the subterranean sea. Every moment I expect one of these monsters to rise from its vast cavernous depths.

I fancy that the worthy Professor in some measure shares my notions, if not my fears, for, after an attentive examination of the crowbar, he cast his eyes rapidly over the mighty and mysterious ocean.

"What could possess him to leave the land," I thought, "as if the depth of this water was of any importance to us. No doubt he has disturbed some terrible monster in his watery home, and perhaps we may pay dearly for our temerity."

Anxious to be prepared for the worst, I examined our weapons, and saw that they were in a fit state for use. My uncle looked on at me and nodded his head approvingly. He, too, has noticed what we have to fear.

Already the uplifting of the waters on the

surface indicates that something is in motion below. The danger approaches. It comes nearer and nearer. It behoves us to be on the watch.

Tuesday, August 18. Evening came at last, the hour, when the desire for sleep caused our eyelids to be heavy. Night there is not, properly speaking, in this place, any more than there is in summer in the arctic regions. Hans, however, is immovable at the rudder. When he snatches a moment of rest I really cannot say. I take advantage of his vigilance to take some little repose.

But two hours after I was awakened from a heavy sleep by an awful shock. The raft appeared to have struck upon a sunken rock. It was lifted right out of the water by some wondrous and mysterious power, and then started off twenty fathoms distant.

"Eh, what is it?" cried my uncle starting up, "are we shipwrecked, or what?"

Hans raised his hand and pointed to where, about two hundred yards off, a huge black mass was moving up and down. I looked with awe. My worst fears were realised.

"It is a colossal monster!" I cried clasping my hands.

"Yes," cried the agitated Professor, "and there yonder is a huge sea lizard of terrible size and shape."

"And farther on behold a prodigious crocodile. Look at his hideous jaws, and that row of monstrous teeth. Ha! he has gone."

"A whale! a whale!" shouted the Professor, "I can see her enormous fins. See, see how she blows air and water!"

Two liquid columns rose to a vast height above the level of the sea, into which they fell with a terrific crash, waking up the echoes of that awful place. We stood still—surprised, stupefied, terror-stricken at the sight of this group of fearful marine monsters, more hideous in the reality than in my dream. They were of supernatural dimensions; the very smallest of the whole party could with ease have crushed our raft and ourselves with a single bite.

Hans seizing the rudder which had flown our of his hand, puts it hard a-weather in order to escape from such dangerous vicinity; but no sooner does he do so, than he finds he is flying from Scylla to Charybdis. To leeward is a turtle about forty feet wide, and a serpent quite as long, with an enormous and hideous head peering from out the waters.

Look which way we will, it is impossible for us to fly. The fearful reptiles advanced upon us; they turned and twisted about the raft with awful rapidity. They formed around our devoted vessel a series of concentric circles. I took up my rifle in desperation. But what effect can a rifleball produce upon the armour scales with which the bodies of these horrid monsters are covered?

We remain still and dumb from utter horror. They advance upon us, nearer and nearer. Our fate appears certain, fearful and terrible. On one side the mighty crocodile, on the other the great sea serpent. The rest of the fearful crowd of marine prodigies have plunged beneath the briny waves and disappeared!

I am about at all risks to fire, and try the effect of a shot. Hans the guide, however, interfered by a sign to check me. The two hideous and ravenous monsters passed within fifty fathoms of the raft, and then made a rush at one another—their fury and rage preventing them from seeing us.

The combat commenced. We distinctly make out every action of the two hideous monsters.

But to my excited imagination the other animals appeared about to take part in the fierce and deadly struggle—the monster, the whale, the lizard, and the turtle. I distinctly saw them every moment. I pointed them out to the Icelander. But he only shook his head.

"Tva," he said.

"What—two only does he say. Surely he is mistaken," I cried, in a tone of wonder.

"He is quite right," replied my uncle coolly and philosophically, examining the terrible duel with his telescope and speaking as if he were in a lecture room.

"How can that be?"

"Yes, it is so. The first of these hideous monsters has the snout of a porpoise, the head of a lizard, the teeth of a crocodile; and it is this that has deceived us. It is the most fearful of all antediluvian reptiles, the world-renowned Ichthyosaurus or Great Fish Lizard."

"And the other?"

"The other is a monstrous serpent, concealed under the hard vaulted shell of the turtle, the terrible enemy of its fearful rival, the Plesiosaurus, or Sea Crocodile."

Hans was quite right. The two monsters only, disturbed the surface of the sea!

At last have mortal eyes gazed upon two reptiles of the great primitive ocean! I see the flaming red eyes of the Ichthyosaurus, each as big, or bigger than a man's head. Nature in its infinite wisdom had gifted this wondrous marine animal with an optical apparatus of extreme power, capable of resisting the pressure of the heavy layers of water which rolled over him in the depth of the ocean where he usually fed. It has by some authors truly

These animals fought with fury.

been called the whale of the Saurian race, for it is as big and quick in its motions as our king of the seas. This one measures not less than a hundred feet in length, and I can form some idea of his girth, when I see him lift his prodigious tail out of the waters. His jaw is of awful size and strength, and according to the best-informed naturalists, it does not contain less than a hundred and eighty-two teeth.

The other was the mighty Plesiosaurus, a serpent with a cylindrical trunk, with a short stumpy tail, with fins like a bank of oars in a Roman galley.

Its whole body covered by the carapace or shell, and its neck, as flexible as that of a swan, rose more than thirty feet above the waves, a tower of animated flesh!

These animals attacked one another with inconceivable fury. Such a combat was never *seen* before by mortal eyes, and to us who did see it, it appeared more like the phantasmagoric creation of a dream than anything else. They raised mountains of water, which dashed in spray over the raft, already tossed to and fro by the waves. Twenty times we seemed on the point of being upset and hurled headlong into the waves. Hideous hisses appeared to shake the gloomy granite roof of that mighty cavern —hisses which carried terror to our hearts. The awful combatants held each other in a tight embrace. I could not make out one from the other. Still the combat could not last for ever; and woe unto us, whichsoever became the victor.

One hour, two hours, three hours passed away, without any decisive result. The struggle continued with the same deadly tenacity, but without apparent result. The deadly opponents now approached, now drew away from the raft. Once or twice we fancied they were about to leave us altogether, but instead of that, they came nearer and nearer.

We crouched on the raft ready to fire at them at a moment's notice, poor as the prospect of hurting or terrifying them was. Still we were determined not to perish without a struggle.

Suddenly the Ichthyosaurus and the Plesiosaurus disappeared beneath the waves, leaving behind them a maelstrom in the midst of the sea. We were very nearly drawn down by the indraught of the water!

Several minutes elapsed before anything was again seen. Was this wonderful combat to end in the depths of the ocean? Was the last act of this terrible drama to take place without spectators?

It was impossible for us to say.

Suddenly, at no great distance from us, an enormous mass rises out of the waters—the head of the great Plesiosaurus. The terrible monster is now wounded unto death. I can see nothing now of his enormous body. All that could be distinguished was his serpent-like neck, which he twisted and curled in all the agonies of death. Now he struck the waters with it as if it had been a gigantic whip, and then again wriggled like a worm cut in two. The water was spurted up to a great distance in all directions. A great portion of it swept over our raft and nearly blinded us. But soon the end of the beast approached nearer and nearer; his movements slackened visibly; his contortions almost ceased; and at last the body of the mighty snake lay an inert, dead mass on the surface of the now calm and placid waters.

As for the Ichthyosaurus, has he gone down to his mighty cavern under the sea to rest, or will he reappear to destroy us?

This question remained unanswered. And we had breathing time.

A Journey to the Centre of the Earth

CHAPTER XXXI.

THE SEA MONSTER

WEDNESDAY, August 19. Fortunately the wind, which at the present blows with great violence, has allowed us to escape from the scene of the unparalleled and extraordinary struggle. Hans with his usual imperturbable calm remained at the helm. My uncle, who for a short time had been withdrawn from his absorbing reverie by the novel incidents of this sea-fight, fell back again apparently into a brown study. All this time, however, his eyes were fixed impatiently on the wide-spread ocean.

Our voyage now became monotonous and uniform. Dull as it has become, I have no desire to have it broken by any repetition of the perils and adventures of yesterday.

Thursday, August 20. The wind is now N.N.E., and blows very irregularly. It has changed to fitful gusts. The temperature is exceedingly high. We are now progressing at the average rate of about ten miles and a half per hour.

About twelve o'clock a distant sound as of thunder fell upon our ears. I make a note of the fact without even venturing a suggestion as to its cause. It was one continued roar as of a sea falling over mighty rocks.

"Far off in the distance," said the Professor dogmatically, "there is some rock or some island against which the sea, lashed to fury by the wind, is breaking violently."

Hans, without saying a word, clambered to the top of the mast, but could make out nothing. The ocean was level in every direction as far as the eye could reach.

Three hours passed away without any sign to indicate what might be before us. The sound began to assume that of a mighty cataract.

I expressed my opinion on this point strongly to my uncle. He merely shook his head. I, however, am strongly impressed by a conviction that I am not wrong. Are we advancing towards some mighty waterfall which shall cast us into the abyss. Probably this mode of descending into the abyss may be agreeable to the Professor, because it would be something like the vertical descent he is so eager to make. I entertain a very different opinion.

Whatever be the truth, it is certain that not many leagues distant there must be some very extraordinary phenomenon, for as we advance the roar becomes something mighty and stupendous. Is it in the water, or in the air?

I cast hasty glances aloft at the suspended vapours, and I seek to penetrate their mighty depths. But the vault above is tranquil. The clouds, which are now elevated to the very summit, appear utterly still and motionless, and completely lost in the irradiation of electric light. It is necessary, therefore, to seek for the cause of this phenomenon elsewhere.

I examine the horizon, now perfectly calm, pure and free from all haze. Its aspect still remains unchanged. But if this awful noise proceeds from a cataract—if, so to speak in plain English, this vast interior ocean is precipitated into a lower basin—if these tremendous roars are produced by the noise of falling waters, the current would increase in activity, and its increasing swiftness would give me some idea of the extent of the peril with which we are menaced. I consult the current. It simply does not exist: there is no such thing. An empty bottle cast into the water lies to leeward without motion.

About four o'clock Hans rises, clambers up the mast and reaches the truck itself. From this elevated position his looks are cast around. They take in a vast circumference of the ocean. At last, his eyes remain fixed. His face expresses no astonishment, but his eyes slightly dilate.

"He has seen something at last," cried my uncle.

"I think so," I replied.

Hans came down, stood beside us and pointed with his right hand to the south.

"Der nere," he said.

"There," replied my uncle.

And seizing his telescope he looked at it with great attention for about a minute, which to me appeared an age. I knew not what to think or expect.

"Yes, yes," he cried in a tone of considerable surprise, "there it is."

"What?" I asked.

"A tremendous spurt of water rising out of the waves."

"Some other marine monster," I cried, already alarmed.

"Perhaps."

A majestic geyser. The geyser of the Central Sea.

"Then let us steer more to the westward, for we know what we have to expect from antediluvian animals," was my eager reply.

"Go ahead," said my uncle.

I turned towards Hans. Hans was at the tiller steering with his usual imperturbable calm.

Nevertheless, if from the distance which separated us from this creature, a distance which must be estimated at not less than a dozen leagues, and this spurting of water proceeded from the pranks of some antediluvian animal, his dimensions must be something preternatural. To fly is, therefore, the course to be suggested by ordinary prudence. But we have not come into that part of the world to be prudent. Such is my uncle's determination.

We, accordingly, continued to advance. The nearer we come, the loftier is the spouting water. What monster can fill himself with such huge volumes of water, and then unceasingly spout them our in such lofty jets?

At eight o'clock in the evening, reckoning as above ground, where there is day and night, we are not more than two leagues from the mighty beast. Its long, black, enormous, mountainous body, lies on the top of the water like an island. But then sailors have been said to have gone ashore on sleeping whales, mistaking them for land. Is it illusion, or is it fear? Its length cannot be less than a thousand fathoms. What, then, is this cetaceous monster of which no Cuvier ever thought?

It is quite motionless and presents the appearance of sleep. The sea seems unable to lift him upwards; it is rather the waves which break on his huge and gigantic frame. The water-spout, rising to a height of five hundred feet, breaks in spray with a dull, sullen roar.

We advance, like senseless lunatics, towards this mighty mass.

I honestly confess that I was abjectly afraid. I declared that I would go no farther. I threatened in my terror to cut the sheet of the sail. I attacked the Professor with considerable acrimony, calling him foolhardy, mad, I know not what. He made no answer.

Suddenly the imperturbable Hans once more pointed his finger to the menacing object.

"*Holme!*"

"An island!" cried my uncle.

"An island?" I replied, shrugging my shoulders at this poor attempt at deception.

"Of course it is," cried my uncle, bursting into a loud and joyous laugh.

"But the water spout?"

"Geyser," said Hans.

"Yes, of course—a geyser," replied my uncle, still laughing, "a geyser like those common in Iceland. Jets like this are the great wonders of the country."

At first I would not allow that I had been so grossly deceived. What could be more ridiculous than to have taken an island for a marine monster? But kick as one may, one must yield to evidence, and I was finally convinced of my error. It was nothing, after all, but a natural phenomenon.

As we approached nearer and nearer, the dimensions of the liquid sheaf of waters became truly grand and stupendous. The island, had, at a distance, presented the appearance of an enormous whale, whose head rose high above the waters. The geyser, a word the Icelanders pronounce geysir, and which signifies fury, rose majestically from its summit. Dull detonations are heard every now and then, and the enormous jet, taken as it were with sudden fury, shakes its plume of vapour, and bounds into the first layer of the clouds. It is alone. Neither spurts of vapour nor hot springs surround it, and the whole volcanic power of that region is concentrated in one sublime column. The rays of electric light mix with this dazzling sheaf, every drop as it falls assuming the prismatic colours of the rainbow.

"Let us go on shore," said the Professor, after some minutes of silence.

It is necessary, however, to take great precaution, in order to avoid the weight of falling waters, which would cause the raft to founder in an instant. Hans, however, steers admirably, and brings us to the other extremity of the island.

I was the first to leap on the rock. My uncle followed, while the eider-duck hunter remained still, like a man above any childish sources of astonishment. We were now walking on granite mixed with silicious sandstone; the soil shivered under our feet like the sides of boilers in which over-heated steam is forcibly confined. It is burning. We soon came in sight of the little central bason from which rose the geyser. I plunged a thermometer into the water which ran bubbling from the centre, and it marked a heat of a hundred and sixty-three degrees!

This water, therefore, came from some place where the heat was intense. This was singularly in contradiction with the theories of Professor Hardwigg. I could not help telling him my opinion on the subject.

"Well," said he sharply, "and what does this prove against my doctrine?"

"Nothing," replied I drily, seeing that I was running my head against a foregone conclusion.

Nevertheless, I am compelled to confess that until now we have been most remarkably fortunate, and that this voyage is being accomplished in most favourable conditions of temperature; but it appears evident, in fact, certain, that we shall sooner or later arrive at one of those regions, where the central heat will reach its utmost limits, and will go far beyond all the possible gradations of thermometers.

Visions of the Hades of the ancients, believed to be in the centre of the earth, floated through my imagination.

We shall however see what we shall see. That is the Professor's favourite phrase now. Having christened the volcanic island by the name of his nephew, the leader of the expedition turned away and gave the signal for embarkation.

I stood still, however, for some minutes, gazing upon the magnificent geyser. I soon was able to perceive that the upward tendency of the water was irregular; now it diminished in intensity, and then, suddenly it regained new vigour, which I attributed to the variation of the pressure of the accumulated vapours in its reservoir.

At last we took our departure, going carefully round the projecting, and rather dangerous, rocks of the southern side. Hans had taken advantage of this brief halt to repair the raft. Not before it was required.

Before we took our final departure from the island, however, I made some observations to calculate the distance we had gone over, and I put them down in my Journal. Since we left Port Gretchen, we had travelled two hundred and seventy leagues—more than eight hundred miles—on this great inland sea; we were therefore six hundred and twenty leagues from Iceland, and exactly under England.

A Journey to the Centre of the Earth

CHAPTER XXXII.

THE BATTLE OF THE ELEMENTS

FRIDAY, August 21st. This morning the magnificent geyser had wholly disappeared. The wind had freshened up, and we were fast leaving the neighbourhood of Henry's Island. Even the roaring sound of the mighty column was lost to the ear.

The weather, if, under the circumstances, we may use such an expression, is about to change very suddenly. The atmosphere is being gradually loaded with vapours, which carry with them the electricity formed by the constant evaporation of the saline waters; the clouds are slowly but sensibly falling towards the sea, and are assuming a dark olive texture; the electric rays can scarcely pierce through the opaque curtain which has fallen like a drop-scene before this wondrous theatre, on the stage of which another and terrible drama is soon to be enacted. This time it is no fight of animals; it is the fearful battle of the elements.

I feel that I am very peculiarly influenced, as all creatures are on land when a deluge is about to take place.

The cumuli, a perfectly oval kind of cloud, piled upon the south, presented a most awful and sinister appearance; with the pitiless aspect often seen before a storm. The air is extremely heavy; the sea is comparatively calm.

In the distance, the clouds have assumed the appearance of enormous balls of cotton, or rather pods, piled one above the other in picturesque confusion. By degrees, they appear to swell out, break, and gain in number what they lose in grandeur; their heaviness is so great that they are unable to lift themselves from the horizon; but under the influence of the upper currents of air, they are gradually broken up, become much darker, and then present the appearance of one single layer of a formidable character; now and then a lighter cloud, still lit up from above, rebounds upon this grey carpet, and is lost in the opaque mass.

There can be not doubt that the entire atmosphere is saturated with electric fluid; I am myself wholly impregnated; my hairs literally stand on end as if under the influence of a galvanic battery. If one of my companions ventured to touch me, I think he would receive rather a violent and unpleasant shock.

About ten o'clock in the morning, the symptoms of the storm became more thorough and decisive; the wind appeared to soften down as if to take breath for a renewed attack; the vast funereal pall above us looked like a huge bag—like the cave of AEolus, in which the storm was collecting its forces for the attack.

I tried all I could not to believe in the menacing signs of the sky, and yet I could not avoid saying, as it were involuntarily—

"I believe we are going to have bad weather."

The Professor made me no answer. He was in a horrible, in a detestable humour—to see the ocean stretching interminably before his eyes. On hearing my words he simply shrugged his shoulders.

"We shall have a tremendous storm," I said again, pointing to the horizon. "These clouds are falling lower and lower upon the sea, as if to crush it."

A great silence prevailed. The wind wholly ceased. Nature assumed a dead calm, and ceased to breathe. Upon the mast, where I noticed a sort of slight *ignis fatuus*, the sail hangs in loose heavy folds. The raft is motionless in the midst of a dark heavy sea—without undulation, without motion. It is as still as glass. But as we are making no progress, what is the use of keeping up the sail, which may be the cause of our perdition if the tempest should suddenly strike us without warning.

"Let us lower the sail," I said, "it is only an act of common prudence."

"No—no," cried my uncle, in an exasperated tone, "a hundred times, no. Let the wind strike us and do its worst, let the storm sweep us away where it will—only let me see the glimmer of some coast—of some rocky cliffs, even if they dash our raft into a thousand pieces. No! keep up the sail—no matter what happens."

These words were scarcely uttered, when the southern horizon underwent a sudden and violent change. The long accumulated vapours were resolved into water, and the air required to fill up the void produced became a wild and raging tempest.

It came from the most distant corners of the mighty cavern. It raged from every point of the compass. It roared; it yelled; it shrieked with

A Hurricane in the centre of the Earth. An electric storm.

glee as of demons let loose. The darkness increased and became indeed darkness visible.

The raft rose and fell with the storm, and bounded over the waves. My uncle was cast headlong upon the deck. I with great difficulty dragged myself towards him. He was holding on with might and main to the end of a cable, and appeared to gaze with pleasure and delight at the spectacle of the unchained elements.

Hans never moved a muscle. His long hair driven hither and thither by the tempest and scattered wildly over his motionless face, gave him a most extraordinary appearance—for every single hair was illuminated by little sparkling sprigs.

His countenance presents the extraordinary appearance of an antediluvian man, a true contemporary of the megatherium.

Still the mast holds good against the storm. The sail spreads out and fills like a soap bubble about to burst. The raft rushes on at a pace impossible to estimate, but still less swiftly than the body of water displaced beneath it, the rapidity of which may be seen by the lines which fly right and left in the wake.

"The sail, the sail!" I cried, making a trumpet of my hands, and then endeavouring to lower it.

"Let it alone!" said my uncle, more exasperated than ever.

"*Nej,*" said Hans, gently shaking his head.

Nevertheless, the rain formed a roaring cataract before this horizon of which we were in search, and to which we were rushing like madmen.

But before this wilderness of waters reached us, the mighty veil of cloud was torn in twain; the sea began to foam wildly; and the electricity, produced by some vast and extraordinary chemical action in the upper layer of cloud, is brought into play. To the fearful claps of thunder are added dazzling flashes of lightning, such as I had never seen. The flashes crossed one another, hurled from every side; while the thunder came pealing like an echo. The mass of vapour becomes incandescent; the hail stones which strike the metal of our boots and our weapons, are actually luminous; the waves as they rise appear to be fire-eating monsters, beneath which seethes an intense fire, their crests surmounted by combs of flame.

My eyes are dazzled, blinded by the intensity of light, my ears are deafened by the awful roar of the elements. I am compelled to hold on to the mast, which bends like a reed beneath the violence of the storm, to which none ever before seen by mariners bore any resemblance.

*   *   *   *   *

Here my travelling notes become very incomplete, loose, and vague. I have only been able to make out one or two fugitive observations, dotted down in a mere mechanical way. But even their brevity, even their obscurity, show the emotions which overcame me.

*   *   *   *   *

Sunday, August 23. Where have we got to? In what region are we wandering? We are still carried forward with inconceivable rapidity.

The night has been fearful, something not to be described. The storm shows no signs of cessation. We exist in the midst of an uproar which has no name. The detonations as of artillery are incessant. Our ears literally bleed. We are unable to exchange a word, or hear each other speak.

The lightning never ceases to flash for a single instant. I can see the zigzags after a rapid dart, strike the arched roof of this mightiest of mighty vaults. If it were to give way and fall upon us! Other lightnings plunge their forked streaks in every direction, and take the form of globes of fire, which explode like bomb shells over a beleaguered city. The general crash and roar do not apparently increase; it has already gone far beyond what human ear can appreciate. If all the powder magazines in the world were to explode together, it would be impossible for us to hear worse noise.

There is a constant emission of light from the storm-clouds; the electric matter is incessantly released; evidently the gaseous principles of the air are out of order; innumerable columns of water rush up like waterspouts, and fall back upon the surface of the ocean in foam.

Whither are we going? My uncle still lies at full length upon the raft, without speaking—without taking any note of time.

The heat increases. I look at the thermometer, to my surprise it indicates—*The exact figure is here rubbed out in my manuscript.*

Monday, August 24. This terrible storm will never end. Why should not this state of the atmosphere, so dense and murky, once modified, again remain definitive?

We are utterly broken and harassed by fatigue. Hans remains just as usual. The raft runs to the south-east invariably. We have now already run two hundred leagues from the newly-discovered island.

About twelve o'clock the storm became worse than ever. We are obliged now to fasten every bit of cargo tightly on the deck of the raft, or everything would be swept away. We tie ourselves to the mast, each man lashing the other. The waves drive over us, so that several times we are actually under water.

We had been under the painful necessity of abstaining from speech for three days and three nights. We opened our mouths, we moved our lips, but no sound came. Even when we placed our mouths to each other's ears it was the same.

The wind carried the voice away.

My uncle once contrived to get his head close to mine after several almost vain endeavours. He appeared to my nearly exhausted senses to articulate some word. I had a notion, more from intuition than anything else, that he said to me, "we are lost."

I took out my note book, from which under the most desperate circumstances I never parted, and wrote a few words as legibly as I could—

"Take in sail."

With a deep sigh he nodded his head and acquiesced.

His head had scarcely time to fall back in the position from which he had momentarily raised it, than a disc or ball of fire appeared on the very edge of the raft—our devoted, our doomed craft. The mast and sail are carried away bodily, and I see them swept away to a prodigious height like a kite.

We were frozen, actually shivered with terror. The ball of fire, half white, half azure coloured, about the size of a ten-inch bombshell, moved along, turning with prodigious rapidity to leeward of the storm. It ran about here, there and everywhere, it clambered up one of the bulwarks of the raft, it leaped upon the sack of provisions, and then finally descended lightly, fell like a foot ball and landed on our powder barrel.

Horrible situation. An explosion of course was now inevitable.

By heaven's mercy, it is not so.

The dazzling disc moves on one side, it approaches Hans, who looked at it with singular fixity; then it approached my uncle, who cast himself on his knees to avoid it; it came towards me, as I stood pale and shuddering in the dazzling light and heat; it pirouetted round my feet, which I endeavoured to withdraw.

An odour of nitrous gas filled the whole air; it penetrated to the throat, to the lungs. I felt ready to choke.

Why is it that I cannot withdraw my feet? Are they rivetted to the flooring of the raft?

No.

The fall of the electric globe has turned all the iron on board into loadstones—the instruments, the tools, the arms are clanging together with awful and horrible noise; the nails of my heavy boots adhere closely to the plate of iron incrustated in the wood. I cannot withdraw my foot.

It is the old story over again of the mountain of adamant.

At last, by a violent and almost superhuman effort, I tear it away just as the ball which is still executing its gyratory motions is about to run round it and drag me with it—if—

O what intense stupendous light! The globe of fire bursts—we are enveloped in cascades of living fire, which floods the space around with luminous matter.

Then all went out and darkness once more fell upon the deep! I had just time to see my uncle once more cast apparently senseless on the flooring of the raft, Hans at the helm, "spitting fire" under the influence of the electricity which seemed to have gone through him.

Whither are we going, I ask? and echo answers, Whither?

Tuesday, August 25. I have just come out of a long fainting fit. The awful and hideous storm still continues; the lightning has increased in vividness, and pours out its fiery wrath like a brood of serpents let loose in the atmosphere.

Are we still upon the sea? Yes, and being carried along with incredible velocity.

We have passed under England, under the Channel, under France, probably under the whole extent of Europe.

*   *   *   *   *

Another awful clamour in the distance. This time it is certain that the sea is breaking upon the rocks at no great distance. Then—

A Journey to the Centre of the Earth

CHAPTER XXXIII.

OUR ROUTE REVERSED

HERE ends what I call My Journal of our voyage on board the raft, which Journal was happily saved from the wreck. I proceed with my narrative as I did before I commenced my daily notes.

What happened when the terrible shock took place, when the raft was cast upon the rocky shore, it would be impossible for me now to say. I felt myself precipitated violently into the boiling waves, and if I escaped from a certain and cruel death, it was wholly owing to the determination of the faithful Hans, who clutching me by the arm, saved me from the yawning abyss.

The courageous Icelander then carried me in his powerful arms, far out of reach of the waves, and laid me down upon a burning expanse of sand, where I found myself some time afterwards in the company of my uncle the Professor.

Then he quietly returned towards the fatal rocks, against which the furious waves were beating, in order to save any stray waifs from the wreck. This man was always practical and thoughtful. I could not utter a word; I was quite overcome with emotion; my whole body was broken and bruised with fatigue; it took hours before I was anything like myself.

Meanwhile, there fell a fearful deluge of rain, drenching us to the skin. Its very violence, however, proclaimed the approaching end of the storm. Some over-hanging rocks, afforded us a slight protection from the torrents.

Under this shelter, Hans prepared some food, which, however, I was unable to touch; and, exhausted by the three weary days and nights of watching, we fell into a deep and painful sleep. My dreams were fearful, but at last exhausted nature asserted her supremacy, and I slumbered.

Next day when I awoke the change was magical. The weather was magnificent. Air and sea, as if by mutual consent, had regained their serenity. Every trace of the storm, even the faintest, had disappeared. I was saluted on my awakening by the first joyous tones I had heard from the Professor for many a day. His gaiety, indeed, was something terrible.

"Well, my lad," he cried, rubbing his hands together, "have you slept soundly?"

Might it not have been supposed that we were in the old house on the König-strasse; that I had just come down quietly to my breakfast, and that my marriage with Gretchen was to take place that very day? My uncle's coolness was exasperating.

Alas, considering how the tempest had driven us in an easterly direction, we had passed under the whole of Germany, under the city of Hamburg where I had been so happy, under the very street which contained all I loved and cared for in the world.

It was a positive fact that I was only separated from her by a distance of forty leagues. But these forty leagues were of hard impenetrable granite!

All these dreary and miserable reflections passed through my mind, before I attempted to answer my uncle's question.

"Why, what is the matter?" he cried, "cannot you say whether you have slept well or not?"

"I have slept very well," was my reply, "but every bone in my body aches. I suppose that will lead to nothing."

"Nothing at all, my boy. It is only the result of the fatigue of the last few days—that is all."

"You appear—if I may be allowed to say so—to be very jolly this morning," I said.

"Delighted, my dear boy, delighted. Was never happier in my life. We have at last reached the wished-for port."

"The end of our expedition?" cried I, in a tone of considerable surprise.

"No; but to the confines of that sea which I began to fear would never end, but go round the whole world. We will now tranquilly resume our journey by land, and once again endeavour to dive into the centre of the Earth."

"My dear uncle," I began, in a hesitating kind of way, "allow me to ask you one question?"

"Certainly, Harry; a dozen, if you think proper."

"One will suffice. How about getting back?" I asked.

"How about getting back? What a question to ask. We have not as yet reached the end of our journey."

"I know that. All I want to know is, how you

The ball of fire.

propose we shall manage the return voyage?''

"In the most simple manner in the world," said the imperturbable Professor. Once we reach the exact centre of this sphere, either we shall find a new road by which to ascend to the surface, or we shall simply turn round and go back by the way we came. I have every reason to believe that while we are travelling forward, it will not close behind us.''

"Then one of the first matters to see to will be to repair the raft," was my rather melancholy response.

"Of course. We must attend to that above all things," continued the Professor.

"Then comes the all-important question of provisions," I urged. "Have we anything like enough left to enable us to accomplish such great, such amazing, designs as you contemplate carrying out."

"I have seen into the matter, and my answer is in the affirmative. Hans is a very clever fellow, and I have reason to believe that he has saved the greater part of the cargo. But the best way to satisfy your scruples, is to come and judge for yourself.''

Saying which, he led the way out of the kind of open grotto in which we had taken shelter. I had almost begun to hope that which I should rather have feared, and this was the impossibility of such a shipwreck leaving even the slightest signs of what it had carried as freight. I was, however, thoroughly mistaken.

As soon as I reached the shores of this inland sea, I found Hans standing gravely in the midst of a large number of things laid out in complete order. My uncle wrung his hands with deep and silent gratitude. His heart was too full for speech.

This man, whose superhuman devotion to his employers, I not only never saw surpassed, nor even equalled, had been hard at work all the time we slept, and at the risk of his life had succeeded in saving the most precious articles of our cargo.

Of course, under the circumstances, we necessarily experienced several severe losses. Our weapons had wholly vanished. But experience had taught us to do without them. The provision of powder had, however, remained intact, after having narrowly escaped blowing us all to atoms in the storm.

"Well," said the Professor, who was now ready to make the best of everything, "as we have no guns, all we have to do is to give up all idea of hunting."

"Yes, my dear sir, we can do without them, but what about all our instruments?"

"Here is the manometer, the most useful of all, and which I gladly accept in lieu of the rest. With it alone I can calculate the depth as we proceed; by its means alone I shall be able to decide when we have reached the centre of the earth. Ha, ha! but for this little instrument we might make a mistake, and run the risk of coming out at the antipodes!''

All this was said amid bursts of unnatural laughter.

"But the compass!" I cried, "without that what can we do?"

"Here it is safe and sound!" he cried, with real joy, "ah, ah, and here we have the chronometer and the thermometers. Hans the hunter is indeed an invaluable man!''

It was impossible to deny this fact. As far as the nautical and other instruments were concerned, nothing was wanting. Then on further examination, I found ladders, cords, pickaxes, crowbars, and shovels, all scattered about on the shore.

There was, however, finally the most important question of all, and that was, provisions.

"But what are we to do for food?" I asked.

"Let us see to the commissariat department," replied my uncle gravely.

The boxes which contained our supply of food for the voyage were placed in a row along the strand, and were in a capital state of preservation; the sea had in every case respected their contents, and to sum up in one sentence, taking into consideration, biscuits, salt meat, schiedam and dried fish, we could still calculate on having about four months' supply, if used with prudence and caution.

"Four months," cried the sanguine Professor, in high glee, "then we shall have plenty of time both to go and to come, and with what remains I undertake to give a grand dinner to my colleagues of the Johanneum.''

I sighed. I should by this time have used myself to the temperament of my uncle, and yet this man astonished me more and more every day. He was the greatest human enigma I ever had known.

"Now," said he, "before we do anything else we must lay in a stock of fresh water. The rain has fallen in abundance, and filled the hollows of the granite. There is a rich supply of water, and we have no fear of suffering from thirst, which in our circumstances is of the last importance. As for the raft, I shall recommend Hans to repair it to the best of his abilities; though I have every reason to believe we shall not require it again.''

"How is that?" I cried, more amazed than ever at my uncle's style of reasoning.

"I have an idea, my dear boy; it is none other

than this simple fact: we shall not come out by the same opening as that by which we entered.''

I began to look at my uncle with vague suspicion. An idea had more than once taken possession of me; and this was, that he was going mad. And yet, little did I think how true and prophetic his words were doomed to be.

"And now," he said, "having seen to all these matters of detail, to breakfast."

I followed him to a sort of projecting cape, after he had given his last instructions to our guide. In this original position, with dried meat, biscuit, and a delicious cup of tea, we made a satisfactory meal—I may say one of the most welcome and pleasant I ever remember. Exhaustion, the keen atmosphere, the state of calm after so much agitation, all contributed to give me an excellent appetite. Indeed, it contributed very much to producing a pleasant and cheerful state of mind.

While breakfast was in hand, and between the sips of warm tea, I asked my uncle if he had any idea of how we now stood in relation to the world above.

"For my part," I added, "I think it will be rather difficult to determine."

"Well, if we were compelled to fix the exact spot," said my uncle, "it might be difficult, since during the three days of that awful tempest I could keep no account either of the quickness of our pace, or of the direction in which the raft was going. Still, we will endeavour to approximate to the truth. We shall not, I believe, be so very far out."

"Well, if I recollect rightly," I replied, "our last observation was made at the Geyser island."

"Harry's Island, my boy! Harry's Island. Do not decline the honour of having named it; given your name to an island discovered by us, the first human beings who trod it since the creation of the world!"

"Let it be so, then. At Harry's Island we had already gone over two hundred and seventy leagues of sea, and we were, I believe, about six hundred leagues, more or less from Iceland."

"Good. I am glad to see that you remember so well. Let us start from that point, and let us count four days of storm, during which our rate of travelling must have been very great. I should say that our velocity must have been about eighty leagues to the twenty-four hours."

I agreed that I thought this a fair calculation. There were then three hundred leagues to be added to the grand total.

"Yes, and the Central Sea must extend at least six hundred leagues from side to side. Do you know, my boy, Harry, that we have discovered an inland lake larger than the Mediterranean?"

"Certainly, and we only know of its extent in one way. It may be hundreds of miles in length."

"Very likely."

"Then," said I, after calculating for some minutes, "if your previsions are right, we are at this moment exactly under the Mediterranean itself."

"Do you think so?"

"Yes, I am almost certain of it. Are we not nine hundred leagues distant from Reykjawik?"

"That is perfectly true, and a famous bit of road we have travelled, my boy. But why we should be under the Mediterranean more than under Turkey or the Atlantic Ocean can only be known when we are sure of not having deviated from our course; and of this we know nothing."

"I do not think we were driven very far from our course: the wind appears to me to have been always about the same. My opinion is that this shore must be situated to the south-east of Port Gretchen."

"Good—I hope so. It will, however, be easy to decide the matter by taking the bearings from our departure by means of the compass. Come along, and we will consult that invaluable invention."

The Professor now walked eagerly in the direction of the rock where the indefatigable Hans had placed the instruments in safety. My uncle was gay and light-hearted; he rubbed his hands, and assumed all sorts of attitudes. He was to all appearance once more a young man. Since I had known him never had he been so amiable and pleasant. I followed him, rather curious to know whether I had made any mistake in my estimation of our position.

As soon as we had reached the rock, my uncle took the compass, placed it horizontally before him and looked keenly at the needle.

As he had at first shaken it to give it vivacity, it oscillated considerably, and then slowly assumed its right position under the influence of the magnetic power.

The Professor bent his eyes curiously over the wondrous instrument. A violent start immediately showed the extent of his emotion.

He closed his eyes, rubbed them, and took another and a keener survey.

Then he turned slowly round to me, stupefaction depicted on his countenance.

"What is the matter?" said I, beginning to be alarmed.

He could not speak. He was too overwhelmed for words. He simply pointed to the instrument.

I examined it eagerly according to his mute directions, and a loud cry of surprise escaped my lips. The needle of the compass pointed due north, in the direction we expected was the south!

It pointed to the shore instead of to the high seas.

I shook the compass; I examined it with a curious and anxious eye. It was in a state of perfection. No blemish in any way explained the phenomenon. Whatever position we forced the needle into, it returned invariably to the same unexpected point.

It was useless attempting to conceal from ourselves the fatal truth.

There could be no doubt about it, unwelcome as was the fact, that during the tempest, there had been a sudden slant of wind, of which we had been unable to take any account and thus the raft had carried us back to the shores we had left, apparently for ever, so many days before!

A Journey to the Centre of the Earth

CHAPTER XXXIV.

A VOYAGE OF DISCOVERY

IT would be altogether impossible for me to give any idea of the utter astonishment which overcame the Professor on making this extraordinary discovery. Amazement, incredulity, and rage were blended in such a way as to alarm me.

During the whole course of my life I had never seen a man at first so chapfallen; and then so furiously indignant.

The terrible fatigues of our sea voyage, the fearful dangers we had passed through, had all, all, gone for nothing. We had to begin them all over again.

Instead of progressing, as we fondly expected, during a voyage of so many days, we had retreated. Every hour of our expedition on the raft had been so much lost time!

Presently, however, the indomitable energy of my uncle overcame every other consideration.

"So," he said, between his set teeth, "fatality will play me these terrible tricks. The elements themselves conspire to overwhelm me with mortification. Air, fire, and water combine their united efforts to oppose my passage. Well, they shall see what the earnest will of a determined man can do. I will not yield, I will not retreat even one inch; and we shall see who shall triumph in this great contest —man or nature."

Standing upright on a rock, irritated and menacing, Professor Hardwigg, like the ferocious Ajax, seemed to defy the fates. I, however, took upon myself to interfere, and to impose some sort of check upon such insensate enthusiasm.

"Listen to me, uncle," I said, in a firm but temperate tone of voice, "there must be some limit to ambition here below. It is utterly useless to struggle against the impossible. Pray listen to reason. We are utterly unprepared for a sea voyage; it is simple madness to think of performing a journey of five hundred leagues upon a wretched pile of beams, with a counterpane for a sail, a paltry stick for a mast, and a tempest to contend with. As we are totally incapable of steering our frail craft, we shall become the mere plaything of the storm, and it is acting the part of madmen if we, a second time, run any risk upon this dangerous and treacherous Central Sea."

These are only a few of the reasons and arguments I put together—reasons and arguments which to me appeared unanswerable. I was allowed to go on without interruption for about ten minutes. The explanation to this I soon discovered. The Professor was not even listening, and did not hear a word of all my eloquence.

"To the raft!" he cried, in a hoarse voice, when I paused for a reply.

Such was the result of my strenuous effort to resist his iron will. I tried again; I begged and implored him; I got into a passion; but I had to deal with a will more determined than my own. I seemed to feel like the waves which fought and battled against the huge mass of granite at our feet, which had smiled grimly for so many ages at their puny efforts.

Hans, meanwhile, without taking part in our discussion, had been repairing the raft. One would have supposed that he instinctively guessed at the further projects of my uncle.

By means of some fragments of cordage, he had again made the raft sea-worthy.

While I had been speaking he had hoisted a new mast and sail, the latter already fluttering and waving in the breeze.

The worthy Professor spoke a few words to our imperturbable guide, who immediately began to put our baggage on board, and to prepare for our departure. The atmosphere was now tolerably clear and pure, and the northeast wind blew steadily and serenely. It appeared likely to last for some time.

What, then, could I do? Could I undertake to resist the iron will of two men? It was simply impossible; if even I could have hoped for the support of Hans. This, however, was out of the question. It appeared to me that the Icelander had set aside all personal will and identity. He was a picture of abnegation.

I could hope for nothing from one so infatuated with and devoted to his master. All I could do, therefore, was to swim with the stream.

In a mood of stolid and sullen resignation, I was about to take my accustomed place on the raft, when my uncle placed his hand upon my shoulder.

"There is no hurry, my boy," he said, "we shall not start until to-morrow."

I looked the picture of resignation to the dire will of fate.

"Under the circumstances," he said, "I ought to neglect no precautions. As fate has cast me upon these shores, I shall not leave without having completely examined them."

In order to understand this remark, I must explain that though we had been driven back to the northern shore, we had landed at a very different spot from that which had been our starting point.

Port Gretchen must, we calculated, be very much to the westward. Nothing, therefore, was more natural and reasonable than that we should reconnoitre this new shore upon which we had so unexpectedly landed.

"Let us go on a journey of discovery," I cried.

And leaving Hans to his important operation, we started on our expedition. The distance between the foreshore at high-water and the foot of the rocks was considerable. It would take about half-an-hour's walking to get from one to the other.

As we trudged along, our feet crushed innumerable shells of every shape and size—once the dwelling-places of animals of every period of creation.

I particularly noticed some enormous shells—carapaces (turtle and tortoise species) the diameter of which exceeded fifteen feet.

They had in past ages belonged to those gigantic glyptodons of the pliocene period, of which the modern turtle is but a minute specimen. In addition, the whole soil was covered by a vast quantity of stony relics, having the appearance of flints worn by the action of the waves, and lying in successive layers one above the other. I came to the conclusion that in past ages the sea must have covered the whole district. Upon the scattered rocks, now lying far beyond its reach, the mighty waves of ages had left evident marks of their passage.

On reflection, this appeared to me partially to explain the existence of this remarkable ocean, forty leagues below the surface of the earth's crust. According to my new, and perhaps fanciful, theory, this liquid mass must be gradually lost in the deep bowels of the earth. I had also no doubt that this mysterious sea was fed by infiltration of the ocean above, through imperceptible fissures.

Nevertheless, it was impossible not to admit that these fissures must now be nearly chocked up, for if not, the cavern, or rather the immense and stupendous reservoir would have been completely filled in a short space of time. Perhaps even this water, having to contend against the accumulated subterraneous fires of the interior of the earth, had become partially vaporised. Hence the explanation of those heavy clouds suspended over our heads, and the super-abundant display of that electricity which occasioned such terrible storms in this deep and cavernous sea.

This lucid explanation of the phenomena we had witnessed appeared to me quite satisfactory. However great and mighty the marvels of nature may seem to us, they are always to be explained by physical reasons. Everything is subordinate to some great law of nature.

It now appeared clear that we were walking upon a kind of sedimentary soil, formed like all the soils of that period, so frequent on the surface of the globe, by the subsidence of the waters. The Professor, who was now in his element, carefully examined every rocky fissure. Let him only find an opening and it directly became important to him to examine its depth.

For a whole mile we followed the windings of the Central Sea, when suddenly an important change took place in the aspect of the soil. It seemed to have been rudely cast up, convulsionised, as it were, by a violent upheaving of the lower strata. In many places, hollows here, and hillocks there, attested great dislocations at some other period of the terrestrial mass.

We advanced with great difficulty over the broken masses of granite mixed with flint, quartz and alluvial deposits, when a large field, more even than a field, a plain of bones, appeared suddenly before our eyes! It looked like an immense cemetery, where generation after generation had mingled their mortal dust.

Lofty barrows of early remains rose at intervals. They undulated away to the limits of the distant horizon and were lost in a thick and brown fog.

On that spot, some three square miles in extent, was accumulated the whole history of animal life—scarcely one creature upon the comparatively modern soil of the upper and inhabited world had there existed.

Nevertheless, we were drawn forward by an all-absorbing and impatient curiosity. Our feet crushed with a dry and crackling sound the remains of these prehistoric fossils, for which the museums of great cities quarrel, even when they obtain only rare and curious morsels. A thousand such naturalists as Cuvier would not have sufficed to recompose the skeletons of the organic beings which lay in this magnificent osseous collection.

I was utterly confounded. My uncle stood for some minutes with his arms raised on high towards the thick granite vault which served us for a sky. His mouth was wide open; his eyes sparkled wildly behind his spectacles (which he had fortunately saved), his head bobbed up and down and from side to side, while his whole attitude and mien expressed unbounded astonishment.

He stood in the presence of an endless, wondrous and inexhaustibly rich collection of antediluvian monsters, piled up for his own private and peculiar satisfaction.

Fancy an enthusiastic lover of books carried suddenly into the very midst of the famous library of Alexandria burned by the sacrilegious Omar, and which some miracle had restored to its pristine splendour! Such was something of the state of mind in which uncle Hardwigg was now placed.

For some time he stood thus, literally aghast at the magnitude of his discovery.

But it was even a greater excitement when, darting wildly over this mass of organic dust, he caught up a naked skull and addressed me in a quivering voice—

"Harry, my boy—Harry—this is a human head!"

"A human head, uncle!" I said, no less amazed and stupefied than himself.

"Yes, nephew. Ah! Mr. Milne-Edwards— ah! Mr. De Quatrefages—why are you not where I am—I, Professor Hardwigg!"

A Journey to the Centre of the Earth

CHAPTER XXXV.

DISCOVERY UPON DISCOVERY

IN order fully to understand the exclamation made by my uncle, and his allusions to these illustrious and learned men, it will be necessary to enter into certain explanations in regard to a circumstance of the highest importance to palaeontology or the science of fossil life, which had taken place a short time before our departure from the upper regions of the earth.

On the 28th of March, 1863, some navigators under the direction of M. Boucher de Perthes, were at work in the great quarries of Moulin-Quignon, near Abbeville, in the department of the Somme, in France. While at work, they unexpectedly came upon a human jawbone buried fourteen feet below the surface of the soil. It was the first fossil of the kind that had ever been brought to the light of day. Near this unexpected human relic were found stone hatchets and carved flints, coloured and clothed by time in one uniform brilliant tint of verdigris.

The report of this extraordinary and unexpected discovery spread not only all over France, but over England and Germany. May learned men belonging to various scientific bodies, and noteworthy among others, Messrs. Milne-Edwards and De Quatrefages, took the affair very much to heart, demonstrated the incontestible authenticity of the bone in question, and became—to use the phrase then recognised in England—the most ardent supporters of the "jawbone question."

To the eminent geologists of the United Kingdom who looked upon the fact as certain—Messrs. Falconer, Buck, Carpenter and others —were soon united the learned men of Germany, and among those in the first rank, the most eager, the most enthusiastic, was my worthy uncle, Professor Hardwigg.

The authenticity of a human fossil of the quaternary period seemed then to be incontestably demonstrated, and even to be admitted by the most sceptical.

This system or theory, call it what you will, had, it is true, a bitter adversary in M. Elie de Beaumont. This learned man, who holds such a high place in the scientific world, holds that the soil of Moulin-Quignon does not belong to the diluvium, but to a much less ancient strata, and, in accordance with Cuvier in this respect,

he would by no means admit that the human species was contemporary with the animals of the quaternary epoch. My worthy uncle, Professor Hardwigg, in concert with the great majority of geologists, had held firm, had disputed, discussed, and finally, after considerable talking and writing, M. Elie de Beaumont had been pretty well left alone in his opinions.

We were familiar with all the details of this discussion, but were far from being aware then that since our departure the matter had entered upon a new phase. Other similar jaw-bones, though belonging to individuals of varied types and very different natures, had been found in the movable gray sands of certain grottoes in France, Switzerland, and Belgium; together with arms, utensils, tools, bones of children, of men in the prime of life, and of old men. The existence of men in the quaternary period became, therefore, more positive every day.

But this was far from being all. New remains, dug up from the pliocene or tertiary deposits, had enabled the more far-seeing or audacious among learned men to assign even a far greater degree of antiquity to the human race. These remains, it is true, were not those of men; that is, were not the bones of men, but objects decidedly having served the human race, shin bones, thigh bones of fossil animals, regularly scooped out, and in fact sculptured—bearing the unmistakeable signs of human handy-work.

By means of these wondrous and unexpected discoveries, man ascended endless centuries in the scale of time; he, in fact, preceded the mastodon; became the cotemporary of the *elephas meridionalis*—the southern elephant; acquired an antiquity of over a hundred thousand years—since that is the date given by the most eminent geologists to the pliocene period of the earth. Such was then the state of palaeontologic science, and what we moreover knew, sufficed to explain our attitude before this great cemetery of the plains of the Hardwigg Ocean.

It will now be easy to understand the Professor's mingled astonishment and joy, when, on advancing about twenty yards, he found himself in the presence of, I may say face to face with, a specimen of the human race actually belonging to the quaternary period!

The plain of bones.

It was indeed a human skull, perfectly recognisable. Had a soil of very peculiar nature, like that of the cemetery of St. Michel at Bordeaux, preserved it during countless ages? This was the question I asked myself, but which I was wholly unable to answer. But this head with stretched and parchmenty skin, with the teeth whole, the hair abundant, was before our eyes as in life!

I stood mute, almost paralysed with wonder and awe before this dread apparition of another age. My uncle, who on almost every occasion was a great talker, remained for a time completely dumbfounded. He was too full of emotion for speech to be possible. After a while, however, we raised up the body to which the skull belonged. We stood it on end. It seemed, to our excited imaginations, to look at us with its terrible hollow eyes.

After some minutes of silence, the man was vanquished by the Professor. Human instincts succumbed to scientific pride and exultation. Professor Hardwigg, carried away by his enthusiasm, forgot all the circumstances of our journey, the extraordinary position in which we were placed, the immense cavern which stretched far away over our heads. There can be no doubt that he thought himself at the Institution addressing his attentive pupils, for he put on his most doctorial style, waved his hand, and began—

"Gentllemen, I have the honour on this auspicious occasion to present to you a man of the quaternary period of our globe. Many learned men have denied his very existence, while other able persons, perhaps of even higher authority, have affirmed their belief in the reality of his life. If the St. Thomases of palaeontology were present, they would reverentially touch him with their fingers and believe in his existence—thus acknowledging their obstinate heresy. I know that science should be careful in relation to all discoveries of this nature. I am not without having heard of the many Barnums and other quacks who have made a trade of such like pretended discoveries. I have, of course, heard of the discovery of the knee-bones of Ajax, of the pretended finding of the body of Orestes by the Spartiates, and of the body of Asterius, ten spans long—fifteen feet—of which we read in Pausanias.

"I have read everything in relation to the skeleton of Trapani, discovered in the fourteenth century, and which many persons chose to regard as that of Polyphemus, and the history of the giant dug up during the sixteenth century in the environs of Palmyra. You are as well aware as I am, gentlemen, of the existence of the celebrated analysis made near Lucerne, in 1577, of the great bones which the celebrated Doctor Felix Plater declared belonged to a giant about nineteen feet high. I have devoured all the treatises of Cassanion, and all those memoirs, pamphlets, speeches, and replies, published in reference to the skeleton of Teutobochus, king of the Cimbri, the invader of Gaul, dug out of a gravel pit in Dauphiny, in 1613. In the eighteenth century I should have denied, with Peter Campet, the existence of the preadamites of Scheuchzer. I have had in my hands the writing called Gigans—"

Here my uncle was afflicted by the natural infirmity which prevented him from pronouncing difficult words in public. It was not exactly stuttering, but a strange sort of constitutional hesitation.

"The writing named Gigans—" he repeated.

He, however, could get no further.

"Giganteo—"

Impossible! The unfortunate word would not come out. There would have been great laughter at the Institution, had the mistake happened there.

"Gigantosteology!" at least exclaimed Professor Hardwigg, between two savage growls.

Having got over our difficulty, and getting more and more excited—

"Yes, gentlemen, I am well acquainted with all these matters, and know, also, that Cuvier and Blumenbach fully recognised in these bones, the undeniable remains of mammoths of the quaternary period. But after what we now see, to allow a doubt is to insult scientific inquiry. There is the body; you can see it; you can touch it. It is not a skeleton, it is a complete and uninjured body, preserved with an anthropological object."

I did not attempt to controvert this singular and astounding assertion.

"If I could but wash this corpse in a solution of sulphuric acid," continued my uncle, "I would undertake to remove all the earthly particles, and these resplendent shells, which are incrusted all over his body. But I am without this precious dissolving medium. Nevertheless, such as it is, this body will tell its own history."

Here the Professor held up the fossil body, and exhibited it with rare dexterity. No professional showman could have shown more activity.

"As on examination you will see," my uncle continued, "it is only about six feet in length, which is a long way from the pretended giants of early days. As to the particular race to which it belonged, it is incontestably Caucasian. It is

Human or not?

of the white race, that is, of our own. The skull of this fossil being is a perfect ovoid without any remarkable or prominent development of the cheek bones, and without any projection of the jaw. It presents no indication of the prognathism which modifies the facial angle.* Measure the angle for yourselves, and you will find that it is just ninety degrees. But I will advance still further on the road of inquiry and deduction, and I dare venture to say that this human sample or specimen belongs to the Japhetic family, which spread over the world from India to the uttermost limits of western Europe. There is no occasion, gentlemen, to smile at my remarks.''

Of course nobody smiled. But the excellent Professor was so accustomed to beaming countenances at his lectures, that he believed he saw all his audience laughing during the delivery of his learned dissertation.

''Yes,'' he continued, with renewed animation, ''this is a fossil man, a contemporary of the mastodons, with the bones of which this whole amphitheatre is covered. But if I am called on to explain how he came to this place, how these various strata by which he is covered have fallen into this vast cavity, I can undertake to give you no explanation. Doubtless, if we carry ourselves back to the quaternary epoch, we shall find that great and mighty convulsions took place in the crust of the earth; the continually cooling operation, through which the earth had to pass, produced fissures, landslips, and chasms, through which a large portion of the earth made its way. I come to no absolute conclusion, but there is the man, surrounded by the works of his hands, his hatchets, his carved flints, which belong to the stony period; and the only rational supposition is, that, like myself, he visited the centre of the earth as a travelling tourist, a pioneer of science. All at events, there can be no doubt of

his great age, and of his being one of the oldest race of human beings.''

The Professor with these words ceased his oration, and I burst forth into loud and ''unanimous'' applause. Besides, after all, my uncle was right. Much more learned men than his nephew would have found it rather hard to refute his facts and arguments.

Another circumstance soon presented itself. This fossilised body was not the only one in this vast plain of bones—the cemetery of an extinct world. Other bodies were found, as we trod the dusty plain, and my uncle was able to choose the most marvellous of these specimens in order to convince the most incredulous.

In truth, it was a surprising spectacle, the successive remains of generations and generations of men and animals confounded together in one vast cemetery. But a great question now presented itself to our notice, and one we were actually afraid to contemplate in all its bearings.

Had these once animated beings been buried so far beneath the soil by some tremendous convulsion of nature, after they had been earth to earth and ashes to ashes, or had they lived here below, in this subterranean world, under this factitious sky, born, married, and given in marriage, and dying at last, just like ordinary inhabitants of the earth?

Up to the present moment, marine monsters, fish, and such like animals, had alone been seen alive!

The question, which rendered us rather uneasy, was a pertinent one. Were any of these men of the abyss wandering about the deserted shores of this wondrous sea of the centre of the earth?

This was a question which rendered me very uneasy and uncomfortable. How, should they really be in existence, would they receive us men from above?

---

*The facial angle is formed by two planes—one more or less vertical, which is in a straight line with the forehead and the incisors; the other, horizontal, which passes through the organs of hearing, and the lower nasal bone. Prognathism, in anthropological language, means that particular projection of the jaw which modified the facial angle.

A Journey to the Centre of the Earth

CHAPTER XXXVI.

WHAT IS IT

FOR a long and weary hour we tramped over this great bed of bones. We advanced regardless of everything, drawn on by ardent curiosity. What other marvels did this great cavern contain—what other wondrous treasures for the scientific man? My eyes were quite prepared for any number of surprises, my imagination lived in expectation of something new and wonderful.

The borders of the great Central Ocean had for some time disappeared behind the hills that were scattered over the ground occupied by the plain of bones. The imprudent and enthusiastic Professor, who did not care whether he lost himself or not, hurried me forward. We advanced silently, bathed in waves of electric fluid.

By reason of a phenomenon which I cannot explain, and thanks to its extreme diffusion, now complete, the light illumined equally the sides of every hill and rock. Its seat appeared to be nowhere, in no determined force, and produced no shade whatever.

The appearance presented was that of a tropical country at midday in summer—in the midst of the equatorial regions and under the vertical rays of the sun.

All sign of vapour had disappeared. The rocks, the distant mountains, some confused masses of far-off forests, assumed a weird and mysterious aspect under this equal distribution of the luminous fluid!

We resembled to a certain extent the mysterious personage in one of Hoffmann's fantastic tales—the man who lost his shadow.

After we had walked about a mile farther, we came to the edge of a vast forest, not however one of the vast mushroom forests we had discovered near Port Gretchen.

It was the glorious and wild vegetation of the tertiary period, in all its superb magnificence. Huge palms, of a species now unknown, superb palmacites—a genus of fossil palms from the coal formation—pines, yews, cypress, and conifers or cone-bearing trees, the whole bound together by an inextricable and complicated mass of creeping plants.

A beautiful carpet of mosses and ferns grew beneath the trees. Pleasant brooks murmured beneath umbrageous boughs, little worthy of this name, for no shade did they give. Upon their borders grew small tree-like shrubs, such as are seen in the hot countries on our own inhabited globe.

The one thing wanted to these plants, these shrubs, these trees—was colour! For ever deprived of the vivifying warmth of the sun, they were vapid and colourless. All shade was lost in one uniform tint, of a brown and faded character. The leaves were wholly devoid of verdure, and the flowers, so numerous during the tertiary period which gave them birth, were without colour and without perfume, something like paper discoloured by long exposure to the atmosphere.

My uncle ventured beneath the gigantic groves. I followed him, though not without a certain amount of apprehension. Since nature had shown herself capable of producing such stupendous vegetable productions, why might we not meet with mammals (animals with breasts) as large, and therefore dangerous.

I particularly remarked, in the clearings left by trees that had fallen and been partially consumed by time, many leguminous (bean-like) shrubs, such as the maple and other eatable trees, dear to ruminating animals. Then there appeared confounded together and intermixed, the trees of such varied lands, specimens of the vegetation of every part of the globe; there was the oak near the palm tree, the Australian eucalyptus, an interesting class of the order *Myrtaceae*—leaning against the tall Norwegian pine, the poplar of the north, mixing its branches with those of the New Zealand kauris. It was enough to drive the most ingenious classifier of the upper regions out of his mind, and to upset all his received ideas about botany.

Suddenly I stopped short and restrained my uncle.

The extreme diffuseness of the light enabled me to see the smallest objects in the distant copses. I thought I saw—no, I really did see with my own eyes—immense, gigantic animals moving about under the mighty trees. Yes, they were truly gigantic animals, a whole herd of mastodons, not fossils, but living, and exactly like those discovered in 1801, on the marshy banks of the great Ohio, in North America!

The vegetation of the tertiary period in all its magnificence.

Yes, I could see these enormous elephants, whose trunks were tearing down large boughs, and working in and out the trees like a legion of serpents. I could hear the sounds of the mighty tusks uprooting huge trees!

The boughs crackled, and whole masses of leaves and green branches went down the capacious throats of these terrible monsters!

That wondrous dream, when I saw the ante-historical times revivified, when the tertiary and quaternary periods passed before me, was now realised!

And there we were alone, far down in the bowels of the earth, at the mercy of its ferocious inhabitants!

My uncle paused, full of wonder and astonishment.

"Come," he said at last, when his first surprise was over, "come along, my boy, and let us see them nearer."

"No," replied I, restraining his efforts to drag me forward, "we are wholly without arms. What should we do in the midst of that flock of gigantic quadrupeds? Come away, uncle, I implore you. No human creature can with impunity brave the ferocious anger of these monsters."

"No human creature," said my uncle, suddenly lowering his voice to a mysterious whisper, "you are mistaken, my dear Henry. Look! look yonder! It seems to me that I behold a human being—a being like ourselves—a man!"

I looked, shrugging my shoulders, decided to push incredulity to its very last limits. But whatever might have been my wish, I was compelled to yield to the weight of ocular demonstration.

Yes—not more than a quarter of a mile off, leaning against the trunk of an enormous tree, was a human being—a Proteus of these sub-terranean regions, a new son of Neptune keeping this innumerable herd of mastodons.

*Immanis pecoris custos, immanis ipse!**

Yes—it was no longer a fossil whose corpse we had raised from the ground in the great cemetery, but a giant capable of guiding and driving these prodigious monsters. His height was above twelve feet. His head, as big as the head of a buffalo, was lost in a mane of matted hair. It was indeed a huge mane, like those which belonged to the elephants of the earlier ages of the world.

In his hand was a branch of a tree, which served as crook for this antediluvian shepherd.

We remained profoundly still, speechless with surprise.

But we might at any moment be seen by him. Nothing remained for us but instant flight.

"Come, come!" I cried, dragging my uncle along; and, for the first time, he made no resistance to my wishes.

A quarter of an hour later we were far away from that terrible monster!

Now that I think of the matter calmly, and that I reflect upon it dispassionately; now that months, years, have passed since this strange and unnatural adventure befell us,—what am I to think, what am I to believe?

No, it is utterly impossible! Our ears must have deceived us, and our eyes have cheated us! we have not seen what we believed we had seen. No human being could by any possibility have existed in that subterranean world! No generation of men could inhabit the lower caverns of the globe without taking note of those who peopled the surface, without com-munication with them. It was folly, folly, folly! nothing else!

I am rather inclined to admit the existence of some animal resembling in structure the human race—of some monkey of the first geological epochs, like that discovered by M. Lartet in the ossiferous deposit of Sansan.

But this animal, or being, whichsoever it was, surpassed in height all things known to modern science. Never mind. However unlikely it may be, it might have been a monkey—but a man, a living man, and with him a whole generation of gigantic animals, buried in the entrails of the earth—it was too monstrous to be believed!

---

*The keeper of gigantic cattle, himself a giant!

Gigantic Inhabitants.

A Journey to the Centre of the Earth

CHAPTER XXXVII.

THE MYSTERIOUS DAGGER

DURING this time, we had left the bright and transparent forest far behind us. We were mute with astonishment, overcome by a kind of feeling which was next door to apathy. We kept running in spite of ourselves. It was a perfect flight, which resembled one of those horrible sensations we sometimes meet with in our dreams.

Instinctively we made our way towards the Central Sea, and I cannot now tell what wild thoughts passed through my mind, nor of what follies I might have been guilty, but for a very serious pre-occupation which brought me back to practical life.

Though I was aware that we were treading on a soil quite new to us, I, however, every now and then noticed certain aggregations of rock, the shape of which forcibly reminded me of those near Port Gretchen.

This confirmed, moreover, the indications of the compass and our extraordinary and unlooked for, as well as involuntary, return to the north of this great Central Sea. It was so like our starting point, that I could scarcely doubt the reality of our position. Streams and cascades, fell in hundreds over the numerous projections of the rocks.

I actually thought I could see our faithful and monotonous Hans and the wonderful grotto in which I had come back to life after my tremendous fall.

Then, as we advanced still farther, the position of the cliffs, the appearance of a stream, the unexpected profile of a rock, threw me again into a state of bewildering doubt.

After some time, I explained my state of mental indecision to my uncle. He confessed to a similar feeling of hesitation. He was totally unable to make up his mind in the midst of this extraordinary but uniform panorama.

"There can be no doubt," I insisted, "that we have not landed exactly at the place whence we first took our departure; but the tempest has brought us above our starting point. I think, therefore, that if we follow the coast we shall once more find Port Gretchen.

"In that case," cried my uncle, "it is useless to continue our exploration. The very best thing we can do is to make our way back to the raft. Are you quite sure, Harry, that you are not mistaken?"

"It is difficult," was my reply, "to come to any decision, for all these rocks are exactly alike. There is no marked difference between them. At the same time, the impression on my mind is, that I recognise the promontory at the foot of which our worthy Hans constructed the raft. We are, I am nearly convinced, near the little port: if this be not it," I added, carefully examining a creek which appeared singularly familiar to my mind.

"My dear Harry—if this were the case, we should find traces of our own footsteps, some signs of our passage; and I can really see nothing to indicate our having passed this way."

"But I see something," I cried, in an impetuous tone of voice, as I rushed forward and eagerly picked up something which shone in the sand under my feet.

"What is it?" cried the astonished and bewildered Professor.

"This," was my reply.

And I handed to my startled relative a rusty dagger, of singular shape.

"What made you bring with you so useless a weapon?" he exclaimed. "It was needlessly hampering yourself."

"I bring it?—it is quite new to me. I never saw it before—are you sure it is not out of your collection?"

"Not that I know of," said the Professor, puzzled. "I have no recollection of the circumstance. It was never my property."

"This is very extraordinary," I said, musing over the novel and singular incident.

"Not at all. There is a very simple explanation, Harry. The Icelanders are known to keep up the use of these antiquated weapons, and this must have belonged to Hans, who has let it fall without knowing it."

I shook my head. That dagger had never been in the possession of the pacific and taciturn Hans. I knew him and his habits too well.

"Then what can it be—unless it be the weapon of some antediluvian warrior," I continued, "of some living man, a contemporary of that mighty shepherd from whom we have just escaped? But no—mystery upon mystery—this is no weapon of the stony epoch, nor even of the bronze period. It is made of excellent steel—"

Ere I could finish my sentence, my uncle stopped me short from entering upon a whole train of theories, and spoke in his most cold and decided tone of voice.

"Calm yourself, my dear boy, and endeavour to use your reason. This weapon, upon which we have fallen so unexpectedly, is a true *dague*, one of those worn by gentlemen in their belts during the sixteenth century. Its use was to give the *coup de grâce*, the final blow, to the foe who would not surrender. It is clearly of Spanish workmanship. It belongs neither to you, nor to me, nor the eider-down hunter, nor to any of the living beings who may still exist so marvellously in the interior of the earth."

"What can you mean, uncle?" I said, now lost in a host of surmises.

"Look closely at it," he continued; these jagged edges were never made by the resistance of human blood and bone. The blade is covered with a regular coating of iron-mould and rust, which is not a day old, not a year old, not a century old, but much more—"

The Professor began to get quite excited, according to custom, and was allowing himself to be carried away by his fertile imagination. I could have said something. He stopped me.

"Harry," he cried, "we are now on the verge of a great discovery. This blade of a dagger you have so marvellously discovered, after being abandoned upon the sand for more than a hundred, two hundred, even three hundred years, has been indented by some one endeavouring to carve an inscription on these rocks."

"But this poignard never got here of itself," I exclaimed, "it could not have twisted itself. Some one, therefore, must have preceded us upon the shores of this extraordinary sea."

"Yes, a man."

"But what man has been sufficiently desperate to do such a thing."

"A man who has somewhere written his name with this very dagger—a man who has endeavoured once more to indicate the right road to the interior of the earth. Let us look around, my boy. You know not the importance of your singular and happy discovery."

Prodigiously interested, we walked along the wall of rock, examining the smallest fissures, which might finally expand into the much wished for gully or shaft.

We at last reached a spot where the shore became extremely narrow. The sea almost bathed the foot of the rocks, which were here very lofty and steep. there was scarcely a path wider than two yards at any point. At last, under a huge overhanging rock, we discovered the entrance of a dark and gloomy tunnel.

There, on a square tablet of granite, which had been smoothed by rubbing it with another stone, we could see two mysterious, and much worn letters, the two initials of the bold and extraordinary traveller who had preceded us on our adventurous journey.

$$\cdot \; \text{⅄} \cdot \text{Ч} \cdot$$

"A. S.," cried my uncle; "you see I was right. Arne Saknussemm, always Arne Saknussemm!"

A Journey to the Centre of the Earth

CHAPTER XXXVIII.

NO OUTLET—BLASTING THE ROCK

EVER since the commencement of our marvellous journey, I had experienced many surprises, had suffered from many illusions. I thought that I was case-hardened against all surprises and could neither see nor hear anything to amaze me again.

I was like a man who, having been round the world, finds himself wholly *blasé* and proof against the marvellous.

When, however, I saw these two letters, which had been engraven three hundred years before, I stood fixed in an attitude of mute surprise.

Not only was there the signature of the learned and enterprising alchemist written in the rock, but I held in my hand the very identical instrument with which he had laboriously engraved it.

It was impossible, without showing an amount of incredulity scarcely becoming a sane man, to deny the existence of the traveller, and the reality of that voyage which I believed all along to have been a myth—the mystification of some fertile brain.

While these reflections were passing through my mind, my uncle, the Professor, gave way to an access of feverish and poetical excitement.

"Wonderful and glorious Genius, great Saknussemm," he cried, "you have left no stone unturned, no resource omitted, to show to other mortals the way into the interior of our mighty globe, and your fellow creatures can find the trail left by your illustrious footsteps, three hundred years ago, at the bottom of these obscure subterranean abodes. You have been careful to secure for others the contemplation of these wonders and marvels of creation. Your name engraved at every important stage of your glorious journey, leads the hopeful traveller direct to the great and mighty discovery to which you devoted much energy and courage. The audacious traveller, who shall follow your footsteps to the last, will doubtless find your initials engraved with your own hand upon the centre of the earth. *I* will be that audacious traveller—*I*, too, will sign my name upon the very same spot, upon the central granite stone of this wondrous work of the Creator. but in justice to your devotion, to your courage, and to your being the first to indicate the road, let this Cape, seen by you upon the shores of this sea discovered by you, be called of all time, Cape Saknussemm."

This is what I heard, and I began to be roused to the pitch of enthusiasm indicated by those words. A fierce excitement roused me. I forgot everything. The dangers of the voyage, and the perils of the return journey, were now as nothing!

What another man had done in ages past, could I felt be done again; I was determined to do it myself, and now nothing that man had accomplished appeared to me impossible.

"Forward—forward," I cried in a burst of genuine and hearty enthusiasm.

I had already started in the direction of the sombre and gloomy gallery, when the Professor stopped me; he, the man so rash and hasty, he, the man so easily roused to the highest pitch of enthusiasm, checked me, and asked me to be patient and show more calm.

"Let us return to our good friend, Hans," he said; "we will then bring the raft down to this place."

I must say that though I at once yielded to my uncle's request, it was not without dissatisfaction, and I hastened along the rocks of that wonderful coast.

"Do you know, my dear uncle," I said, as we walked along, "that we have been singularly helped by a concurrence of circumstances, right up to this very moment."

"So you begin to see it, do you, Harry?" said the Professor, with a smile.

"Doubtless," I responded, "and strangely enough, even the tempest has been the means of putting us on the right road. Blessings on the tempest! It brought us safely back to the very spot from which fine weather would have driven us for ever. Supposing we had succeeded in reaching the southern and distant shores of this extraordinary sea, what would have become of us? The name of Saknussemm would never have appeared to us, and at this moment we should have been cast away upon an inhospitable coast, probably without an outlet."

"Yes, Harry, my boy, there is certainly something providential in that wandering at the mercy of wind and waves towards the south: we have come back exactly north; and what is better still, we fall upon this great discovery of Cape Saknussemm. I mean to say, that it is more than surprising; there is something in it which is far beyond my comprehension. The coincidence is unheard of, marvellous!''

"What matter! It is not our duty to explain facts, but to make the best possible use of them.''

"Doubtless, my boy; but if you will allow me—'' said the really-delighted Professor.

"Excuse me, sir, but I see exactly how it will be; we shall take the northern route; we shall pass under the northern regions of Europe, under Sweden, under Russia, under Siberia, and who knows where—instead of burying ourselves under the burning plains and deserts of Africa, or beneath the mighty waves of the ocean; and that is all, at this stage of our journey, that I care to know. Let us advance, and Heaven will be our guide!''

"Yes, Harry, you are right, quite right; all is for the best. Let us abandon this horizontal sea, which could never have led to anything satisfactory. We shall descend, descend, and everlastingly descend. Do you know, my dear boy, that to reach the interior of the earth we have only five thousand miles to travel!''

"Bah!'' I cried, carried away by a burst of enthusiasm, "the distance is scarcely worth speaking about. The thing is to make a start.''

My wild, mad, and incoherent speeches continued until we rejoined our patient and phlegmatic guide. All was, we found, prepared for an immediate departure. There was not a single parcel but what was in its proper place. We all took up our posts on the raft, and the sail being hoisted, Hans received his directions, and guided the frail barque towards Cape Saknussemm, as we had definitely named it.

The wind was very unfavourable to a craft that was unable to sail close to the wind. It was constructed to go before the blast. We were continually reduced to pushing ourselves forward by means of poles. On several occasions the rocks ran far out into deep water and we were compelled to make a long round. At last, after three long and weary hours of navigation, that is to say, about six o'clock in the evening, we found a place at which we could land.

I jumped on shore first. In my present state of excitement and enthusiasm, I was always first. My uncle and the Icelander followed. The voyage from the port to this point of the sea had by no means calmed me. It had rather produced the opposite effect. I even proposed to burn our vessel, that is to destroy our raft, in order to

completely cut off our retreat. But my uncle sternly opposed this wild project. I began to think him particularly lukewarm and unenthusiastic.

"At any rate, my dear uncle,'' I said, "let us start without delay.''

"Yes, my boy, I am quite as eager to do so as you can be. But, in the first place, let us examine this mysterious gallery, in order to find if we shall need to prepare and mend our ladders.''

My uncle now began to see to the efficiency of our Ruhmkorff's coil, which would doubtless soon be needed; the raft, securely fastened to a rock, was left alone. Moreover, the opening into the new gallery was not twenty paces distant from the spot. Our little troop, with myself at the head, advanced.

The orifice, which was almost circular, presented a diameter of about five feet; the sombre tunnel was cut in the living rock, and coated on the inside by the different material which had once passed through it in a state of fusion. The lower part was about level with the water, so that we were able to penetrate to the interior without difficulty.

We followed an almost horizontal direction; when, at the end of about a dozen paces, our further advance was checked by the interposition of an enormous block of granite rock.

"Accursed stone!'' I cried, furiously, on perceiving that we were stopped by what seemed an insurmountable obstacle.

In vain we looked to the right, in vain we looked to the left; in vain examined it above and below. There existed no passage, no sign of any other tunnel. I experienced the most bitter and painful disappointment. So enraged was I that I would not admit the reality of any obstacle. I stooped to my knees; I looked under the mass of stone. No hole, no interstice. I then looked above. The same barrier of granite! Hans, with the lamp, examined the sides of the tunnel in every direction. But all in vain! It was necessary to renounce all hope of passing through.

I had seated myself upon the ground. My uncle walked angrily and hopelessly up and down. He was evidently desperate.

"But,'' I cried after some moments' thought, "what about Arne Saknussemm?''

"You are right,'' replied my uncle, "he can never have been checked by a lump of rock.''

"No—ten thousand times, no,'' I cried with extreme vivacity. "This huge lump of rock, in consequence of some singular concussion, or process, one of those magnetic phenomena which have so often shaken the terrestrial crust, has in some unexpected way closed up the

The fearful explosion.

passage. Many and many years have passed away since the return of Saknussemm, and the fall of this huge block of granite. Is it not quite evident that this gallery was formerly the outlet for the pent-up lava in the interior of the earth, and that these eruptive matters then circulated freely? Look at these recent fissures in the granite roof; it is evidently formed of pieces of enormous stone, placed here as if by the hand of a giant, who had worked to make a strong and substantial arch. One day, after an unusually strong shock, the vast rock which stands in our way, and which was doubtless the key of a kind of arch, fell through to a level with the soil and has barred our further progress. We are right, then, in thinking that this is an unexpected obstacle, with which Saknussemm did not meet; and if we do not upset it in some way, we are unworthy of following in the footsteps of the great discoverer; and incapable of finding our way to the Centre of the Earth!"

In this wild way I addressed my uncle. The zeal of the Professor, his earnest longing for success, had become part and parcel of my being. I wholly forgot the past; I utterly despised the future. Nothing existed for me upon the surface of this spheroid in the bosom of which I was engulphed, no towns, no country, no Hamburg, no König-strasse, not even my poor Gretchen, who by this time would believe me utterly lost in the interior of the earth!

"Well," cried my uncle, roused to enthusiasm by my words, "let us go to work with pickaxes, with crowbars, with anything that comes to hand—but down with these terrible walls."

"It is far too tough and too big to be destroyed by a pickaxe or crowbar," I replied.

"What then?"

"As I said, it is useless to think of overcoming such a difficulty by means of ordinary tools."

"What then?"

"What else but gunpowder, a subterranean mine? Let us blow up the obstacle that stands in our way."

"Gunpowder!"

"Yes; all we have to do is to get rid of this paltry obstacle."

"To work, Hans, to work!" cried the Professor.

The Icelander went back to the raft, and soon returned with a huge crowbar, with which he began to dig a hole in the rock, which was to serve as a mine. It was by no means a slight task. It was necessary for our purpose to make a cavity large enough to hold fifty pounds of fulminating gun cotton, the expansive power of which is four times as great as that of ordinary gunpowder.

I had now roused myself to an almost miraculous state of excitement. While Hans was at work, I actively assisted my uncle to prepare a long wick, made from damp gunpowder, the mass of which we finally enclosed in a bag of linen.

"We are bound to go through," I cried, enthusiastically.

"We are bound to go through," responded the Professor, tapping me on the back.

At midnight, our work as miners was completely finished; the charge of fulminating cotton was thrust into the hollow, and the match, which we had made of considerable length, was ready.

A spark was now sufficient to ignite this formidable engine, and to blow the rock to atoms!

"We will now rest until to-morrow."

It was absolutely necessary to resign myself to my fate, and to consent to wait for the explosion for six weary hours!

A Journey to the Centre of the Earth

CHAPTER XXXIX.

THE EXPLOSION AND ITS RESULTS

THE next day, which was the twenty-seventh of August, was a date celebrated in our wondrous, subterranean journey.

I never think of it even now, but I shudder with horror. My heart beats wildly at the very memory of that awful day.

From this time forward, our reason, our judgment, our human ingenuity, have nothing to do with the course of events. We are about to become the plaything of the great phenomena of the earth!

At six o'clock we were all up and ready. The dreaded moment was arriving when we were about to seek an opening into the interior of the earth by means of gunpowder. What would be the consequences of breaking through the crust of the earth?

I begged that it might be my duty to set fire to the mine. I looked upon it as an honour. This task once performed, I could rejoin my friends upon the raft, which had not been unloaded. As soon as we were all ready, we were to sail away to some distance to avoid the consequences of the explosion, the effects of which would certainly not be concentrated in the interior of the earth.

The slow match we calculated to burn for about ten minutes, more or less, before it reached the chamber in which the great body of powder was confined. I should therefore have plenty of time to reach the raft and put off to a safe distance.

I prepared to execute my self-allotted task—not, it must be confessed, without considerable emotion.

After a heavy repast, my uncle and the hunter-guide embarked on board the raft, while I remained alone upon the desolate shore.

I was provided with a lantern which was to enable me to set fire to the wick of the infernal machine.

"Go, my boy," said my uncle, "and Heaven be with you. But come back as soon as you can. I shall be all impatience."

"Be easy on that matter," I replied, "there is no fear of my delaying on the road."

Having said this, I advanced towards the opening of the sombre gallery. My heart beat wildly. I opened my lantern and seized the extremity of the wick.

The Professor, who was looking on, held his chronometer in his hand.

"Are you ready?" cried he.

"Quite ready."

"Well, then, fire away!"

I hastened to put the light to the wick, which crackled and sparkled, hissing and spitting like a serpent; then, running as fast as I could, I returned to the shore.

"Get on board my lad, and you, Hans, shove off," cried my uncle.

By a vigorous application of his pole Hans sent us flying over the water. The raft was quite twenty fathoms distant.

It was a moment of palpitating interest, of deep anxiety. My uncle, the Professor, never took his eyes off the chronometer.

"Only five minutes more," he said, in a low tone, "only four, only three."

My pulse went a hundred to the minute. I could hear my heart beating.

"Only two, one! Now, then, mountains of granite, crumble beneath the power of man!"

What happened after that? As to the terrific roar of the explosion, I do not think I heard it. But the form of the rocks completely changed in my eyes—they seemed to be drawn aside like a curtain. I saw a fathomless, a bottomless abyss, which yawned beneath the turgid waves. The sea, which seemed suddenly to have gone mad, then became one great mountainous mass, upon the top of which the raft rose perpendicularly.

We were all thrown down. In less than a second the light gave place to the most profound obscurity. Then I felt all solid support give way, not to my feet, but to the raft itself, I thought it was going bodily down a tremendous well. I tried to speak, to question my uncle. Nothing could be heard but the roaring of the mighty waves. We clung together in utter silence.

Despite the awful darkness, despite the noise, the surprise, the emotion, I thoroughly understood what had happened.

Beyond the rock which had been blown up, there existed a mighty abyss. The explosion had caused a kind of earthquake in this soil, broken by fissures and rents. The gulf, thus suddenly thrown open, was about to swallow the inland

The outlet: The rock must be blasted.

sea, which, transformed into a mighty torrent, was dragging us with it.

One only idea filled my mind. We were utterly and completely lost!

One hour, two hours—what more I cannot say, passed in this manner. We sat close together, elbow touching elbow, knee touching knee! We held one another's hands not to be thrown off the raft. We were subjected to the most violent shocks, whenever our sole dependence, a frail wooden raft struck against the rocky sides of the channel. Fortunately for us, these concussions became less and less frequent, which made me fancy that the gallery was getting wider and wider. There could be now no doubt that we had chanced upon the road once followed by Saknussemm, but instead of going down in a proper manner, we had, through our own imprudence, drawn a whole sea with us!

These ideas presented themselves to my mind in a very vague and obscure manner. I felt rather than reasoned. I put my ideas together only confusedly, while spinning along like a man going down a waterfall. To judge by the air which, as it were, whipped my face, we must have been rushing at a perfectly lightning rate.

To attempt under these circumstances to light a torch was simply impossible, and the last remains of our electric machine, of our Ruhmkorff's coil, had been destroyed during the fearful explosion.

I was therefore very much confused to see at last a bright light shining close to me. The calm countenance of the guide seemed to gleam upon me. The clever and patient hunter had succeeded in lighting the lantern; and though, in the keen and thorough draught, the flame flickered and vacillated and was nearly put out, it served partially to dissipate the awful obscurity.

The gallery into which we had entered was very wide. I was, therefore, quite right in that part of my conjecture. The insufficient light did not allow us to see both of the walls at the same time. The slope of waters, which was carrying us away, was far greater than that of the most rapid river of America. The whole surface of the stream seemed to be composed of liquid arrows, darted forward with extreme violence and power. I can give no idea of the impression it made upon me.

The raft, at times, caught in certain whirlpools, and rushed forward, yet turned on itself all the time. How it did not upset I shall never be able to understand. When it approached the sides of the gallery, I took care to throw upon them the light of the lantern, and I was able to judge of the rapidity of motion by looking at the projecting masses of rock, which as soon as seen were again invisible. So rapid was our progress, that points of rock, at a considerable distance one from the other, appeared like portions of transverse lines, which enclosed us in a kind of net, like that of a line of telegraphic wires.

I believe we were now going at a rate of not less than a hundred miles an hour.

My uncle and I looked at one another with wild and haggard eyes; we clung convulsively to the stump of the mast, which, at the moment when the catastrophe took place, has snapped short off. We turned our backs as much as possible to the wind, in order not to be stifled by a rapidity of motion which nothing human could face and live.

And still the long monotonous hours went on. The situation did not change in the least, though a discovery I suddenly made seemed to complicate it very much.

When we had slightly recovered our equilibrium, I proceeded to examine our cargo. I then made the unsatisfactory discovery that the greater part of it had utterly disappeared.

I became alarmed, and determined to discover what were our resources. My heart beat at the idea, but it was absolutely necessary to know on what we had to depend. With this view, I took the lantern and looked around.

Of all our former collection of nautical and philosophical instruments there remained only the chronometer and the compass. The ladders and ropes were reduced to a small piece of rope fastened to the stump of the mast. Not a pickaxe, not a crowbar, not a hammer, and, far worse than all, no food—not enough for one day!

This discovery was a prelude to a certain and horrible death.

Seated gloomily on the raft, clasping the stump of the mast mechanically, I thought of all I had read as to sufferings from starvation.

I remembered everything that history had taught me on the subject, and I shuddered at the remembrance of the agonies to be endured.

Maddened at the prospect of enduring the miseries of starvation, I persuaded myself that I must be mistaken. I examined the cracks in the raft; I poked between the joints and beams; I examined every possible hole and corner. The result was—simply nothing!

Our stock of provisions consisted of nothing but a piece of dry meat and some soaked and half-mouldy biscuits.

I gazed around me scared and frightened. I could not understand the awful truth. And yet

The torch-light passage.

of what consequence was it in regard to any new danger? Supposing that we had had provisions for months, and even for years, how could we ever get out of the awful abyss into which we were being hurled by the irresistible torrent we had let loose?

Why should we trouble ourselves about the sufferings and tortures to be endured from hunger, when death stared us in the face under so many other swifter and perhaps even more horrid forms?

It was very doubtful, under the circumstances in which we were placed, if we should have time to die of inanition.

But the human frame is singularly constituted.

I knew not how it was; but, from some singular hallucination of the mind, I forgot the real, serious and immediate danger to which we were exposed, to think of the menaces of the future, which appeared before us in all their naked terror. Besides, after all, suggested Hope, perhaps we might finally escape the fury of the raging torrent, and once more revisit the glimpses of the moon, on the surface of our beautiful mother earth.

How was it to be done? I had not the remotest idea. Where were we to come out? No matter, so that we did.

One chance in a thousand is always a chance, while death from hunger gave us not even the faintest glimpse of hope. It left to the imagination nothing but blank horror, without the faintest chance of escape!

I had the greatest mind to reveal all to my uncle, to explain to him the extraordinary and wretched position to which we were reduced, in order that, between the two, we might make a calculation as to the exact space of time which remained for us to live.

It was, it appeared to me, the only thing to be done. But I had the courage to hold my tongue, to gnaw at my entrails like the Spartan boy. I wished to leave him all his coolness.

At this moment, the light of the lantern slowly fell, and at last went out!

The wick had wholly burnt to an end. The obscurity became absolute. It was no longer possible to see through the impenetrable darkness! There was one torch left, but it was impossible to keep it alight. Then, like a child, I shut my eyes, that I might not see the darkness.

After a great lapse of time, the rapidity of our journey increased. I could feel it by the rush of air upon my face. The slope of the waters was excessive. I began to feel that we were no longer going down a slope; we were falling. I felt as one does in a dream, going down bodily—falling; falling; falling!

I felt that the hands of my uncle and Hans were vigorously clasping my arms.

Suddenly, after a lapse of time scarcely appreciable, I felt something like a shock. The raft had not struck a hard body, but had suddenly been checked in its course. A waterspout, a liquid column of water, fell upon us. I felt suffocating. I was being drowned.

Still the sudden inundation did not last. In a few seconds I felt myself once more able to breathe. My uncle and Hans pressed my arms, and the raft carried us all three away.

A Journey to the Centre of the Earth

CHAPTER XL.

THE APE GIGANS

IT is difficult for me to determine what was the real time, but I should suppose, by after calculation, that it must have been ten at night.

I lay in a stupor, a half dream, during which I saw visions of astounding character. Monsters of the deep were side by side with the mighty elephantine shepherd. Gigantic fish and animals seemed to form strange conjunctions.

The raft took a sudden turn, whirled round; entered another tunnel; this time illumined in a most singular manner. The roof was formed of porous stalactite, through which a moon-lit vapour appeared to pass, casting its brilliant light upon our gaunt and haggard figures. The light increased as we advanced, while the roof ascended; until at last, we were once more in a kind of water cavern, the lofty dome of which disappeared in a luminous cloud!

A rugged cavern of small extent appeared to offer a halting place to our weary bodies.

My uncle and the guide moved as men in a dream. I was afraid to waken them, knowing the danger of such a sudden start. I seated myself beside them to watch.

As I did so, I became aware of something moving in the distance, which at once fascinated my eyes. It was floating, apparently, upon the surface of the water, advancing by means of what at first appeared paddles. I looked with glaring eyes. One glance told me that it was something monstrous.

But what?

It was the great *Shark Crocodile* of the early writers on geology. About the size of an ordinary whale, with hideous jaws and two gigantic eyes, it advanced. Its eyes fixed on me with terrible sternness. Some indefinite warning told me that it had marked me for its own.

I attempted to rise—to escape, no matter where, but my knees shook under me; my limbs trembled violently; I almost lost my senses. And still the mighty monster advanced. My uncle and the guide made no effort to save themselves.

With a strange noise, like none other I had ever heard, the beast came on. His jaws were at least seven feet apart, and his distended mouth looked large enough to have swallowed a boatful of men.

We were about ten feet distant, when I discovered that much as his body resembled that of a crocodile, his mouth was wholly that of a shark.

His twofold nature now became apparent. To snatch us up at a mouthful it was necessary for him to turn on his back, which motion necessarily caused his legs to kick up helplessly in the air.

I actually laughed even in the very jaws of death!

But next minute, with a wild cry, I darted away into the interior of the cavern, leaving my unhappy comrades to their fate! This cavern was deep and dreary. After about a hundred yards, I paused and looked around.

The whole floor, composed of sand and malachite, was strewn with bones, freshly-gnawed bones of reptiles and fish, with a mixture of mammalia. My very soul grew sick as my body shuddered with horror. I had truly, according to the old proverb, fallen out of the frying-pan into the fire. Some beast larger and more ferocious even than the Shark-Crocodile inhabited this den.

What could I do? The mouth of the cave was guarded by one ferocious monster, the interior was inhabited by something too hideous to contemplate. Flight was impossible!

One only resource remained, and that was to find some small hiding place to which the fearful denizen of the cavern could not penetrate. I gazed wildly around, and at last discovered a fissure in the rock, to which I rushed in the hope of recovering my scattered senses.

Crouching down, I waited shivering as in an ague fit. No man is brave in presence of an earthquake, or a bursting boiler, or an exploding torpedo. I could not be expected to feel much courage in presence of the fearful fate that appeared to await me.

An hour passed. I heard all the time a strange rumbling outside the cave.

What was the fate of my unhappy companions? It was impossible for me to pause to inquire. My own wretched existence was all I could think of.

Suddenly a groaning, as of fifty bears in a fight, fell upon my ears—hisses, spitting, moaning, hideous to hear—and then I saw—

Never, were ages to pass over my head, shall I forget the horrible apparition.

It was the Ape Gigans!

Fourteen feet high, covered with coarse hair, of a blackish brown, the hair on the arms, from the shoulder to the elbow joints, pointing downwards, while that from the wrist to the elbow pointed upwards, it advanced. Its arms were as long as its body, while its legs were prodigious. It had thick, long, and sharply-pointed teeth—like a mammoth saw.

It struck its breast as it came on smelling and sniffing, reminding me of the stories we read in our early childhood of giants who ate the flesh of men and little boys!

Suddenly it stopped. My heart beat wildly, for I was conscious that, somehow or other, the fearful monster had smelt me out and was peering about with his hideous eyes to try and discover my whereabouts.

My reading, which as a rule is a blessing, but which on this occasion, seemed momentarily to prove a curse, told me the real truth. It was the Ape Gigans, the Antediluvian Gorilla.

Yes! This awful monster, confined by good fortune to the interior of the earth, was the progenitor of the hideous monster of Africa.

He glared wildly about, seeking something—doubtless myself. I gave myself up for lost. No hope of safety or escape seemed to remain.

At this moment, just as my eyes appeared to close in death, there came a strange noise from the entrance of the cave; and turning, the Gorilla evidently recognised some enemy more worthy his prodigious size and strength. It was the huge Shark-Crocodile, which perhaps having disposed of my friends, was coming in search of further prey.

The Gorilla placed himself on the defensive, and clutching a bone some seven or eight feet in length, a perfect club, aimed a deadly blow at the hideous beast, which reared upwards and fell with all its weight upon its adversary.

A terrible combat, the details of which it is impossible to give, now ensued. The struggle was awful and ferocious. I however, did not wait to witness the result. Regarding myself as the object of contention, I determined to remove from the presence of the victor. I slid down from my hiding-place, reached the ground, and gliding against the wall, strove to gain the open mouth of the cavern.

But I had not taken many steps when the fearful clamour ceased, to be followed by a mumbling and groaning which appeared to be indicative of victory.

I looked back and saw the huge ape, gory with blood, coming after me with glaring eyes,

with dilated nostrils that gave forth two columns of heated vapour. I could feel his hot and fetid breath on my neck; and with a horrid jump—awoke from my nightmare sleep.

Yes—it was all a dream. I was still on the raft with my uncle and the guide.

The relief was not instantaneous, for under the influence of the hideous nightmare my senses had become numbed. After a while, however, my feelings were tranquillised. The first of my perceptions which returned in full force was that of hearing. I listened with acute and attentive ears. All was still as death. All I comprehended was silence. To the roaring of the waters, which had filled the gallery with awful reverberations, succeeded perfect peace.

After some little time my uncle spoke, in a low and scarcely audible tone—

"Harry, boy, where are you?"

"I am here," was my faint rejoinder.

"Well, don't you see what has happened? We are going upwards."

"My dear uncle, what can you mean?" was my half delirious reply.

"Yes, I tell you we are ascending rapidly. Our downward journey is quite checked."

I held out my hand, and, after some little difficulty, succeeded in touching the wall. My hand was in an instant covered with blood. The skin was torn from the flesh. We were ascending with extraordinary rapidity.

"The torch—the torch!" cried the Professor, wildly; "it must be lighted."

Hans, the guide, after many vain efforts, at last succeeded in lighting it, and the flame having now nothing to prevent its burning, shed a tolerably clear light. We were enabled to form an approximate idea of the truth.

"It is just as I thought," said my uncle, after a moment or two of silent attention. "We are in a narrow well about four fathoms square. The waters of the great inland sea, having reached the bottom of the gulf, are now forcing themselves up the mighty shaft. As a natural consequence, we are being cast up on the summit of the waters."

"That I can see," was my lugubrious reply; "but where will this shaft end, and to what fall are we likely to be exposed?"

"Of that I am as ignorant as yourself. All I know is, that we should be prepared for the worst. We are going up at a fearfully rapid rate. As far as I can judge, we are ascending at the rate of two fathoms a second, of a hundred and twenty fathoms a minute, or rather more than three and a-half leagues an hour. At this rate, our fate will soon be a matter of certainty."

"No doubt of it," was my reply. "The great

concern I have now, however, is to know whether this shaft has any issue. It may end in a granite roof—in which case we shall be suffocated by compressed air, or dashed to atoms against the top. I fancy, already, that the air is beginning to be close and condensed. I have a difficulty in breathing.''

This might be fancy, or it might be the effect of our rapid motion, but I certainly felt a great oppression of the chest.

"Henry," said the Professor, "I do believe that the situation is to a certain extent desperate. There remain, however, many chances of ultimate safety, and I have, in my own mind, been revolving them over, during your heavy but agitated sleep. I have come to this logical conclusion—whereas we may at any moment perish, so at any moment we may be saved! We need, therefore, prepare ourselves for whatever may turn up in the great chapter of accidents.''

"But what would you have us do?" I cried; "are we not utterly helpless?"

"No! While there is life there is hope. At all events, there is one things we can do—eat, and thus obtain strength to face victory or death.''

As he spoke, I looked at my uncle with a haggard glance. I had put off the fatal communication as long as possible. It was now forced upon me, and I must tell him the truth. Still I hesitated.

"Eat," I said, in a deprecating tone as if there were no hurry.

"Yes, and at once. I feel like a starving prisoner," he said, rubbing his yellow and shivering hands together.

And, turning round to the guide, he spoke some hearty, cheering words, as I judged from his tone, in Danish. Hans shook his head in a terribly significant manner. I tried to look unconcerned.

"What!" cried the Professor, "you do not mean to say that all our provisions are lost?"

"Yes," was my lowly-spoken reply, as I held out something in my hand, "this morsel of dried meat is all that remains for us three.''

My uncle gazed at me as if he could not fully appreciate the meaning of my words. The blow seemed to stun him by its severity. I allowed him to reflect for some moments.

"Well," said I, after a short pause, "what do you think now? Is there any chance of our escaping from our horrible subterreanean dangers? Are we not doomed to perish in the great hollows of the Centre of the Earth?"

But my pertinent questions brought no answer. My uncle either heard me not, or appeared not to do so.

And in this way a whole hour passed. Neither of us cared to speak. For myself, I began to feel the most fearful and devouring hunger. My companions, doubtless, felt the same horrible tortures, but neither of them would touch the wretched morsel of meat that remained. It lay there, a last remnant of all our great preparations for the mad and senseless journey!

I looked back, with wonderment, to my own folly. Fully was I aware that, despite his enthusiasm, and the ever-to-be-hated scroll of Saknussemm, my uncle should never have started on his perilous voyage. What memories of the happy past, what previsions of the horrible future, now filled my brain!

A Journey to the Centre of the Earth

CHAPTER XLI.

HUNGER

HUNGER, prolonged, is temporary madness!

The brain is at work without its required food, and the most fantastic notions fill the mind. Hitherto I had never known what hunger really meant. I was likely to understand it now.

And yet, three months before I could tell my terrible story of starvation, as I thought it. As a boy I used to make frequent excursions in the neighbourhood of the Professor's house.

My uncle always acted on system, and he believed that, in addition to the day of rest and worship, there should be a day of recreation. In consequence, I was always free to do as I liked on a Wednesday.

Now, as I had a notion to combine the useful and the agreeable, my favourite pastime was birds' nesting. I had one of the best collections of eggs in all the town. They were classified, and under glass cases.

There was a certain wood, which, by rising at early morn, and taking the cheap train, I could reach at eleven in the morning. Here I would botanise or geologise at my will. My uncle was always glad of specimens for his herbarium, and stones to examine. When I had filled my wallet, I proceeded to search for nests.

After about two hours of hard work, I, one day, sat down by a stream to eat my humble but copious lunch. How the remembrance of the spiced sausage, the wheaten loaf, and the beer made my mouth water now! I would have given every prospect of worldly wealth for such a meal. But to my story.

While seated thus at my leisure, I looked up at the ruins of an old castle, at no great distance. It was the remains of an historical dwelling, ivy clad, and now falling to pieces.

While looking, I saw two eagles circling about the summit of a lofty tower. I soon became satisfied that there was a nest. Now, in all my collection, I wanted eggs of the native eagle and the large owl.

My mind was made up. I would reach the summit of that tower, or perish in the attempt. I went nearer, and surveyed the ruins. The old staircase, years before, had fallen in. The outer walls were, however, intact. There was no chance that way, unless I looked to the ivy solely for support. This was, as I soon found out, futile.

There remained the chimney, which still went up to the top, and had once served to carry off the smoke from every storey of the tower.

Up this I determined to venture. It was narrow, rough, and therefore the more easily climbed. I took off my coat and crept into the chimney. Looking up, I saw a small, light opening, proclaiming the summit of the chimney.

Up—up I went, for some time using my hands and knees, after the fashion of a chimney sweep. It was slow work, but, there being continual projections, the task was comparatively easy. In this way, I reached half way. The chimney now became narrower. The atmosphere was close, and, at last, to end the matter, I stuck fast. I could ascend no higher.

There could be no doubt of this, and there remained no resource but to descend, and give up my glorious prey in despair. I yielded to fate and endeavoured to descend. But I could not move. Some unseen and mysterious obstacle intervened and stopped me. In an instant the full horror of my situation seized me.

I was unable to move either way, and was doomed to a terrible and horrible death, that of starvation. In a boy's mind, however, there is an extraordinary amount of elasticity and hope, and I began to think of all sorts of plans to escape my gloomy fate.

In the first place, I required no food just at present, having had an excellent meal, and was therefore allowed time for reflection. My first thought was to try and move the mortar with my hand. Had I possessed a knife, something might have been done, but that useful instrument I had left in my coat pocket.

I soon found that all efforts of this kind were vain and useless, and that all I could hope to do was to wriggle downwards.

But though I jerked and struggled, and strove to turn, it was all in vain. I could not move an inch, one way or the other. And time flew rapidly. My early rising probably contributed to the fact that I felt sleepy, and gradually gave way to the sensation of drowsiness.

I slept, and awoke in darkness, ravenously hungry.

Night had come, and still I could not move. I was tight bound, and did not succeed in changing my position an inch. I groaned aloud. Never since the days of my happy childhood, when it was a hardship to go from meal to meal without eating, had I really experienced hunger. The sensation was as novel as it was painful. I began now to lose my head and to scream and cry out in my agony. Something appeared, startled by my noise. It was a harmless lizard, but it appeared to me a loathsome reptile. Again I made the old ruins resound with my cries, and finally so exhausted myself that I fainted.

How long I lay in a kind of trance or sleep I cannot say, but when again I recovered consciousness it was day. How ill I felt, how hunger still gnawed at me, it would be hard to say. I was too weak to scream now, far too weak to struggle.

Suddenly I was startled by a roar.

"Are you there, Henry?" said the voice of my uncle; "are you there, my boy?"

I could only faintly respond, but I also made a desperate effort to turn. Some mortar fell. To this I owed my being discovered. When the search took place, it was easily seen that mortar and small pieces of stone had recently fallen from above. Hence my uncle's cry.

"Be calm," he cried, "if we pull down the whole ruin, you shall be saved."

They were delicious words, but I had little hope.

Soon however, about a quarter of an hour later, I heard a voice *above me*, at one of the upper fireplaces.

"Are you below, or above?"

"Below," was my reply.

In an instant a basket was lowered with milk, a biscuit, and an egg. My uncle was fearful to be too ready with his supply of food. I drank the milk first, for thirst had nearly deadened hunger. I then, much refreshed, ate my bread and hard egg.

They were now at work at the wall, I could hear a pickaxe. Wishing to escape all danger from this terrible weapon I made a desperate struggle, and the belt, which surrounded my waist and which had been hitched on a stone, gave way. I was free, and only escaped falling down by a rapid motion of my hands and knees.

In ten minutes more I was in my uncle's arms, after being two days and nights in that horrible prison. My occasional delirium prevented me from counting time.

I was weeks recovering from that awful starvation adventure; and yet what was that to the hideous sufferings I now endured?

After dreaming for some time, and thinking of this and other matters, I once more looked around me. We were still ascending with fearful rapidity. Every now and then the air appeared to check our respiration as it does that of aëronauts when the ascension of the balloon is too rapid. But if they feel a degree of cold in proportion to the elevation they attain in the atmosphere, we experienced quite a contrary effect. The heat began to increase in a most threatening and exceptional manner. I cannot tell exactly the mean, but I think it must have reached 122 degrees of Fahrenheit.

What was the meaning of this extraordinary change in the temperature? As far as we had hitherto gone, facts had proved the theories of Davy and of Lidenbrock to be correct. Until now, all the peculiar conditions of refractory rocks, of electricity of magnetism, had modified the general laws of nature, and had created for us a moderate temperature; for the theory of the central fire, remained, in my eyes, the only explainable one.

Were we, then, going to reach a position in which these phenomena were to be carried out in all their rigour, and in which the heat would reduce the rocks to a state of fusion?

Such was my not unnatural fear, and I did not conceal the fact from my uncle. My way of doing so might be cold and heartless, but I could not help it.

"If we are not drowned, or smashed into pancakes, and if we do not die of starvation, we have the satisfaction of knowing that we must be burned alive."

My uncle, in presence of this brusque attack, simply shrugged his shoulders, and resumed his reflections—whatever they might be.

An hour passed away, and except that there was a slight increase in the temperature, no incident modified the situation. My uncle at last, of his own accord, broke silence.

"Well Henry my boy," he said, in a cheerful way, "we must make up our minds."

"Make up our minds to what?" I asked, in considerable surprise.

"Well—to something. We must at whatever risk recruit our physical strength. If we make the fatal mistake of husbanding our little remnant of food, we may probably prolong our wretched existence a few hours—but we shall remain weak to the end."

"Yes," I growled, "to the end. That, however, will not keep us long waiting."

"Well, only let a chance of safety present itself,—only allow that a moment of action be necessary,—where shall we find the means of action if we allow ourselves to be reduced to physical weakness by inanition?"

"When this piece of meat is devoured, uncle, what hope will there remain unto us?"

"None, my dear Henry, none. But will it do you any good to devour it with your eyes. You appear to me to reason like one without will or decision, like a being without energy."

"Then," cried I, exasperated to a degree which is scarcely to be explained, "you do not mean to tell me—that you—that you—have not lost all hope?"

"Certainly not," replied the Professor, with consummate coolness.

"You mean to tell me, uncle, that we shall get out of this monstrous subterranean shaft?"

"While there is life there is hope. I beg to assert, Henry, that as long as a man's heart beats, as long as a man's flesh quivers, I do not allow that a being gifted with thought and will can allow himself to despair."

What a nerve! The man placed in a position like that we occupied must have been very brave to speak like this.

"Well," I cried, "what do you mean to do?"

"Eat what remains of the food we have in our hands; let us swallow the last crumb. It will be, heaven willing, our last repast. Well, never mind—instead of being exhausted skeletons, we shall be men."

"True," muttered I in a despairing tone, "let us take our fill."

"We must," replied my uncle, with a deep sigh—"call it what you will."

My uncle took a piece of the meat that remained, and some crusts of biscuit which had escaped the wreck. He divided the whole into three parts.

Each had one pound of food to last him as long as he remained in the interior of the earth.

Each now acted in accordance with his own private character.

My uncle, the Professor, ate greedily, but evidently without appetite, eating simply from some mechanical motion. I put the food inside my lips, and hungry as I was, chewed my morsel without pleasure, and without satisfaction.

Hans the guide, just as if he had been eider-down hunting, swallowed every mouthful, as thought it were a usual affair. He looked like a man equally prepared to enjoy superfluity or total want.

Hans, in all probability, was no more used to starvation than ourselves, but his hardy Icelandic nature had prepared him for many sufferings. As long as he received his three rix-dollars every Saturday night, he was prepared for anything.

The fact was, Hans never troubled himself about much except his money. He had undertaken to serve a certain man at so much per week, and no matter what evils befell his employer or himself, he never found fault or grumbled, so long as his wages were duly paid.

Suddenly my uncle roused himself. He had seen a smile on the face of our guide. I could not make it out.

"What is the matter?" said my uncle.

"Schiedam," said the guide, producing a bottle of this precious fluid.

We drank. My uncle and myself will own to our dying day that hence we derived strength to exist until the last bitter moment. That precious bottle of Hollands was in reality only half-full; but, under the circumstances, it was nectar.

It took some minutes for myself and my uncle to form a decided opinion on the subject. The worthy Professor swallowed about half a pint and did not seem able to drink any more.

"*Förtrafflig*," said Hans, swallowing nearly all that was left.

"Excellent—very good," said my uncle with as much gusto as if he had just left the steps of the club at Hamburg.

I had begun to feel as if there had been one gleam of hope. Now all thought of the future vanished!

We had consumed our last ounce of food, and it was five o'clock in the morning!

A Journey to the Centre of the Earth

CHAPTER XLII.

THE VOLCANIC SHAFT

MAN'S constitution is so peculiar, that his health is purely a negative matter. No sooner is the rage of hunger appeased, than it becomes difficult to comprehend the meaning of starvation. It is only when you suffer that you really understand.

As to any one who has not endured privation having any notion of the matter, it is simply absurd.

With us, after a long fast, some mouthfuls of bread and meat, a little mouldy biscuit and salt beef triumphed over all our previous gloomy and saturnine thoughts.

Nevertheless, after this repast each gave way to his own reflections. I wondered what were those of Hans—the man of the extreme north, who was yet gifted with the fatalistic resignation of Oriental character. But the utmost stretch of the imagination would not allow me to realise the truth. As for my individual self, my thoughts had ceased to be anything but memories of the past, and were all connected with that upper world which I never should have left. I saw it all now, the beautiful house in the Königstrasse, my poor Gretchen, the good Martha; they all passed before my mind like visions of the past. Every time any of the lugubrious groanings which were to be distinguished in the hollows around fell upon my ears, I fancied I heard the distant murmur of the great cities above my head.

As for my uncle, always thinking of his science, he examined the nature of the shaft by means of a torch. He closely examined the different strata one above the other, in order to recognise his situation by geological theory. This calculation, or rather this estimation, could by no means be anything but approximate. But a learned man, a philosopher, is nothing if not a philosopher, when he keeps his ideas calm and collected; and certainly the Professor possessed this quality to perfection.

I heard him, as I sat in silence, murmuring words of geological science. As I understood his object and his meaning, I could not but interest myself despite my pre-occupation in that terrible hour.

"Eruptive granite," he said to himself, "we are still in the primitive epoch. But we are going up—going up, still going up. But who knows?

Who knows?"

Then he still hoped. He felt along the vertical sides of the shaft with his hand, and some few minutes later, he would go on again the following style—

"This is gniess. This is mocashites—silicious mineral. Good again; this is the epoch of transition, at all events, we are close to them—and then and then—"

What could the Professor mean? Could he, by any conceivable means, measure the thickness of the crust of the earth suspended above our heads? Did he possess any possible means of making any approximation to this calculation? No.

The manometer was wanting and no summary estimation could take the place of it.

And yet, as we progressed, the temperature increased in the most extraordinary degree, and I began to feel as if I were bathed in a hot and burning atmosphere. Never before had I felt anything like it. I could only compare it to the hot vapour from an iron foundry, when the liquid iron is in a state of ebullition and runs over. By degrees, and one after the other, Hans, my uncle, and myself had taken off our coats and waistcoats. They were unbearable. Even the slightest garment was not only uncomfortable, but the cause of extreme suffering.

"Are we ascending to a living fire?" I cried; when, to my horror and astonishment, the heat became greater than before.

"No, no," said my uncle, "it is simply impossible, quite impossible."

"And yet," said I, touching the side of the shaft with my naked hand, "this wall is literally burning."

At this moment, feeling as I did that the sides of this extraordinary well were red hot, I plunged my hands into the water to cool them. I drew them back with a cry of despair.

"The water is boiling!" I cried.

My uncle, the Professor, made no reply other than a gesture of rage and despair.

Something very like the truth had probably struck his imagination.

But I could take no share in either what was going on, or in his speculations. An invincible dread had taken possession of my brain and soul. I could only look forward to an immediate

Overpowered by heat.

catastrophe, such a catastrophe as not even the most vivid imagination could have thought of. An idea, at first vague and uncertain, was gradually being changed into certainty.

I tremulously rejected it at first, but it forced itself upon me by degrees with extreme obstinacy. It was so terrible an idea that I scarcely dared to whisper it to myself.

And yet all the while certain, and as it were, involuntary observations determined my convictions. By the doubtful glare of the torch, I could make out some singular changes in the granitic strata; a strange and terrible phenomenon was about to be produced, in which electricity played a part.

Then this boiling water, this terrible and excessive heat? I determined as a last resource to examine the compass.

The compass had gone mad?

Yes, wholly stark staring mad. The needle jumped from pole to pole with sudden and surprising jerks, ran round, or as it is said, boxed the compass, and then ran suddenly back again as if it had the vertigo.

I was aware that, according to the best acknowledged theories, it was a received notion that the mineral crust of the globe is never, and never has been, in a state of complete repose.

The modifications caused by the decomposition of internal matter, the agitation consequent on the flowing of extensive liquid currents, the excessive action of magnetism which tends to shake it incessantly, at a time when even the multitudinous beings on its surface do not suspect the seething process to be going on.

Still this phenomenon would have not alarmed me alone; it would not have aroused in my mind a terrible, an awful idea.

But other facts could now allow any self-delusion to last.

Terrible detonations, like heaven's artillery, began to multiply themselves with fearful intensity. I could only compare them with the noise made by hundreds of heavily-laden chariots being madly driven over a stone pavement. It was a continuous roll of heavy thunder.

And then the mad compass, shaken by the wild electric phenomena, confirmed me in my rapidly-formed opinion. The mineral crust was about to burst, the heavy granite masses were about to rejoin, the fissure was about to close, the void was about to be filled up, and we poor atoms to be crushed in its awful embrace!

"Uncle, uncle!" I cried, "we are wholly, irretrievably lost!"

"What, then, my young friend, is your new cause of terror and alarm?" he said, in his calmest manner. "What fear you now?"

"What do I fear now!" I cried, in fierce and angry tones. "Do you not see that the walls of the shaft are in motion? do you not see that the solid granite masses are cracking? do you not feel the terrible, torrid heat? do you not observe the awful boiling water on which we float? do you not remark this mad needle? every sign and portent of an awful earthquake?"

My uncle coolly shook his head.

"An earthquake," he replied in the most calm and provoking tone.

"Yes."

"My nephew, I tell you that you are utterly mistaken," he continued.

"Do you not, can you not, recognise all the well-known symptoms—"

"Of an earthquake? by no means. I am expecting something far more important."

"My brain is strained beyond endurance—what, what do you mean?" I cried.

"An eruption, Harry."

"An eruption," I gasped. "We are, then, in the volcanic shaft of a crater in full action and vigour."

"I have every reason to think so," said the Professor in a smiling tone, "and I beg to tell you that it is the most fortunate thing that could happen to us."

The most fortunate thing! Had my uncle really and truly gone mad? What did he mean by these awful words—what did he mean by this terrible calm, this solemn smile?

"What!" cried I, in the height of my exasperation, "we are on the way to an eruption, are we? Fatality has cast us into a well of burning and boiling lava, of rocks on fire, of boiling water, in a word, filled with every kind of eruptive matter? We are about to be expelled, thrown up, vomited, spit out of the interior of the earth, in common with huge blocks of granite, with showers of cinders and scoria, in a wild whirlwind of flame, and you say—the most fortunate thing which could happen to us."

"Yes," replied the Professor, looking at me calmly from under his spectacles, "it is the only chance which remains to us of ever escaping from the interior of the earth to the light of day."

It is quite impossible that I can put on paper the thousand strange, wild thoughts which followed this extraordinary announcement.

But my uncle was right, quite right, and never had he appeared to me so audacious and so convinced as when he looked me calmly in the face and spoke of the chances of an eruption—

of our being cast upon mother earth once more through the gaping crater of a volcano!

Nevertheless, while we were speaking we were still ascending; we passed the whole night going up, or to speak more scientifically, in an ascensional motion. The fearful noise redoubled; I was ready to suffocate. I seriously believed that my last hour was approaching, and yet, so strange is imagination, all I thought of was some childish hypothesis or other. In such circumstances you do not choose your own thoughts. They overcome you.

It was quite evident that we were being cast upwards by eruptive matter; under the raft there was a mass of boiling water, and under this was a heaving mass of lava, and an aggregate of rocks which on reaching the summit of the water would be dispersed in every direction.

That we were inside the chimney of a volcano there could no longer be the shadow of a doubt. Nothing more terrible could be conceived!

But on this occasion, instead of Sneffels, an old and extinct volcano, we were inside a mountain of fire in full activity. Several times I found myself asking, what mountain was it, and on what part of the world we should be shot out. As if it were of any consequence!

In the northern regions, there could be no reasonable doubt about that. Before it went decidedly mad, the compass had never made the slightest mistake. From the cape of Saknussemm, we had been swept away to the northward many hundreds of leagues. Now the question was, were we once more under Iceland —should we be belched forth on to the earth through the crater of Mount Hecla, or should we re-appear through one of the other seven fire-funnels of the island? Taking in my mental vision a radius of five hundred leagues to the westward, I could see under this parallel only the little-known volcanoes of the north-west coast of America.

To the east one only existed somewhere above the eightieth degree of latitude, the Esk, upon the island of Jean Mayen, not far from the frozen regions of Spitzbergen.

It was not craters that were wanting, and many of them were big enough to vomit a whole army; all I wished to know was the particular one towards which we were making with such fearful velocity.

I often think now of my folly: as if I should ever have expected to escape!

Towards morning, the ascending motion became greater and greater. If the degree of heat increased instead of decreasing, as we approached the surface of the earth, it was simply because the causes were local and wholly due to volcanic influence. Our very style of locomotion left in my mind no doubt upon the subject. An enormous force, a force of some hundred of combined atmospheres produced by vapours accumulated and long compressed in the interior of the earth, were hoisting us upwards with irresistible power.

But though we were approaching the light of day, to what fearful dangers were we about to be exposed?

Instant death appeared the only fate which we could expect or contemplate.

Soon a dim, sepulchral light penetrated the vertical gallery, which became wider and wider. I could make out to the right and left long dark corridors like immense tunnels, from which awful and horrid vapours poured out. Tongues of fire, sparkling and crackling, appeared about to lick us up.

The hour had come!

"Look, uncle, look!" I cried.

"Well, what you see are the great sulphurous flames. Nothing more common in connection with an eruption."

"But if they lap us round!" I angrily replied.

"They will not lap us round," was his quiet and serene answer.

"But it will be all the same in the end if they stifle us," I cried.

"We shall not be stifled. The gallery is rapidly becoming wider and wider, and if it be necessary, we will presently leave the raft and take refuge in some fissure in the rock."

"But the water, the water, which is continually ascending!" I despairingly replied.

"There is no longer any water, Harry," he answered, "but a kind of lava paste, which is heaving us up, in company with itself, to the mouth of the crater."

In truth, the liquid column of water had wholly disappeared to give place to dense masses of boiling eruptive matter. The temperature was becoming utterly insupportable, and a thermometer exposed to this atmosphere would have marked between 189 and 190 degrees Fahrenheit.

Perspiration rushed from every pore. But for the extraordinary rapidity of our ascent we should have been stifled.

Nevertheless, the Professor did not carry out his proposition of abandoning the raft; and he did quite wisely. Those few ill-joined beams offered, any way, a solid surface—a support which elsewhere must have utterly failed us.

Towards eight o'clock in the morning a new incident startled us. The ascensional movement

The raft floats over the waves of Lava.

suddenly ceased. The raft became still and motionless.

"What is the matter now?" I said, querulously, very much startled by this change.

"A simple halt," replied my uncle.

"Is the eruption about to fail?" I asked.

"I hope not."

Without making any reply, I rose. I tried to look around me. Perhaps the raft, checked by some projecting rock, opposed a momentary resistance to the eruptive mass. In this case, it was absolutely necessary to release it as quickly as possible.

Nothing of the kind had occurred. The column of cinders, of scoriae, of broken rocks and earth, had wholly ceased to ascend.

"I tell you, uncle, that the eruption has stopped," was my oracular decision.

"Ah," said my uncle, "you think so, my boy. You are wrong. Do not be in the least alarmed; this sudden moment of calm will not last long, be assured. It has already endured five minutes, and before we are many minutes older we shall be continuing our journey to the mouth of the crater."

All the time he was speaking the Professor continued to consult his chronometer, and he was probably right in his prognostics. Soon the raft resumed its motion, in a very rapid and disorderly way, which lasted two minutes or thereabout; and then again it stopped as suddenly as before.

"Good," said my uncle, observing the hour, "in ten minutes we shall start again."

"In ten minutes?"

"Yes—precisely. We have to do with a volcano, the eruption of which is intermittent. We are compelled to breathe just as it does."

Nothing could be more true. At the exact minute he had indicated, we were again launched on high with extreme rapidity. Not to be cast off the raft, it was necessary to hold on to the beams. Then the hoist again ceased.

Many times since have I thought of this singular phenomenon without being able to find for it any satisfactory explanation.

Nevertheless, it appeared quite clear to me, that we were not in the principal chimney of the volcano, but in an accessory conduit, where we felt the counter shock of the great and principal tunnel filled by burning lava.

It is impossible for me to say how many times this manoeuvre was repeated. All that I can remember is, that on every ascensional motion, we were hoisted up with ever-increasing velocity, as if we had been launched from a huge projectile. During the sudden halts we were nearly stifled; during the moments of projection the hot air took away our breath.

I thought for a moment of the voluptuous joy of suddenly finding myself in the hyperborean regions with the cold 30 degrees below zero!

My exalted imagination pictured to itself the vast snowy plains of the arctic regions, and I was impatient to roll myself on the icy carpet of the north pole.

By degrees my head, utterly overcome by a series of violent emotions, began to give way to hallucination. I was delirious. Had it not been for the powerful arms of Hans the guide, I should have broken my head against the granite masses of the shaft.

I have, in consequence, kept no account of what followed for many hours. I have a vague and confused remembrance of continual detonations, of the shaking of the huge granitic mass, and of the raft going round and round like a spinning-top. It floated on the stream of hot lava, amidst a falling cloud of cinders. The huge flames roaring, wrapped us around.

A storm of wind which appeared to be cast forth from an immense ventilator roused up the interior fires of the earth. It was a hot incandescent blast!

At last I saw the figure of Hans as if enveloped in the huge halo of burning blaze, and no other sense remained to me but that sinister dread which the condemned victim may be supposed to feel when led to the mouth of a cannon, at the supreme moment when the shot is fired and his limbs are dispersed into empty space.

A Journey to the Centre of the Earth

CHAPTER XLIII.

DAYLIGHT AT LAST

WHEN I opened my eyes I felt the hand of the guide clutching me firmly by the belt. With his other hand he supported my uncle. I was not grievously wounded, but bruised all over in the most remarkable manner.

After a moment I looked around, and found that I was lying down on the slope of a mountain not two yards from a yawning gulf into which I should have fallen had I made the slightest false step. Hans had saved me from death, while I rolled insensible on the flanks of the crater.

"Where are we?" dreamily asked my uncle, who literally appeared to be disgusted at having returned to earth.

The eider-down hunter simply shrugged his shoulders as a mark of total ignorance.

"In Iceland?" said I, not positively but interrogatively.

"*Nej,*" said Hans.

"How do you mean?" cried the Professor; "no—what are your reasons?"

"Hans is wrong," said I, rising.

After all the innumerable surprises of this journey, a yet more singular one was reserved to us. I expected to see a cone covered by snow, by extensive and wide-spread glaciers, in the midst of the arid deserts of the extreme northern regions, beneath the full rays of a polar sky, beyond the highest latitudes.

But contrary to all our expectations, I, my uncle, and the Icelander, were cast upon the slope of a mountain calcined by the burning rays of a sun which was literally baking us with its fires.

I could not believe my eyes, but the actual heat which affected my body allowed me no chance of doubting. We came out of the crater half naked, and the radiant star from which we had asked nothing for two months, was good enough to be prodigal to us of light and warmth—a light and warmth we could easily have dispensed with.

When our eyes were accustomed to the light we had lost sight so long, I used them to rectify the errors of my imagination. Whatever happened, we should have been at Spitzbergen, and I was in no humour to yield to anything but the most absolute proof.

After some delay, the Professor spoke.

"Hem!" he said, in a hesitating kind of way, "it really does not look like Iceland."

"But supposing it were the island of Jean Mayen?" I ventured to observe.

"Not in the least, my boy. This is not one of the volcanoes of the north, with its hills of granite and its crown of snow."

"Nevertheless—"

"Look, look, my boy," said the Professor, as dogmatically as usual.

Right above our heads, at a great height, opened the crater of a volcano from which escaped, from one quarter of an hour to the other, with a very loud explosion, a lofty jet of flame mingled with pumice stone, cinders, and lava. I could feel the convulsions of nature in the mountain, which breathed like a huge whale, throwing up from time to time fire and air through its enormous vents.

Below, and floating along a slope of considerable angularity, the stream of eruptive matter spread away to a depth which did not give the volcano a height of three hundred fathoms.

Its base disappeared in a perfect forest of green trees, among which I perceived olives, fig trees, and vines loaded with rich grapes.

Certainly this was not the ordinary aspect of the Arctic regions. About that there could not be the slightest doubt.

When the eye was satisfied at its glimpse of this verdant expanse, it fell upon the waters of a lovely sea or beautiful lake, which made of this enchanted land an island of not many leagues in extent.

On the side of the rising sun was to be seen a little port, crowded with houses, and near which boats and vessels of peculiar build were floating upon azure waves.

Beyond, groups of islands rose above the liquid plain, so numerous and close together as to resemble a vast bee-hive.

Towards the setting sun, some distant shores were to be made out on the edge of the horizon. Some presented the appearance of blue mountains of harmonious conformation; upon others, much more distant, there appeared a prodigiously lofty cone, above the summit of which hung dark and heavy clouds.

Towards the north, an immense expanse of

water sparkled beneath the solar rays, occasionally allowing the extremity of a mast or the convexity of a sail bellying to the wind, to be seen.

The unexpected character of such a scene added an hundredfold to its marvellous beauties.

"Where can we be?" I asked, speaking in a low and solemn voice.

Hans shut his eyes with an air of indifference, and my uncle looked on without clearly understanding.

"Whatever this mountain may be," he said, at last, "I must confess it is rather warm. The explosions do not leave off, and I do not think it is worth while to have left the interior of a volcano and remain here to receive a huge piece of rock upon one's head. Let us carefully descend the mountain and discover the real state of the case. To confess the truth, I am dying of hunger and thirst."

Decidedly the Professor was no longer a truly reflective character. For myself, forgetting all my necessities, ignoring my fatigues and sufferings, I should have remained still for several hours longer—but it was necessary to follow my companions.

The slope of the volcano was very steep and slippery; we slid over piles of ashes, avoiding the streams of hot lava which glided about like fiery serpents. Still, while we were advancing, I spoke with extreme volubility, for my imagination was too full not to explode in words.

"We are in Asia!" I exclaimed; "we are on the coast of India, in the great Malay islands, in the centre of Oceana. We have crossed the one half of the globe to come out right at the antipodes of Europe!"

"But the compass!" exclaimed my uncle; "explain that to me!"

"Yes,—the compass," I said, with considerable hesitation "I grant that is a difficulty. According to it, we have always been going northward."

"Then it lied."

"Hem—to say it lied is rather a harsh word," was my answer.

"Then we are at the north pole—"

"The pole—no—well—well I give it up," was my reply.

The plain truth was, that there was no explanation possible. I could make nothing of it.

And all the while we were approaching this beautiful verdure, hunger and thirst tormented me fearfully. Happily, after two long hours' march, a beautiful country spread our before us, covered by olives, pomegrantes, and vines, which appeared to belong to anybody and everybody.

In the state of destitution into which we had fallen, we were not particular to a grape.

What delight it was to press these delicious fruits to our lips, and to bite at grapes and pomegrantes fresh from the vine. Not far off, near some fresh and mossy grass, under the delicious shade of some trees, I discovered a spring of fresh water, into which we voluptuously laved our faces, hands, and feet.

While we were all giving way to the delights of new-found pleasures, a little child appeared between two tufted olive trees.

"Ah," cried I, "an inhabitant of this happy country."

The little fellow was poorly dressed, weak and suffering, and appeared terribly alarmed at our appearance. Half naked, with tangled, matted and ragged beards, we did look supremely ill-favoured; and unless the country was a bandit land, we were not unlikely to alarm the inhabitants!

Just as the boy was about to take to his heels, Hans ran after him, and brought him back, despite his cries and kicks.

My uncle tried to look as gentle as possible, and then spoke in German.

"What is the name of this mountain, my friend?"

The child made no reply.

"Good," said my uncle, with a very positive air of conviction, "we are not in Germany."

He then made the same demand in English, of which language he was an excellent scholar.

The child shook its head and made no reply. I began to be considerably puzzled.

"Is he dumb?" cried the Professor, who was rather proud of his polyglot knowledge of languages, and making the same demand in French.

The boy only stared in his face.

"I must perforce try him in Italian," said my uncle, with a shrug.

"*Dove noi siamo?*"

"Yes, tell me where we are?" I added, impatiently and eagerly.

Again the boy remained silent.

"My fine fellow, do you or do you not mean to speak?" cried my uncle, who began to get angry. He shook him, and spoke another dialect of the Italian language.

"*Come si noma questa isola?*"—what is the name of this island?

"Stromboli," replied the rickety little shepherd, dashing away from Hans and disappearing in the olive groves.

We thought little enough about him.

The summit of Stromboli.

Stromboli! What effect on the imagination did these few words produce! We were in the centre of the Mediterranean; amidst the Eastern archipelago of mythological memory; in the ancient Strongylos, where AEolus kept the wind and the tempest chained up. And those blue mountains, which rose towards the rising of the sun, were the mountains of Calabria.

And that mighty volcano which rose on the southern horizon was Etna, the fierce and celebrated Etna!

"Stromboli! Stromboli!" I repeated to myself.

My uncle played a regular accompaniment to my gestures and words. We were singing together like an ancient chorus.

Ah—what a journey—what a marvellous and extraordinary journey! Here we had entered the earth by one volcano, and we had come out by another. And this other was situated more than twelve hundred leagues from Sneffels, from that drear country of Iceland cast away on the confines of the earth. The wondrous chances of this expedition had transported us to the most harmonious and beautiful of earthly lands. We had abandoned the region of eternal snows for that of infinite verdure, and had left over our heads the grey fog of the icy regions to come back to the azure sky of Sicily!

After a delicious repast of fruits and fresh water, we again continued our journey in order to reach the port of Stromboli. To say how we had reached the island would scarcely have been prudent. The superstitious character of the Italians would have been at work, and we should have been called demons vomited from the infernal regions. It was therefore necessary to pass for humble and unfortunate shipwrecked travellers. It was certainly less striking and romantic, but it was decidedly safer.

As we advanced, I could hear my worthy uncle muttering to himself—

"But the compass. The compass most certainly marked north. This is a fact I cannot explain in any way."

"Well, the fact is," said I, with an air of disdain, "we must not explain anything. It will be much more easy."

"I should like to see a professor of the Johannaeum Institution, who is unable to explain a cosmic phenomenon—it would indeed be strange."

And speaking thus; my uncle, half naked, his leathern purse round his loins, and his spectacles upon his nose, became once more the terrible Professor of Mineralogy.

An hour after leaving the wood of olives, we reached the fort of San Vicenza, where Hans demanded the price of his thirteenth week of service. My uncle paid him, with very many warm shakes of the hand.

At that moment, if he did not indeed quite share our natural emotion, he allowed his feelings so far to give way as to indulge in an extraordinary expression for him.

With the tips of two fingers he gently pressed our hands and smiled.

A Journey to the Centre of the Earth

CHAPTER XLIV.

THE JOURNEY ENDED

THIS is the final conclusion of a narrative which will be probably disbelieved even by people who are astonished at nothing. I am, however, armed at all points against human incredulity.

We were kindly received by the Strombolite fishermen, who treated us as shipwrecked travellers. They gave us clothes and food. After a delay of forty-eight hours, on the 31st of September a little vessel took us to Messina, where a few days of delightful and complete repose restored us to ourselves.

On Friday, the 4th October, we embarked in the Volturus, one of the postal packets of the Imperial Messagerie of France; and three days later we landed at Marseilles, having no other care on our minds but that of our precious but erratic compass. This inexplicable circumstance tormented me terribly. On the 9th of October, in the evening, we reached Hamburg.

What was the astonishment of Martha, what the joy of Gretchen! I will not attempt to define it.

"Now then, Harry, that you really are a hero," she said, "there is no reason why you should ever leave me again."

I looked at her. She was weeping tears of joy.

I leave it to be imagined if the return of Professor Hardwigg made or did not make a sensation in Hamburg. Thanks to the indiscretion of Martha, the news of his departure for the Interior of the Earth had been spread over the whole world.

No one would believe it—and when they saw him come back in safety they believed it all the less.

But the presence of Hans and many stray scraps of information by degrees modified public opinion.

Then my uncle became a great man, and I the nephew of a great man; which, at all events, is something. Hamburg gave a festival in our honour. A public meeting of the Johannaeum Institution was held, at which the Professor related the whole story of his adventures, omitting only the facts in connection with the compass.

That same day he deposited in the archives of the town the document he had found written by Saknussemm, and he expressed his great regret that circumstances, stronger than his will, did not allow him to follow the Icelandic traveller's track into the very Centre of the Earth. He was modest in his glory, but his reputation only increased.

So much honour necessarily created for him many envious enemies. Of course they existed, and as his theories, supported by certain facts, contradicted the system of science upon the question of central heat, he maintained his own views both with pen and speech against the learned of every country. Although I still believe in the theory of central heat, I confess that certain circumstances, hitherto very ill defined, may modify the laws of such natural phenomena.

At the moment when these questions were being discussed with interest, my uncle received a rude shock—one that he felt very much. Hans, despite everything he could say to the contrary, quitted Hamburg; the man to whom we owed so much would not allow us to pay our deep debt of gratitude. He was taken with nostalgia; a love for his Icelandic home.

"*Farval*," said he, one day, and with this one short word of adieu, he started for Reykjawick, which he soon reached in safety.

We were deeply attached to our brave eider-duck hunter. His absence will never cause him to be forgotten by those whose lives he saved, and I hope, at some not distant day, to see him again.

To conclude, I may say that our Journey into the Interior of the Earth created an enormous sensation throughout the civilised world. It was translated and printed in many languages. All the leading journals published extracts from it, which were commentated, discussed, attacked, and supported with equal animation by those who believed in its episodes, and by those who were utterly incredulous.

Wonderful! My uncle enjoyed during his lifetime all the glory he deserved; and he was even offered a large sum of money, by Mr. Barnum, to exhibit himself in the United States; while I am credibly informed by a traveller that he is to be seen in waxwork at Madame Tussaud's!

But one care prayed upon his mind, a care which rendered him very unhappy. One fact remained inexplicable—that of the compass.

Our condition at the end of the journey.

For a learned man to be baffled by such an inexplicable phenomenon was very aggravating. But heaven was merciful, and in the end my uncle was happy.

One day, while he put some minerals belonging to his collection in order, I fell upon the famous compass and examined it keenly.

For six months it had lain unnoticed and untouched.

I looked at it with curiosity, which soon became surprise. I gave a loud cry. The Professor, who was at hand, soon joined me.

"What is the matter?" he cried.

"The compass!"

"What then?"

"Why its needle points to the south and not to the north."

"My dear boy, you must be dreaming."

"I am not dreaming. See the poles are changed."

"Changed!"

My uncle put on his spectacles, examined the instrument, and leaped with joy, shaking the whole house.

A clear light fell upon our minds.

"Here it is!" he cried, as soon as he had recovered the use of his speech, "after we had once passed Cape Saknussemm, the needle of this compass pointed to the southward instead of the northward."

"Evidently."

"Our error is now easily explained. But to what phenomenon do we owe this alteration in the needles?"

"Nothing more simple."

"Explain yourself, my boy. I am on thorns."

"During the storm, upon the Central Sea, the ball of fire which made a magnet of the iron in our raft, turned our compass topsy turvy."

"Ah!" cried the Professor, with a loud and ringing laugh, "it was a trick of that inexplicable electricity."

From that hour my uncle was the happiest of learned men, and I the happiest of ordinary mortals. For my pretty Virland girl, abdicating her position as ward, took her place in the house in King Street (König Strasse) in the double quality of niece and wife.

We need scarcely mention that her uncle was the illustrious Professor Hardwigg, corresponding member of all the scientific, geographical, mineralogical and geological societies of the five quarters of the globe.

Jules Verne at Home

Jules Verne at Home

By Marie A. Belloc.

HE author of " Round the World in Eighty Days," "Five Weeks in a Balloon," and many other delightful stories which cannot but have endeared his personality to hundreds of thousands of readers in every part of the world, spends his happy, well-filled working life in Amiens, a quiet, French provincial town situated on the direct route from Calais and Boulogne to Paris.

The humblest Amienois can point out Jules Verne's home. No. 1, Rue Charles Dubois, is a charming, old-fashioned house, situated at the corner of a countrified street leading out of a broad boulevard.

The little door let into a lichen-covered wall was answered by a cheerful-looking old *bonne*. As soon as she heard that I had come by appointment, she led the way across a paved court-yard bounded on two sides by a picturesque, irregular building, flanked by the short tower which is so often a feature of French country houses. As I followed her, I was able to catch a glimpse of Jules Verne's garden, a distant vista of great beeches shading wide expanses of well-kept turf brilliant with flower-beds. Though it was late autumn, everything was exquisitely neat and dainty, and not a stray leaf was to be seen on the broad gravel paths, where the veteran novelist takes every day one of his frequent constitutionals.

A row of shallow stone steps leads to a conservatory hall, which, filled with palms and flowering shrubs, forms a pleasant ante-chamber to the beautiful *salon*, where I was joined a few moments later by my host and hostess.

As the famous author is the first to acknowledge, Mme. Jules Verne has played no small part in each and all of her husband's triumphs and successes; and it is difficult to believe that the bright, active old lady, still so full of youthful vivacity and French *espieglerie*, can really have celebrated over a year ago her golden wedding.

Jules Verne, in his personal appearance, does not fulfil the popular idea of a great author. Rather does he give one the impression of being a cultured country gentleman, and this notwithstanding the fact that he always dresses in the sombre black affected by most Frenchmen belonging to the professional classes. His coat is decorated with the tiny red button denoting that the wearer possesses the high distinction of being an officer of the Legion of Honour. As he sat talking he

From a Photo. by] JULES VERNE'S HOUSE. [*C. Herbert, Amiens.*

did not look his seventy-eight years, and, indeed, appeared but little changed since the large portrait, hanging opposite that of his wife, was painted some twenty odd years ago.

M. Verne is singularly modest about his work, and showed no desire to talk about either his books or himself. Had it not been for the kindly assistance of his wife, whose pride in her husband's genius is delightful to witness, I should have found it difficult to persuade him to give me any particulars about his literary career or his methods of work.

"I cannot remember the time," he observed, in answer to a question, "when I did not write, or intend to be an author; and as you will soon see, many things conspired to that end. You know, I am a Breton by birth—my native town being Nantes—but my father was a Parisian by education and taste, devoted to literature, and, although he was too modest to make any effort to popularize his work, a line poet. Perhaps this is why I myself began my literary career by writing poetry, which—for I followed the example of most budding French litterateurs—took the form of a five-act tragedy," he concluded, with a half-sigh—half-smile.

"My first real piece of work, however," he added, after a pause, "was a little comedy written in collaboration with Dumas *fils*, who was, and has remained, one of my best friends. Our play was called ' Pailles Rompues' (Split Straws), and was acted at the Gymnase Theatre in Paris ; but, although I much enjoyed light dramatic work, I did

not find that it brought me anything in the way of substance or fortune.

"And yet," he continued, slowly, " I have never lost my love for the stage and everything connected with theatrical life. One of the keenest joys my story-writing has brought me has been the successful staging of some of my novels, notably ' Michel Strogoff.'

"I have often been asked what first gave me the idea of writing what, for the want of a better name, may be styled scientific romances.

"Well, I had always been devoted to the study of geography, much as some people delight in history and historical research. I really think that my love for maps and the great explorers of the world led to my composing the first of my long series of geographical stories.

"When writing my first book, ' Five Weeks in a Balloon,' I chose Africa as the scene of action, for the simple reason that less was, and is, known about that continent than any other ; and it struck me that the most ingenious way in which this portion of the world's surface could be explored would be from a balloon. I thoroughly enjoyed writing the story, and, even more, I may add, the researches which it made necessary ; for then, as now, I always tried to make even the wildest of my romances as realistic and true to life as possible.

"Once the story was finished, I sent the manuscript to the well-known Paris publisher, M. Hetzel. He read the tale, was interested by it, and made me an offer which I accepted. I may tell you that this excellent man and his son became, and have remained, my very good friends, and the firm are about to publish my seventieth novel."

"Then you passed no anxious moments waiting on fame?" I asked. "Did your first book become immediately popular, both at home and abroad?"

"Yes," he answered, modestly. "'Five Weeks in a Balloon' has remained to this day one of the most read of my stories, but you must remember that I was already a man of thirty-five when this book was published, and had been married for some eight years," he concluded, turning to Mme. Verne with a charming air of old-fashioned gallantry.

"Your love of geography did not prevent your possessing a strong bent for science?"

"Well, I do not in any way pose as a scientist, but I esteem myself fortunate as having been born in an age of remarkable discoveries, and perhaps still more wonderful inventions."

"You are doubtless aware," interposed Mme. Verne, proudly, "that many apparently impossible scientific phenomena in my husband's romances have come true?"

"Tut, tut," cried M. Verne, deprecatingly, "that is a mere coincidence, and is doubtless owing to the fact that even when inventing scientific phenomena I always try and make everything seem as true and simple as possible. As to the accuracy of my descriptions, I owe that in a great measure to the fact that, even before I began writing stories, I always took numerous notes out of every book, newspaper, magazine, or scientific report that I came across. These notes were, and are, all classified according to the subject with which they dealt, and I need hardly point out to you how invaluable much of this material has been to me.

"I subscribe to over twenty newspapers," he continued, "and I am an assiduous reader of every scientific publication; even apart from my work I keenly enjoy reading or hearing about any new discovery or experiment in the worlds of science, astronomy, meteorology, or physiology."

"And do you find that this miscellaneous reading suggests to you any new ideas for stories, or do you depend for your plots wholly on your own imagination?"

"It is impossible to say what suggests the skeleton of a story; sometimes one thing, sometimes another. I have often carried an idea in my brain for years before I had occasion to work it out on paper, but I always make a note when anything of the kind occurs to me. Of course, I can distinctly trace the beginnings of some of my books: 'Round the World in Eighty Days' was the result of reading a tourist advertisement in a newspaper. The paragraph which caught my attention mentioned the fact that nowadays it would be quite possible for a man to travel round the world in eighty days, and it immediately flashed into my mind that the traveller, profiting by a difference of meridian, could be made to either gain or lose a day during that period of time. It was this initial thought that really made the whole point of the story. You will, perhaps, remember that my hero, Phineas Fogg, owing to this circumstance arrived home in time to win his wager, instead of, as he imagined, a day too late."

"Talking of Phineas Fogg, monsieur: unlike most French writers, you seem to enjoy making your heroes of English or foreign extraction."

"Yes, I consider that members of the English-speaking race make excellent heroes, especially where a story of adventure, or scientific pioneering work, is about to be described. I thoroughly admire the pluck and go-ahead qualities of the nation which have planted the Union Jack on so great a portion of the earth's surface."

"Your stories also differ from those of almost all your fellow-authors," I ventured to observe, "inasmuch that in them the fair sex plays so small a part."

An approving glance from my kindly hostess showed me that she agreed with the truth of my observation.

"I deny that in toto," cried M. Verne, with some heat. "Look at 'Mistress Branican,' and the charming young girls in some of my stories. Whenever there is any necessity for the feminine element to be introduced you will always find it there." Then, smiling: "Love is an all-absorbing passion, and leaves room for little else in the human breast; my heroes need all their wits about them, and the presence of a charming young lady might now and again sadly interfere with what they have to do. Again, I have always wished to so write my stories that they might be placed without the least hesitation in the hands of all young people, and I have scrupulously avoided any scene which, say, a boy would not like to think his sister would read."

" Before daylight wanes, would you not like to come upstairs and see my husband's workroom and study ? " asked my hostess ; " there we can continue our conversation."

And so, with Mme. Verne leading the way, we went once more through the light, airy hall, where a door opened straight on to the quaint winding staircase, which leads up and up till are reached the cosy set of rooms where M. Verne passes the greater

part of his life, and from where have issued many of his most enchanting books. As we went along the passage, I noticed some large maps—dumb testimonies of their owner's delight in geography and love of accurate information—hanging on the wall.

" It is here," remarked Mme. Verne, throwing open the door of what proved to be a tiny, cell-like bed-chamber, " that my husband does his actual writing each morning. You must know that he gets up at five, and by lunch-time, that is, eleven o'clock, his actual writing, proof-correcting, and so on, are over for the day ; but one cannot burn the candle at both ends, and each evening he is generally sound asleep by eight or half-past eight o'clock."

The plain wooden desk-table is situated in front of the one large window, and opposite the little camp bed ; between the pauses of his work on winter mornings M. Verne, by glancing up, is able to see the dawn breaking over the beautiful spire of Amiens Cathedral. The tiny room is bare of all ornamentation, save for two busts of Molière and Shakespeare, and a few pictures, including a water-

colour of my host's yacht, the *St. Michel*, a splendid little boat in which he and his wife spent, some years ago, many of the happiest hours of their long dual life.

Opening out of the bedroom is a fine large apartment, Jules Verne's library. The room is lined with book-cases, and in the middle a large table groans under a carefully sorted mass of newspapers, reviews, and scientific reports, to say nothing of a representative collection of French and English periodical literature. A number of cardboard pigeon-holes, occupying however wonderfully little space, contain the twenty odd thousand notes garnered by the author during his long life.

" Tell me what are a man's books, and I will tell you what manner of man he is," makes an excellent paraphrase of a good old saying, and might well be applied to Jules Verne. His library is strictly for use, not show, and well-worn copies of such intellectual friends as Homer, Virgil, Montaigne, and Shakespeare, shabby, but how dear to their owner; editions of Fenimore Cooper, Dickens, and Scott show hard and constant usage ; and there also, in newer dress, many of the better-known English novels have found their way.

" These books will show you," observed M. Verne, genially, " how sincere is my affection for Great Britain. All my life I have delighted in the works of Sir Walter Scott, and during a never-to-be-forgotten tour in the British Isles, my happiest days were spent in Scotland. I still see, as in a vision, beautiful, picturesque Edinburgh, with its Heart of Midlothian, and many entrancing memories ; the Highlands, world-forgotten Iona, and the wild Hebrides. Of course, to one familiar with the works of Scott, there is scarce a district of his native land lacking some association connected with the writer and his immortal work."

" And how did London impress you ? "

" Well, I consider myself a regular devotee of the Thames. I think the great river is

a translation. It seemed to me, when I read it, to possess extraordinary freshness of style and enormous power. I have not mentioned," he continued, "the English writer whom I consider the master of them all, namely, Charles Dickens," and the face of the King of Storytellers lit up with youthful enthusiasm. "I consider that the author of 'Nicholas Nickleby,' 'David Copperfield,' and 'The Cricket on the Hearth' possesses pathos, humour, incident, plot, and descriptive power, any one of which might have made the reputation of a less gifted mortal; but here, again, is one of those whose fame may smoulder but will never die."

Whilst her husband was concluding these remarks, Mme. Verne drew my attention to a large book-case filled with rows of apparently freshly bound and little-read books. "Here," she observed, "are various French, German, Portuguese, Dutch, Swedish, and Russian editions of M. Verne's books, including a Japanese and Arab translation of 'Round the World in Eighty Days,'" and my kindly hostess took down and opened the strange vellum-bound pages wherein each little Arab who runs may read of the adventures of Phineas Fogg, Esq.

"My husband," she added, "has never re-read a chapter of a single one of his stories. When the last proofs are corrected his interest in them ceases, and this, although he has sometimes been thinking over a plot, and inventing situations figuring in a story, during years of his life."

"And what, monsieur, are your methods of work?" I inquired. "I suppose you can have no objection to giving away your recipe?"

"I cannot see," he answered, goodhumouredly, "what interest the public can find in such things; but I will initiate you into the secrets of my literary kitchen, though

the most striking feature of that extraordinary city."

"I should like to ask you your opinion of some of our boys' books and stories of adventure. Of course, you know England has led the van in regard to such literature."

"Yes, indeed, notably with that classic, beloved alike by old and young, 'Robinson Crusoe'; and yet perhaps I shall shock you by admitting that I myself prefer the dear old 'Swiss Family Robinson.' People forget that Crusoe and his man Friday were but an episode in a seven-volumed story. To my mind the book's great merit is that it was apparently the first romance of the kind ever perpetrated. We have all written 'Robinsons,'" he added, laughing; "but it is a moot question if any of them would have seen the light had it not been for their famous prototype."

"And where do you place other English writers of adventure?"

"Unhappily, I can read only those works which have been translated into French. I never tire of Fenimore Cooper; certain of his romances deserve true immortality, and will I trust be remembered long after the socalled literary giants of a later age are forgotten. Then, again, I thoroughly enjoy Captain Marryat's breezy romances. Owing to my unfortunate inability to read English, I am not so familiar as I should like to be with Mayne Read and Robert Louis Stevenson; still, I was greatly delighted with the latter's 'Treasure Island,' of which I possess

En l'année 1872, la maison portant le numéro 7 de Saville-row, Burlington Gardens — maison dans laquelle Sheridan mourut en 1814, — était habitée par Phileas Fogg, esq., l'un des membres les plus singuliers et les plus remarqués du Reform-Club de Londres, bien qu'il semblât prendre à tâche de ne rien faire qui pût attirer l'attention.

A l'un des plus grands orateurs qui honorent l'Angleterre, succédait donc ce Phileas Fogg, personnage énigmatique, dont on ne savait rien, sinon que c'était un fort galant homme et l'un des plus beaux gentlemen de la haute société anglaise.

On disait qu'il ressemblait à lord Byron — par la tête, car il était irréprochable quant aux pieds — mais un Byron à moustaches et favoris, un Byron impassible, qui aurait vécu mille ans sans vieillir.

FACSIMILE OF JULES VERNE'S HANDWRITING.

I do not know that I would recommend anybody else to proceed on the same plan ; for I always think that each of us works in his or her own way, and instinctively knows what method is best. Well, I start by making a draft of what is going to be my new story. I never begin a book without knowing what the beginning, the middle, and the end will be. Hitherto I have always been fortunate enough to have not one, but half-a-dozen definite schemes floating in my mind. If I ever find myself hard up for a subject, I shall consider that it is time for me to give up work. After having completed my preliminary draft, I draw up a plan of the chapters, and then begin the actual writing of the first rough copy in pencil, leaving a half-page margin for corrections and emendations ; I then read the whole, and go over all I have already done in ink. I consider that my real labour begins with my first set of proofs, for I not only correct something in every sentence, but I rewrite whole chapters. I do not seem to have a grip of my subject till I see my work in print ; fortunately, my kind publisher allows me every latitude as regards corrections, and I often have as many as eight or nine revises. I envy, but do not attempt to emulate, the example of those who from the time they write Chapter I. to the word Finis, never see reason to alter or add a single word."

"This method of composition must greatly retard your work ? "

"I do not find it so. Thanks to my habits of regularity, I invariably produce two completed novels a year. I am also always in advance of my work ; in fact, I am now writing a story which properly belongs to my working year 1897 ; in other words, I have five manuscripts ready for the printers. Of course," he added, thoughtfully, " this has not been achieved without sacrifice. I soon found real hard work and a constant, steady rate of production incompatible with the pleasures of society. When we were younger, my wife and myself lived in Paris, and enjoyed the world and its manifold interests to the full. During the last twelve years I have become a townsman of Amiens ; my wife is an Amienoise by birth. It was here that I first made her acquaintance, fifty-three years ago, and little by little all my affections and interests have centered in the town. Some of my friends will even tell you that I am far prouder of being a town councillor of Amiens than of my literary reputation. I do not deny that I thoroughly enjoy taking my share in municipal government."

"Then, have you never followed the example of so many of your own personages, and travelled, as you easily might have done, here, there, and everywhere?"

"Yes, indeed; I am passionately fond of travelling, and at one time spent a considerable portion of each year on my yacht, the *St. Michel*. Indeed, I may say I am devoted to the sea, and I can imagine nothing more ideal than a sailor's life; but with age came a strong love of peace and quietude, and," added the veteran novelist, half sadly, "I now journey only in imagination."

'Doctor Ox' formed the basis of an operetta at the Varietés some seventeen years ago. I was once able to superintend the mounting of my pieces myself; now, my only glimpse of the theatrical world is seen from the front, in our charming Amiens theatre, on the, I must admit, frequent occasions when some good provincial company honours our town with its presence."

"I suppose," I observed to Mme. Verne, "that your husband receives many communications from his immense English constituency of unknown friends and readers?"

From a Photo. by]　　　　THE DRAWING-ROOM.　　　　[*C. Herbert, Amiens.*

"I believe, monsieur, that you add the dramatist's laurels to your other triumphs?"

"Yes," he answered; "you know we have in France a proverb which declares that a man always ends by returning to his old love. Well, as I told you before, I always took a special delight in everything dramatic, and made my literary début as a playwright, and of the many substantial satisfactions brought me by my labours, none gave more pleasure than my return to the stage."

"And which of your stories were most successful in dramatic form?"

"'Michel Strogoff' was perhaps the most popular; it was played all over the world; then 'Round the World in Eighty Days' was very successful, and more lately 'Mathias Sandorf' was acted in Paris; it may amuse you to know further that my

"Yes, indeed," she cried, brightly; "and the applications for autographs! I wish you could see them. If I were not there to save him from his friends, he would spend most of his time writing out his name on slips of paper. I suppose few people have received stranger epistles than my husband. People write to him about all sorts of things: they suggest plots for new stories, they confide to him their troubles, they tell him their adventures, and they send him their books."

"And do those unknown correspondents ever permit themselves to ask indiscreet questions about M. Verne's future plans?"

My good-natured and courteous host answered for her, "Many are so kind as to be interested in my next book; if you share that curiosity, you may care to know what I have not yet announced to any but my intimates, namely, that my next story will have for title, 'L'Ile Hélice'—in English, 'Screw Island.' It embodies a set of notions and ideas that have been in my mind for many years. The action will take place on a floating island created by the ingenuity of man, a kind of *Great Eastern* magnified 10,000 times, and containing, of course, the whole of what in this case may be truly called a moving population. It is my intention," concluded M. Verne, "to complete, before my working days are done, a series which shall conclude in story

know, I have dealt with the moon, but a great deal remains to be done, and if health and strength permit me, I hope to finish the task."

There was still half an hour left before the Calais-Paris train (once so eloquently described by Rossetti) was due, and Mme. Verne, with the gracious politeness which is so peculiarly the attribute of well-bred French-women, drove me to the beautiful cathedral, Notre Dame d'Amiens, a poem in stone, dating from the twelfth century. Within its stately walls the chance English tourist

From a Photo. by]   JULES VERNE IN THE GARDEN.   [*C. Herbert, Amiens.*

form my whole survey of the world's sur-face and the heavens; there are still left corners of the world to which my thoughts have not yet penetrated. As you

may, all unknowingly, see, any Sunday, the fine old man to whose pen he cannot but have owed many happy hours as boy or man.

Books by Jules Verne

A listing of editions in English, in the order of their publication. The date in brackets is that of the original French edition. All published in London. The titles often completely changed from their French to their English language editions, and several of the re-translations in the 1960s had differing titles from their first translations.

Five Weeks in a Balloon. (1863). Chapman & Hall, London, 1870.

Journey to the Centre of the Earth. (1864). Griffith and Farran, London, 1872.

From the Earth to the Moon direct in 97 Hours 20 Minutes: and a Trip Around It. (1865). Sampson Low, London, 1873.

From the Earth to the Moon . . . and a Trip Around It. (1870). Sampson Low, London, 1873.

Twenty Thousand Leagues under the seas. (1870). Sampson Low, London, 1873.

Meridiana: the Adventures of Three Englishmen and Three Russians in South Africa. (1872). Sampson Low, London, 1873.

The Fur Country: or, Seventy Degrees North Latitude. (1873) (I. *The Sun in Eclipse.* II. *Through The Bering Strait*). Sampson Low, London, 1873.

Around the World in Eighty Days (1873). Sampson Low, London, 1874.

Dr. Ox's Experiment, and Other Stories. (1872). Sampson Low, London, 1874.

English at the North Pole. (1866). Routledge, London, 1874.

The Mysterious Island. (1874). Sampson Low, London, 1875.

Survivors of the Chancelor. (1875). Sampson Low, London, 1875.

A Winter Amid the Ice. (1855). Sampson Low, London, 1876.

The Blockade Runners. (1865). Sampson Low, London, 1876.

Field of Ice. (1866). Routledge, London, 1876.

A Floating City. (1871). Ward, Lock, London, 1876.

Voyage Round the World. (1867). Routledge, London, 1876-7.

Michael Strogoff, The Courier of the Czar. 2 vols. (1876). Sampson Low, London, 1876-7.

The Mutineers: A Romance of Mexico. (1851). Sampson Low, London, 1877.

Child of the Cavern: or, Strange Doings Underground. (1877). Sampson Low, London, 1877. (Also translated as *Black Diamonds*, Arco, London, 1960s).

Hector Servadac. 2 vols. (1877). (I. *Anomalous Phenomena.* II. *Homeward Bound*). Sampson Low, London, 1878.

Dick Sands, The Boy Captain. (1878). 2 vols. Sampson Low, London, 1879.

Celebrated Travels and Travellers. (1870). Sampson Low, London, 1879-81. 3 vols.

The Begum's Fortune. (1878). Sampson Low, London, 1880.

The Mutineers of the Bounty. (1879). Sampson Low, London, 1880.

Tribulations of a Chinaman. (1879). Sampson Low, London, 1880.

The Steam House. (1880). Sampson Low, London, 1881. (I. *Demon of Cawnpore.* II. *Tigers and Traitors.*)

The Giant Raft. (I. *Down the Amazon.* II. *Cryptogram.*) (1881). Sampson Low, London, 1881.

Godfrey Morgan: A Californian Mystery. (1882). Sampson Low, London, 1883. Also translated as *School for Crusoes*, Arco, London, 1964.

The Green Ray. (1882). Sampson Low, London, 1883.

Keraban The Inflexible. (1883). 2 vols. (I. *The Captain of the Guidara.* Sampson Low, London, 1884. II. *Scarpante the Spy.* Sampson Low, London, 1885.

The Vanished Diamond, a Tale of South Africa. (1884). Sampson Low, London, 1885. Also translated as *The Southern Star Mystery*, Arco, London, 1960s.

The Archipelago on Fire. (1884). Sampson Low, London, 1886.

Marthias Sandorf. (1885). Sampson Low, London, 1886.

The Clipper of the Clouds. (1886). Sampson Low, London, 1887.

The Lottery Ticket: A Tale of Tellemarken. (1886). Sampson Low, London, 1887.

Flight to France. (1887). Sampson Low, London, 1888.

North Against South: A Tale of the American Civil War. (1887). (I. *Burbank the Northerner.* II. *Texar the Southerner.*) Sampson Low, London, 1888.

Two Years Holiday. (I. *Adrift in the Pacific.* II. *Second Year Ashore.*) (1888). Sampson Low, London, 1889.

A Family Without a Name. (I. *Leader of the Resistance.* II. *Into the Abyss.*) (1889). Sampson Low, London, 1890.

Purchase of the North Pole. (1889). Sampson Low, London, 1891.

Cesar Cascabel (I. *Travelling Circus.* II. *Show on Ice.*) (1890). Sampson Low, London, 1891.

Mistress Branican. (1881). Sampson Low, London, 1892.

Castle of the Carpathians. (1892). Sampson Low, London, 1893.

Claudius Bombarnac. (1892). Sampson Low, London, 1894.

Foundling Mick. (1893). Sampson Low, London, 1895.

Captain Antifer. (1894). Sampson Low, London, 1895.

The Floating Island. (1895). Sampson Low, London, 1896. Also translated as *Propellor Island,* Arco, London, 1960s.

Clovis Dardentor. (1896). Sampson Low, London, 1897.

For the Flag. (1896). Sampson Low, London, 1897.

An Antarctic Mystery. (1897). Sampson Low, London, 1898. Also translated as *The Mystery of Arthur Gordon,* Arco, London, 1960s.

The Will of an Eccentric. (1899). Sampson Low, London, 1900.

The Chase of the Golden Meteor. (1908). Grant Richards, London, 1909.

Master of the World. (1904). Sampson Low, London, 1914.

Their Island Home. (1900). Sampson Low, London, 1923.

Castaways of the Flag; The Final Adventures of the Swiss Family Robinson. (1900). Sampson Low, London, 1923.

The Lighthouse at the End of the World. (1905). Sampson Low, London, 1923.

Salvage of the Cynthia. (1885). Arco, London, 1960s.

Village in the Tree Tops. (1901). Arco, London, 1960s.

Drama in Livonia. (1904). Arco, London, 1960s.

The Thompson Travel Agency. (1907). 2 vols. (I. *Package Holiday.* II. *End of the Journey.*) Arco, London, 1960s.

Hunt for the Meteor. (1908). Arco, London, 1960s.

The Survivors of the Jonathan. (1909). 2 vols. (I. *Masterless Man.* II. *Unwilling Dictator*). Arco, London, 1960s.

Yesterday and Tomorrow. (1910). Arco, London, 1960s.

The Golden Volcano. (1906). 2 vols. (I. *Claim on Forty Mile Creek.* II. *Flood and Flame*). Arco, London, 1963.

The Secret of Wilhelm Storitz. (1910). Arco, London, 1965.

Into the Niger Bend. (1919). Arco, London, 1965.

City in the Sahara. (1919). Arco, London, 1965.

The Sea Serpent. (1901). Arco, London, 1967.

The Danube Pilot. (1908). Arco, London, 1967.

Books about Jules Verne

Allott, Kenneth. *Jules Verne*. Macmillan (1941).

Allotte de la Fuye, Marguerite. *Jules Verne*. Coward McCann (1956). The author was wife of one of Verne's nephews.

Becker, Beril. *Jules Verne*. G. P. Putnam's Son. (1966).

Born, Franz. *Jules Verne, the Man who Invented the Future*. Prentice-Hall, Englewood Cliffs, N.J. (1964).

Costello, Peter. *Jules Verne: Inventor of Science Fiction*. Scribners. (1978).

Evans, I. O. *Jules Verne Master of Science Fiction*. Sidgwick & Jackson, London (1956). The author translated modern versions of Verne's books.

Evans, I. O. *Jules Verne and his Work*. Arco Books, London (1965).

Freedman, Russell. *Jules Verne, Portrait of a Prophet*. Holiday House (1965).

Jules-Verne, Jean. *Jules Verne*. Macdonald and Jane's, London (1976). Written by Verne's grandson, a retired judge.

Peare, Catherine O. *Jules Verne, his Life*. Holt (1956).

Waltz, George H. *Jules Verne, the Biography of an Imagination*. Holt (1943).

The above were all published in New York, except where otherwise indicated.